ROUTLEDGE HANDBOOK OF THEORY IN SPORT MANAGEMENT

Theory is an essential element in the development of any academic discipline and sport management is no exception. This is the first book to trace the intellectual contours of theory in sport management, and to explain, critique and celebrate the importance of sport management theory in academic research, teaching and learning, and in the development of professional practice.

Written by a world-class team of international sport management scholars, each of whom has taken a leading role in developing a particular theory or framework for understanding sport management, the book covers the full span of contemporary issues, debates, themes and functional approaches, from corporate social responsibility and diversity to strategy, marketing and finance. Every chapter explores a key theoretical approach, including an overview of that theory, a discussion of the process of theory development and of how the theory has been employed in research, practice or teaching, and outlines directions for future research in that area. Each chapter includes cases and examples, as well as short illustrative commentaries from people who have used that particular theory in their work, and attempts to highlight the theory–practice links, or gaps, in that area.

For a fully rounded understanding of what sport management is and how it should be studied, taught and practised, a thorough grounding in theory is essential. The *Routledge Handbook of Theory in Sport Management* is therefore important reading for all advanced students, researchers, instructors, managers and practitioners working in this exciting field.

George B. Cunningham (PhD, The Ohio State University) is a Professor and Associate Dean for Academic Affairs and Research in the College of Education and Human Development at Texas A&M University, USA. He is the Marilyn Kent Byrne Chair for Student Success and the director of the Laboratory for Diversity in Sport. Author of over 180 articles and book chapters, Cunningham conducts research in the area of diversity and inclusion in sport and physical activity, group processes and employee attitudes. He is the author of an award-winning book (*Diversity in Sport Organizations*), recipient of the Dr Earle F. Zeigler award, and former president of the North American Society for Sport Management.

Janet S. Fink is a Professor in the Mark H. McCormack Department of Sport Management at the University of Massachusetts Amherst, USA. Her research interests include the marketing of women's sport and female athletes, sport consumer behaviour and diversity issues in sport. Fink is a NASSM Research Fellow and has published in top sport management journals (including the *Journal of Sport Management* and *Sport Management Review*) as well as outlets outside of sport (e.g., *Sex Roles*, *Group Dynamics*), and her research has been cited in popular press outlets, such as *Elle Magazine*, the *Washington Post*, *Huffington Post Live* and *ESPNW*.

Alison Doherty is a Professor in the Sport Management programme in the School of Kinesiology, Faculty of Health Sciences at Western University in London, Ontario, Canada. Her research focuses broadly on the management of non-profit and community sport, and particularly sport and event volunteerism, group dynamics and organisational capacity and innovation. Doherty is the Editor of *Sport Management Review* and serves on the editorial board of the *Journal of Sport Management*. She is a NASSM Research Fellow and recipient of the Dr Earle F. Zeigler and Dr Garth Paton Distinguished Service awards.

ROUTLEDGE HANDBOOK OF THEORY IN SPORT MANAGEMENT

Edited by
George B. Cunningham, Janet S. Fink
and Alison Doherty

LONDON AND NEW YORK

First published in paperback 2018

First published 2016
by Routledge
2 Park Square, Milton Park, Abingdon, Oxon OX14 4RN

and by Routledge
711 Third Avenue, New York, NY 10017

Routledge is an imprint of the Taylor & Francis Group, an informa business

British Library Cataloguing in Publication Data
A catalogue record for this book is available from the British Library

Library of Congress Cataloging in Publication Data
Routledge handbook of theory in sport management/edited by George B.
Cunningham, Janet S. Fink and Alison Doherty.
pages cm
Includes bibliographical references and index.
1. Sports administration. I. Cunningham, George B.
GV713.R74 2015
796.06'9 – dc23
2015014657

ISBN: 978-1-138-80384-8 (hbk)
ISBN: 978-0-8153-8399-4 (pbk)
ISBN: 978-1-315-75346-1 (ebk)

Typeset in Bembo and Stone Sans
by Florence Production Ltd, Stoodleigh, Devon, UK

CONTENTS

v

Contents

ILLUSTRATIONS

Figures

Tables

CONTRIBUTORS

Eric Anderson is a Professor of Masculinity, Sexuality and Sport at the University of Winchester. His work shows a decline in cultural homohysteria leading to a softening of heterosexual masculinities. This permits heterosexual men to kiss, cuddle and love one another; and promotes inclusive attitudes towards openly gay athletes and the recognition of bisexuality. More can be found on his website: www.ProfessorEricAnderson.com.

Kathy Babiak is an Associate Professor at the University of Michigan (Department of Sport Management). Her most recent research in the area has explored underlying motives and drivers for sport organizations to engage in socially responsible practices, as well as strategic aspects related to social involvement (such as community investment, philanthropy, environmental sustainability) in commercial and non-profit sport organizations. Another dimension of her research explores social entrepreneurship and philanthropy – specifically focusing on elite and professional athletes.

Steve Bien-Aimé is a doctoral candidate in Penn State's College of Communications. His research interests include race and gender portrayals in news and sports media. He has also co-authored an article in the *International Journal of Sport Communication*. Before entering his doctoral studies, Bien-Aimé held various positions in sports journalism.

Jennifer E. Bruening is a Professor of Sport Management and Head of the Department of Educational Leadership at the University of Connecticut. Prior to her academic appointments, she was a volleyball coach and athletics administrator at Kenyon College. Her research focuses on barriers and supports women and under-represented minorities encounter in sport. Bruening is also the founder and director of Husky Sport, a programme allowing students to engage in community capacity building, with an emphasis on sport, physical activity and nutrition.

Packianathan Chelladurai is a founding member of the North American Society for Sport Management (NASSM) and the European Association for Sport Management (EASM). He is the first recipient of the Earle F. Zeigler Award from the North American Society for Sport Management, the Merit Award for Distinguished Service to Sport Management Education from the European Association of Sport Management, and Sport Management Scholar Lifetime Achievement Award from Southern Sport Management Association. On

18 June, 2012, The University of Western Ontario awarded him the honorary degree of Letters of Law (LLD) for his contributions to sport management.

Richard Coleman is a Principal Research Fellow at SIRC with fifteen years of experience evaluating the economic impact of sports events. He has worked extensively for UK Sport (and partners) on the *eventIMPACTS.com* toolkit to deliver consistent impact evaluations for the UK events industry. Recent economic impact studies he has undertaken include: The 2014 Ryder Cup; Ashes Test Cricket at Lord's; ATP World Tour Tennis Finals; The Open Championship; London Marathon; Rally Ireland; Le Tour de France Grand Départ in London and Wimbledon.

T. Bettina Cornwell (PhD in marketing, The University of Texas) is the Edwin E. and June Woldt Cone Professor of Marketing in the Lundquist College of Business at the University of Oregon. Her research has recently appeared in *Journal of Advertising, Journal of the Academy of Marketing Science, Journal of Public Policy & Marketing* and *Journal of Sport Management.* Cornwell's research focuses on marketing communications and consumer behaviour and often includes international and public policy emphases. Her book, *Sponsorship in marketing: Effective communication through sports, arts, and events*, was published by Routledge in 2014.

Veerle de Bosscher is a Professor at the Department of Sports Policy and Management (faculty of Physical Education) in the Vrije Universiteit Brussel (VUB), Belgium and visiting professor at Utrecht University (the Netherlands). Her research expertise is in the area of elite sport, sport development, sport policy and management, effectiveness, benchmarking and competitiveness. She is leading a worldwide international network on research in high-performance sport, called SPLISS (Sports Policy factors Leading to International Sporting Success), which was also the subject of her PhD in 2007.

Marlene A. Dixon is a Professor of Sport Management at Troy University and a former collegiate volleyball and basketball coach. Her primary research interests include examining the multi-level factors that impact sport and life quality for those who work and play in sport. Her work has been published in a variety of journals including the *Journal of Sport Management, Sport Management Review, European Sport Management Quarterly, Research Quarterly for Exercise and Sport* and *Quest.* She continues to coach and manage at the youth level and remains an advocate for positive coach and athlete experiences through innovative design and implementation of sport.

Lesley Ferkins is with the Sports Performance Research Institute, New Zealand (SPRINZ) at AUT University in Auckland, New Zealand. She is a former president of the Sport Management Association of Australia and New Zealand (SMAANZ), and focuses her research and teaching on sport governance and leadership.

Rodney Fort is Professor of Sport Management at the University of Michigan and is recognised internationally as an authority on sports economics and business. In over 100 articles and monographs, and seven books, his work covers sports topics as diverse as sport itself. Fort is author of the best-selling textbook, *Sports economics*, covering pro and college sports, in its third edition (Prentice Hall, 2011). His most recent book, with Jason Winfree, is *15 sports myths and why they are wrong* (Stanford University Press, 2015).

Daniel C. Funk is a world leader in sport consumer behaviour and marketing research. A Professor, Washburn Senior Research Fellow, and Director of Research and PhD Programs at STHM, Dr Funk researches the stage-based development of involvement to enhance sport management and health promotion strategies. He has been recognized as a Research Fellow for the Sport Marketing Association and the North American Society for Sport Management, which recognizes scholars who have shown excellence in the area of research and honours the work they have disseminated through its official journal. Funk has participated in nearly 20 grant-funded projects and has written a refereed scholarly book, a sport marketing textbook, an industry book, and currently serves as Editor for *Sport Marketing Quarterly*. Funk has published over 80 articles in a variety of top journals.

Stephanie Gerretsen is a doctoral student at the University of Michigan and a research assistant in the Center for Sports Management and Policy. Ms Gerretsen's research interests include the role of sports in urban planning and real estate development, and she has been published in *State and Local Government Review*. Ms Gerretsen received her master's degree in Urban Planning from the University of Michigan, a master's degree in Sport Management from the University of Michigan, and a bachelor's degree in International Relations and Anthropology from the University of California, San Diego.

Jay Gladden is the Dean of the School of Physical Education and Tourism Management at IUPUI (Indiana University-Purdue University Indianapolis). Gladden's research expertise lies in the areas of sport brand management, sport sponsorship planning and evaluation, and college athletic fundraising. He has published numerous articles and book chapters on these topics in a wide variety of outlets including the *Journal of Sport Management*, *Sport Marketing Quarterly*, *Sport Management Review* and the *International Journal of Sports Marketing and Sponsorship*, and trade publications such as *Athletic Management* and *Sports Business Journal*. Gladden also brings more than twenty years of experience working with industry, first as a Project Director for DelWilber + Associates (from 1991 to 1994) and then as a faculty member at UMass and IUPUI.

Chris Gratton is Emeritus Professor of Sports Economics and Director of the Sport Industry Research Centre at Sheffield Hallam University. He has an international reputation as a sports economist, a subject which he has played a major role in developing since the late 1970s. He currently has five academic sports books in print in this subject area, the latest being *The global economics of sport*, published in 2012. His main areas of research are the economics of major sports events, measuring the economic value of sport and modelling large sport participation surveys.

Marie Hardin is Dean of Penn State's College of Communications and studies gender, sport journalism and newsroom norms. Previously, she served as associate director of the Curley Center for Sports Journalism at Penn State. Hardin received her PhD in 1998 from the University of Georgia. Before completing her PhD, she worked as a newspaper reporter and editor.

Bob Heere joined the faculty at the University of South Carolina in 2013 as an Associate Professor and PhD Program Director in the Department of Sport and Entertainment. Prior to joining SPTE, he held academic appointments at the University of Texas at Austin, Florida State University, The Cruyff Institute for Sport Studies (the Netherlands) and Auckland University of Technology (New Zealand). His research expertise is on the social impact of sport on society, with a particular focus on social identity theory and community development. He currently serves as the editor of the journal, *Sport & Entertainment Review*.

Kathryn Heinze is an Assistant Professor of Sport Management at the University of Michigan. She earned her PhD in Management and Organizations from Northwestern University.

Heinze's research examines social and institutional change and she has published in the *Journal of Sport Management*, *Sport Management Review* and *Administrative Science Quarterly*.

Kevin Hylton, the first black Professor in over seventy-five years of Carnegie history, brings a voice to the sociology of sport, leisure and education that reflects an intricate engagement with the endemic issues that mark race relations in the UK. Professor Hylton has emerged at the forefront of developments on Critical Race Theory (CRT) nationally and internationally. A team of Routledge academic editors and advisers recommended his book *Race and sport: Critical Race Theory* as one of the top ten resources for teaching undergraduates to think critically about the role of sport in society.

Jeffry D. James is a Professor of Sport Management in the Department of Sport Management at Florida State University, and also serves as Chair. He has focused his research on sport marketing broadly and sport consumer psychology more specifically. James has completed various projects with professional and collegiate sports teams, projects in the community sector and published articles in journals such as the *Journal of Sport Management*, *Sport Management Review*, *Sport Marketing Quarterly* and various other outlets.

Mary Jo Kane is Professor and Director of the Tucker Center for Girls and Women in Sport in the College of Education and Human Development at the University of Minnesota. She is an internationally known scholar who examines issues related to sport, media and gender; her research has been published in such peer-reviewed journals as *Communication and Sport*, *Sociology of Sport Journal*, the *Journal of Sport Management* and *Journal of Sport & Social Issues*. Kane is the recipient of the first Endowed Chair in the nation related to women in sport: The Dorothy McNeill Tucker Chair for Women in Sport and Exercise Science. She has appeared on the *Today Show*, and *National Public Radio*, and had her research cited by the *New York Times*, *USA Today* and *Washington Post*.

Lisa A. Kihl is an Associate Professor of sport management in the School of Kinesiology at the University of Minnesota. She is an Affiliated Scholar with the Tucker Center for Research on Girls and Women in Sport and an editorial board member for the *Journal of Sport Management*. Her research interests primarily focus on the intersection of sport ethics, policy and governance. Kihl has presented her work in numerous national and international conferences and published research on athletes' roles in sport governance, athletic administrators' moral reasoning, sport corporate social responsibility, the consequences of sport corruption and organisational leadership.

Minhong Kim received his Bachelor of Science in Physical Education from Yonsei University in 2008 and earned his Master of Science degree in sport management from the University of Florida in 2011. Currently, he is a doctoral student majoring sport management at the University of Georgia. His research goal is to improve and expand the understanding of sport philanthropy, especially professional and collegiate sport donor behaviour and corporate social responsibility effectiveness in sport-related organisations.

Annelies Knoppers is Professor at the Department of Governance and Organization Studies at the University of Utrecht in the Netherlands. Her research focus is on diversity and gender in (sport) organisations and in positions of leadership. Although she began her research career using positivist approaches, she now uses primarily post structural perspectives to explore these issues.

Alexis Lyras is the founder and CEO of the Olympism4Humanity Alliance and currently holds the Conflict Resolution Fellowship position at Georgetown University's Department of

Government. Lyras is the author of 'Sport for Development Theory (SFDT)', the first and most widely used Applied Olympism humanitarian interdisciplinary theory in the emerging field of Sport for Peace and Development. In January 2013, he was appointed by the International Olympic Academy (IOA) to serve as a special advisor to the IOA on Olympism, Peacebuilding and International Development. His most recent project is Olympism4 Humanity Alliance, a global venture that aims 'to explore and enhance the contribution of Olympism to Humanity' through humanitarian action, capacity building, academic engagement, scholarship and youth-led social entrepreneurship.

Dan Mahony is the President at Winthrop University and a professor of sport management. Prior to coming to Winthrop University in 2015, he spent seven years as the Dean of the College of Education, Health and Human Services at Kent State University and thirteen years as a faculty member and administrator at the University of Louisville. He is an active researcher and has published over fifty articles in various refereed journals, as well as one book and a number of book chapters. Mahony is a NASSM Research Fellow and won the 2007 Earle F. Zeigler Award from the North American Society for Sport Management (NASSM) for his research contributions during his career.

Daniel Mason is a Professor of Physical Education and Recreation and adjunct with the School of Business at the University of Alberta. His research focuses on sports leagues and franchises, cities, events and infrastructure development. His work has been supported by the Social Sciences and Humanities Research Council of Canada and the Alberta Gaming Research Institute, and published in the *Journal of Sport Management*, *Journal of Urban Affairs*, *Economic Development Quarterly*, *Managing Leisure*, *Economic Inquiry*, *Contemporary Economic Policy*, *Tourism Management* and *Urban Studies*. He was named a North American Society for Sport Management Research Fellow in 2004.

Milena M. Parent is an Associate Professor at the University of Ottawa and Norwegian School of Sport Sciences. She is also a professor in the MEMOS (Executive Master in Sport Organizations Management) programme. She is a research fellow of the North American Society for Sport Management and an Early Researcher Award holder of the Government of Ontario. Her research falls within the fields of organisation theory and strategic management as they relate to preparing and hosting major sports events, focusing particularly on stakeholder management, networks and governance aspects.

N. David Pifer is currently a PhD student at the University of Georgia studying Sport Management and Policy. He holds a Master of Science degree in sport administration from Marshall University in 2012 and obtained his Bachelor of Science degree in Business from Covenant College in 2011. His research areas of interest include labour markets for professional sports teams and sport analytics.

Holger Preuss is Professor of Sport Economics and Sport Sociology at the Johannes Gutenberg-University in Mainz, Germany and also at the Molde University College, Norway in the field of Event Management. He is also adjunct professor at the University of Ottawa, Canada and international scholar at the State University of New York (SUNY, Cortland). He is former Editor of *European Sport Management Quarterly* and is an Associate Editor of the *Journal of Sport and Tourism*. In addition to his research directed at economic and socio-economic aspects of sport, he has been a consultant for the Olympic bid of Frankfurt RheinMain 2012, Prague (2016/2014), Budapest (2012), Innsbruck (2014), Munich (2018) and Cairo (2020), Hamburg (2024) as well as Qatar for the FIFA Football World Cup 2022 and Dubai (2020) for the World EXPO.

Mark S. Rosentraub is the Bickner Endowed Professor of Sport Management at the University of Michigan. His most recent articles have appeared in *Applied Economic Letters*, the *Journal of Sports Economics* and *Public Money and Management*. His latest book is *Reversing urban decline: Why and how sports, entertainment, and culture turn cities into major league winners* (2014). Together with Jason Winfree he published *Sports finance and management: Real estate, entertainment, and the remaking of the business* in 2012.

Sally Shaw is a Senior Lecturer in Sport Management at the University of Otago, New Zealand. Her research streams include gender relations and non-profit organisational governance. She has used qualitative methods extensively in her research, underpinned by critical theory and postmodernism. She has supervised students who have utilised indigenous research methods and is interested in challenging taken-for-granted assumptions regarding qualitative methods within sport management research.

Simon Shibli is a graduate in Physical Education, Sport Science and Recreation Management from Loughborough University. Since 2004 he has been the Director of the Sport Industry Research Centre (SIRC) at Sheffield Hallam University, where he is also Professor of Sport Management. In 2003 Simon was admitted to the Chartered Institute of Management Accountants and is one of very few qualified accountants working in sport management in the UK. His main research interests are in the applied use of techniques from the fields of finance and economics to research questions in sport and leisure.

David Shilbury is the Foundation Chair of the Sport Management programme and an associate dean in the School of Business at Deakin University in Melbourne, Australia. He was awarded NASSM's Dr Earle F. Zeigler award in 2011 and has published widely in the area of sport governance and management. Currently, he is Editor-in-Chief of the *Journal of Sport Management* and also holds several directorships of sport and leisure organisations.

Eivind Å. Skille is a Professor of Sport Sociology with the Faculty of Public Health Department of Sport at the Hedmark University College, Elverum, Norway. Skille's main research interests are sport policy, sport organisation and sport participation. Much of his work has focused on the relationship between the state's sport policymaking and the implementation of this policy through the voluntary sport organisations.

Galen T. Trail is a Professor and the Director of the Master's in Sport Administration and Leadership (MASL) programme at Seattle University. He has also taught at The Ohio State University, the University of Florida and Iowa State University, covering a variety of classes (e.g., Sport Consumer Behavior, Sport Business and Finance, Sport Marketing, Sport Branding and Communication and Sport Sponsorship). He has published his research in a variety of academic journals and has been interviewed by Street and Smith's *SportsBusiness Journal*, *Forbes* and other publications regarding sport consumer behaviour many times. In addition, he is president and CEO of a sports marketing consulting agency (Sport Consumer Research Consultants – SCRC) and has worked with the Seattle Seahawks, Arizona Diamondbacks, Baltimore Orioles, Seattle Storm, Philadelphia Phillies, Seattle Thunderbirds, the Boeing Classic and multiple NCAA Division I athletic departments, among other sport organisations.

Kirk Wakefield is the Edwin W. Streetman Professor of Retail Marketing at Baylor University, where he is the Executive Director of the Sports Sponsorship & Sales (S3) programme. He is author of *Team sports marketing* and the publisher/editor of the Baylor S3 Report (www.baylors3.com). His scholarly works appear in the *Journal of Marketing, Journal of*

Consumer Research, Journal of the Academy of Marketing Science, Journal of Retailing, Journal of Advertising and *Journal of Sport Management*, among others.

Stacy Warner is an Associate Professor of Sport Management at East Carolina University. Warner, a Research Fellow of the North American Society for Sport Management, and earned her PhD at the University of Texas at Austin. Her research focuses on the roles that sport and sport culture play in the lives of individuals through communities, families, social networks and work environments. Additionally, Warner has acquired work experience in many facets of the sports industry and often utilises these experiences to critically examine sport and consider how sport *can* build community and have a positive impact on life quality.

Jon Welty Peachey (PhD, The University of Connecticut) is an Assistant Professor in the Department of Recreation, Sport and Tourism at the University of Illinois, whose research centres upon sport for development and social change. He has over twelve years of experience working in the international sport sector and in sport for development, including serving as Vice President of International Operations with the Institute for International Sport, a world-wide non-profit organisation using sport to effect positive social change. Welty Peachey is the author of more than sixty peer-reviewed journal articles and book chapters on sport for development, leadership and change. In addition, Welty Peachey has given over 100 presentations at academic and practitioner-based conferences, symposiums and workshops around the world.

Richard Wolfe is a Professor of Strategic Management and a Winspear Fellow at the Peter B. Gustavson School of Business, the University of Victoria. He holds graduate degrees in organisation theory (PhD, University of Michigan), business administration (MBA, Pennsylvania State University) and physical education (MA, University of Michigan). Much of Wolfe's current research focuses on using sport as a lens through which we can learn about various types of organisations; e.g., by studying innovation, leadership, communication, teamwork and strategy in sport, we can learn about those phenomena in a general sense and, thus, apply learnings from sport to other organisational settings. Wolfe is the past Editor of the *Journal of Sport Management* and has published in such journals as the *Journal of Sport Management, European Sport Management Quarterly, Journal of Management, Organization Science, Human Resource Management* and the *Academy of Management Executive*.

James J. Zhang is a professor of sport management at the University of Georgia. His research interests are applied measurement and applied studies examining sport consumer and organisational behaviours. Zhang has published extensively and is a frequent presenter at international and national conferences. He has received such prestigious recognitions as Fellow of National Academy of Kinesiology, Fellow of NASSM, Dr Earle F. Zeigler Lecture Award, J.B. Nash Scholar from the AAHPERD and University of Florida Research Foundation Professorship. He is a distinguished Oriental Scholar named by the City of Shanghai and was recently named the Honorary Dean of the College of Sport Economics and Management by the Shanghai University of Sport.

PART I

Overview

1

DEVELOPING THEORY IN SPORT MANAGEMENT

George B. Cunningham, Janet S. Fink and Alison Doherty

Introduction

Theory represents a 'statement of constructs and their relationships to one another that explain how, when, why, and under what conditions phenomena take place' (Cunningham, 2013, p. 1). We can think of constructs as approximated units (Bacharach, 1989) representing psychological, economic or social phenomena that cannot be readily observed. Examples include deep-level diversity, workplace creativity, an inclusive organisational climate and the like. Theorists use propositions to help specify how constructs are related to one another. For example, we might expect diversity to be positively associated with workplace creativity, particularly when the work environment is inclusive. In many ways, the constructs offer the descriptive component of theory – the *what* – while the propositions tell the reader the manner in which the constructs relate, thereby satisfy the *how* of theory.

Consistent with Whetten (1989), we suggest good theory moves beyond these elements to also provide the *why*, as well as the *when and under what conditions*. The *why* represents the real meat of the theory and provides the underlying rationale for the propositions. It provides the reason the phenomena occur, offering the underlying rationale so that others might better understand what is taking place. In other cases, the *why* aids in prediction, thereby aiding scholars in their quest to better understand various phenomena and for practitioners to apply the materials (van Knippenberg, 2011; Weick, 1989). In drawing from our aforementioned example, we might expect diversity to positively impact creativity because of the different viewpoints, experiences and perspectives that people from different backgrounds bring to the workplace. When they share these different ways of knowing with one another, the decision-making is likely to improve (for an expanded discussion of these linkages, see Cunningham, 2011; Cunningham and Melton, 2011; Florida, 2012).

Good theory also offers estimations of *when* these relationships might occur and *under what conditions*. These represent boundary conditions and constraints (Bacharach, 1989; Whetten, 1989). Context and time are important elements that potentially affect whether constructs are associated with one another. In again drawing from our example, we might expect diversity to be positively related to creativity when the work environment is inclusive, in which case inclusiveness serves to moderate the relationship between the two constructs. These benefits manifest because, in such environments, employees are likely to feel the psychological safety to express divergent viewpoints, to respectfully disagree with one another, and to flesh out those differences in order to arrive at a quality, creative decision.

Importantly, good theory is falsifiable and has utility (Bacharach, 1989). By falsifiable, we mean that it can be rigorously scrutinised and empirically examined (Popper, 1959). While theories are never proven, they can be supported or refuted. This means that they must be devised in such a way that allows scholars to examine and test them, discover the elements that pass muster, and revise or do away with those parts of the theory that, when empirically tested, are simply not accurate. By utility, we mean that theories must be useful. They should add value to the scholarly enterprise, the educational experience and the practice of sport (Doherty, 2013a; Fink, 2013; Irwin and Ryan, 2013). Absent such practicality, we question why the theory was developed in the first place. We expound upon theory's utility in the following section.

More on theory's utility

Theory's place of preeminence in the academic world is unquestioned. This is particularly the case in the area of research. Authors have described it as 'the bedrock upon which good scholarship rests' (Cunningham, 2013, p. 2), 'the basic aim of science' (Kerlinger and Lee, 2000, p. 11), and 'the currency of our scholarly realm' (Corley and Gioia, 2011, p. 12). Theory ideally undergirds the scholar's research questions and hypotheses, their study design, the analytical approach, the interpretation of the results and conclusions drawn. Absent such connections, the ultimate contribution of the work falls into question (Sutton and Staw, 1995).

A number of scholars have also commented on theory's role in the advancement of an academic discipline (Chalip, 2006; Doherty, 2013a; Fink, 2013; Zhang, 2015). Costa also observed as much in her Delphi study (2005) of sport management leaders. The panelists expressed the belief that a strong theoretical foundation was crucial to successful research endeavours, particularly when the theory had high utility. Shilbury and Rentschler (2007) also noted the importance of theory in their analysis of journal quality. They observed that as the journal's contribution to theory increased, so too did its prestige. These patterns are not unique to sport management, *per se*. Colquitt and Zapata-Phelan (2007) analysed articles published in the *Academy of Management Journal* from 1963 to 2007. They found that as the journal matured, so too did the sophistication of the contributing authors' theorising. Among individual articles within the journal, the degree to which the authors expanded and tested theory positively corresponded with number of times the article was cited – one important measure of an article's impact. Thus, while acknowledging some critics' contention that too much emphasis is placed on theory and theory development (Bennis and O'Toole, 2005; Hambrick, 2007; Weese, 1995), we join the chorus of others who sing theory's praises in the scholarly realm.

And, while theory certainly plays an important role in the research domain, it is also significant in educational endeavours. We have modeled as much in our own work, connecting theory with application in our textbooks (Cunningham, 2015; Taylor, Doherty and McGraw, 2015). Embedding theory into teaching allows students to move beyond a descriptive awareness of phenomena to a deeper understanding of how, why and when activities occur, and as a result, they better understand actions in which they can engage to influence those activities. Teaching can also help the scholar to engage in better theory development. Chelladurai (2013) recognised this connection, noting:

> One other feature of my forays into theorizing is that they have been triggered by my experience in teaching. That is, teaching a particular topic alerted me to the gaps in

4

the literature or the opposing view on a topic. The tension and discomfort of those instances led me to theorize on possible solutions to the issues at hand.

(p. 22)

Finally, theory can help inform practice. Lewin's (1952) famous remark – 'there is nothing more practical than a good theory' (p. 169) – captures these possibilities. If the aim of theory is to better understand and predict phenomena, then certainly good theory can and should help inform practice. The reciprocal can also occur, such that, through engagement with industry professionals, scholars can identify needs in the field, and by melding their understanding of practice with their scholarly expertise, develop theory to help explain and inform these actions (Irwin and Ryan, 2013). Van Knippenberg (2011) also commented on this relationship, suggesting 'theory explains and thus allows practice to move beyond an ill-understood "bag of tricks" to better informed actions, and theory guides the further development of knowledge to develop more sophisticated practice' (p. 3).

Impetus for the current volume

Given the value of theory in research, teaching and practice, we were interested in better understanding how people engaged in the theory-building process. To that end, George Cunningham organised a session on theory and theory development as part of his past-President's workshop at the annual conference for the North American Society for Sport Management in 2011. In building from the fruitful dialogue that ensued, the three of us, along with P. Chelladurai, Richard Irwin and Tim Ryan, took part in a scholarly exchange in an issue of *Sport Management Review* (volume 16, issue 1). We discussed the different thoughts on what constituted theory, its usefulness in sport management, factors that spurred us to develop our theories, and the ways we went about doing so. While commonalities certainly existed, the essays also highlighted the diversity of approaches, viewpoints and processes in which we all engaged.

Thus, in addition to answering some of the questions that drove the scholarly exchange – what is the place of theory in the academy and how do people go about developing it – the writings also led to more questions and a greater sense of curiosity about developing theory. How common were the experiences among those who contributed to the scholarly exchange? Does theory development vary based on the questions asked or disciplinary focus? How have people extended, revised or tweaked their work since the initial iteration, and what is the road they anticipate going forward?

These questions led us to pursue and develop this work: the *Routledge Handbook of Theory in Sport Management*. In assembling the *Handbook*, we adhered to several principles. First, we wanted to understand how scholars had developed theories and frameworks commonly used in sport management, and as such, we limited the scope to contributions from authors who had done just that. This approach differs from others who have written about theories developed in other disciplines but that are nevertheless germane to the field of sport management. As several scholars have accomplished this task admirably (e.g., Chelladurai, 2014; Slack and Parent, 2006), we saw no reason to duplicate these efforts. Instead, the *Handbook* represents the first collection of which we are aware that brings together authors who discuss the genesis and process of developing theory in sport management.

Second, we sought a broad treatment of the field. This includes theories that we broadly classified into four categories: managerial, marketing, sociological and economic. We appreciate that some might take exception with such a broad focus and argue the approach is more in line with a sport *studies* text than a sport management text. We adopt a different lens and suggest the management of sport and sport organisations is best understood by adopting a multi-disciplinary perspective. Otherwise, we limit our scope and capacity to address major issues in sport (Doherty, 2013b; see also Cunningham, 2002).

With these foundational principles in mind, we next needed to decide who to ask to write and about which of their works. In doing so, we first identified highly influential theories, as measured by citations in Google Scholar. While there are many measures of impact, citation counts are regularly used to determine the scholarly influence of specific articles (Colquitt and Zapata-Phelan, 2007) or journals (Podsakoff, MacKenzie, Bachrach and Podsakoff, 2005; but see also Alberts, 2013). Thus, we first identified the theoretical articles with the highest number of citations. Second, we recognised this approach disadvantages newer work and scholarship with a narrower disciplinary focus, and that it might not capture truly novel approaches to theory building. Thus, we also requested contributions from authors who (a) have only recently developed their theories, but who were nonetheless meaningfully impacting the discipline; and (b) used inductive approaches to theory building, such as grounded theory – theory building techniques that, while still relatively rare in our field, hold substantial promise (see also Doherty, 2013a; Locke, 2007; Weed, 2009). Third, we sought an international list of contributors, wary of the pitfalls of having a North American-centric text.

While we believe the list is thorough, it does not include contributions from some scholars who have developed notable and well-cited theories. In one case, this was due to the author's illness and other commitments. In other cases, this was due to the duplication of topic areas. For instance, a number of authors have contributed to the understanding of the under-representation of women in leadership positions, and we certainly valued the contribution of each. However, we also did not necessarily want a book that was over-represented in some topics. In this case, and others like it, we generally relied on the citation count to inform the author from whom we requested a chapter.

Additionally, the reader will see that we have included Application sections for each chapter. In discussing the book with others, we received feedback that it would be helpful to hear from others who have also used the theory in their research, teaching or practice. We agreed. After all, such sentiments are consistent with Bacharach's (1989) notion that good theory has utility, and what better way to learn about its utility than from the very people who have used it?

Finally, with the bones of framework in place, we perceived the need for introductory chapters. We are of the general belief that the research questions should drive the methods one uses, and each of us has employed quantitative and qualitative approaches in our scholarly work. That noted, we have also observed some differences in researchers' use of theory depending on their analytical and methodological approach. Thus, we saw value in asking two scholars we hold in high esteem – Sally Shaw and James Zhang – to write about their use of theory in qualitative and quantitative research, respectively.

Final thoughts

With these principles in mind, we arrived at the final 33-chapter collection. We believe this represents a definitive collection of essays concerning theory and theory development in the field of sport management. The authors offer insightful, reflective, cogent writings, sure to both inform and delight. In reflecting on the chapters, we cannot help but recall Henry Mintzberg's (2005) call to scholars over a decade ago:

So we need all kinds of theories—the more, the better. As researchers, scholars, and teachers, our obligation is to stimulate thinking, and a good way to do that is to offer alternative theories—multiple explanations of the same phenomena. Our students and readers should leave our classrooms and publications pondering, wondering, thinking—not knowing.

(p. 356)

Here's to more theory and its development!

References

Alberts, B. (2013) 'Impact factor distortions'. *Science, 340*(6134): 787.

Bacharach, S.B. (1989) 'Organizational theories: Some criteria for evaluation'. *Academy of Management Review, 14*: 496–515.

Bennis, W.G. and O'Toole, J. (2005) 'How business schools lost their way'. *Harvard Business Review, 83*(5): 96–104.

Chalip, L. (2006) 'Toward a distinctive theory of sport management'. *Journal of Sport Management, 20*: 1–21.

Chelladurai, P. (2013). A personal journey in theorizing in sport management. *Sport Management Review, 16*, 22–8.

Chelladurai, P. (2014). *Managing organizations for sport and physical activity: A systems perspective* (fourth edn). Scottsdale, AZ: Holcomb-Hathaway.

Colquitt, J.A. and Zapata-Phelan, C.P. (2007) 'Trends in theory building and theory testing: A five-decade study of the *Academy of Management Journal*'. *Academy of Management Journal, 50*: 1281–303.

Corley, K.G. and Gioia, D.A. (2011) 'Building theory about theory building: What constitutes a theoretical contribution?' *Academy of Management Review, 36*: 12–32.

Costa, C.A. (2005) 'The status and future of sport management: A Delphi study'. *Journal of Sport Management, 19*: 117–42.

Cunningham, G.B. (in press) *Diversity and inclusion in sport organizations* (third edn). Scottsdale, AZ: Holcomb-Hathaway.

Cunningham, G.B. (2002) 'Removing the blinders: Toward an integrative model of organizational change in sport and physical activity'. *Quest, 54*: 276–91.

Cunningham, G.B. (2011) 'Creative work environments in sport organizations: The influence of sexual orientation diversity and commitment to diversity'. *Journal of Homosexuality, 58*: 1041–57.

Cunningham, G.B. (2013) 'Theory and theory development in sport management'. *Sport Management Review, 16*: 1–4.

Cunningham, G.B. and Melton, E.N. (2011) 'The benefits of sexual orientation diversity in sport organizations'. *Journal of Homosexuality, 58*: 647–63.

Doherty, A.J. (2013a) 'Investing in sport management: The value of good theory'. *Sport Management Review, 16*: 5–11.

Doherty, A.J. (2013b) 'It takes a village: Interdisciplinary research for sport management'. *Journal of Sport Management, 26*: 1–10.

Fink, J.S. (2013) 'Theory development in sport management: My experience and other considerations'. *Sport Management Review, 16*: 17–21.

Florida, R. (2012) *The rise of the creative class, revisited*. New York: Basic Books.

Hambrick, D.C. (2007) 'The field of management's devotion to theory: Too much of a good thing?' *Academy of Management Journal, 50*: 1346–52.

Irwin, R.L. and Ryan, T.D. (2013) 'Get real: Using engagement with practice to advance theory transfer and production'. *Sport Management Review, 16*: 12–16.

Kerlinger, F.N. and Lee, H.B. (2000) *Foundations of behavioral research* (fourth edn). Fort Worth, TX: Harcourt College Publishers.

Lewin, K. (1952) *Field theory in social science: Selected theoretical papers by Kurt Lewin*. London: Tavistock.

Locke, E.A. (2007) 'The case for inductive theory building'. *Journal of Management, 33*: 867–90.

Mintzberg, H. (2005) 'Developing theory about the development of theory'. In K.G. Smith and M.A. Hitt (eds), *Great minds in management: The process of theory development* (pp. 355–72). Oxford: Oxford University Press.

Podsakoff, P.M., MacKenzie, S.B., Bachrach, D.G. and Podsakoff, N.P. (2005) 'The influence of management journals in the 1980s and 1990s'. *Strategic Management Journal, 26*: 473–88.

Popper, K. (1959) *The logic of scientific discovery*. New York, NY: Harper and Row.

Shilbury, D. and Rentschler, R. (2007) 'Assessing sport management journals: A multi-dimensional examination'. *Sport Management Review, 10*: 31–44.

Slack, T. and Parent, M.M. (2006) *Understanding sport organizations: The application of organization theory*. Champaign, IL: Human Kinetics.

Sutton, R.I. and Staw, B.M. (1995) 'What theory is *not*'. *Administrative Science Quarterly, 40*: 371–84.

Taylor, T., Doherty, A. and McGraw, P. (2015) *Managing people in sport organizations: A strategic human resource management perspective* (second edn). London: Routledge.

van Knippenberg, D. (2011) 'Advancing theory in organizational psychology'. *Organizational Psychology Review, 1*: 3–8.

Weed, M. (2009) 'Research quality considerations for grounded theory research in sport and exercise psychology'. *Psychology of Sport and Exercise, 10*: 502–10.

Weese, J. (1995) 'If we're not serving practitioners, then we're not serving sport management'. *Journal of Sport Management, 9*: 237–43.

Weick, K.E. (1989) 'Theory construction as disciplined imagination'. *Academy of Management Review, 14*: 516–31.

Whetten, D.A. (1989) 'What constitutes a theoretical contribution?' *Academy of Management Review, 14*: 490–95.

Zhang, J.J. (2015) 'What to study? That is the question: A conscious thought analysis'. *Journal of Sport Management, 29*: 1–10.

2

IMPORTANCE OF THEORY IN QUANTITATIVE ENQUIRY

James J. Zhang, Minhong Kim and N. David Pifer

Introduction

This chapter illustrates the importance of theory in quantitative enquiry to the selection of an appropriate research paradigm, formation of research questions and hypotheses, development of measures and testing of relationships in the practice of research. These elements are addressed in this chapter, prefaced by an overview of the concept and relevance of theory, and concluded with some closing remarks.

Concept and relevance of theory

In daily life, people have a tendency to loosely refer to personal hunches, speculations, conjectures, insights, assertions and explanations as theory; in a comparatively more rigorous and scientific manner, theory refers to a well-confirmed explanation of *nature* that describes how nature will behave under certain conditions (Zima, 2007). Essentially, the fundamental purpose of scientific enquiries is to develop theories, test theories, modify or revise theories and apply theories. According to Sutton and Staw (1995), theory explains connections among phenomena; it is the answer to queries of why, depicting the rationale behind certain actions, events, structures and thoughts. It emphasises the nature of causal relationships, identifying the sequence of occurrence and interconnectedness in terms of systematic reasons, timing and patterns. Wacker (1998) stated that 'theory-building is important because it provides a framework for analysis, facilitates the efficient development of the field, and is needed for the applicability to practical real world problems' (p. 362). A good theory can be characterised as unique, parsimonious, conversational, generalisable, fruitful, internally consistent, empirically risky and abstract. Generally speaking, a theory should have four basic criteria: conceptual definitions, domain limitations, relationship-building and predictions. Of these, conceptual definitions are fundamental for the reason that a theory starts with its measurements. While domain limitations keep theories applicable to relevant areas, relationship-building implies that theories strive to make connections between two or more concepts. In light of these relationships, theories should also help predict how future events will unfold.

Theories hold strong current and future implications for the growing discipline of sport management. Costa (2005) and Cunningham (2013) gathered the perspectives of leading scholars in sport management, who indicated that there was a general inadequacy and a lack of success in both the areas of adopting theories from parent disciplines and developing sport management theories. According to Chelladurai (1992), Slack (1996) and Doherty (2012), theories adopted by the field of sport management in recent years have originated in mainstream business administration and other social sciences. These theories are then introduced to and tested in the sport management setting, verifying a viable process of knowledge production for sport management. It is important to take into consideration the unique characteristics of the sport industry (e.g., simultaneous production and consumption, synchronised co-operation and competition, monopolistic bargaining and territorial rights, revenue sharing, vicarious identification of consumers, ephemeral experience and, most importantly, uncertainty of game outcomes (Mason, 1999; Mullin, Hardy and Sutton, 2014; Smith and Stewart, 2010). Endeavouring for the establishment of a distinctive sport management discipline (Chalip, 2006), theories, assertions or best practices that are specific to the sport management discipline are now being proposed, tested and even formed. Doherty (2013) noted that 'the strength of an academic discipline is its body of knowledge that is not covered by another discipline' (p. 5). Chalip (2006) emphasised that 'if sport management is to be anything more than the mere application of general management principles to the sport context, then there must be something about sport that renders distinctive concerns, foci, or procedures when sport is managed' (p. 3). Zhang (2015) cautioned that directly adopting the measures derived in general business administration or other social sciences with little to no modification or revision may not adequately capture the unique features of a sport management setting.

Level of theorising and research paradigms

The essence of a profession is knowledge. In human history, there have been numerous habits and methods commonly adopted by people to seek truth, acquire and accumulate knowledge, enquire about the surrounding world and solve problems. These may include, but are not limited to, tenacity, intuition, personal experience and rationalistic inference. However, many of these traditional approaches lack objectivity and control of context and environment, resulting in information that cannot be rigorously scrutinised, replicated and generalised. Instead, it is scientific methods of enquiry that have significantly helped the human race advance its problem-solving capability. Characterised as being systematic, logical, empirical, reductive and replicable, the scientific way of discovery undergoes a meticulous process of defining the question, formulating a hypothesis, collecting and analysing data, and interpreting the results (Baumgartner and Hensley, 2012; Thomas, Nelson and Silverman, 2011).

Following the scientific protocol of research, quantitative, qualitative and mixed methods are the three commonly accepted strategies, approaches or paradigms of enquiries (Creswell, 2003). Originating from natural sciences, a quantitative paradigm assumes that the reality or research parameter is relatively stable, directly measurable, reasonably rational and largely generalisable. A typical quantitative research investigation involves clearly stating the research question(s), rationally developing research hypotheses, carrying out well-conceived research procedures that include controlling extraneous variables, employing statistical or other data-analysis procedures and interpreting the results (Baumgartner and Hensley, 2012). Research questions are usually deducted from an existing theory or combination of related theories, major research findings, or general explanations that apply to a specific setting, which in turn dictates the hypothesis statement, protocol of research investigation for the specified problem and interpretation of the results (Thomas *et al.*, 2011). In quantitative studies, strategies of enquiry usually include the true experiments, less rigorous quasi-experiments and correlational studies via descriptive investigations such as surveys and observations. More recent quantitative strategies involve complex experiments with many variables and treatments (e.g., factorial designs and repeated measure designs) and elaborative structural equation models that incorporate causal paths and the identification of the collective strength of multiple variables. Consistently, data collection is performed via predetermined instrument-based questions, behaviour or performance data, attitude data, observational data or census data (Creswell, 2003).

Although qualitative research methods are not the focus of discussion in this chapter, they need to be briefly defined so as to provide a comparison with quantitative approaches. Qualitative methods, after all, are an integral part of mixed-approach studies, and it is necessary to highlight their importance in this chapter. Unlike quantitative studies, qualitative studies follow an inductive reasoning process by generating research questions, assertions and even answers via information obtained from individual cases. According to Baumgartner and Hensley (2012), Creswell (2003), and Strauss and Corbin (1998), a qualitative approach is one in which the enquirer often makes knowledge claims based primarily on constructivist perspectives or participatory perspectives, where an investigation is often conducted in natural settings without the control of research environment, condition or extraneous variables. A qualitative study is of the assumption that meaning and reality are situational and specific to the case(s) involved. Assertions and themes derived in the study are not ready for forming generalisable statements or theories. This paradigm of research investigation utilises such strategies as narratives, phenomenologies, ethnographies, grounded theory studies or case studies, in which the researcher collects open-ended, emerging data with the primary intent of developing themes from the data. Interviews, observations, focus groups, audio-visual recordings, publications, collections, text and image analyses, and document analyses are often the procedures of data collection in qualitative enquiries. For instance, when conducting a grounded theory study, the investigator attempts to understand the general process, action or interaction grounded in the views of the participants. This process involves conducting multiple stages of data collection, theoretical sampling of different segments of research participants in order to maximise group similarities and differences in information, developing an in-depth understanding of the interrelationships among categorised information, and constantly comparing data with emerging categories of assertions and themes.

Merits exist with both quantitative and qualitative paradigms, and each can be adopted to address research questions unique to a situation. Nonetheless, preferring to adopt one approach over the other would fail to take advantage of the merits of having both. A mixed-approach paradigm is therefore particularly useful for the academic discipline of sport management, where scholars have started to pay attention to the uniqueness of the sport industry and attempted to form a distinctive discipline from the ground up (Rudd and Johnson, 2010; Zhang, 2015). In fact, in today's scientific environment it is less about choosing a quantitative versus qualitative approach and more about choosing the best combination for the research situation and practising research that lies somewhere on a continuum between the two (Bryman, 2007; Newman and Benz, 1998). Adopting a mixed-method approach, the researcher would discover and examine knowledge claims based on pragmatic grounds (e.g., consequence-oriented, problem-centred and/or pluralistic), while adopting research protocols that involve the simultaneous or sequential collection of data to best understand the research problem (Baumgartner and Hensley, 2012; Creswell, 2003). For example, through conducting simultaneous data collection procedures, Cunningham, Ferreira and Fink (2009) carried out a mixed-method study to examine factors that influenced the perceived offensiveness of prejudicial comments made by sport television commentators. After responding to a series of eight experimental scenarios (i.e., quantitative approach), participants were asked to reflect on the pattern of their responses and to explain why they answered as they had (i.e., qualitative approach). Similarly, Rohm, Milne and McDonald (2006) used the mixed-method to develop a consumer segmentation typology by using both demographic variables and self-expressed motivations for sport and fitness participation. In particular, qualitative data were used to help validate quantitative analyses in order to establish the structure of market segmentation. As a final example, Gibson, Qi and Zhang (2008) conducted sequential data collections to investigate the images young Americans held of China as both a tourist destination and host of the 2008 Olympics. The relationships among destination image, travel intentions and tourist characteristics were explored. Qualitative enquiries were first carried out to formulate a preliminary scale to measure images of Beijing as a tourist destination and Olympic Games host. Based on the findings of the qualitative enquiries, a questionnaire was developed to examine the stated research question, appropriately lending a quantitative element to the study.

From theory to forming research questions

A comprehensive review of literature is a prerequisite process for identifying research topics, developing the problem to be investigated, formulating one or more research hypotheses, and designing methods for investigation. In quantitative studies, a related theory or theories, application of these theories and associated research findings play a key role in the rational process for developing the problem and stating the hypotheses. In this process, the investigator generally carries out deductive reasoning as he or she logically constructs a theoretical explanation of a phenomenon in order to form research questions and hypotheses that can be tested for specific situations, practices and/or realities. As Kerlinger (1973) explained, 'hypotheses incorporate the theory, or part of it, in testable or near testable forms' (p. 22). Systematic and progressive testing of hypotheses helps advance research questions and enquiries within the topic area through careful articulation and delimitation of the contextual environment that represents the application parameter of the theory or theories.

For example, Ajzen and Fishbein's (1980) theory of reasoned action is an approach to predict and understand an individual's behaviour. This theory explains that human beliefs refer to knowledge about the attitude object, which could be formed via direct observations, accepting information from outside sources, or self-generated inference processes. To influence people's behaviour, they should be exposed to sufficient information while being able to alter their beliefs in a social environment. These beliefs will in turn determine attitudes and subjective norms, which then determine intentions and their corresponding behaviours. Expectedly, there are strong sequential relationships among beliefs (knowledge), attitudes, behaviour intentions and behaviours. Adopting this theory to deduce research questions, Jin, Zhang, Ma and Connaughton (2011) studied the level of awareness, perceived environmental impact, attitude, behavioural intentions and actual behaviour regarding the support of the Green Olympic initiatives and future hosting of mega-sport events among residents in a host city of the Olympic Games. Specifically, they investigated two research questions:

1   What were the levels of awareness of the Green Olympics, the perceived environmental impact of the event, and the attitudes, behavioural intentions and actual behaviours of supporting the Green Olympic initiative and the future hosting of mega-sport events among local residents?
2   What were the relationships among awareness of Green Olympics, perceived environmental impact, attitude, behavioural intention and actual behaviour of supporting the Green Olympic initiative and future hosting of mega-sport events among local residents?

Based on the theory of reasoned action, and related research findings identified in previous studies, the following hypotheses were tested: There would be sequential relationships among the level of awareness of the Green Olympics, perceived environmental impact of the Olympic Games, attitude towards the Green Olympics, and behavioural intentions and actual behaviour of supporting the Green Olympics initiative and the future hosting of mega-sport events among local residents.

Depending on the nature, complexity and concepts involved, multiple theories may need to be adopted and applied to formulate the theoretical framework for an empirical investigation, which will in turn guide the development of the research problem and hypotheses. For instance, Chen and Zhang (2011, 2012) developed a theoretical framework to examine consumer attributes associated with collegiate athletic facility naming rights sponsorship. As sport facility naming rights is one of the fastest growing and most valuable forms of sponsorship, the limited opportunities in major league professional sports have led corporations to seek marketing opportunities with college sports. Although collegiate athletics has become increasingly attractive for sponsorship investment, it has also been laden with potentially negative side effects. For example, how university stakeholders perceive and respond to stadium naming rights sponsorship is a major concern for both corporations and college administrators. Through a review of literature, a theoretical framework with multidimensional factors (beliefs about naming rights sponsorship, attitudes toward commercialisation, team and stadium identification, perception of financial status and perceived fit) assessing consumers' perspectives of naming rights sponsorship effectiveness was proposed, tested and confirmed. To conduct the study, a number of theories were adopted and related research findings were taken into consideration when developing the research questions and forming the hypotheses. These included, but were not limited to, the planned behaviour theory (Ajzen, 1985), belief-attitude-behaviour intentions hierarchy model (Madrigal, 2001), consumer-based brand equity theory (Keller, 1993), social identity theory (Tajfel and Turner, 1979), team identification (Pease and Zhang, 2001; Trail, Fink and Anderson, 2003; Wann and Branscombe, 1993, 1995) and product match-up hypothesis (Kahle and Homer, 1985; Kamins, 1989, 1990). It was expected that the derived theoretical framework would provide a research direction to comprehensively examine how the stakeholders of intercollegiate athletic programmes perceive and respond to corporate naming rights sponsorship of sport facilities.

From theory to measurement

While a theory generally describes the interrelatedness among concepts and constructs, and how they function together to influence the phenomena, accurately measuring the involved concepts and their constructs is a precondition for utilising the theory in research investigations. Kerlinger (1973) explained that a concept could be constitutively defined by its composing constructs, components or ingredients. According to Zhang, Connaughton, Byrd, Cianfrone, Byon and Kim (2007), various theories are often adopted by researchers to conduct empirical investigations to identify the constructs or perspectives (i.e., dimensions or factors) of a concept as their first step of testing relationships among different concepts or even developing a new theory. For instance, Sloan (1989) and Zillmann and Paulus (1993) postulated the concept of social motivation for sport spectatorship. Conducting a comprehensive review of literature and deducing from general motivation theories, they identified five theoretical categories that could be used to explain the social motivations of sport fans, including (a) salubrious effect theories (recreation theory and diversion theory), (b) stress and stimulation seeking theories, (c) catharsis and aggression theories (catharsis theory, frustration–aggression theory and social learning theory), (d) entertainment theories and (e) achievement-seeking theories. Closely following these components for assessing the concept of spectators' social motivation, Pease and Zhang (2001) developed the Spectator Motivation Scale, with a total of thirty-five items measuring these components, or sub-concepts, from different perspectives and written items. Other researchers have developed similar scales (e.g., Trail *et al.*, 2003; Trail and James, 2001; Trail, Robinson, Dick and Gillentine, 2003; Wann and Branscombe, 1993, 1995).

When stringently following the quantitative research paradigm, deduction for measuring different perspectives of a concept is necessarily based on the theoretical definition of the concept and the related research findings of previous studies. For instance, by following Schofield's (1983) arguments and applying the theory of reasoned action (Ajzen and Fishbein, 1980), Zhang, Pease, Hui and Michaud (1995) and Zhang, Lam and Connaughton (2003) defined the concept of market demand as consumer expectations towards the attributes of the core product. In essence, it is a cluster of pull factors associated with the game event that a sport team can offer to its new and returning spectators/consumers. Market demand factors may vary among different settings or sectors within the sport industry. After the Spectator Decision Making Inventory (SDMI) with four factors (Game Promotion, Home Team, Opposing Team and Schedule Convenience) was first developed by Zhang *et al.* (1995), Zhang, Lam, Bennett and Connaughton (2003) conducted a replication study to confirm the composition of these constructs. In this study, the hypotheses were deducted from the theory that originally guided the development of the SDMI and also from the research findings of related studies. A survey form containing the SDMI and consumption variables was administered to sport game spectators and re-examination of SDMIs construct and predictive validity and testing of the stated hypotheses were carried out by conducting a confirmatory factor analysis and a structural equation modelling analysis. Essentially, this replication study rigorously carried out the principles of a deductive reasoning process.

In sport management studies, there are a variety of situational factors that require mixed-method investigations containing both quantitative and qualitative approaches. These include, but are not limited to, the following: (a) adopting theories from mainstream business or social science studies and adapting or modifying them for sport settings; (b) expanding upon the rather small number of theories or measurement models that originate in the field of sport management for applications in various research settings within the sport industry; and (c) developing new measures or revising available measures to account for the diverse segments and settings of the sport industry. For instance, through both qualitative (i.e., interviews, observations, focus–group studies and review of literature) and quantitative investigations (i.e., survey administration, test of content validity, exploratory and confirmatory factor analyses, calculation of reliability coefficients), Byon, Zhang and Connaughton (2010) developed the Scale of Market Demand by following the theory of reasoned action (Ajzen and Fishbein, 1980) to assess consumers' general market demand factors associated with professional team sports. Similarly, Byon and Zhang (2010) developed the Scale of Destination Image by following the cognitive-affective attitude theory (Bagozzi and Burnkrant, 1985) to assess perceived destination images by sport tourists. Adopting the uses and gratifications theory (Katz, Blumler and Gurevitch, 1974), Cianfrone, Zhang and Ko (2011) modified and extended the Sport Video Game Motivation Scale (SVGMS) that was developed by Kim and Ross (2006). The original scale had seven factors (Competition, Diversion, Enjoyment, Fantasy, Interest with Sport, Social Interaction and Sport Knowledge Application); however, after conducting a comprehensive review of literature and taking into consideration multiple perspectives of motivational theories and research findings in general motivation, sport spectator motivation, sport participation motivation and media usage motivation, three new factors (Challenge, Arousal and Team Identification) were added to the revised SVGMS.

After a measure is preliminarily developed from original formulation, modification or revision, it is necessary to first establish content validity that adequately represents the concept and its specified constructs, regardless of the enquiry approach adopted for the measurement study. To have good content validity, a measure should assess what it purports to assess according to the defined concept, which would in turn help support, develop, change and improve theory or theories, decrease inferential errors, enhance confidence in the internal validity of the study and increase the generalisability of research findings (Wood, 1989). Unlike measures in psycho-motor and behavioural domains, many cognitive and affective concepts in sport management studies cannot be directly assessed, as they are latent. Instead, they are often estimated from observable and manifested indications, typically referred to as items or statements. Essentially, these tangible items are indirect indications of various constructs constituting the concept (Zhang, Lam and Williamson, 2002). With an intention to measure a particular construct (i.e., factor) under a concept, the items need to be relevant to the delineation of the construct, representative of the universe of the construct and clear enough to describe the construct in a uni-dimensional fashion (Baumgartner, Jackson, Mahar and Rowe, 2006; Wood, 1989).

Traditionally, a panel of experts, consisting of related theorists, practitioners and even participants for whom the measure is designed, are involved in testing the content validity of the newly developed or revised measure. Based on the percentage of agreement, each item is judged in a dichotomous fashion (e.g., 'Yes' or 'No'; 'Match' or 'Not Match') by the experts with respect to the concept or at times its constructs. Judgment is made in terms of each item's relevance, representativeness and clarity. An alternative format asks experts to place an item into the most appropriate construct. Sometimes, the Delphi technique with multiple rounds of surveys of the expert panel is adopted to define a concept, specify the constructs constituting the concept, write items and verify the content validity. Other times, conducting focus group interviews and pilot studies can help strengthen the content of the measure (Zhang *et al.*, 2002). While the traditional approach focuses on the concept, a more contemporary approach focuses on the constructs of the concept and simultaneously evaluates the three aspects of content validity. Experts judge how well each item represents the corresponding construct using a Likert scale (e.g., from 1 = *not match* to 5 = *match*). Then, validity evidence, reliability and homogeneity coefficients are calculated (Aiken, 1985, 1996; Dunn, Bouffard and Rogers, 1999; Messick, 1989). Nonetheless, it is necessary to re-emphasise that both the theoretical concept and its defined constructs dictate the entire testing procedures of content validity, which is particularly true in quantitative or mixed-method studies. This practice is also true when choosing statistical procedures to examine the construct validity evidence (i.e., factor, convergent and discriminant validity), criterion-related validity evidence (i.e., concurrent and predicative validity) and reliability. For instance, a preliminary scale developed through mixed-method procedures would likely need both exploratory and confirmatory factor analyses; whereas, a scale developed strictly through deductive reasoning and quantitative procedures would need only confirmatory factor analyses.

From theory to testing relationships

Ultimately, theory explains the nature, pattern and strength of interconnectedness among concepts and phenomena (Sutton and Staw, 1995). As a theory or set of theories provides directions and parameters for the formulation of research questions, hypotheses and measurement, it also offers hints for forming research designs, methods and even analytical procedures. As such, numerous studies in the field of sport management have adhered to theory while testing the relationships among a set of constructs.

For example, Cianfrone and Zhang (2006) followed the Attention, Interest, Desire and Action (AIDA) theoretical model (Pitts and Stotlar, 2012; Mullin *et al.*, 2014) while conducting an experimental study to examine the differential effectiveness of television commercials, athlete endorsements, venue signage and combined promotions, as assessed by Generation Y consumers. The researchers conducted a 2 × 4 independent-group experiment consisting of two experimental conditions (experimental and control) and four video footage interventions with different promotional procedures (television commercial, athlete endorsement, venue signage and combined promotion). Research participants were randomly assigned to the eight groups and then responded to a questionnaire that measured brand awareness in terms of unaided recall, aided recall and recognition. A factorial MANCOVA revealed that after controlling for differences in the action sport consumption backgrounds of the subjects, all four promotional procedures effectively increased the participants' brand awareness during a televised action sports event. Television commercials were the most effective, followed by combined promotion, athlete endorsement and venue signage.

In another study, Cianfrone, Zhang, Lutz and Trail (2008) followed multiple theories, including Lavidge and Steiner's (1961) Hierarchy of Effects Model of Advertising, Tajfel and Turner's (1979) social identity theory, Madrigal's (2001) belief-attitude-intentions sponsorship model and Oliver's (1997) customer loyalty framework while conducting an experimental study to examine the effectiveness of a sport video game's (SVG) in-game advertisements in the cognitive, affective and conative consumption domains. Participants were gamers who were randomly assigned to one of two conditions: (a) experimental – playing a SVG with advertisements, and (b) control – playing a SVG without advertisements. Consumption background and identification level were incorporated as covariates to ensure group equivalence. The participating gamers responded to a questionnaire measuring brand awareness, brand attitude and purchase intentions. Results from the MANCOVA revealed that after controlling for the effect of the covariates, the experimental group had a significantly greater mean brand awareness score than the control group. Mean brand attitude and purchase intention scores were not significantly different among groups.

Through deductive reasoning and the implementation of a structural equation modelling analysis, Braunstein, Zhang and Trail (2011) followed Fishbein and Ajzen's (1975) expectancy-value model and the multiple aspects of identity theory (Stryker and Burke, 2000) to develop an explanatory model that analysed athlete endorser effectiveness in promoting non-sport products. The sequential relationships of identification with an athlete and sport to product-endorser congruency, perceived value and purchase intentions were examined, providing a preliminary overview of key socio-psychological factors that may influence the purchase intentions of endorsed products.

Kim, Zhang, Jackson, Connaughton and Kim (2013) and Kim, Zhang and Ko (2009) first developed and revised the Scale of Market Demand for Taekwondo schools by conducting both qualitative and quantitative studies. Then, the researchers followed the concept of the Yale Attitude Change Model (Hovland, Janis and Kelley, 1953; Zimbardo, Ebbesen and Maslach, 1977), which explains that human attitudes (the affective component) are usually influenced or changed by altering the opinions or beliefs of people (the cognitive or knowledge component) and, in turn, can be a powerful driving force that impacts consumer behaviour (Fazio, Powell and Williams, 1989). The researchers were able to use this theory to examine the structural relationships of market demand factors to member satisfaction and commitment factors of Taekwondo schools. Testing the proposed structural model revealed good fit of the model to the data, and the market demand factors were found to have positive effects on member satisfaction and member commitment. Member satisfaction also had a positive influence on member commitment. The market demand factors directly and indirectly affected member commitment and all direct and indirect paths were statistically significant. The indirect effect was substantially larger than the magnitude of the direct effect, indicating that the addition of member satisfaction as a mediating construct to the direct effect enhanced the predictive power of the market demand factors on member commitment.

Closing remarks

In addition to guiding the formulation of the research question, measurement, design, procedures and, the ever-important, testing of the relationships among concepts, theory and related empirical findings derived from previous research investigations should serve as the focal point in the discussion section of a research report. In this process, a number of key questions need to be answered, including but not limited to the following: (a) how consistent or different the research findings are in the current study from the stated theory and those of related previous studies; (b) what reasonable explanations are for the identified consistence or difference; (c) how the findings of the current study contribute to the confirmation, strengthening, addition, modification or even rejection of the theory; and (d) how the findings of the current study provide implications for the application of the stated theory.

In sport management studies, theories developed in mainstream business administration and social psychological studies are often adopted. Sometimes, due to a lack of empirical evidence for the applicability of these theories or inter-concept relationships in specific segments of sport organisations, a co-ordinated theoretical framework is developed to guide the research investigation. Even so, earlier discussions on the relevance and importance of theory in quantitative and mixed-method studies would be equally pertinent to these situations.

All in all, theory plays a pivotal role in quantitative or mixed-method studies. It is prevalent in every step of a research investigation and is in every part of a research report. After all, the advancement, confirmation or rejection of theory is one of the main goals of research. Nonetheless, challenging tasks remain for sport management scholars, the least of which include the following two perspectives: (a) how to best apply and interpret general business administration and social psychology theories in specific sport management settings; and (b) how to best, thoroughly and unambiguously, develop theories in specific sport management settings and make them generalisable within or beyond a larger realm of the sport industry.

References

Aiken, L.R. (1985) 'Three coefficients for analyzing the reliability and validity of ratings'. *Educational & Psychological Measurement*, 45: 131–42.

Aiken, L.R. (1996) *Rating scales and checklists: Evaluating behavior, personality, and attitude.* New York: Wiley.

Ajzen, I. (1985) 'From intentions to actions: A theory of planned behavior'. In J. Kuhl and J. Beckmann (eds), *Action control: From cognition to behavior* (pp. 11–39). New York: Springer-Verlag.

Ajzen, I. and Fishbein, M. (1980) *Understanding attitudes and predicting social behavior.* Englewood Cliffs, NJ: Prentice-Hall.

Bagozzi, R.P. and Burnkrant, R.E. (1985) 'Attitude organization and the attitude-behavior relation: A reply to Dilon and Kumar'. *Journal of Personality & Social Psychology*, 49: 47–57.

Baumgartner, T.A. and Hensley, L.D. (2012) *Conducting and reading research in health and human performance* (fourth edn). Boston, TX: McGraw-Hill.

Baumgartner, T.A., Jackson, A.S., Mahar, M.T. and Rowe, D.A. (2006) *Measurement and evaluation in physical education and exercise science* (eighth edn). Boston, MA: McGraw-Hill.

Braunstein, J.R., Zhang, J.J. and Trail, G.T. (2011) 'Athlete endorser effectiveness: Model development and analysis'. *Sport, Business & Management*, 1(1): 93–114.

Bryman, A. (2007) 'Barriers to integrating quantitative and qualitative research'. *Journal of Mixed Methods Research*, 1: 8–22.

Byon, K.K. and Zhang, J.J. (2010) 'Development of a scale measuring destination image: Sport tourist perspective'. *Marketing Intelligence & Planning*, 28(4): 508–32.

Byon, K.K., Zhang, J.J. and Connaughton, D.P. (2010) 'Dimensions of general market demand associated with professional team sports: Development of a scale'. *Sport Management Review*, 13(2): 142–57.

Chalip, L. (2006) 'Toward a distinctive discipline'. *Journal of Sport Management*, 20: 1–21.

Chelladurai, P. (1992) 'Sport management opportunities and obstacles'. *Journal of Sport Management*, 6: 215–19.

Chen, K.K. and Zhang, J.J. (2011) 'Examining consumer attributes associated with collegiate athletic facility naming rights sponsorship: Development of a theoretical framework'. *Sport Management Review*, 14: 103–16.

Chen, K.K. and Zhang, J.J. (2012) 'To name it or not? Consumer perspectives of collegiate athletic facility naming rights sponsorship'. *Journal of Issues in Intercollegiate Athletics*, 5: 119–48.

Cianfrone, B.A. and Zhang, J.J. (2006) 'Differential effects of television commercials, athlete endorsements, and event sponsorships during a televised action sports event'. *Journal of Sport Management*, 20: 321–43.

Cianfrone, B.A., Zhang, J.J. and Ko, Y.J. (2011) 'Dimensions of motivation associated with playing sport video games: Modification and extension of the sport video game motivation scale'. *Sport, Business & Management*, 1(2): 172–89.

Cianfrone, B.A., Zhang, J.J., Lutz, R.J. and Trail, G.T. (2008) 'Effectiveness of sponsorships in sport video games: An experimental inquiry on current gamers'. *International Journal of Sport Communication*, 1: 195–218.

Costa, C.A. (2005) 'The status and future of sport management: A Delphi study'. *Journal of Sport Management*, 19: 117–42.

Creswell, J.W. (2003) *Research design qualitative, quantitative, and mixed methods approaches* (second edn). Thousand Oaks, CA: Sage.

Cunningham, G.B. (2013) 'Theory and theory development in sport management'. *Sport Management Review*, 16: 1–4.

Cunningham, G.B., Ferreira, M. and Fink, J.S. (2009) 'Reactions to prejudicial statements: The influence of statement'. *Group Dynamics: Theory, Research, & Practice*, 13: 59–73.

Doherty, A. (2012) ' "It takes a village:" Interdisciplinary research for sport management'. *Journal of Sport Management*, 26: 1–10.

Doherty, A. (2013) 'Investing in sport management: The value of good theory'. *Sport Management Review*, 16: 5–11.

Dunn, J.G., Bouffard, M. and Rogers, W.T. (1999) 'Assessing item content-relevance in sport psychology scale construction research: Issues and recommendations'. *Measurement in Physical Education & Exercise Science*, 3: 15–36.

Fazio, R.H., Powell, M.C. and Williams, C.J. (1989) 'The role of attitude accessibility in the attitude-to-behavior process'. *Journal of Consumer Research*, 16: 280–8.

Fishbein, M. and Ajzen, I. (1975) *Belief, attitude, intention, and behavior: An introduction to theory and research*. Reading, MA: Addison-Wesley.

Gibson, H., Qi, C.X. and Zhang, J.J. (2008) 'Destination image and intent to visit China, and the 2008 Beijing Olympic Games'. *Journal of Sport Management*, 22: 427–50.

Hovland, C., Janis, I.L. and Kelley, H.H. (1953) *Communication and persuasion: Psychological studies of opinion change*. New Haven, CT: Yale University.

Jin, L., Zhang, J.J., Ma, X. and Connaughton, D.P. (2011) 'Residents' perceptions of environmental impacts of the 2008 Beijing Green Olympic Games'. *European Sport Management Quarterly*, 11: 275–300.

Kahle, L.R. and Homer, P.M. (1985) 'Physical attractiveness of celebrity endorser: A social adaptation perspective'. *Journal of Consumer Research*, 11: 954–61.

Kamins, M.A. (1989) 'Celebrity and non-celebrity advertising in a two-sided context'. *Journal of Advertising Research*, 29(3): 34–42.

Kamins, M.A. (1990) 'An investigation into the match-up-hypothesis in celebrity advertising: When beauty be only skin deep'. *Journal of Advertising*, 19(1): 4–13.

Katz, E., Blumler, J.G. and Gurevitch, M. (1974) 'U & G research'. *The Public Opinion Quarterly*, 37: 509–23.

Keller, K.L. (1993) 'Conceptualizing, measuring, and managing customer-based brand equity'. *Journal of Marketing*, 57(1): 1–22.

Kerlinger, F.N. (1973) *Foundations of behavioral research: Educational, psychological and sociological inquiry* (second edn). New York: Holt Rinehart & Winston.

Kim, M.K., Zhang, J.J. and Ko, Y.J. (2009) 'Dimensions of market demand associated with Taekwondo schools in North America: Development of a scale'. *Sport Management Review*, 12: 149–66.

Kim, M.K., Zhang, J.J., Jackson, E.N., Connaughton, D.P. and Kim, M. (2013) 'Modification and revision of the Scale of Market Demand for Taekwondo'. *Measurement in Physical Education & Exercise Science*, 17: 187–207.

Kim, Y. and Ross, S. (2006) 'An exploration of motives in sport video gaming'. *International Journal of Sport Marketing & Sponsorship*, 8(1): 34–46.

Lavidge, R.J. and Steiner, G.A. (1961) 'A model for predictive measurements of advertising effectiveness'. *Journal of Marketing*, 25(6): 59–62.

Madrigal, R. (2001) 'Social identity effects in a belief-attitude-intentions hierarchy: Implications for corporate sponsorship'. *Psychology & Marketing*, 18(2): 145–65.

Mason, D.S. (1999) 'What is the sports product and who buys it? The marketing of professional sports leagues'. *European Journal of Marketing*, 33: 402–18.

Messick, S. (1989) 'Validity'. In R.L. Linn (ed.), *Educational measurement* (third edn, pp. 13–103). New York: American Council on Education.

Mullin, B.J., Hardy, S. and Sutton, W.A. (2014) *Sport marketing* (fourth edn). Champaign, IL: Human Kinetics.

Newman, I. and Benz, C.R. (1998) *Qualitative-quantitative research methodology: Exploring the interactive continuum*. Carbondale, IL: University of Illinois.

Oliver, R.L. (1997) *Satisfaction: A behavioral perspective on the consumer*. New York: Irwin/McGraw-Hill.

Pease, D.G. and Zhang, J.J. (2001) 'Socio-motivational factors affecting spectator attendance at professional basketball games'. *International Journal of Sport Management*, 2: 31–59.

Pitts, B.G. and Stotlar, D.K. (2012) *Fundamentals of sport marketing* (fourth edn). Morgantown, WV: Fitness Information Technology.

Rohm, A.J., Milne, G.R. and McDonald, M.A. (2006) 'A mixed-method approach for developing market segmentation typologies in the sports industry'. *Sport Marketing Quarterly*, 15: 29–39.

Rudd, A. and Johnson, R.B. (2010) 'A call for more mixed methods in sport management research'. *Sport Management Review*, 13: 14–24.

Schofield, J.A. (1983) 'Performance and attendance at professional team sports'. *Journal of Sport Behavior*, 6: 196–206.

Slack, T. (1996) 'From the locker room to the board room: Changing the domain of sport management'. *Journal of Sport Management*, 10: 97–105.

Sloan, L.R. (1989) 'The motives of sports fans'. In J.H. Goldstein (ed.), *Sports, games, and play: Social and psychological viewpoints* (second edn) (pp. 175–240). Hillsdale, NJ: Lawrence Erlbaum.

Smith, A.C.T. and Stewart, B. (2010) 'The special features of sport: A critical revisit'. *Sport Management Review*, 13: 1–13.

Strauss, A. and Corbin, J. (1998) *Basics of qualitative research: Techniques and procedures for developing grounded theory* (second edn). Thousand Oaks, CA: Sage.

Stryker, S. and Burke, P.J. (2000) 'The past, present and future of identity theory'. *Social Psychology Quarterly*, 63: 284–97.

Sutton, R.I. and Staw, B.M. (1995) 'What theory is not'. *Administrative Science Quarterly*, 40: 371–84.

Tajfel, H. and Turner, J. (1979) 'An integrative theory of intergroup conflict'. In W. Austin and S. Worchel (eds), *The social psychology of intergroup relations* (pp. 33–47). Monterey, CA: Brooks/Cole.

Thomas, J.R., Nelson, J.K. and Silverman, S. (2011) *Research methods in physical activity* (sixth edn). Urbana-Champaign, IL: Human Kinetics.

Trail, G.T. and James, J. (2001) 'The Motivation Scale for Sport Consumption: Assessment of the scale's psychometric properties'. *Journal of Sport Behavior*, 24: 108–27.

Trail, G.T., Fink, J.S. and Anderson, D.F. (2003) 'Sport spectator consumption behavior'. *Sport Marketing Quarterly*, 12: 8–17.

Trail, G.T., Robinson, M.J., Dick, R.J. and Gillentine, A.I. (2003) 'Motives and points of attachment: Fans versus spectators in intercollegiate athletics'. *Sport Marketing Quarterly*, 12: 217–27.

Wacker, J.G. (1998) 'A definition of theory: Research guidelines for different theory-building research methods in operations management'. *Journal of Operations Management*, 16: 361–85.

Wann, D.L. and Branscombe, N.R. (1993) 'Sports fans: Measuring degree of identification with their team'. *International Journal of Sport Psychology*, 24: 1–17.

Wann, D.L. and Branscombe, N.R. (1995) 'Influence of identification with a sports team on objective knowledge and subjective beliefs'. *International Journal of Sport Psychology*, *26*(4): 551–67.

Wood, T.M. (1989) 'The changing nature of norm-referenced validity'. In M.J. Safrit and T.M. Wood (eds), *Measurement concepts in physical education and exercise science* (pp. 23–44). Champaign, IL: Human Kinetics.

Zhang, J.J. (2015) 'What to study? That is a question: A conscious thought analysis'. *Journal of Sport Management*, *29*: 1–10.

Zhang, J.J., Connaughton, D.P., Byrd, C.E., Cianfrone, B.A., Byon, K.W. and Kim, D.H. (2007) 'Formulating a questionnaire for marketing studies of professional basketball game attendance: A review of literature'. In J. James (ed.), *Sport marketing in the new millennium* (pp. 193–212). Morgantown, WV: Fitness Information Technology.

Zhang, J.J., Lam, E.T.C., Bennett, G. and Connaughton, D.P. (2003) 'Confirmatory Factor Analysis of the Spectator Decision Making Inventory (SDMI)'. *Measurement in Physical Education & Exercise Science*, *7*(2): 57–70.

Zhang, J.J., Lam, E.T.C. and Connaughton, D.C. (2003) 'General market demand variables associated with professional sport consumption'. *International Journal of Sport Marketing & Sponsorship*, *5*(1): 33–55.

Zhang, J.J., Lam, E.T.C. and Williamson, D.P. (2002, May) *Contemporary approach for examining validity and reliability of scales in sport management.* Paper presented at North American Society for Sport Management Annual Conference, Canmore, Canada.

Zhang, J.J., Pease, D.G., Hui, S.C. and Michaud, T.J. (1995) 'Variables affecting the spectator decision to attend NBA games'. *Sport Marketing Quarterly*, *4*(4): 29–39.

Zillmann, D. and Paulus, P.B. (1993) 'Spectators: Reactions to sports events and effect on athletic performance'. In R.N. Singer, M. Murphey and L.K. Tennant (eds), *Handbook of research on sport psychology* (pp. 600–19). New York: McMillan.

Zima, P.V. (2007) *What is theory? Cultural theory as discourse and dialogue.* London: Continuum.

Zimbardo, P.G., Ebbesen, E.B. and Maslach, C. (1977) *Influencing attitudes and changing behavior: An introduction to method, theory and applications of social control and personal power* (second edn). Boston: Addison-Wesley.

3

IMPORTANCE OF THEORY IN QUALITATIVE ENQUIRY

Sally Shaw

Introduction

When I was asked to write this chapter my immediate reaction was, 'what a strange request'. Surely we all know why theory is important and why it is central to academic research. It is, as I often tell my students, the difference between a chat in the pub and an academic discussion. There have been many debates and special issues on this exact question, most recently in *Sport Management Review* in 2013. So, I thought, why have this conversation when the importance of theory is fundamental, discussion over, job done?

Reflection is a wonderful thing. Once I'd had a chance to think about the editors' request, some ideas began to percolate. The question changed a little in my mind, to 'why is it that we need to keep this conversation about theory in sport management going?' and 'what can that conversation offer us?' My perspective changed, revealing a desire not just to answer the question 'why is theory important?' but also what can theory offer us in our quest to do better research with outcomes that are connected to our field of practice, and that stretches us beyond our normal range of intellectual engagement in sport management? What is theory's *capacity* within qualitative approaches to sport management and how can we harness and develop that capacity?

There is no doubt in my mind that we need to use theory to challenge ourselves to engage better with the raft of methodological opportunities open to us. Qualitative researchers in sport management rely heavily on case studies, usually formed through semi-structured interviews and focus groups. Such research has taken us to a certain level of knowledge but we can go further. With this in mind, I will attempt to examine the following in this chapter. First, while reluctant to get mired in the 'what is theory?' question, I will provide a brief outline of my perspective on theory for the purpose of this chapter, along with an overview of recent sport management research using qualitative research. I will then discuss the purpose of theory in qualitative research and the potential for developing its capacity. In the final section, I will unpack my crystal ball and outline a utopian future of research, in which multiple theoretical and methodological approaches are interlinked in sport management research, regardless of qualitative or quantitative approaches.

A perspective on theory in sport management

I stand by my comment above that theory is what differentiates a chat about sport in the pub or the coffee bar from an academic discussion. This is hardly an academic definition but it allows us to start to put the argument together that theory is something different from the everyday. We know that we are not just describing when we engage in theory; rather, we are analysing or examining something that we find interesting in sport (Doherty, 2013). Simply, it 'explains how things work and why' (Doherty, 2013, p. 5). So far, so good. I start to diverge from both Cunningham's (2013) and Doherty's (2013) definitions of theory, however, when the discussion turns to testing. Testing implies an objective measure. This is impossible in qualitative research, as its job is to describe, analyse and explain. This process is undertaken by researchers interpreting participants' experiences, whether through interviews, focus groups, ethnographic or auto-ethnographic engagement, pictorial analysis or a myriad of other methods. This may sound subjective, because it is. Contrary to the claims of many graduate students and faculty, this subjective process is not a limitation of the research; rather, it is a feature of qualitative research. We look for similarities and differences between themes and compare them with our chosen theory, not relationships among variables. We paint a picture of a social phenomenon to the best of our abilities, guided by the rigours of our research paradigm.

If not used for testing, then what is good theory in the realms of qualitative research? Doherty (2013) lists three characteristics of theory: the foundation of research, of teaching and of practice. I agree, in part, as theory is at the forefront of everything researchers do. Where I disagree is with the word *foundation*. Yes, theory is a key, integral part of qualitative research but is it the foundation, or is it something that is woven into the research as we progress? Do we need to identify our theoretical position before we start research and use it as an unshakeable foundation, or can we use theory more flexibly? Fink (2013) discusses her approach to theory, which involves finding out about the context of the topic being researched and then investigating what theories might be useful in analysing the topic. She outlines how the topics she has researched have been those that sustain her interest, not necessarily the most 'fundable' (Fink, 2013). I extend this again, and say that by having a solid knowledge about the research context before deciding what theory to use to analyse it encourages not only personal motivation but avoids a slavish adherence to one theory over others, when a previously unused theory, or combination of theories, might be more appropriate (Barbour, 2001). I argue that a stronger position is to choose a topic then examine theories to see which ones usefully explain it. We are not searching for *the* theory, rather one or many that may help us to understand a little bit more than we did.

To summarise, my position on theory in qualitative research is as follows. It makes us think in a different way from how we might in a casual conversation (Frisby, Maguire and Reid, 2009). It helps to explain social phenomena within sport management. It sets a rigorous framework through which we can examine similarities and differences between themes within our research. And finally, it is integral to the development of academic research: not only as a foundation, but as a feature that is woven in throughout the research. As with any weaving, there may be mistakes, changes of pattern or colour, or unpicking in order to create the pattern as clearly as we can. Theory gives us the opportunity to create a pattern, with the freedom to reflect as accurately as we can the vagaries and contradictions of our participants' stories.

Theory and qualitative research in sport management

From 2011–13, twenty-eight articles using qualitative research were published in *Sport Management Review*, thirty-five in the *Journal of Sport Management* and seventeen in *European*

Sport Management Quarterly. These figures represent a healthy engagement in qualitative research, in part due to the calls for such research by Amis and Silk (2005), Frisby (2005) and others, as well as a broader recognition of the value of qualitative research.

Multiple theoretical approaches were used in these articles, ranging from grounded theory (Warner and Dixon, 2011), gender theory (Hardin and Whiteside, 2012), resource dependency (Morrow and Robinson, 2013) and capacity theory (Casey, Payne and Eime, 2012), to name a few. How these theories were used differed, which raises an interesting point regarding the use of theory in qualitative research. For some (e.g., Fairley and Tyler, 2012), theory is distinct from method; that is, the theory is presented and the methods outlined but the connections between those sections, and in turn the discussion, are not fully articulated. For others (e.g., Spaaij, 2012), the theoretical framework is integrated into the method and discussion, an approach that I will expand on shortly.

I favour this latter approach as a reviewer and in my own research. A long time ago, my PhD supervisor, Professor Trevor Slack, told me that theory should be used as a framework (hence the term theoretical framework) for the whole project. As I have noted above, this theoretical approach does not need to be firmly decided at the start of the project. Indeed, a theoretical approach may change as the project progresses and its focus shifts. The theory we thought would help us answer our questions may not do so fully, so we may shift our focus into a complementary theoretical approach. For example, when I was writing my dissertation, I thought that a traditional gender theory would suffice for examining questions about gender relations in sport organisations. As I progressed, I realised that it would, to a point. If I wanted to explore the nuances of gender relations, however, and get into the murkiness of multiple masculinities and femininities, then I would need something more subtle. That is why I turned to discourse analysis. If we take this tack as scholars, it should be documented and explained, presenting an honest, consistent picture of our engagement with theory.

The purpose of a theoretical framework

In this section, I provide an overview of a theoretical framework's utility. A project's theoretical framework does three things for qualitative researchers: it integrates and strengthens methodological choices; it gives us rigour and close distance from our work; and it allows us to compare our work with others.[1]

Methodological choices

At the beginning of the chapter, I suggested that theory is the difference between a chat in the pub and an academic opinion. Qualitative research is a process underpinned by personal choices based on gender, class, race, sexuality, culture and ethnicity, among other individual differences. Those personal choices include choice about theory and its relationship to method, or the tools we use to undertake our research. While method refers to the tools used to collect data, methodology is interwoven with theory, and the term is used by qualitative researchers to indicate a tight, symbiotic relationship (Denzin and Lincoln, 2000). For example, research on gender relations in sport organisations might be undertaken using a discourse analysis approach informed by feminism. It would be impossible to pull apart where the theory of feminism ended and the practice of discourse analysis started because feminism is integral to discourse analysis in this case.

It is therefore almost impossible to differentiate between theory and method. Discourse analysis, for example, is a methodology that is intrinsically bound to ideas of power. Yet it is also a method and analytical tool. It allows researchers to bring their own political positions to research as well as a focus on the discourses that influence and are influenced by participants. Discourse analysis represents a framework that articulates power relations, examines them and possibly suggests alternative practices. Researchers who have used such an approach effectively include Annalies Knoppers and Anton Anthonissen. In particular, their work on gender in sport organisations has frequently asked different questions about women's and men's positions in those organisations (Knoppers and Anthonissen, 2008). For researchers such as Knoppers and Anthonissen, discourse analysis, with power at its centre, provides a platform on which they can acknowledge their career-long commitment to understanding gender and organisations.

The discourse analysis framework challenges researchers too, because power comes in multiple, complex and conflicting forms (Foucault, 1979). Researchers using this approach must recognise that the power dynamics and relationships that they observe may not always fit with what they believe or expect. For example, gender is not straightforward, and although we may expect men to have the upper hand in most sport organisations, there are other social dimensions, such as race, sexuality, disability and class (Frisby, 2011), and structural dimensions, such as funding, sponsorship appeal or policy decisions, which may ensure that men are marginalised within their organisations (Kihl, Shaw and Schull, 2013). Theory, in this case discourse analysis, makes us think about our choices of method and analysis, challenge ourselves and recognise and value the times when our research doesn't quite fit the way we thought it might.

Rigour and theory

In qualitative research, methodology's unique relationship between theory and method enables rigorous research. Rigour is often confused with objectivity and validity, which have little bearing in qualitative research. Qualitative researchers cannot claim objectivity or validity because 'we have no direct knowledge of our accounts and thus no independent entity to which to compare these accounts' (Maxwell, 1992, p. 283). Our research cannot be validated against an objective measure because there isn't one. Importantly, we shouldn't go looking for one. Some qualitative researchers will try to reproduce quantitative procedures by having independent researchers outside the interviewing team check their coding or thematic development. This is a pointless exercise because the purpose of qualitative research is to represent what was said or done in data collection as accurately as possible. If an independent expert was not present at the data collection, they cannot validate the findings. The only people who can come close to validating anything are the participants themselves, and even their accounts may change over time. We need to accept this and not force our data into non-existent validity.

What qualitative researchers can do, however, is ensure descriptive rigour; that is, compare one participant's experiences against another, take field notes to ensure that context is clear, and have the participants read transcripts for accuracy. Where there is disconnect or disagreement, they can comment on this as a feature of an individual's recollections of events. This is a subjective process and researchers recognise that subjectivity in the form of individuals' experiences (whether they are participants or the researchers) will influence a project. How else can we be interested, passionate, enthused or sometimes disillusioned or bored by our research? Why else would participants agree to be part of our research unless they had some personal or related interest? Acknowledging subjectivity, and working with it, is a strength of qualitative research.

This is where the use of theory becomes vital. Theory means that the research process is not a 'free for all' of opinions, ideas and agendas. Indeed, qualitative researchers need to be acutely aware of their position as researchers in order to conduct rigorous research, so that their 'personal baggage [that is] emotional, political and intellectual positioning' (Knowles, 2006, p. 403) is acknowledged and worked into the research but does not take it over.

A notable example of this is Hoeber and Kerwin's (2013) self-ethnography as female sport fans. The authors diligently present their position as researchers and fans as they investigated the phenomenon of female sport fans. Hoeber and Kerwin have multiple identities – as women, sport fans, critical researchers, wives and sisters. They argue that their identities put them in an enviable position to research female sport fandom (Hoeber and Kerwin, 2013). Their methodology was a narrative construction informed by theories of hegemonic masculinity. Hoeber and Kerwin shared their experiences, journals and thoughts with each other and opened themselves to mutual, theoretically informed critique. These processes gave the research rigour and credibility.

An area of particular interest with Hoeber and Kerwin's work is the analysis of voice. Widening the discussion, White and Drew (2011) have described the pitfalls and difficulties of dealing with voice in qualitative research. They outline the dangers of the 'romantic or literal notion of voice and tak[ing] at face value stories that are told by research participants. Here, voice and story are hived off as providing some sort of special truth rather than being subject to critical research analysis' (White and Drew, 2011, p. 5). They highlight the importance of understanding the researchers' role in creating knowledge by the questions they ask (or don't), the topics that they choose at the start of the research, and the prompts and follow-up questions that they choose. Knowledge in qualitative research is not some single truth that is out there to be harvested. As researchers, we commit time and energy to shaping the kinds of knowledge that we expect and want to hear.

Qualitative researchers need to be able to examine and reflect on that process. White and Drew (2011) openly describe that they were 'plagued by doubt and methodological unease' (p. 3) as they began their study on young people's social connectedness. What held them together, gave them confidence in their process and ultimately decided the success of the project was their commitment to a communal, reflective, critical theoretical framework to determine their approach to analyse voice. They did not strive to develop procedures to validate their data. Rather, their use of theory supported Maxwell's (1992) argument. In this, Maxwell calls for the development of rigour 'of an account as inherent, not in the procedures used to produce and validate it, but in its relationships to those things that it is intended to be an account *of*' (Maxwell, 1992, p. 281). If qualitative research is to be accurate in its representation of data, then we are better served by ensuring our data represent participants' views and analyse them with relation to theory, rather than testing them against arbitrary measures of reliability that have little to do with the context of our research.

Close distance and theory

It is not only researchers who benefit from theory in qualitative research. Much qualitative research has a critical, or even emancipatory, focus. It is conducted with participants who may see some value to changing their social, cultural or political position. There is some danger that researchers become so involved in such work that they lose the academic distance needed to ensure rigour. I call the protection of that distance, while recognising personal, political and social interest and connection to the research, close distance. A good example of this in sport research is Frisby, Reid, Millar and Hoeber's (2005) and Frisby's (2011) work with women on low incomes and immigrant women's access to leisure. In both studies, Frisby and her team used a methodology informed by a feminist participatory action framework. While personally and politically engaged in the work, feminist theory informed the methodology that enabled the researchers to work towards describing some common themes with their participants and also to recognise their own personal stance in the research (Frisby *et al.*, 2005). Moreover, a feminist-informed participatory action framework ensured that the participants were involved in a partnership between the 'people with problems to solve, the researchers, and those who control public services' (Frisby *et al.*, 2005, p. 370). Feminist theory provided a framework for participants and researchers alike. Participants were intrinsically involved in the project, giving it more meaning for them and working towards their goals. Similarly, in her work with immigrant women, Frisby (2011) created a project using feminist informed participatory action research, in which those women set the research agenda with a view to influencing policy. Theory, in these two cases, was used to provide a close distance to the research: recognising the connectedness and politicality of, and researchers' closeness to, research but not allowing those features to swamp its rigour.

Comparing our research with others'

Our research does not stand alone and the pattern that we weave as we undertake our research needs to be able to be compared with other patterns, however disharmonious we think that may look. This is not generalisability. Qualitative research does not normally seek to generalise to a wider population; rather, it focuses on individuals' expressions of their experiences in a given time frame. The use of theory does allow us to make comparisons across different projects and paradigms. Williams (2004) has argued that if we acknowledge the potential for limited comparisons, we may be able to expand the utility of qualitative research, by creating a larger picture of our topic. He has argued for a much more open discussion about generalisability in qualitative research, stating 'it is rather like the attitude of the Victorian middle class to sex. They do it, they know it goes on, but they rarely admit to either' (Williams, 2004, p. 210). If we do admit to it, we may be able to engage in a process that Williams (2004) has dubbed 'moderatum generalization', or moderate generalisation through qualitative research. These generalisations depend on two features: the cultural and social similarities of the phenomenon being investigated (e.g., funding of non-profit sport organisations in Commonwealth countries) and ontological similarities. These generalisations (and I'm not sure I agree with them being called generalisations, preferring the term comparisons) can only ever be moderate, they may well change, and they cannot be considered long term (Williams, 2004).

Fairweather and Rime (2012) have extended Williams' concept, arguing that cultural modelling may provide an avenue for generalisation in qualitative research. They suggest that research that analyses discourses that are evident in 'taken-for-granted models of knowledge and thought that are used in the course of everyday life to guide a person's understanding of the world and their behaviour' (Fairweather and Rime, 2012, p. 478) may be open to comparison and generalisability with similar projects. Unhelpfully, however, they then note that 'in contexts in which such a claim is likely to be contested it may be necessary to provide additional analysis to support such claims' (p. 478).

I find Williams' (2004) and Fairweather and Rime's (2012) arguments fairly limited. They shy away from showing how the complex, political, subjective world of qualitative work can be improved by *moderatum generalization*. What they do show is a willingness to engage in the discussion regarding generalisation, which seems to be missing from qualitative research. I think that there is an added element to their ideas, which is the consistency of a theoretical approach. If the theories used in a variety of research projects are justifiably compatible, then it makes sense to me that some limited form of generalisation or comparison *might* be possible in qualitative research. Conceptualising this approach and working towards achieving it may be one way to push this conversation forward.

In this section, I have outlined the usefulness of theory in contemporary qualitative research. Drawing on sport management and wider literature, I have shown how theory demands rigour and encourages us to define our close distance. It also allows us to compare our work with similar others. The arguments of Williams (2004) and Fairweather and Rime (2012) provide thought-provoking suggestions regarding the moderate generalisability of qualitative research. I see merit in this direction because it codifies what many of us already do; for example, making research-based suggestions for change is a form of generalisation. Their arguments are not yet fully developed, though, and I would like to see more engagement in theory's place in this moderate generalisation. Finally, understanding theory as a tool by which we can rigorously interrogate our methodological choices and critique our own position is central to the enhancement of our choices regarding methods in qualitative research.

The crystal ball moment: theory and qualitative research in twenty years' time!

To go forward, we need to move into a more imaginative, engaged and reflective space. Others in this book may argue that we need to develop sport-specific theory to investigate our field. Personally, I do not agree with this perspective. I think that while sport management has some unique factors – for example, the passion for a sport that often overrides normal business-making processes – it shares more similarities than differences with other organisations in the commercial, public and non-profit sectors.

So, I believe that we should utilise the theories that serve other disciplines well and adapt them when necessary for sport. For example, Hoeber and Kerwin's (2013) and Kodama, Doherty and Popovic's (2013) engagement with autoethnography as a theoretically informed methodology achieves this. Autoethnography is a well-established methodology. It allows authors to reflect on their position as a participant and observer; in these cases, as a fan or a volunteer (Hoeber and Kerwin, 2013; Kodama *et al.*, 2013). It enables the research to account for the things that are often positioned as special in sport (Chalip, 2006); in this case, fandom and volunteering. There may, of course, be limits in how well some theories stand up to the application to sport, but that is how we create new theoretical knowledge: by identifying those limits and discovering where our research takes us as we try to investigate them. Is sport special? Yes, but only in the same way that other distinct organisational fields are special, too.

My point here is that if we spend too much time debating the specialness of sport and devising tricky ways to produce new theories, then we run the risk of chasing down false alleyways. To butcher a familiar metaphor: rather than the narrative (statistical) tail wagging of the conceptual dog, we may spend time and energy breeding a new type of designer conceptual dog that looks attractive but achieves little more than its old mongrel cousin.

The question that should drive the future of sport management research is not, 'how can we develop theories to best understand our world?' but, 'what are the problems we are trying to examine?' and 'whose interests are served by our research?'. If we recognise that we are trying to examine problems that are of value to people working in sport, then the development of theory for theory's sake becomes much less important than developing existing theories to better suit our research task. Theory may well develop as a result of this, but theoretical development is not the purpose of our research.

So, what are the theoretical approaches and methodologies with which we can we start? Critical Theory ensures that we examine, critique and offer alternatives to organisational norms

(Alvesson and Willmott, 1992). Post-structuralism critiques the very discourses, power relations and paradigms on which we base our assumptions about organisational life (Knoppers and Anthonissen, 2008). Hegemony examines power relations, specifically those of influential groups. These are only three approaches among many, that are highly critical of the norms of organisational life, and which lend themselves to the use of qualitative methods. They have all been used to some degree within sport management but none have been fully played out to see what the outcomes of their approach might be. For example, Frisby and I asked whether 'gender equity could be more equitable' (Shaw and Frisby, 2006, p. 483) and presented a fourth frame for putting critiques of gender relations into practice in sport organisations. Yet there has been no follow up regarding what that practice might look like. This is but one example of a good idea not pushing through to see whether it works in practice. In twenty years' time, I would like to see this sort of project becoming commonplace.

Such a movement requires input from more than some interested academics. This research requires acceptance from organisations, whether the NCAA or governmental organisations such as Sport New Zealand, Sport England, The Australian Sport Commission or Sport Canada. Many of us know from previous experience that obtaining this sort of support can be problematic and political (McKay, 1997). Yet, change is possible. That change, though, must start with us; sport management scholars from all sides of the argument. If our research is going to be useful, then we need to work together to promote that research widely. There will always be paradigmatic and philosophical differences between and within qualitative and quantitative research groups. The debate is a useful one, pushing both sides to reflect on the rigour and applicability of their respective research. Stalling on this argument, however, does not benefit anyone and certainly does not progress our field.

At the beginning of this chapter, I asked what theory's capacity was to develop qualitative research. A way of moving forward on this discussion (and bringing this chapter full cycle) is to go back once again to the analogy of theory being the difference between a casual conversation and academic endeavour. Qualitative researchers have a responsibility to ensure that our use of theory is as rigorous and informed as possible. In short, it helps us to do good research. Good research is not looking for praise for copying our quantitatively orientated colleagues and claiming authenticity for using procedures that have nothing to do with qualitative approaches. It is about using theory to create an argument that informs our methodology and analysis, and working with theory to ensure that we represent our data as thoroughly as possible. Working with our colleagues across the spectrum of sport management, we can support research that makes a difference using theoretically informed methods, whether they are qualitative or quantitative. By embracing difference in theories that challenge our research norms, we can stretch our boundaries and increase the relevance of our research. That is what I would like to see in twenty years' time, and that is why I think theory is important to qualitative research.

References

Alvesson, M. and Willmott, H. (eds) (1992) *Critical management studies*. London: Sage.

Amis, J. and Silk, M. (2005) 'Rupture: Promoting critical and innovative approaches to the study of sport management'. *Journal of Sport Management, 19*: 355–66.

Barbour, R.S. (2001) 'Checklists for improving rigour in qualitative research: A case of the tail wagging the dog?' *British Medical Journal, 322*: 1115–17.

Casey, M.M., Payne, W.R. and Eime, R.M. (2012) 'Organisational readiness and capacity building strategies of sporting organisations to promote health'. *Sport Management Review, 15*: 109–24.

Chalip, L. (2006) 'Toward a distinctive sport management discipline'. *Journal of Sport Management, 20*: 1–21.

Cunningham, G.B. (2013) 'Theory and theory development in sport management'. *Sport Management Review*, *16*: 1–4.

Denzin, N.K. and Lincoln, Y.S. (eds) (2000) *Handbook of qualitative research* (second edn). Thousand Oaks, CA: Sage Publications.

Doherty, A.J. (2013) 'Investing in sport management: The value of good theory'. *Sport Management Review*, *16*: 5–11.

Fairley, S. and Tyler, B.D. (2012) 'Bringing baseball to the big screen: Building sense of community outside of the ballpark'. *Journal of Sport Management*, *26*: 258–70.

Fairweather, J. and Rime, T. (2012) 'Clarifying a basis for qualitative generalization using approaches that identify shared culture'. *Qualitative Research*, *12*: 473–85.

Fink, J.S. (2013) 'Theory development in sport management: My experience and other considerations'. *Sport Management Review*, *16*: 17–21.

Foucault, M. (1979) *The will to knowledge: The history of sexuality, volume 1* (R. Hurley, trans.). London: Penguin.

Frisby, W. (2005) 'The good, the bad, and the ugly: Critical sport management research'. *Journal of Sport Management*, *19*: 1–12.

Frisby, W. (2011) 'Promising physical activity inclusion practices for Chinese immigrant women in Vancouver, Canada'. *Quest*, *63*: 135–47.

Frisby, W., Maguire, P. and Reid, C. (2009) 'The 'f' word has everything to do with it: How feminist theories inform action research'. *Action Research*, *7*: 13–29.

Frisby, W., Reid, C., Millar, S. and Hoeber, L. (2005) 'Putting "participatory" into participatory forms of action research'. *Journal of Sport Management*, *19*: 367.

Hardin, M. and Whiteside, E. (2012) 'Consequences of being the "team mom": Women in sports information and the friendliness trap'. *Journal of Sport Management*, *26*: 309–21.

Hoeber, L. and Kerwin, S. (2013) 'Exploring the experiences of female sport fans: A collaborative self-ethnography'. *Sport Management Review*, *16*: 326–36.

Kihl, L., Shaw, S. and Schull, V. (2013) 'Fear, anxiety and loss of control: Analyzing an athletic department merger as a gendered political process'. *Journal of Sport Management*, *27*: 146–57.

Knoppers, A. and Anthonissen, A. (2008) 'Gendered managerial discourses in sport organizations: Multiplicity and complexity'. *Sex Roles*, *58*: 93–103.

Knowles, C. (2006) 'Handling your baggage in the field. Reflections on research relationships'. *International Journal of Social Research Methodology*, *9*: 404.

Kodama, E., Doherty, A.J. and Popovic, M. (2013) 'Front line insight: An autoethnography of the Vancouver 2010 volunteer experience'. *European Sport Management Quarterly*, *13*: 76–93.

McKay, J. (1997) *Managing gender. Affirmative action and organizational power in Australian, Canadian, and New Zealand Sport*. New York: State University of New York.

Maxwell, J. (1992) 'Understanding and validity in qualitative research'. *Harvard Educational Review*, *62*: 279–301.

Morrow, S. and Robinson, L. (2013) 'The FTSE-British Olympic Association Initiative: A resource dependence perspective'. *Sport Management Review*, *16*: 413–23.

Shaw, S. and Frisby, W. (2006) 'Can gender equity be more equitable? Promoting an alternative frame for sport management research, education, and practice'. *Journal of Sport Management*, *20*: 483–509.

Spaaij, R. (2012) 'Cultural diversity in community sport: An ethnographic inquiry of Somai Australians' experiences'. *Sport Management Review*, *16*: 29–40.

Warner, S. and Dixon, M.A. (2011) 'Understanding sense of community from the athlete's perspective'. *Journal of Sport Management*, *25*: 257–71.

White, J. and Drew, S. (2011) 'Collecting data or creating meaning?' *Qualitative Research Journal*, *11*: 3–12.

Williams, M. (2004) 'Interpretivism and generalisation'. *Sociology*, *34*: 209–24.

PART II

Managerial theories

4

DEVELOPING A THEORY OF SUFFERING AND ACADEMIC CORRUPTION IN SPORT[1]

Lisa A. Kihl

Overview

The generation of a theory of suffering and academic corruption was initiated by asking how organisational stakeholders are impacted by corruption. At the time, within the academic business literature, a growing dialogue featured a macro-level organisational analysis about the consequences of corruption (e.g., impact on firm performance). However, I was employed at an institution that had experienced one of the most extensive cases of academic corruption in the history of intercollegiate athletics (National Collegiate Athletic Association (NCAA) Infractions Committee, 2000). I noticed a reoccurring theme of the effect of the corruption on various programme stakeholders (e.g., sanctions, negative reputation and consistent reference to the case). I therefore sought a micro-level organisational analysis to gain an understanding of how specific sport organisational stakeholders who were not involved in corrupt acts but were required to perform their roles and responsibilities post corruption were affected. I engaged in a conversation with a fellow university colleague, who at the time was my doctoral student and worked as the academic counselor for men's basketball (MBB), about my observations and how the MBB programme at the University of Minnesota was impacted by the 1999 case of academic fraud (details of the case are presented later in the chapter). The result of that conversation was his offer to ask the head coach if he would grant us access and participate in a study about how the programme was impacted by the academic corruption. Three months later we were granted access to conduct our research!

While negotiating entry, I engaged in a literature review to learn about the consequences of corruption. As a result of the review, I discovered a lack of theory and empirical research about the consequences of corruption on organisational stakeholders not involved in malfeasant acts. While conceptual frameworks exist in the business literature relating to organisational models of corruption (e.g., Ashforth and Anand, 2003; Luo, 2004), these frameworks mostly provided a macro-level overview of corruption's antecedents, consequences and reform efforts in general, rather than detailed theoretical accounts of the micro-level consequences of corruption on organisational stakeholders and how specific types of corruption impact stakeholders. The corruption literature was therefore limited in providing explanatory insights into post-corruption experiences and the implications for management. Furthermore, the sport management literature was absent in documenting micro-level explanations of the impact of corruption on sport organisational stakeholders. At this point, I realised that I needed to generate a theory that addressed my research question, which required using grounded theory methodology. The theory is called *suffering and academic corruption* and conceptualises the consequences of academic corruption on organisational stakeholders within an intercollegiate setting. This chapter documents the process used to generate this theory using a qualitative methodology – grounded theory (Glaser and Strauss, 1967; Corbin and Strauss, 2008). Fundamental characteristics of grounded theory, and the methods used to develop the theory along with its application, and future directions are presented.

Process

The process for developing a theory of suffering and academic corruption involved first defining theory in relation to grounded theory, then understanding grounded theory methodology and its key methodological characteristics. The methodological procedures were then followed to generate a theory of suffering and academic corruption.

My understanding of theory in relation to grounded theory

To generate a theory of suffering and academic corruption required a firm understanding of what is meant by theory, how theory can be generated, and how theory can be applied. Post-positivists' definitions generally conceptualise theory as seeking causes, deterministic explanations, predictions and emphasising generality and universality (Creswell, 2014). From this perspective, theory is created by verifying theoretical relationships of operationalised variables through hypothesis testing with the end result of providing reductionist explanations of the world. In contrast, my conception of theory is based on Hage (1972), who defines theory as a 'set of well-developed categories (themes, concepts) that are systematically interrelated through statements of relationship to form a theoretical framework that explains some phenomenon' (p. 34). Corbin and Strauss (2008) adopt Hage's definition and add that cohesive theory 'occurs through the use of an overarching explanatory concept, one that stands above the rest . . . and incorporated with other concepts explains the what, how, when, where, and why of something' (p. 55).

Theory generated through grounded theory assumes 'theory as process' (Glaser and Strauss, 1967, p. 32), meaning that concepts (categories) are derived from the data and systematically produced through the research process. Grounded theory can generally generate two levels of theory: substantive or formal (Glaser and Strauss, 1967). Substantive theory is founded on research from one specific area and does not seek explanations outside the existing area of study (e.g., suffering from academic corruption). Formal theory is more applicable to a wider range of disciplinary concerns and less related to a specific group or context. Glaser and Strauss maintain that substantive theories are used as 'a springboard or stepping stone to the development of a grounded formal theory' (p. 79).

Grounded theory methodology

Grounded theory is a 'general methodology for developing theory that is grounded in data systematically gathered and analyzed' (Strauss and Corbin, 1994, p. 273). It has utility as a methodology for examining previously under-studied social phenomenon and is useful in researching and capturing the complexity of organisational behaviour (Locke, 2001), such as how corruption can impact a men's basketball programme. Grounded theory methodology has three main characteristics: contextual, inductive and procedural (Corbin and Strauss, 1998, 2008).[2] Grounded theory is generated from a context-based and process-orientated explanation of social phenomenon, which is illustrated through representative examples of data (Glaser and Strauss, 1967). Theory generation is an inductive process where data collection and analysis are emergent processes where the intent is to build from local understandings that, without enquiry, remain implicit and unexplained. Theory generation is procedural in that the researcher alternates between data collection and analysis that involves systematic abstraction and conceptualisation of empirical data to generate, develop and verify concepts. The end product is conceptual theory that fits, is relevant and can be used in practice.

The essential distinctive characteristics of grounded theory are the systematics in the methodology (including theoretical sampling, data analysis process and theoretical sensitivity) and the constant comparative method, which are explained next.

Theoretical sampling

Theory generation from data requires theoretical sampling. It is a data collection process where emerging theory guides collection of data, analysis and posing questions to assist in formulating categories and their properties and dimensions (Glaser and Strauss, 1967). The aim is to select sources of data that can extend theory development (Corbin and Strauss, 2008) and thus, after initial data collection, the continued process of data gathering is guided by seeking categorical saturation and the development of a substantive theory. This makes grounded theory data collection different from conventional qualitative data methods because theoretical sampling is a circular process of data collection, analysis and categorical development; category development leads to question regeneration, which guides further data collection. The researcher asks what data sources (e.g., people, places, situations, archival documents) will help lead to a point of theoretical saturation where all concepts and their properties and dimensions are defined and explained (Corbin and Strauss, 1998, 2008).

Data analysis process

The key to grounded theory data analysis is a process of conceptualisation: thinking about what the data mean, learning to think abstractly and assigning words that describe conceptually what the data means (Corbin and Strauss, 2008). Conceptualisation is carried out through coding where concepts are extracted from raw data to develop conceptual categories and their respective properties (characteristics) and dimensions (location on a dimensional continuum; Corbin and Strauss, 2008, p. 159), and an explanation of the generalised relationships between each category. A category is 'a conceptual element of a theory' (Glaser and Strauss, 1967, p. 36) and ranges in level of abstraction from higher level to lower level. Lower-level categories are grouped under higher-level concepts according to their shared properties.

Grounded theory coding involves three hierarchical coding processes: open coding, axial coding and selective coding (Corbin and Strauss, 1998, 2008). These coding processes all entail using the constant comparative method, where codes, categories, properties and dimensions are constantly compared to identify variations, similarities and differences in the data (Corbin and Strauss, 1998, 2008). Open coding involves a line-by-line reading of the data where they are broken down analytically into categories and subcategories. During this process, incidents (i.e., events/actions/interactions) are compared with other incidents together to establish fundamental likenesses and differences to delineate the categories and their respective properties and dimensions. Axial coding involves conceptualising how the categories and subcategories are related to each other. Categories are compared with more incidents to generate new theoretical categorical properties. The purpose is theoretical explanation and categorical saturation through property development. Selective coding occurs in the latter phase of analysis and involves unifying all the categories around a core category. The core category represents the central phenomenon of the study – in this case, the core category was suffering. Categories are compared with other categories to further explain the theory. Identifying a core category is one of the most challenging aspects of conceptualisation and unique to grounded theory analysis. Corbin and Strauss (1990, p. 14) suggest consideration of the following to assist in identifying the core category: 'What is the main analytic idea presented in this research? If my findings are to be conceptualized in a few sentences, what do I say? What does all the action/interaction seem to be about? How can I explain the variation that I see between and among the categories?' Diagramming is an important analytical strategy that helps map out the core category and its relationship with the other categories and subcategories.

Theoretical memoing is another important strategy that is performed throughout the conceptualisation process. Memoing is 'theorizing write-up of ideas about codes and their relationships' as they come to the researcher's mind (Glaser, 1978, p. 83). A detailed account of conceptual ideas, associations and theoretical reflections related to the categories, properties and dimensions are kept throughout the analytical process.

Theoretical sensitivity

Theoretical sensitivity is the 'ability to generate concepts from data and to relate them according to normal models of theory in general' (Glaser, 2004, para. 43). Sensitivity requires the researcher to have disciplinary professional knowledge and analytical competence (Corbin and Strauss, 1998, 2008). Typically, sensitivity is frowned upon in data analysis as we are taught to be objective, or qualitative researchers are taught to present our researcher stance (Marshall and Rossman, 2010). However, grounded theory generation requires 'a personal and temperamental bent to maintain analytic distance, tolerate confusion and regression while remaining open, trusting to preconscious processing and to conceptual emergence' (Glaser, 2004, para. 43). Analytical competence requires developing theoretical insights, conceptualising and organising, and making abstract connections from the data. Theoretical sensitivity therefore requires entering a research project with little to no predetermined hunches in order to generate a theory from the data.

Generating a theory of suffering and academic corruption

In an effort to generate a substantive theory of suffering and academic corruption within the context of an intercollegiate MBB programme, I used a grounded theory research approach within the boundaries of a single revelatory case study (Yin, 2014). This afforded me the opportunity to observe and analyse the impact of the University of Minnesota's case of academic corruption and thus generate a substantive theory.

The case of academic corruption

Between 1994 and 1998, the University of Minnesota MBB programme was involved in one of the most extensive cases of academic fraud in the history of intercollegiate athletics (NCAA Infractions Committee, 2000). Broadly conceived, academic corruption is the abuse of authority and misuse of trust by a public official and/or private actor for personal or material gain. In this case, academic fraud was conceived of and supported by the Head Men's Basketball Coach, his staff, the team's academic counsellor and the sport's secretary. The infractions report (NCAA Infractions Committee, 2000) stated that the former secretary in the Academic Counseling Office had written approximately 400 pieces of coursework (homework assignments, preparing take-home exams, typing and composing theme papers) for at least eighteen MBB. Both institutional and NCAA investigations found copious rules violations (e.g., extra benefits, academic eligibility, unethical conduct and lack of institutional control) had occurred, with academic fraud being the most serious. Furthermore, the violations were deemed 'significant, widespread and intentional' and 'undermined the bedrock foundation of a university' as relates to realising institutional integrity (NCAA Infractions Committee, 2000, p. 2). Numerous sanctions were imposed by the University and the NCAA on the MBB programme and the athletic department as a whole.[3] In an effort to regain institutional control, major organisational restructuring and enhanced institutional governance were implemented. A new basketball staff was hired four months after the corruption was exposed and was assigned the challenging task of overcoming the corruption.

Data gathering and initial data analysis

As previously noted, prior to data collection I conducted a brief review of the literature to gain a general understanding of the theoretical and empirical consequences of corruption. Gaining an understanding of the phenomenon within the context of intercollegiate athletics and business organisations was included in this review. Based on the literature search, the original research question posed was: 'how was the MBB programme impacted by the incidence of academic corruption?' Theoretical sampling steered preliminary data collection and analysis of documents. An extensive search of archival documents about the Minnesota case of academic corruption was then conducted and included newspaper articles, popular sports magazines, news magazines, institutional meeting minutes and official reports from both the NCAA and institution.

Initial data were openly coded and organised into major categories and subcategories. Major categories (and their respective subcategories) at this point in the analysis included: (a) negative treatment (public criticism and guilt by association), (b) sanctions (recruiting, loss of records and ban on post-season competition) and (c) reform policies (increased University oversight, University restructuring and increased academic assistance policies and procedures). Research team members consulted with each about the initial codes, categories and subcategories, and written memos they had developed. Discussions aimed at gaining clarity about the meaning of the data. The biggest challenge for the researchers was focusing on conceptualising the data and not describing the data. That is, it was important to centre on what the raw data represented and how these representations were connected. This conceptualisation process was challenging, as we naturally wanted to describe the data, which is not an aspect of grounded theory methodology.

Using the constant comparative method, the initial categories (i.e., negative treatment, sanctions and reform policies) were further delineated. Memo writing, for example, focused on developing paragraphs of conceptual thoughts of the respective characteristics of each category, including what humiliation meant, who was humiliated, how they were humiliated and the intensity of the humiliation. This theoretical sampling activity led to asking more research questions, requiring additional data collection and further analysis. Based on the preliminary data collected and initial open coding, the following four questions were posed: How did the instance of academic corruption impact the newly hired MBB coaching staff? How did the instance of academic corruption impact the players not involved in the corruption? What were the specific consequences of the academic corruption on both the newly hired MBB coaching staff and the players? And how did the consequences of the academic corruption affect the newly hired MBB coaching staff and the players?

Data collection and analysis from this point on was steered by identifying and seeking to refine the gaps in the respective categorical properties and dimensions. For example, each piece of raw data was read and re-read. Memos were written where they were first labelled with a concept name and then reflections were made about what the data meant. I asked questions such as 'what types of consequences were evident?' 'Who experienced the consequences?' 'Did the athletes and coaches experience similar or different consequences?' And 'did the consequences differ among athletes and coaches?' As the data-guided memo writing was assessed I answered these questions. I initially identified that athletes and coaches experience different consequences as a result of the corruption. Consequences were a higher-level concept and the specific type of consequence that either athletes (e.g., negative treatment) or coaches (e.g., sanctions) experienced were lower-level concepts. Athletes experienced negative treatment (associated guilt, lack of communication, lack of support and public criticism and humiliation, including racism) and coaches experienced sanctions (unknown and recruiting). However, based on this particular cycle of data collection and analysis, the concepts were underdeveloped in terms of their properties and dimensions. Coaches experienced recruiting sanctions, but it was not evident what type of sanctions impacted the coaching staff and how, the degree of impact, the consistency of impact across coaches and how long the sanctions impacted the coaches. Future data collection and analysis therefore aimed to delineate the respective properties and dimensions of the concept recruiting.

Theoretical sample

Participants and sources of data that could extend theory development were identified. Interviewee selection criteria included: (a) first-hand knowledge of the consequences of academic corruption, (b) willingness to speak about the consequences, (c) ability to help explain categorical properties and dimension, and (d) ability to clarify any relationships between emerging categories. Semi-structured face-to-face and phone interviews were conducted with nineteen participants, including MBB coaches ($n = 4$), former MBB student-athletes ($n = 2$), athletic department and university administrators ($n = 5$), compliance staff ($n = 1$), academic counselling services for intercollegiate athletics staff ($n = 3$) and faculty ($n = 4$). Given that interview participants were not involved in the academic corruption but experienced the post-corruption first-hand, overall they were open to share their experiences. For certain participants, sharing their stories appeared to be a form of therapy because they had withheld their experiences and rarely opened up to outsiders about what they were enduring. Participants negatively portrayed in either the public or media also requested that we tell the truth. One athlete specifically asked, 'you will tell the truth, right?'. Interviews ranged from 45–120 minutes in duration, were audio-taped, transcribed verbatim, and a summary research report was submitted to all participants. Noteworthy, when the head coach received the research report, he called me and thanked me for telling the truth.

Data collection

Interview questions were posed that would advance categorical development. Based on our initial four research questions, interview participants were asked three open-ended questions: what happened after the scandal was exposed; what were the specific consequences of the scandal;

and how did these consequences impact individuals and the overall MBB programme? The data generated from these interview questions prompted the development of novel categories and subcategories. For example, in relation to coaches' suffering, the categories of stakeholder separation (i.e., team and university units) and managing multiple roles (i.e., publicly dealing with issue, meeting athletic and academic expectations, and media and public scrutiny) were established. Athlete suffering categories and subcategories identified were sanctions (loss of records and ban on post-season play) and loss (step-father syndrome, team and reputation).

The higher-level category (harmful outcomes) and respective categories and subcategories were also identified in analysing the raw data during this cycle of data collection and analysis. For example, the coaches' category (stakeholder separation) and its associated subcategories (team and university units generated harmful outcomes including anger, associated guilt, conflict, distrust, disrupted team dynamics and insular behaviour) emerged. In addition, the data collected helped delineate initial categories identified from the previous cycles of data collection and analysis. Examples include coaching staff consequences, such as sanctions, and athlete consequences, such as sources of negative treatment and negative treatment.

Following this next round of data analysis, it became evident that the interview questions needed further revision to enhance our understanding about coaches and student-athlete suffering. The lower-level concepts related to coach and athlete higher-level concepts (consequences and harmful outcomes) required further delineation. It needed to be determined explicitly what kinds of harmful outcomes were associated with which particular lower-level consequences. Therefore, interview questions from this point on involved asking how coaches suffered. Questions included: how had the corruption affected the coaches' relationships with faculty, administrators, players and the media; what was it like coaching the team the season after the incident occurred; what was it like coaching the team in subsequent years; how did the sanctions impact the coaching staff; and how did the recruiting sanctions impact the coaches' ability to carry out their jobs? Student-athlete suffering questions included: describe what it was like immediately after the story broke; describe what it was like being on the team that first year with Coach; and describe what it was like being a student and going to class.

The semi-structured nature of the interviews also allowed the flexibility in pursuing unexpected paths and cues suggested by theoretical sensitivity in theory development (Corbin and Strauss, 1998). For example, in one of the initial interviews with one of the coaching staff members, we learned that the student-athletes *suffer* and experience the brunt of negative treatment by a case of academic fraud. This interview and subsequent document data collection led to asking questions about: how were MBB student-athletes treated by faculty and the student body after the scandal broke; how did the media treat the MBB student-athletes after the scandal broke; how did the MBB student-athletes react; what was it like playing on the team the following season; and how did the sanctions impact the team? The result of this particular theoretical sampling and analysis was delineating the category of *athlete negative treatment*, which included a subcategory of *public criticism and humiliation* that had racial overtones (Kihl, Richardson and Campisi, 2008).

Theory building required seeking multiple sources of data (e.g., documents, observations and interviews) that assisted in the conceptualisation process. Two examples help illustrate. First, the category *negative treatment* and its related subcategory – *associative guilt of MBB student-athletes* – were initially generated by the student-athlete participant interviews. This led to the further collection of various news media documents to assist in providing a detailed explanation of the properties and dimensions of the concept of *student-athlete negative treatment and associative guilt*. Second, interview, archival and observational data were sought and analysed to thoroughly delineate the category *coaching harmful outcomes* and the relationship (i.e., axial coding) with the consequences subcategory *managing multiple roles*. The data analysis involved identifying what kinds of harmful outcomes were related to the coaches experiencing by managing multiple roles. Three concepts were identified, including *distrust, insular behaviours* and *stress*. Each type of data was analysed through comparing incidents with incidents to help abstract this harmful outcome concept and further explain the nature of suffering in terms of understanding who and why they distrusted individuals, how they reacted and how the stress impacted carrying out their day-to-day operations.

One of the researchers served in a participant observation role as a complete insider working within a support unit for intercollegiate athletics, specifically with the MBB programme. Research questions and emergent theoretical categories as shared above directed his observations. Observations were guided by both the broad initial research question initially posed and the additional research questions that evolved as a result of data collection and analysis, which aimed at explaining the emergent categories found during theory generation. Informal and formal interactions with players, coaches and faculty; planned activities (student tables, road trips, meetings); and communications (with student-athletes, faculty, support staff, coaches and administrators) were documented for the duration of data collection (one year). As the research progressed, the refined questions shifted observational foci to assist in defining categorical properties and dimensions as well as determining relationships among categories. Observational data were therefore compared with the interview and textual data and contributed to the saturation of categories and subcategories. In all, data collection occurred over a twelve-month period that generated an extensive amount of data, including over 300 single-spaced pages of interview text, 200 pages of documents and 30 single-spaced pages of observational text.

Analysis and writing

All data were downloaded into the qualitative data analysis software Atlas.ti (Scientific Software Development, 1997). Data were coded both by hand and using the software. First notes were written by hand and then coding was carried out using the software. Data were then openly coded where codes were conceptualised by inductively labelling phenomenon. The data were micro-analysed and codes were named based on what was suggested by the context in which an event, action/interaction and object occurred and through in vivo coding. Examples of conceptualised codes for student-athlete suffering were *dual consciousness, racism, stakeholder separation, anger* and *empowerment*. Coaches' conceptual codes were *conservative recruiting, dysfunctional relationships* and *insular behaviours*. Student-athlete in vivo code examples included *suffer, hurt, felt bad, bothered me, disappointment, embarrassed, pretty bad* and *real uncomfortable*, and examples of coaches in vivo codes were *the virus, negative recruiting* and *behind the eight ball*. The constant comparison method of comparing incidents with incidents to help define categories and delineating properties and dimensions was carried out at both the dimensional and property level until a point of theoretical saturation was reached where no new properties, dimensions, consequences, conditions or actions were evident in the data.

Axial coding was then performed to describe the relationship between the core categories and respective subcategories and to further demarcate properties and dimensions. The various categories and subcategories were conceptually integrated to explain the theoretical conditions, actions and consequences of how a MBB programme is affected by an instance of academic corruption. For example, the category *sanctions* and respective subcategory *recruiting* were examined to determine the relationship with the specific harmful outcome of recruiting challenges for coaches. A limitation on the number of days a prospective student-athlete can be evaluated and official on-campus visits alters a coaching staff's recruiting philosophy that leads to conservative recruiting. These theoretical comparisons allowed for an in-depth understanding of critical post-corruption incidents and participants' perceptions of their experiences of these events.

Theoretical memoing was performed throughout the analysis process, where documented thoughts about the data and the conceptual connections between categories were recorded. This sample memo shows my thoughts about how the sanctions impacted the coaching staff:

> Coaches' perspective – until working within the post scandal period one might under-estimate the magnitude of how the sanctions, reform policies and the scandal itself will affect one's working conditions and relationships with co-workers within the respective athletic department units, athletic administration, faculty oversight committees and the student-athletes.
>
> Held to a higher standard – MBB staff impacted as it is perceived that they are held to a different standard – success, academic assistance and conservative compliance and interpretations.

Note taking assisted in the elevation of the data to a conceptual level to help define properties and dimensions of categories. Selective coding was lastly carried out where categories were integrated at the dimensional level to identify a core category (i.e., *suffering*) and refine the theory. Validation of statements of relationships among concepts and completion of categories that required further refinement was important during this process. A theoretical diagram (see Figure 4.1) was developed, illustrating the major concepts, subcategories and their connections leading to a substantive theory of a MBB programme's suffering and academic corruption, conceptualised next.

A theory of suffering and academic corruption

In the context of intercollegiate athletics and the occurrence of extreme academic fraud, team personnel (i.e., student-athletes and coaches) who were not involved in the corruption are subject to, and endure, enormous and assorted forms of suffering that are produced by various consequences and subsequent harmful outcomes (Kihl and Richardson, 2009). The respective consequences and harmful outcomes on team personnel are depicted in Figure 4.1. The nature and degree of suffering experienced will vary in relation to one's role on the team, time elapsed after the corruption is exposed, who initiated the suffering and the various consequences of the corruption itself. The players and coaching staff will generally experience distinctive consequences (e.g., players – negative treatment, and loss; coaching staff – stakeholder separation, reform policies and managing multiple roles). These consequences, however, appear to produce both similar and unique forms of suffering for both coaches and players as reported in Kihl *et al.* (2008). Coaches and players will experience similar harmful outcomes of distrust, anger, conflict, disrupted team dynamics and stress. Unique forms of suffering experienced by players will include devastation, embarrassment, ostracism, feelings of discomfort, stereotyping, pain and disappointment. Coaches, however, experience unique harmful outcomes of associative guilt, insular behaviour, micromanagement and a lack of stakeholder separation where different university units and players showed a reluctance to trust the MBB staff, which can lead to stress and dysfunctional team dynamics.

In general, sanctions and media scrutiny will affect both stakeholder groups; however, the penalties and public examination will impact them both through different means, which subsequently generates contrasting forms of suffering. 'The suffering is most acute at the

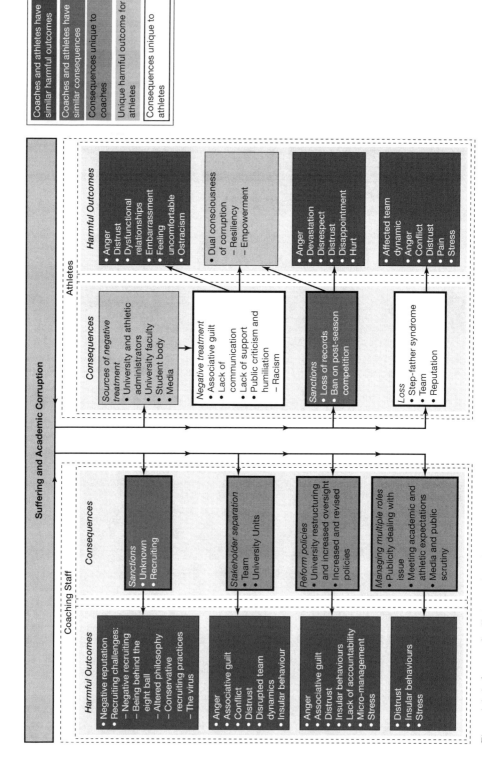

Figure 4.1 A theory of suffering and academic corruption

exposure of the academic fraud and during the subsequent 12–24 months' (Kihl *et al.*, 2008, p. 283). In time, the 'intensity of the anguish felt by the athletes dissipates' and to some degree the coaching staff's anguish lessens; however, the consequences of corruption (i.e., negative treatment, stakeholder separation and reform policies) appear to linger well into the post-corruption period where the coaches and players continue to experience distrust, ostracism and embarrassment (Kihl *et al.*, 2008, p. 283). While individuals are able to cope with their suffering, it appears that the coaching staff hired to fix the mess can never restore the programme to its original health.

Extensions and applications

Quality grounded theory is evaluated in terms of fit, workability and relevance (Glaser and Strauss, 1967). The categories created in the theory of suffering and academic corruption should fit and explain conceptually all data collected. The theory must also be relevant in terms of accurately explaining the phenomenon of how academic corruption impacts a MBB programme post-corruption. The theory must also work or have practical application that would first add to coaches' and administrators' knowledge base, as well as assist decision-makers to develop policy and change practice to provide support for individuals as they deal with the after-effects of academic corruption. Assuming that the theory generated from the data meets these criteria, I have not sought to alter or revise the theory of suffering and academic corruption.

Through conversations with my colleagues about the theory, I have learned that several use the Kihl and Richardson (2009) article in qualitative methods courses. The article is used to help their students learn about grounded theory as a methodology. They learn how to do it, how data collection and analysis differs between grounded theory and other types of qualitative methodologies (e.g., phenomenology and case studies), and it provides a good example of the write-up of grounded theory categories and conceptualising of a theory. It has also been shared with me that the article has practical implications for athletic administrators, coaches and student-athletes, in that it is used to understand the nature and impact of academic corruption in the context of intercollegiate athletics. In particular, understanding the types of consequences and harmful outcomes a coaching staff and their players might endure post-corruption can assist athletic administrators in providing the necessary support and resources to help them overcome their respective suffering. Furthermore, the theory can help explicate to coaches and players the types of consequences they might encounter and how they might be managed.

I have also discovered that the Kihl and Richardson (2009) study has been cited in several publications to document unethical behaviour in sport (e.g., Bell-Laroche, MacLean, Thibault and Wolfe, 2014), in discussions about what constitutes grounded theory in the field of Kinesiology (e.g., Weed, 2009), in connecting theory and practice through qualitative research (Nite and Singer, 2012) and as an example of developing good theory (Doherty, 2013). Of note, what I find important about these citations is that my research is drawn upon to help discuss and debate how to improve our field of sport management in terms of theory, research and practice.

Future directions

To date, I have not had the opportunity to extend this substantive theory to develop a formal theory. This is partly due to the challenges in gaining access to organisations to conduct research, and particularly issues of corruption. However, my plan is to conduct research in different sporting contexts (governing bodies, international contexts, sports) that would examine different forms, types and extent of corruption cases across the different contexts. The main aim in carrying out this process is to develop a *formal* theory of suffering and corruption. A formal theory would be at a higher level of abstraction that extends beyond a specific stakeholder group and/or organisation to generalise across a discipline.

In practice, I hope faculty members continue to use my work as a teaching tool for students to gain an understanding of the grounded theory generation process. Ultimately, I would also like to see the theory assist sport programmes in managing the challenges caused by academic fraud. However, realistically, the practical application of the theory would require first re-writing it into a more accessible/user friendly language and format for athletic administrators. In its current form, I am not so sure if it is as useful as it could be.

Notes

1 This chapter is a reflection on Kihl, Richardson and Campisi (2008), Kihl and Richardson (2009), and the works related to them.
2 The authors acknowledge the different methodological perspectives between Glaser (1992, 2004) and Corbin and Strauss (1998, 2008). Although drawing from both Glaser, and Strauss and Corbin, the grounded theory methodology relied more on Corbin and Strauss (1998).
3 A detailed account of the Minnesota case and the sanctions is outlined in Kihl *et al.* (2008).

References

Ashforth, B.E. and Anand, V. (2003) 'The normalization of corruption in organizations'. *Research in Organizational Behavior, 25*: 1–52.

Bell-Laroche, D., MacLean, J., Thibault, L. and Wolfe, R. (2014) 'Leader perceptions of management by values within Canadian national sport organizations'. *Journal of Sport Management, 28*: 68–80.

Corbin, J.M. and Strauss, A. (1990) 'Grounded theory research: Procedures, canons, and evaluative criteria'. *Qualitative sociology, 13*: 3–21.

Corbin, J. and Strauss, A. (1998) *Basics of qualitative research: Techniques and procedures for developing grounded theory* (second edn). Thousand Oaks, CA: Sage.

Corbin, J. and Strauss, A. (2008) *Basics of qualitative research: Techniques and procedures for developing grounded theory* (third edn). Thousand Oaks, CA: Sage.

Creswell, J.W. (2014) *Research design: Qualitative, quantitative, and mixed methods approaches* (third edn). Thousand Oaks, CA: Sage.

Doherty, A. (2013) 'Investing in sport management: The value of good theory'. *Sport Management Review, 16*: 5–11.

Glaser, B.G. (1978) *Theoretical sensitivity: Advances in the methodology of grounded theory*. Mill Valley, CA: Sociology Press.

Glaser, B.G. (1992) *Basics of grounded theory analysis: Emergence vs. forcing*. Mill Valley, CA: Sociology Press.

Glaser, B.G. (with the assistance of Judith Holton) (2004) 'Remodeling grounded theory'. *Forum Qualitative Sozialforschung/ Forum: Qualitative Social Research, 5*(4). Available at http://nbn-resolving.de/urn:nbn: de:0114-fqs040245 (accessed on 1 September, 2014).

Glaser, B.G. and Strauss, A.L. (1967) *The discovery of grounded theory: Strategies for qualitative research*. New York: Aldine de Gruyter.

Hage, J. (1972) *Techniques and problems of theory construction in sociology*. New York, NY: John Wiley.

Kihl, L.A., Richardson, T. and Campisi, C. (2008) 'Toward a grounded theory of student-athlete suffering and dealing with academic corruption'. *Journal of Sport Management, 22*: 273–302.

Kihl, L.A. and Richardson, T. (2009) '"Fixing the mess": A grounded theory of a men's basketball coaching staff's suffering as a result of academic corruption'. *Journal of Sport Management, 23*: 278–304.

Locke, K. (2001) *Grounded theory in management research*. Thousand Oaks, CA: Sage.

Luo, Y. (2004) 'An organizational perspective of corruption'. *Management and Organization Review, 1*: 119–54.

Marshall, C. and Rossman, G.B. (2010) *Designing qualitative research* (fourth edn) Thousand Oaks, CA: Sage.

National Collegiate Athletic Association Division I Committee on Infractions, George Washington University (2000) *University of Minnesota, Twin Cities: Public infractions report*. Indianapolis, IN: National Collegiate Athletic Association.

Nite, C. and Singer, J.N. (2012) 'Qualitative inquiry: Quality research for connecting with and affecting change in sport populations'. *Qualitative Research Journal*, 12: 88–97.

Scientific Software Development (1997) *Atlas ti: The knowledge workbench visual qualitative data analysis management model building (Version 4.1)*. Berlin, Germany: Author. [Computer software].

Strauss, A. and Corbin, J. (1994) 'Grounded theory methodology: An overview'. In N.K. Denzin and Y.S. Lincoln (eds), *Handbook of qualitative research* (pp. 273–85). Thousand Oaks, CA: Sage.

Weed, M. (2009) 'Research quality considerations for grounded theory research in sport and exercise psychology'. *Psychology of Sport and Exercise*, 10: 502–10.

Yin, R.K. (2014) *Case study research: Design and methods* (fifth edn). Thousand Oaks, CA: Sage.

Applying the theory of suffering and academic corruption in sport

Calvin Nite[1]

I was first introduced to Dr Kihl's work when I was a doctoral student searching for research topics. Given my background in intercollegiate athletics, I was drawn to her work investigating the effects of the scandals at the University of Minnesota. I was specifically interested in her research that looked into how academic corruption affected college athletes and coaches (Kihl and Richardson, 2009). As my research has evolved, I have also incorporated her work regarding morality within athletic departments into my research (Kihl, 2007). I have drawn upon her work as the foundation for much of my understanding of the complexities of athletic programmes on college campuses. Further, I have found Dr Kihl's work on corruption and morality to be invaluable in the classroom. Although she has specifically situated her research in college athletics, I have found her grounded theories of academic corruption to be transferrable to other managerial, and even marketing, contexts outside of intercollegiate athletics.

Dr Kihl's research on corruption and ethics has been influential in shaping my own research from a foundational standpoint. As my research interests have evolved since my time as a doctoral student, I have drawn on Dr Kihl's work in a variety of ways. First, her work provides an excellent example and guide to implementing grounded theory. Second, I have consulted her work in both research and classroom settings as I have sought to further understand the complexities of intercollegiate athletics. Specifically, her work has informed my understanding of how athletes as well as athletic department employees are affected by the competing ideals within the institution (Nite and Bopp, 2015). Although I have not directly built upon her theory of suffering and academic corruption (Kihl, Richardson and Campisi, 2008; Kihl and Richardson, 2009), I have used her research as a reference point for suggesting that competing logics within organisations may result in ethical dilemmas for employees and manifest into hardships for both employees and athletes alike (see also Kihl, 2007). In future research endeavours, I envision coupling research of competing institutional logics with Kihl's research of corruption and ethics as means for better understanding how and why organisational scandals come to fruition.

Dr Kihl's research has also proved useful in a variety of classroom activities. I have found her studies of academic corruption (Kihl *et al.*, 2008; Kihl and Richardson, 2009), along with her research into leader morality (Kihl, 2007), to be impactful across a variety of contexts and disciplines. Although much of her work is situated within the context of college athletic departments, it translates well into teaching the impacts of corporate scandals on organisational employees and organisational reputation. I have implemented her work to demonstrate to students how corruption within the leadership of an organisation can have lasting consequences that may result in years of recovery efforts. This also shows students that the actions of a few can damage the entirety of the organisation. Incorporation of Dr Kihl's research into the classroom has been an effective teaching tool for students in my classroom.

Note

1   Calvin Nite is an assistant professor in sport management in the Department of Kinesiology and Sport Management at Texas Tech University.

References

Kihl, L. (2007) 'Moral codes, moral tensions and hiding behind the rules: A snapshot of athletic administrators' practical morality'. *Sport Management Review, 10*: 279–305.

Kihl, L. and Richardson, T. (2009) ' "Fixing the mess": A grounded theory of a men's basketball coaching staff's suffering as a result of academic corruption'. *Journal of Sport Management, 23*: 278–304.

Kihl, L., Richardson, T. and Campisi, C. (2008) 'Toward a grounded theory of student-athlete suffering and dealing with academic corruption'. *Journal of Sport Management, 22*: 273–302.

Nite, C. and Bopp, T. (2015) 'Conflicting prescriptions for "ethical" leadership in complex institutions: Perspectives from U.S. college athletic administrators'. Unpublished manuscript.

5

BUILDING THEORETICAL FOUNDATIONS FOR STRATEGIC CSR IN SPORT[1]

Kathy Babiak, Kathryn Heinze and Richard Wolfe[2]

Overview

The term Corporate Social Responsibility (CSR) has become an important feature of the management lexicon. CSR and related terms (e.g., strategic philanthropy, corporate citizenship, sustainability, social entrepreneurship, corporate governance) are underpinned by the belief that modern business has a responsibility to society that extends beyond the shareholders of a firm and, more specifically, focuses on minimising or eliminating harmful effects on society and maximising long-term beneficial impact (Mohr, Webb and Harris, 2001). Serious discussion concerning CSR gained momentum in the early 1970s when Milton Friedman suggested, 'there is one and only one social responsibility of business – to use its resources and engage in activities designed to increase its profits so long as it stays within the rules of the game, which is to say, engages in open and free competition without deception or fraud' (Friedman, 1970, p. 33), and scholars began debating the role of business in society (Friedman, 1962, 1970). From that time, the interest in, and significance of, CSR has grown and has gained broad acceptance as a legitimate aspect of business practice. Today, organisations across industries engage in CSR practices. In the sport setting, CSR has become a central and strategic feature encompassing an array of activities and objectives for sport organisations.

From a scholarly perspective, the theoretical conceptualisation of CSR has developed over time. Early management research focused on delineating and defining the concept of CSR, understanding its components and articulating its purpose (c.f., Carroll, 1979; Davis, 1973; Drucker, 1984; Sethi, 1975). Academic activity in this area shifted in the mid-1980s to examine and understand the linkage between CSR and financial performance (e.g., the business case for CSR; Aupperle, Carroll and Hatfield, 1985; McGuire, Sundgren and Schneeweis, 1988). It was also during this time that Freeman (1984) further embedded the notion of the responsibility of corporations to attend not only to shareholders, but also other relevant stakeholders who are affected by, and can affect, business activities. More recent literature on CSR emphasises a fit between a company's core strategy and its CSR efforts (Bruch and Walter, 2005; Porter and Kramer, 2006, 2011). Scholars in this area contend that it is appropriate – and indeed advantageous – for organisations to engage in CSR activities. These efforts not only contribute to societal beneficiaries, and enhance business performance, but are more sustainable. These latter perspectives augmented the theoretical conceptualisation of CSR.

While the concept of CSR has been present in the management literature for forty to fifty years (Carroll, 1979; Margolis and Walsh, 2003; McWilliams and Siegel, 2000), the focus on CSR in the sport management domain is much more recent. Early work on CSR in sport described different types and forms of sport organisations' CSR programmes (Babiak and Wolfe, 2006; Robinson, 2005), and examined the perceptions and intentions of customers concerning CSR, including cause-related marketing efforts (Irwin, Lachowetz, Cornwell and Clark, 2003). The development of our framework (Babiak and Wolfe, 2009) emerged from this milieu in an effort to contribute to the broader theoretical and practical development of CSR in sport. In our article (Babiak and Wolfe, 2009), we sought to ground CSR in sport within the broad and deep extant understandings of CSR in business (Margolis and Walsh, 2003), but with sensitivity to the unique elements of sport. Our aim was to uncover the contextual forces – both internal and external to the firm – that lead sport organisations to be socially responsible. In essence, we wanted to shift the scholarly conversation and understand *why* sport organisations were becoming increasingly focused on CSR as a strategic management practice (as opposed to descriptions of *what* they were doing). We also suspected that different motives and resources of sport organisations would lead to different forms or types of CSR engagement. Thus, we designed our framing to consider such linkages.

Based on the findings from our study, our prior research and themes in the broader management literature (c.f., Bruch and Walter, 2005; Porter and Kramer, 2006), we developed a conceptual framework that integrates the external pressures and internal motives of organisations to engage in CSR. We suggested that the nature of a professional sport organisation's CSR efforts depends upon the organisation's focus on external pressures (e.g., societal issues, stakeholder concerns) and/or internal resources (Babiak and Wolfe, 2009). The four types of CSR initiatives we identified in the framework include: stakeholder-centric CSR, corporate-centric CSR, ad hoc CSR and strategic CSR. We argued:

> When external pressures are the essential determinants of a sport organization adopting CSR, it is classified as practicing *stakeholder-centric CSR*. Such initiatives are certainly ethically appropriate as the organization meets societal needs. However, such initiatives usually cannot be sustained in the long run as they are not based on the organization's core competencies.
>
> *(p. 734)*

Corporate-centric CSR is defined as activities based on high internal resource orientation. Here we claimed:

> Teams adopting such an orientation emphasize synergies between their core business activities and CSR. This approach, however, largely neglects societal needs. Since this type of CSR does not address a company's key stakeholders, it lacks a strategic orientation and its impact on a team's competitive position tends to be limited.
>
> *(p. 735)*

Ad hoc CSR has neither a strong resource orientation nor a strong external motivation. Finally, we contended that *strategic CSR* represents both a high internal and external orientation and is evident in teams that 'align their CSR efforts with their core competencies using the organisation's unique abilities to benefit society, thus enabling the team to fully realise the potential of CSR both for its beneficiaries and for the team' (p. 735). From these four CSR orientations, we developed several propositions, including the notion that given corporate-centric CSR's emphasis on corporate competencies, it may lead to a neglect of societal needs, and therefore have a more limited effect on society in general. We also proposed that stakeholder-centric CSR 'will not serve external constituents as well as initiatives of organizations that have capabilities more directly related to the societal issue being addressed' (p. 736), given that it does not leverage important organisational resources and competencies. Our final proposition stated that as strategic CSR activities leverage competencies and resources as well as take into account key stakeholder (societal) needs and expectations, these CSR initiatives will have the optimum impact for both society and the corporation.

Our CSR framework was developed through studying the specific context of professional sport. As we argue in the paper, compared with other industries, sport has more visibility and distinctive resources to bring attention to social issues. We differentiate sport-focused CSR based on: the *passion* of fans or customers for the product and organisations; *transparency* of management practices, decisions and outcomes; *economics* (unique perceived and actual protections and support from public coffers); and its unique *stakeholder management* needs (i.e., its complex set of stakeholder relationships, and a team's reliance on the co-operation of many organisations). These factors are particularly salient in professional sport, where there is an increased emphasis on CSR by teams and leagues. Thus, the unique nature of organisations in this area of the sport industry both indicates the significance of our work and forms a boundary condition. An organisational lens also bound our framework, as we do not consider consumer reactions and views of team and league CSR and cause-related marketing efforts (c.f., Irwin, Lachowetz, Cornwell and Clark, 2003; Walker and Kent, 2009).

The notions we originally developed concerning strategic CSR in sport have been discussed, applied and advanced in subsequent research. For instance, in research examining CSR efforts around environmental sustainability, Babiak and Trendafilova (2011) and Trendafilova, Babiak and Heinze (2013) examined institutional pressures leading organisations to adopt environmental practices. In these studies, the authors found that sport organisations adapted to both outside forces and internal interests, with the outcome of an increasing focus on environmentally responsible management practices. Trendafilova *et al.* (2013), for example, found institutional theory helpful in determining the external forces, as well as internal social controls and interests, related to the adoption of environmentally focused business practices. This study drew on the concepts outlined in Babiak and Wolfe (2009) to examine more broad internal interests, values and controls. The findings suggested that 'scrutiny and regulation, and normative and associative pressures are playing a role in adopting environmentally friendly behaviors' (Trendafilova *et al.*, 2013, p. 310). Our work continues to demonstrate that strategic considerations regarding the design and implementation of CSR are underlying drivers of these activities in the professional sport setting.

Other extensions and applications of our framing are evident in the work of Hamil and Morrow (2011), who examined the context and motivation of CSR in the Scottish Premier League (SPL). Using a stakeholder approach, they described some of the key CSR efforts of these organisations. The authors considered external pressures, internal organisational attributes, and the management motivations and orientation to adopt a CSR focus. Their findings suggest that CSR in SPL organisations maps to CSR categories found in the Babiak and Wolfe (2009) framework. More specifically, Hamil and Morrow find CSR initiatives that fit our *stakeholder-oriented CSR* drivers, our *corporate-centric* approach, as well as *strategic CSR* motives.

In more recent work, Heinze, Soderstrom and Zdroik (2014) sought to uncover the processes and mechanisms of strategic CSR – extending the context elements described in Babiak and Wolfe (2009). In particular, their research examined a unique positive outlier sport organisation (a professional team) to gain a deeper understanding of the evolution to strategic CSR. The authors looked to our framework to define strategic CSR in sport, and how it applied to the subject of their case study. They determined the existence of strategic CSR by identifying a match between internal resources and external needs (citing our framework) and examined the implementation process from the decision phase to the development of strategic community partnerships. Further, to motivate this study, Heinze and colleagues drew on our rationale around the platform of sport for CSR and benefits of CSR for both sport organisations and society. The authors concluded by noting that their work takes inspiration from, and builds on, our conceptualisation of strategic CSR by uncovering the mechanisms that enable sports teams to implement strategic CSR.

Finally, concepts from our framing have been discussed, applied and extended in a number of related research efforts examining CSR in various settings with different foci. For example, Anagnostopoulos and Shilbury (2013) integrated and extended strategic CSR perspectives by considering different levels of analysis (e.g., individual and organisational) in the examination of how CSR was implemented in professional football organisations via charitable foundations. Their results suggested that external pressures (what they termed environmental determinism) as well as internal resources (key board trustees, relevant expertise and intangible resources) were key factors in the implementation and execution of charitable efforts in European professional football.

Process of developing our framework

Our curiosity of CSR in professional sport began with extended conversations related to developing our research programmes and our common interests. As colleagues working together in the same department (Sport Management at the University of Michigan), we were keen to collaborate on research that would be personally and professionally interesting and rewarding. We found that we had overlapping scholarly interests in the areas of collaborations and part-nerships, strategy and general ethical and moral business practices, and that these merged around the concept of social responsibility. This background served as the foundation to inform and develop our thinking concerning CSR. Once we had established our common motivation and our common ground, we then engaged in further conversations and reading on the topic of CSR and began thinking about its application to professional sport. Together, in 2005, we attended a lecture from a colleague in the business school at the University of Michigan (Jim Walsh), who spoke about the need for scholars to dig deeper into corporate social initiatives (c.f., Margolis and Walsh, 2003). He identified key gaps that the management literature had overlooked in this area, including the context, process and outcomes of CSR efforts. Following this presentation we had an 'ah ha' moment. We decided to extend the extant theoretical knowledge concerning CSR to professional sport. As discussed earlier, we believed that this was a worthy endeavour given the unique elements of sport. We thus set about to better understand CSR in the sport industry with a focus on key gaps in the CSR literature that Jim Walsh had identified: the context and processes of CSR. We then began to seriously pursue questions concerning the phenomenon of CSR in sport, including: in what types of CSR activities are sport organisations engaging; why are they interested in CSR; what is motivating particular types of CSR activities; what are the processes by which teams and leagues engage in CSR; and what perceptions decision-makers had concerning the benefits of CSR to the sport organisations and to society more broadly.

We thought that it was important to leverage extant knowledge concerning CSR – from scholars as well as practitioners. From a scholarly perspective, we organised symposia at both the Academy of Management Annual Meeting, as well as NASSM, to share and develop our ideas around CSR and the unique setting of professional sport. Given our location, we reached out, and were able to develop relationships with executives of teams in each of the major professional sport leagues in the Midwest. We also had extensive discussions with executives from the Sports Philanthropy Project and the Robert Wood Johnson Foundation (who around the same time had begun efforts to building the field of CSR and philanthropy in sport), which helped crystallise our thinking of the internal resources that sport teams and leagues might leverage to engage in impactful CSR. Our relationships with practitioners, as well as other academics, were instrumental in informing our efforts to develop concepts and processes related to CSR in professional sport.

At the time we were doing the research resulting in our framework, literature in management was advancing beyond simple descriptions of CSR initiatives, to one of understanding the rationale for, and the benefit of, these activities (c.f., Bruch and Walter, 2005; Campbell, 2007; Porter and Kramer, 2006). This more strategic CSR focus seemed to be in line with our findings. Given that, we revisited whether there is something unique about sport organisations as it relates to CSR. If not – what would our contribution be? This question about whether there is something unique about sport organisations, is, of course, not unique to our efforts (Chalip, 2006; Doherty, 2013; Slack, 1998). We had our own perspective concerning how sport *is different* from a CSR perspective that we presented in detail in Babiak and Wolfe (2009) and briefly above. That is, the key dimensions of transparency, passion, economics and stakeholder management are somewhat unique in sport and each has an effect on CSR. Thus, the momentum and growth of CSR efforts in sport organisations, along with the increasing focus in the scholarly management literature, and our common research interests, led us to begin our research programme in this area.

Our first step in building a framework that would have broad practical and scholarly impact was to scan and review CSR theories and approaches in the academic literature and consider the variety of perspectives to set the bounds for our research question – why are sport organisations engaging in CSR? We believed that not only were there external pressures driving organisations to behave socially responsibly, but also internal values, competencies and resources that would determine in what types of CSR organisations engaged.

Carroll's (1979, 1999) writing on CSR was instrumental in helping us conceptualise the key areas of obligation of CSR. He argued that there are four areas of CSR. These are: economic responsibility, legal responsibility, ethical responsibility and discretionary/philanthropic responsibility. In our framing, we focused primarily on facets of CSR related to ethical and discretionary forms of responsibility. We also sought out and considered various other theoretical perspectives evident in the literature to explain and extend knowledge generated about CSR. We were particularly interested in certain theoretical perspectives, including instrumental theories, where the corporation is viewed as an instrument for wealth creation and CSR is viewed as a tool to create financial and strategic benefits for the organisation; political theories, that emphasise the social power of corporations and their political responsibility to society; and theories in which businesses integrate their social demands and expectations given the dependence, growth and continuity of business on society (Garriga and Melé, 2004). These theoretical perspectives helped us narrow our framing to answer our questions of interest. While our research was primarily inductive and grounded, this theoretical background served as the foundation from which to initiate our study.

In developing our framework, we first conducted a qualitative study to explore what forces sport practitioners deem central to the adoption and integration of CSR efforts in their organisations (Babiak and Wolfe, 2009). The empirical findings provided the foundation for our conceptual framework and we connected these with existing theoretical perspectives. In particular, to situate and describe the external pressures faced by professional sports teams that emerged from our findings, we drew on Oliver's (1991) framing with the concepts: cause, constituents, control, context and content. Oliver's work integrates institutional, stakeholder and resource dependence theories; we found this work helpful in explaining the reasons outside of the organisation that CSR practices were adopted by sport organisations. However, in our study, we found that the external pressures only told part of the story. An internal perspective was missing, as we found that organisations leverage key resources that are rare, valuable or inimitable to bring about CSR benefits to both the organisation and society. Thus, we drew theoretically on the resource based view of the firm (c.f., Barney, 1991; Barney, Wright and Ketchen, 2001) to consider whether relevant resources of professional sport teams provided them with advantages in implementing CSR. We were particularly interested in 'whether or not, and the extent to which, our respondents framed the rationale for adopting CSR as being related to internal resources' (Babiak and Wolfe, 2009, p. 731).

Extensions and applications of our framework

The central tenets of our framework have remained relatively consistent since we developed them. However, we have further refined our conceptualisation of CSR. The early literature on CSR in sport tended to focus primarily on community relations efforts. However, as we have further immersed ourselves in the area, we realised that CSR in sport is more nuanced and complex. A recent book chapter we wrote (Babiak and Wolfe, 2013) highlights the industry-specific indicators (or what we termed *pillars*) of CSR in sport; these are: labour relations, community relations, philanthropy, diversity, environmental sustainability and corporate governance. We believe that this fine-tuning of CSR in sport is very much related to our determinants of the adoption of CSR in professional sport framework, as each CSR pillar would have different and unique rationales and the engagement in each of these would be driven by different motives. We discuss the relationship of the pillars to our framework in the Future Directions section.

From a practical perspective, our research has helped to define and direct the work of practitioners and the evaluation of CSR and philanthropy practices in professional sport. For instance, with our involvement, the Steve Patterson Sport Philanthropy Award (co-ordinated through the Robert Wood Johnson Foundation) has integrated into its criteria for assessing team and league philanthropy, how internal resources are leveraged to deliver philanthropy, as well as the key links and relationships built with stakeholders in the environment.

Future directions

The framing we developed in Babiak and Wolfe (2009) offered a foundation from which to launch further exploration of the phenomenon of CSR in sport. While we believe that our thinking around strategic CSR in sport is robust, there are some gaps and clarifications that might advance deeper theoretical and empirical understanding of CSR in this context. Below, we highlight some of these areas.

As previously indicated, in Babiak and Wolfe (2013) we outline six pillars of CSR in sport. An interesting research direction would be to determine where each pillar (labour relations, community relations, philanthropy, diversity, environmental sustainability and corporate governance) tends to be situated within the cells of our framework – i.e., stakeholder-centric, corporate-centric, ad hoc, strategic, cells – and how such situating is related to outcomes.

The framework we developed considers the context in which CSR is emerging in sport. We know less about the processes and outcomes of these efforts in sport management. In particular, the relationship between institutional environments and organisational variation in the scope and scale of CSR efforts needs further attention. Organisations are exposed to multiple, sometimes conflicting, institutional pressures across nested fields (c.f., Dacin, Goodstein and Scott, 2002; Kraatz and Block, 2008; Greenwood, *et al.*, 2011). Corresponding uncertainty may decelerate or halt the process of adoption or implementation of CSR. Thus, we suggest that future research explore how sport organisations make sense of, and respond to, institutional pressures from different levels (e.g., team, league, community; Babiak and Wolfe, 2013). This line of questioning may illuminate what leads to variation in the degree to which sport organisations engage in CSR behaviours – an area not explained fully by our framing. Further, by examining heterogeneity in CSR activities across organisations, we can also gain a better understanding of the internal and external impacts. So far, researchers have mostly struggled to evaluate the impact of different types of CSR to organisations and society broadly. Developing better metrics to assess both financial and non-financial outcomes will improve scholars' ability to make causal claims about CSR, and its particular forms.

Our framework can also be extended to other contexts. Applying our framing to other settings will provide a deeper understanding of social responsibility in the sport domain and what makes sport organisations similar to, and different from, each other. Furthermore, as Gardberg and Fombrun (2006) suggest, it is important to examine CSR in the global context. For globalising companies, CSR serves as a strategic investment similar to advertising or traditional marketing. CSR can also be an important tool to quickly gain legitimacy. Engaging in the communities they come into allows businesses to overcome cultural barriers and build a local advantage in these communities. This has not been an area of focus for the sport CSR literature – but one which is gaining traction in practice with the global expansion of professional sport leagues. We expect that the external pressures for engaging in CSR in a global setting are different with a broader set of stakeholders. Additionally, internal resources may shift in value and utility from one country context to another. Understanding how resources are employed and the rationales for sport teams and leagues to engage in CSR globally will add important nuance to our framework.

Notes

1   This chapter is a reflection on Babiak and Wolfe (2009) and the work related to it.
2   This chapter was written by the three authors Kathy Babiak, Kate Heinze and Richard Wolfe. While Dr Heinze arrived at the University of Michigan after this framework was developed, she has collaborated on projects linked to CSR with us and has extensively employed and extended the framing described herein.

References

Anagnostopoulos, C. and Shilbury, D. (2013) 'Implementing corporate social responsibility in English football: Towards multi-theoretical integration'. *Sport, Business and Management: An International Journal*, 3: 268–84.

Aupperle, K.E., Carroll, A.B. and Hatfield, J.D. (1985) 'An empirical examination of the relationship between corporate social responsibility and profitability'. *Academy of Management Journal, 28*: 446–63.

Babiak, K. and Trendafilova, S. (2011) 'CSR and environmental responsibility: Motives and pressures to adopt green management practices'. *Corporate Social Responsibility and Environmental Management, 18*: 11–24.

Babiak, K. and Wolfe, R. (2006) 'More than just a game? Corporate social responsibility and Super Bowl XL'. *Sport Marketing Quarterly, 15*: 214.

Babiak, K. and Wolfe, R. (2009) 'Determinants of corporate social responsibility in professional sport: Internal and external factors'. *Journal of Sport Management, 23*: 717–42.

Babiak, K. and Wolfe, R. (2013) 'Perspectives on CSR in sport'. In J.L. Paramio, K. Babiak and G. Walters (eds). *The handbook of corporate responsibility in sport: Principles and practice* (pp. 17–34). London: Routledge.

Barney, J. (1991) 'Firm resources and sustained competitive advantage'. *Journal of Management, 17*: 99–120.

Barney, J., Wright, M. and Ketchen, D.J. (2001) 'The resource-based view of the firm: Ten years after 1991'. *Journal of Management, 27*: 625–41.

Bruch, H. and Walter, F. (2005) 'The keys to rethinking corporate philanthropy'. *MIT Sloan Management Review, 47*: 49–55.

Campbell, J.L. (2007) 'Why would corporations behave in socially responsible ways? An institutional theory of corporate social responsibility'. *Academy of Management Review, 32*: 946–67.

Carroll, A. (1979) 'A three dimensional conceptual model of corporate social performance'. *Academy of Management Review, 4*: 497–505.

Carroll, A. (1999) 'Corporate social responsibility: Evolution of a definitional construct'. *Business and Society, 38*: 268–95.

Chalip, L. (2006) 'Toward a distinctive sport management discipline'. *Journal of Sport Management, 20*: 1–21.

Dacin, M.T., Goodstein, J. and Scott, W.R. (2002) 'Institutional theory and institutional change: Introduction and special research forum'. *Academy of Management Journal, 45*: 45–57.

Davis, K. (1973) 'The case for and against business assumptions of social responsibilities'. *Academy of Management Journal, 16*: 312–22.

Doherty, A. (2013) '"It takes a village": Interdisciplinary research for sport management'. *Journal of Sport Management, 27*: 1–10.

Drucker, P.F. (1984) 'The new meaning of corporate social responsibility'. *California Management Review, 26*: 53–63.

Freeman R.E. (1984) *Strategic management: A stakeholder approach.* Marshfield, MA: Pitman Publishing.

Friedman, M. (1962) *Capitalism and freedom.* Chicago, IL: The University of Chicago Press.

Friedman, M. (1970) 'A Friedman doctrine – The social responsibility of business is to increase its profits'. *The New York Times Magazine*, Sept. 13, 32–3, and 123–5.

Gardberg, N.A. and Fombrun, C.J. (2006) 'Corporate citizenship: Creating intangible assets across institutional environments'. *Academy of Management Review, 31*: 329–46.

Garriga, E. and Melé, D. (2004) 'Corporate social responsibility theories: Mapping the territory'. *Journal of Business Ethics, 53*(1–2): 51–71.

Greenwood, R., Raynard, M., Kodeih, F., Micelotta, E.R. and Lounsbury, M. (2011) 'Institutional complexity and organizational responses'. *The Academy of Management Annals, 5*: 317–71.

Hamil, S. and Morrow, S. (2011) 'Corporate social responsibility in the Scottish Premier League: context and motivation'. *European Sport Management Quarterly, 11*: 143–70.

Heinze, K.L., Soderstrom, S. and Zdroik, J. (2014) 'Toward strategic and authentic corporate social responsibility in professional sport: A case study of the Detroit Lions'. *Journal of Sport Management, 28*: 672–86.

Irwin, R.L., Lachowetz, T., Cornwell, T.B. and Clark, J.S. (2003) 'Cause-related sport sponsorship: An assessment of spectator beliefs, attitudes, and behavioral intentions'. *Sport Marketing Quarterly, 12*: 131–9.

Kraatz, M.S. and Block, E.S. (2008) 'Organizational implications of institutional pluralism'. In R. Suddaby, R. Greenwood and K. Sahlin (eds), *Handbook of organizational institutionalism.* New York: Sage.

McGuire, J.B., Sundgren, A. and Schneeweis, T. (1988) 'Corporate social responsibility and firm financial performance'. *Academy of Management Journal, 31*: 854–72.

McWilliams, A. and Siegel, D. (2000) 'Corporate social responsibility and financial performance: Correlation or misspecification?' *Strategic Management Journal, 21*: 603–09.

Margolis, J.D. and Walsh, J.P. (2003) 'Misery loves companies: Rethinking social initiatives by business'. *Administrative Science Quarterly, 48*: 268–305.

Mohr, L.A., Webb, D.J. and Harris, K.E. (2001) 'Do consumers expect companies to be socially responsible? The impact of corporate social responsibility on buying behavior'. *Journal of Consumer Affairs, 35*: 45–72.

Oliver, C. (1991) 'Strategic responses to institutional processes'. *Academy of Management Review*, 16: 145–79.

Porter, M.E. and Kramer, M.R. (2006) 'Strategy and society: The link between competitive advantage and corporate social responsibility'. *Harvard Business Review*, 84: 78–92.

Porter, M.E. and Kramer, M.R. (2011) 'Creating shared value'. *Harvard Business Review*, 89: 62–77.

Robinson, R. (2005) 'Sports philanthropy: An analysis of the charitable foundations of major league teams'. Unpublished master's thesis. University of San Francisco.

Sethi, S.P. (1975) 'The dimensions of corporate social performance: An analytic framework'. *California Management Review*, 17: 58–64.

Slack, T. (1998) 'Is there anything unique about sport management'. *European Journal for Sport Management*, 5: 21–9.

Trendafilova, S., Babiak, K. and Heinze, K. (2013) 'Corporate social responsibility and environmental sustainability: Why professional sport is greening the field'. *Sport Management Review*, 16: 298–313.

Walker, M. and Kent, A. (2009) 'Do fans care? Assessing the influence of corporate social responsibility on consumer attitudes in the sport industry'. *Journal of Sport Management*, 23: 743–69.

Applying strategic CSR in sport

Yuhei Inoue[1]

As a doctoral student, I paid close attention to Kathy Babiak's research because her foundational work in 2006 (Babiak and Wolfe, 2006) on sport and corporate social responsibility (CSR) played a critical role in my decision to pursue a doctoral degree. I further drew from Babiak and Wolfe (2009) in my literature review on CSR for my dissertation. Introduced to the concept of CSR through these works, I was inspired by the idea that academic research can advance the development of socially responsible practices among professional sport organisations.

The main contribution of Babiak and Wolfe (2009) to my academic development is to clarify the uniqueness of CSR in professional sport. Early in the paper, Babiak and Wolfe identified four factors that make CSR in professional sport distinctive: passion, economics, transparency and stakeholder management. Their framework regarding the adoption of CSR also built on unique elements that determine the decisions of professional sport organisations. Through theoretical discussions and empirical findings, they successfully challenged the contention that 'there is no need for research to examine the determinants of CSR in professional sport, as they would not differ from those in other industries' (Babiak and Wolfe, 2009, p. 722).

In identifying the uniqueness of CSR in professional sport, Babiak and Wolfe (2009) revealed that 'given the passion and interest that sport generates . . . athletes promoting, for example, healthful living, may generate a larger, more attentive audience than would employees in other fields' (p. 722). I took this revelation seriously. I designed my dissertation project to understand whether and how professional sport organisations promote socially responsible behaviours through their corporate social marketing effort, which is one type of CSR initiative (Inoue, 2011). I also conducted related research projects to address this research agenda (Inoue and Kent, 2012; Inoue, Mahan and Kent, 2013). Babiak and Wolfe's framework has been helpful for my teaching as well. For my courses on CSR, I have used their framework to explain why professional sport organisations have increased CSR efforts since the late 1990s.

Babiak and Wolfe (2009) concluded their paper by suggesting that 'a further, future, direction in which to embark would be to address intended CSR outcomes; i.e., to what extent do programs have the intended influence?' (p. 737). My future research aligns with these sentiments.

Through empirical evidence, I hope to demonstrate that professional sport organisations' CSR programmes are impactful for improving given social issues. I further aim to identify the factors that affect the social impact of such programmes as Babiak and Wolfe's framework has shown that any CSR activity is constrained by both internal resources and external pressures.

In conclusion, Babiak and Wolfe have made a clear case for why the specific examination of CSR in professional sport is worthy of academic investigation. Their work has contributed to the development of a unique body of knowledge in sport management and has inspired a number of researchers, including myself, to conduct research on this topic.

Note

1   Yuhei Inoue is an Assistant Professor of Sport Management in the School of Kinesiology at the University of Minnesota.

References

Babiak, K. and Wolfe, R. (2006) 'More than just a game? Corporate social responsibility and super bowl'. *Sport Marketing Quarterly*, *15*: 214–22.

Babiak, K. and Wolfe, R. (2009) 'Determinants of corporate social responsibility in professional sport: Internal and external factors'. *Journal of Sport Management*, *23*: 717–42.

Inoue, Y. (2011) 'Investigating the role of corporate credibility in corporate social marketing: A case study of environmental initiatives by professional sport organizations' (Unpublished doctoral dissertation). Temple University, Philadelphia, PA.

Inoue, Y. and Kent, A. (2012) 'Sport teams as promoters of pro-environmental behavior: An empirical study'. *Journal of Sport Management*, *26*: 417–32.

Inoue, Y., Mahan, J.E. and Kent, A. (2013) 'Enhancing the benefits of professional sport philanthropy: The roles of corporate ability and communication strategies'. *Sport Management Review*, *16*: 314–25.

6

STAKEHOLDER MANAGEMENT FOR SPORT ORGANISATIONS[1]

Milena M. Parent

Overview

In this chapter, I explore the framework I developed in my paper titled 'Evolution and issue patterns for major-sport-event organizing committees and their stakeholders', published in the *Journal of Sport Management* (Parent, 2008). The purpose of the article was 'to develop a framework of how an organising committee operationally evolves over time and the types of issues with which it and its stakeholders must deal' (p. 136). This study was part of my doctoral dissertation, in which I took an organisation theory perspective to understand the type of organisation (temporary, project, business, passion, adrenaline, etc.) an organising committee is, how it changes or evolves, who surrounds the organising committee, and what do they want/need.

To do so, I drew on stakeholder theory and issues management, sister theories under the corporate social responsibility (CSR) banner (Carroll, 1999; Wood, 1991). I also considered what literature was available in terms of organisational evolution and issues pertaining to sports events. These theoretical underpinnings helped guide methodology decisions and resulted in the empirically derived sport event organising committee and stakeholder framework, which answered the study's purpose.

In the first part of this chapter, I discuss the theoretical basis of my study, followed by the final framework itself, boundary considerations and how I have applied the framework in subsequent research. I then move on to describing the process I used to derive the theoretical underpinnings and the final framework, as well as extensions and applications of that framework. I end the chapter with some future directions that I trust will benefit theory, research, practice and teaching.

Stakeholder theory

Stakeholder theory took form with Freeman's (1984) book *Strategic management: A stakeholder approach*. He used strategic organisational planning, systems theory and organisation theory to build his argument for a stakeholder theory of the firm. Since then, thousands of articles and books have been published related to stakeholder theory (e.g., Donaldson and Preston, 1995; Mitchell, Agle and Wood, 1997; Parmar *et al.*, 2010). Freeman (1984) described a stakeholder as any group or person who can affect or who is affected by an organisation's actions. Since then, researchers have argued that this definition of a stakeholder is too broad (e.g., Donaldson and Preston, 1995; Mitchell *et al.*, 1997; Phillips, 2003; Post, Preston and Sachs, 2002). Nevertheless, as the sport event literature had not determined who the sport event stakeholder groups were, I followed Freeman's broad definition for my study.

Stakeholder theorists are interested in a given (focal) organisation, its stakeholders, as well as the relationship between the focal organisation and its stakeholders, examining both process and outcome. The key is the focal organisation–stakeholder relationship. As Post *et al.* (2002) noted, 'The stakeholder view of the corporation recognises these reciprocal interdependencies, which constitute the stakeholder network of each firm' (p. 255). Stakeholder theorists focus on managerial decision-making and strategies to meet stakeholder needs (Jones and Wicks, 1999). Donaldson and Preston (1995) suggest that there are three ways to use stakeholder theory:

1   *Empirical/descriptive approach*: describing the nature and type of organisation, how board members consider the interests of stakeholders, how managers understand managing, and how organisations are truly managed;
2   *Instrumental approach*: identifying factors associated with stakeholder management that lead to organisational success (usually traditionally defined as profit and corporate social performance or CSP); and
3   *Normative approach*: examining and providing the moral/philosophical guidelines associated with the management/operation of the focal organisation, as well as analysing the functions of an organisation.

While strategic management researchers may use stakeholder theory's instrumentalist approach, some argue that the descriptive and normative core are the key to stakeholder theory (e.g., Donaldson and Preston, 1995; Rowley, 1998), especially with the debate surrounding the impact of stakeholder management on CSP (see Clarkson, 1995; Gerde, 2000; Orlitzky and Swanson, 2012; Rowley and Berman, 2000). As I was beginning to explore the world of sport event organising committees, the empirical/descriptive approach seemed most appropriate. Clarkson (1995) suggested that the key generic stakeholders include the company itself, its employees, customers, shareholders and suppliers. However, these did not necessarily fit with what I understood the world of sport event stakeholders to be – organising committees are an entirely different beast from the for-profit organisations usually scrutinised in stakeholder theory and management research. Thus, finding out who the stakeholders were and what they wanted would become an essential starting point. I knew from the literature that stakeholder groups have different needs and wants, both between these groups and within a given stakeholder group – what is termed stakeholder heterogeneity (see Wolfe and Putler, 2002). Reichart (2003) suggested that stakeholders have a combination of the following interests: affiliative, informational, material, political and symbolic. These would be used as part of the theoretical underpinnings to understand sport event stakeholder needs and wants. It is noteworthy that when Freeman and colleagues (2010) reviewed and updated the thinking on stakeholder theory, they argued that stakeholder theory was about creating value for all stakeholders of an organisation.

Issues management

Along with stakeholder management and crisis management, issues management is seen as a proactive managerial activity where managerial involvement is high (Oomens and van den Bosch, 1999). Wartick and Mahon (1994) defined a corporate issue as:

(a) a controversial inconsistency based on one or more expectational gaps, (b) involving management perceptions of changing legitimacy and other stakeholder perceptions of changing cost/benefit positions, (c) that occur within or between views of what is and/or what ought to be corporate performance or stakeholder perceptions of corporate performance, and (d) imply an actual or anticipated resolution that creates significant, identifiable present or future impact on the organization.

(p. 306)

Of interest for my study was the concept of gaps. If stakeholders had different expectations from what the organising committee (or vice versa) was thinking, planning and/or undertaking in relation to one of their interests (see Reichart, 2003), an expectational gap occurred, which I would then be able to identify in the study as an issue.

The resulting framework

Stakeholder theory combined with issues management provided me with a lens to examine the world of an organising committee to (a) understand what an organising committee is (e.g., how it evolves from beginning to end and the types of issues or expectational gaps with which it must deal); and (b) to identify and characterise the stakeholders that surround the organising committee. These theoretical underpinnings guided my methodological choices (e.g., types of data to gather and initial guide for coding the qualitative data).

The resulting findings shaped the sport event management framework. More precisely, the results of the data analysis indicated there are three modes of operation for an organising committee: (a) planning (including bid and transition phases, business plan, operational plan and divisional plans), (b) implementation (including venuisation and Games-time) and (c) wrap-up (including decommissioning the venues, writing the final reports, closing the books and organisation, and managing the legacies). Throughout these modes, the organising committee deals with a number of issues, categorised as follows: politics, visibility, financial, organising, relationships, operations, sport, infrastructure, human resources, media, interdependence, participation and legacy. Taking the organising committee board of directors as the focal organisation, the stakeholder groups to be managed include: the volunteers and paid staff composing the organising committee, host governments, various levels of sports organisations, community (including residents, local businesses/sponsors, community groups and schools), media and delegations (athletes, mission staff). Finally, I found intra- and inter-stakeholder group heterogeneity regarding the types of issues and interests.

Boundary conditions

Following Whetten (1989), the boundaries of generalisability or range of a theory are the temporal (when) and contextual (who, where) factors forming the theory. The sport event management framework I developed must be understood as one that was advanced with events held before the explosion of new technologies (e.g., smartphones, Wi-Fi and social media). As well, it was developed based on non-mega sport event data, which has meant some extensions have been needed for mega events (see the 'Extensions and applications' section, below). Still, the stakeholder approach and resulting stakeholder map is general enough to be adaptable to other types of events (see next section).

Application of the framework in subsequent research

In effect, the framework I developed in Parent (2008) has become the starting point for most, if not all, of my research on sports events since then. For example, with Christopher Hautbois and Benoit Séguin (Hautbois, Parent and Séguin, 2012), we used stakeholder analysis (specifically the power-legitimacy-urgency framework developed by Mitchell *et al.*, 1997) to see how the stakeholder network factored into the national bid process of an Olympic Winter Games. With Norwegian colleagues (Hanstad, Parent and Kristiansen, 2013; Parent, Kristiansen, Skille and Hanstad, 2015), I moved from examining dyadic stakeholder ties to the ties in the overall stakeholder network ties in the 2012 Winter Youth Olympic Games.

These studies have mainly used stakeholder theory's empirical/descriptive approach. I have also used the two other approaches described by Donaldson and Preston (1995). From an instrumental perspective, the stakeholder theory approach to sports events and the organising committee modes have been used to examine decision-making (Parent, 2010), leadership (Parent, Beaupre and Séguin, 2009; Parent, Olver and Séguin, 2009), brand creation in one-off (Parent and Séguin, 2008) and recurring events (Parent, Eskerud and Hanstad, 2012), risk management (Leopkey and Parent, 2009a, 2009b), specific issues and strategies for a particular stakeholder group the governments bringing in the concept of multi-level governance (Parent, Rouillard and Leopkey, 2011) and organisational culture and member performance (Parent and MacIntosh, 2013). From a normative standpoint, the stakeholder approach has been used in relation to the Olympic Games Organizing Committee and International Olympic Committee CSR (Walker, Heere, Parent and Drane, 2010) as well as partners' or sponsor CSR (Séguin, Parent and O'Reilly, 2010).

The process of developing the framework

My interest in sport event organising committees and stakeholders was spurred by my practical experience. During my master's degree internship with the 2001 Games of la Francophonie (GF), I felt I did not know much about the area, as I had been in the field of sport management for less than eight months. I had undertaken a career and field change from physiology and biochemistry to sport management the previous fall. Prior to the change, I had had no course/theoretical knowledge in management, let alone sport management – though I had been a competitive figure skater, coach and volunteer, and so had the practical experience. Like a good student, I endeavoured to find some research and general information on who/what organising committees were to help me in my tasks at the 2001 GF. Yet, I could not find empirical papers (as opposed to to-do lists) on the topic, as odd as that seemed. I thought someone should do research on this, maybe even me, to ensure I would not repeat the same mistakes I made the first time around. This thought eventually led to my admission into a doctoral programme, and examination of these issues. A key concern in this Handbook is how theory in sport management is developed. There are a variety of ways this can be undertaken. I describe mine below.

Contribution of theory to the study of sport event management includes borrowing and adapting existing theories (cf., Doherty, 2013). So let's start with borrowing. When I was exposed to stakeholder theory during a doctoral course in strategic management theories, I realised that I, as a 2001 GF manager, and the rest of the organising committee, had grouped clients (stakeholders) by category (e.g., athletes and media) in order to deal with them. So, when I learned about stakeholder theory, it seemed to be an appropriate theory to help explain how organising committees work. Stakeholder theory's attractiveness resided in it, ironically, not being a fully formed theory. Rather, it is (a) an umbrella framework, for lack of a better word, that allows for other concepts and theories to be included, or conceptual blending as Oswick, Fleming and Hanlon (2011) suggest; (b) practitioner-derived and constantly applied in the broader management field; and (c) general enough to be rather easily applied in a different/new context. As a framework it is 'a set of ideas from which a number of theories can be derived' (Parmar *et al.*, 2010, p. 406). In terms of adapting a theory, further examination of stakeholder theory, its premises and origins, made me realise that to understand how the organising committee worked – an organisation that seems (on the outside) to plan the event (be proactive) and balance or respond to (be reactive) stakeholder needs, demands and situations – I needed to look for a way to add to stakeholder theory. This is where issues management came in (see also Friedman, Parent and Mason, 2004). By borrowing and adapting stakeholder theory and issues management, I was able to have a theoretical basis upon which to organise and analyse my data, such as identifying the stakeholders, grouping data/findings by stakeholders and identifying issues.

Next, contributions to theory also entail extending and generating (new) theory (Doherty, 2013). In my case, the research actually started with a simple, yet too broad question: how do organising committees work? My doctoral supervisor at the time, Professor Trevor Slack, and I both knew this was a large and very complex issue to study (cf., Cunningham, 2013), but neither of us knew where to start and what was feasible to do. So I took a very exploratory approach (akin to grounded theory, see Charmaz, 2006; Glaser and Strauss, 1967) by conducting a pilot study in 2002 on the 2001 GF; a retrospective case study that included a rather lengthy discussion on the topic with a former 2001 GF colleague, who had many sport events and festivals under his belt, as well as discussing ideas with other former 2001 GF colleagues through pilot interviews. These discussions focused my work for the ensuing retrospective and full case study of the 1999 Pan American Games. Key ideas were taking shape (i.e., generating new theory through empirical observations in the natural setting, see Doherty, 2013), including the concept of time (or lack thereof) being important in a potential sport event management framework, and multiple issues (including, in particular, image and identity management, see Parent and Foreman, 2007) and stakeholders to negotiate. During my studies, I was advised by a prominent researcher in management that, if I could illustrate in one image the various theories and concepts to be examined in my study, then I was on the right track. Figure 6.1, therefore, depicts the evolution from the research question to pilot study (2001 GF) to the actual research I undertook for the Parent (2008) study on the 1999 Pan American Games.

Going back to the baseline theories, I could see links between what stakeholder theorists examine (the focal organisation–stakeholder relationship) and the topics in which I was interested. Figure 6.2 was the result of linking the two ideas and the starting point for data collection related to the 1999 Pan American Games, which would lead to the empirically derived sport event management framework.

The ideas in the pilot study were explored and refined in the 1999 Games case. First, I looked at the temporal aspect; how organising committees evolve. By comparing the terms and explanations found in the data, I was able to come up with the three modes of organising committees. The second piece was figuring out how stakeholders should be grouped. Interviewees' responses as to whom they dealt with were compared, which provided me with the aggregated stakeholder map found in the article (Parent, 2008). Admittedly, this was a rather descriptive approach, though one which was needed before being able to move to instrumental and normative aspects.

Using the issues management portion of the theoretical framework or more precisely the expectational gaps, helped me determine what an issue would be, so I was able to identify issues faced by organising committees and their stakeholders. A long list of initial issues was created, which I then aggregated into broader compatible issue categories.

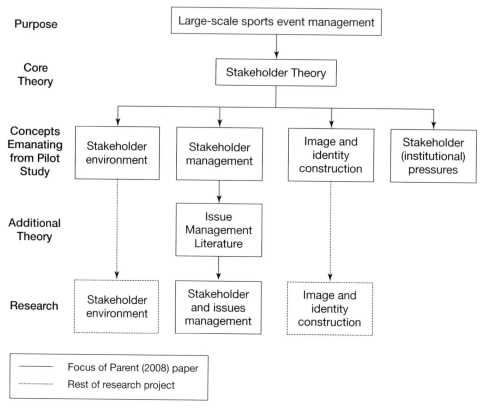

Figure 6.1 Purpose, theory, pilot study and (proposed) research flow chart

With the modes (the *what* and *when*), issues (also part of the *what*) and stakeholder map (the *who*), in addition to the theoretical underpinnings, I now had a working, empirically derived framework from which to further build theory in sport event management (cf., Whetten, 1989). For example, I was able to link the issue categories list to the modes of the organising committee, to the managerial level of organising committee members and to the stakeholders. So the study contributed to theory, for example, by demonstrating that perceived stakeholder salience depends on the manager (managerial level and the cognitive perception or map of his/her world), the issue and time. Essentially, I found that any stakeholder can be critical at one particular time for one particular issue.

Extensions and applications

Since 2008, the framework has evolved as we have learned more about event organising committees. For instance, sponsors have become a distinct category of stakeholders for larger sports events and new/social media has emerged. The workforce has been expanded to include other types of members, such as those who are seconded from their workplace and contract workers. An 'Other Stakeholders' category has been added to reflect the fact that many event organising committees will engage with non-traditional stakeholders, such as non-governmental organisations (e.g., United Nations) and consultant organisations. So, the updated list of

Organising Committee	Relationship	Stakeholders

- Description of sport event and its organising committee (o);
- How is the organising committee viewed (s);
- Event management issues (o).

- Management strategies used by the organising committee and stakeholders (o/s);
- Partnership characteristics (o/s);
- Partnership issues (o/s);
- Issues management (o/s);
- Partnership success (o/s).

- Who are the stakeholders (o);
- How are the stakeholders viewed (o);
- What do the stakeholders want and why enter into a partnership (s);
- Which stakeholders are more important (o).

(o) – Organising committee questions
(s) – Stakeholders' questions
(o/s) – Question asked to both the organising committee and the stakeholders

Figure 6.2 Relationship between the theory and research questions

stakeholders should read: the organising committee workforce, the host governments, the various levels of sport organisations (including the event rights holder), the community, the media (including internet and new/social media), sponsors, the delegations and other stakeholders (see Parent and Smith-Swan, 2013).

Others have also applied parts of the framework in their research. Some researchers have taken the stakeholder perspective to examine partnerships or bilateral relationships, as well as by adopting a stakeholder approach to their study. For example, Heere *et al.* (2012) based the premise of their study on bilateral relationships on a key idea of the Parent (2008) article that effective stakeholder management is at the core of a successful sport event. In turn, Dowling, Robinson and Washington (2013) have extended thoughts from my study, arguing that:

> given the very cyclical nature of major sporting events, and congruent with the mega-event decision-making literature (see for example, Parent, 2008, 2010), *timing and context matters*, with sport being inherently more attractive in the lead up to mega-events. This research shows that that there may be better times than others for sport organisations to seek CSR and partnership arrangements.
>
> *(p. 288, emphasis added)*

Finally, Kihl, Leberman and Schull (2010) took a stakeholder approach to examine how leadership is constructed in intercollegiate athletics.

More broadly, though, the use of stakeholder theory in sport management has blossomed since 2008. For instance, in 2011 there was a special issue on stakeholders in *European Sport Management Quarterly* (e.g., Russo and Vito, 2011; Xue and Mason, 2011). Interestingly, Esteve and colleagues (2011), who set out to empirically examine 'the impact of stakeholder relations on the resources that a non-profit sports organization is able to attract' (p. 424), found that:

the quality of relations between sports clubs and their external stakeholders relate positively to the financial and non-financial contributions of stakeholders. A club's financial resources are also positively linked to the amount of time its Board of Directors is willing to invest.

(p. 423)

Clearly, the organising committee and stakeholder approach has been a useful one for research. However, it has also been useful in informing teaching and practice, at least for me. I organise my sport events and festivals class according to the three modes of organising committees. The modes, stakeholders and issues identified also formed the basis (the skeleton) for the *Managing major sports events: Theory and practice* book (Parent and Smith-Swan, 2013), which is used as a reference by a variety of practitioners, such as those at Sport Canada, as well as the International Olympic Committee.

Future directions

So what lies ahead for the framework? In terms of theoretical/empirical extensions of the sport event organising committees and stakeholders framework, it is important to move from dyadic ties to inter-stakeholder relationships; that is, the network of stakeholders (Rowley, 1997). For instance, which stakeholders are more important and why, across each mode? What is the impact on the network of the newly added stakeholders (e.g., new/social media, non-governmental organisations and security organisations)? It is also important to further examine the transition from bid to organising committee to foster organisational effectiveness and efficiency, but also the organising committee members' transition from headquarters to the venues come event-time (for the same reasons). Transitions and change are difficult in any context; in this high-stress situation, it becomes even more critical to manage properly. In turn, continuing to examine the various issues/issue categories is important to show interrelationships and influences between issues. There is also a need to expand the type of event examined to smaller events and to recurring events, as these events are more likely to be hosted by more cities worldwide in their events portfolios. Due to the practical perspective of the sport event management framework, in that it is meant not only to help frame a study but also to inform event managers' decisions, each of these future directions should be undertaken with both theory and practice rationales.

One final thought: it is not easy to develop theory properly, and there are multiple ways to do so. Following proper methodological procedures (e.g., Bacharach, 1989; Suddaby, 2006; Whetten, 1989) is critical. But just as important is to have people around you (e.g., doctoral supervisor, journal editors and book editors) who believe in what you do and want to publish it in order to truly advance the field.

Note

1   This chapter is a reflection on Parent (2008) and the work related to it.

References

Bacharach, S.B. (1989) 'Organizational theories: Some criteria for evaluation'. *Academy of Management Review*, *14*: 496–515.
Carroll, A.B. (1999) 'Corporate social responsibility: Evolution of a definitional construct'. *Business & Society*, *38*: 268–95.

Charmaz, K. (2006) *Constructing grounded theory: A practical guide through qualitative analysis*. Thousand Oaks, CA: Sage Publications.

Clarkson, M.B.E. (1995) 'A stakeholder framework for analyzing and evaluating corporate social performance'. *Academy of Management Review*, 20: 92–117.

Cunningham, G.B. (2013) 'Theory and theory development in sport management'. *Sport Management Review*, 16: 1–4.

Doherty, A. (2013) 'Investing in sport management: The value of good theory'. *Sport Management Review*, 16: 5–11.

Donaldson, T. and Preston, L.E. (1995) 'The stakeholder theory of the corporation: Concepts, evidence, and implications'. *Academy of Management Review*, 20: 65–91.

Dowling, M., Robinson, L. and Washington, M. (2013) 'Taking advantage of the London 2012 Olympic Games: Corporate social responsibility through sport partnerships'. *European Sport Management Quarterly*, 13: 269–92.

Esteve, M., Di Lorenzo, F., Inglés, E. and Puig, N. (2011) 'Empirical evidence of stakeholder management in sports clubs: The impact of the board of directors'. *European Sport Management Quarterly*, 11: 423–40.

Freeman, R.E. (1984) *Strategic management: A stakeholder approach*. Boston, MA: Pitman.

Freeman, R.E., Harrison, J.S., Wicks, A.C., Parmar, B.L. and de Colle, S. (2010) *Stakeholder theory: The state of the art*. New York: Cambridge University Press.

Friedman, M.T., Parent, M.M. and Mason, D.S. (2004) 'Building a framework for issues management in sport through stakeholder theory'. *European Sport Management Quarterly*, 4: 170–90.

Gerde, V.W. (2000) 'Stakeholders and organization design: An empirical test of corporate social performance'. In J.M. Logsdon, D.J. Wood and L.E. Benson (eds), *Research in stakeholder theory, 1997–1998. The Sloan Foundation Mini-grant Project* (pp. 7–19). Toronto, ON: The Clarkson Centre for Business Ethics.

Glaser, B. and Strauss, A.M. (1967) *The discovery of grounded theory: Strategies for qualitative research*. New York: Dr Gruyter.

Hanstad, D.V., Parent, M.M. and Kristiansen, E. (2013) 'The Youth Olympic Games: The best of the Olympics or a poor copy?' *European Sport Management Quarterly*, 13: 315–38.

Hautbois, C., Parent, M.M. and Séguin, B. (2012) 'How to win a bid for major sporting events? A stakeholder analysis of the 2018 Olympic Winter Games French bid'. *Sport Management Review*, 15: 263–75.

Heere, B., Kim, C., Yoshida, M., Nakamura, H., Ogura, T., Chung, K.S., *et al.* (2012) 'The impact of World Cup 2002 on the bilateral relationship between South Korea and Japan'. *Journal of Sport Management*, 26: 127–42.

Jones, T.M. and Wicks, A.C. (1999) 'Convergent stakeholder theory'. *Academy of Management Review*, 24: 206–21.

Kihl, L.A., Leberman, S. and Schull, V. (2010) 'Stakeholder constructions of leadership in intercollegiate athletics'. *European Sport Management Quarterly*, 10: 241–75.

Leopkey, B. and Parent, M.M. (2009a) 'Risk management issues in large-scale sporting events: A stakeholder perspective'. *European Sport Management Quarterly*, 9: 187–208.

Leopkey, B. and Parent, M.M. (2009b) 'Risk management strategies by stakeholders in Canadian major sporting events'. *Event Management*, 13: 153–70.

Mitchell, R.K., Agle, B.R. and Wood, D.J. (1997) 'Toward a theory of stakeholder identification and salience: Defining the principle of who and what really counts'. *Academy of Management Review*, 22: 853–86.

Oomens, M.J.H. and van den Bosch, F.A.J. (1999) 'Strategic issue management in major European-based companies'. *Long Range Planning*, 32(1): 49–57.

Orlitzky, M. and Swanson, D.L. (2012) 'Assessing stakeholder satisfaction: Toward a supplemental measure of corporate social performance as reputation'. *Corporate Reputation Review*, 15(2): 119–37.

Oswick, C., Fleming, P. and Hanlon, G. (2011) 'From borrowing to blending: Rethinking the processes of organizational theory building'. *Academy of Management Review*, 36: 6–11.

Parent, M.M. (2008) 'Evolution and issue patterns for major-sport-event organizing committees and their stakeholders'. *Journal of Sport Management*, 22: 135–64.

Parent, M.M. (2010) 'Decision making in major sport events over time: Parameters, drivers, and strategies'. *Journal of Sport Management*, 24: 291–318.

Parent, M.M., Beaupre, R. and Seguin, B. (2009) 'Key leadership qualities for major sporting events: The case of the world aquatics championships'. *International Journal of Sport Management & Marketing*, 6: 367–88.

Parent, M.M., Eskerud, L. and Hanstad, D.V. (2012) 'Brand creation in international recurring sports events'. *Sport Management Review, 15*: 145–59.

Parent, M.M. and Foreman, P.O. (2007) 'Organizational image and identity management in large-scale sporting events'. *Journal of Sport Management, 21*: 15–40.

Parent, M.M., Kristiansen, E., Skille, E.Å. and Hanstad, D.V. (2015) 'The sustainability of the Youth Olympic Games: Stakeholder networks and institutional perspectives'. *International Review for the Sociology of Sport, 50*: 326–348.

Parent, M.M. and MacIntosh, E.W. (2013) 'Organizational culture evolution in temporary organizations: The case of the 2010 Olympic Winter Games'. *Canadian Journal of Administrative Sciences, 30*: 223–37.

Parent, M.M., Olver, D. and Séguin, B. (2009) 'Understanding leadership in major sporting events: The case of the 2005 World Aquatics Championships'. *Sport Management Review, 12*: 167–84.

Parent, M.M., Rouillard, C. and Leopkey, B. (2011) 'Issues and strategies pertaining to the Canadian Governments' coordination efforts in relation to the 2010 Olympic Games'. *European Sport Management Quarterly, 11*: 337–69.

Parent, M.M. and Séguin, B. (2008) 'Toward a model of brand creation for international large-scale sporting events: The impact of leadership, context, and nature of the event'. *Journal of Sport Management, 22*: 526–49.

Parent, M.M. and Smith-Swan, S. (2013) *Managing major sports events: Theory and practice*. London: Routledge.

Parmar, B.L., Freeman, R.E., Harrison, J.S., Wicks, A.C., Purnell, L. and de Colle, S. (2010) 'Stakeholder theory: The state of the art'. *Academy of Management Annals, 4*: 403–45.

Phillips, R. (2003) *Stakeholder theory and organizational ethics*. San Francisco, CA: Berrett-Koehler Publishers.

Post, J.E., Preston, L.E. and Sachs, S. (2002) *Redefining the corporation: Stakeholder management and organizational wealth*. Stanford, CA: Stanford University Press.

Reichart, J. (2003) 'A theoretical exploration of expectational gaps in the corporate issue construct'. *Corporate Reputation Review, 6*(1): 58–69.

Rowley, T.J. (1997) 'Moving beyond dyadic ties: A network theory of stakeholder influences'. *Academy of Management Review, 22*: 887–910.

Rowley, T.J. (1998) 'A normative justification for stakeholder theory'. *Business & Society, 37*: 105–7.

Rowley, T.J. and Berman, S. (2000) 'A brand new brand of corporate social performance'. *Business and Society, 39*: 397–418.

Russo, A. and Vito, G. (2011) 'Introduction'. *European Sport Management Quarterly, 11*: 327–35.

Séguin, B., Parent, M.M. and O'Reilly, N. (2010) 'Corporate support: A corporate social responsibility alternative to traditional event sponsorship'. *International Journal of Sport Management & Marketing, 7*: 202–22.

Suddaby, R. (2006) 'From the editors: What grounded theory is not'. *Academy of Management Journal, 49*: 633–42.

Walker, M., Heere, B., Parent, M.M. and Drane, D. (2010) 'Social responsibility and the Olympic Games: The mediating role of consumer attributions'. *Journal of Business Ethics, 95*: 659–80.

Wartick, S.L. and Mahon, J.F. (1994) 'Toward a substantive definition of the corporate issue construct'. *Business & Society, 33*: 293–311.

Whetten, D.A. (1989) 'What constitutes a theoretical contribution?' *Academy of Management Review, 14*: 490–5.

Wolfe, R.A. and Putler, D.S. (2002) 'How tight are the ties that bind stakeholder groups?' *Organization Science, 13*: 64–80.

Wood, D.J. (1991) 'Corporate social performance revisited'. *Academy of Management Review, 16*: 691–718.

Xue, H. and Mason, D.S. (2011) 'The changing stakeholder map of Formula One Grand Prix in Shanghai'. *European Sport Management Quarterly, 11*: 371–95.

Applying stakeholder theory

Dag Vidar Hanstad[1]

For the last decade, I have focused my research on anti-doping (Hanstad, Skill and Thurston, 2009), media (Kristiansen, Hanstad and Roberts, 2011), top-level sport (Andersen and Hanstad, 2010) and events (Hanstad, 2012). A common thread seen in these areas is that many individuals and organisations are involved. It has been a challenge to find a theoretical framework in order to provide a good analysis, particularly when it comes to power and influence among the different actors. Parent's (2008) paper about organising committees and their stakeholders served as an analytical tool that gave me ideas and inspiration. Her article provided an expanded list of categories with details of the specific issues dealt with depending on the organising committee's evolution, the stakeholders involved and the organising committee members' hierarchical level and role.

I have applied this framework in varied ways. As one example, my colleagues and I utilised a stakeholder approach to examine the similarities and differences between the winter editions of the Youth Olympic Games (YOG) and Olympic Games (OG; Hanstad, Parent and Kristiansen, 2013). We revealed four main groupings of the YOG that differed in relative salience as compared with the OG: the host core stakeholders, international core stakeholders, sponsors and media, and parents and other stakeholders. Given that a multitude of stakeholders are required to host such events (Parent, 2008), using a stakeholder approach helped to organise and analyse the data, provide an overview of the YOG world, and thereby assist in developing an understanding of the YOG. While the basic list of stakeholders may be the same between the YOG and OG, the relative salience levels changed. OGs usually present the media and sponsors as primary, critical stakeholders; for the YOG, however, these two stakeholders were lower in salience, in favour of the parents who gained salience in part because of their legal responsibilities for their under-aged children and because they formed a significant portion of the tourists/spectators.

Further direction for research utilising stakeholder theory may include how the YOG is changing the relationship dynamics between the IOC and other stakeholders. Whereas prominent sponsors and media dominate the OG network of relationships by providing significant funding to the IOC and the Olympic Movement (e.g., through sponsorship deals and the purchase of host broadcasting rights), the relationship changes in the context of the YOG as the sponsors and media obtain additional visibility opportunities and broadcasting material/information, respectively, without having to pay for these benefits.

Note

1   Dr. Dag Vidar Hanstad is an Associate Professor in Sport Management and Head of the Department of Cultural and Social Studies at the Norwegian School of Sport Sciences.

References

Andersen, S.S. and Hanstad, D.V. (2010) 'Organizing for optimal performance: Norway's participation in Vancouver Olympics'. Presented at the 'Conference on Organizational mechanisms for knowledge creation in projects', Maltera, Italy 24–25 June 2010.

Hanstad, D.V. (2012) 'Risk management in major sporting event. A participating team's perspective'. *Event Management, 16*: 189–201.

Hanstad, D.V., Parent, M.M. and Kristiansen, E. (2013) 'The Youth Olympic Games: The best of the Olympic Games or a poor copy?' *European Sport Management Quarterly*, *13*: 315–38.

Hanstad, D.V., Skille, E.Å. and Thurston, M. (2009) 'Elite athletes' perspectives on providing whereabouts information: A survey of athletes in the Norwegian Registered Testing Pool'. *Sport und Gesellschaft*, *6*: 1–16.

Kristiansen, E., Hanstad, D.V. and Roberts, G.C. (2011) 'Coping with media at the Vancouver Winter Olympics: "We all make a living out of this"'. *Journal of Applied Sport Psychology*, *23*: 443–58.

Parent, M.M. (2008) 'Evolution and issue patterns for major-sport-event organizing committees and stakeholders'. *Journal of Sport Management*, *22*: 135–64.

7

A THEORY OF MEGA SPORT EVENT LEGACIES[1]

Holger Preuss

Overview

The general phenomenon of interest in this chapter is the transformation left by a mega sport event. Event-related changes to a city cannot be disregarded as it is hard to justify spending billions of dollars on a brief sport event, despite its entertainment and worldwide promotional value.

Many of the motives for staging a mega event are focused not so much on the event itself but on possible beneficial development. The city's transformation becomes of greater interest the more public money is used. Citizens do not always welcome events such as the Olympic Games, so planning a legacy before the event and evaluating it afterwards is critical for policymakers, administrators, the population of the host country and the international sport governing bodies. In 2014, the International Olympic Committee (IOC) acknowledged this, and many of the Olympic Agenda 2020's decisions are aimed at more flexible management of the Games and more attention to sustainable development of the host city.

Six key propositions frame my legacy theory work presented in this chapter:

1 The value of a legacy is measured by how much it improves quality of life.
2 Legacy must be distinguished from sustainability, impact and leveraging.
3 The identification of a legacy depends on the host city's long-term development plans.
4 A legacy may be positive or negative and it must be evaluated in the context of a particular stakeholder group.
5 Legacies change in importance over time and can even be latent.
6 A legacy is the result of event-related changes to the host city's location factors.

The boundary conditions of the legacy theory are that a legacy must be identified and evaluated on the basis of its spatial, temporal and stakeholder limits. The outcome of any legacy calculation will depend on how these are defined.

What I present in this chapter is the evolution of my original legacy theory (Preuss, 2007) to my most recent theorising about legacy (Preuss, 2015). My propositions have evolved from the consideration of five dimensions of legacy (value, intention, positive/negative and tangibility, as confined by time and space) to a more holistic consideration of the value and size of event-related changes (according to *what* should be considered as legacy, *who* is affected by the changes, *how* the legacy will affect the quality of life in a host city or country, and *when* a legacy starts to create value). The evolution from the original legacy 'cube' to my most recent theorising is outlined below.

Process of theory development

The event that spurred my interest in legacy and made me aware of the importance of sustainable changes to a host city was the IOC-initiated congress on 'The Legacy of the Olympic Games: 1984–2000' in Lausanne in 2002. It was only around 2000 that legacy research began, and until 2002 there was no satisfactory definition of the term *legacy*. A congress delegate observed that 'there are several meanings of the concept' and that some speakers' contributions had 'high-lighted the convenience of using other expressions and concepts that can mean different things in different languages and cultures' (Moragas, Kennett and Puig, 2003, p. 491).

Much of the legacy literature focuses on either economic or infrastructural effects (Gratton and Preuss, 2008; Hodges and Hall, 1996; Preuss, 2007; Silvestre, 2009). Leopkey and Parent (2012) show how legacy became institutionalised within the Olympic Movement. Thomson, Schlenker and Schulenkorf (2013) comprehensively review legacy definitions from 1991 to 2008. From 2005, scholars began to take a more complex view of legacy and to place more emphasis on social, environmental and political legacies (Chappelet, 2012; Griffiths and Armour, 2013; Minnaert, 2012; Preuss, 2007; Silvestre, 2009). Mangan and Dyreson (2012) provide a broad overview of legacies.

Barget and Gouguet (2007) focus on the long-term nature of legacy and consider *legacy value* as the people's satisfaction associated with the mega event being passed to future generations. This definition meets the requirement of focusing on the quality of life but is unsatisfactory because it is limited to future generations. Conceptual models of tourism legacy have been developed by Li and McCabe (2013) and Fourie and Santana-Gallego (2011). Taylor and Edmondson (2007) examine the nature of legacy planning and suggest six ways to secure legacy benefits for major sporting events. Girginov and Hills (2008), Frawley and Cush (2011) and Griffiths and Armour (2013) investigate sport legacy to see whether an event stimulates participation in sport.

The springboard for the theory presented here was my attendance at the 2005 European Association for Sport Management conference in Newcastle to present a keynote lecture entitled 'The legacy of major sporting events: More than expensive buildings'. Despite con-siderable research interest in legacy, the scientific community had failed to produce a clear, commonly accepted definition of legacy (Lienhard and Preuss, 2014). Since 2000 the focus has tended to be on either specific pieces of legacy or an incomplete selection of legacies, and the concept of 'legacy' has often been confused with 'sustainability', 'impact' or 'leveraging'.

I felt there was a need for a broader perspective that captured the range of soft (e.g., knowledge, culture) and hard (e.g., infrastructure) event-related changes (event structures) being touted. Thus, I framed my original work by five dimensions captured in a comprehensive definition of legacy:

> Irrespective of the time of production and space, legacy is all planned and unplanned, positive and negative, tangible and intangible structures created for and by a sport event that remain longer than the event itself.
>
> *(Preuss, 2007, p. 211)*

Thus, I characterised legacy by:

1   The intention of the change: the degree of planned and unplanned structure.
2   The value of the change: the degree of positive and/or negative structure.
3   The tangibility of the change: the degree of tangible and intangible structure.
4   Time: the timing and duration of a changed structure.
5   Space: the actual space affected by the changed structure.

The first three dimensions framed a *legacy cube*, together outlining eight smaller cubes that prompt researchers and bid committees to direct their focus to more than, typically, the planned, positive and tangible legacy(s) of an event; rather, the cube highlights the possibility of, for example, an unplanned, positive, intangible legacy, and an unplanned, negative, tangible legacy, and so on. A narrower focus means that 'many of the pre-event feasibility and economic impact studies that consider legacies are potentially biased' (Preuss, 2007, p. 211).

The complexity, yet limitations, of the legacy cube are further highlighted by the notion that it can only be used to evaluate change at a particular time and in a particular space (dimensions 4 and 5). However, change may occur well in advance of an event, and legacy may be of short or long duration. Thus, the intention, value and tangibility of a legacy must be measured for a given time and space, and by extension for each time and space. To address this, I argued that two additional aspects needed to be considered 'for a valuation of "net" mega event legacy' (Preuss, 2007, p. 212). I referred to these as 're-distributions', or the consideration that resources invested in the event may have been invested to create other benefits (legacy), and 'crowding-out', or the notion that some anticipated benefits may not happen because of limited capacity and so must be deducted from the expected event legacy.

A further consideration is that any change in soft and hard event structures (whether planned/unplanned, positive/negative and tangible/intangible) will change the quality of the host site (location). I identified key locations that may be changed as a legacy of a mega sporting event: industry, tourism, living, events, conferences and fairs/exhibitions. The quality of location depends on the quality of its location factors and those are changed by staging an event. Therefore the location factors must be considered in the assessment of net legacy of a mega sporting event.

This legacy model can be used for both (net) legacy evaluation and event legacy planning, ensuring that intention and value of all changes of location factors due to the event are considered, each with regard to a particular time and space. My original model framed legacy as a change in soft and hard event structures that were partly overlapping concepts, at given times and in given spaces. However, I felt I was just beginning to tap into the sense of time and space, and that I needed to also capture a sense of legacy value in this process.

Extensions and applications

Thus, my most recent work (Preuss, 2015) systematically identifies the value and timing of event-related changes, and also the size or magnitude of that change. Perhaps the most notable advancement in this extension of my original theorising about legacy is that it takes into account four aspects: *what* should be considered as legacy, *who* (i.e., which stakeholders) is affected by the changes, *how* the legacy will affect the quality of life in a host city or country, and *when* a legacy starts to create value (which happens when it is used and no longer latent). Figure 7.1 illustrates the *how* and *when* aspects and Figure 7.2 gives an overview of the whole process.

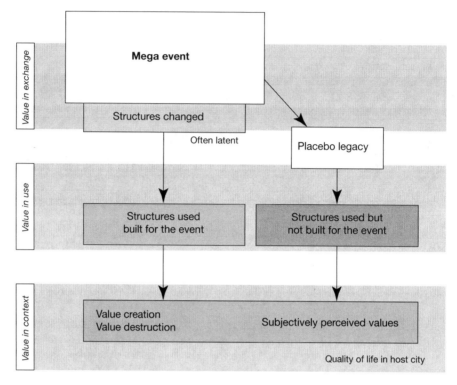

Figure 7.1 Value creation through legacy
Source: Adapted from Preuss, 2015.

First conceptual extension

As I outlined originally (Preuss, 2007), all legacies develop from structural change. After an event, almost all event-related change (both soft and hard changes) will still exist but will often be latent (not used). Latent legacies make it more likely that upcoming opportunities will be used.

The creation of a structure intended only for the duration of the event is referred to as *value in exchange*. In other words, the event organisers and the city pay for structures that are only for short-term (event time) use. Structural changes will lead to positive or negative impacts only when the structures are used after the event. This is called *value in use*, referring to the integration and application of resources in a specific context (Vargo, Maglio and Akaka, 2008). How the event affects the quality of life depends on the context, so when deciding whether a legacy is positive (creation) or negative (destruction) we refer to *value in context*. Value is solely determined by the beneficiary and in sport we often find value co-creation (Woratschek, Horbel and Popp, 2014), which means that the addition of another stakeholder can change the context of a value.

Sometimes what appears to be a legacy of an event may in fact just be normal change in the city, but citizens may subjectively attribute the change to the event (a placebo legacy) (Preuss, in press). Even though we can see they are mistaken, the effect is real because their behaviour and happiness are influenced by their belief (Meyer, 2003). This is known as the Thomas Theorem: 'If men define situations as real, they are real in their consequences' (Thomas and Thomas, 1928, p. 572).

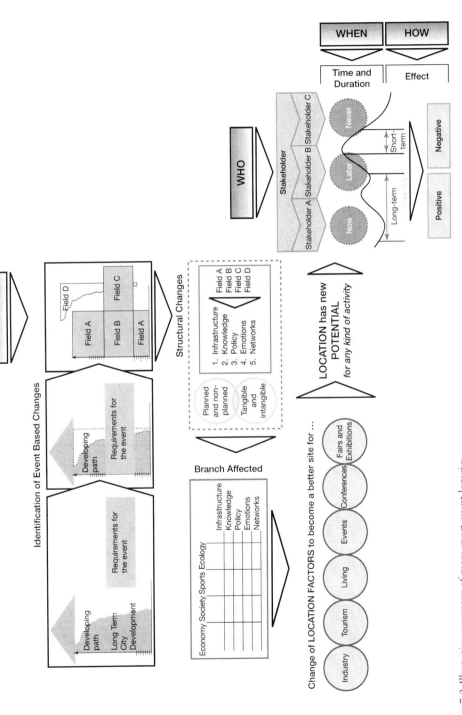

Figure 7.2 Illustrative summary of mega sport event legacies

Source: Reprinted from Preuss (2015) with permission from Taylor & Francis Ltd. (www.tandfonline.com)

Second conceptual extension

What can be counted as legacy is represented by how the required event structures fit in with the host city's long-term development plans. I distinguish four fields of event-related development (Figure 7.2, top part), each having different legacy effects:

Field A   Represents the non-event-related development of the host city. Here the legacy is the negative effect where event development hampers normal development; for example, if money spent on the event was needed for hospitals or schools.

Field B   Represents the changes the city would have experienced without a mega event. An event may speed up changes (acceleration effect) and help politicians to budget public money or develop policies for structures (political effect), and some changes will be externally financed (financial effect). In this field, the legacy consists not of the change itself (which would have happened anyway) but of the accelerated development, the way an event can remove barriers, or the financial support for change. This kind of indirect legacy can be either positive or negative.

Field C   Represents the changes that are needed only for the mega event and not for the city's long-term development. To avoid a negative legacy, the host should try to limit investments in this field, either by avoiding them (for example by constructing fewer stadiums) or reducing long-term impact (for example by using temporary structures or renting existing ones).

Field D   This field represents developments the city does not plan at the time of the event but would plan in the future. For example, the event may alert the city to the need for more transport facilities, and the development of these will thus be brought forward. The earlier the event is awarded to a city, the larger this field will be, since the development is further in the future and planning will be more long term. The event may force the city to analyse its structures, revealing inappropriate or late and therefore expensive development. Intelligent legacy planning will use the overlap of Field D with Field B to create event structures that can be used later for development that is needed anyway.

Third conceptual extension

Many studies consider legacy only indirectly. They study specific developments, such as enhancement of the host city or the country's image, or more efficient local governance or improved communal well-being, rather than the concept of legacy as a whole. The legacy literature reveals many opinions on what legacy is. Table 7.1 lists some typologies, mostly related to particular industries such as sport or tourism.

Unlike the views of legacy presented in Table 7.1, my theory views legacy as constituting five event factors (infrastructure, knowledge, policy, emotions or networks) within an industry or branch (economy, society, sport or ecology) that undergo change. This is visualised as a matrix (Figure 7.2, middle, left side). With this extension, the theory avoids the missing and overlapping categories prevalent in the literature (Table 7.1) and makes it possible to identify the legacies of a past event and plan for the legacies of a future one.

The typologies used in earlier research often either fail to identify a legacy or combine two or more legacies into one. A tourism legacy consists of tourism infrastructure (hotels, iconic buildings, museums) and knowledge about the city's history. This brings lasting revenue streams from post-event consumers. A sport legacy consists of sport infrastructure and knowledge about

Table 7.1 Typologies of event legacies (adapted from Preuss, 2015)

	Thorpe (2002)	Hiller (2003)	Cashman (2005)	Chappelet and Junod (2006)	House of Commons (2007)	Taylor and Edmondson (2007)	IOC (2009)	Cornelissen, Bo and Swart (2011)	Mayor of London (2013)	Minnaert (2012)	Veal, Toohey and Frawley (2012)	Sum
Economic		X	X	X	X	X	X	X	X		X	9
Infrastructure		X	X	X	X	X	X		X		X	8
Social		X	X	X		X	X	X	X		X	8
Sport			X	X	X	X	X	X	X		X	8
Culture			X	X	X	X	X	X			X	7
Urban				X	X			X		X		4
Communities		X			X					X		3
Image, branding					X			X	X	X		4
Information, knowledge			X					X		X	X	4
Political						X	X	X		X	X	5
Psychological, emotional	X						X	X		X		4
Environment						X	X	X				3
Networks							X	X		X		3
Trust fund	X					X						2
Education, skills			X							X		2
Symbols, memory, history			X								X	2
Tourism						X						1
Health										X	X	2

coaching and may bring lasting consumption of sport goods and therefore also an economic legacy. Clearly, infrastructural legacy is not limited to sport venues, knowledge legacy not only to coaching, and economic legacy not only to the immediate profit from the event.

The legacy theory described here largely avoids these overlaps. A city planner or event manager wanting to plan an event legacy could use Figure 7.2 by reading the middle section from left to right. For example, to use an event to develop a sport legacy, one could take sport and plan to develop sport infrastructure, sport knowledge, sport policy, sport networks and sport emotions (Sallent, Palau and Guia, 2011). Each of these five event factors can, in turn, leave several legacies. Infrastructure in sport includes venues, training sites, tracks and clubhouses. One must check each factor to see whether it constitutes a legacy or not. One must also ask whether the particular infrastructure was planned anyway (Field A), or developed quicker (Field B), or was not planned but is now available (Field C), or was simply an opportunist use of the event to fit in with the city's long-term sport development planning (Field D).

In this theory, a wide variety of industries or branches can be considered, depending on the purpose of a study or a practical application. The structural changes remaining after the event can be attributed to the five event factors, and whether they affect a stakeholder positively or negatively depends on the context.

Fourth conceptual extension

The third major change extension to my legacy theory was to narrow the aim of legacy to improved quality of life for the host city population (see Figure 7.1), as suggested by Kaplanidou (2012) and Karadakis and Kaplanidou (2012). However, it was important to distinguish precisely how legacy affects particular stakeholders. Conflicting legacies cause disagreements between mega-event opponents and protagonists. It is thus virtually impossible to study event legacy as a general phenomenon; any study must define its stakeholder perspective, as the following example from the London 2012 Olympic Games makes clear:

> More than 11,000 new properties will be built on the site of the Olympic Park in the next 20 years but despite assurances that more than a third would be allocated to 'affordable housing' there are fears that recent changes to social housing policy will mean that the majority of local people will be frozen out by the high cost.
>
> *(Cooper, 2012, np)*

This gentrification of East London made affordable homes more widely available to middle-class citizens, who could rent the subsidised properties at up to 80 per cent of market rates (Cooper, 2012). For them this was a positive legacy. But it was negative for the poorer population of East London, some of whom had to relocate because of the increased rents, thus losing their neighbourhood and having to travel further to work (Bernstock, 2014). For the rich Londoners, or those not looking for a new house, there was no legacy, as they were not affected by the change in housing prices.

Fifth conceptual extension

The final extension of the theory was a more exact definition of the time and duration of a legacy (see Figure 7.2, bottom, right side). 'Time' refers to the moment when a legacy occurs and starts creating value. When structures are built long before the event, and the location factors are thus changed before the event, we have what we may call a *pregnancy effect*; in other words, a legacy not of the event itself but of the preparation for the event.

A legacy may affect the quality of life only long after the event. The event creates the event factors (value in exchange), but the legacy may only be used (value in use) when other circumstances occur. For example, knowledge about how to bid for and prepare a mega event is acquired long before the event is staged but does not become a legacy unless it is needed – it will only become valuable if the city bids for another event. This latent legacy is illustrated in Figure 7.1, which shows a structural change built up for an event but not used, thus only value in exchange. Events create opportunities, but until an opportunity is used, the legacy that will develop from it remains latent (Barget and Gouguet, 2007, p. 169, call this 'potential use value'). Latent legacies may exist for all five event factors. For example, a network is only activated when a contact is used for co-operation of some kind.

The other temporal aspect is the duration of a legacy. This is different for each stakeholder. Some legacies, such as emotions or political reputation, are short-lived while others, such as infrastructure, last much longer.

Regarding duration, I should also note that a positive legacy can turn negative and vice versa. A new stadium may at first be economically positive (non-sport events are staged, tourists visit, a tenant team uses it as their home stadium), but later become a financial burden (the venue deteriorates, tourists stop coming because memories of the event have faded, the tenant team finds another venue).

Another kind of temporal legacy is the retro legacy (Preuss, 2015), where rundown areas or buildings are renovated, extending the life span of the structure. The Maracanã stadium in Rio de Janeiro, a prestigious symbol of the 1950s, was restored to its former glory at least partly as a result of the FIFA World Cup 2014. A similar concept is the reincorporation of brownfields or a polluted environment into city development. However, unlike the 'retro legacy', here the refurbishment changes rather than restores the character of the area. These examples demonstrate that both new and redeveloped infrastructure create legacies.

In the long run most legacy loses its power and therefore its utility. People get older and networks and memories disappear. Knowledge and skills become outdated. The older infra-structure may no longer satisfy modern demands. But regardless of the time and duration of the legacy, it is critical that legacy benefits be considered well in advance of the event (Taylor and Edmondson, 2007).

An overview of the current theory

The legacy theory as it stands today makes it possible to identify the value and size of event-related changes systematically. Again, four aspects are considered:

- *What* constitutes an event-related change?
- *Who* is affected by the change?
- *How* does a legacy affect a particular stakeholder?
- *When* does a legacy occur, how long does the legacy last and how constant is it over time?

Figure 7.2 illustrates the difficulty of taking into account all legacies for all stakeholders over a prolonged period.

The grey bar in the figure illustrates the flow of legacy, starting with 'What is a legacy?' To measure an event legacy we must first isolate it from non-event-related city development. In my original theorising (Preuss, 2007), I suggest that the most workable way to measure legacy is to start with the event changes (a bottom-up approach).

The event itself is of short duration but it can be a catalyst for change, with important consequences for the host city. An event energizes the political, economic and social systems of a city and helps to break stale patterns that are difficult to change by ordinary political means. The 1992 Olympics changed Barcelona from a mundane industrial city with extremely high unemployment into the cultural and tourist centre it is today. In Athens, the 2004 Olympics finally moved the airport out of the city and infrastructure investments improved the traffic flow. However, breaking through formal systems can also destroy systems that were functioning well. The time pressure and the argument that 'we need this for the event' may result in structures that benefit only a small stakeholder group (Lenskyj, 2014). Last-minute construction may bypass public procurements or expropriate property, as happened in Athens 2004 (defeating anti-corruption legislation) and also during preparation for the FIFA World Cup in Brazil in 2014.

Centrally, the theory states that legacy should be seen as structural changes that affect the city's location factors – positively or negatively. A location factor is a given strength or weakness to consider when searching for an ideal location for industry or other purposes. The event-related structural change in the city strengthens or weakens its location factors to make it a different kind of destination. Positive changes then trigger new impacts, such as event tourists' expenditure, which we categorise as an economic impact, not as a legacy for the tourism industry. We can identify a legacy only if the event leads to continually increased economic activity, which will happen only if the event changes the tourism-relevant location factors (such as new iconic buildings, new museums, better access to a beach) and makes the destination more attractive, thus bringing more tourists to the city (Stevenson, 2012). In other words, a legacy depends on changes on the supply side.

Future directions

For practice

The theory can be used in practice to guide event organisers in planning a legacy. It was introduced to the organising committees for Qatar 2022 (FIFA Football Word Cup), and to the government in Brazil regarding the IFA World Cup 2014 and Olympics in Rio 2016, as well as to the Japan Sports Council concerning the Tokyo 2020 Olympic Games.

Importantly, any evaluation of an event legacy must take the following into account:

- The net legacy must be distinguished from the gross legacy. We must establish whether a development in a city was driven by the event or not.
- Had the event not been staged, some investments would been made differently. These investments would also leave legacies. Such opportunity costs must not be missed.
- Developments that get crowded out by an event legacy must not be overlooked (for example, if a school cannot be built because the money was spent on a stadium).
- It is difficult to decide whether a legacy is positive or negative, because sometimes it is both, depending on which stakeholders are being studied. An evaluation of legacy must therefore be based on a social welfare function defined by the decision-makers. A welfare function ranks social status and thus helps politicians to aim for a legacy that may benefit a needy group, although a less-needy group may perceive it as negative.
- It is essential to define the region under consideration, since different legacies occur for different spaces.
- The measurement of legacy over time is challenging. Because a mega event changes the location factors, it stimulates social change, environmental improvements and economic activities only indirectly. Legacy, therefore, cannot be identified in isolation from the general development of the city. For example, it is impossible to determine to what degree a business that runs conferences in Barcelona is a legacy of the 1992 Olympic Games. The choice of Barcelona as a conference destination is partly based on the now-available Olympic facilities, but also on the city's overall attractiveness.
- Improved quality of life is the main target that politicians hope to achieve through legacies. As explained above, this can be achieved by transforming the location factors of a city. Measurement of quality of life must be assessed by citizen surveys. But citizens often cannot distinguish between change stemming from an event and normal city development. They may attribute any changes to the event. If they are wrong, we can call this the 'placebo legacy' (Figure 7.1).

Overall, legacy results from changes in a host city's structures and therefore its location factors. However, these changes are latent if they are only value in exchange (Figure 7.1). The changes only leave a legacy if the opportunity arises and the location factors attract social or economic activity (value in use). The better the location factors, the more likely they are to trigger social or economic impacts. A legacy increases the city's ability to use future opportunities but can be costly if no one takes advantage of the opportunities. A newly constructed stadium triggers a positive economic impact if it is used for another event or by a tenant home team but a negative impact if it is not used or cannot be filled regularly but still has to be maintained.

The municipal government is the most appropriate entity to be in charge of stimulating legacies (Leopkey and Parent, 2012). The government must start with good city planning, to fit the event into the long-term city development. Then it must optimise the way structures are created or changed by the event and sometimes it must make additional investments to produce optimal structures. Finally, its task must be ongoing – it must stimulate a succession of new impacts by exploiting the location factors that have been enhanced by the event.

For research

An important next step to be taken is the development of methods to measure the changes of soft location factors. A measurement tool to evaluate networks or to measure a change of emotions is extremely difficult, yet it will be important to capture this aspect effectively. As well, to fully use this model some additional research is needed on how to better distinguish the event related changes from other changes in the city. The bottom-up approach is the only way to do this, however, often during the event preparation there is no time and there are no resources to observe all changes based on the event. While there are many important applications for the model in practice now, it nevertheless requires further operationalisation in an empirical setting, and continued refinement as appropriate.

Note

1   This chapter is a reflection on Preuss (2007) and the work related to it.

References

Barget, E. and Gouguet J. (2007) 'The total economic value of sporting events: Theory and practice'. *Journal of Sports Economics*, 8: 165–82.

Bernstock, P. (2014) *Olympic housing. A critical review of London 2012's Legacy*. Surrey: Ashgate.

Cashman, R. (2005) *The bitter-sweet awakening: The legacy of the Sydney 2000 Olympic Games*. Sydney: Walla Walla Press.

Chappelet, J-L. (2012) 'Mega sporting event legacies: A multifaceted concept'. *Papers of Europe/Papeles de Europa*, 25: 76–86.

Chappelet, J.-L. and Junod, T. (2006) 'A tale of 3 Olympic cities: What can Turin learn from the Olympic legacy of other Alpine cities?'. In D. Torres (ed.), *Major sport events as opportunity for development, proceedings of the Valencia Summit 2006* (pp. 83–9). Valencia: Instituto Nóos.

Cooper, J. (2012) 'Price rise for "affordable" housing puts Olympic legacy under threat'. *The Independent* (2.6.2012), available online at: www.independent.co.uk/news/uk/home-news/price-rise-for-affordable-housing-puts-olympic-legacy-under-threat-7902915.html (accessed on 12 June, 2014).

Fourie, J. and Santana-Gallego, M. (2011) 'The impact of mega-sport events of tourist arrivals'. *Tourism Management: Research, Policies, Practice*, 32: 1364–70.

Frawley, S. and Cush, A. (2011) 'Major sport events and participation legacy: The case of the 2003 Rugby World Cup'. *Managing Leisure: An International Journal*, 16: 65–77.

Girginov, V. and Hills, L. (2008) 'A sustainable sports legacy: Creating a link between the London Olympics and sports participation'. *International Journal of the History of Sport*, 25: 2091–116.

Gratton, C. and Preuss, H. (2008) 'Maximising Olympic impacts by building up legacies'. *The International Journal of the History of Sport*, 25: 1922–38.

Griffiths, M. and Armour, K. (2013) 'Physical education and youth sport in England: Conceptual and practical foundations for an Olympic legacy?' *International Journal of Sport Policy & Politics*, 5: 213–27.

Hiller, H. (2003) 'Towards a science of Olympic outcomes: The urban legacy'. In M. de Moragas, C. Kennett and N. Puig, (eds), *The legacy of the Olympic Games, 1984–2002* (pp. 102–9). Lausanne: International Olympic Committee.

Hodges, J. and Hall, C. (1996) 'The housing and social impacts of mega events: Lessons for the Sydney 2000 Olympics'. In G. Kearsley (ed.), *Tourism down under II: Towards a more sustainable tourism* (pp. 152–166). Dunedin: Centre for Tourism, University of Otago.

House of Commons, culture, Media and Sport Committee (2007) *London 2012 Olympic Games and Paralympic Games: Funding and legacy*: Secondary Report, Vol I (HC 69-1). London: Stationary Office.

IOC (2009) *2018 Candidature acceptance procedure*. Lausanne: International Olympic Committee.

Kaplanidou, K. (2012). 'The importance of legacy outcomes for Olympic Games four summer host cities residents quality of life: 1996–2008'. *European Sport Management Quarterly*, *12*: 397–433.

Karadakis, K. and Kaplanidou, K. (2012). 'Legacy perceptions among host and non-host Olympic Games residents: A longitudinal study of the 2010 Vancouver Olympic Games'. *European Sport Management Quarterly*, *12*: 243–64.

Lenskyj, J.H. (2014) *Sexual diversity and the Sochi 2014 Olympics*. Basingstoke: Palgrave Macmillan.

Leopkey, B. and Parent, M.M. (2012) 'The (neo) institutionalization of legacy and its sustainable governance within the Olympic Movement'. *European Sport Management Quarterly*, *12*: 437–55.

Li, S. and McCabe, S. (2013) 'Measuring the socio-economic legacies of mega events: Concepts, propositions and indicators'. *International Journal of Tourism Research*, *15*: 388–402.

Lienhard, P. and Preuss, H. (2014) *Legacy, sustainability and CSR at mega sport events*. Wiesbaden: Springer Gabler Verlag.

Mangan, J.A. and Dyreson, M. (2012) *Olympic legacies: Intended and unintended; political, cultural, economic and educational. Sport in the global society*. London: Routledge.

Meyer, W.-U. (2003) 'Einige grundlegende Annahmen und Konzepte der Attributionstheorie'. Available online at: www.uni-bielefeld.de/psychologie/ae/AE02/LEHRE/Attributionstheorie.pdf (accessed on 23 November, 2014).

Minnaert, L. (2012) 'An Olympic legacy for all? The non-infrastructural outcomes of the Olympic Games for socially excluded groups (Atlanta 1996 – Beijing 2008)'. *Tourism Management Journal*, *33*: 361–70.

Moragas M. de, Kennett, C. and Puig, N. (2003) 'Conclusions and recommendations', in M. de Moragas, C. Kennett and N. Puig (eds), *The legacy of the Olympic Games 1984–2000* (pp. 489–94). Lausanne: International Olympic Committee.

Preuss, H. (2007). 'The conceptualization and measurement of mega sport event legacies'. *Journal of Sport & Tourism*, *12*, 207–227.

Preuss, H. (2015) 'A framework for identifying the legacies of a mega sport event'. *Leisure Studies*. DOI. 10.1080/02614367.2014.994552.

Sallent, O., Palau, R. and Guia, J. (2011) 'Exploring the legacy of sport events on sport tourism networks'. *European Sport Management Quarterly*, *11*: 397–421.

Silvestre, G. (2009) 'The social impacts of mega events: towards a framework'. *Esporte e Sociedade*, *4*(10): 1–25.

Stevenson, N. (2012) 'Culture and the 2012 Games creating a tourism legacy?' *Journal of Tourism & Cultural Change*, *10*(2): 137–50.

Taylor, M. and Edmondson, I. (2007) 'Major sporting events: planning for legacy'. *Proceedings of the Institution of Civil Engineers – Municipal Engineer*, *160*(4): 171–6.

Thomas, W.I. and Thomas D.S. (1928) *The child in America: Behavior problems and programs*. New York: A.A. Knopf.

Thomson, A., Schlenker, K. and Schulenkorf, N. (2013) 'Conceptualizing sport event legacy'. *Event Management*, *17*(2): 111–22.

Thorpe, R. (2002) *The economic impact of the Winter Olympic and Paralympic Games. Initial estimates*. A Report prepared for Honourable Ted Nebbeling Minister of State for Community Charter and 2010 Olympic Bid.

Vargo, S.L., Maglio, P.P. and Akaka, M.A. (2008) 'On value and value co-creation: A service systems and service logic perspective'. *European Management Journal*, *26*: 145–52.

Woratschek, H., Horbel, C. and Popp, B. (2014) 'The sport value framework: A new fundamental logic for analyses in sport management'. *European Sport Management Quarterly*, *14*: 6–24.

Applying the theory of mega sport event legacies

Nola Agha[1]

In the early 2000s, there was an explosion of research on mega event legacy that produced multiple competing, yet incomplete, typologies (e.g., Cashman, 2003). It was in this environment in 2010 that I began researching the concept in order to write a case study about Olympic legacy (Agha,

Fairley and Gibson, 2012). Immediately, the brilliance of Preuss's (2007) model was apparent in its ability to distil a complex phenomenon into multiple measurable dimensions. Those dimensions (time, space, tangibility, planning, and positivity) illustrate the complex nature of the concept in a way that is simple, yet thorough; making it accessible to both students and scholars. The model allows the total legacy impact of an event to be estimated over time by netting out positive and negative legacies. By implicitly including perspective as a necessary variable to measure the positive/negative dimension, Preuss created the first framework that gives equal weight to the non-dominant legacy views of marginalized populations. Whereas event organizers promote the dominant narrative of planned, positive, tangible legacies, Preuss's conceptualization requires that total legacy is a function of all perspectives of all types of legacies.

Researchers often do not include all of the dimensions when applying Preuss's legacy framework; focusing, for example, on only one positive legacy from a single stakeholder, with or without the dimension of time (e.g., Knott, Fyall and Jones, 2013; Sallent, Palau and Guia, 2011). While the analysis is simplified by allowing variation in fewer dimensions, in reality one should account for all five dimensions, and the implicit variable of perspective, that allow the net effect to be calculated.

For example, I used multiple perspectives to assess variation in legacy dimensions while analysing the decade-long process of obtaining public funding for a new NBA arena (Agha, 2014). North American team owners view this process as the *de facto* standard of business that results in a positive, planned, tangible new facility. This view fails to take into account known cases where battles for public funds reduce fan support and catalyse teams to move away. My analysis found legacy is not always positive or tangible from the perspective of fans. In fact, the fans' views of the owners, team, and arena are both positive and negative, and fluctuate over time. To determine the net legacy of a new facility, the additional perspectives of developers, housing advocates, non-fans, and so on should also be considered.

I believe Preuss's model can apply to nearly anything designed to create a long-term transformation. Beyond mega events, this includes smaller events, structures, team moves, and the process of obtaining public funds to build new facilities. There is incredible opportunity to extend Preuss's framework even further by applying all five dimensions simultaneously to determine the true net legacy of a variety of phenomena.

Note

1   Dr. Nola Agha is an Assistant Professor in the Sport Management Program, University of San Francisco.

References

Agha, N. (2014, September) 'Legacy effects of a new sports venue'. In *Book of Abstracts, 22nd Annual Conference of the European Association of Sport Management* (pp. 7–8). Coventry, UK: EASM.

Agha, N., Fairley, F. and Gibson, H. (2012) 'Considering legacy as a multi-dimensional construct: The legacy of the Olympic Games'. *Sport Management Review*, 15: 125–39.

Cashman, R. (2003) 'What is "Olympic Legacy"?' In M. Moragas, C. Kennett and N. Puig (eds), *The legacy of the Olympic Games 1984–2000: International Symposium Lausanne, 14th, 15th and 16th November 2002* (pp. 31–42). Lausanne: International Olympic Committee.

Knott, B., Fyall, A. and Jones, I. (2013) 'The nation-branding legacy of the 2010 FIFA World Cup for South Africa'. *Journal of Hospitality Marketing & Management*, 22(6): 569–95.

Preuss, H. (2007) 'The conceptualisation and measurement of mega sport event legacies'. *Journal of Sport & Tourism*, 12(3–4): 207–27.

Sallent, O., Palau, R. and Guia, J. (2011) 'Exploring the legacy of sport events on sport tourism networks'. *European Sport Management Quarterly*, 11(4): 397–421.

8

SPORT POLICY IMPLEMENTATION[1]

Eivind Å. Skille

Overview

In Skille (2008) I developed a framework for the analysis of sport policy implementation via local and voluntary sport clubs or, as the title of the article indicates, for 'understanding sport clubs as sport policy implementers'. Thus, the general phenomenon of interest was sport policy, and the specific phenomenon of interest was the implementation process (of sport policy). My intent was to find or create a framework for a specific empirical research project regarding Norwegian sport clubs. In that respect, the framework is both focused upon and limited to a sport club point of view. To my knowledge, the use of this specific theoretical framework was new in sport management – and sport (social) sciences in general – when I introduced it in 2008.

The specific constructs and key propositions of the framework are taken from neo-institutionalism, especially from an updated and 'agency-friendly' version of neo-institutionalism, as opposed to what I label the classic and reproductive-oriented institutionalism. From classic neo-institutionalism, I had earlier used the key concepts of rationalised myths and the three versions of isomorphism (see more details on the process in the next section). I had used, first, the concepts of Meyer and Rowan (1977) to analyse how the Norwegian confederation of sports (NIF), as the monopolistic and relatively independent (from the state) sport organisation in Norway, reproduces its monopolistic and relatively independent position in the field of sport also during phases of claimed change. It does so by leaning on the rationalised myth of being the best and only provider of sport activity in Norway (Skille, 2004b). I had used, second, the concepts from DiMaggio and Powell (1983) to show how inventions in the sport field (which was an empirical example of the claimed change), referred to as alternative sports (alternative in organisation, with a less competitive focus and more adolescent-controlled as opposed to adult-controlled, in comparison with conventional sports) underwent isomorphic processes and resembled conventional sport (Skille, 2005c).

At the outset of the focal paper it was, therefore, crucial to search for a theoretical framework which focused on how organisations respond to external pressure and at the same time focused on how internal strategies of organisations were created. It could be claimed that I then searched for rather contradicting theoretical perspectives, and that a combination of very different theories would be needed in order to fulfil the two foci.[2] I turned, however, to relatively recent developments within neo-institutional theory, rather than combining with other theories.

These developments are based on a critique of the classic neo-institutionalism and its focus on how organisations resemble each other in an institutional field, and how external influence is seen as a more important reason for organisational behaviour than internal agency. I leaned on earlier theoretical developments in sport management, with various positions on the structure-agency axis (Kikulis, Slack and Hinings, 1995; Stevens and Slack, 1998). In line with, for example, Kikulis (2000), I claimed that there are fundamental elements of agency implicit in the institutional perspective; the establishment and sustaining of institutions depend on individual agents' behaviour (Berger and Luckmann, 1991).

The key concept in the proposed theoretical framework is translation. The concept of translation focuses upon organisational change, where type and degree of change in an organisation depends on how the focal organisation adapts to institutional elements in the institutional environment. The adaption process is about importing institutional elements from other fields or successful parts of its own field. Important here is how translation is seen as a more appropriate denomination than diffusion. When diffusion is used, the process is associated with a passive sense, as it is a metaphor stemming from a chemical and biological process of a movement of a substance from one side of a membrane to the other, based purely on the pressure difference on the two sides of a membrane (Berry and Berry, 1999). Hence the concept of translation was introduced in order to indicate an active process where, such as in my empirical case, the local sport club and its relation to central sport policy were conceived as active processes conducted by active agents (individual representatives of sport clubs).

After criticising former paradigms within institutionalism for not clarifying their criteria for the analysis of institutional change, and for not clarifying the underlying mechanisms for institutional change, Campbell (2004) identifies two such mechanisms: *bricolage* and *translation*. In short, the former is about being innovative and recombining intrinsic institutional elements into new forms, thereby creating change from within the focal organisation. According to Campbell (2004), 'actors often craft new institutional solutions by recombining elements in their repertoire through an innovative process of *bricolage*' (p. 69). The latter refers to the import of new elements from the outside of the focal organisation. About translation, he explains:

> More specifically, new ideas are combined with already existing institutional practices and, therefore, are *translated* into local practice in varying degrees and in ways that involve a process very similar to bricolage. The difference is that translation involves the combination of *new* externally given elements received through diffusion as well as old locally given ones inherited from the past.
>
> *(Campbell, 2004, p. 80)*

Translation is a process with several steps, of which each has an active aspect. Translation implies, first, that there is a new institutional element taken from outside the focal organisation, which is actively imported. When imported it is, second, actively treated by individual agents within the receiving organisation to fit into the focal organisation. The treatment includes a translation step. It is this translation, of fitting the imported element into the receiving and focal organisation, which challenges classic neo-institutionalism seeing diffusion as a passive process leading to resemblance and hence homogeneity of organisations within an institutional field (Campbell, 2004). In other words, the overall concept of translation refers to recombination of internal *and* external institutional elements. According to Czarniawska and Joerges (1996) translation 'comprises what exists and what is created; the relationship between humans and ideas, ideas and objects, and humans and objects – all needed in order to understand what in shorthand we call "organizational change"' (p. 24).

Translation not only implies but requires agency in the behaviour of the individual agents representing the receiving and focal organisation. However, individual agency does not equalise randomness, as it is regulated by culture. Cultures vary across contexts; in the focal article, I made this point by utilising Rottenburg's (1996) ball–game metaphor:

> [I]n order to bring an idea into a local cosmos from any part of the outside world, one has to use a cultural code . . . each culture has several mutually contradicting codes which are made available to individual people like alternative repertoires for thought. . . . [I]t is . . . accurate to imagine this process as a kind of ball game. Only if the actors catch the ball and pass it on, i.e. they collaborate, can the game continue. . . in this way, we move from the *trans-mission* . . . to the *trans-formation* of a thing.
>
> *(pp. 214–215, emphasis original)*

When I was searching for a theoretical framework to analyse how Norwegian sport clubs were related to national sport policy, it was important to find a concept that took into account the fact that there were active agents within – individual representatives of – the sport clubs. In that respect, I followed Spyberg (1996) who claimed that, 'it is important to retain the view of the individual as a human agent routinely engaged in the reproduction of social institutions, but with the capacity to translate them in the course of day-to-day activities' (p. 189). For example, one objective of the empirical study of Norwegian sport clubs was to analyse if/how the health element of national sport policy influenced the local sport clubs. The point was that:

> If the health argument of central sport policy influences the local sport clubs, it relies on the sport club representatives' interpretation of it; health (or any element of the sport policy) will only be empirically observable as an interpreted and implemented version of that health-as-part-of-sport policy.
>
> *(Skille, 2008, p. 193)*

On this point I followed Rottenburg (1996) who claimed: 'Translation aims at the appropriation of the external thing, which is then given another function, an altered meaning and often a new shape in the new context' (p. 214). Based on the need for a theoretical framework for one specific empirical study, the translation perspective was chosen. Moreover, the translation perspective makes it possible to discuss larger sociological issues, as it takes into account the issue of structure and agency as well as the relationship between the global or national and the local.

With regard to boundary conditions, the framework was developed in order to focus on the local sport clubs as the last link in the chain for delivering sport policies. In that respect, it could be seen as a boundary condition that the framework lacks the possibility for a larger view on the policy process. It should be noted that in Skille (2008), I go through other theories used in sport policy analysis. I judge these as not as appropriate for the analysis of the local sport clubs as the proposed and applied framework. I acknowledge, however, that other theories are fruitful for other sport policy analyses. This is especially true because each level and each context of sport policy analysis is specific; therefore, various theories are better on one level than another (Skille, 2008). For example, the advocacy coalition framework, as employed by Houlihan (2005), is an appropriate framework to apply in analyses of how different actors involved with national level sport policy form coalitions and compete with other coalitions in order to get their arguments through in a decision-making process. A criticism of the translation perspective is 'that the central policy is conceived as something "out there", which may be or may not be imported, translated and implemented' (Skille, 2008, p. 194). The translation perspective does not cover the complexity and wholeness of a sport policy field where various policy organisations and/or sport organisations negotiate and/or co-operate to influence decision-making processes of sport policy making. (The above mentioned advocacy coalition framework can work for such purposes.)

As the above article was the theoretical part of a larger, empirically based study into Norwegian sport clubs, the framework has been cited in several empirical articles (Skille, 2009, 2010a, 2011a) and one book (Skille, 2010b).[3] In the first of the empirical articles (Skille, 2009), I reflect upon the sport clubs' role and sport clubs representatives' experiences in a specific sport programme (Skille, 2005c; see more about the programme and the research in the following sections). Applying both the isomorphic and the translation perspectives of neo-institutionalism, it was shown that sport clubs on the one hand resemble the (universal) competitive logic of sport; on the other hand, representatives of sport clubs translate the social policy incentives of the programme (made in the state sport policy) and combine these with responses to perceived requirements in their local communities when implementing their programme activities.

In another empirical project, I studied three ordinary sport clubs. Ordinary sport takes place during leisure time, it is voluntarily conducted, competitively oriented, and participation is based on membership in a sport club that is organisationally linked to the central policy through the Norwegian confederation of sports (NIF) system. The study's focus was on if/how the health elements of national sport policy influence local sport clubs. It identified processes going on in the sport clubs, where sport club representatives were concerned with recombining existing institutional elements. This process is the bricolage referred to earlier (Campbell, 2004; Skille, 2010a). Treating the question about how different, and apparently contradictory, elements such as competitiveness and healthy upbringing were integrated parts of the sport clubs' institutional context, I turned to the distinction between substantive and symbolic bricolage (Campbell, 2004; Skille, 2010a). I elaborate by citing from one of the empirical articles:

> Substantive bricolage is applied in order to find solutions to specific problems, '. . . and thus follows a logic of instrumentality' (Campbell, 2004: 63). Specific problems here refer to issues related to how achievement in sport competitions should be improved. In the case of the football club, this is manifested in the sport development plan which provides a guideline on how to train, and what to focus upon regarding certain skills levels and for the various age groups. Following this logic, competitiveness and sport development seem to be substantive elements because they refer to the practice of the sport club. Second, symbolic bricolage basis on '. . . a logic of appropriateness' and that '. . . the solutions that actors devise must be acceptable and legitimate within the broad social environment' (Campbell, 2004: 70). Thus, arguments related to sport clubs' role in the upbringing of young people to enjoy healthy lifestyles may be considered as a symbolic element: it is utilized for legislative purposes in a broader societal setting. Sport club representatives emphasised the possible positive outcome of sport provision in order to gain symbolic and financial support from the public sector. Because everybody agrees on the positive connotations of the concept of health (St. meld. nr. 14, 1999–2000), the link between sport and health may be considered as a '. . . utilization of symbolic language, rhetorical devices, lofty and culturally accepted principles . . .' (Campbell, 2004: 70).
>
> *(Skille, 2010a, p. 81)*

In the third empirical article (Skille, 2011a), I studied one single sport club (a football/soccer club) by considering it as a mixture of rational, natural and open systems (Scott, 2001) and by employing the perspective of translation from neo-institutionalism. When change took place in the soccer club it was based on an interaction between pressure from external sources and discussions about strategy within the club. For example, if the 'club should develop a model for development of players, aiming at taking into account both elite orientation and mass participation, the solution was found by mimicking ideas from other organisations in the institutional field' (Skille, 2011a, p. 79). Hence, the specific empirical case shows how the real world consists of reproduction – as described by classic neo-institutionalism – as well as change – described by modern neo-institutionalism. The isomorphic processes described in classic neo-institutionalism (DiMaggio and Powell, 1983) were explained by translation as suggested by updated and agency-oriented neo-institutionalism (Campbell, 2004). To be specific, it is shown that representatives of a soccer club's board are inspired by ideas stemming from other soccer clubs that are conceived as successful in the regional institutional field. In that respect, something that, from the outside, can be observed as pure mimicking, was actually an institutional idea that is actively imported, treated and implemented (Skille, 2011a).

Process

The process that spurred my interest in the topic was simply a continuation or a follow up of former research. In my dissertation (Skille, 2005c), I studied a specific sports programme that was initiated in a state sport policy document (St. meld. nr. 41, 1991–1992), organised through the Norwegian confederation of sports (NIF) and aimed at adolescents who were not active in ordinary sport (leisure time, organised, competitive sport activities in local sport clubs).[4] When studying such a programme I focused, first, on the policymaking and its organisation at the national level; this was done by document analysis, observation in meetings and interviews by key personnel in the state's sport bureaucracy and in the NIF (Skille, 2004a, 2004b). Second, I measured the outcome of the programme on an individual adolescent level; I measured participation in programme activities compared with participation in ordinary sports in specific geographical areas (Skille, 2005a) and preferences for participation in programme activities compared with ordinary sport (Skille, 2005b). Both were conducted with a quantitative survey. In addition, I studied adolescents' experiences of participation in programme activities, with qualitative interviews with sport programme participants and observations at strategically sampled programme sites (Skille, 2007; Skille and Waddington, 2006).

The point is, as stated in the concluding remarks of my dissertation, that 'more research is needed' that, among other things, addresses 'how the leaders and coaches of sport clubs perceive public incentives like program funding for defined target groups' (Skille, 2005c, p. 56). When defining a new research project, the level of sport clubs appeared as a clearly needed focus as this was identified as a missing link in my earlier research and in sport management research in general.[5] Moreover, I moved on from focusing particularly on programme sport. Programme sport refers to sport with specific policy aims (for example social integration) for specific target groups (for example immigrants) followed by specific funding in order to provide alternatives to ordinary sports (for example demand less volunteering from parents, make it less competitive, and fewer membership demands). In other words, I took a more general sport organisational perspective when studying ordinary sport clubs.

Thus, the manner in which I thought about and developed the theoretical tenets and relationships among constructs was based on a clear idea of having the acting organisation as the point of departure for analysis. The 'acting organisation' refers to where the sport activity takes place; it is the context where policy is put into practice. Regarding practice, it refers to sport activity and provision of sport activity. With the exception of national teams and regional teams in various sports, sport activity takes place solely in sport clubs. In that respect, I found representatives of sport clubs to be the ultimate interviewees, as they can say something about internal and external elements of the acting organisation. These elements include how or whether the sport club is informed by sport policy from above in any respect. Considering the sport club as both a formal organisation as part of an institutional field and as a unit with or collection of individuals of whom each has a free will, I needed what I felt was a relatively complete theory. A complete theory here refers to a framework taking into account stability and change, as well as structure and agency. In that respect, the stability and reproduction part is taken care of by the institutional field level where resemblance can be discovered (DiMaggio and Powell, 1983; Meyer and Rowan, 1977); the part about agency and individuals with a free will and their desire and ability to make change is covered by what I call an updated and agency-oriented version of neo-institutionalism (Campbell, 2004; Sahlin and Wedlin, 2008).

The felt need to have a more nuanced theory stems, first, from earlier research where the isomorphic processes were highlighted (Skille, 2004b). With a theoretical focus upon isomorphic processes, it is easy to get into an empirical trap of only finding what you are looking for; namely, actors in compliance with an institutional field's norms (competitiveness within the sport organisational field) and organisations resembling each other so that the field as such (understood as the aggregation of organisations) becomes homogenous. Second, the need for a more nuanced theory stems from the simple observation that organisations in the sport field differ and change. Why is that? The assumption was that there were active agents in the sport clubs.

Extensions and applications

Alterations I have made to the theory since its first iteration can be summed up as follows: I have added a concept to describe the consequences of agency and hence more change. With Bodemar I have added two elements from neo-institutional literature to the above-mentioned translation perspective (see Bodemar and Skille, 2014). The first is another step in the direction of acknowledging agency in organisations: namely, the concept of institutional entrepreneurship (Hardy and Maguire, 2008; Maguire, Hardy and Lawrence, 2004). The other is more about pinpointing that a consequence of change in organisations is actually pluralism (Kraatz and Block, 2008); this is contrary to resemblance and homogeneity as proposed as a consequence of isomorphism in classic neo-institutionalism.

Institutional entrepreneurship deals with how individual players are able to change the institutional field through innovation of new institutional elements (Hardy and Maguire, 2008). Institutional entrepreneurship is often defined as 'activities of actors who have interest in particular institutional arrangements and who leverage resources to create new institutions or to transform existing ones' (Maguire et al., 2004, p. 657). The introduction of the concept of institutional entrepreneurship can be seen as a response to critics of the focus on static and reproductive elements of organisational fields found in classic neo-institutionalism. A main aspect of this solution is thus to reintroduce 'considerations of agency, power and interests into analyses of institutional fields' (Hardy and Maguire, 2008, p. 198). Most of the literature on institutional entrepreneurship has focused on how the individual player is capable of changing the institutional field and how this is solved by considerations of power and interest in the analysis of the institutional field. However, there are disagreements in the literature about how much power the individual entrepreneur actually has to possess in order to implement institutional changes (Hardy and Maguire, 2008).

The result of processes of change, regardless of being bricolage, translation or entrepreneurship, is a pluralisation of the institutional field (Kraatz and Block, 2008); hence pluralisation is a framework that analyses the results of the changes and refers to how new institutional elements are created. If many people are supporters of new approaches or viewpoints, this will have a different impact or focus as opposed to if there were no majority for new solutions. I have used the pluralisation idea offered by Kraatz and Block (2008) in a fourth empirical article from the mentioned project into sport clubs, together with Enjolras' (2006) ideas of institutional regimes. The idea of institutional regimes has clear similarities to the idea of institutional pluralism; institutional regimes refer to arrangements where there are several actors and several conventions. For example, with different institutional regimes, some people within organisations, such as sport clubs, may idolise competitiveness as the main convention while others may cultivate a sport for health convention (Skille, 2011b).

Ways in which others have applied and revised the theory in their research are always interesting. Donaldson and various colleagues have used a similar approach to mine, and cited the focal article on several occasions (e.g., Donaldson and Poulus, 2014; Poulus and Donaldson, 2012) when studying sport policy implementation in Australia, as have Vos *et al.* (2011) in the study of sport policy implementation in Flanders (a region in Belgium). More specifically, Donaldson and colleagues referred to Skille (2008) when they studied how local sport club representatives in Australian football interpret central trainer policy developed by the Australian Football League; in that respect they claim that: 'The way from national policy development to local implementation is "long and uneasy" (Skille, 2008: 181), requiring implementers (e.g., community sports clubs) to interpret and modify the centrally developed policy to suit their local context' (Donaldson, Leggett and Finch, 2011, p. 744). Moreover, in a study of implementation and translation of sport policy, Donaldson and Finch (2012) conclude that it is important to understand the end users: 'sports participants, volunteer administrators and coaches respond first and foremost to their own needs and the needs of those they are responsible for', as these local actors 'interpret and implement centrally or top–down developed sports policy within the context of their daily experience and local environment' (p. 307).

Vos and colleagues (2011) clearly apply the same perspective as I advocated in Skille (2008), employing neo-institutional theory (but not the complete theoretical framework as sketched above); they, for example, emphasised how the relationship between state sport policymaking and grassroots implementing is influenced by 'the autonomy of voluntary sport clubs', which in turn 'is reinforced by the strong dependence on volunteers (Skille, 2008)' (Vos *et al.*, 2011, p. 273). They conclude that state subsidies as a coercive mechanism to execute pressure from the state on the local sport clubs is low, indicating that processes in the local sport clubs and their immediate context are of much higher importance for local sport clubs' work than governmental pressure via subsidies. The perspective of local sport clubs as the point of departure for policy implementation can, of course, be taken with the application of the Skille (2008) theoretical framework, but can also be taken with the (further) application of, for example, symbolic interactionism, as applied by Donaldson *et al.* (2011). In sum, the overall perspective permeated in Skille (2008) can also be seen in other theories.

I use the theoretical framework in my teaching of public health as well. I find the framework especially interesting when asking the students to compare the public sector's health service and the voluntary sport sector with a focus upon the implementing process. The students have various approaches to the study of public health at the graduate level: health professions (such as nursing, physiotherapy), school professions (general teacher, PE teacher) and bachelor of sport and bachelor of public health. When they start they share a belief in the role they will have as public health actors, usually seen as agents for change in society (e.g., changing deviant habits among people). It is therefore interesting to observe their discussions, across backgrounds and professions, when they reflect upon the institutionalised environment their specific contexts represent. A common outcome is, interestingly, that they see the need for co-operation across sectors (when, for example, analysing how physical activity levels could be raised); it seems as if they want to eliminate institutional barriers in one sector by adding another sector.[6]

Future directions

Theoretical or empirical extensions of this theory or the general phenomena of interest are huge topics. Theoretically, I want to make two interrelated emphases. First, in general, sport management researchers should be up to date on the institutional theory field (and other theories). In that respect, I want to mention an emerging academic at the University of Utah, Patricia Bromley. She has written much lately with colleagues, among others, John Meyer and Walter Powell (Bromley and Powell, 2012; Meyer and Bromley, 2013). After reading her work, I have generated new ideas for research into my own field, sport policy. Second, moving on more systematically in my own research, I plan a comparison between the public sector's health service and the voluntary sector's sport system in order to extend the knowledge into the public health and sport relationship (which seems to be overwhelmingly on a political level these days). I think organisational sociologists and sport management researchers have something to contribute in that respect.

Notes

1   This chapter is a reflection on Skille (2008) and the work related to it.
2   In Bodemar and Skille (2014), a totally different theory was combined with neo-institutionalism to account for the individual and agency element of leadership.
3   The book is in the Norwegian language.
4   Further descriptions of the programme are not given, as the point here is the policy and organisation levels studied, in order to explain why I developed the framework in the focal article. For those interested, see Skille (2004a, 2004b, 2005c).
5   An important exception is Heinemann's (1999) *Sport Clubs in Various European Countries*. It should also be mentioned that there is a new book on sport clubs in Europe in process (eds: van der Werff *et al.*, 2015).
6   These are just a teacher's observations during class discussions. Research is needed in order to say more about the exemplified issues.

References

Berger, P. and Luckmann, T. (1991 [1966]) *The social construction of reality*. London: Penguin Books.

Berry, F.S. and Berry, W.D. (1999) 'Innovation and diffusion models in policy research'. In P.A. Sabatier (ed.) *Theories of the policy process* (pp. 169–200). Boulder, CO: Westview Press.

Bodemar, A. and Skille, E.A. (2014) 'Young leadership. An exploration using neo-institutionalism and authentic leadership theory'. In D.V. Hanstad, M. Parent and B. Houlihan (eds) *The Youth Olympic Games* (pp. 75–90). London: Routledge.

Bromley, P. and Powell, W.W. (2012) 'From smoke and mirrors to walking the talk: The causes and consequences of decoupling in the contemporary world'. *Academy of Management Annals*, 6(1): 483–530.

Campbell, J.L. (2004) *Institutional change and globalization*. Princeton, NJ: Princeton University Press.

Czarniawska, B. and Joerges, B. (1996) 'Travels of ideas'. In B. Czarniawska and G. Sevón (eds) *Translating organizational change* (pp. 13–48). Berlin: Walter de Gruyter.

DiMaggio, P. and Powell, W.W. (1983) 'The iron cage revisited: Institutional isomorphism and collective rationality in organizational fields'. *American Sociological Review*, 48: 147–60.

Donaldson, A. and Finch, C.F. (2012) 'Sport as a setting for promoting health'. *British Journal of Sports Medicine*, 46(1): 4–5.

Donaldson, A. and Poulus, R.G. (2014) 'Planning the diffusion of a neck-injury prevention programme among community rugby union coaches'. *British Journal of Sports Medicine*, 48: 151–8.

Donaldson, A., Leggett, S. and Finch, C.F. (2011) 'Sports policy development and implementation in context: Researching and understanding the perceptions of community end-users'. *International Review for the Sociology of Sport*, 47(6): 743–60.

Enjolras, B. (2006) *Conventions et institutions* [Conventions and institutions]. Paris: L'Harmattan.

Hardy, C. and Maguire, S. (2008) 'Institutional entrepreneurship'. In R. Greenwood, C. Oliver, K. Sahlin and R. Suddaby (eds) *The Sage handbook of organizational institutionalism* (pp. 198–217). Los Angeles, CA: Sage.

Heinemann, K. (1999) (ed.) *Sport clubs in various European countries*. Schorndorf, Germany: Hofmann.

Houlihan, B. (2005) 'Public sector sport policy developing a framework for analysis'. *International Review for the Sociology of Sport*, 40: 163–85.

Kikulis, L., Slack, T. and Hinings, B. (1995) 'Does decision making make a difference? Patterns of change within Canadian national sport organizations'. *Journal of Sport Management*, 9: 273–99.

Kikulis, L. (2000) 'Continuity and change in governance and decision making in national sport organizations: Institutional explanations'. *Journal of Sport Management*, 14: 293–320.

Kraatz, M. and Block, E. (2008) 'Organizational implications of institutional pluralism'. In R. Greenwood, C. Oliver, K. Sahlin and R. Suddaby (eds) *Handbook of organizational institutionalism* (pp. 243–75). London: Sage.

Maguire, S., Hardy, C. and Lawrence, T. (2004) 'Institutional entreperneurship in emerging fields: HIV/AIDS treatment advocacy in Canada'. *Academy of Management Journal*, 47: 657–79.

Meyer, J.W. and Bromley, P. (2013) 'The worldwide expansion of "organization"'. *Sociological Theory*, 31: 366–89.

Meyer, J.W. and Rowan, B. (1977) 'Institutionalized organizations: Formal structure as myth and ceremony'. *American Journal of Sociology*, 83: 340–63.

Poulus, R.G. and Donaldson, A. (2012). 'Is sports safety policy being translated into practice: What can be learnt from the Australian rugby union Mayday procedure?' *British Journal of Sports Medicine*, 46: 585–90.

Rottenburg, R. (1996) 'When organization travels: On intercultural translation'. In B. Czarniawska and G. Sevón (eds) *Translating organizational change* (pp. 191–240). Berlin, Germany: Walter de Gruyter.

Sahlin, K. and Wedlin, L. (2008) 'Circulating ideas: Imitation, translation and editing'. In R. Greenwood, C. Oliver and R. Suddaby (eds) *The Sage handbook of organizational institutionalism* (pp. 218–42). Thousand Oaks, CA: Sage.

Scott, W.R. (2001) *Institutions and organizations*. New York: Sage.

Skille, E.Å. (2004a) 'Sport for All? The 'Sports City Programme' in Norway'. *Sport in Society*, 7(2): 192–210.

Skille, E.Å. (2004b) 'Revisiting myths of Norwegian Sport – Case of the sports city program'. *International Journal of Applied Sport Science*, 16(1): 29–40.

Skille, E.Å. (2005a) 'Individuality or reproduction'. *International Review for the Sociology of Sport*, 40: 307–20.

Skille, E.Å. (2005b) 'Adolescents' preferences for participation – Alternative versus conventional sports. A Norwegian case'. *Sport und Gesellschaft/Sport and Society*, 2(2): 107–24.

Skille E.Å. (2005c) *Sport policy and adolescent sport*. Oslo: Norwegian School of Sport Sciences.

Skille, E.Å. (2007) 'The meaning of social context: experiences of and educational outcome of participation in two different sport contexts'. *Sport, Education and Society*, 12: 367–82.

Skille, E.Å. (2008) 'Understanding sport clubs as sport policy implementers: A theoretical framework for the analysis of the implementation of central sport policy through local and voluntary sport organizations'. *International Review for the Sociology of Sport*, 43: 181–200.

Skille, E.Å. (2009) 'State sport policy and the voluntary sport clubs: The case of the Norwegian Sports City Program as social policy'. *European Sport Management Quarterly*, 9: 63–79.

Skille, E.Å. (2010a) 'Competitiveness and health – the work of sport clubs seen from the perspectives of Norwegian sport club representatives'. *International Review for the Sociology of Sport*, 45: 73–85.

Skille, E.Å. (2010b) *Idrettslaget – helseprodusent eller trivselsarena?* Vallset: Oplandske Bokforlag.

Skille, E.Å. (2011a) 'Change and isomorphism – a case study of translation processes in a Norwegian sport club'. *Sport Management Review*, 14: 79–88.

Skille, E.Å. (2011b) 'The conventions of sport clubs: Enabling and constraining the implementation of social goods through sport'. *Sport, Education and Society*, 16: 241–53.

Skille, E.Å. and Waddington, I. (2006) 'Alternative sport programmes and social inclusion in Norway'. *European Physical Education Review*, 12: 251–70.

Spyberg, T. (1996) 'Global transformations'. In B. Czarniawska and G. Sevón (eds) *Translating organizational change* (pp. 173–190). Berlin: Walter de Gruyter.

Stevens, J.A. and Slack, T. (1998) 'Integrating social action and structural constraints'. *International Review for the Sociology of Sport*, *33*: 143–54.

St. meld. nr. 41 (1991–1992). Innledning. Oslo: Kulturdepartementet.

St. meld. nr. 14 (1999–2000) *Idrettslivet i endrng*. Oslo: Kulturdepartementet.

van der Werff, H., Hoekman, R., Breuer, C. and Nagel, S. (2015) *Sport clubs in Europe*. Frankfurt: Springer Verlag.

Vos, S., Breesch, D., Késenne, S., Van Hoecke, J., Vanreusel, B. and Scheerder, J. (2011) 'Governmental subsidies and coercive pressures. Evidence from sport clubs and their resource dependencies'. *European Journal for Sport and Society*, *8*: 257–80.

Applying a neo-institutional translational theory of policy implementation

Alex Donaldson[1]

I became aware of Eivind Skille's (2008) theoretical framework in 2009 while developing the protocol for, and conducting a study of, how Australian community football clubs interpret safety policy developed by the central governing body for their sport (the Australian Football League – AFL). The AFL had commissioned me to develop a first aid policy for community Australian football that was both evidence-based and implementable by their affiliated community clubs. Completing the first part of this brief was relatively straightforward and involved reviewing the available community-level Australian football-related injury epidemiological data, consulting with relevant experts, and examining the contents of existing sports' first aid training courses (Donaldson and Finch, 2012a). It was while designing and conducting the more challenging second part of the brief that I came across Skille's theoretical framework. What attracted me to this framework was that it addressed the issue of sports policy implementation from the perspective of the community clubs that actually do the implementing, and it placed understanding the complex implementation context at the centre of the implementation challenge. Skille also acknowledged that sport policy outcomes depend heavily on the volunteers who run community sports clubs. These volunteers have an overriding allegiance to their local environment, and they interpret centrally developed policy through the filters of the local context, organisational characteristics and their personal experiences. In addition, Skille's framework was developed to interpret sport policy implementation within the Nordic model of sport, which is very similar to the Australian federated model. Finally, Skille's framework expanded on Stage 5 (*'Describe intervention context to inform implementation strategies'*) of the Translating Research into Injury Prevention Practice (TRIPP) framework (Finch, 2006) and complemented Step 5 of the Intervention Mapping health promotion programme planning protocol (Bartholomew *et al.*, 2011) I had previously used to guide much of my research.

I have used Skille's theoretical framework in my research to assist me to establish the significance of understanding the end-users' perspective of centrally developed sports policy as a critical factor to policy implementation success (Donaldson and Finch, 2012b). Most Australian sports governing bodies operate under a hierarchical structure using a centralised model of policy development and a top-down, directed implementation process. This often results in the development of safety policies and programmes that do not reflect the needs, motivations or capacities of the community sports clubs that eventually become the policy and programme implementers and agents of change. As a consequence, safety policies and programmes are frequently poorly implemented and rarely complied with at the community level (Hollis *et al.*, 2012; Poulos and Donaldson, 2012). Skille's framework has been particularly useful for me when working in partnership with national sporting organisations on policy development and implementation-related projects specifically when negotiating with these organisations to invest in time consuming research that requires engagement and consultation with community sports club stakeholders (administrators, coaches, athletes, etc.) (Donaldson and Poulos, 2014). To assist those tasked with facilitating the implementation of sports policy in the community sports setting, it would now be helpful if Skille's framework were extended to describe and empirically measure the nature and strength of the major influences on the sports policy implementation actions of community sports clubs.

Note

1   Dr. Alex Donaldson is a Research Fellow at the Australian Centre for Research into Injury in Sport and its Prevention (ACRISP), Federation University Australia.

References

Bartholomew, L.K., Parcel, G.S., Kok, G., Gottilieb, N.H. and Fernandez, M.E. (2011) *Planning health promotion programs. An Intervention Mapping approach* (third edn). San Francisco, CA: Jossey-Bass.

Donaldson, A. and Finch, C.F. (2012a) 'Identifying context-specific competencies required by community Australian Football sports trainers'. *British Journal of Sports Medicine, 46*: 759–66.

Donaldson, A. and Finch, C.F. (2012b) 'Planning for implementation and translation: Seek first to understand the end-users' perspectives'. *British Journal of Sports Medicine, 46*: 306–07.

Donaldson, A. and Poulos, R. (2014) 'Planning the diffusion of a neck-injury prevention programme among community rugby union coaches'. *British Journal of Sports Medicine, 48*: 151–9.

Finch, C. (2006) 'A new framework for research leading to sports injury prevention'. *Journal of Science and Medicine in Sport, 9*: 3–9.

Hollis, S.J., Stevenson, M.R., McIntosh, A.S., Shores, E.A. and Finch, C.F. (2012) 'Compliance with return-to-play regulations following concussion in Australian schoolboy and community rugby union players'. *British Journal of Sports Medicine, 46*: 735–40.

Poulos, R.G. and Donaldson, A. (2012) 'Is sports safety policy being translated into practice: What can be learnt from the Australian rugby union Mayday procedure?' *British Journal of Sports Medicine, 46*: 585–90.

Skille, E.A. (2008) 'Understanding sport clubs as sport policy implementers: A theoretical framework for the analysis of the implementation of central sport policy through local and voluntary sport organisations'. *International Review for the Sociology of Sport, 43*: 181–200.

9

THEORY OF SPORTS POLICY FACTORS LEADING TO INTERNATIONAL SPORTING SUCCESS (SPLISS)[1]

Veerle de Bosscher

Introduction

The elite sports policies of nations have one common aim: to perform successfully against the best athletes, mostly during international competitions. In spite of increasing competition and high investments in elite sports systems by many countries, an optimum strategy for delivering international success is still unclear and complicated to realise. This makes it difficult for sports managers and policymakers to prioritise and to make the right choices in elite sports policy. In this chapter, we present an overview and account of the development of a conceptual framework: the Sports Policy factors Leading to International Sporting Success, also known as the SPLISS model (De Bosscher, De Knop, van Bottenburg and Shibli, 2006). This model is the result of joint efforts of a consortium group of international researchers established in 2002. That group wanted to develop a model that could be used by policymakers and high-performance managers to compare and benchmark nations in elite sport; to measure the performances of their organisations; and to evaluate the effectiveness of national elite sport policies (De Bosscher *et al.*, 2006). The model was subsequently tested in an empirical environment first with six and then later with fifteen nations. While the model addresses the evaluation at the national level of elite sport policy, how it can be implemented at other levels has also been explored; for example, by national governing bodies (in specific sports), for regional elite sport development, in cities or by digging deeper into specific policy areas (Pillars).

The basic ideas of this model are related to the generic competitiveness literature, in which researchers seek to determine what makes one firm or nation more successful than its competitors. The measurement of world competitiveness is routinely used in economic studies to provide a framework 'to assess how nations manage their economic future' (Garelli, 2008, p. 1). In the SPLISS project, we attempted to replicate this approach in an elite sport setting. Accordingly, we developed a framework and explored a method 'to assess how nations can manage their future success in international sporting competitions' (De Bosscher, Shibli, van Bottenburg, De Knop and Truyens, 2010, p. 568). The term *manage* indicates that the focus is at the meso-level factors, or those determinants that can be influenced by human intervention; in this case, by national elite sport policies.

The SPLISS model: overview

Problem definition

Three research issues lay at the root of the SPLISS model; namely, theoretical, methodological and political issues. A theoretical issue appeared because of the lack of an empirically grounded, coherent theory on the factors determining international sporting success. There are a range of studies that show that macro-level factors – of which population and wealth were identified as the most important – explain more than 50 per cent of international sporting successes (e.g., Bernard and Busse, 2004; De Bosscher, De Knop and Heyndels, 2003; Kiviaho and Mäkelä, 1978; Morton, 2002; Suen, 1992; van Bottenburg, 2000). Nonetheless, at the meso-level (i.e., the level of sports policies), statistical relationships are hard to determine, and theory development was, and is still, at an early stage of development.

The nature of international sporting success also raised a methodological issue. Elite sports are international by definition. International comparative research between nations can therefore be seen as the only means by which one can detect the variables that explain international success. Among others, Chalip, Johnson and Stachura (1996), Henry, Amara, Al-Tauqi and Lee (2005), and Houlihan (1997) noted that there were relatively few comparative studies in sport and studies are often restricted to a descriptive level. This is largely due to the complexity of comparing nations on a like-for-like basis and a lack of international comparable research data.

A third issue concerned policymakers. Governmental authorities across the globe spend large sums of money to compete against other countries to achieve superior sport performances. There is a lack of literature and data to explain how nations can sustain their competitive position amidst increasing competition and how the efficiency and effectiveness of their elite sport investments can be enhanced.

During the past few years, a plethora of studies (e.g., Andersen and Ronglan, 2012; Bergsgard *et al.*, 2007; Digel, Burk and Fahrner, 2006; Green and Houlihan, 2005; Houlihan and Green, 2008; Oakley and Green, 2001) have increased the knowledge on elite sport development in different nations and contributed to a better understanding of elite sport systems and the factors that shape policy. According to Bergsgard *et al.* (2007), many international comparative studies fail to establish analytical relationships between variables. The SPLISS project strived to complement these studies by examining the interaction between policy inputs (resources/money), policy throughputs (processes) and outputs (results during international competitions, e.g., medals, medal points, number of elite athletes qualifying, etc.) in elite sport more closely. Therefore, we developed a model during the first phase and tested it in an empirical environment by comparing it in six nations (2004–2008, SPLISS 1.0), and subsequently in fifteen nations (2010–2014, SPLISS 2.0), to refine and further validate the model.

The SPLISS model: Sports Policy factors Leading to International Sporting Success

The SPLISS model clusters all factors within sport policy that can contribute to success (outputs) in nine policy dimensions, called Pillars, situated at two levels: inputs (Pillar 1) and throughputs (Pillars 2–9). This is presented graphically in Figure 9.1 (De Bosscher *et al.*, 2006).

- Inputs are reflected in Pillar 1, as the financial support for sport and elite sport. Countries that invest more in (elite) sport can create more opportunities for athletes to train under ideal circumstances to develop their talent.

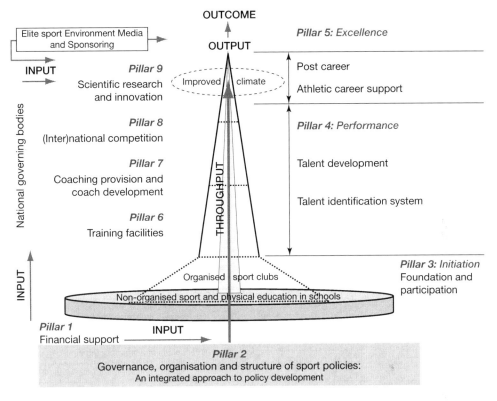

Figure 9.1 The SPLISS model: theoretical model of nine Pillars of sports policy factors influencing international success

Source: De Bosscher, V., De Knop, P., Van Bottenburg, M. and Shibli, S. (2006) 'A conceptual framework for analyzing sports policy factos leading to international sporting success.' *European Sport Management Quarterly*, 6: 185–215. Copyright European Association for Sport Management, reprinted by permission of Taylor & Francis Ltd, www.tandfonline.com, on behalf of European Association for Sport Management.

- Throughputs are the policy actions that script and deliver the processes in elite sport policies ('what' is invested and 'how' it is used) that may lead to increasing success in international sport competitions. They refer to the efficiency of sport policies; that is, the optimum way the inputs can be managed to produce the required outputs. All of the Pillars 2–9 are indicators of the throughput stage: We have thus used a multidimensional approach to evaluate effectiveness of organisations (Chelladurai, 2001) and applied this literature to a national sport policy context at the level of inputs (the system-resource model), throughputs (the internal process approach), outputs (the 'goals' model) and feedback on the system (the multiple constituency model or the participant satisfaction model.

One of the key characteristics of the SPLISS model is that each Pillar is operationalised into measurable sub-dimensions. These are the critical success factors (CSFs) that identify *what* characterises successful elite sport policies, and also *how* these different dimensions (Pillars) can be developed. The unique feature of this model is that in addition to measuring easily quantifiable variables, such as inputs and outputs, it also delves into understanding the 'black box' of throughputs (De Bosscher *et al.*, 2008, p. 35). The nine Pillars in the SPLISS model try to capture all the factors that can be managed by national sports policies or national sport

Table 9.1 Overview of the number of critical success factors (CSFs) in the 9 Pillars measured in the SPLISS 2.0 project (2014)

	CSF	*Sub-factors*
Pillar 1: Financial support	8	9
Pillar 2: Governance, organisation and structure	18	119
Pillar 3: Sports participation	10	31
Pillar 4: Talent identification and development	12	169
Pillar 5: Athletic and post-athletic career support	7	122
Pillar 6: Training facilities	9	84
Pillar 7: Coach provision and development	16	100
Pillar 8: (Inter)national competition	7	51
Pillar 9: Scientific research and innovation	9	65
TOTAL	**96**	**750**

Source: De Bosscher, Shibli, Westerbeek and van Bottenburg, 2015.

organisations, and that may influence the potential for athletes to perform at the international level. CSFs within each Pillar are elements that can drive the Pillar forward. They should not be confused with Key Performance Indicators (KPIs), which are measures that quantify management objectives to measure strategic progress and performance. In the SPLISS model, a total of 144 CSF were initially determined in nine Pillars and later reduced to 96 CSF, as will be explained further. Table 9.1 provides an overview of the number of CSFs within each Pillar. We refer to previous publications for an overview of CSFs (De Bosscher *et al.*, 2009; www.SPLISS.net/publications).

Process: how the SPLISS model was developed

To address the multifaceted research problems of this study (the lack of an existing theoretical model, the scarcity of data on elite sport policies of nations, and the lack of a method to compare nations), and in order to answer the complicated research question on the possible relationship between elite sport policies and international sporting success, triangulation of qualitative and quantitative methods was applied. The basic principles of economic competitiveness studies are quite similar in design (OECD, 2008). Linssen (1998) used the following four steps to measure 110 indicators clustered in ten determinants and compared across six nations: (a) generating the determinants of competitiveness; (b) expressing relevant factors in indicators and sub-indicators; (c) scoring each indicator and in some cases applying weightings; and (d) comparing the scores and, if possible, explaining differences between nations. Similar methods can be found in the IMD *World competitiveness yearbook* or the *Global competitiveness report* (World Economic Forum, 2008). For example, in the *World competitiveness yearbook*, fifty-five economies are analysed and ranked on 331 criteria that are grouped into twenty factors and then regrouped into four competitiveness determinants (Rosselet, 2008). Reflecting these studies, this chapter details the SPLISS design, with a specific focus on process, without going into depth on the scoring system methodology.

The SPLISS project used a three-phase exploratory sequential design (cf. Creswell and Plano Clark, 2007), as shown in Table 9.2. As suggested by Creswell and Plano Clark, the design is exploratory because of the premise that 'an initial qualitative exploration is needed for the reason that measures or instruments are not available, there is no guiding framework or theory and the variables are unknown' (p. 75). This was the first (mainly) qualitative phase, where the SPLISS model was developed because of a lack of an existing theory.

Table 9.2 Research phases and the process of development

		Aim and outcome	Method (process)
Sequential exploratory design (phase 1–2–3)	Concurrent triangulation design	**Phase 1:** SPLISS model	A conceptual model of the Sports Policy factors Leading to International Sporting Success • Nine Pillars to evaluate effectiveness of elite sport policies at the input-throughput-output level • Operationalised by 144 CSF (critical success factors)	*Data collection* QUALITATIVE • literature review: macro–meso–micro • two experimental preliminary studies – consumer perspective: athletes (n=114), coaches (n=99) and performance directors (n= 26) in Flanders – expert perspective: international tennis experts *Data analysis* • inductive content analysis, thematic development – consortium group discussion (validation)
		Phase 2: Pilot study in six sample nations **SPLISS 1.0**	Test the model in an empirical environment, resulting in theory development supported by pattern recognition: • Insights into the relationship between policies and success • Insights into elite sport systems of nations in nine Pillars • Instrument/method to: – Compare elite sport policies of nations more objectively – Evaluate effectiveness of elite sport policies and measure the competitive position from a resource-based view (RBV)	*Data collection* • QUANTITATIVE (+qual): Elite sport climate survey with 1090 elite athletes, 253 coaches and 71 performance directors (1/3 of the scores) • QUALITATIVE (+quan): overall elite sport policy inventory (about 30 pages per nation) (2/3 of the scores) *Data analysis* • QUAN: Develop a scoring system – 103 CSF measured: composite indicators – transform qualitative data into competitive position from a resource-based view (RBV) quantitative 1–5 scores aggregated into final percentage score and presented as traffic lights – develop weights for each CSF – consortium group discussion • QUAL: Descriptive analysis to support/ explain the scores
	Concurrent triangulation design	**Phase 3:** Comparison in 15 nations **SPLISS 2.0**	Further validation of the nine Pillars and CSFs • Reduction to 96 CSFs in 9 Pillars • Deeper insights in elite sport systems of more nations worldwide • Deeper insights in the relationship between each Pillar, each CSF (policies) and success: 6 Pillars and 22 CSFs with significant Spearman's rank correlation • Progressed method to compare nations, evaluate effectiveness and measure competitiveness	*Data collection* Collaboration of 58 researchers and 33 policymakers, collecting data in 15 nations: • QUANTITATIVE (+qual): Elite sport climate survey with 3142 elite athletes (18 pages, 57 questions), 1376 coaches (18 pages, 60 questions) and 241 performance directors (22 pages, 62 questions) (1/3 of the scores) • QUALITATIVE (+quan): overall elite sport policy inventory (over 3000 pages) (2/3 of the scores) – (174 pages and 212 questions in total, per country) *Data analysis* • QUAN: Develop a scoring system – 96 CSF measured: composite indicators • transform qualitative data into quantitative 1/0 scores aggregated into final percentage score and presented as traffic lights • QUAL: Descriptive analysis to support/ explain the scores

The second mixed phase builds on the results obtained in the first phase and is therefore sequential (Creswell and Plano Clark, 2007). This stage consisted of obtaining concurrent qualitative and quantitative data on the elite sport policies of six sample nations to implement and test a conceptual framework of nine Pillars and 144 CSFs in an empirical environment. Subsequently, mirroring economic competitiveness studies, the data were translated into a quantitative scoring system. The third phase is a follow-up phase, developed between 2010–14, that aims to apply and further validate the SPLISS model and the scoring methods in an international comparison with fifteen nations. The processes involved with these three phases are outlined in Table 9.2 and will be further explained in the next section.

The development process of the SPLISS model

The development of the SPLISS model was based mainly on three kinds of sources (De Bosscher *et al.*, 2006):

1   A comprehensive body of literature on the organisational context of countries in elite sport, elite sport systems (such as the former Soviet Union and East Germany), and policy analysis. This literature was supplemented by studies at the micro-level, which attempted to understand the determinants of success for individual athletes rather than nations.[2]
2   A survey with international coaches from twenty-two nations to approach key success drivers from an expert perspective.
3   A survey with 114 Flemish (i.e., the northern, Dutch-speaking part of Belgium) elite athletes, ninety-nine coaches and twenty-six performance directors to approach key success drivers from a consumer perspective.

These surveys used simple open-ended questions to identify the external factors that make the most significant contribution to the international sport success of athletes.

Two independent researchers employed inductive procedures to cluster relevant raw data into first order and second order themes until interpretable and meaningful key categories were found (Gliner and Morgan, 2000). Subsequently, to increase validity and interpretive consistency (Tashakkori and Teddlie, 2003), the list of different items and themes, derived from both the literature and preliminary research, was presented to an international consortium group of seven researchers with expertise in elite sport policy research (the SPLISS group), who were asked, independently, to cluster the items into categories. This categorisation was compared and discussed during a two-day meeting. Where different interpretations emerged, the items were regrouped and discussed until consensus was achieved.

Finally, we concluded that a total of 144 key success drivers – or critical success factors (CSFs) that can be influenced by policies – can be distilled down into nine key areas in elite sport policy, or Pillars, situated at two levels: (a) inputs (financial support) for elite sport, which are quantitative and are reflected in Pillar 1; and (b) throughputs, or the processes of how inputs can be managed to produce the required success (outputs), reflected in the remaining eight Pillars. This model, presented graphically in Figure 9.1, was the starting point of the international comparative study in Phase 2 in Table 9.2.

We undertook different steps to increase the validity of the model and methods used (face, content, criterion, construct validity). The Appendix provides an overview of the processes related to validity that are inherent to the development of theory.

Testing the model in an empirical environment in six nations: SPLISS 1.0

In a second phase of the SPLISS project, the conceptual framework was tested empirically in an international comparative pilot study with six nations (De Bosscher *et al.*, 2008): Belgium (treated separately as two regions, Flanders and Wallonia), Canada, Italy, the Netherlands, Norway and the United Kingdom. In order to collect data on each CSF, two different research instruments were used:

1   An overall elite sport policy inventory was used to collect mainly qualitative data on all Pillars identified. It was completed by the partner researchers in each country through interviews with policy agencies and analysis of existing secondary sources such as policy documents. This inventory contained eighty-four open-ended and closed questions in the nine Pillars, including their evolution in the past ten years. Open-ended questions primarily sought to gain insight into each country's policy system for each Pillar. Closed questions were added to ensure a degree of comparability across nations for the various sub-criteria. Space was left for additional comments that might be helpful in refining the conceptual model.

2   The second instrument was called the 'Elite Sport Climate Survey', completed by athletes, coaches and performance directors (national governing bodies) of each nation as main stakeholders in elite sport. In the six countries combined, a total of 1090 athletes, 253 coaches and 71 performance directors completed these questionnaires. Here, mainly quantitative information was collected through objective dichotomous (yes/no) questions to assess availability (i.e., as in the example above, the kind of information the stakeholders had received and whether they were involved in policies); and subjective questions on a five-point Likert scale, to assess how stakeholders perceived the CSF (i.e., in the example above whether their involvement in policy and the information they received was suffi-cient). This survey served two purposes: first, to gather information through stakeholders on objective indicators that cannot easily be measured (De Pelsmacker and Van Kenhove, 1999); and second, to assess the quality of elite sport development as it is perceived by the primary users.

For the data analysis, one of the key elements in the SPLISS study was that the qualitative and quantitative data on the CSFs were transformed into a 1–5 scale scoring system. The scores for different CSFs in one Pillar were then aggregated into one final percentage score for each Pillar for the six sample nations. Subsequently, each nation was allocated a colour-coded score or traffic light (black and white here), varying from a policy area 'very well developed' to 'little or no development'. This is illustrated in Figure 9.2, which presents a summary of the 126 CSFs that were measured in nine Pillars used in SPLISS 1.0. We echoed economic studies such as those previously mentioned to develop the scoring system and measure competitiveness from a resource-based view (Truyens *et al.*, 2013). The methodology is pretty similar to these studies in terms of the mixed quantitative and qualitative data, the use of surveys with stakeholders (with hard data and perceived data) to develop scores, and the conversion into a scale for scoring. Contrary to the economic competitiveness studies, SPLISS did not use relative rankings and standardised measures based on averages or quartiles due to the small sample size of only six nations.

The scoring system aimed to express the general assessment of each Pillar for each nation by consolidating different criteria into one final percentage score, which is suggested by

	ITA	UK	NED	CAN	NOR	FLA	WAL
1a. Financial support for elite sport	○	○	◍	●	●	●	●
1b. Financial support for national sport organisations	○	◎	○	●	⬤	⬤	⬤
2. Governance, organisation and structure of sport policies	◍	◎	○	◍	○	◍	◍
3. Sport participation	●	○	◍	NA	◍	◍	●
4. Talent identification and development	⬤	●	◍	●	◍	◍	●
5. Athletic career and post career support	○	◎	◎	○	○	●	●
6. Training facilities	○	○	○	◍	○	○	NA
7. Coaching provision and coach development	○	◎	○	NA	NA	●	●
8. International competitions	◍	◎	◎	○	◍	◍	●
9. Scientific research and innovation	◍	●	◍	◍	○	◍	⬤

◎ Very well developed ○ Good level of development ◍ Moderate level of development ● Limited development ⬤ Little or no development

NA: Insufficient data were available to retrieve a total score

Figure 9.2 Evaluation of six sample nations against nine Pillars (nations ranked in order of performances in Athens)

Source: De Bosscher, 2007.

De Pelsmacker and Van Kenhove (1999) as a typical methodology for measuring competitiveness in market research. This measurement system served two purposes: (a) to move beyond the descriptive level of comparing the elite sport policies of nations in order to objectify comparison in nine Pillars and to recognise patterns of well-developed elite sport policies; and (b) to find possible relationships between elite sport policies (independent variables) and sporting success (dependent variable), or to increase criterion validity on the conceptual model. This approach was primarily to facilitate interpretation and comparison; to simplify the presentation of results; and to identify any specific characteristics in the overall results for the nine Pillars. We refer the reader to De Bosscher *et al.* (2010) for a fuller explanation of this scoring system methodology.

In summary, the SPLISS 1.0 project resulted in a conceptual model of sports policy factors contributing to international sporting success, consisting of 9 Pillars and 144 CSFs (of which 126 were measured). It also contained a methodology to measure effectiveness in elite sport policies objectively (De Bosscher *et al.*, 2010) and competitiveness of nations from a resource-based view (Truyens *et al.*, 2013) by involving main stakeholders in elite sport (elite athletes, elite coaches, performance directors) in the process.

Extensions and applications of the SPLISS model

Further validation: SPLISS 2.0

Despite advancing our knowledge about theory, methodology and policies, the SPLISS 1.0 study also delivered numerous new research questions. Irrespective of anecdotal evidence about the relationship between policy actions and elite sport success, SPLISS 1.0 did not provide much conclusive evidence on the relationship between policies and success. In policy research it is hard to conduct an experiment where the impact of a single or series of policy factor(s) on outcome measures is determined in a controlled policy environment. It also became clear that various research paradigms deliver multiple (causal) models that may explain the production of elite sporting success. Country-specific context based on, for example, history or culture may provide nations with various options to design and implement successful elite sport systems. This has led to a research focus on government funded, mainly Olympic sports and to a lesser extent commercialised sports. The SPLISS model and its CSFs may be less applicable to countries where elite sport policy is the remit of NGOs or private organisations. SPLISS has therefore been typified as a functionalistic approach to elite sport (Bogerd, 2010).

To address these issues, the SPLISS methodology has further developed to take in more nations and delve deeper into the different CSFs and their relationship with success, reflected in the name SPLISS 2.0. This large-scale project includes fifteen nations: ten European countries (including three separate regions: Flanders and Wallonia representing Belgium and Northern Ireland representing Great Britain), two countries in Asia, two in America, and Australia (Oceania). The CSFs were clustered and reduced to ninety-six CSFs measured in SPLISS 2.0 (as shown in Table 9.1) and 750 sub-factors. Similar to SPLISS 1.0, the data were collected by means of an inventory on nine Pillars (data collected by the partner researchers) and three elite sport climates with elite athletes, elite coaches and performance directors. These surveys have been translated in twelve languages: English, Dutch, Danish, Estonian, Finnish, French, Portuguese (including Brazil), Spanish, Japanese, Italian, German and Korean.

Individual researchers, or teams in research institutes, are the drivers of the SPLISS 2.0 project, involving a total of fifty-eight researchers and thirty-three policymakers. To triangulate our findings we use the insights of 3142 elite athletes, 1376 coaches and 241 performance directors.

The objective of the SPLISS 2.0 project is to better understand which (and how) sport policies lead to international sporting success throughout the nine Pillars and CSFs. There are a number of sub-objectives that can be formulated (De Bosscher *et al.*, 2015). First, we want to improve and refine the theoretical model that helps explain how sport policy factors lead to international sporting success, and we want to improve the methodological approach for making valid international comparisons. Second, we aim to use our new found theoretical and methodological knowledge to inform policymakers and researchers about international policy developments in an increasingly competitive environment. This should also allow (participating) nations to better benchmark themselves against others. Ultimately, we hope to identify which are the policy factors that lead to performance improvement across nations and which are those that may deliver scope for nation-specific competitive advantage. Finally, we want to develop knowledge that can be used by policymakers to evaluate the effectiveness of elite sport policies.

The SPLISS 2.0 project builds on the model and methodologies developed in SPLISS 1.0. We take this project beyond SPLISS 1.0 by collecting more information about certain Pillars, and sampling more nations and more respondents. This has allowed us to develop a more comprehensive scoring methodology and to obtain deeper insights into the relationship between elite sport policies and sporting success of nations. The SPLISS 2.0 study has resulted in: (a) a refined model of sports policy factors contributing to international sporting success, consisting of nine Pillars and ninety-six CSFs; (b) identification of the characteristics of efficient sporting nations, and elements of convergence and divergence in elite sport policies; (c) a relationship between Pillars and success (criterion validity); (d) a relationship between CSFs and success (criterion validity); (e) the identification of different configurations of CSFs within each Pillar and different Pillar strengths; and (f) a methodology to measure effectiveness in elite sport policies objectively and competitiveness of nations from a resource-based view, both accomplished by involving main stakeholders in elite sport (elite athletes, elite coaches, performance directors) in the process.

As an example, Figure 9.3 is an illustration of summarised scores in nine Pillars and two nations (Japan and Brazil, two Olympic host nations) compared with the sample average and maximum scores. This figure presents a summary of the results of over 3000 pages of inventory information, and the responses from more than 3100 elite athletes, 1300 elite coaches and 240 performance directors. What this figure shows, looking at the nine Pillars for Brazil, is that Brazil is only above the average of the other fifteen nations in Pillar 1 (financial support) and around the average in Pillar 8 (access to international competition). There is significant funding available in Brazil (Pillar 1) but the allocation of funding remains quite undirected. The magnitude of the gaps between the scores for Brazil and the sample average are the greatest in Pillars 7 (coaches), 4 (talent) and 6 (facilities). Sport participation is a long-term development

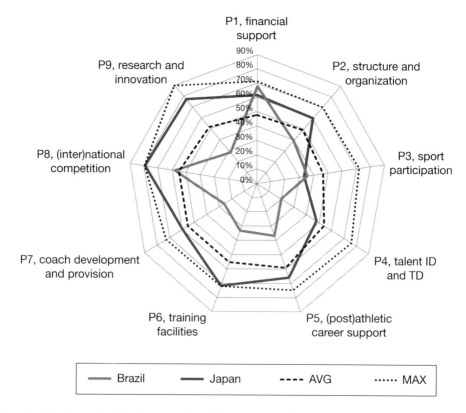

Figure 9.3 Radar graph of Brazil compared with Japan in nine Pillars, in comparison with the average and maximum scores of fifteen nations

that also scores low. Japan performs far better than Brazil on the nine Pillar scores, except for sports participation (Pillar 3). It has a maximum score of the fifteen nations in training facilities (Pillar 6) and (international) competition (Pillar 8), and has a relative strength in research and innovation (Pillar 9).

Without dwelling on the comparison of these nations and their scores, the main point of note in the SPLISS study was that the transformation of qualitative data into quantitative scores improved our understanding of the extent to which nations are developed in managing their elite sport success. As indicated by Sandelowski, Voils and Knafl (2009), the scoring system helps to test hypotheses addressing relationships between independent and dependent variables. It facilitates the recognition of patterns and extracts meaning from qualitative data, accounts for all data, document analytic moves and verifies interpretations. The full study will be published in a book in 2015 (De Bosscher *et al.*, 2015).

Applications to other contexts and future directions

In the SPLISS study, we maintained a focus at the national sport policy level. We did not go into sport-by-sport comparisons, nor did we consider the policy systems that drive the development of commercial sport success. As stated by Porter (1990), commenting on the competitive advantage of nations: 'No nation can be competitive in everything . . . A high level of competitiveness in all areas is very unlikely in the economy and therefore nations may specialize in one domain' (p. 8).

Sport-by-sport comparisons may reveal that certain Pillars are more conditional to success than others. Clusters of policy success models may be found, for example, for early versus late (talent) specialisation sports, or for team sports versus individual sports. Accordingly, to address these issues, several SPLISS studies that are underway and partly completed are looking into sport specific comparisons and from different viewpoints:

- Athletics: A resource-based perspective on countries' competitive advantage in elite athletics (Jasper Truyens, PhD, Vrije Universiteit Brussel, Belgium; Truyens *et al.*, 2013).
- Tennis: The examination of the tennis policy factors that influence the tennis performance of a country (Jessie Brouwers, PhD, Griffith University (AUS) in collaboration with Vrije Universiteit Brussel; Brouwers, Sotiriadou and De Bosscher, 2015).
- Judo: Organisational determinants for international sporting success (Leandro Mazzei, PhD, University of Sao Paulo (BRA) in collaboration with Vrije Universiteit Brussel; Mazzei, Bastos, De Bosscher and Böhme, 2013).
- Snow sports: A market-based view of nations on the medal market of the Winter Olympic Games (Andreas Christophe Weber, PhD, Swiss Federal Institute of Sport Magglingen SFISM/Vrije Universiteit Brussel, SUI).
- Canoe: Elite sport culture and policy interrelationships: the case of Sprint Canoe in Australia (Sotiriadou, Gowthorp and De Bosscher, 2013).
- Equestrian: Key success determinants in sports policies (Clara Van Laer, 2012, master's thesis at Vrije Universiteit Brussel 2012).
- Commercial speed-skating teams: Key figures in the development of branding teams in speed skating for the elite sport climate and talent development in particular, a case study in the Netherlands (Renneke Bogerd, master's thesis at Utrecht University 2011).
- Swimming: Comparing elite sport policy factors leading to international sporting success in Flanders and the Netherlands (Sepp Meyers, master's thesis at Vrije Universiteit Brussel 2010).

Furthermore, the SPLISS model is being or has been applied in other contexts, such as:

- Examining Pillar 2: A network approach to elite sport policies (Susana Rodrigues, PhD, Lisbon University (POR) in collaboration with Vrije Universiteit Brussel).
- Regional/state level: Analysis of the policies and the climate/environment for elite sport on the different organisational levels of Brazil: governmental and non-governmental – with emphasis on the relations of school sport and participative sport with sports talents identification and development programmes (led by Maria Thereza Ter Böhme, Universidade de Sao Paulo).
- Elite sport and cities: A comparison between five Dutch and three Belgian cities (Fenke van Rossum, 2012, master's thesis at Vrije Universiteit Brussel).

Projects regarding elite sport policies in Paralympic Sports, elite sport policies in developing countries, and military participation in international sporting success are also under development, together with other researchers that have shown interest. More information about these projects can be consulted at the website: www.SPLISS.net.

Valorisations and applications by practitioners

The SPLISS knowledge has been valorised to a variety of contexts and made suitable to policymakers, high-performance directors, national governing bodies and ministries of sport. Some end-user agreements have been made with other institutions, which entitles external partners (e.g., in Thailand, Denmark, Brazil) to use the non-published SPLISS instruments and surveys; for example, an analysis of the policies and the climate/environment for elite sport on the different organisational levels of Brazil, with emphasis on the relations of school sport and participative sport with sports talent identification and development programmes.

Furthermore, using the SPLISS instruments, research partners and policymakers have produced their own national policy reports, as well as numerous other publications and presentations at sport policy conferences. The countries represented by this work include: Brazil, Canada, Denmark, Estonia, Japan, Finland, the Netherlands, Northern Ireland, Portugal, Spain and Switzerland. For an overview and for additional publications by the researchers, we refer the reader to the website: www.SPLISS.net.

Last but not least, the SPLISS model and its methodology is a helpful tool in developing elite sport policies and it has been applied in many nations to evaluate their effectiveness. The model is used by policymakers at various levels and in different countries; for example, in Belgium (Ministry of Sport), Brazil (Federal Department of Sport, Elite Sport department), Canada (Sport Canada), the Netherlands (NOC★NSF) and Switzerland (Swiss Olympic). Obviously, not all valorisations of the SPLISS model are known to us, but its use is perhaps illustrated by two quotes from policymakers in the UK and Belgium:

> In the UK, it has been difficult to answer the frequently-asked question: how does our sports system compare with that of other nations? However, as a result of the SPLISS project, we finally have some robust comparative information on this subject. Looking across the nine policy areas that comprise the SPLISS framework, the results for the UK are generally encouraging, providing us with a degree of assurance that we are doing the right things. The two policy areas in which we appear to have performed less well are those of talent development and the coordination of scientific

research. In reality, we have already identified these as areas needing attention, and the new investment we are now making in them may be seen as a test of the reasonableness of the SPLISS analysis.

(Jerry Bingham, Research Director UKSport,
personal communication, 2008)

In Belgium (Flanders), the SPLISS research has had an enormous impact on the direction of future policy choices. It has given policy makers and federations very useful insights into the strengths and weaknesses of our elite sports policies compared with other nations. The study has made policy makers aware of the determinants of competitiveness and the nine pillars model is now used as a basic framework for our 2009–2012/16 policy plan. Most of all, the study keeps policy makers alert to international developments, and has given insights into the characteristics of effective elite sport policies and how nations can develop a competitive advantage. We have also learned that it is difficult to implement good practice from other nations directly, but nonetheless it inspires us to innovate and develop our own ideas.

(Bert Anciaux, Flemish Minister of Sport and Ivo Van Aken,
elite sports manager, personal communication, 2008)

Reflections

This chapter showed how SPLISS was designed and used. The various building blocks that lead to elite sport success are complex, multi-faceted and multi-layered. Although the SPLISS model and its constituting CSFs is comprehensive, it is not an all-embracing model that can be applied to any situation, any country or any context. It is impossible to create one single model for explaining international success and different systems may lead to similar levels of success. Furthermore, policy instruments are often dependent on politics and policy regimes, which implies that similar policy actions may have different outcomes in different nations. Therefore, international comparative studies are one of the most complicated areas of research (Henry *et al.*, 2005; Porter, 1990). In this regard, some well-considered choices had to be made prior to the start of the SPLISS project. These are related, for example, to its specific focus at the 'national level' of comparison, and in particular the meso-level or those factors that can be influenced by policies. We are well aware of the caveats this also encompasses. While historical data are collected and described, so are contextual factors; they are not the key focus point of the SPLISS study and are inherent to the pathways of elite sport development.

The SPLISS study has only touched the surface of the factors influencing international sporting success. It will therefore never be possible in comparative elite sport policy studies to reduce all success factors to one all-embracing theory. The key point of note, as stated by Hofstede (1998), is to identify how one can pare down typical problems to an extent that a common language can be found for those factors that can be compared. Hofstede (1998) provided the metaphor that every comparison of values and norms between nations is like a comparison between apples and oranges, and it is important to find a common language (De Bosscher, 2007):

Popular wisdom deems that one cannot compare apples with oranges. But what do we mean by 'compare'? Scientifically speaking, apples and oranges come under the general category of 'fruits' and can be compared on many criteria, such as availability, price, colour, vitamin content or keeping quality. Comparing apples with oranges, cross-cultural psychologist Harry Triandis once said, is okay as long as we possess a fruitology, a theory of fruits.

(Hofstede, 1998, p. 16)

The SPLISS's fruitfulness is its nine Pillars and CSFs. The scoring system should not be seen as a stand-alone evaluation of elite sport policies. It is a useful tool to move beyond the descriptive level of comparison, to facilitate pattern recognition and to extract meaning from qualitative data and to verify interpretations; to investigate the black box of policy throughput, not only in regard to what happens between input and outputs, but also get a sense of the usefulness and quality of those actions by having them rated by stakeholders.

The danger arises when nations benchmark themselves transferring best practices, Pillars and CSFs from one setting to another. The global sporting arms race, and the subsequent pressures to be seen to succeed on the world stage, has led to a drive towards the exchange and transfer of sporting practices between nations. One of the most significant obstacles in the implementation, as has been indicated with the policy learning, lesson drawing and policy transfer by Houlihan and Green (2008), is the inherent difficulty of translating ideas and strategies from one context into another. The exchange of information between sporting nations is rarely reciprocal or bidirectional (Collins and Bailey, 2013). Furthermore, Collins and Bailey (2013) add to this the scienciness, the illusion of scientific credibility and validity of scientific principles behind a sport system, which are highly technical and specialist, and usually lacking the underpinning evidence. In line with these concepts, one of the major conclusions in the SPLISS 2.0 project and the different scores (De Bosscher *et al.*, 2015) was that despite the search for a common (similar) path towards elite sport development, the reality seems there is no generic blueprint – no sets of Pillars, critical success factors or recognised best practices that can be copied and pasted between different contexts and that will guarantee success. There are, however, a set of broad principles around a common framework that can be adapted to local circumstances in a culturally appropriate manner. Accordingly, the key challenge for nations remains to find the right blend of system ingredients and processes that work best in their own context and culture, encouraging them to benchlearning, rather than benchmarking against other competitors, and to seek for the best broad principles of efficient and effective elite sport policies, rather than copying best practices.

Notes

1   This chapter is a reflection on De Bosscher, De Knop, Van Bottenburg and Shibli (2006), and the work related to it.

2   In this research, inductive procedures were used to consolidate all relevant sources from a comprehensive body of literature on the former Soviet Union and East Germany (e.g., Broom, 1991; Douyin, 1988; Krüger, 1984; Riordan, 1989; Semotiuk, 1990) and more recently on the organisational context of countries in elite sport (e.g., Clumpner, 1994; Digel *et al.*, 2003; Digel and Barra, 2004; Green and Houlihan, 2005; Larose and Haggerty, 1996; Oakley and Green, 2001; Stamm and Lamprecht, 2000). It was found that the one crucial element missing in all the previous attempts to model sports policy influences on success was the involvement of athletes and coaches who are the key stakeholders responsible for delivering their nation's success. This literature was, therefore, supplemented by studies at the micro-level, which attempt to understand success determinants for individual athletes instead of nations (e.g., Conzelmann and Nagel, 2003; Duffy *et al.*, 2001; Gibbons *et al.*, 2003; Greenleaf, Gould and Diefen, 2001; Nys, De Knop and De Bosscher, 2002; Van Bottenburg, 2000). We refer to De Bosscher *et al.* (2006) for a fuller explanation.

References

Andersen, S.S. and Ronglan, L.T. (2012) *Nordic elite sport: Same ambitions, different tracks.* Copenhagen: Copenhagen Business School Press.

Bergsgard, N.A., Houlihan, B., Mangset, P., Nødland, S.I. and Rommetvedt, H. (2007) *Sport policy: A comparative analysis of stability and change.* London: Elsevier.

Bernard, A.B. and Busse, M.R. (2004) 'Who wins the Olympic Games? Economic resources and medal totals'. *Review of Economics & Statistics, 86:* 413–17.

Bogerd, J. (2010) 'Twee kanten van de medaille. Sleutelfiguren uit de schaatssport over de gevolgen van de ontwikkeling van de merkenteams voor het topsportklimaat van het langebaanschaatsen en talentontwikkeling in het bijzonder [Two sides of the medal. Key figures from speed skating about the consequences of the development of branding teams, for the elite sport climate and talent development in particular]'. Unpublished master's thesis, Utrecht University, the Netherlands.

Broom, E.F. (1991) 'Lifestyles of aspiring high performance athletes: A comparison of national models'. *Journal of Comparative Physical Education and Sport, 8*(2): 24–54.

Brouwers, J., Sotiriadou, P. and De Bosscher, V. (2015) 'Sport-specific policies and factors that influence international success: The case of tennis'. *Sport Management Review, 18:* 343–358.

Burk, V. and Fahrner, M. (2006) *High-performance sport. An international comparison* (Vol. 9). Weilheim/Teck, Tubingen: Bräuer.

Chalip, L., Johnson, A. and Stachura, L. (1996) *National sport policies: An international handbook.* London: Greenwood Press.

Chelladurai, P. (2001) *Managing organizations for sport and physical activity: A systems perspective.* Scottsdale, AZ: Holcomb-Hathaway.

Clumpner, R.A. (1994) '21st century success in international competition'. In R. Wilcox (ed.) *Sport in the global village* (pp. 298–303). Morgantown, WV: FIT.

Collins, D. and Bailey, R. (2013) '"Scienciness" and the allure of second-hand strategy in talent identification and development'. *International Journal of Sport Policy & Politics, 5:* 183–91.

Conzelmann, A. and Nagel, S. (2003) 'Professional careers of the German Olympic athletes'. *International Review for the Sociology of Sport, 38:* 259–80.

Creswell, J.W. and Plano Clark, V.L. (2007) *Designing and conducting mixed methods research.* London: Sage.

De Bosscher, V. (2007) *Sports policy factors leading to international sporting success.* Belgium: VUBPRESS, Brussels.

De Bosscher, V., De Knop, P. and Heyndels, B. (2003) 'Comparing tennis success among countries'. *International Sports Studies, 25:* 49–68.

De Bosscher, V., De Knop, P., Van Bottenburg, M. and Shibli, S. (2006) 'A conceptual framework for analysing sports policy factors leading to international sporting success'. *European Sport Management Quarterly, 6:* 185–215.

De Bosscher, V., Shibli, S., Westerbeek, H. and van Bottenburg, M. (2015) *Successful elite sport policies. An international comparison of the Sports Policy factors Leading to International Sporting Success (SPLISS 2.0) in 15 nations.* Aachen: Meyer & Meyer.

De Bosscher, V., Bingham, J., Shibli, S., Van Bottenburg, M. and De Knop, P. (2008) *The global sporting arms race. An international comparative study on sports policy factors leading to international sporting success.* Aachen: Meyer & Meyer.

De Bosscher, V., De Knop, P., van Bottenburg, M., Shibli, S. and Bingham, J. (2009) 'Explaining international sporting success. An international comparison of elite sport systems and policies in six nations'. *Sport Management Review, 12:* 113–36.

De Bosscher, V., Shibli, S., van Bottenburg, M., De Knop, P. and Truyens, J. (2010) 'Developing a methodology for comparing the elite sport systems and policies of nations: A mixed research methods approach'. *Journal of Sport Management, 24:* 467–600.

De Pelsmacker, P. and Van Kenhove, P. (1999) *Marktonderzoek: methoden en toepassingen [Market research: methods and applications]* (third edn). Leuven Apeldoorn, BE: Garant.

Digel, H. and Barra, M. (2004) *Hochleistungssport in Italien.* Weilheim/Teck: Bräuer.

Digel, H., Miao, J. and Utz, A. (2003) *Hochleistungssport in China.* Weilheim/Teck: Bräuer.

Digel, H., Burk, V. and Fahrner, M. (2006) 'High-performance sport: An international comparison'. *Edition Sports International,* 9. Weilheim/Teck, Tubingen, DE: Bräuer.

Douyin, X. (1988) 'A comparative study on the competitive sports training systems in different countries'. *Journal of Comparative Physical Education and Sport, 2:* 3–12.

Duffy, P., Lyons, D., Moran, A., Warrington, G. and Macmanus, C. (2001) *Factors promoting and inhibiting the success of high performance players and athletes in Ireland.* National coaching & Training Centre: Ireland.

Garelli, S. (2002) 'Competitiveness of nations: The fundamentals'. Available online at: http://members.shaw.ca/compilerpress1/Anno%20Garelli%20CN%20Fundamentals.htm

Gibbons, T., McConnel, A., Forster, T., Riewald, S.T. and Peterson, K. (2003) *Reflections on success: US Olympians describe the success factors and obstacles that most influenced their Olympic development*. Report phase II from United States Olympic Committee (USOC).

Gliner, J.A. and Morgan, G.A. (2000) *Research methods in applied settings: An integrated approach to design and analysis*. Mahwah, NJ: Lawrence Erlbaum Associates.

Green, M. and Houlihan, B. (2005) *Elite sport development. Policy learning and political priorities*. New York: Routledge.

Greenleaf, C., Gould, D. and Diefen, K. (2001) 'Factors influencing Olympic performance with Atlanta and Nagano US Olympians'. *Journal of Applied Sport Psychology*, *13*: 154–84.

Henry, I., Amara, M., Al-Tauqi, M. and Chao Lee, P. (2005) 'A typology of approaches to comparative analysis of sports policy'. *Journal of Sport Management*, *19*: 480–96.

Hofstede, G. (1998) 'A case for comparing apples with oranges: International differences in values'. *International Journal of Comparative Sociology*, *39*: 16–31.

Houlihan, B. (1997) *Sport, policy and politics. A comparative analysis*. London: Routledge.

Houlihan, B. and Green, M. (2008) *Comparative elite sport development. Systems, structures and public policy*. London: Elsevier.

Kiviaho, P. and Mäkelä, P. (1978) 'Olympic success: A sum of non-material and material factors'. *International Review of Sport Sociology*, *2*: 5–17.

Krüger, A. (1984) 'To Moscow and back: international status of comparative research in regard to physical activity outside of schools'. Proceedings of the fourth international seminar on comparative physical education and sport (pp. 213–27). Malente-Kiel, Germany.

Larose, K. and Haggerty, T.R. (1996) 'Factors associated with national Olympic success: an exploratory study'. Unpublished master's thesis, Universiteit Brunswick, Canada.

Linssen, G.W.J.M. (1998) 'Benchmarking. De concurrentietoets 1997: Een voorbeeld van benchmarken [An example of benchmarking]'. *Beleidsanalyse*, *1*: 14–22.

Mazzei, L.C., Bastos, F.C., De Bosscher, V. and Böhme, M.T.S. (2013) 'Who is the best? Performance evaluation of countries in international Judo'. In: VIII International Judo Research Symposium, 2013, Rio de Janeiro. VIII International Judo Research Symposium. Rio de Janeiro: International Judo Federation, v. 1. p. 16–19.

Meyers S. (2010) 'Explorour onderzoek naar het zwembeleid in Vlaanderen en Nederland. [Explorative research in swimming policies in Flanders and the Netherlands]'. Unpublished master's thesis, Vrije Universiteit Brussels.

Morton, H. (2002) 'Who won the Sydney 2000 Olympics? An allometric approach'. *The Statistician, 51*: 147–55.

Nys, K., De Knop, P. and De Bosscher, V. (2002) 'Prestatiebepalende factoren in topsport' [Factors determining international success in elite sports]. Unpublished master's thesis, Vrije Universiteit Brussel, Belgium. Unierzyski, 2002.

Oakley, B. and Green, M. (2001) 'The production of Olympic champions: International perspectives on elite sport development system'. *European Journal for Sport Management*, *8*: 83–105.

OECD (Producer) (2008) *Handbook on constructing composite indicators: Methodology and user guide*. Available at www.oecd.org/std/42495745.pdf (accessed on 1 September, 2014).

Porter, M.E. (1990) *The competitive advantage of nations*. London: Macmillan.

Riordan, J. (1989) 'Soviet sport and perestroika'. *Journal of Comparative physical Education and Sport*, 6(2): 7–18.

Rosselet, S. (2008) *Methodology and principles of analysis*. International Institute for Management Development World Competitiveness yearbook. Available online at www02.imd.ch/wcc/yearbook (accessed on 2 August, 2008).

Sandelowski, M., Voils, C.I. and Knafl, G. (2009) 'On quantitizing'. *Journal of Mixed Methods Research, 3*: 208–22.

Semotiuk, D. (1990) 'East bloc athletics in the Glasnost era'. *Journal of Comparative Physical Education & Sport*, 9(1): 26–9.

Sotiriadou, P., Gowthorp, L. and De Bosscher, V. (2013) 'Elite sport culture and policy interrelationships: The case of Sprint Canoe in Australia'. *Leisure Studies*, *32*: 598–617.

Stamm, H. and Lamprecht, M. (2001) 'Sydney 2000, the best games ever? World sport and relationships of structural dependency'. Summary of a paper presented at the First World Congress of the Sociology of Sport, Seoul, Korea. Available at www.lssfb.ch/download/ISSA_Seoul.pd (accessed March, 2002).

Suen, W. (1992) *Men, money and medals: an econometric analysis of the Olympic Games.* Discussion Paper from the University of Hong Kong.

Tashakkori, A. and Teddlie, C. (2003) *Handbook of mixed methods in social and behavioral research.* Thousand Oakes, CA: Sage.

Truyens, J., De Bosscher, V., Heyndels, B. and Westerbeek, H. (2013). 'A resource-based perspective on countries' competitive advantage in elite athletics'. *International Journal of Sport Policy & Politics,* 6: 459–89.

van Bottenburg, M. (2000) *Het topsportklimaat in Nederland [The elite sports climate in the Netherlands].* Hertogenbosch, Netherlands: Diopter-Janssens and van Bottenburg bv.

Van Laer, C. (2012) 'Een exploratieve studie naar de prestatiebepalende factoren in het paardrijden: een benchmarkstudie in Vlaanderen en Nederland [Explorative research to the sports policy factors influencing success in equestrian]'. Unpublished master's thesis, Vrije Universiteit Brussels.

Van Rossum, F. (2012) 'Stedelijke topsportondersteuning. Een vergelijking tussen Vlaanderen en Nederland. [Elite sport support by cities. A comparison between Flanders and the Netherlands]'. Published masters thesis, Vrije Universiteit Brussel and abstract published in V. De Bosscher (ed.) 'Elite sport success: Society boost or not?' Proceedings of the first SPLISS conference, pp. 12–13, Nieuwegein: Arko Sports media & VUB. Antwerp, 13 – 14/11. ISBN 978–90–5472–261–8

World Economic Forum (2007). *The global competitiveness report 2007. World Economic Forum.* New York: Palgrave Macmillan.

Applying the theory of SPLISS

David Legg[1]

In 2001, I was introduced to Veerle De Bosscher, then a doctoral student in Belgium, who was pursuing an ambitious research agenda for her PhD dissertation. She was attempting to develop an empirically based model that would help clarify the sport policies under an administrator's influence that could lead to sporting success. De Bosscher was looking for other nations to participate, so with funding support from Sport Canada (the governing body for amateur sport in Canada), I graciously accepted. The methodology was extremely detailed and in-depth, and required considerable time and energy, but with this was the concomitant hope that the results would be meaningful and relevant. More specifically, we completed detailed questionnaires on various aspects of the national sport system. This included items such as coaching, funding and athlete support services. We then surveyed all national athletes, national team coaches and national high-performance directors for all sports that competed in the summer Olympic Games. The first iteration of the SPLISS study was led by a consortium of sport management researchers and practitioners from Belgium, the Netherlands and the United Kingdom. Along with myself, researchers from Norway and Italy also participated. After the publication of a book and several articles, a second iteration of this study was initiated in 2010, this time with fifteen nations participating, and once again I was fortunate to be the Canadian researcher.

During this time, I saw the acceptance of SPLISS in the sport industry flourish. In Canada, SPLISS is now being used by Sport Canada officials, who supported both studies, to align the roles and responsibilities of its partners in the Canadian high-performance sport system. Sport Canada is also hoping that future SPLISS research will focus on Paralympic sport so that a similar guiding framework can be incorporated.

A second way in which SPLISS is being used practically is via Canadian Sport for Life (www.cs4l.ca) and its Long-Term Athlete Development (LTAD) model:

Canadian Sport for Life is a movement to improve the quality of sport and physical activity in Canada. CS4L links sport, education, recreation and health and aligns community, provincial and national programming. Canadian Sport for Life's Long-Term Athlete Development framework is a seven-stage training, competition and recovery pathway guiding an individual's experience in sport and physical activity from infancy through all phases of adulthood.

(http://canadiansportforlife.ca/)

SPLISS, while focusing primarily on elite sport, still falls within the CS4L framework and its athlete pathway approach. The nine SPLISS pillars identified as leading to international sporting success can thus be used by sport leaders to serve as benchmarks and guides. Only a small portion of the LTAD system focuses on elite sport performance, but the nine pillars allow one to see how the other stages that are more focused on physical literacy, play and training interrelate and can mutually benefit.

Additionally, I use the SPLISS model in my own teaching. For first-year students, I use the model to help direct them to the various intersecting realms within our industry. For fourth-year students, I use the model to help guide them when writing their senior theses and to remind them of the interdependences of a myriad of players and organisations.

For the future I am hopeful that a similar study can address the policies leading to international sporting success in Paralympic sport. As well, it would behoove sport leaders to address whether the same Pillars noted in both iterations of the SPLISS study are applicable in other national contexts. To date, the majority of participating nations have been western European and financially stable.

Note

1   Dr. David Legg is a Professor of Sport and Recreation Management at Mount Royal University.

Table 9.3 Research steps and evaluation of validity and reliability

Validity and reliability	*Research procedures*

Stage 1: Development of a conceptual model (competitiveness determinants)

Face validity

Does the model measure what we want it to measure at first glance?
- Literature review

Content validity:
- nine Pillars
- detailed CSFs

Are the nine Pillars the right competitiveness/elite sport policy determinants?
- Literature review: macro-meso-micro (factors influencing international sporting success); economic studies (methodological)
- Preliminary research, survey with:
  Stakeholders (athletes, coaches, performance directors in Flanders)
  International experts (tennis)
- International consortium group (experts' opinions)

Criterion validity

Is success clearly defined?
Define criterion (outputs): different methods to measure success (absolute, relative, summer and winter sports, different events, medals or top eight places . . .)
Are the CSFs related with success?
- Literature review: macro-meso-micro
- Preliminary research, survey with:
  Stakeholders (athletes, coaches, performance directors in Flanders)
  International experts (tennis)
- International consortium group (experts' opinions)

Construct validity

Are the concepts measured correctly and with all its facets?
- See above, for completion of the nine Pillars and their CSF
- clustering of items by two independent researchers
- International consortium group (experts' opinions) – two-day meeting: to classify the CSF, to define CSF clearly, eventually add and delete CSF

Stage 2: Pilot study with six nations (SPLISS 1.0) and follow up study with fifteen nations (SPLISS 2.0)
A. Transformation of Pillars and CSF into questions and data collection procedures

Validity (internal)

Has the theory been correctly transformed into practice? Are the questions sufficiently covering the nine Pillars and their CSF? (construct validity) Were the questions correctly defined; can they be misinterpreted? (internal validity)
- Literature on transnational studies in different areas (methodology)
- Transformation of nine Pillars and its CSF into measurement questions: discussed with consortium group (meetings, emails and conference calls) to avoid translation and interpretative difficulties; increase the validity of direct comparisons
- Careful sample selection
Two surveys
- Elite sport climate survey (operationalisation of 1/3 of the CSF)
  Aim: (1) collect data on questions that are difficult to measure and (2) stakeholders' perspective in elite sport
  Prior to the Athens Olympic Games
  Measures objective (facts) and subjective (satisfaction) indicators; these are kept separated
  Pre-tested in two nations (Flanders and the Netherlands) and adapted where necessary

Table 9.3 continued

Validity and reliability	*Research procedures*
	• Overall sport policy questionnaire (operationalisation of 2/3 of the CSF) Aim: measure objective indicators or 'facts' and get insights into international elite sport policies of nations Researchers' questionnaire: a comprehensive research by itself, collected through secondary sources and (eventually) interviews (for each Pillar) questions: open-ended (to gain insight) and closed (comparability); strengths and weaknesses and past ten years' evolutions Pre-tested in three consortium nations Clarifications through emails and telephones
Internal and external reliability (interpretive consistency and inter-rater reliability)	• Careful selection of researchers in the sample nations (knowledgeable, precise, good relations with policy, find funds) • Organisation of initial meetings, to explain the methods • Procedures in the elite sport climate survey • Research protocol and definitions (athlete, coach, co-ordinator, elite sports discipline); • Questions can be added, but remain unchanged • Advise to conduct local interviews (reproduce data to own context) • Procedures in the overall sport policy questionnaire • Guidelines and flow chart with information • Two examples of completed questionnaires as an example • Asked for sufficiently comprehensive detail and not fill in if unclear • Further clarification later through email and telephone • Analysis: elite sport climate survey • word template, SPSS file and manual

Stage 2: Pilot study with six nations (SPLISS 1.0) and follow up study with fifteen nations (SPLISS 2.0)

B. data-analysis: development of a scoring system and the introduction of 'measurement'

Reliability	*Is the sample representative?* • There are only six sample nations, because the aim was to explore a measurement tool and to refine a conceptual model Overall sports policy questionnaire: • completed by each nation (N=7) Elite sport climate survey: • Intervening variables on the sample are mentioned in the paper; • It should therefore be noted that results may be biased by non-response The response rate is below 30 per cent for Canadian athletes (16 per cent, N=116) and Dutch coaches (28 per cent) Walloon coaches (19 per cent, N=6) and UK coaches (8 per cent, N=23) were excluded; data from performance directors were excluded Remark: the Netherlands did a non-response check for their athletes and coaches and found a high correlation (r>0.8)
Construct validity of the measurement instrument	*Have scores and weights adequately been assigned?* • Standards to develop scores in the overall sport policy questionnaire are to some extent arbitrary (they are expressed in terms of 'availability' – the more, the better). Weights are added to 'lock in' the impact of each CSF on the overall score

Table 9.3 continued

Validity and reliability	*Research procedures*
	to increase validity of this procedure, all standards and weights were discussed with a group of experts (consortium group) during several longstanding meetings
	the standards were finally checked by the researchers of each nation and their policymakers
	• The elite sport climate (quantitative information) allowed to create objective standards for comparison and develop five point categories
	Is the score adequate for the concept measured? Are all facets of the factors leading to success measured?
	• The profoundly defined set of CSFs, and the use of two different instruments, intend to increase construct validity of the measurement instrument
	2/3 of the CSF derive from the overall sports policy questionnaires, 1/3 from the elite sport climate survey
	To increase construct validity hard data were separated from perceived data.
	• The definition of relative success allows inclusion of macro-level factors to some extent (wealth, population, political system, religion, geography)
	Boundaries:
	• Some data should be measured at other levels (sport specific, local policies and sponsorships)
	• Representativeness of the pilot study and the sample; n/a (not available) scores for some nations on certain CSF
	• Small sample (six nations) does not allow the use of relative values or averages for missing values
	• Not all Pillars have an assessment
	• Many extraneous factors that can't be measured in quantitative terms (cultural, historical)
Criterion validity	*Are the results related to an external criterion or is there a relation between success (outputs) and the scores on nine Pillars (inputs and throughputs)? Is each indicator related to success?*
	• The development of a scoring system is especially important to increase criterion validity
	• The study can not be conclusive on a possible input–output relationship because:
	– it is not possible to make statistical relations with only six sample nations; no causalities
	– Definition of success is ambiguous: absolute, relative, winter sports, summer sports . . . all giving different rankings for the nations
	– There are many extraneous factors, that influence success
	– Further research is needed at other levels (e.g., sport by sport)

10

DEVELOPING A THEORY OF BOARD STRATEGIC BALANCE[1]

Lesley Ferkins and David Shilbury

Overview

Why sport governance?

Our interest in sport governance came about because of our belief in the potential impact and influence of those involved in the oversight of sport organisations. At best, those who govern set the future course of the organisation. In a collective sense, the potential to set the future course of the sport sector resides with those who are ultimately accountable for the performance of sport organisations. Our aspiration was to contribute to the way sport is organised, managed and led, and we considered there was no better way to do this than to work with those who govern and, by definition, lead. We also saw the development of theory focused on the board's strategic role as an important building block in this aspiration.

We began in the early 2000s by focusing on what is commonly referred to as organisation governance (Cornforth, 2012; i.e., the work of the board of a single organisation), and concerned ourselves with the governance of specific sports (also referred to as sport codes; e.g., tennis, golf, etc). In this way, national and state sport organisations became the subject of our interest. As we got deeper into the issues of governing a sport code, we became increasingly engaged with the interplay *between* organisations, variously referred to as systemic governance or network governance (Henry and Lee, 2004). This also involved the dynamics between volunteer directors and the increasing influence of paid staff. The transition of the sport sector inexorably towards professionalisation raised a multitude of challenges for sport organisations, all of which demanded further enquiry.

In recognising the curious nature of the sport sector where non–profit (e.g., national sport organisations), public (e.g., government agencies) and commercialised entities (e.g., professional teams) coalesce, and in drawing on Kikilus (2000), we positioned our work to reflect the following conceptualisation. Sport governance is 'the responsibility for the functioning and overall direction of the organization and is a necessary and institutionalized component of all sport codes from club level to national bodies, government agencies, sport service organizations and professional teams around the world' (Ferkins, Shilbury and McDonald, 2009, p. 245). Once established, this definition has remained constant throughout our topic of investigation and subsequent theory development process.

Our specific curiosity: board strategic capability

Sport governance was the starting point for the general phenomenon that attracted our interest. As detailed later, our specific curiosity emerged as a result of wide-ranging discussions with sport practitioners, as well as finding a gap in the literature that revealed *board strategic capability* as an under-researched area. We identified this gap in a 2005 article titled, 'The role of the board in building strategic capability: Towards an integrated model of sport governance research' (Ferkins *et al.*, 2005). In that paper, we argued that the state of governance research was 'still largely shaped by a normative and prescriptive approach that may not fully explain the diversity that exists in sport' (Ferkins *et al.*, 2005, p. 218). An excerpt from the conclusion of that paper illustrates our assessment of the field at that time, highlighting the essence of the problem and how a systematic analysis of the issue might lead to a better understanding of sport governance, and eventually how to enhance the strategic capabilities of sport boards:

> The small but growing body of knowledge on sport boards indicates that the evolutionary process of bureaucratisation and professionalisation has resulted in changing board roles and relationships with paid executives. The contribution of the board in strategic activities such as developing the vision and mission, engaging in strategic planning including monitoring and responding to external environmental influences, and considering long-term, big picture issues as and when needed, is a topic superficially explored by sport management scholars. Understanding the factors that both constrain and enable sport boards to think and act strategically may provide an empirical basis for sports to build their strategic capabilities. It may also contribute to the wider governance and sport management literature in this critical area of knowledge development.
>
> *(Ferkins et al., 2005, p. 219)*

We argued that board strategic capability is the *ability* of the board to function strategically, and recognises the *development potential* of the board to think and act in a strategic manner. The concept of capabilities in the organisational studies literature is not new and has been extensively discussed in the domains of human resource management (Maatman, Bondarouk and Looise, 2010) and strategic management (Wheelen and Hunger, 2012). The term *capability* is known to have come from the middle French word *capabilité* and late Latin word *capābili* (Merriam-Webster, 2002), and has come to mean *implied* abilities or abilities to be developed (Merriam-Webster, 2002). Lenz (1980) brought the notion of capability into the sphere of strategic management, arguing that there was a need for a more relevant concept to identify an organisation's *potential* for strategic action and that a label 'sufficient for discussing this aspect of organization is that of *strategic capability*' (p. 226).

It also emerged from this work that governance across organisations, such as that required in a federal model of governance, was perhaps the single most important constraint on good governance. Cornforth (2012), for example, argued that, 'most research has focused on the boards of unitary organizations and has neglected the governance of organizations that have more complex governance structures' (p. 3). Traditionally, the influence of the wider governance system has been ignored, yet remains a central governance issue for the non-profit sector (Cornforth, 2012). Consequently, we incorporated the broader governance system in our research in relation to sport board strategic capability and it is this focus that forms the 'heart' of our theory of board strategic balance. In practical terms, Australian and New Zealand national and state sport organisations became the focus of the research programme and the quest to better understand how boards could enhance their strategic capability.

How our framework evolved

Using developmental action research, our studies of five non-profit national and state sport organisations typically lasted between 12–24 months each, depending on the magnitude of the issue and the readiness of the sport organisations to accept and implement the intervention designed in conjunction with each individual board. Each of the five studies witnessed the evolution of a quite distinct and relevant governance issue, as indicated in Table 10.1. The table shows that four of the studies focused, in differing ways, on issues related to structure as a consequence of a federal or regional model of governance. The main theoretical perspective in which each study was grounded is also shown in Table 10.1.

To date, the five research studies have been reported in ten articles detailing key findings. Figure 10.1 illustrates the progression from the review of literature and conceptual model at the base of Figure 10.1 through to the roof depicting the final theory of board strategic balance developed as a result of these sport governance studies. The identification of a research gap, followed by the formulation of a research question and study design, is a traditional approach to building a study plan and ultimately leading to theory development. Following the initial conceptual paper published in *Sport Management Review* in 2005 identifying the research gap, Figure 10.1 shows how three distinct issues were explored and reported on (shared leadership,

Table 10.1 Participating research sites, issues and theoretical concepts

Sport organisation	Time frame	Issue	Theoretical concepts
Squash New Zealand	July 2005– February 2007	Need to deliver strategic priorities at district level (the regions). Best articulated by the inability to achieve participation goals	Theoretical work relating to governing structures (Shilbury, 2001)
New Zealand Football	July 2005– December 2006	Need to establish a frame of reference for the board to steer the organisation, and address the balance of leadership between the board and CEO to ensure board involvement in strategy	Theoretical work on board strategy and shared leadership (Inglis, 1994; McNulty and Pettigrew, 1999; Shilbury, 2001)
Tennis New Zealand	July 2005– January 2007	Need to design a regional governance structure that allowed greater ability for the national board to enact its strategic priorities	Theoretical work on board power and governing structure (Pettigrew and McNulty, 1995)
Squash Vic	August 2010– April 2012	Need to change the governing structure to enable greater stakeholder engagement so that the board can better perform its governing role. Who do we govern?	Theoretical work on stakeholder theory (Freeman, 1984, 1999), leading to notion of Stakeowners (Fassin, 2012)
Bowls Australia	August 2011– April 2013	Need to overcome an amateur culture and lack of aspiration to grow and professionalise the sport and to ensure state member associations implement an agreed strategy	Collaborative governance and leadership (Ansell and Gash, 2008, 2012)

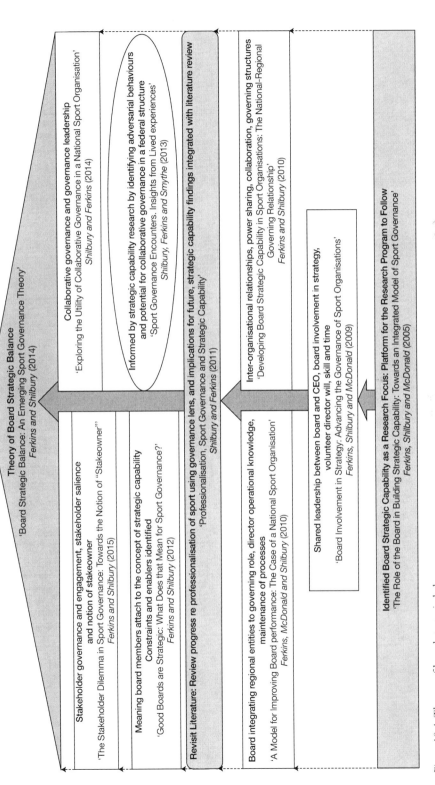

Figure 10.1 Theory of board strategic balance

inter-organisational relationships, board integrating regional entities) before we once again revisited the literature to synthesise the current state of sport governance research while at the same time infusing findings from the first three completed studies. This synthesis of literature was published six years after the original literature overview and conceptual model on the role of the board in building strategic capability. The long shaded box entitled Professionalisation, Sport Governance and Strategic Capability shows this.

Further empirical papers followed, with one, depicted as an oval shape in Figure 10.1, not directly a result of the governance capability studies, but its emergence was informed by findings from this work pointing to the need to examine more closely governance in federal structures and the influences of the transition from amateur to professionalised sport management and governance. Interestingly, two key concepts emerged from this work shaping the two studies published in 2012/13. The first of these concepts was adversarial behaviours and how they were manifest in a federal model. The second was the potential for collaborative governance to overcome the barriers created by a federal model and associated behaviours. With this overview and introduction to the focus of our theory development, we now turn our attention to a more detailed insight to the process of examining board strategic capability that ultimately led to our emerging theory of board strategic balance, which we believe explains how boards might develop their strategic capability.

Process

Initial milestones of our theory development

Having established the nature of our topic and focus in the previous section, this section explains the intellectual contours of our process of theory development. While Figure 10.1 might suggest a chronological sequence in terms of publication dates, in reality, there were many hills and dales, peaks and troughs, and perhaps it is only in hindsight that we have been able to plot the milestones of this journey with any real clarity.

As signalled earlier, the beginning phase of the process, which enabled us to settle on board strategic capability as our specific topic, came about by widely canvassing both a practical need and theoretical gap. We talked with over twenty different sport organisation board members, CEOs and senior staff, government agency personnel charged with leading sport organisation capability, as well as leaders outside of the sector. Not part of any fieldwork, these conversations were a critical part of the process to understand the issues and find a topic that would benefit current and future practice. In essence, we were seeking answers to: what aspect of sport governance do we need to better understand; what are we not doing well and what do we need to know more about; and what topic of governance will resonate into the future? Responses often focused on board composition, the skills and understanding of those who sat on the board, and how they came to be elected or appointed. On several occasions, the response simply came back as, 'board members need to add value; we need to figure out how they can do that'.

We intentionally oscillated between this process of practical enquiry and our search of relevant literature to find what was missing, and how *we* could add value to the practice and theory of sport governance. It was this interchange between our reading and conversations with practitioners, as well as the act of involving and moving beyond the sport management literature, that ultimately provided us with what we were seeking. The corporate governance literature (i.e., scholarship situated within the for-profit, often large organisation context) was heavily dominated by studies on board composition, many of which were quantitative, questionnaire based and derived from an outsider perspective. Agency theory featured strongly in this approach as concerns about ownership and control of corporations were debated. While we considered the board composition to be a critical part of the equation based on our practical conversations, and issues of control (between CEO as agent, and the board) were relevant for sports (sport codes), we were unclear as to how we could add significant value to this particular theoretical and practical debate.

The non-profit literature (outside of the sport context) contained some interesting strands of research on board roles but, as we saw it, tended to be flavoured by a prescriptive how-to style. The theoretical basis for this body of work appeared to be most commonly drawn from the application of social constructionism to board and organisational effectiveness. Stewardship theory, a contrasting theory to agency theory, also appeared to be favoured by non-profit scholars to explain a more collaborative leaning between the board and CEO. Finally, in the absence of an established body of knowledge (at that stage) in the governance of sport organisations, we drew heavily on the organisational theory literature specific to sport. Our intention in involving this body of work was to connect existing knowledge of sport organisations to sport governance. As also highlighted earlier, much of the impetus for studies engaging organisational theory and sport had come from an interest in examining the changing nature of sport and its transition towards greater professionalisation and bureaucratisation. This motivation provided a valuable foundation for understanding sport governance issues.

How we developed our theory of board strategic balance

So, how did we make sense of these strands of knowledge? How could we possibly narrow down a relevant focus for the governance of sport organisations with a theoretical basis that we could build upon to become a useful conceptualisation for governance practitioners? We concentrated on looking for the connections – looking for the useful, relevant gems from each body of work or context that might advance current practice and understanding of sport governance. In this, we also organised and synthesised. If we were to put our ideas into a model with boxes and arrows, what elements would we place where and with what connections? The outcome of this early process is represented in Figure 10.2 showing a 'Thematic schema of sport governance' (Ferkins *et al.*, 2005). In the first or upper third of Figure 10.2 we presented the environmental conditions that were driving much of the sport organisation theory work (i.e., professionalisation and bureaucratisation). In the second or middle third of Figure 10.2, we identified four themes that emerged from the few studies on sport governance, as well as the broader context of organisation governance (i.e., shared leadership, board motivation, board roles, board structure). In the final or lower third of Figure 10.2 we captured the four areas that we expressed as Governance Capabilities, essentially four generic themes that cut across the corporate and non-profit governance domains (i.e., performance, conformance, policy, operations).

It was the work of Cornforth (2003), McNulty and Pettigrew (1999) and Nadler (2004) that guided our next move. Carver (2010) too had a profound impact. His mantra that the board's job is to create the future, not mind the shop, encapsulated the issue. For us, the golden thread in this search was the board's *strategic* contribution. In considering strategists on the board within the corporate context, Pettigrew and McNulty (1995, 1998) also emphasised the importance of board processes in their work, and Nadler (2004) gave us the idea of strategic capability. Boards are charged with looking ahead, thinking strategically and creating the future. Where was the body of research, knowledge and insight on this? Very few studies existed that addressed the board's strategic role across any of the domains (corporate, non-profit, sport). A further excerpt from our 2005 paper illustrates the synthesis of this thinking across the corporate,

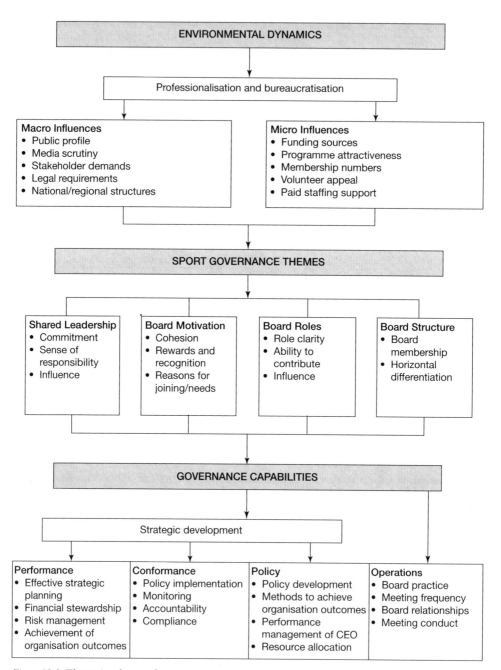

ENVIRONMENTAL DYNAMICS

Professionalisation and bureaucratisation

Macro Influences
• Public profile
• Media scrutiny
• Stakeholder demands
• Legal requirements
• National/regional structures

Micro Influences
• Funding sources
• Programme attractiveness
• Membership numbers
• Volunteer appeal
• Paid staffing support

SPORT GOVERNANCE THEMES

Shared Leadership
• Commitment
• Sense of responsibility
• Influence

Board Motivation
• Cohesion
• Rewards and recognition
• Reasons for joining/needs

Board Roles
• Role clarity
• Ability to contribute
• Influence

Board Structure
• Board membership
• Horizontal differentiation

GOVERNANCE CAPABILITIES

Strategic development

Performance
• Effective strategic planning
• Financial stewardship
• Risk management
• Achievement of organisation outcomes

Conformance
• Policy implementation
• Monitoring
• Accountability
• Compliance

Policy
• Policy development
• Methods to achieve organisation outcomes
• Performance management of CEO
• Resource allocation

Operations
• Board practice
• Meeting frequency
• Board relationships
• Meeting conduct

Figure 10.2 Thematic schema of sport governance

non-profit and sport literature, and how we arrived at the place from which we were to subsequently contribute theoretically and practically:

> The themes and ideas discussed in this paper underscore a gap in our knowledge and understanding about the strategic function of the board. Gaps exist in the sport management literature on strategy development, while the corporate governance literature has not fully explored the role of the board in terms of its strategic contribution. Finally, the non-profit governance literature acknowledges the importance of strategic input by the board, but indicates that boards may not be active enough.
>
> *(Ferkins et al., 2005, p. 219)*

Finally, in utilising an action research approach, we investigated sport governance in a way that offered the ability to situate ourselves *inside* the boardroom in asking how boards of sport organisations could develop their strategic capability. A little-used approach in sport management scholarship or governance literature, action research also presented the opportunity to address the theory–practice divide in our theory development process. Widely recognised as the father of action research, Kurt Lewin designed the approach with the specific intent to produce the dual outcomes of improving practice and developing theory (Coghlan and Brannick, 2010). We drew on Lewin (1948) as well as later proponents (Cardno, 2003; Coghlan and Brannick, 2010; Heron and Reason, 2006) to employ a specific style of action research designated by Cardno (2003) as developmental action research. We also founded our approach on the interpretive research paradigm (Denzin and Lincoln, 2011), which meant that our method for generating data was underpinned by the notion of multiple realities, co-constructed by the interpretations of the researchers and research participants (Ferkins *et al.*, 2009).

This approach emphasised collaboration with our chosen national and state sport organisation governing personnel, with the intention of creating positive change in governance practice, engaging in multiple iterations of change in order to enhance learning, and throughout, intentionally integrating theoretical constructs drawn from the literature described above. This created the opportunity to produce knowledge derived and tested in the rich setting of governance practice – inside the boardroom – as well as the chance to improve current boardroom practice (Ferkins and Shilbury, in press).

In adopting developmental action research we moved through a four-staged process:

- phase one: issue identification;
- phase two: context analysis;
- phase three: intervention and action; and
- phase four: evaluation of action.

In this way, developmental action research has been instrumental in fuelling our theory development process, and, with its emphasis on cyclical, iterative elements, has allowed for refinement and deepening in understanding of the issues presented by the research participants (Heron and Reason, 2006). In each instance of fieldwork, this entailed collaboration with sport boards to jointly determine the barriers and enablers of board strategic capability; to determine and enact possible solutions, and to evaluate the outcomes for theory and practice.

By engaging action research in this way, we worked with our five different national and state sport organisations over the course of just over seven years (between 2005 and 2013) to investigate the development of board strategic capability and, more broadly, sport governance capability. We continued to move back and forth between developments in the governance literature across the three domains (corporate, non-profit, sport) and, in doing so, have worked with established governance theories, namely managerial hegemony (Stiles, 2001), institutional (DiMaggio and Powell, 1983), stakeholder (Freeman, 1984), agency (Fama and Jensen, 1983) and stewardship theory (Davis, Schoorman and Donaldson, 1997). In this we have been advocates of the use of a multi-theoretical approach, considering that not one of these theories fully explains the governance phenomenon. We also continue to argue that the sport setting offers an insightful context to employ and develop these theories and we have maintained our focus on national and state sport organisations as our setting of choice. Table 10.1 shows the outcomes of our theoretical work, where each of the five different case study organisations concentrates on a particular aspect of board strategic capability and, consequently, governance capability.

Of this work set out in Table 10.1, we consider our primary theoretical contribution to date to be the development of a theory that considers, in a holistic way, how boards might develop their strategic capability. Referred to as board strategic balance, our process of theory development involved an analysis of the findings across all our fieldwork settings in concert with other published empirical and conceptual work on governance and the board's strategic role. In this, we considered influences on board strategic capability within the context of non-profit national and state sport organisations. We theorised about the relationships between six characteristics, derived from our work with the five national and state sporting organisations (i.e., increasing contribution of volunteer board members; board operational knowledge; board integrating regional entities into the governing role; board maintaining the monitoring and control function; board co-leading strategy development; and board co-leading integration of strategy into board processes).

With the benefit of hindsight, we have been able to pinpoint three key elements that have converged to drive our theory development process, which began with an interest in sport governance; moved to a focus on the study of board strategic capability; and led to the theory of board strategic balance. The first was our determined engagement with the literature from across the three contexts noted above. In this we mined for new knowledge, worked with the major theories that informed the practice of governance, and continually sought to contribute to the existing foundation of knowledge.

The second was the use of developmental action research, which allowed us to bring the ideas and theories from the literature into boardroom practice. In essence, an action research approach allowed us to become the conduit between theory and practice, and to build working relationships with sport governance practitioners. This interaction enabled our theory development work to be firmly grounded in issues of practice. As previously noted, in each instance we worked with non-profit sport organisations to identify their views on the constraints and enablers to strategic capability and what, in their specific circumstances, could be done to enhance the strategic capability of the board. From this, our theory of board strategic balance emerged.

The final element is that our work has been longitudinal. To date, it has spanned twelve years and engaged constant interaction with the literature and the conduct of five different case studies, each taking approximately two years in the field. Over this period of time, we have been highly influenced by the thinking of sport governance exponents, accumulating wisdom and experience from them as we have influenced their practice. In a similar way, we have also drawn on the thinking of our fellow governance scholars and, in turn, have had the opportunity to influence scholarship in sport governance.

Extensions and applications

Beyond conceptual and empirical work

Twelve years on from our first tentative steps in seeking to contribute to the way sport is organised, managed and led by focusing on those who govern, we moved beyond conceptual and empirical work to establishing a theory indigenous to the sport governance setting. The extensions and applications of our original topic of board strategic capability have occurred in a highly iterative manner. We began with existing theory, borrowed from other settings, which we used to add insight and explain the sport governance phenomenon. In using it as a tool of analysis, the amalgamation of existing theory with insights from the boardroom situation created new thinking and, ultimately, a new theory.

Albeit an *emerging* theory (i.e., yet to be rigorously examined and employed by others), we distinguish the theory of board strategic balance from our previous conceptual work because it not only identifies concepts but it also explains how and why the concepts relate to each other; in other words, as Doherty (2013) explains, 'a theory is a set of concepts and the relationship among them' (p. 6). Thus, in board strategic balance, we identified a set of concepts as well as the relationships among them as factors *influencing* board strategic capability within our chosen setting. We have been careful to propose this theory, not as a definitive approach, but as a per-spective that has potential explanatory power to provide insight into the relationships between influences of board strategic capability. We are hopeful that our emerging theory will also provide guidance for future research that will go on to contribute to the governance of sport and beyond.

Influencing the scholarly conversation

While the study of sport governance remains a small, but emerging field of enquiry, we have been intrigued to see the ways in which others have applied and revised our work in their research. To begin, our emphasis on board strategic capability was picked up by Hoye and Cuskelly (2007) in their textbook *Sport governance*. Situated within the chapter on strategic governance, the authors note that, 'Ferkins, Shilbury, and McDonald (2005) highlighted the significant gap in the knowledge and understanding of the strategic function of non-profit sport boards' (p. 116).

Others who have incorporated our thinking on the role of the board and the importance of the strategic aspect have included Yeh and Taylor (2008), and Yeh, Taylor and Hoye (2009) in relation to their investigation of Taiwanese boards. In considering how national governing bodies of sport should be governed in the United Kingdom, Taylor and O'Sullivan (2009) drew on our assertion for the need to consider structural aspects as part of their exploratory study of board structure. In a publication in *Nonprofit and Voluntary Sector Quarterly*, Balduck, Van Rossema and Buelens (2010) used our contention about the need to understand board motivation in their discussion of competencies of volunteer board members within community sports clubs.

More recently, Jansen van Rensburg, Venter and Krie (2013) undertook an exploratory study of boards and governance in African national cricket organisations. In this, they employed the conceptualisation we put forward on the board's strategic role (Ferkins *et al.*, 2005; Ferkins and Shilbury, 2012) in order to help explain board functioning of twenty-three cricket associations affiliated with the African Cricket Association (ACA). In doing so, they determined that:

> The overall impression is that the governance and strategic management process is, in most cases, geared towards compliance rather than deriving real benefit for the

organisation. The danger is that if compliance is the goal, the process becomes a burden rather than an asset. What is required is a culture change from mainly amateur sporting bodies (at least in spirit) to professional sport organisations that realise the benefits of good governance and professional management.

(Jansen van Rensburg et al., 2013, p. 40)

Although undertaken in a context quite distinct from the setting of our work (i.e., Africa versus Australasia), this outcome is remarkably consistent with the issues we found in seeking to develop governance capability in national and state sport boards (Ferkins and Shilbury, 2015; Shilbury and Ferkins, 2014). The combination of the African and Australasian work helps to offer a more global picture of the challenges related to strategic sport governance.

Influencing teaching and learning

Besides the use of our conceptual and empirical work within our own teaching context, our work has also made its way to over a dozen textbook chapters where we hope it provides a helpful resource for students and teachers alike. Of note is a useful resource by Sam Young, an academic at the Nelson Marlborough Institute of Technology in New Zealand, who developed an undergraduate teaching case on shared leadership within Tennis New Zealand (one of our action research case studies), based on Ferkins and Shilbury (2010). In the postgraduate teaching context, a number of PhD and masters students have adopted our conceptual frameworks, findings and calls for future research as a resource in the design of their studies. This has included diverse settings such as the governance of community health centers in Canada (Greening, 2013), volunteers in Canadian sport organisations (Mrak, 2010), Maori and Pasifika voices in New Zealand sport governance (Holland, 2012), theoretical explanations of governance in Australian sport (Shimeld, 2012), strategic preparation for CEO succession in Australian sport (Schoenberg, 2011), corporate governance in the Australian Football League (Foreman, 2006) and tennis event impact on clubs in New Zealand (Hoskyn, 2011). In many of these studies the need for greater focus on board strategic functioning has been the common element derived from our work.

In perhaps one of the deepest applications and extensions of our conceptual work, as presented in Ferkins and Shilbury (2012), a student at the University of Kentucky in the US analysed the strategic capability of the Rolex Kentucky Three Day Event's board (Burrows, 2014). In following our framework (Ferkins and Shilbury, 2012), the student then applied key success factors from this event to the governance of world-class annual sport championships in the Bahamas. In so doing, Burrows (2014) has potentially demonstrated how a conceptual framework borne from one context can be introduced into other settings in order to enrich the theorising process.

Influencing practice

From the outset, our interest in sport governance came about because of our belief in the potential impact and influence of those involved in the oversight of sport organisations. How has our theorising impacted and influenced those who are charged with this oversight? At a local level, the two-year in-field immersion with each of the boards and CEOs of our five case study organisations has meant that we have had this opportunity and our evaluation phase of the action research process has provided evidence of this for us. This has involved tangible impacts such as major change to the governing structure (see Ferkins, McDonald and Shilbury, 2010; Shilbury and Ferkins, 2014), changes to board activity, meeting processes and agenda (see

Ferkins *et al.*, 2009), and less tangible influence on individual board member thinking: 'I've learnt more about what our aim is to the members – why we are here – what our role really is for our members' (Ferkins and Shilbury, 2015, p. 105); 'there's been quite a shift in thinking from . . . [being] focused on your own backyard at a national level. Now there's this philosophy and thinking of shared services' (Shilbury and Ferkins, 2014); 'For me, the exercise . . . forced me to think long term. I enjoyed the process of going through it. It helped my thinking and I think it forced us to question what we thought were priorities' (Ferkins *et al.*, 2009, p. 265). We consider that this kind of impact and influence has been facilitated by the action research approach and the theorising embedded within it, which may not have been possible otherwise.

Our work has also prompted contact by CEOs and board members of national and state sport organisations situated in a range of countries with similar sport systems; namely, Ireland, Canada, Scotland, as well as New Zealand and Australia. Our findings related to shared leadership between the board and CEO with respect to the strategic role has been of particular interest. The vexed issue of governance across organisations (federal model), in relation to strategic function, has also resonated with CEOs. We are speculating, however, that the impact and influence on these practitioners of what they have read, versus the experiences of those we have collaborated with, is much less powerful. We are also mindful that this impact has been restricted to our conceptual work associated with board strategic capability. Yet to make an impact is our emerging theory of board strategic balance.

Future directions

To conclude, it is appropriate to illustrate the theory of board strategic balance, shown as the roof of Figure 10.1. What commenced as an investigation into board strategic capability was transformed into a theory of board strategic balance as it conceptualised a series of ideas and how and why they relate to each other (Doherty, 2013). Figure 10.3a depicts the six component parts identified from this ongoing investigation of board strategic capability. On their own, and as independent component parts, Figure 10.3a remains a depiction of the concept of board strategic capability; however, Figure 10.3b transforms these six static components of board strategic capability into a dynamically fluctuating set of interrelated parts that together form the theory of board strategic balance in the quest to understand the idea of equilibrium between these six areas.

The notion of equilibrium is important to board strategic balance. This is illustrated in Figure 10.3b, which shows how balance, or inter-relationship, between inputs and processes needs to occur in order for the board to perform optimally. It is theorised that board equilibrium is rarely achieved, but that it would swing back and forth, with different inputs and outputs receiving varying levels of attention as a consequence of the range of issues confronting a board at any given time. Recognising the unrealistic quest for sustained equilibrium, Figure 10.3b indicates a tolerance range acknowledging the natural fluctuations in board functions in the ebb and flow of organisational life.

Theoretically, sub-optimisation of board performance could occur should an imbalance in the attention given to inputs or processes or, indeed, any of the six components transpire over a sustained period of time. For example, how would the will and skill of elected volunteer board members (Circle 1) influence its ability to lead strategy and set strategic direction (Circle 5)? As an input, the collective knowledge and skills of board members is important in shaping its understanding of the need to strike a balance between strategy development and performance, and spending too much time on monitoring operational control in relation to the sport. In this

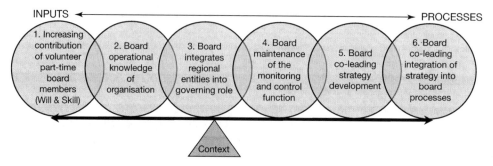

Figure 10.3a Components of board strategic capability

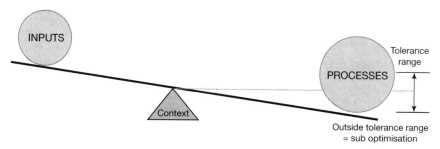

Figure 10.3b Equilibrium in board strategic balance
Source: Ferkins and Silbury (2014).

example, input component parts clearly influence process component parts, demonstrating relationships that need to be recognised and understood.

As may be expected with theory (Doherty, 2013), many questions arise despite the theory explaining how and why concepts are related. A good theory also explains what might happen and why under certain circumstances. Although this theory of board strategic balance helps explain board strategic capability and what might happen if equilibrium is not achieved over a sustained period of time, it also raises many questions that could shape future research directions in the sport governance domain. For example, what we cannot answer at this time is:

- How can boards create optimum strategic balance and what might constitute optimum strategic balance for their situation?
- How quickly do boards need to respond to correct an imbalance in the six strategic components?
- What role does context (e.g., NSO, SSO, or professional sport organisation) play in defining the range of tolerance and the time afforded to recognise and correct an imbalance?

The main questions to emerge from this theory relate to the concept of tolerance, and it is here that further work is envisaged to delve more deeply into the theory of board strategic balance. The following questions are examples of where future research could be focused:

- What range of tolerance is afforded boards in terms of time, in relation to a concentration on one or more of the six components?
- What might be the tolerance range for boards in terms of optimal board strategic function and in what contexts?

- Could a scale be developed to guide or measure this tolerance range?
- What might constitute over-emphasis on one component over another and over what time period, resulting in sub-optimisation?
- How might varying situations, such as a crisis or change in personnel, influence board strategic balance?

Metaphorically, the roof overlaying Figure 10.1 depicts more than ten years of theory building and construction, ultimately leading to a theory of board strategic balance. This theory helps explain sport governance behaviour in the context of national and state sport organisations. It also assists in shaping our thinking in planning future sport governance-related research studies. We also believe that it has, and will, assist board members elected and appointed to the challenging role as a director, to better understand their role and range of responsibilities. The empirical studies leading to the construction of the roof have, each in their own way, formed the pillars leading to an enhanced understanding of board strategic capability. The theoretical perspectives encapsulated in the five empirical studies conducted in New Zealand and Australia demonstrates the multi-theoretical approach that characterises governance research.

These perspectives (shown in Table 10.1), including governing structures, shared leadership, board power, stakeholder theory and collaborative governance, represent a small insight to the range of theories used to explain governance behaviour. Significantly, it was these theoretical labels that best described the problems identified by the participating sport boards as the best way to enhance the strategic capability of their respective boards. In our quest to achieve the dual aim of improving practice and developing theory we believe the choice of developmental action research was instrumental to that outcome. Moreover, it led to relevant research for and with participants working directly in the sport governance domain. It also identified governing structures as a consistent constraint in the governance of sport organisations embedded in a federal structure. Ultimately, this approach led to a theory of board strategic balance crafted to provide theoretical and practical direction through the maze that is sport governance.

Note

1   This chapter is a reflection on Ferkins, Shilbury and McDonald (2005) and the work related to it.

References

Ansell, C. and Gash, A. (2008) 'Collaborative governance in theory and practice'. *Journal of Public Administration Research and Theory*, 18: 543–71.

Ansell, C. and Gash, A. (2012) 'Stewards, mediators and catalysts: Towards a model of collaborative leadership'. *The Innovation Journal: The Public Sector Innovation Journal*, 17(1): 1–21.

Balduck, A., Van Rossem, A. and Buelens, M. (2010) 'Identifying competencies of volunteer board members of community sports clubs'. *Nonprofit and Voluntary Sector Quarterly*, 39: 213–35.

Burrows, E.V. (2014) *Board governance of world-class annual sport championships: Learning from Kentucky to create tourism opportunities in the Bahamas*. Unpublished masters dissertation. University of Kentucky, Lexington, USA.

Cardno, C. (2003) *Action research: A developmental approach*. Wellington, NZ: New Zealand Council for Educational Research.

Carver, J. (2010) 'A case for global governance theory: Practitioners avoid it, academics narrow it, the world needs it'. *Corporate Governance: An International Review*, 18: 149–57.

Coghlan, D. and Brannick, T. (2010) *Doing action research in your own organization* (third edn). Thousand Oaks, CA: Sage.

Cornforth, C. (ed.) (2003) *The governance of public and non-profit organizations: What do boards do?* London: Routledge.

Cornforth, C. (2012) 'Nonprofit governance research: Limitations of the focus on boards and suggestions for new directions'. *Nonprofit and Voluntary Sector Quarterly, 41*: 1116–35.

Davis, J., Schoorman, D. and Donaldson, L. (1997) 'Toward a stewardship theory of management'. *Academy of Management Review, 22*: 20–48.

Denzin, N.K. and Lincoln, Y.S. (eds) (2011) *The SAGE handbook of qualitative research* (fourth edn). Thousand Oaks, CA: Sage.

DiMaggio, P. and Powell, W. (1983) 'The iron cage revisited: Institutional isomorphism and collective rationality in organizational fields'. *American Sociological Review, 48*: 147–60.

Doherty, A. (2013) 'Investing in sport management: The value of good theory'. *Sport Management Review, 16*: 5–11.

Fama, E. and Jensen, M. (1983) 'Separation of ownership and control'. *Journal of Law & Economics, 26*: 307–25.

Fassin, Y. (2012) 'Stakeholder management, reciprocity and stakeholder responsibility'. *Journal of Business Ethics, 109*: 83–96.

Ferkins, L. and Shilbury, D. (2010) 'Developing board strategic capability in sport organizations: The national-regional governing relationship'. *Sport Management Review, 13*: 235–54.

Ferkins, L. and Shilbury, D. (2012) 'Good boards are strategic: What does that mean for sport governance?' *Journal of Sport Management, 26*: 67–80.

Ferkins, L. and Shilbury, D. (2014) 'Board strategic balance: An emerging sport governance theory'. *Sport Management Review.* http://dx.doi.org/10.1016/j.smr.2014.12.002.

Ferkins, L. and Shilbury, D. (2015) 'The stakeholder dilemma in sport governance: Toward the notion of "stakeowner"', *Journal of Sport Management, 29*: 93–108.

Ferkins, L., Shilbury, D. and McDonald, G. (2005) 'The role of the board in building strategic capability: Towards an integrated model of sport governance research'. *Sport Management Review, 8*: 195–225.

Ferkins, L., Shilbury, D. and McDonald, G. (2009) 'Board involvement in strategy: Advancing the governance of sport organizations'. *Journal of Sport Management, 23*: 245–77.

Ferkins, L., McDonald, G. and Shilbury, D. (2010) 'A model for improving board performance: The case of a national sport organization'. *Journal of Management & Organization, 16*: 633–53.

Freeman, E. (1984) *Strategic management: A stakeholder approach.* Boston, MA: Pitman.

Freeman, R.E. (1999) 'Response: divergent stakeholder theory'. *Academy of Management Review, 24*: 233–6.

Foreman, J. (2006) 'Corporate governance in the Australian Football League: A critical evaluation'. Unpublished doctoral dissertation. Victoria University of Technology, Melbourne, Australia.

Greening, S. (2013) 'Community health centres: Board governance and stakeholder relations during service expansion'. Unpublished masters dissertation. University of Alberta, Canada.

Henry, I. and Lee, P.C. (2004) 'Governance and ethics in sport'. In J. Beech and S. Chadwick (eds) *The business of sport management* (pp. 25–41). Essex: Pearson Education.

Heron, J. and Reason, P. (2006) 'The practice of co-operative inquiry: Research "with" rather than "on" people'. In P. Reason and H. Bradbury (eds) *Handbook of action research: Participative inquiry and practice* (pp. 171–8). Thousand Oaks, CA: Sage.

Holland, R. (2012) 'Governance of New Zealand national sport organisations: Pasifika and Māori voices'. Unpublished doctoral dissertation. Massey University, Palmerston North, Auckland New Zealand.

Hoskyn, K. (2011) 'Major sports events and their ability to benefit local sports clubs: A case study of the Auckland professional tennis tournaments'. Unpublished masters dissertation. Auckland University of Technology, New Zealand.

Hoye, R. and Cuskelly, G. (2007) *Sport governance.* Sydney: Elsevier.

Inglis, S. (1994) 'Exploring volunteer board member and executive director needs: Importance and fulfillment'. *Journal of Applied Recreation Research, 19*: 171–89.

Jansen van Rensburg, M., Venter, P. and Krie, H.S. (2013) 'Boards and governance in African national cricket organizations: An exploratory study'. *South African Business Review, 17*(2): 23–44.

Kikulis, L. (2000) 'Continuity and change in governance and decision making in national sport organizations: Institutional explanations'. *Journal of Sport Management, 14*: 293–320.

Lenz, R. (1980) 'Strategic capability: A concept and framework for analysis'. *Academy of Management Review, 5*: 225–34.

Lewin, K. (1948) *Resolving social conflicts.* New York: Harper & Row.

Maatman, M., Bondarouk, T. and Looise, J. (2010) 'Conceptualizing the capabilities and value creation of HRM shared service models'. *Human Resource Management Review, 20*: 327–39.

McNulty, T. and Pettigrew, A. (1999) 'Strategists on the board'. *Organization Studies, 20*: 47–74.

Merriam-Webster (2002) *Merriam-Webster's concise dictionary of English usage*. Springfield, MA: Author.

Mrak, J. (2010) 'Managing volunteers in Canadian community sport organizations'. Unpublished masters dissertation. Brock University, Ontario, Canada.

Nadler, D. (2004) 'What's the board's role in strategy development? Engaging the board in corporate strategy'. *Strategy & Leadership*, *32*(5): 25–33.

Pettigrew, A. and McNulty, T. (1995) 'Power and influence in and around the boardroom'. *Human Relations*, *48*: 845–73.

Pettigrew, A. and McNulty, T. (1998) 'Sources and uses of power in the boardroom'. *European Journal of Work & Organizational Psychology*, 7: 197–214.

Schoenberg, G. (2011) 'Examining strategic preparation for CEO succession'. Unpublished masters dissertation. Deakin University, Melbourne, Australia.

Shilbury, D. (2001) 'Examining board member roles, functions and influence: A study of Victorian sporting organizations'. *International Journal of Sport Management*, 2: 253–81.

Shilbury, D. and Ferkins, L. (2014) 'Exploring the utility of collaborative governance in a national sport organization'. *Journal of Sport Management*. http://dx.doi.org/10.1123/jsm.2014-0139.

Shimeld, S. (2012) 'Seeking a theoretical explanation of governance in not-for-profit sporting organizations'. Unpublished doctoral dissertation. University of Tasmania, Hobart, Australia.

Stiles, P. (2001) 'The impact of the board on strategy: An empirical examination'. *Journal of Management Studies*, *38*: 627–50.

Taylor, M. and O'Sullivan, N. (2009) 'How should national governing bodies of sport be governed in the UK? An exploratory study of board structure'. *Corporate Governance: An International Review*, 17: 681–93.

Wheelen, T. and Hunger, D. (2012) *Strategic management and business policy: Toward global sustainability*. (thirteenth edn). Sydney: Prentice Hall.

Yeh, C. and Taylor, T. (2008) 'Issues of governance in sport organizations: A question of board size, structure and roles'. *World Leisure*, 1: 33–45.

Yeh, C., Taylor, T. and Hoye, R. (2009) 'Board roles in organisations with a dual board system: Empirical evidence from Taiwanese non-profit sport organisations'. *Sport Management Review*, 12: 91–100.

Applying a theory of board strategic balance

Neil Dalrymple[1]

Bowls Australia became aware of the research paper by Ferkins, Shilbury and McDonald (2005) through an approach from Dr David Shilbury and Dr Lesley Ferkins from Deakin University regarding a potential research partnership in the area of sport governance and the role of boards. At the time, the governance structure of Bowls Australia was volunteer-based, with the majority of directors coming from a bowls administration background. The governance of the sport also contained a number of layers that inhibited decision-making and progress, including a council structure that had the ability to override decisions made by directors and staff of the national body. Therefore, the themes detailed in the 2005 paper resonated strongly with the state of the sport at the time.

Using the theories detailed in that article, and other related work by the research team, Bowls Australia was able to better educate its directors to understand their roles and responsibilities on the board, specifically in determining the strategic direction of bowls in Australia. In the years following the release of the 2005 article, the governance of the sport of bowls had undergone a number of changes, including: (a) the creation of a number of appointed director positions on the Bowls Australia Board for persons with specific skill sets; (b) the transition from a Council of State/Territory Association delegates, with decision-making powers, to a consultative body to Bowls Australia; and (c) analysis of the governance capability of the Bowls Australia Board.

This last point, the analysis of the governance capability of the Bowls Australia Board, was the focus of the action research study facilitated by Drs Shilbury and Ferkins. It was also a direct response to the 2005 article in which enhancing the strategic capability of sport boards was identified as a key challenge. The major recommendation emanating from the problem identification phase of the action research was to work more collaboratively with state member associations in order to grow the sport of bowls in Australia. This outcome was the result of the board addressing the following aim as posed by the research team: to explore how boards of non-profit sport organisations can develop their governance capability.

The recommendation to adopt and implement collaborative governance was the means to enhance the governance capability of the Bowls Australia Board. This approach, adopted in conjunction with state member association boards, was put into practice through the development of the 2013–17 *Bowls in Australia* strategic plan. The formulation of the new strategic plan was an ideal vehicle through which to adopt a collaborative approach. The process commenced in April 2012 with a consultative planning workshop involving fifty stakeholders from all levels of the sport, which ultimately led to the development and agreement of six key strategic priorities underpinning the strategic plan. This workshop also led to the creation of a common vision, mission and values.

The concept of collective and shared leadership also emerged as an important outcome, not only between the board and paid staff, but significantly with and between the boards of the state member associations. The collaborative nature of the process resulted in the *Bowls in Australia* strategic plan, agreed to in April 2013 by Bowls Australia and its member associations. Its use was intended for all member associations as the basis of their individual state plans rather than solely for Bowls Australia as the national governing organisation.

Future organisational plans aim to expand governance capabilities and practices throughout the sport, with the long-term aim of implementing a standardised set of good governance principles at all levels of the sport. Education of boards and committees at lower levels of the bowls structure, in terms of recognising the roles and skills set required and the establishment of appropriate structures, is seen as a vital step towards enhancing future governance capabilities for the sport. The theory-based research and consultation undertaken by Drs Shilbury and Ferkins has been extremely valuable for the sport of Bowls in Australia and, without this, evidence-based governance change in our sport would not have been possible.

Note

1   Neil Dalrymple is the Chief Executive Officer of Bowls Australia.

Reference

Ferkins, L., Shilbury, D. and McDonald, G. (2005) 'The role of the board in building strategic capability: Towards an integrated model of sport governance research'. *Sport Management Review*, 8: 195–225.

11

THE CONCEPTION, DEVELOPMENT AND APPLICATION OF SPORT-FOR-DEVELOPMENT THEORY[1]

Alexis Lyras and Jon Welty Peachey

Overview

In this journey, universities and practitioners will have to create the conditions and real life examples of transforming existing 'Sport . . . cheer'(leading) institutions into 'Change leading' agencies where the 'score' is kept on scholarship and programs produced in service of improving human condition.

Alexis Lyras (2013)

In early 2000, the concept of sport-for-development and peace building was irrelevant and non-existent in traditional sport management teaching and scholarship. The existing social challenges we face in local communities across the globe makes it critically important to understand, advance and improve the functions of sport and olympism. The way we perceive, theorise and practise sport is relevant to each one of us, no matter our role or cultural context. Based on the axiom that 'there is nothing more practical than a good theory' (Lewin, 1952, p. 169), every stakeholder engaged in this movement has a responsibility to shift the existing paradigm by changing current frameworks and visions in order to improve the way we address humanitarian challenges. This rationale was the main drive and vision of my (Lyras) personal, professional and academic journey that led to (a) the conception of Sport-for-Development Theory (SFDT) (Lyras, 2007); (b) the implementation of human-centred global initiatives; and (c) integrated teaching, research and service endeavours.

While the first part of this chapter will use the word 'I' to indicate the first author, we will move from 'I' the individual into 'we' – the collective – to demonstrate how theory can be used for diversified collaborations, new programming, scientific testing, tenure, promotion, teaching, publications, student engagement and in service of humanitarian goals and objectives. The main purpose of this chapter is to share personal narratives in order to better understand how ideas related to Sport-for-Development Theory (Lyras, 2007) were conceived and how this framework has evolved and been put in practice over time. Hopefully, this personal expression will make the process of theory building and testing transparent and informative for other scholars.

Theory development process

Born and raised in Cyprus (referring to Lyras), a country that is still divided due to inter-ethnic conflict and military occupation, the way I think and understand is influenced by the complexities of war, division and separation. When I recall my memories of war in my home country, and while I travel in my mind over time, I am often upset from the realisation that cognitions are strongly influenced by theory, and that the interpretation of personal narratives are often biased by personal, institutional or cultural constraints. The duality and yin-yang oneness of our existence is often lost or trapped in the over-simplification of the way we theorize, interpret, describe and explain phenomena.

Growing up in an educational system and country that had recent wounds from war has helped me become sensitive in understanding the complexity of transforming hatred into reconciliation; feelings, cognitions and behaviours of a militaristic patriotic mindset into proactive peacebuilding and development interventions as a philosophy of life. I begin with sharing my personal journey and an overview of how SFDT was conceived, my drive and various incidences and experiences in life that pushed me to the existing theory and practice (Lyras 2001, 2003, 2004, 2005, 2007, 2009, 2012a, 2012b, 2014). While this chapter is not a biography, I believe that the geo-political and cultural context of my identities served as personal drives of a life journey, personal and academic. My attempt is to provide the foundations of this journey for further constructive criticism that can potentially challenge the way we think and handle SFDT and practice.

'I know one thing: that I know nothing' – Socrates

I have broken down my professional and personal journey into three chapters (so far). The first was the chapter on sport development, where I had the opportunity to work as a coach for youth and professional national basketball teams, and with national and international policy and coaching certification programmes. The second chapter was fully dedicated to sport *for* development, initiating and implementing integrated Applied Olympism teaching, research and service. The latest chapter is more integrated and in progress – trying to understand and merge both worlds, Sport-for-Development (SFD) and sport development. The first chapter was filled with sport-industry-related experience, the second one with work related to sport for peace and applied Olympism theory building and testing through the Doves Olympic Movement model, and the last one through Olympism4Humanity and integrated teaching, research and service. All three chapters intersect with one another. Looking back, I realise each chapter has its yin-yang aspects, and that every one of us can play a significant role in finding a balance between both aspects of sport and development.

While I was in perceived heaven during my sport development chapter, the last pages were hiding experiences and situations that pushed me from the false consciousness of the bright side and the power of sport into the awareness of the darkest sides of the sport industry. After spending approximately two years on a personal journey, I started writing thoughts on principles and values that could potentially give me hope out of that darkness and disappointment. My thoughts were kept in a form of journal, and formed the personal GPS system that had human progress, anti-racism, peacebuilding and development as a final destination (Lyras, 2001). The final destination and my GPS entry was 'Applied Olympism theory and praxis' that can be integrated in academic teaching, research and service.

Looking back, I realise that the yin-yang context of life exists in every aspect of our social, personal and institutional settings and experiences. Inter-group dynamics, and intra-personal and inter-personal thoughts and behaviours are often guided by positivism or negativity. I came to a conclusion that the default of human thinking and interaction, many times, leans to simplistic linear recollections of pre-existing memories and interpretations. Socratic Wisdom and positivism, with its ongoing and persistent enquiry-oriented mindset, can potentially serve as the anti-virus for the problematic default of the human function. This foundation can also help us understand that certain conditions (educational, organisational, cultural and institutional) can either promote or hinder positive thinking, growth and development. How does this thinking apply to SFD? I strongly believe we should start with the assumption that the purpose, conditions, intentions and context of the phenomena around us can define either positive or negative outcomes. Therefore, if we refer to a vague statement such as the 'power of sport', we have to start with the assumption that this power can lead to both good and bad. It is therefore essential to integrate theories and wisdom from various frameworks to first gain an intentional, interventionist, enquiry-oriented scientific mindset that will continually be open to identifying and controlling the conditions that lead to targeted objectives and assessing the actual impact over time and space.

In early 2000, influenced by the excitement surrounding the 2004 Olympic Games in Athens, the conceptual framework that I had developed as my 'Olympism for Humanity' exploration and academic journey served as the foundation for multiple proposals, projects and a long-term vision (e.g., Doves Olympic Movement, Sport-for-Development Global Initiative, Youth IDEALS, International Sport for Peace and Development Association, Olympism4Humanity Alliance, SFDT, graduate and undergraduate courses that integrate teaching, research and service). In 2002, I started my graduate work under Dr Andrew Yiannakis, who was very supportive in giving me freedom to take classes beyond the traditional sport management and sociology of sport courses. This freedom created the conditions for self and academic exploration to answer non-sport related questions and look for answers in disciplines and frameworks with a long history of related scholarship. Through this exploration, I was always trying to integrate theory with practice, by translating organisational theory, human development theory and contact theory into practical propositions and foundations of a longitudinal field experimental design. The rationale was that if I could create a model that utilised ancient Hellenic philosophical wisdom with the foundations of the Ancient Olympic Games as a vehicle for community building, this model could (a) serve as a foundation for field experimental projects; (b) be tested with real data; (c) be used in non-idealistic but adverse conditions such as conflict; (d) over time could be modified to ensure the delivery of positive outcomes in various settings and with different groups; and (e) potentially serve as a universal model for resolving targeted social challenges. The logic behind this model was if I could create some type of social medicine and a prescription that could work in adverse conditions, a more mild treatment could also serve as a treatment in less adverse conditions. Parallel to my integrated and applied coursework, I was submitting grant proposals to secure funding for operationalising this conceptual framework.

In the summer of 2005, I received my first grant to implement the Doves Olympic Movement project, the operational part of SFDT, a four-year long initiative and the first peacebuilding inter-group educational sport initiative on the island of Cyprus. The programme was the first step towards implementing replicable applied Olympic education initiatives on the island and around the globe. The initial objectives were to provide the new generation of Greek and Turkish Cypriot youth on the island with the essential resources to help them overcome long-held negative beliefs and practices. The purpose of the programme was to utilise Olympic ideals to encourage Greek and Turkish Cypriots to develop 'a better understanding for each other's needs; inter-ethnic tolerance and acceptance; friendships among members of both communities; and patterns of working together in the pursuit of common goals'

(Lyras, 2005, p. 2). The formalisation and design of the initial concept of the Doves Olympic Movement project were made feasible with support from the Olympic Solidarity (International Olympic Committee). The implementation of the Doves Project's activities was funded by UNDP-ACT and USAID, and the Cyprus Research Foundation supported the research arm of the project (theory building and theory testing).

'Non?' Existing sport for peacebuilding body of knowledge and Sugden's pioneer fieldwork

In early 2000, while I was navigating in various sport-related bodies of knowledge to identify guidelines for successful sport for peace and development interventions, I found the body of knowledge to be non-existent and the concept of sport for peace just emerging. While a number of researchers have investigated the relationship between political and religious violence and sports in countries experiencing conflict, each study suggested that the structures, practices and dynamics of organised sports in places with a long history of conflict reflect the problems of division that exist in those countries (Saunders and Sugden, 1997; Sugden and Harvie, 1995). Sugden and Harvie (1995) examined how sports influence stability and conflict in Northern Ireland and concluded that sport can 'be both fraternal and sectarian; to promote harmony and widen community division' (p. 91). They also reported that the most influential inter-ethnic interaction in sport was observed in non-traditional, non-institutionalised sport settings, which were not managed by governing bodies or organisations (Sugden and Harvie, 1995).

Sugden (1991) conducted the first field experimental inter-ethnic sport for conflict resolution intervention in 1989 with the Belfast United Project. His pioneer work brought together sixteen young Irish football (soccer) players who participated in a twenty-three-day tour in the US that included football tournaments, outdoor activities, participation in an adventure summer camp, and staying in a mixed ethnic and religious residential setting. Sugden identified general characteristics that can contribute to positive impacts as a result of cross-cultural contact and emphasised the necessity for: (a) designing research-based and well-structured sport programmes; (b) employing sport activities that promote teamwork and mutual reliance; (c) incorporating social activities as part of sport programmes; (d) employing sport activities that challenge both mentally and physically to contribute to peak experiences; (e) implementing follow-up activities after the end of the sport initiative to sustain positive outcomes; and (f) providing detailed documentation at all stages of the programme.

Doves Olympic Movement project and Sport-for-Development Theory

These guidelines and general characteristics were among the first components that I considered as the initial pillars to be used towards the development of a theoretical basis for understanding sport interventions in cross-cultural settings. The initial framework of SFDT was built from the first-ever published programme components of a sport for peace intervention advanced by Sugden (1991) and enriched with non-sport theoretical frameworks derived from principles and propositions of inter-group contact theory (Allport, 1954; Pettigrew, 1998; Pettigrew and Tropp, 2006) and human development (Maslow, 1970; Ryan and Deci, 2000). My first propositions were built on the assumptions that the foundation of successful sport and social change initiatives should cultivate human development frameworks and inter-group contact theory conditions before, during and after implementing the programmes.

Given the absence of a theoretical framework, I utilised grounded theory methodology to design and assess a number of Applied Olympism initiatives, known as the Doves Olympic

Movement model (DOM), aimed at providing an interdisciplinary approach to better understand the conditions under which sport, education and cultural enrichment (Olympism) can promote personal and social change and development as a vehicle for peacebuilding and reconciliation. In other words, the DOM model's programme components and theoretical foundations served as the conceptual framework for developing SFDT, which was a result of cumulative programme design and delivery, manuscripts, training manuals and reports grounded on theory (Lyras, 2001, 2003, 2004, 2005) that were then operationalised, tested and validated with evidence from the field (Lyras, 2007, 2009, 2012a, 2012b, 2014).

As a component of the DOM model, which played an integral role in developing SFDT, I implemented a five-year, longitudinal action research project (2005–10), also known as The Doves Project, which aimed to promote inter-group acceptance and collaboration between Greek and Turkish Cypriot youths (Lyras, 2003, 2007). The Doves Project served as a platform for theory building based on an interdisciplinary theoretical foundation drawn from organisational theory, humanistic psychology, inter-group contact theory, educational psychology and theory and methods of research (Lyras, 2007), which provided evidence and programme recommendations about the context and the conditions under which sport and Olympic education programmes can leverage positive social change. These theoretical frameworks were selected because they could provide a foundation that would help SFD researchers and practitioners best design programmes and policy; understand important principles and frameworks (how people learn, grow and develop); understand implications, foundations, limitations and the process of change (organisational change theory); and promote inter-group acceptance, collaboration and cohesiveness (inter-group contact theory). Theory and methods of research were considered the main foundation for programme assessment, promoting in this way evidence-based programming. In other words, due to the fact that none of the sport-for-development and peace initiatives had scientific assessment of their impact as an integrated part of their programme implementation, the application of novel methods of assessment was, and is, essential for the advancement of our understanding of the conditions under which sport-based interventions can serve as a platform for peacebuilding and development. I found no examples of such design efforts in the sport management literature or sport for peacebuilding and development practice. There was a need, therefore, for adopting a scientific impact assessment mindset as an integral part of a sport or Olympism in action intervention. Grounded theory methodology and mixed methods design served as the foundations for the assessment of the impact and programme component of The Doves Project to evaluate: (a) the effectiveness of the organisational, educational, sport and cultural components; (b) the impact of the programme on peacebuilding and development indicators across time and space; (c) with validated social-psychological scales; and (d) based on a robust, human-centred conceptual framework.

The Doves Project was designed with the objective to advance SFD theory and practice by providing theoretical foundations and empirical evidence on how sport researchers and practitioners can promote evidence-based programme development with positive educational and social outcomes. Beyond the educational benefits, The Doves Project had a significant positive impact on ethnic and gender groups, and girls and boys benefited equally from the project (e.g., inter-group acceptance and collaboration, social perspective taking, active citizenship and change agent self-efficacy). Such findings have significant practical implications, since evidence and theory suggest that inter-group acceptance can be better facilitated by (a) creating an inclusive educational sport setting, and (b) following certain conditions and assumptions (Lyras, 2007).

The Sport-for-Development Theory (SFDT)

Based upon the above theoretical foundations and assumptions (inter-group contact and humanistic psychology), through SFDT (Lyras, 2007), I suggest that sport initiatives can facilitate personal development and social change by embracing Applied Olympism and non-traditional sport management practices through an interdisciplinary framework, blending sport with cultural enrichment (the mix of sport with cultural and educational activities). In particular, SFDT suggests that the blend of sport with cultural enrichment activities (e.g., arts, dance and music) and global citizenship education (e.g., global issues awareness, human rights and environmental issues) can provide a framework for personal development, cross-cultural acceptance and collaboration, and social change. These components can then be used to identify factors that facilitate, as well as forces that inhibit, positive change, as well as to set objectives to assess social, psychological and societal change across time and space. One of the most significant outcomes related to SFDT is an Olympism-in-action intervention template that was tested and refined over time and space through a mixed methods field experimental design. The ultimate goal was to provide guidelines for further testing in various populations, in different contexts and with various social challenges.

Once SFDT was established, I wanted to disseminate and further validate the universality of this theory. To this end, I was interested in initiating global ventures, further testing and evidence from the field, related scholarship, programme evaluation reports, workshops, academic courses, professional training and capacity building endeavours and collaborations with scholars, students and practitioners interested in programmes and initiatives with similar structure and objectives. My vision was to utilise SFDT to provide sound applied Olympism for humanity (O4H) theoretical foundations and practical recommendations that can be used in the real world to address current social challenges through related programme design, delivery and evaluation of preventive interventions, curriculum design, professional/vocational training, academic courses and student engagement initiatives. The following sections provide more information on how SFDT and the work developed through The Doves Project served as a platform for joint ventures with related scholarship, teaching, research and service.

First extension of SFDT in praxis: the Lyras and Welty Peachey (2011) milestone

The first key published co-authored article that utilised the application of SFDT for programme evaluation, beyond the Cypriot context, was the conceptual comparison of The Doves Project and the World Scholar Athlete-Games (WSAG) (Lyras and Welty Peachey, 2011). Both were Olympic Education programmes working at peacebuilding and cultural understanding through sport, but at different levels (local and global respectively). This article was instrumental in demonstrating how the blueprint of the SFDT elements of effective programming (Lyras, 2007) can be used to evaluate organisational, cultural, educational, sport and impact assessment components of existing Olympic education-based programmes or events. This work was a result of a number of conversations, joint presentations and close friendship between Lyras and Welty Peachey that was based on shared vision and desire to advance applied scholarship and service. These conversations began while Welty Peachey was serving as a vice president of the WSAG, when we both observed the gaps and opportunities due to the absence of an evaluation mechanism in the WSAG's already successful endeavours.

The ultimate goal of our collaboration, initiated with the 2011 work, was to test the applicability of SFDT in different contexts and to provide recommendations for more effective programming. This foundation, research methodology and rationale served as a platform for multiple inter-institutional collaborations that aimed to provide: (a) instrumentation and long-term evaluation of sport for peace and development programmes; (b) evidence from the field; (b) related scholarship; (c) capacity building and service to SFD and Olympism in action organisations; and (d) integrated teaching, research and service. Based on the principles of SFDT, we formed partnerships and strategic planning agreements with the WSAG and Street Soccer USA (SSUSA). In other words, the Lyras and Welty Peachey (2011) publication was the first tangible example of how SFDT can be utilised in practice, and this framework and shared vision served as a platform for programme evaluation and comparison, launching collaborations with other scholars, practitioners and graduate and undergraduate students. Through our close collaboration utilising SFDT and its programme evaluation model we have published thirteen co-authored journal articles and book chapters and presented eighteen papers at academic conferences in collaboration with other noted scholars, received three grants, developed four impact assessment reports and provided training and oversight for twelve master's and doctoral students applying SFDT in various contexts.

Further extensions and applications

Since SFDT's development in the Cypriot context, and its application to the WSAG, we decided to utilise the existing theory for further application and testing in several different arenas. Our next application and testing of SFDT was with the SSUSA National Cup and SSUSA local teams. SSUSA is a non-profit organisation with a mission to use soccer to help individuals suffering from homelessness in the US make positive changes in their lives. In this instance, we were interested in ascertaining the applicability of SFDT in a setting focused on a social cause much different from facilitating cultural understanding at the local level in Cyprus. Our purpose was to investigate the short- and long-term impact of SSUSA and the SSUSA Cup on its homeless participants and to identify the event's structures and processes that can facilitate positive outcomes (Welty Peachey, Lyras, Borland and Cohen, 2013).

This study with the SSUSA Cup revealed that participants generally experienced a positive impact through the event by building a sense of community, creating hope, cultivating an outward focus, fostering goal achievement and enhancing personal development (Welty Peachey *et al.*, 2013). As a direct result of this study and application of SFDT, SSUSA Cup organisers revamped the competition structure to pay closer attention to matching teams of similar calibre in the round-robin phase of the tournament, and in subsequent iterations of the Cup, organisers de-emphasised winning, and focused much more on the educational and cultural aspects of the event surrounding the competition. Thus, this research directly informed practice and also was an important testing of the applicability of SFDT to inform research in a sport intervention context focused on marginalised and disenfranchised individuals.

Further, we wished to ascertain the applicability of SFDT in a larger, international sport intervention setting, and test the applicability of SFDT with the 2011 WSAG, a ten-day sport-for-development and peace event held in Hartford, Connecticut (US) designed to bring together young people from around the world to promote understanding, peace and social change. Our evaluation and long-term research plan was a continuation of our first joint publication (Lyras and Welty Peachey, 2011). Held every four or five years since 1993, the 2011 WSAG attracted 525 participants, ages 14–20, from forty countries. Participants had to be talented in academics and a sport or fine arts activity.

Our initial work situated within the WSAG examined the impact of the event on prejudice and change agent self-efficacy, and the structures and processes of the event that facilitated this impact (Welty Peachey, Cunningham, Lyras, Cohen and Bruening, 2015). Here, the results indicated that it was the inclusive, team-based sport environment that contributed to prejudice reduction, while the educational platform was critical for increasing change agent self-efficacy, or the belief that one had the power and capacity to effect social change upon returning home from the event. This work was critical, as it was one of the first studies beyond The Doves Project connecting programme design components of SFDT with programme outcomes, a stream of research that has been called for by SFD scholars (Coalter, 2007, 2013; Lyras, 2007, 2012; Lyras and Welty Peachey, 2011; Schulenkorf and Edwards, 2012). In addition, this work is important because it extended SFDT into a new application, that of a large, international SFD event working at cultural understanding and peacebuilding between youth from different cultural contexts.

Welty Peachey and colleagues also extended SFDT into the service-learning environment of a university sport management programme in the US (Bruening *et al.*, 2015). The aim of this study was to gain an understanding of the design, structure and management of a sport-based service-learning project with a SFD mandate situated in the inner-city environment. This programme, City Sport, integrates SFD service opportunities for college students with class-based training, education and reflection. The important theoretical extension and application of SFDT in this study is that it was the first work to examine the design, structures and management of a sport-based service-learning project with a SFD mission. Importantly, it was shown that the tenets of SFDT were useful and applicable in this context.

Aside from our investigations utilising and extending SFDT, other scholars have begun to apply this theoretical lens in their conceptual and empirical work. Edwards (2015) recently published a conceptual piece on the role of sport in community capacity building, utilising SFDT as a grand theoretical framework (Henderson, Presley and Bialeschki, 2004) from which to build a smaller range theoretical framework of sport's role in community capacity building. In another theoretical extension, Inoue, Funk and Jordan (2013) built upon SFDT to incorporate a logic model for evaluating the Back on My Feet programme, which helps those experiencing homelessness to develop self-sufficiency through running. In a logic model, a programme is deconstructed into inputs, activities, outputs, outcomes and impact (W.K. Kellogg Foundation, 2004). Findings of this study indicated that enhanced involvement in sport, in particular running, created important psychological benefits for individuals suffering from homelessness (Inoue *et al.*, 2013).

In terms of other empirical applications, Marshall and Barry (2015) applied SFDT as the theoretical lens to examine the Kicking AIDS Out Network in Southern Africa to test SFDT's applicability in this context. The Kicking AIDS Out Network strives to enhance life skills through sport, to foster youth development, to raise HIV/AIDS awareness and to promote behavioural change, emphasising a balance between sport and education to achieve positive change. The findings suggest that SFDT offers an appropriate framework to enhance project design and delivery that integrates the features of sport, education, life skills development, use of leaders as change agents and participation that are key to Kicking AIDS Out programmes and other community sport programmes promoting behaviour and social change.

Another investigation examined trends in 440 SFD programmes for girls and women aimed at promoting health, gender equity and social integration, using SFDT as the guiding framework (Hancock, Lyras and Ha, 2013). SFDT was also used as a framework to assist in evaluating the use of football (soccer) as a tool for promoting the development of marginalised groups of people in South Africa, most notably women and youth (Chiyapo, 2014). The results of this study demonstrated that sport has the potential to empower women and girls and to encourage personal growth, but it is the processes and experiences of playing the sport, not the actual sport, that contribute to positive impact. Finally, Ha and Lyras (2013) utilised SFDT to explain the construct of acculturation within the framework of the sport for development and peace movement and how these programmes can be utilised as a vehicle for refugee youth in acculturating into a host country. Based on the acculturation literature and SFDT, the authors provided recommendations for practitioners who work with refugee youth in a new country.

As has been illustrated, SFDT has been theoretically extended and applied through both our own work and the scholarship of others since its initial development. There remain, however, many avenues for continued testing and refining of SFDT across multiple cultures and contexts.

SFDT has also informed our teaching at the undergraduate, graduate and professional training levels. For instance, Lyras designed and taught ten courses and has given multiple guest lectures (graduate, undergraduate and study abroad) at universities in Europe, the US, Africa, Asia and the Caribbean for the purpose of introducing undergraduate and graduate students to SFD and its underlying theoretical foundations. Lyras also developed the first Applied Olympism professional training called Olympism4Humanity (O4H) Praxis Program in Ancient Olympia, Greece, a joint venture between the International Olympic Academy, Georgetown University and the Olympism4Humanity (O4H) Alliance, a global consortium of prominent experts and agencies in conflict resolution, global health, international development, human rights, global citizenship, disability and Olympism Legacy. O4H's current endeavours are being implemented under the patronage of the European Union Commissioner for Education, Culture, Multilingualism and Youth. O4H aims to create a world-leading interdisciplinary academic consortium to build human-centred bridges between disciplines, academic agencies, educational systems and practitioners. O4H as a global venture is considered the extension and the platform where SFDT serves as a validated framework for integrated and applied Olympic education teaching, research and service. All graduate, undergraduate and professional training initiated through O4H utilises SFDT as the main pillars of the skills and proficiencies needed in programming and scholarship. All courses have integrated and applied project-based structures where individuals design and implement projects back home that address local challenges. In addition, Welty Peachey has taught a graduate class with a SFD focus using SFDT as the foundation, and out of this class, students are using SFDT to construct a sport- and cultural arts-based intervention with a local Boys and Girls Club aimed at helping girls and boys in a disadvantaged neighbourhood reach their full potential.

Future directions

There are a number of theoretical and empirical extensions of SFDT that scholars may wish to pursue within and outside of the SFD and Olympic education arena. First, as suggested by numerous scholars (Coalter, 2007, 2013; Lyras, 2007, Lyras, 2012a; Lyras and Welty Peachey, 2011; Schulenkorf and Edwards, 2012), there is still a critical need for more research connecting SFD programme design features and components with specified outcomes. In this regard, more work is needed to investigate how and which components of SFDT are related to specific outcomes. Second, SFDT needs to be applied with longitudinal research, as most of the research on SFD interventions and impacts has been short-term in nature (Coalter, 2013; Darnell, 2012; Lyras, 2007, Lyras and Welty Peachey, 2011). The impacts of these interventions and events over time and space need to be further explored. Third, there is opportunity to test and apply SFDT not only within other SFD contexts not previously explored (e.g., interventions with prisoners, gangs, immigrants, refugees and different cultural contexts experiencing conflict), but also within more mainstream sport industry sectors, such as non-governmental organisations, non-profit sport, professional sport, intercollegiate athletics and within the Olympic movement. SFDT could also be helpful in negotiating the terrains of corporate social responsibility, fan identity and organisational commitment. We invite scholars to join us in these efforts.

Note

1   This chapter is a reflection on Lyras (2007) and Lyras and Welty Peachey (2011), and the related works.

References

Allport, G.W. (1954) 'The historical background of modern social psychology'. *Handbook of Social Psychology*, 1: 3–56.

Bruening, J.E., Welty Peachey, J., Evanovich, J.M., Fuller, R.D., Murty, C.J.C., Percy, V.E., Lauren, A.S. and Chung, M. (2015) 'Managing sport for social change: The effects of intentional design and structure in a sport-based service learning initiative'. *Sport Management Review*, 18: 69–85.

Chiyapo, T. (2014) 'Football as an agent or tool to promote women and girls' empowerment: A case study of coaching for hope – Cape Town'. Unpublished master's thesis, University of Cape Town, South Africa.

Coalter, F. (2007). 'Sports clubs, social capital and social regeneration: "Ill-defined interventions with hard to follow outcomes?"' *Sport in Society*, 10: 537–59.

Coalter, F. (2013) '"There is loads of relationships here": Developing a program theory for sport-for-change programs'. *International Review for the Sociology of Sport*, 48: 594–612.

Darnell, S.C. (2012) 'Global citizenship and the ethical challenges of sport for development and peace'. *Journal of Global Citizenship & Equity Education*, 2(1): 2–17.

Edwards, M. (2015) 'The role of sport in community capacity building: An examination of sport for development research and practice'. *Sport Management Review*, 18: 6–19.

Ha, J. and Lyras, A. (2013) 'Sport for refugee youth in a new society: The role of acculturation in SFDP programming'. *South African Journal for Research in Sport, Physical Education & Recreation*, 35: 121–40.

Hancock, M.G., Lyras, A. and Ha, J. (2013) 'Sport for development programs for girls and women: A global assessment'. *Journal of Sport for Development*, 1(1): 15–24.

Henderson, K.A., Presley, J. and Bialeschki, M.D. (2004) 'Theory in recreation and leisure research: Reflections from the editors'. *Leisure Sciences*, 26: 411–25.

Inoue, Y., Funk, D. and Jordan, J. (2013) 'The role of running involvement in creating self-sufficiency for homeless individuals through a community-based running program'. *Journal of Sport Management*, 27: 439–52.

Kellogg, W.K. (2004) *Logic model development guide*. Battle Creek, MI: WK Kellogg Foundation.

Lewin, K. (1952) *Field theory in social science: Selected theoretical papers by Kurt Lewin*. London: Tavistock.

Lyras, A. (2001) 'Sport for development: The philosophy of sport of the millennium'. Unpublished manuscript, Nicosia, Cyprus.

Lyras, A. (2003) 'Doves Olympic Movement: Pilot study for interethnic conflict management and cultural development'. Unpublished manuscript, University of Connecticut, Storrs, CT.

Lyras, A. (2004) 'Multidimensional sport development: An investigation of the educational aspects and psycho-social impact of sports'. Grant awarded from the Cyprus Research Foundation, Nicosia, Cyprus.

Lyras, A. (2005) 'Doves Olympic Movement Summer Camp 2005: Training manual'. Unpublished manuscript submitted to UNOPS/UNDP, Nicosia, Cyprus.

Lyras, A. (2007) 'Characteristics and psycho-social impacts of an inter-ethnic educational sport initiative on Greek and Turkish Cypriot youth'. Unpublished dissertation, University of Connecticut, Storrs.

Lyras, A. (2009) 'Sport for peace and development theory'. Unpublished manuscript.

Lyras, A. (2012a) 'The Doves Olympic Movement Project: Integrating Olympism, development, and peace'. In R. Schinke and S. Hanrahan (eds) *Sport for development, peace, and social justice*. Morgantown, WV: Fitness Information Technology.

Lyras, A. (2012b) 'Olympism in practice: Psycho-social impacts of an educational sport initiativeon Greek and Turkish Cypriot Youth'. *ICHPER-SD Journal of Research*, 7: 46–54.

Lyras, A. (2013, November 20) 'Earning respect and recognition'. Retrieved from www.alexislyras.com/blog/e-debate-earning-respect-and-recognition-sport-and-development-platform-20-november-2013 (accessed on 1 September, 2014).

Lyras, A. (2014) 'Olympic education in practice: Educational components of a sport for peacebuilding intervention'. In D. Chatziefstathiou and M. Muller (eds) *Olympism, Olympic education and learning legacies* (pp. 245–59). Cambridge, MA: Cambridge Scholars Publishing.

Lyras, A. and Welty Peachey, J. (2011) 'Integrating sport-for-development theory and praxis'. *Sport Management Review, 14*: 311–26.

Maslow, A.H. (1970) *Motivation and personality* (second edn). New York, NY: Harper & Row.

Marshall, S.K. and Barry, P. (2015) 'Community sport for development: Perceptions from practice in Southern Africa'. *Journal of Sport Management, 29*: 109–21.

Pettigrew, T.F. (1998) 'Intergroup contact theory'. *Annual Review of Psychology, 49*: 65–85.

Pettigrew, T.F. and Tropp, L. (2006) 'A meta-analytic test of intergroup contact theory'. *Journal of Personality & Social Psychology, 90*: 751–83.

Ryan, M.R. and Deci, L.E. (2000) 'Self-determination theory and the facilitation of intrinsic motivation, social development and well-being'. *American Psychologist, 55*: 68–78.

Saunders, E. and Sugden, J. (1997) 'Sport and community relations in Northern Ireland'. *Managing Leisure, 2*: 39–54.

Schulenkorf, N. and Edwards, D. (2012) 'Maximizing positive social impacts: Strategies for sustaining and leveraging the benefits of inter-community sport events in divided societies'. *Journal of Sport Management, 26*: 379–90.

Sugden, J. (1991) 'Belfast United: Encouraging cross-community through sport in Northern Ireland'. *Journal of Sport & Social Issues, 15*(1): 59–80.

Sugden, J. and Harvie, S. (1995) *Sport and community relations in Northern Ireland*. Coleraine: University of Ulster.

Welty Peachey, J., Lyras, A., Borland, J. and Cohen, A. (2013) 'Street Soccer USA Cup: Preliminary findings of a sport-for-homeless intervention'. *ICHPER-SD Journal of Research, 8*(1): 3–11.

Welty Peachey, J., Cunningham, G., Lyras, A., Cohen, A. and Bruening, J. (2015) 'The influence of a sport-for-peacet event on prejudice and change agent self-efficacy'. *Journal of Sport Management, 29*, 229–244.

Applying Sport-for-Development Theory

Adam Cohen[1]

Lyras and Welty Peachey's (2011) publication has certainly been influential in my academic career regarding my research, teaching and service. Prior to re-entering academia, I worked for a number of public policy initiatives and non-profit organisations. One of the most frustrating aspects of this industry, in my mind, was the lack of ability to properly assess or quantify the grandiose claims my respective workplaces would assert. When I decided to pursue a PhD degree in Sport Management and focus my research efforts in the field of sport-for-development, the work of these two authors really stood out to me. After speaking with them about their research and collaborations, I learned about the value that quality research could provide the practitioner world. While the idea of theory and theory development began as a foreign concept to me as a first-year PhD student, one thing I began to understand was the intersection of practice and academia.

In their 2011 article, the authors attempt to answer the call of many sport-for-development scholars who have stressed the need for greater monitor and evaluation efforts (Coalter, 2010; Schulenkorf and Sugden, 2011), along with increased rigor, both in method and theory. Specifically, the authors suggest five components that can serve as a model to analyse and evaluate a sport-for-development initiative: impact assessment, organisational, sport, educational and cultural enrichment. These components, in some capacity, have steered my work as a professor and a scholar.

At the time of this writing, every single one of my publications has involved the collaboration with a practitioner in the sport-for-development field, each of which had several factors in common: a passionate leadership, a mission to create change on and off the field of play, and a need for expert analysis of their outcomes. Whether it was writing an executive summary or an impact report for Street Soccer USA (a homeless soccer initiative), evaluating the intersection of pop culture and sport with the International Quidditch Association, or interviewing participants of the World Scholar Athlete Games on their experience off the field and in the classroom, my work constantly seems to revolve around Lyras and Welty Peachey's (2011) recommendations for monitoring and evaluating a sport-for-development programme.

This has carried over to my teaching and service. Practising what I (and this article) preach in a classroom setting, my latest project is to conduct an impact assessment of a service learning class I recently implemented. Specifically, I aim to gauge the impact my students have working with a local Special Olympics chapter, along with assessing the impact the initiative has on them. This evaluation aims to enhance the efforts of a sport-for-development initiative and in turn increase the effectiveness of a unique classroom setting.

Note

1   Adam Cohen is with the Department of Health, Exercise and Sports Sciences at Texas Tech University.

References

Coalter, F. (2010) 'The politics of sport-for-development: Limited focus programmes and broad gauge problems?' *International Review for the Sociology of Sport, 45*(3): 295–314.

Lyras, A. and Welty Peachey, J. (2011) 'Integrating sport-for-development theory and praxis'. *Sport Management Review, 14*: 311–26.

Schulenkorf, N. and Sugden, J. (2011) 'Sport for development and peace in divided societies: Cooperating for inter-community empowerment in Israel'. *European Journal for Sport and Society, 8*: 235–56.

12

LEADERSHIP[1]

Packianathan Chelladurai

Prologue

Although every scholar of renown has researched and written on several topics, that scholar is likely to be identified with a singular work. I am personally proud of inspiring and initiating several new lines of research in sport management; yet I am most often identified with the Multidimensional Model of Leadership (MML) that I developed. This is particularly true in the field of sport and exercise psychology more so than in sport management. In fact, several textbooks in sport psychology have included a section on the Multidimensional Model (e.g., Jowett and Lavallee, 2007; LeUnes, 2008; Weinberg and Gould, 2015). Similarly, my Leadership Scale for Sports (LSS), developed in conjunction with the Multidimensional Model, has been quite popular with researchers around the world. Its significance is highlighted by the fact that the 1980 publication detailing the development of the scale (Chelladurai and Saleh, 1980) is included as one of the essential readings in sport psychology twenty-five years later (reprinted as Chelladurai and Saleh, 2007).

The little theorizing I have done on leadership has been based on my own experiences as a player and coach. I tended to favour some theories of leadership because they related to some of my experiences and explained/justified my actions as a coach. In turn, I offered an integrated model of leadership, once again reflecting my background in coaching. That one's experiences and the thinking associated with those experiences can lead to theorizing is supported by Albert Einstein's statement that 'the whole of science is nothing more than a refinement of everyday thinking' and Kurt Lewin's view that 'there is nothing so practical as a good theory'.

Multidimensional Model of Leadership

The Multidimensional Model of Leadership (Chelladurai, 1978, 1993; Chelladurai and Carron, 1978) is illustrated in Figure 12.1a. The model incorporates three sets of antecedent factors (situational characteristics, member characteristics, and leader characteristics) influencing three states of leader behaviours (required, preferred and actual), and the congruence among them is expected to result in higher levels of performance of and satisfaction among members.

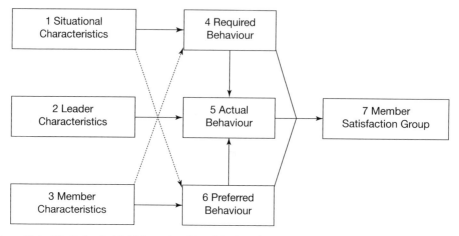

Figure 12.1a Chelladurai's Multidimensional Model of Leadership

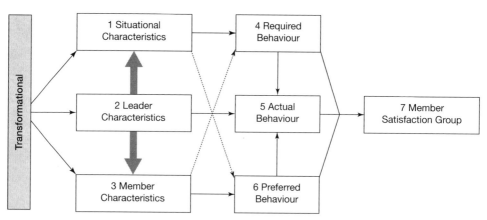

Figure 12.1b Transformational effects of leader behaviour in the Multidimensional Model

Required behaviour

The situational characteristics (Box 1 in Figure 12.1a) that influence required behaviour (Box 4) include the goals of the group, the type of task (e.g., individual versus team, closed or self-paced versus open or externally paced tasks) and the social and cultural context of the group. It must be noted that these situational characteristics may prescribe certain leader behaviours (i.e., what ought to be done) or proscribe certain behaviours (i.e., what ought not to be done). The leader is also cognizant of the nature of the members of the group that he or she is leading and thus their characteristics would also influence what is required in the situation as indicated by the dotted line from Box 3 to Box 4.

Preferred behaviour

Member preferences for specific forms of leader behaviours (i.e., preferred behaviours, Box 6) are influenced by member characteristics. These include individual difference factors (Box 3)

such as task relevant ability, and personality traits and needs (e.g., need for achievement, need for affiliation, cognitive structure, attitude towards authority). In addition, as individual members are aware of the situational demands and constraints, their preferences are likely to be influenced by situational characteristics as well (dotted arrow from Box 1 to Box 6).

Actual behaviour

The third and final state of leader behaviour is the leader's actual behaviour (Box 5). While the leader's personal characteristics of personality, ability, experience and so on (Box 2) are likely to influence actual leader behaviour, the leader is also expected to be attuned to, and accommodate the requirements of, the situation (Box 4) and preferences of members (Box 6).

Outcomes

In my original formulation of the model, I included performance and satisfaction of the members as the outcome variables. Given that the primary goal of an athletic team is to enhance performance so as to secure victories against opponents in organised competitions, it is only reasonable to include performance as a primary outcome of the leadership model. But this global notion of performance can be broken down into individual performance and team performance. We can also consider improvements in performances at the individual or team level as outcomes.

As individuals freely engage in prolonged and agonistic training, their satisfaction with their experiences in such pursuits is a critical outcome variable. And the facets of such satisfaction may relate to their own performance, the team's performance, the leadership provided by the coach and the interactions among team members, and so on. Riemer and I (Riemer and Chelladurai, 1998) developed the *Athlete Satisfaction Questionnaire* (ASQ), which measures fifteen facets of athlete satisfaction – individual performance, team performance, ability utilisation, strategy, personal treatment, training and instruction, team task/social contribution, ethics, team integration, personal dedication, budget, medical personnel, academic support services and external agents. Readers should recognise that some of the facets listed above do not relate to coaching, *per se* (e.g., budget, medical personnel, academic support services), but refer to decisions by superior authorities. It must also be noted that the inclusion of performance and satisfaction in the multidimensional model does not preclude consideration of other team-related outcomes as indicated by our facets of satisfaction.

Congruence hypothesis

A critical thrust within the multidimensional model is the hypothesis that the congruence among the three states of leader behaviour would lead to performance and satisfaction. That is, the leader/coach is expected to balance the requirements of the situation, preferences of the members, and his or her personal inclinations in behaviour towards the members. The model also includes feedback from performance and satisfaction back towards actual leadership. That is, the coach is likely to alter her or his leader behaviours based on the feedback related to performance and satisfaction. If the coach perceives performance to be lower than expected, the coach may become more focused on task accomplishment and engage in task-oriented behaviours. If the members are seen to be less cohesive and disjointed, the coach may begin to engage in those behaviours that foster warm interpersonal interactions between the leader and members, and among the members.

Why the interest in leadership

As noted, my experience as a player, referee and coach in basketball while in India provided the impetus to study the phenomenon of leadership in sports. Although I had been quite a successful coach at the university level, I had very little knowledge about the psychological aspects of athletics. When I began my graduate studies at the University of Western Ontario, I started reading about coaching of athletic teams. My teachers were very critical of coaches who were demanding and autocratic. However, this view was inconsistent with the presence of several successful coaches who were authoritarian in their treatment of their teams and their players. Further, as a coach I had been quite demanding and autocratic myself. My teams were successful, and my players liked me and respected me. This disconnect between what was taught and what was happening in everyday life triggered my interests in the study of leadership. As Bandura (2005) noted, 'Discontent with the adequacy of existing theoretical explanations provides the impetus to search for conceptual schemes that can offer better explanations and solutions to phenomena of import' (p. 10). As the existing models of leadership in sports did not explain the observed phenomenon adequately, I was looking for better explanations.

Genesis of the model

As I was doing my doctoral work, I was quite excited about studying the existing leadership models. Of most interest to me was Fiedler's (1967) *Contingency Model of Leadership Effectiveness* because some of the tenets of the theory were consistent with my own experiences as a basketball coach. The elements of situational favourableness (leader–member relations, task-structure and position power) are really applicable to coaching an athletic team, and I had enjoyed all of them in my coaching career. His proposition that task-oriented leaders would be more effective in more favourable situations is certainly true in the case of athletic coaching. Another theory that related to my coaching experience was House's (1971; House and Dessler, 1974) *Path-goal Theory of Leadership*. The theory posits that the main role of a leader is to clarify the goals of the group, the path to achieve those goals and to facilitate members' efforts towards those goals. Such facilitation involves enhancing the abilities of members and providing social support during the effort phase. This is what coaches do during those prolonged and arduous training sessions. The third theory that reflected the coaching situation was Osborn and Hunt's (1975) *Adaptive-Reactive Theory*, which stipulates that a successful leader is one who adapts to the requirements of the situation and reacts to member preferences. Typically, a coach is operating within the confines of a larger institution (e.g., an educational institution, a national sports organisation, a professional sports franchise) that has its own requirements. In addition, the athletes being coached may have their own preferences, which at times may contravene the regulations of the larger institution. The coach has to adapt to these regulations of the higher unit and react positively to member preferences. In sum, I was able to reflect back on my own experiences and relate them to the principles enunciated by these three theories.

But, I was also uncomfortable with these theories because each one of them emphasised only one of the three aspects of leadership – the leader (Fiedler's *Contingency Theory*), the members (House's *Path-goal Theory*) and the situation (Osborn and Hunt's *Adaptive-Reactive Theory*). This discomfort was the stimulant for me to think of amalgamating these three approaches into a single model, resulting in the MML.

Applications and extensions of the model

Current status of the Multidimensional Model

My MML continues to be recognised as 'one of the most significant models of sporting leadership and has generated extensive empirical attention' (Fletcher and Roberts, 2013; p. 90). As noted, leading psychology textbooks include the model in their treatise on leadership in sports (e.g., Weinberg and Gould, 2015). The incorporation of transformational leadership into the MML has begun to have an impact on sport leadership. For example, Din and Paskevich (2013) labelled my approach as *Chelladurai's Pursuit of Excellence in Sport Model* and have incorporated it into their integrated research model of Olympic podium performance.

While the MML has relevance to this day, much of the research regarding the multidimensional model of leadership has been largely descriptive wherein the influence of selected antecedent variables on preferred and/or perceived leadership have been investigated. Such antecedent variables have included individual difference factors such as gender (Chelladurai and Saleh, 1978; Garba, 2011; Liukkonen and Salminen, 1990; Serpa, Pataco and Santos, 1991); personality and psychological characteristics (Chelladurai and Carron, 1981; Erle, 1981; Horn *et al.*, 2011); age, experience and maturity (Chelladurai and Carron, 1983; Erle, 1981; Serpa, 1990); and ability (Liukkonen and Salminen, 1990; Garland and Barry, 1988; Toros, Türksoy and Doğaner, 2013). The situational characteristics examined have included organisational goals (Erle, 1981); task type (Chelladurai, 1978; Garba, 2011; Kim, Lee and Lee, 1990; Liukkonen and Salminen, 1990; Serpa, 1990); culture (Chelladurai *et al.*, 1988; Chelladurai *et al.*, 1987; Terry, 1984); and the distinction between offensive and defensive squads in football (Riemer and Chelladurai, 1995). The statistical procedures in these studies have been largely correlational and/or analysis of variance procedures.

Another approach has been the study of congruence between the perceived and preferred leadership and its effect on one of the consequences specified in the model, such as satisfaction with leadership, team performance and/or individual performance (Chelladurai, 1978, 1984; Chelladurai *et al.*, 1988; Schlieshman, 1987; Weiss and Friedricks, 1986). The general conclusion emerging from these studies is that 'athletes are satisfied with leadership to the extent that the coach emphasises (a) training and instruction that enhances the ability and coordinated effort by members, which in turn contributes to task accomplishment; and (b) positive feedback that recognizes and rewards good performance' (Chelladurai, 1993, p. 654). The attempts to relate leadership to performance have been limited (e.g., Chelladurai, 1978; Gordon, 1988; Serpa, Pateo and Santos, 1991; Weiss and Friedrichs, 1986).

One of the difficulties with respect to the Multidimensional Model is in operationalising the required behaviour. That would explain why only one study included required leader behaviour along with actual and preferred leader behaviours (Chelladurai, 1978). My approach was to treat the mean preferences of all basketball players included in the study as the required behaviour and the mean of the perceptions of players of a particular team as the actual behaviour. The hypothesis that congruence between required behaviour and actual behaviour would be related to performance was not supported. That could have been a function of the low number of teams ($n = 10$) in the study. Overall, the model has not been subjected to strict empirical verification in its entirety.

Transformational leadership in the Multidimensional Model

Given that athletics is the pursuit of excellence and that athletes are constantly striving to improve their performance capabilities, one could conclude that they are in the transformational mode.

Accordingly, coaches are constantly attempting to enhance their charges' beliefs, self-esteem, self-confidence, self-discipline and ultimately their performances. These are the essential effects of transformational leadership. So, one can say that coaches are in the business of transforming their athletes. In other words, all of coaching is based on transformational leadership.

Accordingly, I incorporated the notion of transformational leadership on the Multidimensional Model (Chelladurai, 2007), as shown in Figure 12.1b. In those cases where there is a chief coach and several assistant coaches, the chief coach can be seen as influencing/transforming not only the athletes but also the assistants who, in turn, interact with the athletes. In the absence of assistants between the coach and the athletes, the transformational process would take the form of the coach altering member characteristics as well as the situational characteristics as indicated by the arrows from leader characteristics (Box 2) to situational characteristics (Box 1) and member characteristics (Box 3).

In the transformational process, coaches are expected to (a) incite the higher order needs of members (b) motivate them to perform beyond expectations, (c) express confidence in members, and (d) empower them (e.g., Bass, 1985). The coach creates a new *Vision* for the athlete or team as a great performer(s), convinces them of the viability of the vision and expresses confidence in them reaching that vision. Transformational leadership also involves *Inspirational Communication* where the coach inspires the athletes to extend themselves to achieve excellence, stimulates enthusiasm, builds confidence, instills pride, enhances morale, sets examples of courage and dedication and shares the hardships. In *Intellectual Stimulation*, the coach engages the intellect, thus enabling the athletes to see their activity in its totality and understand the scheme of things surrounding the performance. The coach also engages in *Individualised and Supportive Leadership* by bestowing individualised attention on the athletes. *Personal Recognition* is a critical component of transformational leadership. While the public, media and other athletes recognise better performances, the coach's recognition takes centre stage in practice sessions where incremental improvements are achieved. Achievement of simple and specific practice goals are the bricks on which excellence is built. The coach needs to recognise those smaller achievements.

Leadership Scale for Sports (LSS)

Any theoretical model is only meaningful and useful if the constructs included in the model are measurable. Further, the model can be verified only if there are scales to measure the constructs contained in the model. Stated otherwise, anyone advancing a new model with new con-structs has also the responsibility to develop scales to measure those new constructs. Accordingly, I developed the Leadership Scale for Sports (LSS).

The development of the LSS is described in Chelladurai and Saleh (1978). In the first stage, I selected and modified ninety-nine items from existing leadership scales (i.e., LBDQ – Halpin, 1957; SBDQ – Fleishman, 1957a; LOQ – Fleishman, 1957b; LBDQ Form XII – Stogdill, 1963). The stem for the items was 'The coach should . . .' with the response categories of 'always', 'often', 'occasionally', 'seldom' and 'never'. The data from 160 Canadian university physical education students (equal number of males and females) were subjected to a principal components analysis with varimax (orthogonal) rotation[2]. I selected a five-component solution (training, autocratic, democratic, social support and rewarding behaviours) as the most meaningful. The selected items ($n = 37$) loaded high on the focal component (i.e., >.40) and loaded low on every other component (i.e., <.30).

As none of the selected items referred to the coaching behaviour of teaching skills and strategies, I added seven more items reflecting this behaviour for the second stage (Chelladurai and Saleh,

Table 12.1 Dimensions of leader behaviour in sports

Dimension	Description
Training and instruction	Coaching behaviour aimed at improving the athletes' performance by emphasising and facilitating hard and strenuous training; instructing them in the skills, techniques and tactics of the sport; clarifying the relationship among the members; and by structuring and coordinating the members' activities
Democratic behaviour	Coaching behaviour that allows greater participation by the athletes in decisions pertaining to group goals, practice methods, and game tactics and strategies
Autocratic behaviour	Coaching behaviour that involves independent decision making and stresses personal authority
Social support	Coaching behaviour characterised by a concern for the welfare of individual athletes, positive group atmosphere, and warm interpersonal relations with members
Positive feedback	Coaching behaviour which reinforces an athlete by recognising and rewarding good performance

Source: From Chelladurai, P. (1989). Adapted with permission.

1980). In addition, six more items reflecting social support were added. I also modified the response format to (a) always, (b) often – 75 per cent of the time, (c) occasionally – 50 per cent of the time, (d) seldom – 25 per cent of the time, to (e) never. This modified scale was administered to samples of 102 physical education students (45 males and 57 females) and 223 varsity athletes (all male). The students and athletes completed the preference version with the stem 'I prefer my coach to . . .' and the perception version with the stem 'My coach . . .' Once again, five factors were extracted from the principal components analysis with varimax rotation in each of the three data sets and the items that (a) had their highest loading on the same factor for all three solutions, and (b) loaded at least .30 in two of the solutions were selected. The forty retained items make up the current version of the scale and measure *training and instruction* (thirteen items), *democratic behaviour* (nine items), *autocratic behaviour* (five items), *social support* (eight items) and *positive feedback/rewarding behaviour* (five items). These dimensions of leader behaviour are described in Table 12.1. With different opening stems the scale can be used to measure (a) athletes' preferences for specific leader behaviours (with the stem of 'I prefer my coach to . . .'), (b) athletes' perceptions of their coaches' leader behaviours (with the stem of 'My coach . . .') and/or (c) coaches' perceptions of their own behaviour (with the stem of 'In coaching, I . . .').

LSS dimensions and individual motivation

While the derivation of the LSS dimensions was based on factor analysis of items collected from different existing scales and some self-generated items, later I provided a theoretical justification for the scales as follows (Chelladurai and Carron, 1981): Three of the dimensions of the LSS – training and instruction, positive feedback and social support – could be placed in juxtaposition with Porter and Lawler's (1968) model of individual motivation. That is, training and instruction increase members' ability and role perceptions, which are instrumental to improved performance. Positive feedback reflects equitable distribution of rewards based on performance, which is fundamental to feelings of equity and satisfaction. Social support becomes critical to the effort phase, which is much more prolonged and agonistic in athletics than in other spheres. The remaining two dimensions refer to the manner in which the coach makes decisions that should be distinguished from the substance of those decisions.

Psychometric properties of the LSS

In the development stage reported earlier, the test–retest (after four weeks) reliability estimates derived from the data of fifty-three physical education students were .72 for training and instruction, .82 for democratic behaviour, .76 for autocratic behaviour, .71 for social support and .79 for positive feedback (Chelladurai and Saleh, 1980). These values were considered adequate (Nunnally, 1978). The internal consistency estimates reported by various authors were all well above .70, the usual cut-off point for all versions of the LSS (Chelladurai, 1990), except for autocratic behaviour with considerably lower estimates. In general, the alpha values are relatively higher for the perception version than for the preference version, although the items are identical with only a change in the stem. This is understandable as perceptions are likely to dominate when respondents report both their preferences and perceptions (White, Crino and Hatfield, 1985). Accordingly, it is expected that the expression of those perceptions is to be more consistent across the various items of a sub-scale than would be the case in the expression of preferences.

Recent research carried out in different national contexts and/or using LSS in different languages attests to the robustness of the psychometric properties of the LSS (e.g., Aristotelis, Kaloyan and Evangelos, 2013; Durujlal and Dhurup, 2012; Fletcher and Roberts, 2013; Kwon, Pyunb, Han and Ogasawara, 2011; Thon *et al.*, 2012; Wałach-Bista, 2013). Fletcher and Roberts (2013) noted, 'the weak factorial invariance achieved when testing the LSS over four time points provides good evidence that the LSS is consistently measuring perceptions of leadership behavior over time' (p. 100). Similarly, Kwon *et al.* (2011) tested the multi-group invariance of the LSS (without the dimension of autocratic behaviour) with middle and high school student-athletes in Japan and found that the configural, metric, scalar and factor variance-covariance to be invariant across the two groups.

The low alpha values for the sub-scale of autocratic behaviour in several studies are a continuing concern. The problem may be due to the five items in the scale representing distinct domains of behaviour (Chelladurai and Riemer, 1998). Two of the items refer to the aloofness of the coach (i.e., work relatively independent of the athletes; keep to him/herself), two refer to how the coach handles decisions (i.e., not explain his/her action; refuse to compromise a point) and one seems to deal with how the coach addresses players (i.e., speak in a manner not to be questioned). They certainly do not reflect autocratic behaviour in the traditional sense (i.e., the opposite end of the continuum from democratic behaviour). Further, the LSS does not tap into the transformational leadership that has been recently incorporated into the Multidimensional Model. The proposed dimensions of transformational leadership were described earlier. Future research needs to refine the existing sub-scales and develop new sub-scales to reflect transformational leadership.

Revised leadership scale for sports (RLSS)

I am aware of only one attempt to revise the LSS – that of Zhang, Jensen and Mann (1997). However, their modified version includes the original five dimensions, the instructions and the response format of the original LSS, as well as the same three versions. The only new dimension – *Situational Consideration Behaviours* – was described as behaviours 'aimed at considering the situation factors (such as the time, individual, environment, team and game); setting up individual goals and clarifying ways to reach the goals; differentiating coaching methods at different stages; and assigning an athlete to the right position' (Zhang *et al.*, 1997, pp. 109–10). I had noted elsewhere (Chelladurai, 2007, 2012) that the only new dimension in the revised scale is subsumed by the five dimensions of the original LSS. Accordingly, I suggested that parsimony would indicate the use of the shorter original LSS.

Epilogue

As indicated, the Multidimensional Model has not been tested in its entirety. This lapse is a direct result of the difficulty of measuring the excluded variable (i.e., required leadership) and assessing the congruence among the three states of leader behaviour. Thus, future studies should be focused on testing the model in its entirety, which would necessitate devising a method of estimating what is required behaviour in a given situation and measuring the degree of congruence among the three states of leader behaviour. In addition, it is also necessary that the LSS be revised to include more relevant dimensions of leader behaviours pertinent to the sporting context including various aspects of transformational leadership.

In summary, the formulation of the MML and the development of the LSS were a function of the dearth of literature on those topics and an urgent need for me to get a doctorate degree. Even though my work was simply an integration of streams of previous work, it is still satisfying and flattering that both the MML and the LSS have stood the test of time, continue to be popular with scholars and teachers and were the foundations of considerable research on leadership in sports. But the ground has just been scratched. There is so much work to be done in terms of refining the model and developing better and more comprehensive measures of leadership. As noted, better analytical techniques have to evolve to determine required leadership in a given situation and to measure congruence among the three states of leader behaviour.

Notes

1   This chapter is a reflection on the works of Chelladurai (1990, 2007, 2012) and Chelladurai and Saleh (1980).
2   At that time, I had to use the mainframe computer in my university, which occupied a fairly large room. That computer could not handle more than sixty items in a factor analysis. So I was forced to go the neighbouring university, where I did my doctorate. Even that computer could not carry out factor analysis of more than ninety-nine items. So I had to drop thirty-one items from the original list of 120 items. Further, confirmatory factor analysis was not available in the universities with which I was associated.

References

Aristotelis, G., Kaloyan, K. and Evangelos, B. (2013) 'Leadership style of Greek soccer coaches'. *Journal of Physical Education & Sport*, *13*: 348–53.

Bandura, A. (2005) 'The evolution of social cognitive theory'. In K.G. Smith and M.A. Hitt (eds) *Great minds in management*. (pp. 9–35). New York: Oxford University Press.

Bass, B.M. (1985) *Leadership and performance beyond expectations*. New York: The Free Press.

Chelladurai, P. (1978) 'A contingency model of leadership in athletics'. Unpublished doctoral dissertation, Department of Management Sciences, University of Waterloo, Canada.

Chelladurai, P. (1984) 'Discrepancy between preferences and perceptions of leadership behavior and satisfaction of athletes in varying sports'. *Journal of Sport Psychology*, *6*(1): 27–41.

Chelladurai, P. (1990) 'Leadership in sports: A review'. *International Journal of Sport Psychology*, *21*: 328–54.

Chelladurai, P. (1993) 'Leadership'. In R.N. Singer, M. Murphey and L.K. Tennant (eds) *Handbook of research on sport psychology* (pp. 647–71). New York: Macmillan.

Chelladurai, P. (2007) 'Leadership in sports'. In G. Tenenbaum and R.C. Eklund (eds) *Handbook of sport psychology* (third edn, pp. 113–35). New York: John Wiley.

Chelladurai, P. (2012) 'Leadership and manifestations of sport'. In S. Murphy (ed.) *The handbook of sport and performance psychology* (pp. 328–42). New York: Oxford University Press.

Chelladurai, P. and Carron, A.V. (1978) *Leadership*. Ottawa: CAHPER, Sociology of Sport Monograph Series.

Chelladurai, P. and Carron, A.V. (1981) 'Applicability to youth sports of the leadership scale for sports'. *Perceptual & Motor Skills*, 53: 361–2.

Chelladurai, P. and Carron, A.V. (1983) 'Athletic maturity and preferred leadership'. *Journal of Sport Psychology*, 5: 371–80.

Chelladurai, P., Imamura, H., Yamaguchi, Y., Oinuma, Y. and Miyauchi, T. (1988) 'Sport leadership in a cross-national setting: The case of Japanese and Canadian university athletes'. *Journal of Sport & Exercise Psychology*, 10: 374–89.

Chelladurai, P. Malloy, D., Imamaura, H. and Yamaguchi, Y. (1987) 'A cross-cultural study of preferred leadership in sports'. *Canadian Journal of Sport Sciences*, 12(2): 106–10.

Chelladurai, P. and Riemer, H. (1998) 'Measurement of leadership in sports'. In J.L. Duda (ed.) *Advancements in sport and exercise psychology measurement* (pp. 227–53). Morgantown, WV: Fitness Information Technology.

Chelladurai, P. and Saleh, S.D. (1978) 'Preferred leadership in sports'. *Canadian Journal of Applied Sport Sciences*, 3(2): 85–92.

Chelladurai, P. and Saleh, S.D. (1980) 'Dimensions of leader behavior in sports: Development of a leadership scale'. *Journal of Sport Psychology*, 2: 34–45.

Chelladurai, P. and Saleh, S.D. (2007) 'Dimensions of leader behavior in sports: Development of a leadership scale'. In D. Smith and M. Bar-Eli (eds) *Essential readings in sport and exercise psychology* (pp. 185–9). Champaign, IL: Human Kinetics (reprint of the 1980 article).

Din, C. and Paskevich, D. (2013) 'An integrated research model of Olympic podium performance'. *International Journal of Sports Science & Coaching*, 8(2): 431–44.

Durujlal, J. and Dhurup, M. (2012) 'Athlete preference of coaches' leadership style'. *African Journal for Physical, Health Education, Recreation & Dance*, 18(1): 111–21.

Erle. F.J. (1981) 'Leadership in competitive and recreational sport'. Unpublished master's thesis. University of Western Ontario. London, Canada.

Fiedler, F.E. (1967) *A theory of leadership effectiveness*. New York: McGraw-Hill.

Fleishman, E.A. (1957a) 'A leader behavior description for industry'. In R.M. Stogdill and A.E. Coons (eds) *Leader behavior: Its description and measurement* (pp. 103–19). Columbus, OH: The Ohio State University.

Fleishman, E.A. (1957b) 'The leadership opinion questionnaire'. In R.M. Stogdill and A.E. Coons (eds) *Leader behavior: Its description and measurement* (pp. 120–33). Columbus, OH: The Ohio State University.

Fletcher, R.B. and Roberts, M.H. (2013) 'Longitudinal stability of the Leadership Scale for Sports'. *Measurement in Physical Education & Exercise Science*, 17: 89–104.

Garba, Y.M. (2011) 'Type and gender as predictors of sports leadership behavior patterns in northern Nigeria'. *International Journal of Sports Sciences & Fitness*, 1(2): 188–97.

Garland, D.J. and Barry, J.R. (1988) 'The effects of personality and perceived leader behavior on performance in collegiate football'. *The Psychological Record*, 38: 237–47.

Gordon, S. (1988) 'Decision styles and coaching effectiveness in university soccer'. *Canadian Journal of Sport Sciences*, 13: 56–65.

Halpin, A.W. (1957) 'The leader behavior and effectiveness of aircraft commanders'. In R.M. Stogdill and A.E. Coons (eds) *Leader behavior: Its description and measurement* (pp. 52–64). Columbus, OH: The Ohio State University, Bureau of Business Research.

Horn, T.S., Bloom, P., Berglund, K.M. and Packard, S. (2011) 'Relationship between collegiate athletes' psychological characteristics and their preferences for different types of coaching behavior'. *The Sport Psychologist*, 25: 190–211.

House, R.J. (1971) 'A path-goal theory of leader effectiveness'. *Administrative Science Quarterly*, 16: 321–38.

House, R.J. and Dessler, G. (1974) 'The path-goal theory of leadership: Some post hoc and a priori tests'. In J.G. Hunt and L.L. Larson (eds) *Contingency approaches to leadership* (pp. 29–55). Carbondale, IL: Southern Illinois University Press.

Jowett, S. and Lavallee, D. (2007) *Social psychology in sport*. Champaign, IL: Human Kinetics.

Kim, B.H., Lee, H.K. and Lee, J.Y. (1990) 'A study on the coaches' leadership behavior in sports'. Unpublished manuscript. Korea Sport Science Institute, Seoul.

Kwon, H.H., Pyunb, D.Y., Han, S. and Ogasawara, E. (2011) 'Testing for factorial invariance of the Modified Leadership Scale for Sports: Using a Japanese version'. *Asia Pacific Journal of Education, 31*(1): 65–76.

LeUnes, A. (2008) *Sport psychology* (fourth edn). New York: Psychology Press.

Liukkonen. J. and Salminen, S. (1990, June) 'The athletes' perceptions of leader behavior of Finnish coaches'. Paper presented at the World Congress on Sport for All, Tampere, Finland.

Nunnally, J.C. (1978) *Psychometric theory* (second edn). New York: McGraw-Hill.

Osborn, R.N. and Hunt, J.G. (1975) 'An adaptive-reactive theory of leadership: The role of macro variables in leadership research'. In J.G. Hunt and L.L. Larson (eds) *Leadership frontiers* (pp. 27–44). Kent, OH: Kent State University.

Porter, L.W. and Lawler, E.E. (1968) *Managerial attitudes and performance*. Homewood, IL: Irwin-Dorsey.

Riemer, H.A. and Chelladurai, P. (1995) 'Leadership and satisfaction in athletics'. *Journal of Sport & Exercise Psychology, 17*: 216–93.

Riemer, H.A. and Chelladurai, P. (1998) 'Development of the Athlete Satisfaction Questionnaire (ASQ)'. *Journal of Sport & Exercise Psychology, 20*: 127–56.

Schliesman, E.S. (1987) 'Relationship between the congruence of preferred and actual leader behavior and subordinate satisfaction with leadership'. *Journal of Sport Behavior, 10*: 151–66.

Serpa, S. (1990) 'Research work on sport leadership in Portugal'. Unpublished manuscript. Lisbon Technical University.

Serpa, S., Pataeo, V. and Santos, E. (1991) 'Leadership patterns in handball international competition'. *International Journal of Sport Psychology, 22*: 78–89.

Stogdill, R.M. (1963) *Manual for the leader behavior description questionnaire-form XII*. Columbus. OH: The Ohio State University, Bureau of Business Research.

Terry, P.C. (1984) 'The coaching preferences of elite athletes competing at Universiade '83'. *The Canadian Journal of Applied Sport Sciences*, 9: 201–8.

Thon, R.A., Passos, P.C.B., da Costa, L.C.A., Prates, M.E.F., do Nascimento, Jr, J.R.A. and Vieira, L.F. (2012) 'Leadership style in the context swimming coaches in the state of Paraná'. *Brazilian Journal of Kinanthropometry & Human Performance, 14*: 527–34.

Toros, T., Türksoy, A. and Doğaner, S. (2013) 'The comparison of basketball coaches' leadership and motivation according to length of experience'. *Nigde University Journal of Physical Education & Sport Sciences*, 7(1): 9–15.

Wałach-Bista, Z. (2013) 'A Polish adaptation of leadership scale for sports – A questionnaire examining coaching behavior'. *Human Movement, 14*: 265–74.

Weinberg, R. and Gould, D. (2015) *Foundations of sport and exercise psychology* (sixth edn). Champaign, IL: Human Kinetics.

Weiss, M.R. and Friedrichs, W.D. (1986) 'The influence of leader behaviors, coach attributes, and institutional variables on performance and satisfaction of collegiate basketball reams'. *Journal of Sport Psychology, 8*: 332–46.

White, M.C., Crino, M.D. and Hatfield, J.D. (1985) 'An empirical examination of the parsimony of perceptual congruence scores'. *Academy of Management Journal, 28*: 732–7.

Zhang, J., Jensen, B.E. and Mann, B.L. (1997) 'Modification and revision of the Leadership Scale for Sport'. *Journal of Sport Behavior, 20*: 105–21.

Applying the Multidimensional Model of Leadership

Aubrey Kent[1]

I came by my interest in leadership – and Chelladurai's (Chella) Multidimensional Model of Leadership (MML) – early in my studies. As an undergraduate at the University of Toronto, I studied with emeritus professor Juri Daniel, who introduced me to the concept of leading in organisations, and with whom I conducted my first research study, utilising the leader behaviour description questionnaire (LBDQ). From there, I was fortunate to work with several leading leadership scholars through my graduate studies, including Bob Boucher and Jim Weese at the University of Windsor, and Chella himself at the Ohio State University. Long a hotbed of cutting-edge leadership scholarship, Ohio State is also, ironically, where the LBDQ originated. My first published work emanated from my master's thesis, which investigated the influence of leadership on the cultures and ultimate performance of sport governing bodies (Kent and Weese, 2000). From there, under Chella's guidance, my investigations of leadership became more incisive as I became very interested in the MML tenet of 'congruence' and in the value of self-other analysis. Together, we endeavoured to understand the nature of how leadership interactions can have a 'cascading' effect on followers (Kent and Chelladurai, 2001, 2003).

While my interests have broadened to attitudes in a more general sense, leadership and the MML have remained central to my teaching of undergraduate and graduate students. Chella's MML evolved to encapsulate the idea that a truly transformational leader can shape their antecedents – which is a central theme in teaching about the value of leadership to any organisation. I talk often about the congruence hypothesis and how leaders can work towards ensuring it by seeing the big picture impact of their management of antecedents, as defined by the MML. This leads to lessons in understanding the competitive environment (situation), the value of self-awareness and authenticity (leader), and all manner of discussions about understanding the person-side of organisations (group) such as personality, attitudes and group dynamics.

As for the future of the MML, I think that it remains as relevant and instructive today as it ever has – a testament to its quality. While the genesis of the MML was taking several mainstream leadership theories and representing them more holistically, an opportunity to break away from traditionally derivative work exists in studying the possibility of distinct characteristics and/or impacts of leadership within certain sporting contexts. With the MML as a foundational theory for any sport management scholar to understand, indeed this work has already begun (e.g., Swanson and Kent, 2014).

Note

1   Aubrey Kent is with the School of Tourism and Hospitality Management at Temple University.

References

Kent, A. and Chelladurai, P. (2001) 'Leadership and employee attitudes: A case study in intercollegiate athletics'. *Journal of Sport Management, 15*: 135–59.

Kent, A. and Chelladurai, P. (2003) 'Multiple sources of leadership and employee reactions in a State parks and recreation department'. *Journal of Park & Recreation Administration, 21*: 39–61.

Kent, A. and Weese, W.J. (2000) 'Do effective sport organizations have better executive leadership and/or organizational cultures? A study of selected sport organizations in Canada'. *European Journal for Sport Management, 17*(2): 4–21.

Swanson, S. and Kent, A. (2014) 'The complexity of leading in sport: Examining the role of domain expertise in assessing leader credibility and prototypicality'. *Journal of Sport Management, 28*: 81–93.

13

ORGANISATIONAL JUSTICE THEORY DEVELOPMENT[1]

Dan Mahony

Overview

In this chapter, I am going to discuss my interest and work in organisational justice. Although organisational justice has a long history of research in other settings, the first study in sport management was published only about twenty years ago. My initial goal was to extend the theory by applying it to sport, but I also believe some of our findings, including the identification of sub-principles of need, could be applied outside of sport. While I will focus primarily on our efforts to apply this theory in a sport setting, we have recently begun to examine organisational justice in higher education. I will discuss that work and the reason for this change of focus briefly at the end of the chapter.

Before discussing my work with my colleagues, it is important to first provide a general explanation of organisational justice. Organisational justice research examines perceptions of fairness and their impact on the workplace (Greenberg, 1990). These perceptions can be based on a variety of factors and can vary across individuals. In other words, different people can come to different conclusions about whether a particular organisation is acting fairly and the factors they examine in making this determination may be different. While individuals may not agree on what determines fairness, there are some general patterns and this is the focus of organisational justice research. In addition, research has found perceptions of organisational justice impact a number of key organisational variables, including job satisfaction, organisational commitment, organisational citizenship behaviours, trust, turnover intentions and ultimately job performance (e.g., Colquitt *et al.*, 2001; Cropanzano *et al.*, 2001; Fitzgerald, Mahony and Crawford, 2014).

Although the issue of fairness is not new, research on organisational justice did not start until recently. Scholars have identified three major aspects of organisational justice: distributive justice, procedural justice and interactional justice (Greenberg, 1990). The development of these three areas all pre-dated the work focused on sport and my work that began in the 1990s. Because all of our work in sport used research from other settings, it is important to first discuss this research and the major aspects of organisational justice.

Distributive justice

The research on organisational justice began with the focus on the fairness of the distributions. While there was some earlier work (Stouffer *et al.*, 1949), the research on distributive justice increased after the development of Adams' (1963, 1965) Equity Theory. This theory suggests individuals engage in a comparison of their inputs and outcomes relative to others' in order to determine if what they received was fair. Adams believed that when the ratios were equal, then individuals perceived the distributions as fair. However, if they perceived the ratios as unfair, individuals would perceive the distributions as unfair and would then do something to restore fairness (e.g., work harder, work less hard, ask for a raise). Overall, the theory suggests individuals believe they should be rewarded based on their contributions to the organisation. This became known as the equity or contribution principle in the literature. The next question was 'what is considered a valuable contribution to the organisation?' Tornblom and Jonsson (1985) identified three possible contributions, labelled as sub-principles of equity: productivity, effort and ability. However, as I will discuss later, there are more sub-principles of equity across organisation types and any research on distributive justice should first determine these possible contributions in the setting being examined.

In addition, later research suggested there are other ways resources can be distributive that do not involve examining the contribution of an individual or group. Deutsch (1975) suggested two other possibilities: equality and need. He further argued the use of equality or need instead of equity was often based on the goals of the organisation. For example, organisations are more likely to base distributions on equality when positive relationships among employees and co-operation among employees are important (Deutsch, 1975). Like equity, there were several methods or sub-principles when making distributions based on equality. According to Tornblom and Jonsson (1985), distributions could be made to all groups or individuals equally in a given distribution (equality of treatment), distributions could be equalised over time across more than one distribution (equality of results), or all groups or individuals could have an equal chance to receive a particular resource (equality of opportunity). Need is also used when co-operative relationships and survival of members of the group are important (Deutsch, 1975). Originally, need was considered to be a fairly clear principle with those having fewer resources being seen as having greater needs. However, as will be discussed, the examination of sport distributions suggested need was far more complex and this complexity has also been found in other settings.

Procedural justice

While distributions are important, later research focused on procedural justice. Procedural justice examined perceptions of the fairness of the procedures used to make distributions (Greenberg, 1990). Work in this area began with Thibault and Walker (1975), who focused on procedural justice in dispute resolution and found that control within the process of making decisions was important when people were determining if it was fair. Later research in an organisational setting found a number of aspects of the procedures were important when assessing procedural justice, including consistency, suppression of bias, use of accurate information, opportunities to correct for mistakes, and allowing for input when developing the process and making the decisions (Greenberg, 1986; Leventhal, 1980). Although there is sometimes a relationship between perceptions of distributive justice and procedural justice, they are distinct variables and can impact key organisational variables differently. For example, research suggests that distributive justice is a better predictor of satisfaction, while procedural justice is a better predictor of organisational commitment (e.g., Dailey and Kirk, 1992; Folger and Konovsky, 1989; McFarlin and Sweeney, 1992).

Interactional justice

The third aspect of organisational justice to be examined was interactional justice. Interactional justice focuses on the perceptions of fairness based on the interpersonal treatment received by the employee and the methods used for communicating throughout the decision-making process (Bies and Moag, 1986). Bies and Moag suggested there were a number of factors that impacted employees' perceptions of interactional justice, including truthfulness, justifications used for decisions, respect from management and avoiding inappropriate comments. While there has been some disagreement about whether interactional justice is distinct from distributive justice and procedural justice, an overall assessment of the research in this area suggests that it is distinct (Cohen-Charash and Spector, 2001; Colquitt *et al.*, 2001). Greenberg (1993) suggested that interactional justice should actually be split into two dimensions: interpersonal justice and informational justice. While there is some support for Greenberg's (1993) model (Colquitt *et al.*, 2001), it is not yet widely accepted or used (Bies, 2005).

Process

My interest in organisational justice in sport began when I was a doctoral student in sport management at Ohio State University in 1992. Dr Mary Hums was a presenter in one of our graduate classes and she discussed her dissertation, which was the first attempt at examining organisational justice in a sport management setting. I found the theory, as well as her study, very interesting. However, my primary research focus was on sport consumer behaviour, so I did not explore organisational justice further until a year and half later. In the spring of 1994, I was preparing for my comprehensive exams and Dr Packinathian Chellardurai gave me two options for his question. One of those options was to focus on expanding the application of organisational justice in sport management. Because I was already interested in organisational justice, this was the more appealing option. When preparing for this question, I spent a considerable amount of time examining the literature and developing a number of future research questions. By the time I completed my comprehensive exam, I decided to utilise what I had done with this exam question and develop another line of research after completing my dissertation.

Reason for interest

I believe my interest in organisational justice as a theoretical framework was closely tied to my experience and interest in serving in leadership roles. I have been in leadership roles for most of my life, starting with serving as class president when I was eleven years old. I learned early on that I could accomplish very little on my own and in order to be successful, it was important to have others actively engaged. This perspective has only increased as I have managed larger and more complex operations. Over time, I have come to realise that my role is largely about managing morale and keeping people motivated towards achieving the organisation's goals. Because organisational justice impacts a number of key organisational variables, including job satisfaction, organisational commitment, organisational citizenship behaviours, trust, turnover intentions and ultimately job performance (e.g., Colquitt *et al.*, 2001, Cropanzano *et al.*, 2001; Fitzgerald *et al.*, 2014), it has always been clear to me that understanding organisational justice perceptions and their impact is important to those in leadership roles.

Moreover, the organisational justice framework has always made intuitive sense to me. I believe organisations send messages about what is important by how they distribute resources. So, these distributions are not only important because of their direct impact on employees (e.g., increase in salary), but also because the distributions let people know about the organisation's priorities. In addition, I believe the procedures and the interactions have an important impact and have found this to be the case in my various leadership roles. However, prior researchers have also suggested that organisational setting is important and has an impact on what is perceived as being fair (Deutsch, 1975), so one cannot assume perceptions are consistent across settings. I have certainly found this to be the case in my own experiences. For example, the expectation of faculty regarding their level of involvement in the process of making salary distribution decisions of colleagues is considerably different from the expectations among my fellow employees when I worked for the accounting firm of Peat Marwick Main. Faculty members expect to be involved, and sometimes very involved, while the accountants did not expect to be involved at all in the decisions regarding the compensation of other accountants at the same level. Therefore, I saw value in examining organisational justice in sport organisations, and primarily in intercollegiate athletics. More recently, I have begun to examine higher education for similar reasons.

Early organisational justice research in sport management

My research really built from the research project Dr Hums presented to our class in 1992. Hums and Chelladurai (1994) focused on intercollegiate athletics and examined the distribution of a variety of resources (facilities, support services and money) and differences based on gender, NCAA division and position (e.g., coach, administrator). They also began the process of revising the distribution principles for college athletics by defining productivity as wins and adding spectator appeal as a new principle. Hums and Chelladurai found that while there were some group differences, the respondents in all groups consistently indicated a preference for equality of treatment, need and equality of results over the other principles.

These results surprised me. As a former athletic department employee and a scholar who had examined resource distribution in intercollegiate athletics, at least at a cursory level, this seemed completely inconsistent with what I had observed. While it is hard to examine facility and support service distributions, the distribution of financial resources is easier. So, I decided to examine the actual distribution of resources in intercollegiate athletics as a next step in this line of research (Mahony and Pastore, 1998). Fortunately, the NCAA has been collecting data from institutions about revenues and expenses, as well as number of sports and participation opportunities by gender, since the 1970s.

While there had been a shift in resources and opportunities that favour women during the twenty-year period we examined, this shift appeared to be more related to legislation (e.g., Title IX, Civil Rights Restoration Act of 1988) than a belief that distributions based on equality or need were most fair (Mahony and Pastore, 1998). In fact, during the period between the *Grove City v. Bell* (1984) and the Civil Rights Restoration Act of 1988, when Title IX's implications for intercollegiate athletics was essentially removed, resource shifts to women's sports stopped. This shift began again only after the Civil Rights Restoration Act re-established Title IX's impact on intercollegiate athletics. In addition, the shift to women's sports appeared to have no impact on the revenue-generating sports of football and men's basketball, which continued to be the largest growth area in the budget, and had a much greater impact on men's non-revenue sports (Mahony and Pastore, 1998). This clearly indicated an emphasis on the importance of spectator appeal in distributing resources, as opposed to equality or need.

Attempts to understand inconsistencies

The inconsistency between the findings of Hums and Chelladurai (1994) and my first organisational justice study (Mahony and Pastore, 1998) led to our next research project. We did several things in the next study to see if we could better understand the inconsistency in the results (Mahony, Hums and Riemer, 2002). First, we decided to focus on only the distributions of money. This is the resource for which we could clearly see the difference between the two studies, so it made sense to focus on it. Second, we decided to focus on only those in the decision-making positions regarding financial resource distributions. We surveyed athletic directors and athletic board chairs, because athletic boards ultimately approve budgets. Third, we added several principles. Revenue production was added as a sub-principle of equity. While spectator appeal and revenue production are closely related, we thought the term revenue production would elicit a different reaction among respondents. The principle of equal percentages (i.e., all receive the same percentage increase or decrease) was added based on feedback from respondents in the prior study. We also believed there may be more to the principle of need than simply the concept that those who have less need more. Therefore, we had three need sub-principles – need to survive (women's sport), need to survive (men's non-revenue sport) and need to be successful. Fourth, we asked about the likelihood of each principle being used. We believed this might be the most important question because it is possible one may believe a particular principle is most fair (e.g., equality, need), but feel compelled to make distributions based on another principle (e.g., revenue production). This could alone explain the differences in the results in the prior studies. All of these changes were examples of theory building in an effort to better understand the operations of intercollegiate athletics.

Although we made these changes from the Hums and Chelladurai (1994) study, the results did not differ considerably (Mahony *et al.*, 2002). In this study, the need sub-principles were considered to be the most fair and only equality of treatment was also considered to be fair (i.e., past the mid-point on the seven-point scale). Moreover, respondents indicated the three need sub-principles were also more likely to be used. In fact, the respondents indicated strong consistency between what they perceived as being fair and what was likely to be used. On one level this made sense. Our respondents were the decision-makers, so there should be consistency between what they perceive as being fair and what is actually done in the organisation. On the other hand, the findings still suggested a conflict with the findings in Mahony and Pastore (1998). In particular, the support for need to survive (men's non-revenue sports) was in direct conflict with the actual decisions that were being made.

Because we believed understanding the need principle was important, we added a few open-ended questions at the end of the survey used for the Mahony *et al.* (2002) study. The analysis of these questions led to the Mahony, Hums and Riemer (2005) study, which I believe may have been a more important contribution to theory development and the organisational justice literature. The questions simply asked what men's and women's sports were perceived as having the greatest need and why. At both the NCAA Division I-A (FBS) and Division III levels, the sport with the greatest need was football. This suggested at least some consistency between the strong support for need in Mahony *et al.* (2002) and Hums and Chelladurai (1994) and the actual distributions examined in Mahony and Pastore (1998).

More importantly, we identified three sub-principles of need. The first, need due to lack of resources, was aligned with the traditional definition of need in the literature (i.e., those with less need more). However, the second two sub-principles, need due to high costs and need to be competitively successful, were additions to the literature. These principles explain how participants could perceive football as having the greatest needs. The sport has higher costs for several reasons (e.g., more players, high equipment costs) and could be perceived as needing to spend more because competing institutions are also spending more on football.

Moreover, while our focus was on developing sub-principles of need for the college athletics setting, the three sub-principles identified could be useful in studying other organisational types.

One could imagine why leaders in a wide variety of organisations may make allocation decisions based on the naturally higher costs associated with activities in some areas of their organisations or on the need to be successful in competing with rival organisations. For example, higher education academic leaders often allocate more resources to those departments with higher costs associated with the work of faculty in the area (e.g., lab space, equipment) and pay different salaries to faculty in departments in which the salaries at competing organisations are higher (e.g., law, medicine, business). Therefore, I believe we expanded the organisational justice literature beyond sport in this particular study.

As a follow-up to this study, we examined the fairness of three sub-principles of need developed in Mahony et al. (2005), as well as the most popular sub-principles of equality (e.g., equality of treatment) and equity (e.g., revenue production) (Patrick, Mahony and Petrosko, 2008). In this study, we also changed the scenarios. In the prior studies, the reasons for distributions and budget reductions were related to a neutral source (e.g., increased donations and bad economy; Hums and Chelladurai, 1994; Mahony et al., 2002). We believed it was possible that one of the reasons there was less support for revenue production and spectator appeal was that the change in funding was not related to the activities of the sports producing more revenue. Therefore, we added scenarios in which the changes were described as being directly related to the success or failures of these sports. We again focused on those in higher administration positions (i.e., athletic directors and senior women's administrators) at Division I and III institutions.

The results indicated that need due to lack of resources was viewed positively across scenarios, divisions and genders, so we again found support for a principle that did not appear to be used frequently, particularly at the Division I level. There were the predicted differences based on gender, with women preferring equality and men preferring revenue production, and on division, with Division I perceiving revenue production and need to be competitively successful as more fair. However, while there were also some differences across scenarios, the general preference across groups and scenarios for need due to lack of resources was consistent.

While these studies were informative, we consistently found some inconsistencies between what was actually done and the responses regarding fairness and likelihood of use. We decided to conduct a study examining the perspectives of college students (Mahony, Riemer, Breeding and Hums, 2006). There were several reasons for this study. We questioned the honesty of the responses in the previous studies and believed participants were simply providing the socially appropriate responses as opposed to what they truly believed. We thought students might be more honest when answering the questions. We also focused on those who would be future leaders in sport organisations (i.e., sport management students) and those who were impacted by the distribution decisions (i.e., student athletes). We divided them into five groups: (a) male non-athletes, (b) male revenue sport athletes, (c) male non-revenue sport athletes, (d) female non-athletes, and (e) female athletes. In addition, we were interested in examining if the results would be different in a for-profit sport organisation, so we examined their perceptions of distributive justice principles for a sporting goods company (i.e., New Balance).

In many ways, the results were similar to those we had found in the earlier studies with coaches and administrators. The students preferred equality of treatment and need over all of the other principles and this was consistent for all five groups. There were some group differences, but in contrast to prior research in organisational justice they were not simply gender differences. Male revenue sport athletes and male non-athletes tended to prefer equity or contribution more, while male non-revenue athletes and women athletes tended to prefer equality more. The responses appear to be based on self-interest. Male revenue sport athletes would benefit if revenue production and spectator appeal were used, while the other athletes would do better under a system that focuses on equality. Moreover, in the sporting goods scenarios, which eliminated any self-interest, there were no significant differences between the groups. Therefore, self-interest did appear to impact responses.

We believe this finding could have important implications for organisational justice literature in general. When prior research found women tended to prefer equality and men preferred equity (e.g., Hums and Chelladurai, 1994; Major, Bylsma and Cozzarelli, 1989), the explanation provided was that women tend to be more compassionate and are more concerned with looking out for the best interests of all, while men are more competitive. However, the results in Mahony *et al.* (2006) suggest another possibility. The preference by women for equality in distributions may be because they perceive the equity based systems to be biased against them and the only way to get a 'fair' share is through a system that has no subjectivity (i.e., equality of treatment). While more research is still needed to determine the impact of gender and self-interest on perceptions of fairness of distributive justice principles, this study suggests such research is warranted.

Extensions and applications

After these studies, I continued to be involved in research on organisational justice in intercollegiate athletics (Andrew *et al.*, 2009; Kim *et al.*, 2008) and applications of organisational justice in other sport settings (Dittmore *et al.*, 2009). However, my interest in examining organisational justice in sport organisations began to decline and the new studies were student initiated. Frankly, I was continually frustrated by the clear differences between the realities we observed (Mahony and Pastore, 1998) and the respondents' indication of what they perceived as fair and what their athletic departments would be likely to do. Despite these frustrations, I do think some of our findings added to the literature in sport and beyond. As previously discussed, I think the development of different sub-principles for need has wide applications (Mahony *et al.*, 2005). I also believe the findings in Mahony *et al.* (2006) related to gender and self-interest have the potential to change a widely accepted theory regarding gender differences related to fairness perceptions. Overall, I believe this line of research has made a contribution to the literature and I have seen others expand the work and believe there is still potential to do more.

In fact, the inconsistences raise many questions that could be examined. While this would go beyond research on organisational justice, I suspect there may be something within the culture of intercollegiate athletics that has impacted the responses in this line of research. There appears to be a strong need within this culture to 'stick to the story'. The 'story' impacting this line of research is that athletic departments are not businesses and are not about generating revenue, and their main goal is to treat all student athletes equally and provide them what they need to have a great experience. Regardless of which group we asked or how we changed the scenarios or options, all groups kept to this story. In his book, former NCAA executive director Walter Byers (1995) discussed the related attempt to create and then maintain the myth of amateurism and the student-athlete over many years. More recently, those involved with intercollegiate athletics have continued this approach and frequently discuss the collegiate model in contrast to the professional model. The fact that this 'story' is being challenged at the time this is being written in 2014, by the O'Bannon case and Northwestern football players' attempt to unionize, will likely strengthen the need to be consistent when stakeholders describe the goals and practices of intercollegiate athletics. I believe examining the culture of intercollegiate athletics and the consistency of beliefs within this culture, and perhaps comparing it with different cultures across organisational types, would be an interesting direction for research.

Transitioning to examinations of higher education

Regardless, my curiosity about distributive justice has been moving in a new direction. By 2004, I was a full-time higher education administrator and became more interested in organisational justice in this setting. This interest increased when I moved in to the role of dean and was responsible for making distribution decisions on a daily basis. I saw clear applications for organisational justice in the higher education setting and thought research would be valuable to the literature and to my daily work. In addition, I believed the responses would be very different from what we found in intercollegiate athletics. While consistency of thought and group mentality is valued in intercollegiate athletics, I find the opposite to be true in the academic world. Faculty members frequently and openly question decisions of administrators as well as the direction of the university and higher education in general. Moreover, even mid-level administrators openly disagree with the upper administration. In my experiences, consistency of thought is simply not valued in this setting.

We began this line of research by ascertaining the key contributions in this setting. Because contributions and their importance vary across organisational types, this appeared to be a logical first step. The study involved interviewing several deans and identified five possible contributions or sub-principles of equity: (a) quantity and quality of research publications, (b) external research funding, (c) quality of teaching, (d) impact on students and (e) quality service (Bradley Hnat, Mahony, Fitzgerald and Crawford, 2015).

As a follow-up to this study, we surveyed university administrators (deans and department chairs). In the first study from this dataset, we were interested in examining the perceptions of fairness of various distributive justice principles and the likelihood they would be used (Fitzgerald, Mahony, Crawford and Bradley Hnat, 2014). This was similar to the study we did with administrators in intercollegiate athletics (Mahony *et al.*, 2002). We had two scenarios – one involved distributing resources to faculty and the other involved distributing resources to academic programmes. When examining the distributive justice principles, we used the principles identified in Bradley Hnat *et al.* (2015) and added two other equity principles in the academic programme scenario based on a review of the literature (i.e., enrolment growth, student credit hours produced). We used only equality of treatment to assess equality because it is the equality sub-principles that received the strongest support in prior research (Patrick *et al.*, 2008). We also used all three need sub-principles identified in Mahony *et al.* (2005). This gave us an opportunity to examine if these need sub-principles could be used in another setting.

We found academic administrators generally believed that compensating faculty members and allocating resources to departments based on the quality of teaching and impact on students was most fair (Fitzgerald *et al.*, 2014). While there were some differences across institution types (i.e., research universities vs. other institutions), these principles were consistently at the top of the list. However, they believed factors such as research productivity, funding secured and need to be competitively successful were more likely to be used. Need due to high costs, enrollment growth and student credit hours produced were also perceived as fair in the academic programme scenario. The results also indicated that equal distributions and distributions based on need due to less resources were not perceived as fair or likely to be used.

These results were interesting in a couple of ways. First, the responses were very different from what occurred in the intercollegiate athletic studies. In this case, the principles perceived as fair and those identified as most likely to be used were the opposite (i.e., not equality and need due to less resources). Second, there were large differences between what was perceived as being fair and likely to be used. This was not the case in the intercollegiate athletics studies (Mahony *et al.*, 2002). Moreover, the administrators being surveyed appear to be in decision-making positions, but still did not believe resources would be distributed the way they thought was most fair. This may support my earlier suggestion that the culture in these two organisations is very different.

Future directions

The initial findings in higher education have encouraged us to explore this further. We are currently working on two additional papers from the survey of administrators exploring the impact of organisational justice on organisational commitment, job satisfaction and turnover intentions. We have also begun to collect data from faculty using a similar survey and will likely explore other higher education stakeholders in the future. As a former dean of an education college, I have also become interested in exploring organisational justice in K-12 education settings. Again, this has largely been ignored and the rapid changes in teacher evaluation and compensation plans make this an ideal time for such research. I have also discussed the possibility of exploring the interaction between organisational justice and social justice in various education settings. Overall, while I have moved this line of research away from sport, my interest in organisational justice remains and I am excited about all of the future possibilities.

Note

1   This chapter is a reflection on Mahony *et al.* (2010) and the work related to it.

References

Adams, J.S. (1963) 'Toward an understanding of inequity'. *Journal of Abnormal & Social Psychology*, 67: 422–36.

Adams, J.S. (1965) 'Inequity in social exchange'. In L. Berkowitz (ed.) *Advances in experimental social psychology* (Vol. 2, pp. 267–99). New York: Academic Press.

Andrew, D.P.S., Kim, S., Mahony, D.F. and Hums, M. (2009) 'Outcomes of distributive justice: Perceptions in intercollegiate athletics'. *International Journal of Sport Management*, 10: 474–98.

Bies, R.J. (2005) 'Are procedural and interactional justice conceptually distinct?' In J. Greenberg and J.A. Colquitt (eds) *Handbook of organizational justice* (pp. 85–112). Mahwah, NJ: Lawrence Erlbaum.

Bies, R.J. and Moag, J.S. (1986) 'Interactional justice: Communication criteria of fairness'. *Research on Negotiation in Organizations*, 1: 43–55.

Bradley Hnat, H., Mahony, D., Fitzgerald, S. and Crawford, F. (2015) 'Organizational justice and higher education resource allocation: Perceptions of fairness'. *Innovative Higher Education*, 40: 79–93.

Byers, W. (1995) *Unsportsmanlike conduct: Exploiting college athletes*. Ann Arbor, MI: University of Michigan Press.

Cohen-Charash, Y. and Spector, P.E. (2001) 'The role of justice in organizations: A meta-analysis'. *Organizational Behavior and Human Decision Processes*, 86: 278–321.

Colquitt, J.A., Conlon, D.E., Wesson, M.J., Porter, C.O.L.H. and Ng, K.Y. (2001) 'Justice at the millennium: A meta-analytic review of 25 years of organizational justice review'. *Journal of Applied Psychology*, 86: 425–45.

Cropanzano, R., Rupp, D.E., Mohler, C.J. and Schminke, M. (2001) 'Three roads to organizational justice'. In Ferris, G.R. (ed.) *Research in personnel and human resources management* (vol. 20, pp. 1–113). Oxford, UK: JAI Press/Elsevier Science.

Dailey, R.C. and Kirk, D.J. (1992) 'Distributive and procedural justice as antecedents of job dissatisfaction and intent to turnover'. *Human Relations*, 45: 305–17.

Deutsch, M. (1975) 'Equity, equality, and need: What determines which value will be used as the basis of distributive justice?' *Journal of Social Issues*, 31: 137–49.

Dittmore, S.W., Mahony, D.F., Andrew, D.P.S. and Hums, M.A. (2009) 'Examining fairness perceptions of financial resource allocations in U.S. Olympic sport'. *Journal of Sport Management*, 23: 429–56.

Fitzgerald, S., Mahony, D. and Crawford, F. (2014) 'The relationship between organizational justice perceptions and organizational commitment, job satisfaction, and turnover intentions'. Presented at the Eastern Educational Research Association Conference, Jacksonville, Florida.

Fitzgerald, S.M., Mahony, D., Crawford, F. and Bradley Hnat, H. (2014) 'Distributive justice in higher education: Perceptions of administrators'. *Innovative Higher Education, 39*: 401–15.

Folger, R. and Konovsky, M.A. (1989) 'Effects of procedural and distributive justice on reactions to pay raise decisions'. *Academy of Management Journal, 32*: 115–30.

Greenberg, J. (1986) 'Determinants of perceived fairness of performance evaluations'. *Journal of Applied Psychology, 71*: 340–2.

Greenberg, J. (1990) 'Organizational justice: Yesterday, today, and tomorrow'. *Journal of Management, 16*: 399–432.

Greenberg, J. (1993) 'Stealing in the name of justice: Informational and interpersonal moderators of theft reactions to underpayment inequity'. *Organizational Behavior and Human Decision Processes, 54*: 81–103.

Hums, M.A. and Chelladurai, P. (1994) 'Distributive justice in intercollegiate athletics: The views of NCAA coaches and administrators'. *Journal of Sport Management, 8*: 200–17.

Kim, S., Andrew, D.P.S., Mahony, D.F. and Hums, M.A. (2008) 'Distributive justice in intercollegiate athletics: Perceptions of student athletes'. *International Journal of Sport Management, 9*: 379–93.

Leventhal, G.S. (1980) 'What should be done with equity theory? New approaches to the study of fairness in social relationships'. In K.S. Gergen, M.S. Greenberg and R.H. Willis (eds) *Social exchange: Advances in theory and research* (pp. 27–55). New York: Plenum Press.

McFarlin, D.B. and Sweeney, P.D. (1992) 'Research notes. Distributive and procedural justice as predictors of satisfaction with personal and organizational outcomes'. *Academy of Management Journal, 35*: 626–37.

Mahony, D.F. and Pastore, D.M. (1998) 'An examination of participation opportunities, revenues, and expenses at NCAA institutions – 1973–1993'. *Journal of Sport & Social Issues, 22*: 127–52.

Mahony, D.F., Hums, M.A. and Riemer, H. (2002) 'Distributive justice in intercollegiate athletics'. *Journal of Sport Management, 16*: 31–356.

Mahony, D.F., Hums, M.A. and Riemer, H. (2005) 'Bases for determining need: Perspectives of intercollegiate athletic directors and athletic board chairs'. *Journal of Sport Management, 19*: 170–92.

Mahony, D.F., Riemer, H.A., Breeding, J.L. and Hums, M.A. (2006) 'Organizational justice in sport organizations: Perceptions of student-athletes and other college students'. *Journal of Sport Management, 20*: 159–88.

Mahony, D.F., Hums, M.A., Andrew, D.P. and Dittmore, S.W. (2010) 'Organizational justice in sport'. *Sport Management Review, 13*: 91–105.

Major, B., Bylsma, W.H. and Cozzarelli, C. (1989) 'Gender differences in distributive justice principles: The impact of domain'. *Sex Roles, 21*: 478–97.

Patrick, I.S.C., Mahony, D.F. and Petrosko, J.M. (2008) 'Distributive justice in intercollegiate athletics: Perceptions of equality, revenue production, and need'. *Journal of Sport Management, 22*: 165–83.

Stouffer, S.A., Suchman, E.A., DeVinney, L.C., Star, S.A. and Williams, R.M., Jr (1949) *The American soldier: Adjustment during Army life* (Vol. 1). Clinton, MA: Colonial Press.

Thibault, J. and Walker, L. (1975) *Procedural justice: A psychological analysis*. Hillsdale, NJ: Erlbaum.

Tornblom, K.Y. and Jonsson, D.R. (1985) 'Subrules of the equality and contribution principles: Their perceived fairness in distribution and retribution'. *Social Psychology Quarterly, 48*: 249–61.

Applying organisational justice theory

Jeremy S. Jordan[1]

The substantial body of work examining organisational justice in sport organisations by Mahony and his various co-authors has had a significant impact on my research and the advancement of organisational justice research in sport management. Research by Mahony and Pastore (1998), along with Hums and Chelladurai (1994), is generally considered some of the first in sport management and was foundational for subsequent work by other scholars in the field.

Similar to the evolution of organisational justice research outside of sport management, Mahony's initial focus was on the dimension of distributive justice, the perceived fairness of resource allocations. His work was based on that of Adams (1965), Homans (1961) and Greenberg (1990), among others, and focused on how and why resources were allocated in intercollegiate athletics. This line of research examined the distribution principles of equity, equality and need and the relative fairness of each method when allocating resources. To understand the impact of each distribution process, Mahony and colleagues sampled coaches, athletic administrators, athletic board chairs and sport management students throughout a variety of studies (see Mahony, Hums, Andrew and Dittmore, 2010). In addition to understanding the allocation principles of distributive justice that were deemed most fair by each of these groups, Mahony *et al.* (2002; 2005; 2006) deconstructed the principle of need by identifying sub-principles of need that seemed to be operating in intercollegiate athletics (2005). This work, along with that of Hums and Chelladurai (1994), did much to advance understanding of distributive justice in sport management and also contributed to the broader examination of organisational justice in non-sport settings.

The work by Mahony and colleagues has informed my research on organisational justice and that of many other scholars in sport management who have worked to expand not only understanding of distributive justice but also the other dimensions of justice. The thorough examination of how distributive justice operates in sport organisations undertaken by Mahony has allowed other researchers, including me, to build upon his work by examining how procedural, interactional and informational justice interact with distributive justice and the influence these interactions have on organisational relevant attitudes and behaviours. Additionally, review of work completed by Mahony and his co-authors provides an example of a systematic line of research that tests theory by building upon previous findings to develop appropriate hypotheses moving forward. The development of a systematic line of enquiry is critical to extending understanding of theory in a coherent and organised manner. Sport management as a discipline continues to mature, based on the development of systematic lines of enquiry such as that initiated by Mahony and colleagues.

Finally, Mahony *et al.* (2010) provided a comprehensive overview of organisational justice research in sport management and synthesised findings from various studies into an organised review. This study represented a first attempt to consolidate the work done by multiple scholars into a single narrative that identified what is known and what type of research needs to be done in order to move this line of enquiry forward. This study will benefit current and future sport management scholars by identifying lines of research necessary to advance what we know about organisational justice in sport management.

Note

1 Jeremy S. Jordan is with the School of Tourism and Hospitality Management at Temple University.

References

Adams, J.S. (1965) 'Inequity in social exchange'. In L. Berkowitz (ed.) *Advances in experimental social psychology* (Vol. 2, pp. 267–99). New York: Academic Press.

Greenberg, J. (1990) 'Organizational justice: Yesterday, today, and tomorrow'. *Journal of Management*, 16: 399–432.

Homans, G.C. (1961) *Social behavior: Its elementary forms*. Oxford: Harcourt.

Hums, M.A. and Chelladurai, P. (1994) 'Distributive justice in intercollegiate athletics: The views of NCAA coaches and administrators'. *Journal of Sport Management*, 8: 200–17.

Mahony, D.F. and Pastore, D.M. (1998) 'An examination of participation opportunities, revenues, and expenses at NCAA institutions – 1973–1993'. *Journal of Sport & Social Issues*, 22: 127–52.

Mahony, D.F., Hums, M.A., Andrew, D.P. and Dittmore, S.W. (2010) 'Organizational justice in sport'. *Sport Management Review*, 13: 91–105.

Mahony, D.F., Hums, M.A. and Riemer, H. (2002) 'Distributive justice in intercollegiate athletics'. *Journal of Sport Management*, 16: 31–356.

Mahony, D.F., Hums, M.A. and Riemer, H. (2005) 'Bases for determining need: Perspectives of intercollegiate athletic directors and athletic board chairs'. *Journal of Sport Management*, 19: 170–92.

Mahony, D.F., Riemer, H.A., Breeding, J.L. and Hums, M.A. (2006) 'Organizational justice in sport organizations: Perceptions of student-athletes and other college students'. *Journal of Sport Management*, 20: 159–88.

14

MANAGING DIVERSITY[1]

Janet S. Fink

Introduction

In this chapter, I will provide a brief overview of the original work in the diversity management literature to provide a backdrop for the framework we developed in Fink and Pastore (1999). From there, I will discuss the reasons for my initial interest in the topic and the process I utilised in the development of the framework. I will explain how I have used the framework in my own work and highlight a sample of others' applications and extensions of the framework. I will conclude the chapter with an examination of possible directions for future research.

When I began to research it, the topic of managing diversity was relatively new to the field of sport management. Some of the earliest work utilising the term 'managing diversity' tackled the problem of corporate divisional relationships as firms began to diversify their industrial composition (e.g., Hall, 1987). The movement away from single industry corporations to conglomerates brought a variety of challenges for management relative to the different industries, structures, operations and policies the various enterprises brought to the firm (Farr, 1973; Nystrom, 1976). The perspective of this diversity management had little to do with employees beyond the industry or unit to which they belonged.

However, by the late 1980s and early 1990s, recognition of the rapidly changing personal characteristics of the workforce and marketplace manifested in a focus on managing employee diversity to obtain a competitive advantage for organisations (Cox, 1993; Loden and Rosener, 1991; Morrison, 1992; Thomas, 1991). Thomas defined managing diversity as 'a comprehensive managerial process for developing an environment that works for all employees' (p. 10). Though the topic of managing employee diversity was spurred by the changing demographics of the workplace, Thomas (1990) positioned the managerial practice as dissimilar to affirmative action policy. He argued that affirmative action was meant to be a temporary, corrective process that was artificial in nature and, therefore, unable to substantially alter the fundamental work environment to produce the opportunity for success for *all* employees. In contrast, those advocating for the management of diversity envisioned the process as a comprehensive overhaul of typical work environments, not merely the addition of ancillary practices/policies aimed to counteract the current work environment's negative outcomes for certain employees (e.g., Cox, 1991; Thomas, 1990). As Thomas (1991) noted, managing diversity 'begins with taking a look at the system and asking the questions that were not asked: Why doesn't the system work naturally for everyone? What has to be done to allow it to do so?' (p. 26).

Admittedly, implementing the answers to these questions would require an incredible amount of change for most organisations. To sell the idea to industry leaders, scholars argued that diversity, if managed well, substantially improves organisational performance (Robinson and Dechant, 1997). While many advocates for diversity agreed with the social justice argument that organisations should be *obligated* to treat all employees fairly (e.g., Cox, 1991; DeSensi, 1995; Morrison, 1992), it was recognised that establishing a business case for diversity would likely resonate more strongly with organisational leaders (Robinson and Dechant, 1997; Thomas, 1991). That is, if the organisational changes necessary to effectively manage diversity could be directly tied to positive organisational outcomes and a true competitive advantage, organisational leaders would be more likely to provide the commitment necessary for such changes to occur.

However, research regarding the benefits of a diverse workforce was somewhat ambiguous. There was clear evidence that a diverse workforce would not *automatically* result in positive work outcomes; in fact, many studies found that heterogeneity in workgroups often led to poorer group functioning and negative work outcomes (e.g., Milliken and Martens, 1996). Conversely, other research demonstrated that the *effective* management of diversity resulted in many positive organisational outcomes including: reduced discrimination lawsuits (Robinson and Dechant, 1997); increased worker satisfaction and reduced employee turnover (Morrison, 1992); a more diverse customer base (Johnson and O'Mara, 1992); and increased organisational productivity and stock returns (Morrison, 1992; Wright, Ferris, Hiller and Kroll, 1995). Thus, in my mind, it seemed imperative to understand the characteristics of organisations that most effectively managed diversity. Below I describe why I felt this was so important.

Origin of interest

The origin of my interest in managing diversity began long before I entered the doctoral programme at the Ohio State University. And, truthfully, my attraction to the concept was driven less by the positive *organisational* outcomes that could be derived, and much more from how people of colour and women in intercollegiate athletics could benefit from such practices. My venture into the development of our diversity framework was the result of a combination of lived experiences, exposure to key literature and my inner perspectives at that time.

During one of my practicum experiences prior to entering the doctoral programme, I worked in an intercollegiate athletic department. I was thrilled to be assigned to work under a very established and high-ranking female administrator who served as my supervisor. Overall, I had a fantastic experience – she gave me meaningful assignments, a great deal of independence and support when I needed it. She was incredibly good at her job. However, it became clear to me that, in many ways, she was suppressed in her work environment. The mostly (White) male administrative team failed to interact with her much, although they often interacted with one another both formally and informally. They were not overtly uncivil, but they were not at all inclusive. They would often ask each other (and some younger female workers) to join them for lunch, but never stopped in to ask my supervisor. This exclusion went beyond lunch, it was as though she mainly operated in a separate sphere – she got a great deal accomplished, but for the most part, she did it on her own. Admittedly, I do not know the history of personnel interactions within the department before I arrived; perhaps she behaved in ways to create this isolation. However, from my vantage point, it appeared that she was treated this way because she was deemed different. Those differences went beyond demographics (gender, age, marital status), as she often harboured thoughts about priorities, strategies or assessments within the department that were dissimilar to the majority of other administrators'.

This experience stayed with me as I entered my doctoral programme and was exposed to a wide variety of popular press and academic articles regarding the lack of women and people of colour employed in intercollegiate athletics, particularly in positions of leadership. I was appalled by the statistics; however, many of my friends and colleagues did not have the same sense of urgency to remedy the problem. They felt that progress was just a matter of time, as indeed, the ideal of meritocracy is firmly entrenched in the world of sport (Smith, 2000). I lacked their optimism as I was keenly aware of the disparity in power, status and access for these groups. That is, I had much less faith in the ideal of meritocracy and thought such disparities often rendered an unfair playing field that definitely impaired progress for women and people of colour. Consequently, I strongly believed in the social justice argument that sport organisations should sense an *ethical obligation* to provide opportunities for qualified people of color and women. However, I was also quite cognizant of the criticisms of government-mandated or voluntary affirmative action programmes aimed towards social justice and witnessed how qualified candidates often endured unfair stigmas that their hiring and/or promotions were merely the result of a quota system.

Thus, I was very interested in the working environments of sport organisations, particularly (at the time) Division IA intercollegiate athletic programmes and, more specifically, the lack of women and people of colour in leadership positions. I read a great deal of literature that was sociologically based, described the problems and offered various explanations for why women and people of colour did not advance (e.g., Knoppers, 1987; Lapchick, 1984; Lovett and Lowrey, 1994; Stangl and Kane, 1991). However, these offered few suggestions for how to bring about change. After consulting some of my general exam committee members, I undertook an independent study project on the topics of organisational culture and change and how they related to my interest. I spent the entire summer after my first year of doctoral work reading about organisational culture and change from a variety of perspectives, but I never felt comfortable with those theoretical paradigms relative to my interests. (Several years later, Doherty and Chelladurai (1999) expertly wove the organisational culture and diversity management literature together and developed a model for the management of cultural diversity in sport organisations.) It was after that failed summer project that I took a human resource management class as an elective. In the course, I was exposed to the concept of managing diversity for the first time. I remember thinking to myself, 'finally, something that gets at the research ideas that have been percolating in my mind'.

So, you see, I was not interested in managing employee diversity to enhance organisational outcomes *as an end in and of itself* – I saw it as a managerial strategy that could positively impact the work environment for women and people of colour. Furthermore, because the effective management of diversity was tied to advantageous business outcomes, I thought it offered the best probability of activating real social change and the greatest likelihood for progress for women and people of colour in intercollegiate athletics. My thought at the time was that, given the research regarding the positive organisational benefits stemming from effective diversity management, how could those in positions of power *not* want to transform their management tactics?

Developing the framework

Thus, I wanted to learn everything there was to know about the effective management of diversity. What strategies did this require, what did organisations that effectively managed diversity look like, and how did they function? This became the topic of my dissertation. At the time, there was very little in the sport management literature that related to the topic. However,

I was greatly influenced by DeSensi's Dr. Earle F. Zeigler lecture (1994) as well as her 1995 publication in *Quest*. While she was focused on changes to education and curricula to spur *individual* appreciation for multiculturalism, and I was more interested in strategies for *organisational* transformation, we shared an interest in the same end goal – a desire for 'a true multicultural understanding within sport' (DeSensi, 1994, p. 73).

I read as much as I could relative to the topic of managing diversity, but with a particular eye towards an overall structure, or underlying characteristics, of organisations that effectively managed diversity. As I read, I noted where there seemed to be consistency among authors' thoughts (although they often used different terminologies), as well as unique concepts that seemed important to effective diversity management. As I analysed all this information, slowly the framework began to take form. Though I had read as much as I could find on the topic, in the end, the framework mainly integrated the ideas of Cox (1991), DeSensi (1995), Golembiewski (1995), Johnson (1992) and Thomas (1991).

To briefly summarise, the framework was conceived as a diamond continuum with non-compliant organisations at the bottom, followed by compliant organisations, reactive organisations and proactive organisations (Fink and Pastore, 1999). The framework also pictured three dimensions along which organisations change as they progress from bottom to top. Organisations at the bottom of the diamond perceive employee diversity to be a liability, while those at the top perceive it to be an asset. Similarly, organisations falling on the bottom of the diamond perceive managing diversity as merely a compliance issue but those at the top envision it as an integrated management issue. Finally, non-compliant organisations exhibit rigid organisational structures and lines of communication, while those at the top display much greater flexibility in these areas.

Originally, only the diamond in its entirety was envisioned as a continuum. That is, we anticipated that the stages of the diamond would be (mostly) successive. For example, if non-compliant, an organisation would first focus on becoming compliant before engaging in reactive strategies. However, we soon realised that organisations probably would not fit nicely into one distinct category. For example, an organisation might comply with most laws, engage in a several reactive strategies, but exhibit no proactive strategies. Thus, we restructured the framework to denote three distinct dimensions (compliance, reactive, proactive) each of which had its own continuum. We envisioned it as a diamond as we suspected organisations would engage in far fewer diversity management strategies at the very top (proactive strategies) and bottom (non-compliance) points of the continuum, with the most diversity efforts falling within compliance and reactive diversity management, the middle portions of the diamond (Golembiewski, 1995; Thomas, 1991).

The defining characteristics of each of these dimensions were thoroughly described and examples of sport organisations, or sport organisations' practices, were used to highlight each dimension. I provide a brief summary of each dimension here. Non-compliant organisations view diversity as a liability and attempt to keep their workforce as homogeneous as possible. These organisations fail to follow city, state and federal legislation, possess strict hierarchical structures and engage in unilateral (top-down) decision-making. Compliant organisations still view diversity as a liability, but they comply with legislation in order to avoid costly lawsuits. Still, they do nothing beyond this to make the work environment for diverse employees more accommodating. Organisations that reactively manage diversity view employee diversity as an asset, and they recognise that differences can bring advantages to the organisation. However, reactive organisations tend to view diversity in terms of gender and race only and often wait for a problem to arise before implementing piecemeal strategies designed to alleviate the difficulty. Proactive organisations strongly believe in the benefits of a diverse workforce and their leaders show their commitment through financial and personnel resources. They 'look at their policies, practices, and procedures and attempt to shape them in order to attain and utilize employee diversity from the start' (Fink and Pastore, 1999, p. 324). Leaders in these organisations typically view diversity as a social justice issue and supply resources for continuing endeavours aimed towards an appreciation of individual differences among the workforce. These organisations view diversity more broadly (i.e., beyond race and gender) and demonstrate flexibility in organisational structure.

Extensions and applications

As the framework began to take shape, it was my hope that it could be utilised to assess a sport organisation's status relative to its management of employee diversity. Towards that end, we began to operationalise the dimensions via a survey instrument. Thus, my dissertation also included the development of this instrument, which was used to obtain perceptions from Division IA intercollegiate athletic employees regarding how their organisations managed diversity, whether these perceptions differed based on demographic variables, and how the management of diversity related to positive organisational outcomes. This resulted in the Fink, Pastore and Riemer (2001) publication in the *Journal of Sport Management*. Interestingly, the original submission of that piece did not include the demographic difference variable. At the time I was working on the revisions to the original manuscript, Harold Riemer was my colleague at the University of Texas. We were discussing the paper and he suggested that, rather than merely looking at how demographics impact perceptions of diversity management, we should also assess how relational demography (i.e., the level of dissimilarity between an employee and supervisor) impacts these perceptions. It was a substantial addition to the study.

We found that compliance was the most used diversity management strategy in intercollegiate athletics at the time, followed by proactive strategies. Reactive strategies obtained the lowest mean score (Fink *et al.*, 2001). While we were pleasantly surprised that sport organisations engaged in some proactive strategies, we were concerned that the focus on issues of gender and race was primarily reactive. As we stated, 'while a broad definition of diversity is certainly the terminal goal of effective diversity management, women and minorities have been disadvantaged throughout history' (p. 41), and we warned against failing to create progress for some (i.e., women and people of colour) by utilising limited resources on too broad a range of diverse characteristics.

We also found that people of colour and lesbian, gay and bisexual employees perceived that their organisations engaged in less reactive diversity management relative to other employees, and people of colour perceived that less proactive strategies were employed. Thus, it appeared that employees different from the status quo perceived organisational efforts to managing diversity as less effective than majority members. However, relational demography predicted a greater amount of variance in diversity management perceptions than demographic variables alone; further, we found that the more similar the athletic director (AD) was to the employee in terms of race and gender, the greater the perceptions of effective diversity management. As we stated, 'This is a disturbing finding and one which intimates that current efforts to manage diversity have done little to nudge people toward greater understanding and appreciation of differences' (Fink *et al.*, 2001, p. 42).

Proactive diversity management strategies were the most predictive of the majority of positive work outcomes, while compliance strategies predicted some positive outcomes as well. However, reactive diversity management strategies did not contribute a significant amount of variance to any of the measured outcomes. Though we did not discuss this (non) finding in the manuscript, we speculated that this could be a combination of two factors: (a) reactive diversity strategies may be seen by majority members as similar to affirmative action programmes, thus leading to negative perceptions; and (b) too few of these strategies were utilised to make a significant impact.

Because there are substantial differences between Division I and Division III intercollegiate athletic environments, we decided to replicate aspects of the initial study with Division III employees (Fink, Pastore and Riemer, 2003). The findings were similar to Fink *et al.* (2001) in that employees perceived compliance strategies to be the most utilised, followed by proactive strategies, while reactive strategies were the least utilised (with a mean score below the mid-point of the scale). Further, proactive diversity management strategies predicted the greatest amount of variance in all of the organisational outcome measures. Compliance strategies also contributed significantly to several outcome measures; however, as in Fink *et al.* (2001), reactive strategies did not contribute to positive organisational outcomes, which led us to question the value of reactive diversity management strategies. As we noted, 'majority group members may perceive these types of strategies as non-inclusive and advantageous only for minority members. On the other hand, minority groups may see them as "quick fixes" or "window dressings" to long-term problems' (Fink *et al.*, 2003, p. 162).

Soon after the publication of that manuscript, I became aware of a wave of research utilising a more critical lens relative to managing diversity. It questioned the diversity management discourse and its utility relative to improving workplace conditions for those groups that have been historically discriminated against (Prasad, Pringle and Konrad, 2006). Such researchers argued that diversity had been appropriated by those in positions of power in order to resist true change and maintain the status quo. As Embrick (2011) noted:

> Specifically, corporations have systematically and strategically co-opted the notions of diversity that were established by the civil rights movement and helped to perpetuate a diversity ideology that has enabled them to advocate racial and gender equality, yet maintain highly inequitable work environments and an even more inequitable chain of command [. . .] By increasing the number of categories of people that fall under the umbrella of diversity, companies are able to effectively escape close examination of racial and gender inequalities that might occur in their workplaces. As long as no one brings it up, it can be ignored.
>
> *(pp. 544–7)*

Given my initial reason for the study of diversity management, I found this contention interesting. Our *ideal* of proactive diversity management certainly embodied the notion that managing diversity was an issue of social justice and that an organisation exemplifying such strategies would inherently help employees who have been historically discriminated against. However, while proactive diversity management was predictive of positive organisational outcomes, demographic and relational differences (race, gender, sexual orientation) led to differences in perceptions of the extent to which diversity was being managed. If proactive diversity management worked as we envisioned, *all* employees would have relatively similar assessments of the strategies utilised. Still, it must be kept in mind that while athletic departments did engage in *some* proactive strategies, the mean scores in both studies indicated they could be doing *much more* in terms of proactive diversity management. Thus, perhaps the proactive diversity management practised by these organisations was not robust enough to work entirely as we envisioned.

Interestingly, Cunningham (2009, 2011) provided evidence that it is important to foster *both* demographic diversity and proactive diversity management. In a study of Division 1A athletic departments, he discovered that race diversity positively impacted organisational performance directly; however, when high racial diversity was coupled with an environment high in pro-active diversity management, performance was improved even further (Cunningham, 2009). In another study that included all Division 1 athletic departments, he found that sexual orienta-tion diversity was not directly related to organisational performance, but once again found an interaction effect with proactive diversity management (Cunningham, 2011). As Cunningham (2011, p. 458) stated:

> when the department did not follow a proactive diversity strategy, sexual orientation diversity did not influence NACDA points earned [an indicator of organisational performance]. However, when the department did follow a proactive diversity strategy, there was a strong, positive association between sexual orientation diversity and NACDA points earned. In fact, departments with high sexual orientation diversity and a high proactive diversity strategy accrued nearly 7 times the NACDA points than did departments that had low sexual orientation diversity and a high proactive diversity strategy.

While employees' perceptions of the work experience were not directly examined in these studies, it seems unlikely that such positive organisational outcomes would occur if the work environments were highly inequitable. Further, it is obvious that organisations' management of diversity must be twofold: there must be efforts made to recruit and retain demographically diverse employees while also engaging in proactive diversity management.

Further applications

We have been pleased to see our framework referenced throughout the years in studies of various diversity issues in sport. It is incredibly rewarding to realise that future generations of sport management scholars are committed to improving the work experiences for diverse employees, and it is my hope that the continued scholarly scrutiny will result in more equitable sport environments. I am particularly honoured that it was utilised to produce measures for the Diversity in Athletics Award established in 2005 and offered for several years by the Laboratory for Diversity in Sport at Texas A&M University. The award was developed to recognise athletic departments with exemplary diversity practices across eight categories: diversity strategy (measured based on our framework); sex diversity; race diversity; attitudes and values diversity; graduation rate of African American male athletes; graduation rate of African American female athletes; Title IX compliance; and overall diversity excellence. In 2006, the Laboratory for Diversity in Sport partnered with NCAA's Office of Diversity and Inclusion to expand the award to all three intercollegiate athletic divisions. It was a highly imaginative and effective way to bring attention to diversity management practices in intercollegiate athletic departments. Each year the award was announced in a variety of media outlets and winning schools widely publicised the results. It served to publicly illustrate that diverse and equitable work environments are possible within intercollegiate athletics. The establishment of the award is a great exemplar of bridging scholarship and practice. Indeed, as Dan Dutcher, NCAA vice president for Division III remarked:

This award is significant because it demonstrates that diversity is more than a theoretical concept. These institutions have demonstrated that diversity can be achieved on a very practical and personal level, further enhancing the educational experience of our student–athletes. These institutions can serve as a model and guide for the rest of our membership.

(NCAA News Release, 2009, para. 5)

Directions for future research

My initial interest in studying the management of diversity stemmed in large part from the lack of women and people of colour in leadership positions in sport. The 2012 *Racial and Gender Report Card* confirms that this remains a problem. Only 18.6 per cent of all head coaches were African American, the lowest percentage since 1995–6, and women held only 36.8 per cent of head coaching jobs in Division 1. Only fifteen people of colour and only four women held athletic director positions in the Football Bowl Subdivision (FBS, N = 127). Further, all FBS conference commissioners were White men (Lapchick, 2012). Given this lack of progress, it seems imperative to conduct in–depth examinations of the recruitment, development and retention practices of university athletic departments (and other sport organisations) relative to women and people of colour, a call previously identified by Cunningham (2009, 2011). Indeed, athletic administrators may claim to value diversity and purport to have diversity practices in place, but it is important to critically examine such claims, particularly in light of evidence that demographic differences impact perceptions of how diversity is managed (Fink *et al.*, 2001). Prasad *et al.* (2006) warned that diversity researchers have failed to provide adequate attention to *employees'* experiences related to diversity and have relied too heavily on top management's views. Relatedly, Embrick (2011) studied upper-level managers in Fortune 1000 companies. Seventy-five percent of the participants revealed that their company had a formal diversity policy, yet 70 per cent could not explain or elaborate on the policy when queried. Further, when asked about their personal definitions of diversity, less than a quarter of them mentioned race or gender in their definitions. Thus, it appears that in order to truly understand an organisation's diversity practices and their impact, we must seek out all employees' assessments of their environments and engage in more critical analyses of purported diversity management practices.

Issues of diversity are complex and messy – they are impacted by the historical and socio-political contexts of organisations, as well as the interplay among multiple identities and inequities in organisations. As such, I encourage more multi-level (e.g., Cunningham, 2010; Melton and Cunningham, 2014) examinations of diversity issues in order to more fully tease out the complexity of mechanisms related to these topics. Similarly, multiple dimensions of diversity undoubtedly interact to form even more nuanced forms of oppression (e.g., gendered racism; gendered, racist homophobia) and thus, more research needs to account for such intersectionality (e.g., Borland and Bruening, 2010; Melton and Cunningham, 2014; Walker and Sartore-Baldwin, 2013). Given this complexity, we must incorporate a variety of research methods and investigative paradigms to produce a robust collective flow of research aimed to positively transform the working environment of sport organisations (Cunningham and Fink, 2006).

Note

1   This chapter is a reflection on Fink and Pastore (1999) and the work related to it.

References

Borland, J.F. and Bruening, J.E. (2010) 'Navigating the barriers: A qualitative examination of the under-representation of Black females as head coaches in collegiate basketball'. *Sport Management Review*, 13: 407–21.

Cox, T. (1991) 'The multicultural organization'. *Academy of Management Executive*, 5: 34–47.

Cox, T. (1993) *Cultural diversity in organizations: Theory, research and practice*. San Francisco, CA: Berrett-Koehler Publishers.

Cunningham, G.B. (2009) 'The moderating effect of diversity strategy on the relationship between racial diversity and organizational performance'. *Journal of Applied Social Psychology*, 36: 1445–60.

Cunningham, G.B. (2010) 'Understanding the under-representation of African American coaches: A multilevel perspective'. *Sport Management Review*, 13: 395–406.

Cunningham, G.B. (2011) 'The LGBT advantage: Examining the relationship among sexual orientation diversity, diversity strategy, and performance'. *Sport Management Review*, 14: 453–61.

Cunningham, G.B. and Fink, J.S. (2006) 'Diversity issues in sport and leisure: Introduction to a special issue'. *Journal of Sport Management*, 20: 455–65.

DeSensi, J.T. (1994) 'Multiculturalism as an issue in sport management'. *Journal of Sport Management*, 8: 63–74.

DeSensi, J.T. (1995) 'Understanding multiculturalism and valuing diversity: A theoretical perspective'. *Quest*, 47: 34–43.

Doherty, A.J. and Chelladurai, P. (1999) 'Managing cultural diversity in sport organizations: A theoretical perspective'. *Journal of Sport Management*, 13: 280–97.

Embrick, D.G. (2011) 'The diversity ideology in the business world: A new oppression for a new age'. *Critical Sociology*, 37: 541–56.

Farr, J.L. (1973) 'Managing diversity and interdependence (book)'. *Personnel Psychology*, 26(4): 640–4.

Fink, J.S. and Pastore, D.L. (1999) 'Diversity in sport? Utilizing the business literature to devise a comprehensive framework of diversity initiatives'. *Quest*, 51: 310–27.

Fink, J.S., Pastore, D.L. and Riemer, H.A. (2001) 'Do differences make a difference? Managing diversity in Division IA intercollegiate athletics'. *Journal of Sport Management*, 15: 10–50.

Fink, J.S., Pastore, D.L. and Riemer, H.A. (2003) 'Managing employee diversity: Perceived practices and organisational outcomes in NCAA Division III athletic departments'. *Sport Management Review*, 6: 147–68.

Golembiewski, R.T. (1995) *Managing diversity in organizations*. Tuscaloosa: The University of Alabama Press.

Hall, G.E. (1987) 'Reflections on running a diversified company'. *Harvard Business Review*, 65: 84–92.

Johnson, R.B. and O'Mara, J. (1992) 'Shedding new light on diversity training'. *Training and Development*, 46(5): 44–52.

Johnson, S. (1992) 'Valuing and managing diversity in business and industry. Literature reviews and models'. *Training and Development Research Center Project #59*. St Paul, MN: Microform.

Knoppers, A. (1987) 'Gender and the coaching profession'. *Quest*, 39: 9–22.

Lapchick, R.E. (1984) *Broken promises: Racism in American sports*. New York: St Martins Publishing.

Lapchick, R.E. (2012) *The 2012 racial and gender report card*. Orlando, FL: The Institute for Diversity and Ethics in Sport.

Loden, M. and Rosener, J.B. (1991) *Workforce America! Managing employee diversity as a vital resource*. New York: McGraw-Hill.

Lovett, D.J. and Lowry, C.D. (1994) '"Good old boys" and "Good old girls" clubs: myth or reality?' *Journal of Sport Management*, 8: 27–36.

Melton, N.E. and Cunningham, G.B. (2014) 'Who are the champions? Using a multilevel model to examine perceptions of employee support for LGBT inclusion in sport organizations'. *Journal of Sport Management*, 28: 189–207.

Milliken, F.J. and Martins, L.L. (1996) 'Searching for common threads: Understanding the multiple effects of diversity in organizational groups'. *Academy of Management Review*, 21: 402–33.

Morrison, A.M. (1992) *The new leaders*. San Francisco, CA: Jossey-Bass.

NCAA News Release (2009) 'Texas A&M University's Laboratory for Diversity in Sport and the NCAA announce the 2009 Diversity in Athletics Awards'. Available online at: www.ncaa.org (accessed on 1 September, 2014).

Nystrom, P.C. (1976) 'Managing diversity and interdependence: An organizational study of multidivisional firms'. *Industrial & Labor Relations Review*, 29: 628–30.

Prasad, P., Pringle, J.K. and Konrad, A.D. (2006) *Handbook of workplace diversity*. London: Sage Publications.

Robinson, G. and Dechant, K. (1997) 'Building a case for diversity'. *The Academy of Management Executive*, *11*: 21–31.

Smith, E. (2000) 'There was no golden age of sport for African American athletes'. *Society*, *37*: 45–9.

Stangl, J.M. and Kane, M.J. (1991) 'Structural variables that offer explanatory power for the underrepresentation of women coaches since Title IX: The case of homologous reproduction'. *Sociology of Sport Journal*, *8*: 47–61.

Thomas, R.R. (1990) 'From affirmative action to affirming diversity'. *Harvard Business Review*, *March-April*: 107–17.

Thomas, R.R. (1991) *Beyond race and gender*. New York: AMACOM.

Walker, N.A. and Sartore-Baldwin, M. (2013) 'Hegemonic masculinity and the institutionalized bias of women in men's collegiate basketball: What do men think?' *Journal of Sport Management*, *27*: 303–15.

Wright, P., Ferris, S.P., Hiller, J.S. and Kroll, M. (1995) 'Competitiveness through the Management of diversity: Effects on stock price valuation'. *Academy of Management Journal*, *38*: 272–87.

Applying the theory of managing diversity

George B. Cunningham[1]

I first became aware of Fink and Pastore's (1999) model during graduate school. My dissertation work focused on ways managers could reduce the biases, such as stereotyping, prejudice and discrimination, that sometimes accompany people working in diverse groups, so Fink and Pastore's model was attractive to me. I also had the good fortune of studying at the Ohio State University, and both of the authors served on my committee. Thus, my understanding of their work was enhanced through personal interactions and debates with them. The theoretical grounding of the work, coupled with the real-world applications, were appealing to me, and given the work's continued citation rate, I suspect others concur. In fact, even now, fifteen years after its publication, I still re-read the original publication, drawing new insights. While I ultimately focused my dissertation efforts on the group level of analysis and social psychological approaches to reducing bias (see Cunningham, 2004, 2006; Cunningham and Chelladurai, 2004), I continued to draw from Fink and Pastore's writing in other work and in my research since that time.

My application of Fink and Pastore's framework largely began with service projects I undertook at my current institution as part of our research laboratory, the Laboratory for Diversity. For several years, we awarded the Diversity in Athletics Award, which recognised National Collegiate Athletic Association (NCAA) athletic departments for their diversity and inclusion efforts. We collected archival and survey data to determine the recipients. One category included diversity strategy, and in drawing from Fink and Pastore's model, we developed vignettes representing departments that followed a compliance, reactive or proactive strategy. Survey respondents then rated how characteristic each vignette was of their athletic department. We found the framework useful in differentiating between those departments following inclusive strategies from those that did not.

In addition to facilitating the award decisions, the data collected during that process allowed us to examine how diversity strategies affected organisational outcomes. Specifically, we drew from Fink and Pastore's writings, as well as those of Doherty and Chelladurai (1999), to underscore the importance of having an inclusive culture when the sport organisation had a diverse work-force. We theorised that employee diversity interacted with an inclusive work culture to predict subsequent outcomes. Our results largely supported this premise. Sport organisations that couple employee diversity with an inclusive culture outpace their counterparts across various outcomes, including creativity, human resource outcomes and objective measures of performance (Cunningham, 2008, 2009, 2011a, 2011b; Singer and Cunningham, 2012). Inclusive organisations also signal a commitment to diversity that is attractive to prospective customers and employees (Cunningham and Melton, 2014; Melton and Cunningham, 2012).

Finally, I have used Fink and Pastore's framework in my teaching. I discuss their work in my textbook (Cunningham, in press) and students are frequently drawn to it when seeking to understand how organisations develop strategies to create inclusive workplaces.

Moving forward, I suspect researchers will continue to draw from the principles undergirding Fink and Pastore's framework to understand the influence of strategy in the work environment. I am particularly interested in understanding how inclusive workplaces impact people who have traditionally been in the minority, such as women, religious minorities, sexual minorities, racial minorities and so on. How does inclusiveness allow them to express unique identities important to them while still feeling the sense of connectedness to the workplace? Further, how do inclusive sport organisations differentiate themselves from their competitors to attract and retain talented athletes, coaches and administrators? Diving further into the *why* components of their framework will further strengthen the understanding of diverse and inclusive workplace cultures.

Note

1   Dr. George B. Cunningham is a Professor and Associate Dean for Academic Affairs and Research in the College of Education and Human Developments, at Texas A&M University.

References

Cunningham, G.B. (2004) 'Strategies for transforming the possible negative effects of group diversity'. *Quest*, *56*: 421–38.

Cunningham, G.B. (2006) 'The influence of group diversity on intergroup bias following recategorization'. *The Journal of Social Psychology*, *146*: 533–47.

Cunningham, G.B. (2008) 'Commitment to diversity and its influence on athletic department outcomes'. *Journal of Intercollegiate Sport*, *1*: 176–201.

Cunningham, G.B. (2009) 'The moderating effect of diversity strategy on the relationship between racial diversity and organizational performance'. *Journal of Applied Social Psychology*, *36*: 1445–60.

Cunningham, G.B. (2011a) 'Creative work environments in sport organizations: The influence of sexual orientation diversity and commitment to diversity'. *Journal of Homosexuality*, *58*: 1041–57.

Cunningham, G.B. (2011b) 'The LGBT advantage: Examining the relationship among sexual orientation diversity, diversity strategy, and performance'. *Sport Management Review*, *14*: 453–61.

Cunningham, G.B. (in press) *Diversity and inclusion in sport organizations* (third edn). Scottsdale, AZ: Holcomb Hathaway.

Cunningham, G.B. and Chelladurai, P. (2004) 'Affective reactions to cross-functional teams: The impact of size, relative performance, and common in-group identity'. *Group Dynamics: Theory, Research, and Practice*, *8*: 83–97.

Cunningham, G.B. and Melton, E.N. (2014) 'Signals and cues: LGBT inclusive advertising and consumer attraction'. *Sport Marketing Quarterly*, *23*: 37–46.

Doherty, A.J. and Chelladurai, P. (1999) 'Managing cultural diversity in sport organizations: A theoretical perspective'. *Journal of Sport Management*, *13*: 280–97.

Fink, J.S. and Pastore, D.L. (1999) 'Diversity in sport? Utilizing the business literature to devise a comprehensive framework of diversity initiatives'. *Quest*, *51*: 310–27.

Melton, E.N. and Cunningham, G.B. (2012) 'The effect of LGBT-inclusive policies, gender, and social dominance orientation on organizational attraction'. *International Journal of Sport Management*, *13*: 444–62.

Singer, J.N. and Cunningham, G.B. (2012) 'A case study of the diversity culture of an American university athletic department: Implications for educational stakeholders'. *Sport, Education & Society*, *17*: 647–69.

15

WORK–LIFE INTERFACE IN SPORT[1]

Marlene A. Dixon and Jennifer E. Bruening

Overview

The theoretical model of work–family conflict in sport is a multi-level approach to understanding the antecedents and outcomes of work–family interactions in a sport context. The theory essentially poses that individual lives and work–life choices are shaped and constrained by the organisational and socio-cultural structures and norms surrounding them. It asserts that by examining individuals within the contexts in which they live and work, we can understand and manage work–life conflict and work–life balance pursuant to better individual, organisational and socio-cultural outcomes. This chapter provides a look at this theory – its constructs, major propositions and how it was developed. We then examine what we and others have learned in our investigations of work–life conflict among coaches, as well as ways that we can extend the theory in the future.

Specific constructs

There are a number of constructs utilised to build the model, which we list below with their basic definitions:

- *Work*. Understanding that there are multiple forms and structures of work, within the work–family literature work is typically defined as paid employment.
- *Family*. Again, this is a broad concept, but a working definition is offered by Eby *et al.* (2005) as 'two or more individuals occupying interdependent roles with the purpose of accomplishing shared goals' (p. 126).
- *Work–family conflict*. Work–family conflict is defined as a type of inter-role conflict wherein at least some work and family responsibilities are not compatible and have resultant effects within each domain (Boles, Howard and Donofrio, 2001; Greenhaus and Beutell, 1985). It has become largely accepted that work and family interact, and that this interaction is bi-directional. Work can affect family, and family can affect work (Boles *et al.*, 2001; Greenhaus and Beutell,1985; Greenhaus *et al.*, 1997; Parasuraman *et al.*, 1996).
- *Work–family balance*. Although our original theoretical framework in 2005 examined only work–family conflict, the work–family literature (in general and our own) has expanded

to a greater understanding that the work–family interface can have both negative (conflict) and positive (balance, enrichment) outcomes (see Schenewark and Dixon, 2012). In addition, it is understood that conflict and balance may not necessarily be the opposite ends of the same continuum, but each has distinct antecedents and consequences (Eby *et al.*, 2005).

- *Work–life.* Much like the constructs of conflict and balance, the construct of work–family has expanded to understand that even those without a 'family' will still experience conflict and enrichment from work and non-work domains. For example, Mazerolle and Goodman (2013) have explored the ways that organisations can support athletic trainers who have life pursuits including hobbies, exercise and personal athletic pursuits.
- *Role theory.* This is the basic set of theories undergirding work–life research. These theories purport that individuals hold multiple life roles and that these roles interface with each other. Some approaches operate out of a scarcity assumption (e.g., Greenhaus and Powell, 2003), which assumes that individuals hold finite resources such as time, energy and money, and that choices in one role come at a cost to another. Other role theories, such as those from Grzywacz and Marks (2000), Greenhaus and Powell (2003) and Greenhaus and Brummelhuis (2013), suggest that work and family can actually have an enriching effect, whereby resources in one role enhance those within the other role. Our collective work supports both approaches.
- *Multi-level.* One major tenet that is often not central in work–family conflict theory is that it is multi-level. This means that it allows for simultaneous examination and analysis of individual and organisational behaviours (e.g., Kozlowski and Klein, 2000). It allows the researcher to address the complexity of relationships among variables and within changing contexts and to specify relationships between constructs and behaviours at various levels.
- *Top-down.* A top-down perspective suggests that higher levels (e.g., organisations, cultural assumptions) shape and constrain lower levels. To paraphrase Kanter (1977), the workplace shapes the worker.
- *Bottom-up.* A bottom-up perspective suggests that individual behaviours can collectively influence higher levels. For example, worker demand for work–life balance policies can alter those policies at the organisational level.

Major propositions

We put forth four major propositions. These are described below:

1 Work and family interact for those working in a sport context, and those interactions are somewhat distinct to that context due to the organisational and social structures and cultural assumptions within sport;
2 Individual behaviours are shaped and constrained by both organisational and socio-cultural properties;
3 Organisational behaviours are shaped by individual attitudes and behaviours regarding work–family; and
4 Work–life issues impact both men and women, although the antecedents, experiences and outcomes may look different. Boundary conditions regarding gender, while acknowledged, were not specified in the original theoretical model.

How has it been tested?

The model has been applied and tested somewhat broadly in the sport management literature in particular. We completed the initial testing of the model (Bruening and Dixon, 2007; Bruening and Dixon, 2008; Dixon and Bruening, 2007), setting out to examine both the top-down and bottom-up processes and relationships within the model. To that end, we conducted online focus groups with forty-one women (nine focus groups with four to five members each). Then, we conducted additional individual interviews with seventeen of those women who coached at the NCAA Division I level and also were mothers. We asked them about their experiences with work and family, how organisations helped and hindered their work–family conflict, and how they were coping and seeking change through their experiences.

The data confirmed that top-down and bottom-up processes were at work, and that antecedents and outcomes could be identified at all three levels within the model (individual, structural and socio-cultural). At the individual level, coaching mothers' drive (many of them self defined as Type A personalities) and values impacted their level of work–family conflict and their abilities and mechanisms for coping with it. Most coaching mothers reported that they valued both their family and their work, which increased work–family conflict, but also increased their resiliency. Organisational practices, such as flexible scheduling and a family-friendly culture, also impacted work–family conflict. Finally, socio-cultural norms, such as expectations that women handle the majority of child-rearing duties, strongly impacted coaching mothers' work–family conflict.

Our two studies confirmed the general viability of the model, which has been extended and applied to other contexts, individuals and research questions in the ten years following publication of the original piece. These extensions and applications will be addressed in a later section.

Process

The development of the theory was a blend of our personal and professional experiences and backgrounds. On a scholarly level, Dixon had a human-resource-management background, so the questions of improving employee satisfaction and performance within an organisational context fit nicely within her overall research framework (see also Dixon, Noe and Pastore, 2004, 2008; Dixon and Warner, 2010). Thus, the model flowed from original questions about the factors impacting coaching satisfaction (Dixon and Warner, 2010), whereby work–life balance emerged as one of the most salient factors impacting the satisfaction of current college coaches.

Bruening had a strong background in qualitative research, sociology and women's studies. She had written extensively on the experiences of African-American women in sport and on creating inclusive participation and work environments (see Bruening, Borland and Burton, 2008; Bruening, Dover and Clark, 2009). Thus, this area of research flowed naturally from her examinations of barriers to persistence in sport for women.

On a personal level, we had been college coaches, leaving the profession partly due to anticipation of work–family conflict issues. As such, our own backgrounds resonated with the participants in our studies and made powerful connections and motivations for the study of work–life balance in general. At the time of the creation of the model, we both had young children and were experiencing fairly high levels of work–family conflict. This experience motivated us to find new pathways for career and life success for ourselves and others. It also, however, created challenges for remaining objective as scholars, something we constantly had to check within both thinking and writing.

In conducting the interviews, we felt that our own background created an atmosphere of trust with the study participants, such that they were willing to share their struggles and experiences at more than a surface level. As we spoke to them, the mothers brought up many points that were salient to our own lives. For example, they mentioned exhaustion and feelings of guilt, which resonated with us as we travelled (leaving our children at home) to conduct the interviews. As researchers, it was extremely valuable that both of us were in similar life stages. We could discuss the similarities and differences of our lives to the participants, we could support each other in the sometimes arduous research process, and we were able to de-brief often such that we could ensure that we were approaching the participants' stories and our interpretation of those stories with proper perspective.

The theory was built on previous work on the lives of coaches. This work had either theorized or utilised quantitative methods to demonstrate high levels of work–life conflict in coaches from a variety of contexts. For example, Chalip (1978) examined the experiences of swimming coaches in New Zealand and found that there was tremendous pressure to choose sport over family. Knoppers (1992) found vast differences in the support systems for male and female coaches. For example, most female coaches had to carry their own career and family, while male coaches had spouses who not only took sole responsibility for home care, but also supported the coach's career through actions such as hosting recruits and donors, and attending team events. Pastore, Inglis and Danylchuk (1996) and Weiss and Stevens (1993) echoed these findings, demonstrating that work–life conflict was a significant source of burnout among female coaches. We sought to add to this literature with in-depth interviews with the coaches, and with a specific focus on work–life conflict, rather than the overall experience or satisfaction of coaches.

The larger body of literature on work–life experiences, and three pieces of work in particular, also informed our efforts. Garey's (1999) in-depth examination of the lives of nurses was provocative in that she wrote that many women did not see work and life as separate realms, nor did they portion off stages of their own and their children's lives. Instead they worked to weave a life into what may, at the time, have looked like a jumbled mess. Yet, when they looked back, they could see the beautiful tapestry they had created. Garey's study led us to question if coaches saw their lives similarly – a woven mess of children, athletes, games, events, years – none of which they were willing to leave. This work provided a focal point on the individual experiences of coaching women.

Rapoport, Fletcher and Pruitt (2002) examined work–life conflict within organisations. Their work was influential in that it demonstrated not only the work–life issues that arise in organisations, but also that something could be done to change organisations when the policies and culture were not working for the employees. This work provided direction towards the organisational factors impacting coaching mothers, and it influenced a focus on bottom-up processes that lead to organisational transformation.

Hewlett and Luce's (2005) work built a case for the pressures on young mothers to maintain a ridiculous work schedule even in the face of mounting home challenges, or desires to spend more time with their families. This article, both compelling and true to others' experiences, was influential in informing enquiry in the sport realm. We found that female coaches felt they could not exit the profession or they would never re-enter. Hewlett and Luce highlighted the socio-cultural pressures that influence the work–life experiences of mothers, and aided in us in revealing the hidden assumptions behind working, coaching and motherhood.

Processing Hewlett and Luce's (2005) findings also represented a culmination of our thinking regarding multi-level theories, as did studying an entire edited text on the topic by Kozlowski and Klein (2000). These authors grappled with the idea that human behaviours take place within a context – both organisational and social – and that in order to adequately understand and measure human behaviours, scholars need to develop conceptual and measurement models within contexts. They explained that the scholarly community had embraced the idea of top-down processes, but had done little to explain or measure those that emerged from the bottom, or individual level. Thus, work–family conflict theory in sport was somewhat an answer to Kozlowski and Klein's challenge for more work on emergent or bottom-up processes, particularly within organisations.

Therefore, in developing the theory, we reached into the psychological, sociological, human resource management, family studies and organisational behaviour literatures to uncover the factors that might be related at the various levels as antecedents and outcomes. With attention to theoretical developmental principles outlined by Whetton (1989), we wanted to develop a theory that was comprehensive yet parsimonious, contextually flexible and, most of all, useful for predicting and explaining attitudes, behaviour and relationships within a complex framework.

Individual factors included personality, values, family structure and gender. Organisational factors included job pressure, work hours, work scheduling and organisational culture. Socio-cultural factors included gender ideology and cultural norms and expectations. Subsequent testing of the theory, qualitatively in particular, has demonstrated that these factors all play a part in work–family conflict to varying degrees, with organisational and individual factors being the most salient (see Dixon and Sagas, 2007).

The outcomes examined were drawn largely from the human resource management, organisational behaviour and family studies literature bases. Using the principles of multi-level theory, the outcomes can be experienced at any level, but we wanted to demonstrate that outcomes at lower levels could also influence those at higher levels. For example, if worker satisfaction and performance increased due to work–life balance, then organisations might be prompted to enhance policies and practices that facilitate work–life balance. If more working mothers assert influence in organisations, such that the labour force composition were altered, then cultural norms and gender roles within society could also shift.

Extensions and applications

The original framework presented in 2005 has been extended and applied in various contexts and samples. It was first tested empirically with college coaching mothers (Bruening and Dixon, 2007; Dixon and Bruening, 2007) in a two-part study that examined the top-down and bottom-up processes that impacted the experience of work and family for these women. Since then, several scholars have extended and applied the model both directly and tangentially.

One of the extensions of the theory was an examination of the work–life balance of young professional baseball players (Dixon et al., 2006). We demonstrated that it was incredibly taxing on young men to pursue career and family at the same time. In fact, one baseball player described having a 'Double A' clause on any serious relationship – that is, he would not enter into one until he had made at least the Double A level in the minor leagues. Results also showed, however, that men who were married and who had a robust support system (spouse, family of origin) were more satisfied with their lives, even in the midst of difficulty. This study, which supported the findings for college coaches, pointed to the importance of a strong support system in navigating work–life conflict.

Another extension was a systematic examination of the work–life balance practices and policies within college athletic departments (Bruening, Dixon, Tiell, Osbourne, Lough and Sweeney, 2008; Tiell et al., 2008). This series of studies demonstrated that while numerous work–life practices and policies are available to coaches, often they are not applicable or otherwise go unused. For example, universities may offer maternity leave. However, most coaches said they would never take six weeks away from their team, even in the off-season. So, the policy is on the books but does not impact the coaches' lives. Of equal importance, these studies pointed to the supervisor as the most immediate determinant of the work–life climate with an organisation and the subsequent work–life conflict for college coaches.

Dixon and Sagas (2007) conducted a large-scale quantitative study of both male and female college coaches, examining the role of perceived organisational and supervisor support in the work–life conflict, and work and life satisfaction. They found that work–life conflict was a significant predictor of both work and life satisfaction. High levels of work–life conflict were associated with decreased satisfaction – a relationship mediated by perceived supervisor support. Specifically, increased support helped mitigate the impact that conflict had on satisfaction. Extending the work of Dixon and Sagas (2007), Ryan and Sagas (2011) gathered data from a large number of college coaches and confirmed the role a supervisor can have in facilitating a positive work environment.

Our previous work with coaching mothers, along with work from Garey (1999) and Hewlett and Luce (2005), collectively suggests that work–life challenges might change over a person's life course. We blended this thinking with Sweet and Moen's life course theory to examine how this may apply to coaching mothers (Bruening and Dixon, 2008). The participants indicated that career, family and support systems changed over time, and impacted their work–life experiences and the interpretation of those experiences. They suggested that work–life balance did not get easier with time, but it changed and morphed into new challenges and new support needs. The implications were that organisations must be aware that work–life challenges extend beyond childcare for young children into a supportive culture that values people's entire life course.

The work to date has largely focused on work–life conflict as its central construct. While this construct captured the experiences and frustrations of many of the participants, some suggested that it inherently left one with the feeling that 'some conflict' was probably inevitable, and that 'no conflict' was the best possible outcome. Given that perspective, it was difficult to see the benefits of adopting dual roles of worker and family member (Ryan and Sagas, 2011). Schenewark and Dixon (2012), therefore, examined the dual concept of work–family conflict and work–family balance among college coaches. Ryan and Sagas revealed that both constructs provided unique explanatory value, and that both should be utilised in future studies to provide more explanatory power.

A number of researchers have also extended the theory beyond college coaches to other contexts. In a series of compelling articles, Leberman and Palmer (Leberman and Palmer, 2008, 2009; Palmer and Leberman, 2009) explored the lives of mothers in New Zealand who are also elite athletes (and sometimes coaches as well). They found that the mothers relish their dual roles, and value participation in multiple roles as making significant contributions to their lives, yet find a constant struggle in balancing the time and the emotional and financial demands of their multiple roles. These authors highlight the gender differences in navigating multiple roles for elite male athletes and female athletes. They recommend, in particular, financial support systems for the elite athletes, such that they do not also have to work full-time while training and tending to their families.

Mazerolle and colleagues have also extended the work–family theory to the context of athletic trainers (e.g., Mazerolle, Bruening and Casa, 2008; Mazerolle, Bruening, Casa and Burton, 2008; Mazerolle, Pitney, Casa and Pagnotta, 2011; Mazerolle and Goodman, 2013). Their work has demonstrated that work–family conflict is also a significant contributor to the satisfaction and retention of athletic trainers. Additionally, Mazerolle and colleagues' work has revealed that work–life conflict and balance are significant issues for both men and women, and that both have left the profession as a result. Their work echoes the need for more investigation of the work–life balance of fathers (see also Dixon *et al.*, 2006). Towards that end, Graham and Dixon have developed a research agenda to investigate the work–family experiences of coaching fathers. An initial review article (Graham and Dixon, 2014) examines the tensions of coaching fathers stemming from contrasting perspectives on work and family in larger society versus those in the coaching subculture. These expectations and values create tensions for coaching fathers as they simultaneously seek to be 'good fathers' and 'good coaches'.

Future directions

To expand the existing work, theory building in the area of the work–life interface could take a number of different directions. The three most pressing include expanded examination of fathers in sport, life course applications and experimental designs for reducing conflict/increasing balance.

First, there is clearly an emergent trend and a need to examine the work–life experiences of fathers within sport. As Graham and Dixon (2014) indicated, there is a clear tension for men between traditional notions of work and family (e.g., those outlined by Knoppers, 1992) and emergent social expectations of fathers, particularly to be more involved and engaged in their children's lives. These tensions have implications for individual level stress, coping and career choices, but may also inform work design and organisational culture in sport. Clearly, coaching fathers must be studied and, since a vast majority of management positions in both college and professional sport are also held by men, examinations must extend to those positions as well. As such, the following research questions should be central: (a) what are the work–life experiences of fathers working in the sport industry; and (b) how do gender roles shape those experiences?

Another important direction for the future of this theoretical agenda is the further exploration of the work–life interface over the life course. Clearly both life and career stages need to be part of the equation in an effort to address these questions: (a) how do work–life experiences change over the life-course of employees in the sport industry; (b) how do professional expectations change; and (c) how to familial expectations change?

Finally, while models of work–life conflict and work–life enrichment have been expanded qualitatively (Bruening and Dixon, 2007, 2008; Dixon and Bruening, 2007) and through survey-based research (Kacmar, Crawford, Carlson, Ferguson and Whitten, 2014; Odle-Dusseau, Britt and Greene-Shortridge, 2012), we could not identify any research testing designs to reduce conflict and increase balance, and even enrichment. Scholars could consider the following questions: (a) what conditions optimise the presence of work–family balance and minimise conflict; and (b) how can a supervisor facilitate work–family enrichment in the sport workplace? It might be possible to introduce work–family policy or practice interventions and examine their effects. This could involve more controlled quasi-experimental designs or in-depth cross-case comparisons. The idea is that we have little insight into direct cause-effect relationships of policies and practices. Research designs that would illumine these relationships more strongly would be helpful for creating practical applications.

To date, scholars developing the theoretical model of work–family conflict in sport have focused on a multi-level approach. Work–family interactions of individuals are impacted by the sport organisations in which they work and the socio-cultural context in which they find themselves. Moving forward, scholars need to continue to acknowledge the complex and unique nature of the work–family interface within sport, expanding to include research on fathers, work–family conflict, balance and enrichment over the life course, and utilising experimental designs to better understand and manage work and life roles. The result can be better individual, organisational and socio-cultural outcomes.

Note

1   This chapter is a reflection on Dixon and Bruening (2005) and the work related to it.

References

Boles, J., Howard, W.G. and Donofrio, H. (2001) 'An investigation into the inter-relatioinships of work–family conflict, family-work conflict, and work satisfaction'. *Journal of Managerial Issues*, 13: 376–91.

Bruening, J.E., Borland, J.F. and Burton, L.J. (2008) 'The impact of influential others on the sport participation patterns of African American female student-athletes'. *Journal for the Study of Sports & Athletes in Education*, 3: 379–417.

Bruening, J.E. and Dixon, M.A. (2007) 'Work–family conflict in coaching II: Managing role conflict'. *Journal of Sport Management*, 21: 471–96.

Bruening, J.E. and Dixon, M.A. (2008) 'Situating work–family negotiations within a life course perspective: Insights on the gendered experiences of NCAA Division I head coaching mothers'. *Sex Roles*, 58: 10–23.

Bruening, J.E., Dixon, M.A., Tiell, B., Osbourne, B., Lough, N. and Sweeney, K. (2008) 'The role of the supervisor in the work–life culture of collegiate athletics'. *International Journal of Sport Management*, 9: 250–72.

Bruening, J.E., Dover, K.M. and Clark, B.S. (2009) 'Pre-adolescent female development through sport and physical activity: A case study of an urban afterschool program'. *Research Quarterly for Exercise & Sport*, 80: 87–101.

Chalip, L. (1978) 'Role conflicts in a coaching subculture'. In J. Hinchcliff (ed.) *The nature and meaning of sport in New Zealand* (pp. 62–5). Auckland, NZ: University of Auckland.

Dixon, M.A. and Bruening, J.E. (2005) 'Perspectives on work–family conflict in sport: An integrated approach'. *Sport Management Review*, 8: 227–53.

Dixon, M.A. and Bruening, J.E. (2007) 'Work–family conflict in coaching: A top-down perspective'. *Journal of Sport Management*, 21: 377–406.

Dixon, M.A., Bruening, J., Mazerolle, S., Davis, A., Crowder, J. and Lorsbach, M. (2006) 'Career, family, or both? A case study of young professional baseball players'. *Nine: Journal of Baseball*, 14: 81–101.

Dixon, M.A., Noe, R.A. and Pastore, D.L. (2004) 'Impacting athletic department effectiveness through human resource management: A multi-level model and review of practices'. *Journal of Contemporary Athletics*, 1: 71–98.

Dixon, M.A., Noe, R. and Pastore, D.L. (2008) 'Human resource management systems and organizational effectiveness in non-profit sport organizations: A multilevel approach'. *International Journal of Sport Management*, 9: 22–45.

Dixon, M.A. and Sagas, M. (2007) 'The relationship between organizational support, work family conflict, and the job-life satisfaction of university coaches'. *Research Quarterly for Exercise & Sport*, 78: 236–47.

Dixon, M.A. and Warner, S. (2010) 'Employee satisfaction in sport: Development of a multi-dimensional model in coaching'. *Journal of Sport Management*, 24: 139–68.

Eby, L., Casper, W., Lockwood, A., Bordeaux, C. and Brinley, A. (2005) 'Work and family research in IO/OV: Content analysis and review of the literature (1980–2000)'. *Journal of Vocational Behavior*, 66: 124–97.

Garey, A.I. (1999) *Weaving work and motherhood*. Philadelphia, PA: Temple University Press.

Graham, J. and Dixon, M.A. (2014) 'Coaching fathers in conflict: A review of the tensions surrounding the work–family interface'. *Journal of Sport Management*, 28: 447–56.

Greenhaus, J.H. and Beutell, N.J. (1985) 'Sources of conflict between work and family roles'. *Academy of Management Review*, 10: 76–88.

Greenhaus, J.H., Collins, K.M., Singh, R. and Parasuraman, S. (1997) 'Work and family influences on departure from public accounting'. *Journal of Vocational Behavior*, 50: 249–70.

Greenhaus, J.H. and Brummelhuis, L.L. (2013) 'Models and frameworks underlying work–life research'. In D.A. Major and R. Burke (eds) *Handbook of work–life integration among professionals* (pp. 14–34). Northampton, MA: Elgar Publishing.

Greenhaus, J.H. and Powell, G.N. (2003) 'When work and family collide: Deciding between competing role demands'. *Organizational Behavior & Human Decision Processes*, 90: 291–303.

Grzywacz, J.G. and Marks, N.F. (2000) 'Reconceptualizing the work–family interface: An ecological perspective on the correlates of positive and negative spillover between work and family'. *Journal of Occupational Health Psychology*, 5: 111–26.

Hewlett, S. and Luce, C. (2005) 'Off-ramps and on-ramps: Keeping talented women on the road to success'. *Harvard Business Review*, 83(3): 43–53.

Kacmar, K.M., Crawford, W.S., Carlson, D.S., Ferguson, M. and Whitten, D. (2014) 'A short and valid measure of work–family enrichment'. *Journal of Occupational Health Psychology*, 19: 32–45.

Kanter, R.M. (1977) *Men and women of the corporation*. New York: Basic Books.

Knoppers, A. (1992) 'Explaining male dominance and sex segregation in coaching: Three approaches'. *Quest*, 44: 210–27.

Kozlowski, S.W.J. and Klein, K.J. (2000) 'A multilevel approach to theory and research in organizations: Contextual, temporal, and emergent processes'. In K.J. Klein and S.W.J. Kozlowski (eds) *Multilevel theory, research, and methods in organizations: Foundations, extensions, and new directions* (pp. 3–90). San Francisco, CA: Jossey-Bass.

Leberman, S.I. and Palmer, F.R. (2008) 'Mothers realising choices as leaders in elite sport'. In C. Obel, S. Thompson and T. Bruce (eds) *Women and sport in New Zealand* (pp. 31–50). Hamilton, NZ: Waikato University Press.

Leberman, S.I. and Palmer, F.R. (2009) 'Motherhood, sport leadership and domain theory: Experiences from New Zealand'. *Journal of Sport Management*, 23: 303–34.

Mazerolle, S.M., Bruening, J.E. and Casa, D.J. (2008) 'Work–family conflict, part I: antecedents of work–family conflict in national collegiate athletic association division I-A certified athletic trainers'. *Journal of Athletic Training*, 43: 505–12.

Mazerolle, S.M., Bruening, J.E., Casa, D.J. and Burton, L.J. (2008) 'Work–family conflict, part II: Antecedents of work–family conflict in national collegiate athletic association division I-A certified athletic trainers'. *Journal of Athletic Training*, 43: 513–22.

Mazerolle, S.M., Pitney, W.A., Casa, D.J. and Pagnotta, K.D. (2011) 'Assessing strategies to manage work and life balance of athletic trainers working in the National Collegiate Athletic Association Division I setting'. *Journal of Athletic Training*, 46: 194–205.

Mazzerolle, S.M. and Goodman, A. (2013) 'Fulfillment of work–life balance from the organizational perspective: a case study'. *Journal of Athletic Training*, 48: 668–77.

Odle-Dusseau, H.N., Britt, T.W. and Greene-Shortridge, T.M. (2012) 'Organizational work–family resources as predictors of job performance and attitudes: The process of work–family conflict and enrichment'. *Journal of Occupational Health Psychology*, 17: 28–40.

Parasuraman, S., Purohit, Y.S., Godshalk, V.M. and Buetell, N.J. (1996) 'Work and family variable, entrepreneurial career success and psychological well-being'. *Journal of Vocational Behavior*, 48: 275–300.

Palmer, F. and Leberman, S. (2009) 'Elite athletes as mothers: Managing multiple identities'. *Sport Management Review*, 12: 241–5.

Pastore, D., Inglis, S. and Danylchuk, K. (1996) 'Retention factors in coaching and athletic management: Differences by gender, position, and geographic location'. *Journal of Sport & Social Issues*, 20: 427–41.

Rapoport, R., Fletcher, L. and Pruitt, B. (2002) *Beyond work–family balance*. San Francisco, CA: Jossey-Bass.

Ryan, T.D. and Sagas, M. (2011) 'Coaching and family: the beneficial effects of multiple role membership'. *Team Performance Management*, 17: 168–86.

Schenewark, J. and Dixon, M. (2012) 'A dual model of work–family conflict and enrichment in collegiate coaches'. *Journal of Issues in Intercollegiate Athletics*, 5: 15–39.

Sweet, S. and Moen, P. (2007) 'Integrating educational careers in work and family: Women's return to school and family life quality'. *Community, Work and Family*, 10: 231–50.

Tiell, G., Sweeney, K., Lough, N., Dixon, M. and Bruening, J. (2008) 'The work/life interface in intercollegiate athletics: An examination of policies, programs and institutional climate'. *Journal for the Study of Sports and Athletes in Education*, 2: 137–59.

Weiss, M. and Stevens, C. (1993) 'Motivation and attrition of female coaches: An application of social exchange theory'. *The Sport Psychologist*, 7: 244–61.

Whetten, D. (1989) 'What constitutes a theoretical contribution?' *Academy of Management Review*, 14: 490–5.

Applying work–family conflict theory

Rachel Madsen[1]

I first became aware of Marlene Dixon and Jennifer Bruening's (2005) research on work–family conflict in 2007 when I was a doctoral student researching the lack of women as collegiate head coaches. I had just completed a twelve-year career as a head collegiate basketball coach where the glaring lack of female head coaches was impossible to ignore, but the reasons for the gender gap were not as obvious. Like many others, I assumed that the problem was simply a factor of time, even though more than forty years had passed since Title IX was introduced. However, the statistics had been telling a very different story over the years as the percentage of women as head collegiate coaches had dropped almost steadily since the 1970s and reached an all-time low in 2006 (Acosta and Carpenter, 2014). It became clear to me that time was not the solution and there were certainly other factors at play preventing women from becoming head coaches.

When digging deeper to explore the problem of so few women in coaching, work–family conflict quickly arises as an explanation because coaching careers require very long, non-traditional hours and a great deal of travel away from home and family. However, work–family conflict had often been presented as a single-level theory and, therefore, did not satisfy me as an explanation. In critiquing such simplistic explanations, Dixon and Bruening explained, 'While single-level perspectives have some explanatory value, alone they cannot adequately address behavior in organizations and social contexts' (2005, p. 246). Thus, they expanded work–family conflict into a multi-level theory, which then became very useful in my research on the lack of women in collegiate coaching.

To be specific, when looking at the issue more critically, I began asking why work–family conflict seemed to keep women out of coaching but it did not have the same negative effect on male coaches. Those following a single-level, bottom-up work–family conflict approach would suggest that the women analysed the situation and made rational, individual choices to spend more time with their family. However, as Dixon and Bruening point out, 'we must be cognizant of the potential constraints – both structural and social – that impact individual choices' (2005, p. 232). The description of these multi-level constraints was very important to me, and in particular the explanation that work–family conflict acts on women in very complicated and often unconscious ways.

I have applied Dixon and Bruening's multi-level theory to several projects: my dissertation research exploring why high-level female athletes choose to not pursue coaching careers (Madsen, 2010) and investigating why women are increasingly pursuing careers as assistant coaches, but not head coaches (Madsen, Clark and Burton, 2013). In each project, the participants consistently described multi-level factors (societal, structural and individual) impacting their perception of work–family conflict in coaching careers.

The problem of too few women in coaching is a complicated issue that requires a thorough understanding of the problem. Dixon and Bruening have provided a lens through which to examine the multiple factors acting on women as they navigate athletic careers. Perhaps even more importantly, through discussing a multi-level interactive theory, Dixon and Bruening (2007) also propose that women need not be passive observers of a system that excludes them, but rather they can work from the bottom-up to make college athletics more inclusive. It is this latter point that I stress to students with my current teaching; they recognise college athletics as a somewhat flawed system, closed off to many. With greater awareness and encouragement they can bring about some long overdue positive change.

Note

1   Rachel Madsen is with the College of Hospitality and Tourism Management at Niagara University.

References

Acosta, V. and Carpenter, R. (2014) *A longitudinal, national study: Thirty-seven year update.* West Brookfield, MA: The project on women and social change of Smith College and Brooklyn College of the City University of New York.

Dixon, M.A. and Bruening, J.E. (2005) 'Perspectives on work–family conflict in sport: An integrated approach'. *Sport Management Review,* 8: 227–53.

Dixon, M.A. and Bruening, J.E. (2007) 'Work–family conflict in coaching II: Managing role conflict'. *Journal of Sport Management, 21:* 471–96.

Madsen, R.M. (2010) 'Female student-athletes' intentions to pursue careers in college athletic leadership: The impact of gender socialization'. Unpublished doctoral dissertation, University of Connecticut.

Madsen, R.M., Clark, B.S. and Burton, L.J. (2013, May) 'Gender role expectations and the prevalence of women as assistant coaches'. Presented to the North American Society for Sport Management, Austin, TX.

16

SPORT AND SENSE OF COMMUNITY THEORY[1]

Stacy Warner

Introduction

Sport managers are often concerned with ways to improve the sport experience for their stakeholders. The Sport and Sense of Community Theory, like the other theories presented in this text, provides a guide for sport managers to improving one avenue of the sport experience. Specifically, the theory addresses how community can be built or enhanced within a sport setting. In this chapter, I will provide an overview of the Sport and Sense of Community Theory, along with a description of individual constructs involved in the theory. Next, I highlight the boundary conditions, testing and applicability of the theory. Finally, I discuss the process of developing the theory, extensions, applications and future directions.

Overview

Martene Dixon and I define sense of community as 'community characteristics that lead to members feeling a sense of belonging, attachment, and shared faith and interest in common goals or values' (Warner and Dixon, 2011, p. 258; see also McMillan and Chavis, 1986; Sarason, 1974). Sport stakeholders often assert that fostering a sense of community is a fundamental outcome of the sport experience. There is considerable evidence of such among sport participants (Glover and Bates, 2006; Lyons and Dionigi, 2007), fans and spectators (Chalip, 2006; Clopton, 2009; Swyers, 2010; Warner, Shapiro, Ridinger, Dixon and Harrison, 2011), volunteers (Costa et al., 2006; Green and Chalip, 2004) and even sport/leisure employees (McCole et al., 2012; Kellett and Warner, 2011). However, little work has been done on how and under what conditions this sense of community is cultivated. My work with Dixon resulted in a Sport and Sense of Community Theory. Our theory addresses *how* this phenomenon of fostering a sense of community occurs within a sporting environment.

We identified seven constructs and/or factors that work in concert with one another to facilitate the development of community and, thus, the ensuing sense of community. Based on extensive grounded theory data from a wide array of current and former athletes, we (Warner and Dixon, 2011, 2013) theorize that *administrative consideration, common interest, competition, equity in administrative decisions, leadership opportunities, social spaces* and *voluntary action* are the essential factors or community characteristics that are needed for a sense of community to be fostered among athletes. Creating a sense of community is an important outcome in sport settings because doing so not only helps justify the need and demand for sport, but is associated with programme retention (Kellett and Warner, 2011; Warner, Kerwin and Walker, 2013) and numerous life-quality enhancing benefits, such as improved health (Berkman, Glass, Brissette and Seeman, 2000) and civic participation (Albanesi, Cicognani and Zani, 2007). Thus, capturing how a sense of community is fostered within sport is key to better managing sport and justifying its importance.

Constructs

Administrative consideration involves the expression of care, concern and intentionality by administrators. It has been noted that this consideration from administrators needs to extend beyond that of the athletes' sport experience and also involve a genuine concern for the athlete/person's overall well-being. An example of this would be when a coach or administrator enquires about an athlete's family or an off-the-field endeavour, such as their schooling, jobs or hobbies. *Common interest* is defined as group dynamics, social networking and friendships that result from individuals being brought together by the common interest of the sport, combined with a common goal, shared values or other unifying factors (Warner and Dixon, 2013). We further highlighted that community starts with this common interest, but in order to activate this factor, members must find additional points of attachment, values or goals that extend beyond the actual sporting experience.

Competition reflects the challenges people encounter in seeking to better their rivals. Our initial work revealed that this factor varied by gender. That is, *competition* seemingly enhanced the sense of community for males and detracted for females. Our later work (Warner and Dixon, in press) more clearly distinguished that *external* competition enhanced the sense of community experienced for both males and females; consequently, it is only the *internal* competition that negatively detracted for females. Thus, the rivalry against a common opponent outside of the team and overall competitive atmosphere contributes to the promotion of community for both male and female sport participants.

Next, *equity in administrative decisions* is also a factor that contributes to fostering a sense of community for athletes. This factor is composed of the decisions and practices by administrators that establish that all community members are treated equitably. In other words, when members feel that administrators make fair decisions, the overall sense of community is enhanced. *Leadership opportunities* include both the formal and informal roles and occasions for community members to lead and direct other community members. Thus, this entails holding formal roles, such as team captain or more informally leading a drill during practice or being in charge of a fundraising event. When such leadership roles or positions are available, the sense of community is further cultivated.

Social spaces, or a common area or facility where individuals could interact with one another, is also a key component to fostering a sense of community. This often includes locker rooms, designated cafeteria tables, or lounge areas in or near practice fields or arenas. *Voluntary action* entails the actions related to being in a community when little external pressure exists. That is, when community members join on their own free will without tangible external incentive or peer pressure, a greater sense of community is fostered. In sum, our work found that the seven aforementioned constructs are the fundamental components to the Sport and Sense of Community Theory.

Boundary conditions

Bacharach (1989) stated, 'A theory is a statement of relations among concepts with a set of boundary assumptions and constraints' (p. 496). Consequently, it is important to note the constraints surrounding any theory. The Sport and Sense of Community Theory is based on eighty current and former athletes' sport experiences. While the theory could likely be applied to other stakeholder groups in sport, the data used to construct the theory was specific to the athletes' experience; it was developed and grounded in solely the athletes' words and reflection on their personal experiences.

Our work (Warner, Dixon and Chalip, 2012) noted that while all of the seven identified factors contribute to the creation of a sense of community, the salience of some factors were context specific. This specific work compared US athletes in formal (i.e., varsity athletics) and more informal (i.e., club sports) settings and revealed that all of the factors influenced sense of community, despite not being prominent or readily observable in initial interviews. Thus, when all seven factors were probed in an interview setting, it became evident that they are indeed underlying and influential to the experience. In many cases, the Sport and Sense of Community factors were found to be taken for granted, because they were expected or assumed by the sport participants to be present.

Scholars have defined such factors that are assumed or expected to be present as *must-be* components; they are expected to be present and are only noted when they are not present and consequently often detrimental or dissatisfying to the experience (e.g., Kano *et al.*, 1984; Warner, Newland and Green, 2011). The Sport and Sense of Community factors all fell into this category of being must-be components. For example, our early work suggested that *voluntary action* was salient to athletes in informal club sport settings (Warner and Dixon, 2013). This factor emerged from interviews of the informal club sport athletes, but not initially from varsity athletes in more formal (i.e., professionalised) sport systems (Warner, 2010). When prompted about this in the subsequent study (Warner *et al.*, 2012), the athletes in the more formal setting agreed *voluntary action* is indeed important to their sense of community. These athletes noted that the *voluntary action* is essential and expected, and that its absence led to dissatisfaction and a decreased sense of community. Thus, *voluntary action's* presence and absence impacts the sense of community experienced. We argue that the same holds true for all seven of the identified Sport and Sense of Community Theory factors. That is, all seven factors are essential or 'must-be' factors to fostering a sense of community for athletes.

Testing and application of theory

All theory must be refutable and testable (e.g., Bacharach, 1989; Platt, 1964), while also providing utility (Chalip, 2006; Doherty, 2013; Fink, 2013; Van de Ven, 1989) and answering the 'so what?' question (e.g., Davis, 1971; Whetton, 1989). Although the community psychology, education and sport management literature provide support for the factors that emerged from data to formulate the Sport and Sense of Community Theory, my work with Shannon Kerwin and Matt Walker (Warner, Kerwin and Walker, 2013) further tested and refined the theory. This study empirically assessed and validated the theory (and its factors) through the development of a quantitative scale. It also provided and demonstrated the much-needed utility of the theory.

Using a youth sport population and following the steps outlined by DeVellis (2003), we (Warner, Kerwin and Walker, 2013) put forth a valid and reliable twenty-one-item instrument with six sub-scales (i.e., *administrative consideration, common interest, competition, equity in administrative decisions, leadership*, and *social spaces*) to measure sense of community in sport. The resulting

Sense of Community in Sport scale (SCS) provided empirical support for six of our original seven factors. *Voluntary action* was not supported by the quantitative findings, which we attributed to the age and dependence of the participants on others (i.e., youth participants are heavily dependent on adults for transport, support and resources necessary for their sport participation; consequently, we concluded that *voluntary action* was not relevant to them.). We removed this factor to create a more parsimonious scale that could be applicable across sport settings. That is, *voluntary action* was removed so that the scale would be applicable to both youth and adult sport participants.

The resulting twenty-one-item SCS (Warner, Kerwin and Walker, 2013) was an important contribution to the Sense of Community and Sport Theory, because it tested and demonstrated the utility and applicability of the theory. The SCS provides practitioners and researchers with a means to measure, evaluate and assess the sense of community experienced in sport. Of equal importance, it also demonstrates the usefulness of a theory built from data grounded in the sport realm rather than from borrowed theory. Chalip (2006) advocated that such a sport-focus aids in probing the distinctiveness of sport management and Doherty (2013) suggested that this could narrow the gap between research and practice.

Process

As a doctoral student, who had spent several years working in the sport industry, I had a specific drive to understand the distinctiveness of sport and narrow the gap between research and practice. A class-assigned consumer behaviour article initially spurred the idea that I would attempt to tackle this through exploring a sense of community within a sport setting theory. Specifically, an ethnographic fieldwork of Harley-Davidson motorcycle owners and their community helped initiate the idea (Schouten and McAlexander, 1995). While the article was centred on marketing, brand community and a sub-culture of consumption and was far from my (and PhD advisor, Marlene Dixon's) research interests, it resonated with me. I agreed with the first line of the article and contemplated the parallels to sport. 'The most powerful organizing forces in modern life are the activities and associated interpersonal relationships that people undertake to give their lives meaning' (p. 43). Sport is indeed a powerful organising force in modern life, and from my work in the sport industry, I understood the importance of the interpersonal relationships that develop around sport. More importantly, the development of community or collective group clearly plays an important role in individuals' lives and overall life quality, which *is* fundamental to both Dixon's and my individual research agendas.

Also from my previous work experience in collegiate athletics and campus recreation, I was well aware that creating community was a frequently used, and rarely rebutted, justification for having sport on university campuses. At this point, I began to notice it was not just university sports, but other sport organisations' websites, and even their mission statements, were focused on this idea that they are fostering community. It was evident that many assume and take for granted that sport serendipitously fosters some sense of collective togetherness for individuals. After many conversations with Marlene Dixon, Laurence Chalip and Chris Green and reading numerous articles and books they had suggested, I began to identify this idea of sport fostering a sense of community as an overlooked shared paradigm in the field of sport management (cf. Kuhn, 1996). That is, a shared paradigm is a discipline's specific way of answering or explaining phenomena. It was a paradigm that needed to be challenged, because while many would agree that sport *could* foster a sense of community, it was not readily apparent how or under what conditions it occurs. Chalip's (2006) work was especially influential at this point, as he put forth that community development was one of five common legitimations of sport. He pointed out that because economic impact analyses often fail to demonstrate sport's economic benefit, governmental investments in sport are then justified based on community development in terms of the social and psychological gains. Chalip emphasised that, 'The value of sport in each case depends on the ways that sport is managed. Factors that facilitate and that inhibit optimization of sport's contribution to each [legitimation] must be identified and probed' (p. 1). It became evident that 'whether sport fosters or thwarts community depends on how it is designed and implemented' (p. 8).

Thus, a grounded theory approach seemed like an appropriate avenue, because a resulting sport and sense of community theory would likely challenge a fundamental assumption and justification of sport. In the words of Davis (1971), 'All interesting theories, at least all interesting social theories, then, constitute an attack on the taken-for-granted world of their audience' (p. 311). Chalip's (2006) work clearly pointed to the need to explore the assumption and justification that sport fosters community and heavily influenced the process of building a sport and sense of community theory.

After thorough consultation with existing community psychology literature on sense of community theories, it became evident that a sport-focused and grounded theory approach could indeed contribute to the literature. While Sarason (1974) has been credited with coining the term 'sense of community' and calling for the new discipline of community psychology to develop with this concept at its core, surprisingly this discipline offered few formal theories on a sense of community. The theory derived from McMillian and Chavis' (1986) conceptual work continues to be the most widely used and accepted sense of community theory within the community psychology discipline. This work contends that membership, influence, integration and fulfillment of needs, and shared emotional connections are the four elements of sense of community. However, Hill (1996) and Puddifoot (1996) highlighted the context-specific nature of sense of community and, consequently, lent credence to the value of studying sense of community in different contexts such as sport. As a result, a grounded theory approach was used to explain how a sense of community is fostered in a sport setting. Such an approach is most beneficial when little is known about a topic and the goal is to develop a framework or theory that captures social processes in an effort to explain human behaviour (Glaser and Strauss, 1967).

The first step to building the theory involved the interviewing of twenty former collegiate varsity athletes (Warner and Dixon, 2011). While it would have been appropriate to initially study any specific stakeholder group in sport, I chose to focus on former athletes, 1–5 removed from their playing experience. This was ideal because they were able to reflect on their sport experiences and discuss factors that resonated beyond their sport experiences rather than just proximal experiences (Warner, 2010).

After using an on-going inductive and constant comparison coding process, an initial theory emerged. *Administrative consideration, leadership opportunities, equity in administrative decisions, competition* and *social spaces* were the five factors found to work in concert with one another to foster a sense of community for former varsity athletes. Using the same interview guide, a follow-up studied was conducted with twenty-one former club sport athletes (Warner and Dixon, 2013). This sample was similar, yet distinct, to collegiate athletes from the first study. In the USA, the collegiate varsity athletes' experience is highly structured, regulated, more professionalised and coach-directed. However, the club sport athletes' experiences tend to be more flexible, open and athlete-directed. The results from the club sport athletes revealed that *common interest, leadership opportunities, voluntary activity* and *competition* were the most critical components to creating a sense of community for these participants.

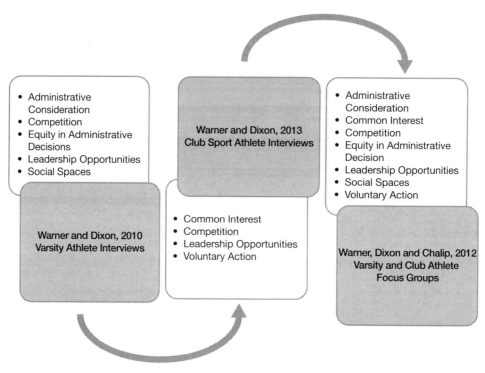

Figure 16.1 Sense of Community Theory development

Since two differing theoretical models emerged, I conducted a third study to triangulate the data (Warner, Dixon and Chalip, 2012[2]). Eight focus groups composed of thirty-nine current varsity and club sport athletes, none of whom were involved in the previous studies, were then conducted. The focus groups were presented with both emergent models. This allowed a new group of participants to cross-validate and then compare and contrast the previous results found in both the varsity and club settings. Ultimately, this work resulted in seven factors. I offer an illustrative summary of this process in Figure 16.1.

Extensions and application

In sum, the Sport and Sense of Community theoretical framework emerged after three unique qualitative investigations that involved eighty current and former adult athletes. The theory was grounded in the experiences of adult athletes. However, its broad application to various stakeholders in and outside of sport is likely (Warner, 2012).

To give an example of application of the theory within sport, Kellett and I (2011) utilised the theory to provide a theoretical framework for our study on umpire retention. After reviewing the data from the umpires regarding their retention, it became clear that the factors that they discussed (e.g., administrative consideration, social spaces, common interest, competition, inequity) that added and detracted from their experiences were all related to the felt sense of community, or lack thereof. Thus, the Sport and Sense of Community Theory provided the theoretical framework for the work. My work with Shannon Kerwin and Matt Walker (Warner, Kerwin and Walker, 2013) lent support to the model for its applicability within a youth athlete population. This study used the Sport and Sense of Community Theory to produce a quantitative tool (i.e., the previously discussed SCS) to measure the felt community among youth archers and swimmers. In doing so, it extended the theory to a youth sport population. We (Kerwin, Warner, Walker and Stevens, in press) subsequently used the theory and modified version of SCS with sport event volunteers. In that study, the six-factor SCS (*voluntary action* was not tested) indicated that the initially identified Sport and Sense of Community factors, except *competition* showed a statistical fit with the event volunteer data. Consequently, this yielded further support of a refined iteration of the initial Sport and Sense of Community Theory (Warner and Dixon, 2011, 2013). More importantly, like the umpiring study, it extended the theory's application beyond just athletes. Furthermore these works suggested that more testing and refinement, with special attention regarding the *voluntary action* and *competition* factors, would likely result in a more parsimonious and broadly applicable theory.

The work done thus far has focused on individuals' experiences in communities; however, more work is also needed at the group or macro level. Comparing and contrasting sport communities versus other communities of interest and understanding the nuances and different outcomes would extend this line of research. For example, comparing the experiences of members of a participatory sport club versus members of a political support group could yield further insight on the distinctiveness (or lack thereof) of sport settings and the development of communities. We also needed to know more about the outcomes and consequences of being in a community. For the most part, scholars focus on the positive outcomes related to the improvement in life quality for those that experience a sense of community. However, it can be argued that gangs and those involved in hooliganism experience strong sense of community, but reap many negative outcomes.

Potential extension and applications of the Sport and Sense of Community Theory outside of sport are also possible. Maslow's Theory of Motivation (1943) tells us that after the basic physiological and safety needs are met, individuals have an innate desire for interpersonal interaction and to feel a sense of belonging. Thus, understanding the environmental characteristics necessary to create this atmosphere for individuals in various contexts could potentially have widespread implications. While the SCS and/or the theory have not be tested outside of sport, many of the factors may likely apply to not just athletes or those in a sport setting, but outside of sport, as all individuals have an innate desire for community.

Future directions

Data and support have been found for the Sport and Sense of Community Theory; however, the strength of a theory rests in its utility for practice. Steps to apply the theory to individuals in and outside of sport have begun. Because sense of community is theoretically and empirically linked to retention (Kellett and Warner, 2011; McCole *et al.*, 2012; Warner, Kerwin and Walker, 2013), the framework could impact various groups and individuals concerned with participant retention and, subsequently, improve life quality. Sport is highly dependent upon volunteer labour (Costa *et al.*, 2006; Doherty and Carron, 2003; Green and Chalip, 2004) and sport officials (e.g., Tingle, Warner and Sartore-Baldwin, 2014; Warner, Tingle and Kellett, 2013). Consequently, using the framework to study these key personnel and their retention provides the initial steps towards that end. That is, this work provided the groundwork for potentially using the theory to explore other groups concerned with retention and life quality. For example, work environments that are especially concerned with employee retention would likely be a suitable place to extend the applicability of this theory.

In addition to studying employees, hedonic rewards and opportunities for social interaction (and the ensuing sense of community experienced) are two overlooked, yet primary, benefits sought by participants in physical activity programmes (Berg, Warner and Das, 2015). This indicates that extending and testing the Sport and Sense of Community theory in programmatic settings may lead to better-designed programmes, which may provide a meaningful public health impact. That is, if we can use the Sport and Sense of Community Theory as a guide to better designing physical activity programmes, it is possible that more participants can be retained in these programmes such that greater health results are achieved. Considering physical activity, participants explicitly noted in Berg and colleagues' (2015) recent work that they are looking for opportunities for social interaction, so creating an environment that fosters a greater sense of community would help in retaining more participants in these programmes.

Notes

1   In this chapter, the author reflects on the development of the Sport and Sense of Community Theory (Warner and Dixon, 2011, 2013).
2   This study was conducted following the varsity athlete (Warner and Dixon, 2011) and club athlete (Warner and Dixon, 2013) work, but was published in 2012.

References

Albanesi, C., Cicognani, E. and Zani, B. (2007) 'Civic involvement, sense of community and social well being in adolescence', *Journal of Community & Applied Social Psychology, 17*: 387–406.

Bacharach, S.B. (1989) 'Organizational theories: Some criteria for evaluation'. *Academy of Management Review, 14*: 496–515.

Berg, B., Warner, S. and Das, B. (2015) 'What about sport? A public health perspective on leisure-time physical activity'. *Sport Management Review, 18*: 20–31.

Berkman, L.F., Glass, T., Brissette, I. and Seeman, T.E. (2000) 'From social integration to health: Durkheim in the new millennium'. *Social Science & Medicine, 51*: 843–57.

Chalip, L. (2006) 'Toward a distinctive sport management discipline'. *Journal of Sport Management, 20*: 1–21.

Clopton, A. (2009) 'Students as spectators: Their academic and social integration'. *New Directions for Higher Education, 148*: 83–9.

Costa, C.A., Chalip, L., Green, B.C. and Simes, C. (2006) 'Reconsidering the role of training in event volunteers' satisfaction'. *Sport Management Review, 9*: 165–82.

Davis, M. (1971) 'That's interesting: Towards a phenomenology of sociology and a sociology of phenomenology'. *Philosophy of the Social Sciences, 1*: 309–44.

DeVellis, R.F. (2003) *Scale development: Theory and applications* (second edn). Thousand Oaks, CA: Sage.

Doherty, A. (2013) 'Investing in sport management: The value of good theory'. *Sport Management Review, 16*: 5–11.

Doherty, A.J. and Carron, A.V. (2003) 'Cohesion in volunteer sport executive committees'. *Journal of Sport Management, 17*: 116–41.

Fink, J.S. (2013) 'Theory development in sport management: My experiences and other considerations'. *Sport Management Review, 16*: 17–21.

Glaser, B. and Strauss, A. (1967) *The discovery of grounded theory strategies for qualitative research.* New York, NY: Aldine.

Glover, T.D. and Bates, N.R. (2006) 'Recapturing a sense of neighborhood since lost: Nostalgia and the formation of First String, a Community Team Inc'. *Leisure Studies, 25*: 329–51.

Green, B.C. and Chalip, L. (2004) 'Paths to volunteer commitment: Lessons from the Sydney Olympic Games'. In R.A. Stebbins and M. Graham (eds) *Volunteering as leisure/leisure as volunteering* (pp. 49–67). Oxfordshire, UK: Cambi Publishing.

Hill, J. (1996) 'Psychological sense of community: Suggestions for future research'. *Journal of Community Psychology, 24*: 431–8.

Kano, N., Nobuhiko, S., Takahashi, F. and Shinichi, T. (1984) 'Attractive quality and must-be quality'. *Journal of the Japanese Society for Quality Control*, *14*: 39–48.

Kellett, P. and Warner, S. (2011) 'Creating communities that lead to retention: The social worlds and communities of umpires'. *European Sport Management Quarterly*, *11*: 475–98.

Kerwin, S., Warner, S., Walker, M. and Stevens, J. (in press) 'Exploring sense of community among small-scale sport event volunteers'. *European Sport Management Quarterly*.

Kuhn, T.S. (1996) *The structure of scientific revolutions* (third edn). Chicago, IL: University of Chicago Press.

Lyons, K. and Dionigi, R. (2007) 'Transcending emotional community: A qualitative examination of older adults and masters' sports participation'. *Leisure Sciences*, *29*: 375–89.

McCole, D. Jacobs, J., Lindley, L. and McAvoy, B. (2012) 'The relationship between seasonal employee retention and sense of community: The case of summer camp employment'. *Journal of Parks & Recreation Administration*, *30*: 85–191.

McMillan, D. and Chavis, D. (1986) 'Sense of community: A definition and theory'. *Journal of Community Psychology*, *14*: 6–23.

Maslow, A. (1943) 'A theory of human motivation'. *Psychological Review*, *50*: 370–96.

Platt, J.R. (1964) 'Strong inference'. *Science: New Series*, *146*: 347–53.

Puddifoot, J.E. (1996) 'Some initial considerations in the measurement of community identity'. *Journal of Community Psychology*, *24*: 327–36.

Sarason, S.B. (1974) *The psychological sense of community: Prospects for a community psychology*. San Francisco, CA: Jossey-Bass.

Schouten, J.W. and McAlexander, J.H. (1995) 'Subcultures of consumption: An ethnography of the new bikers'. *Journal of Consumer Research*, *22*: 43–61.

Swyers, H. (2010) *Wrigley regulars: Finding community in the bleachers?* Champaign, IL: University of Illinois Press.

Tingle, J., Warner, S. and Sartore-Baldwin, M. (2014) 'The experience of former women referees and the community level impact'. *Sex Roles*. DOI: 10.1007/s11199–014–0366–8.

Van de Ven, A.H. (1989) 'Nothing is quite so practical as a good theory'. *Academy of Management Review*, *14*: 486–9.

Warner, S. (2010) 'Sport and social structures: Building community on campuses'. Doctoral dissertation. Available from University of Texas at Austin.

Warner, S. (2012) 'Sport and community'. In G.B. Cunningham and J.N. Singer (eds) *Sociology of sport and physical activity* (second edn, pp. 237–54). College Station, TX: Center for Sport Management Research and Education.

Warner, S. and Dixon, M.A. (in press) 'Competition, gender, and the sport experience: An exploration among collegiate athletes'. *Sport, Education and Society*.

Warner, S. and Dixon, M.A. (2011) 'Understanding sense of community from an athlete's perspective'. *Journal of Sport Management*, *25*: 258–72.

Warner, S. and Dixon, M.A. (2013) 'Sport and community on campus: Constructing a sport experience that matters'. *Journal of College Student Development*, *54*: 283–98.

Warner, S., Dixon, M.A. and Chalip, L.C. (2012) 'The impact of formal versus informal sport: Mapping the differences in sense of community'. *Journal of Community Psychology*, *40*: 983–1003.

Warner, S., Kerwin, S. and Walker, M. (2013) 'Examining sense of community in sport: Developing the multidimensional 'SCS' Scale'. *Journal of Sport Management*, *27*: 349–62.

Warner, S., Newland, B. and Green, B.C. (2011) 'More than motivation: Reconsidering volunteer management tools'. *Journal of Sport Management*, *25*: 391–407.

Warner, S., Shapiro, S., Dixon, M.A., Ridinger, L.L. and Harrison, S. (2011) 'The football factor: Shaping community on campus'. *Journal of Issues in Intercollegiate Athletics*, *4*: 236–56.

Warner, S., Tingle, J. and Kellett, P. (2013) 'Officiating attrition: The experiences of former referees'. *Journal of Sport Management*, *27*: 316–28.

Whetton, D. (1989) 'What constitutes a theoretical contribution?' *Academy of Management Review*, *14*: 490–5.

Applying Sport and Sense of Community Theory

Emily Sparvero[1]

I was first introduced to Warner's ideas about sport and sense of community while she was still a doctoral student and we were engaging in a favourite pastime of academics: discussing the big ideas in the field over cheap burgers. In my own work, I was primarily focused on the potential economic benefits attributable to sport. However, the idea of exploring the associated sense of community was intriguing and seemed to constitute an important missing piece in discussions about the value of sport. The economic arguments for sport have consistently been disproved (c.f. Siegfried and Zimbalist, 2000) and, as a result, there has been increasing emphasis on non-economic benefits, including those benefits associated with community. Although there are frequent references in the academic literature to the community benefits associated with both participant and spectator sport (Crompton, 2004; Eckstein and Delaney, 2002; Misener and Mason, 2006; Schulenkorf and Edwards, 2012), there had not been coherent efforts to define community benefits specific to the sport context. Thus, Warner's attempts to contextualise sense of community within sport were especially appealing when considered in concert with efforts in the field to establish sport management as a distinctive discipline.

I have used Warner's work (Warner and Dixon, 2011; Warner and Dixon, 2013; Warner, Dixon and Chalip (2012) in a variety of sport management classes and have found it to be especially relevant to courses with a managerial focus (e.g., strategic management, organisational behaviour, sport policy). When teaching these courses, I emphasise the importance of alignment between an organisation's mission/vision and its structure, systems and processes. Warner's work allows for measurement of sense of community, but perhaps more importantly, it identifies specific organisational factors that either enable or inhibit sense of community in sport settings. Thus, students are encouraged to consider the following: (a) the importance of sense of community to a sport organisation; (b) the extent to which its pursuit is consistent with broader strategic goals, and (c) how sport organisations can implement processes and functions to promote sense of community. In management-oriented courses, I challenge students to consider whether sport is more or less efficient in creating a sense of community than other alternatives (e.g., does participation in high school athletics create greater/superior sense of community as compared with high school theatre? For whom is the sense of community created?) Additionally, from a policy perspective, students are encouraged to consider sense of community as not only an end unto itself, but as a means to achieving other desirable policy goals.

To date, Warner has focused on athletes, officials and volunteers and their sense of community. I believe that a natural extension of this work is the examination of the sense of community among sport fans and spectators. Additionally, a comparative approach could be used to determine the most efficient ways to build sense of community through sport. There are varied sport systems, even within the same institutions (e.g., varsity, club and intramural sport at the university level). A better understanding of the full range and scale of benefits delivered through these systems could have significant impacts on the way sport is delivered and funded.

Note

1   Emily Sparvero is with the Department of Kinesiology and Health Education and the University of Texas at Austin.

References

Crompton, J. (2004) 'Beyond economic impact: An alternative rationale for the public subsidy of Major League sports facilities'. *Journal of Sport Management, 18*: 40–58.

Eckstein, R. and Delaney, K. (2002) 'New sports stadiums, community self-esteem, and community collective conscience'. *Journal of Sport & Social Issues, 26*: 235–47.

Misener, L. and Mason, D. (2006) 'Creating community networks: Can sporting events offer meaningful sources of social capital?' *Managing Leisure, 11*: 39–56.

Schulenkorf, N. and Edwards, D. (2012) 'Maximizing positive social impacts: Strategies for sustaining and leveraging the benefits of intercommunity sport events in divided societies'. *Journal of Sport Management, 26*: 379–90.

Siegfried, J. and Zimbalist, A. (2000) 'The economics of sport facilities and their communities'. *Journal of Economic Perspectives, 14*: 95–114.

Warner, S. and Dixon, M.A. (2011) 'Understanding sense of community from an athlete's perspective'. *Journal of Sport Management, 25*: 258–72.

Warner, S. and Dixon, M.A. (2013) 'Sport and community on campus: Constructing a sport experience that matters'. *Journal of College Student Development, 54*: 283–98.

Warner, S., Dixon, M.A. and Chalip, L. (2012) 'The impact of formal versus informal sport: Mapping the differences in sense of community'. *Journal of Community Psychology, 40*: 983–1003.

PART III

Marketing theories

17

SPONSORSHIP-LINKED MARKETING[1]

T. Bettina Cornwell

Overview

Phenomenon of interest

I coined the term 'sponsorship-linked marketing' early on in order to distinguish marketing *via* sports from the marketing *of* sports (Cornwell, 1995). Sponsoring was coming into the business limelight and terms were being used pell-mell. At the time, I also needed a term that focused not on the sponsorship deal or contract, but on the marketing surrounding it. Thus, defining 'sponsorship-linked marketing as the orchestration and implementation of marketing activities for the purpose of building and communicating an association (link) to a sponsorship' (Cornwell, 1995, p. 15) served a descriptive purpose. My research interest has largely been about how one goes about building and communicating associations between the sponsor and the sponsored. At this point, sponsorship-linked marketing could be termed approximate theory, or what Merton (1945) described so long ago as general orientation towards substantive material because it serves to 'indicate types of variables which are somehow to be taken into account rather than specifying determinate relationships between particular variables' (p. 464).

Under the general umbrella of sponsorship-linked marketing many particular theoretical orientations are possible. In subsequent work with colleagues and students (e.g., Chien, Cornwell and Pappu, 2011; Cornwell, Humphreys, Maguire, Weeks and Tellegen 2006; Weeks, Cornwell and Humphreys, 2006) there has been effort to advance and test theory. In my 2008 paper titled, 'State of the art and science in sponsorship-linked marketing', one particular theoretical orientation was developed. The history and growth of sponsorship was reviewed in this paper, but the main theoretical discussion orients on how sponsorship works and, at times, *does not work as we expect.*

Constructs and key propositions

The conceptual understanding presented in the 2008 paper builds on work regarding associative networks (Anderson and Bower, 1973) and spreading activation (Collins and Loftus, 1975). Briefly, the thinking is that knowledge is stored in memory in the form of linked nodes of information and activation of a node through some stimulation spreads and, in doing so, supports retrieval of stored information. Jumping forward, this conceptualisation of memory, and others like it, have informed marketing for decades. For example, in a conceptual model of brand knowledge, Keller (1993) shows that sponsorship activities become linked to the brand node in memory in an associative network. He further argues that experience with the brand results in greater associative strength. These associations and their strength are what drive much of what is subsequently measured as success in sponsoring (e.g., brand-event relationship recall, brand awareness given the event as a cue and brand attitudes). It should be noted that despite these roots in psychology and theory they imply, it is the case that in marketing and sponsorship we often do not measure empirically the processes we posit.

Nonetheless, to describe how memories and, in particular, brand knowledge are developed gives clues as to how sponsorship's contribution to knowledge might best be measured and understood; however, to take it a step further and begin to make predictions, one must consider more particular aspects of how associations are developed and made strong via sponsoring. To that end, six propositions were put forward in that 2008 paper, and are reviewed here with the briefest possible introduction.

As a starting point, research must consider how pre-existing memories might contribute to recall. Researchers have shown that when recall is cued with an associate (in the sponsorship case, the event) for the target (the sponsor), the network of associations emanating from both the cue and the target are involved in the recall process (Nelson, Bennett and Leibert, 1997; Nelson and McEvoy, 2002). For instance, if one were familiar with Oscar Myer products and also United States baseball then a natural connection of 'hot dogs' might come to mind. Following is the first proposition:

Proposition 1: Natural mediators arise and influence memory for sponsorship-linked communications.

If natural links could not be capitalised upon, communication managers could supply a concept to support the link between the sponsor and activity. For example, an insurance company may not have much in common with little league baseball but if the team were located in the same city as the firm, this shared aspect could be brought forward and made salient. This example is, however, not strongly distinctive if there are many insurance companies in the city and moreover less distinctive if several of them sponsor little league baseball teams. This suggests a second testable proposition:

Proposition 2: Plausible (yet distinctive) supplied mediating associations can help individuals form better memories for sponsor-event linkages and may also influence formation of positive attitudes.

Further, articulation or reasons to form an explicit memory for the sponsor-event relationship (Cornwell *et al.*, 2006) may support memory and differentiate this relationship from other plausible event-brand partnerships. Keeping with the example of an insurance company and sponsor-ship of child participation baseball, it might be possible to articulate the value of child sport participation as a pathway to health and as a way to avoid obesity, something in everyone's best interest. Thus, the following proposition is derived:

Proposition 3: Providing a link of information relating to the sponsor and event may help establish memory for the sponsor as contrasted to any direct competitors.

The first three propositions dealt with providing a link and developing memory for it. The next two propositions delve into a different theoretical base and present different study design challenges. Based on the conceptual discussion in Weeks *et al.* (2006), both item information and relational information may be useful in sponsorship communications. An oversimplification of the work of Einstein and Hunt (1980; Hunt and Einstein, 1981) suggests that distinctiveness encoding applies to the processing of item information, while similarity encoding applies to the processing of relational information. Relational information helps to activate a general class, or category, to which a specific stimulus belongs. Item information is then used to search within this delimited group of representations. Einstein and Hunt propose that relational and item information both contribute to memory retrieval, but in different ways. If someone is asked, 'Which brand is the title sponsor of the Little League Baseball World Series?' relational processing is required to activate memories related to the category of 'Little League Baseball World Series', then item processing would be used to discriminate among all activated representations to identify the one with the distinctive feature of major sponsor. If a huge number of matches still occur due to their fit with baseball, an individual will still have problems plucking the right answer from memory. This theorising leads to two propositions:

Proposition 4: A brand with a diffuse image (and many varied associations) might be congruent with, and fit with, more sponsorship opportunities, but memory for sponsorship relationships would be expected to be poor.

Proposition 5: A brand with a very distinctive image might have to work to develop fit with a sponsorship opportunity but would then be expected to have a stronger relationship in memory due to the distinctiveness of the association.

The final proposition from the 2008 paper deals with the generalisability of the proposed thinking beyond sponsorship to brand placement, buzz marketing and social media marketing. Importantly, this final proposition questions the nature and quality of indirect communications such as sponsorship. While on the one hand, they may be richer in some ways due to their connection with the passion of sport or more focused in terms of demographics, they will likely also be more variable. Individuals experiencing a sponsor's message during a sporting event, live or broadcast, will not be provided with a singular interpretation of their presence there. There are advantages and disadvantages to sponsoring as a communication platform and this is one possible disadvantage that is shared with all forms of indirect marketing.

Proposition 6: Indirect marketing communications result in context-dependent associations that are more variable and idiosyncratic than associations developed via traditional advertising messages.

Boundaries

This thinking about how sponsorship-linked marketing works is focused on communications and is primarily consumer-oriented. Areas such as integrated communications, brand image, collateral communications, promotion and, of course, sponsorship leveraging and activation all work with the basic premise of developing strong linkages. While research on sponsorship-linked marketing has been primarily located in mass communication, it applies equally well to grassroots (small scale) sponsoring. It is even relevant to sales management and business networking. After all, managers have memories too and associations to an organisation held in memory influence them as well. Managerial issues, planning and control of sponsorship programmes, as well as areas such as proposal development and pricing were not within the ambit of this paper in 2008 but do, in many ways, contribute to sponsorship communication success.

Testing and application in subsequent research

One of the most direct applications of the theoretical thinking presented in the 2008 paper is found in a 2012 study of free recall (Cornwell, Humphreys, Quinn and McAlister, 2012). This counterintuitive research shows that sponsorship exposures can indeed support memory for sponsors but under certain conditions the mention of direct competitors can also facilitate recall of sponsors and events. Competitors are natural associations. The brand Adidas brings to mind the brand Nike and vice versa. These associates, depending on how they are presented, might form a distinction in one's mind (e.g., 'this one is the sponsor because I know the other one did that outrageous ambushing'). This is not to say that the competitor or ambusher was not also remembered, but rather, that to understand how memory-based characteristics influence sponsorship-linked marketing measurement requires accepting and anticipating possible hidden associations. When major competitors in a category (think Gatorade and Powerade, for example) take up sport sponsorships, unless there is some distinctiveness in marketing (e.g., sideline orange drink dispensers utilised by Gatorade) the associative network is largely interchangeable.

Process

How I became interested in sponsorship

The Men's Tennis Open was in town and I met the Vice President North America for Volvo. He said Volvo felt their sponsorships in tennis were valuable but they wanted evidence to take to decision-makers, and asked if I had any recommendations. I did. Marketing leaders had already been talking for some time about the 'death of advertising' at the hand of new technology (Rust and Oliver, 1994) and observers could feel the great sea change in marketing communications that would take place in the next decades. In this mix, I could see the birth of sponsorship-linked marketing and I had some ideas about how to measure the value.

I already had some thoughts about the appalling, yet fascinating, ways in which tobacco companies had circumnavigated advertising bans through sponsorship (Cornwell, 1997). Tobacco companies had been forced by law to reach markets in new ways. On the grounds of health and environment, I am categorically opposed to the production and consumption of tobacco, but you have to hand it to them, they made the best of a difficult situation. Tobacco companies invested heavily in sponsorship and still do in many countries in order to circumnavigate bans on broadcast advertising. Some observe that in advance of proposed limits and bans for unhealthy food and drink, producers in these categories are moving into sponsorship.

Companies in other industries also moved away from traditional advertising in the last two decades, but not by mandate – rather because of the narrowing relevance traditional advertising had to their goals and markets. These companies began to reach their markets in new ways. Volvo was early in this trend through the happenstance, as reported to me, of their leadership having noted the striking similarity between Volvo owner demographics and tennis participant demographics. There were many more of these patterns out there and brand managers were about to make use of them. This fascinating context for consumer research and applied psychology would have endless interesting questions to investigate.

Not to sound overly rosy, I must add that initial thinking about the importance of sponsorship, as a marketing communications platform, was not well received. My excitement for the topic was dampened a bit when an 'A+' marketing journal returned a reviewer comment that read 'sponsorship is a topic tangential to marketing and will never see the light of day in a top quality journal'. I include this comment for junior authors that may face harsh critique in the review process. If something is inherently interesting to you, listen to what reviewers say but don't be put down by them. They could possibly be wrong.

The manner in which I thought/think

Some of my favourite thinking on theory actually comes from management. Sutton and Staw (1995) wrote about 'what theory is not' in an effort to help authors avoid the criticism of inadequate theory development. While they admitted what constitutes strong theory is not readily agreed upon (which is still the case today), they argued that references, data, variables, diagrams and hypotheses are not theory. A favourite sentence is 'listing references to existing theories and mentioning the names of such theories is not the same as explicating the causal logic they contain' (Sutton and Staw, 1995, p. 372). It is true and we are guilty of this in marketing, especially when 'borrowing theory' from psychology.

My PhD from the University of Texas was from the business school and concentrated in marketing, but my minor areas were in statistics and cognitive psychology. I came to admire the clever designs that experimental researchers use to disclose process. Many applied topics do not need to nail down exact processing but I think in terms of processes even when they are not being measured. While it is possible to capture a great scree of variables and to look for correlations between them, this approach is context dependent. Fishing for variance can bring a catch, but not consistently. Theory helps one to rise above the particular and to see and predict general patterns.

Extensions and applications

The term 'sponsorship-linked marketing' is utilised extensively in research in keeping with the original definition as outlined. Under this approximate theoretical construct many applications and several extensions can be found. As an application example, Chien *et al.* (2011) utilised social cognition and categorisation theory to understand how brand personalities from sport and charity become part of the brand's image. During the experiments, a sponsorship portfolio communicated images and associations that were found to influence brand meaning clarity and consistency for the sponsoring brand. Interestingly, when the sport was rugged (Rugby) and the charity was also rugged (in this example Greenpeace – known for their Rainbow Warriors) the sponsoring brand received a 'spike' in brand personality from association. This research shows the importance of available associates in building brand meaning.

Sponsorship-linked advertising

Kelly, Cornwell, Coote and McAlister (2012) extended sponsorship-linked marketing to sponsorship-linked advertising. Discussed ratios in sponsorship suggest that brands spend the same, or more, beyond the sponsorship deal in advertising and promotion. Much of this is sponsorship-linked or thematically tied to sponsorships. Kelly *et al.* (2012) examined the extent to which linked advertising was ambushing from organisations not having a legitimate sponsor role.

Findings across two studies and hundreds of advertisements showed that thematically tied ads were largely from ambushers (Kelly *et al.*, 2012). Returning to the theoretical reasoning about the use of item and relational information, the researchers found evidence that ambushers utilise relational cues, such as timing and context, to imply a relationship to an event. Interestingly, actual sponsors often do not exercise their opportunities to link to events in advertising and develop relational information, but rather utilise product-focused advertising without mention of their major investment in sponsorship.

Sponsorship-linked internal marketing

Farrelly and Greyser (2012) extended sponsorship-linked marketing to the internal audience. They explained sponsorship-linked internal marketing (SLIM) as encompassing 'all activities associated with the conceptualization and leveraging of sport sponsorship to better satisfy employee needs as a way of preparing them to serve customers more effectively' (p. 507). Their research, based on twenty-two in-depth interviews with senior marketing and sponsorship managers from six countries, found that many corporate identity and performance programmes were built around sport sponsorships. Programmes emphasised sport-related topics such as reaching for one's personal best or building a team. The programmes had one or more of the following orientations: identity and performance enhancing, strategy and planning-oriented, organisation engagement development, leadership development, and rewards and goal setting. Farrelly and Greyser's SLIM departed from the communications orientation of the original work but retained the emphasis on linking. This research could be applied beyond sport and could be conceptualised and measured as a contributor to brand or corporate equity.

Use in teaching and practice

The University of Michigan offers a course titled 'Sponsorship-Linked Marketing' in the Sport Management major taught by Dr Dae Hee Kwak. This is a legacy course in that it was established and named when I was there. Given that it continues as a part of the curriculum and has been developed and extended by Dr Kwak is testament to the value it offers students. Dr Jörg Königstorfer at the Technische Universität München also offers a course titled 'Sponsorship-Linked Marketing' in their Department of Sport and Health Management. In correspondence with him I have learned that the 'State of the art and science in sponsorship-linked marketing' paper and others regarding sponsorship-linked marketing are used extensively in the class. Further, the 2008 paper was also included in the *Handbook of research on sport and business* (Elgar, 2013).

It is more difficult to capture the extent to which an academic article, or even a series of them, influences practice. One indicator is that books for practitioners cite the work. In this case, the 2008 paper has been cited in Sten Söderman's *Football and management: Comparisons between sport and enterprise* (Söderman, 2013). I have utilised ideas from the 2008 paper in my book titled *Sponsorship in marketing: Effective communication through sports, arts, and events* (Cornwell, 2014). This book is a 'cross-over' book designed for business professionals and students alike. Another indicator of application would be that the ideas are utilised in a case oriented to practice such as that by Cianfrone and Zhang (2013) on in-game advertising effectiveness in sport video games.

The clearest indicator that one's work has informed practice comes when practitioners contact you. For example, Mr Royce Wolfe, Vice President of Experiential Marketing, Sponsorship Strategy at Wells Fargo reads academic work on sponsorship, including mine. He seeks to continuously improve the value of sponsorship at Wells Fargo and utilises academic work in developing strategy.

Future directions

Sponsorship and social media

As I have mentioned elsewhere (Cornwell, 2014), the melding of social media and sponsorship is one of the most important trends in sponsoring. People are not that interested in the typical brand on Facebook. Sponsoring teams, athletes, performers and the arts provides the story, or the content, for social interaction that is lacking in many corporate social media attempts. On the other hand, social media interactions provide the tracking that sponsorship currently lacks. There are myriad ways to link, and articulate a link, between a brand and an event or activity and to measure the strength of this developed relationship. Brand managers are keenly interested in understanding the link between on-field and online in sports.

Internal marketing via sponsorship

We are only beginning to explore the values of sponsorship-linked marketing within firms that sponsor. Internal marketing, or marketing activities directed to those inside the firm, is a largely unaccounted value of sponsoring that brand managers naturally do not consider. Nonetheless, employees and future employees are influenced by the sponsorships held by a firm. For example, Hickman, Lawrence and Ward (2005) studied a NASCAR partnership held by a major trucking company and found that affinity for the firm's NASCAR sponsorship was related to feelings of identification with the firm, commitment to the firm and customer satisfaction.

While not an internal market, *per se*, potential future employees reached via a firm's sponsorship engagement are of interest. For example, Enterprise, a car rental company with a huge US presence, sponsors the National Collegiate Athletic Association and views sponsorship-linked advertising to be effective for consumer–employee engagement and employee recruitment. The extent to which sport attributes (e.g., 'fairness' or 'fun') become associated with the employer is another sponsorship-linked marketing effect that should be taken into account.

Sponsorship and corporate social responsibility

Sponsorship of sport is globally the activity that receives the majority of spending; however, there has been a trend towards more social and cause sponsorships since the great recession of 2007–8. Sponsoring causes, or activities that could be thought of as socially responsible, works similarly to sponsoring in other areas. However, cause sponsorship is designed to develop goodwill and this often means that the brand or corporate relationship with the event or activity should be remembered and be authentic (Pappu and Cornwell, 2014). When sales are the goal, as is often the case with fast-moving consumer goods, one may not, and in fact should not, be oriented to the recall of the sponsor–event relationship (Cornwell and Humphreys, 2013). In contrast, for-cause related marketing is not enough to just influence sales, rather the goal is to build an image and to connect with the cause in a way that brings goodwill to the sponsor. This typically requires memory for the sponsor–cause relationship.

An additional challenge is in understanding of sponsorship-linked marketing effects when sport entities include their own beneficiary charities, which is evermore the case (e.g., National Football League and Play60 for youth sport participation). Today's sponsorship landscape is increasingly a complex fabric of associations found not only with sports and charities, but also the individual athletes and celebrities having developed ties to charitable causes to cultivate their own brand identity. To gain traction and break through a wall of cluttered communications, a brand must focus on a set of associations. The corporate sponsor, the sport, the charity and each individual celebrity bring a host of associations to the brand. These associations are so numerous that the challenge is to identify those to build upon and those to ignore.

Sponsorship-linked marketing has served up an endless set of research opportunities. As the practice of sponsoring has evolved and matured new questions have arisen. Approaches and measurements from only a few decades ago have been revisited (Pappu and Cornwell, 2014). The dynamic nature of sponsorship makes it inherently interesting as a place to study communications, corporate social responsibility and brand building into the future.

Note

1   This chapter is a reflection on Cornwell (2008) and the work related to it.

References

Anderson, J.R. and Bower, G.H. (1973) *Human associative memory: A brief edition*. Hillsdale, NJ: Erlbaum and Associates.

Chien, M., Cornwell, T.B. and Pappu, R. (2011) 'Sponsorship portfolio as brand image creation strategy'. *Journal of Business Research, 64*: 142–49.

Cianfrone, B.A. and Zhang, J.J. (2013) 'The impact of gamer motives, consumption, and in-game advertising effectiveness: A case study of football sport video games'. *International Journal of Sport Communication, 6*: 325–47.

Collins, A.M. and Loftus, E.F. (1975) 'A spreading-activation theory of semantic processing'. *Psychological Review, 82*: 407–28.

Cornwell, T.B. (1995) 'Sponsorship–linked marketing development'. *Sport Marketing Quarterly, 4*: 13–24.

Cornwell, T.B. (1997) 'The use of sponsorship-linked marketing by tobacco firms: international public policy issues'. *Journal of Consumer Affairs, 31*: 238–54.

Cornwell, T.B. (2008) 'State of the art and science in sponsorship-linked marketing'. *Journal of Advertising, 37*: 41–55.

Cornwell, T.B. (2014) *Sponsorship in marketing: Effective communication through sports, arts and events*. London: Routledge.

Cornwell, T.B. and Humphreys, M.S. (2013) 'Memory for sponsorship relationship: A critical juncture in thinking'. *Psychology & Marketing, 30*: 394–407.

Cornwell, T.B., Humphreys, M.S., Maguire, A.M., Weeks, C.S. and Tellegen, C.L. (2006) 'Sponsorship-linked marketing: The role of articulation in memory'. *Journal of Consumer Research, 33*: 312–21.

Cornwell, T.B., Humphreys, M.S., Quinn, E. and McAlister, A.R. (2012) 'Memory of sponsorship-linked communications: The effect of competitor mentions'. *SAGE Open*: 1–14.

Einstein, G.O. and Hunt, R.R. (1980) 'Levels of processing and organization: Additive effects of individual-item and relational processing'. *Journal of Experimental Psychology: Human Learning & Memory, 6*: 588–98.

Farrelly, F. and Greyser, S. (2012) 'Sponsorship linked internal marketing (SLIM): A strategic platform for employee engagement and business performance'. *Journal of Sport Management, 26*: 506–20.

Hickman, T.M., Lawrence, K.E. and Ward, J.C. (2005) 'A social perspective on the effects of corporate sport sponsorship on employees'. *Sport Marketing Quarterly, 14*: 148–57.

Hunt, R.R. and Einstein, G.O. (1981) 'Relational and item-specific information in memory'. *Journal of Verbal Learning & Verbal Behavior, 20*: 497–514.

Keller, K.L. (1993) 'Conceptualizing, measuring and managing customer-based brand equity'. *Journal of Marketing, 57*: 1–22.

Kelly, S.J., Cornwell, T.B., Coote, L.V. and McAlister, A.R. (2012) 'Event related advertising and the special case of sponsorship-linked advertising'. *International Journal of Advertising, 31*: 15–37.

Merton, R.K. (1945) 'Sociological theory'. *American Journal of Sociology, 50*: 462–73.

Nelson, D.L. and McEvoy, C.L. (2002) 'How can the same type of prior knowledge both help and hinder recall?' *Journal of Memory & Language, 46*: 652–63.

Nelson, D.L., Bennett, D.J. and Leibert T.W. (1997) 'One step is not enough: Making better use of association norms to predict cued recall'. *Memory & Cognition, 25*: 785–96.

Pappu, R. and Cornwell, T.B. (2014) 'Corporate sponsorship as an image platform: Understanding the roles of relationship fit *and* sponsor-sponsee similarity'. *Journal of the Academy of Marketing Science, 42*: 490–510.

Rust, R.T. and Oliver, R.W. (1994) 'The death of advertising'. *Journal of Advertising, 23*(4): 71–7.

Söderman, S. (2013) *Football and management: Comparisons between sport and enterprise.* New York: Palgrave MacMillan.

Söderman, S. and Dolles (2013) *Handbook of research on sport and business.* Gloucestershire, UK: Edward Elgar.

Sutton, R.I. and Staw, B.M. (1995) 'What theory is not'. *Administrative Science Quarterly, 40*: 371–84.

Weeks, C.S., Cornwell, T.B. and Humphreys, M.S. (2006) 'Conceptualizing sponsorship: An item and relational information account', in L.R. Kahle And Chung-Hyun Kim (eds) *Creating images and the psychology of marketing communications* (pp. 257–76). Mahwah, NJ: Lawrence Erlbaum Associates.

Applying sponsorship-linked marketing theory

Christopher Rumpf[1]

I came across Cornwell's (2008) paper when I was an early-career researcher in 2009. At that time, I was spending innumerous hours browsing research databases to discover innovative research topics in the vast literature on sponsorship-linked marketing. Soon I realised that there was a large variety of empirical studies dealing with sponsorship effectiveness, but a definite shortage of theoretical explanations for how sponsorship works in the minds of consumers. Cornwell's paper provided me with an inspiring framework that elaborates on one of the most fascinating questions in sponsorship research: how do consumers process sponsorship messages?

Cornwell's paper set a milestone in the literature on sponsorship-linked marketing, as it extends our knowledge on the formation of associative memory networks in the consumer's mind. The main achievement of the paper is the comprehensive composition of theoretical approaches from basic psychology, which significantly adds to our understanding about how sponsorship functions inside the black box. In contrast to most other contributions in the field, Cornwell puts emphasis on the *process* of sponsorship effectiveness instead of the *outcome* of sponsorship activities.

The theoretical framework encouraged me to perform research on sponsorship information processing with regard to the psychological concepts of attention and working memory capacity. It is well known from the psychology literature that attention plays a critical role in the formation of associative memory networks, since there is no information processing if the message is unattended. That is, sponsor messages that do not capture attention among the audience cannot get access to the declarative memory of consumers and, thus, will not be remembered. Building on Cornwell's framework, attention to sponsorship messages was found to be a necessary, but not sufficient, condition for the creation of sponsor-event linkages.

Whereas most other frameworks analyse sponsorship effectiveness as a simple input-output model, Cornwell highlights the cognitive processes occurring between the input and output stage. Since cognitive processes are influenced by the individual's ability to control her or his mental resources, we examined the influence of working memory capacity on the formation of associative networks (Rumpf, Noël, Breuer and Memmert, 2014). By doing so, we identified a correlation between the receiver's capacity to process information in general and the associative strength between sponsor and event. This finding builds on Cornwell's argumentation that the encoding and retrieval of sponsorship information 'depends not only on the nature of the exposure, but also on the nature of the receiver' (Cornwell, 2008, p. 47).

So far we have gained valuable understanding about how sponsorship-linked marketing forms accessible memory structures for sponsor-event pairings: that is, conscious associations. In future research, it would be interesting to test Cornwell's framework with regard to the formation of implicit associative networks. Since indirect marketing communications can be assumed to be processed on pre-conscious levels, it remains to be seen how sponsorship messages build underlying associations in the consumer's mind.

Note

1 Dr Christopher Rumpf is a Lecturer and Researcher at the German Sport University Cologne.

References

Cornwell, T.B. (2008) 'State of the art and science in sponsorship-linked marketing'. *The Journal of Advertising*, 37: 41–55.
Rumpf, C., Noël, B., Breuer, C. and Memmert, D. (2015) 'The role of context intensity and working memory capacity in the consumer's processing of brand information in entertainment media'.

18

TEAM IDENTITY THEORY[1]

Bob Heere

Elaine: *What is that?*
Puddy: *I painted my face.*
Elaine *(still in disbelief): You painted your face?*
Puddy: *Yeah.*
Elaine: *Why?*
Puddy: *You know, support the team.*

('*The Facepainter*' – *Seinfeld, broadcast on May 11, 1995)*

Introduction

The starting point for a theory is that single puzzling observation, one that challenges the observer towards a better understanding. Such an observation can be tiny, originated in daily life and so eloquently portrayed by the comedy of Jerry Seinfeld, yet sometimes it evolves from bigger issues that we encounter when we move outside of our own comfort zone and experience something with which we are not familiar. For me, that moment came when I moved to another country, and I realised that the way 'we do things' did not necessarily apply anymore. I am among those people who believe that every social scientist should at some point in her or his life live in a different nation, so as to gain an understanding and appreciation of the fact that many of the norms and values we have agreed upon as a society are negotiable and differ from nation to nation. It allows a researcher to quite literally 'step outside the box'. Making such a move at first might blind a researcher because of all the differences, thus forcing the individual to focus exclusively on these differences. Yet, after a while the researcher does not notice only the differences, but more importantly, also starts noticing the similarities between the current and previous surroundings. It is my opinion that, in order to understand the world around us, we should not only understand the differences, but also the similarities. In my case, I needed both elements to develop my observations into something bigger: a theory.

My first observation came when I attended my first American sport event, during a trip to the United States back in 1999. I was visiting a friend in Orlando and went to an NBA basketball game, in which the rebuilding Magic were scheduled to play a very strong Trailblazers team. Despite the expected uneven match-up, the game went down to the wire and was won by a

213

Trailblazer buzzer beater (last second basket). It was one of the most entertaining sport events I had witnessed until that day and made me realise that, unlike European football, American sports were all about entertainment. The lights, the music, the dancers, the promotions – I was enthralled by it all. I walked away with my first perception of the general difference between the United States and Europe: professional sport teams in the United States provide entertainment first and foremost, while professional sport teams in Europe are primarily about the sport and the need to identify with your local community. In hindsight, this observation was too straightforward, providing evidence to the statement that in order to make accurate observations one should understand both the differences and similarities between occurrences. So, while there was merit in the observation – and I would find empirical support for the American view of sports in the work of Wann (1995) and his colleagues (Wann, Brewer and Royalty, 1999; Wann, Schrader and Wilson, 1999) in which they demonstrated constructs such as entertainment and eustress were more salient than group affiliation and family (Wann *et al.*, 2001) – it was not as straightforward as I believed it to be. It would take me a few more years to gain a better understanding of the similarities between European and American sport, which was essential to proposing my theory.

In the fall of 2002 I started my doctoral training at Florida State University, and in my quest to assimilate into American culture, I began to attend the college football and basketball games. At first I was again taken by the differences between the American and the European game day experience, yet after some time I started to see the similarities. First, people identified quite strongly with the team and their performance and, to many, this identification meant that they would endure a less entertaining game as long as their team was winning. This observation itself was not a very innovative one. Cialdini *et al.* (1976) had discussed this phenomenon back in the 1970s and had coined the term 'basking in reflected glory', which was followed by the reverse, 'cutting off reflected failure' (Snyder, Lassegard and Ford, 1986). Wann (1995) also captured this phenomenon in the motive of self-esteem. Moreover, Wann and Branscombe (1990, 1991) had introduced the term 'team identification' to our field to discuss this phenomenon and they would embark on a search to better understand this term. As such, my observation – that in the US, sport was not just about entertainment but, similar to Europe, also offered people the opportunity to identify with their sport team – did not offer anything unique.

Similarly, my realisation that many people, as with European sport fans, primarily attended games to spend time with their friends, family or colleagues was not new, and captured in the same line of research as discussed by the authors mentioned before, as well as my own doctoral advisor Jeffrey James, who had published several articles on this issue (Funk and James, 2001; James, Kolbe and Trail, 2002; Trail and James, 2001). Yet, it was my third observation of a 'similarity' for which I could not find any supporting literature. I noticed people wearing university-related merchandise but with no reference to the sports team, something I had noticed at many different sport events. Fans at Green Bay Packers would wear foam cheeses as hats, Dutch national team soccer fans would wear windmill hats, and Australian fans would burst out in Waltzing Matilda in support of their sport teams. The focal point of these rituals and traditions did not seem to be the team, but the associated community: the state of Wisconsin and the nations of the Netherlands and Australia. It made me realise that for many people, the team itself was not necessarily the focal point in their search for community; instead, it was seen as an instrument to fulfill the need to express their belonging to a larger community. Anderson (1983) described nations as imagined communities, too large and abstract to identify with directly; thus, we use symbols and smaller sub-communities to help us with the identity process. While Anderson limited his discussion to nations, it did not seem far-fetched to me that the same idea applied to cities, states, universities and others; all communities that might be too large to identify with directly. Sport teams are among the most powerful symbols that allow us to identify with the larger community. Thus, at Florida State University, the quest of spectators for group affiliation resulted in a community of people whose focal point of identity was not necessarily the football team, but the university itself. Many of these fans did not even care about football; the team was an instrument to identify with the university. Interestingly, this similarity between the United States and Europe helped me to clarify my view on the European fan experience. Until then, I had not realised that this was a distinguished feature of European football: we support our team because it represents our community, whether that is our neighbourhood (e.g., FC Chelsea, Tottenham Hotspurs), our city (e.g., Feyenoord Rotterdam, FC Liverpool, Club Brugge), our region (e.g., FC Barcelona, FC Napoli, FC Twente) or our nation (e.g., the Dutch National football team – the Orange). It was this realisation that pushed me to gain a stronger understanding of team identity, and set me on my path as a researcher.

Defining team identity

Terminology to study the phenomenon of the psychological connection between an individual and a sports team has been diverse and has included terms such as social identity, commitment, attachment, awareness, loyalty and, more recently, engagement (Funk and James, 2001; Wann and Branscombe, 1993; Yoshida, Gordon, Nakazawa and Biscaia, 2014). To confuse matters even more, this terminology is grounded in different fields, which often uses multi-dimensional models that incorporate some of the other terminology. For instance, loyalty researchers have discussed identity and awareness as dimensions within loyalty (Pritchard, Havitz and Howard, 1999), while social identity researchers propose the opposite, and incorporate attachment and commitment as dimensions within social identity (Ashmore, Deaux and McLaughlin-Volpe, 2004). Neither approach is necessarily invalid, yet the different terminology does complicate and hinder the understanding of people who study the psychological connection between individuals and sport teams. Even within the spectrum of social identity research in sports, several different terms have been used, sometimes seemingly interchangeably, such as fan identity, team identity and team identification (in addition to the different terminology within social psychology, which includes social identity, community identity, collective, organisational identity and group identity).

I prefer the term team identity because of my background in social psychology and my perception that the grounded theory in this field, built over the last half century, serves the purposes of sport marketers quite well. Moreover, the terminology introduced in the field of marketing is ultimately derived from the same line of research in social psychology. In essence, all the other terms imply identity, while the other is not necessarily the case. I identify with the Dutch National football team; thus, I have a commitment to them, I am aware of them, I have developed an attachment to them, I am loyal to them and I am engaged with the team. This is not necessarily the case if you would reverse the connection between the different terms. I am committed to my students, yet I do not have a shared identity with them; I am attached to my favourite television shows, yet lack identification with them; and so on.

Lastly, I have used the term team identity over fan identity, as my focus has always been on the team and team-related outcomes (e.g., attendance, media consumption, merchandise), rather than fan-related outcomes. While the difference between these two terms might be primarily semantic, I believe that fan identity refers to the role we play as a fan, while team identity refers to the group, which forms the object of that identification process (see Deaux, Reid, Mizrahi, and Ethier (1995) for a good discussion on role versus group). Thus if the purpose of the study is to examine the fan and what that role means to them, fan identity might be appropriate, while team identity is a better term if one is trying to understand organisational outcomes, such as attendance, merchandise sales and media consumption.

Over the last decade I have defined team identity by adapting the social identity theory definition of Tajfel (1978, 1981), yet I still find it somewhat lacking. Thus, for the purpose of this chapter, I would like to propose a new definition, based on the work my colleagues and I have been conducting:

> Team identity is that part of an individual's self-concept which derives from membership into a community anchored around a sports team, based on the emotional value attached to that membership, and the knowledge of, engagement with, and evaluation of the community itself.

The value of this new definition is that it acknowledges several findings on team identity since we started examining it (Heere and James, 2007b; Heere, James, Yoshida and Scremin, 2011; Heere, Walker, Yoshida, Ko, Jordan and James, 2011; Heere, Walker, Gibson, Thapa, Geldenhuys and Coetzee, 2013). First, it recognises that the concept of social identity is directly related to the sociological concept of community, and that the sport team merely functions as an anchoring point (Clopton and Finch, 2011). Social identity is a process that inherently describes the bond between an individual and a community. When I started this line of research, this linkage was so apparent and logical to me that I never thought about writing about it in depth, explaining why I believed that team identity was an indicator for how one identified with a community. After years of fighting with reviewers, I started to realise that this was a mistake and that the linkage between team identity and community needed elaboration. The connection between team identity and community moves this construct very closely to the related construct of 'sense of community' (see also Warner's work in this area, Chapter 16), yet conceptually I believe them to be different. Community identity might describe a much stronger connection between individual and community than sense of community, which does not include the notion of membership. Social identity theory includes the notion of self-categorisation (Henderson-King and Stewart, 1994), which means that people need to identify themselves first as a member of the community before they are asked to evaluate their social identity. In all my data collections, I rigorously implemented such an approach and deleted anyone who did not self-identify as a community member (Heere and James, 2007b; Heere and Katz, 2014; Heere et al., 2013; Heere, James, Yoshida and Scremin, 2011; Heere, Walker, Yoshida, Ko, Jordan and James, 2011). Empirical assessments of sense of community do not incorporate self-categorisation as a way to eliminate non-group members and includes responses from people who do, and people who do not, identify with the team (Warner, Kerwin and Walker, 2013).

Second, the definition implies that there is nothing unique about our identification process with the team compared with other communities and that we can examine it through the same measures we use to measure our social identity with other communities, such as universities, nations, cities and organisations. Reviewing the first team identity scale proposed by Wann and Branscombe (1993) supports such a view, as some of their items are directly related to constructs grounded in social identity theory, such as importance, evaluation and behavioural involvement (see Ashmore et al., 2004 for an overview of social identity constructs). Other researchers have made use of Mael's (1988) organisational identity instrument to measure team identity, which was also grounded in social identity theory. Both approaches support the view that the term 'team identity' merely serves to indicate an anchoring point for community identity, and that our psychological connection with the team is best measured if we use social identity theory to do so. Again, this separates community identity from sense of community, as Warner and colleagues (2013) propose to measure sense of community through constructs that are specific to the field of sport management and might not necessarily transcend beyond the boundaries of a sport team. I also deemed the choice to measure team identity through social identity theory as beneficial since it allowed me to measure team identity through the same instrumentation as the measurement of university, city and state identity. This decision increased the validity evidence of testing relationships between different community identities, which ultimately I set out to do when I started my journey into team identity.

Third, this definition emphasises that team identity is a multi-dimensional construct that is best captured through the measurement of different processes. Grounding the team identity scale I developed for my dissertation in social identity theory (Heere and James, 2007b) allowed for a more in-depth perspective on what team identity truly means and what constructs drive the identity process. While doing so delayed my quest to find empirical evidence for the linkages between different community identities (since I needed to develop the multi-dimensional team identity scale first), it did allow me to gain a strong understanding of team identity as a focal point for social identity formation.

Grounding team identity in social identity: a multi-dimensional view on team identity

Early on in my search for a valid team identity scale, I realised that the concept of social identity had become so many things to so many different people that it might be almost impossible to capture it accurately through a one-dimensional scale. The best example I have for these limitations is when I would ask someone how strongly they identified with the United States of America – invariably they would answer 'very strongly' (e.g., 7 on a 7-point Likert scale). Similarly, if you would ask me how strongly I identify with the Netherlands, I would give a similar response. However, how Dutch people identify with their nation is entirely different from how Americans identify with their nation. Whereas in the United States patriotism is encouraged and citizens have maintained deference to the national anthem and flag, Dutch people in general showcase discomfort doing so. Even the Dutch national sport teams demonstrate this reluctance to embrace the national flag as the fans have embraced the colour orange (symbolic of the Royal house rather than the Dutch nation), instead of the red, white and blue of the national flag (despite the fact that this flag is one of the oldest in the world and precedes any other flag using these colours). The fact that the Dutch national anthem contains references to German origin and Spanish royalty does not help either. The differences do not limit themselves to symbolism, as the Dutch are comfortable paying high taxes to maintain the welfare state, while Americans do not show similar attitudes towards the support of their nation and their fellow citizens.

Thus, my main concern was that the one-dimensional scale would not pick up on these differences and that if I asked them about how strongly they identified with the university or team, they would respond with 'very strongly' regardless. This does not mean I believe that our current one-dimensional team identity scales (Kwon and Armstrong, 2002; Wann and Branscombe, 1993) lack evidence of validity. For many purposes, particularly in those instances where team identity merely functions as a mediator or outcome, the use of a one-dimensional scale might be preferential since they are so much more practical to use. Yet, for those instances where we would like to gain an in-depth understanding of team identity, we need to incorporate a more complex measure of team identity.

My intuitive concern that a one-dimensional scale of team identity was insufficient for my purposes was confirmed when I started to review the existing work on social identity theory.

I came to realise that scholars in this field had been viewing social identity as a multi-dimensional construct existing of many different processes. One of the most instrumental articles that helped me review the diversity in this field was Ashmore *et al.*'s (2004) previously noted work. They published a review of the decades of work in this field and listed the following elements as part of social identity: self-categorisation, evaluation, importance, attachment and sense of inter-dependence, social embeddedness, behavioural involvement, and content and meaning. To com-plicate matters further, many of these elements consisted of several dimensions (e.g., evaluation included both a private and public element).

Most of my dissertation was then focused on developing a multi-dimensional scale based on the conceptual work of Ashmore and colleagues (2004). Ultimately, we proposed a seven-dimensional scale, consisting of six Likert-based scales and one open-ended question that allowed people to self-categorise themselves as members of the community. The first dimension pro-posed was the element of private evaluation (Luhtanen and Crocker, 1992) in which the respond-ent would indicate how they felt about their membership to the group. While instinctively one might think that this is always positive, this is not necessarily the case. For example, sport fans of unsuccessful sport teams (in my own case: Feyenoord Rotterdam) are not always happy about their membership to the community yet remain identified with the team, resisting the lure of CORFing (cutting off reflected failure). A second evaluative element within social identity is public evaluation (Luhtanen and Crocker, 1992), which describes how we think non-members (out-group) feel about our community. In general, people care about how others feel about them, and team identity is no exception to this rule. A negative public evaluation can bring us to suppress or hide our identity with the team, or vice versa, to increase our tendency to act upon that identity as we feel threatened in our identity and thus try to defend it.

The third dimension is the interconnection we feel with the community. To some extent, I have come to understand this dimension to be at the core of social identity, and it shows the most overlap with the more traditional one-dimensional team identity scales (Mael and Tetrick, 1992). Ultimately, interconnection measures to what extent we accept the group membership to be a part of ourselves. The fourth element, sense of interdependence to the group, is one of the most debated dimensions of team identity. Sense of interdependence measures to what extent we believe that our own faith is intertwined with the faith of the team (Gurin and Townsend, 1986). In our first article on team identity (Heere and James, 2007a), we noted the lack of dis-criminant validity evidence between this construct and the construct of interconnection of self with group. Ashmore and colleagues (2004) also discussed these two concepts as being highly related. Lock, Funk, Doyle and McDonald (2014) argued that sense of interdependence should not be part of the team identity model, and they proposed a five-dimensional scale without it. Yet to me, conceptually these two dimensions do indicate a difference, particularly in the context of a sport team, as it is one of the few settings in which we acknowledge one without the other. When we measured group identity for university, city or state (Heere, James, Yoshida and Scremin, 2011) we noticed that people rated their sense of interdependence as high, if not higher, than their interconnection of self with group. However, in the context of the sport team, sense of interdependence was the only construct that consistently received average scores below 3.0, indicating that while people might feel a connection to the team, they lacked a sense of interdependence. I believe this makes our identification process with a sport team somewhat unique (thus validating the dimension of sense of interdependence), and perhaps even explains why sport fandom is so popular. When the team performs well, we identify strongly with it (see BIRGing in Cialdini *et al.*, 1976), yet when they perform poorly, we quite easily cut off our identity with the sport team (e.g., CORFing; Snyder *et al.*, 1986), as we do not feel a sense of interdependence to the team community. This is unlike our identification with other communities, such as the ones measured in our 2011 study (Heere, Walker, Yoshida, Ko, Jordan and James, 2011), as we realise that it is much harder to cut off those ties, since we work or live there, and the costs of giving up that membership is much harder.

The fifth dimension is behavioural involvement (Phinney, 1992), in which we examine the extent to which people act within the community. This dimension has been viewed as controversial as sense of interdependence, as many scholars have discussed some elements of behavioural involvement as an outcome of social identity, rather than an element within the social identity process (Schau, Muñiz and Arnould, 2009). Yet, there is a difference between behaviour as an outcome of the identity process and behavioural involvement with the community as an element of the team identity process. What we measured within this dimension is not how people act upon their identity, which is what Schau and colleagues discussed under the label brand practices, but rather how involved they are with the community, other group members and how often they interact with them. The emphasis in behavioural involvement is not on consumer behaviour, but on the involvement part. Ultimately, when we tested our final model (Heere, James, Yoshida and Scremin, 2011), we included both the behavioural involvement items to measure team identity, as well as behavioural outcomes, such as attendance, merchandise purchases and media consumption. Despite the overlap between the two components, we do believe that behavioural involvement is a crucial part of the social identity process, and more than just an outcome. A study I did with Matthew Katz among college football fans (Katz and Heere, 2013) confirmed that idea, as many people who were part of the tailgate did not initially identify with the team, but were there to socialise with other people; yet, their behavioural involvement with the tailgate event allowed them to develop a sense of team identity.

The sixth and final element is cognitive awareness, which measures the cognitive part of our identity process and asks respondents how much they know about the community, their traditions and history, and their successes and failures. Ashmore and colleagues (2004) did not offer any existing measures to examine this concept and described qualitative work to review the dimension. However, we included this construct based on attitudinal research that acknowledges that cognition is a crucial element of an attitude (Eagly and Chaiken, 1993), and the items developed were based on some of the characteristics of community as proposed by Muñiz and O'Guinn (2001).

Since then, we have used this six-dimensional scale many times to measure not only team identity, but also other social identities, such as city identity, state identity, university identity (Heere, James, Yoshida and Scremin, 2011; Heere, Walker, Yoshida, Ko, Jordan and James, 2011; Heere and Katz, 2014), national identity (Heere et al., 2013; Bogdanov, 2011), ethnic identity (Heere et al., 2013) and gender identity (Heere and Newland, 2013), and found evidence of scale reliability and validity in the different contexts. This work allowed us to finally test the theory with which I started: To what extent do our identity processes with the larger communities to which we belong (e.g. city, state, nation, university, gender, etc.) affect our identity with the sport team? Examining this question would allow us to better understand if the team itself is a goal for community fulfillment, or whether people see the sport team simply as an instrument to identify with a larger community.

Leaving the vacuum: empirical support for the associated group identity model

Seven years after I first proposed the theory that how we identify with the larger, associated communities of the team affects our identity process with the team, we were able to publish it in the *Journal of Marketing Theory and Practice* (*JMTP*) (Heere, Walker, Yoshida, Ko, Jordan and

James, 2011). In between, we had been able to publish the conceptual work that outlined this model (Heere and James, 2007a), and the aforementioned articles that discussed the psychometrics of the group identity scale (Heere and James, 2007b; Heere, James, Yoshida and Scremin, 2011). Additionally, we were already in the midst of setting up several other studies that used the multi-dimensional group identity scale to gain an indication of the strength of the community. I perceived the publication in *JMTP* as a culmination of the work we had been doing all those years, and I was excited about the extent to which our model confirmed our conceptual thinking on this issue. The data that we had collected from students at universities with the three most prominent college football programmes ($n = 872$) in the state of Florida demonstrated how strong the linkage was between the different identity processes, with correlations between the second order constructs of team, university, city and state identity ranging from .41 to .80. Moreover, the three combined associated group identities explained 60 per cent of the variance in team identity, emphasising the importance of the associated communities to how people identified with the team. Finally, it underpinned the importance of these identity processes to consumer behaviour as, combined, these identity processes were able to explain 84 per cent of the variance in reported merchandise buying, 89 per cent of the variance in media consumption, and 56 per cent of the variance in reported attendance. It provided very powerful empirical support for the theory that our team identity processes do not operate in a vacuum and are strongly affected by how we identify with the larger communities we perceive the team to be representative of.

Directions moving forward

Most of the work reviewed in this chapter is based on cross-sectional survey research, which limits our understanding of how predictive team identity is of consumer behaviour. Ultimately, cross-sectional research can only provide insight on correlations between team identity and other related constructs. Multiple regression analysis and structural equation modelling can give some indication of the direction and importance of the relationship, yet they fail to provide a true indication of the predictive value of team identity, as both methods are ultimately still correlational in nature. Thus, there is a need for studies that either incorporate a (quasi-) experimental approach to the examination of team identity, which would allow for a better understanding of what drives team identity, or a longitudinal approach. It is time to move beyond the basic cross-sectional survey approach as by now we have demonstrated the importance and centrality of team identity to the field of consumer behaviour.

A good example of a quasi-experimental approach is our study on the effect of the World Cup 2010 on the national identity of South African citizens (Heere *et al.*, 2013), which measured national identity prior to and after the World Cup. Yet, this study did not incorporate an assessment of team identity, and instead focused on the effect of a sport event on national identity. Our study on the effect of a triathlon event on the organisational identity with a charity also incorporated such an approach (Woolf, Heere and Walker, 2013) but, again, it did not incorporate team identity itself as a construct.

Lock and colleagues (2014) did collect longitudinal data on team identity, yet their approach only used two data points, which hinders the usage of longitudinal data analysis methods, requiring three data points at a minimum. As that study was part of a larger research project, it is hopefully only a matter of time before these scholars publish data based on more than two time points, allowing them to conduct growth curve analyses and similar methods. Similar to their work, we have been collecting team identity data over a period of three years with a large Southwestern university in the United States, and published our baseline data of the first year (Heere and

Katz, 2014), with the goal of publishing our longitudinal data in the years to come. In a longitudinal study among spectators of a J-League soccer team (Yoshida, Heere and Gordon, in press), we found that team identity was not directly predictive of continued attendance, which countered our cross-sectional findings previously (Heere, Walker, Yoshida, Ko, Jordan and James, 2011). Whether this was because the study implemented a one-dimensional team identity scale or whether this was a first sign that we might overestimate the importance of team identity is uncertain. The same study also found game satisfaction, service satisfaction and behavioural intentions to be insignificant, which might indicate the limitations of relying on a single source data collection and suggests additional data collections into this issue are necessary. Regardless, this study did signify that the time to rely on cross-sectional survey research to measure attitudinal constructs such as team identity has come to an end. We need more rigorous methods to gain a better understanding of the importance of team identity to consumer behaviour.

Note

1   This chapter is a reflection on Heere and James (2007a) and the work related to it.

References

Anderson, B. (1983) *Imagined communities*. New York: Verso.

Ashmore, R.D., Deaux, K. and McLaughlin-Volpe, T. (2004) 'An organizing framework for collective identity: Articulation and significance of multidimensionality'. *Psychological Bulletin*, *130*(1): 80–114.

Bogdanov, D. (2011) 'Influence of national sport team identity on national identity'. Unpublished Doctoral Dissertation. Tallahassee, FL: The Florida State University.

Cialdini, R.B., Borden, R.J., Thorne, A., Walker, M.R., Freeman, S. and Sloan, L.R. (1976) 'Basking in reflected glory: Three (football) field studies'. *Journal of Personality & Social Psychology*, *34*: 366–75.

Clopton, A.W. and Finch, B.L. (2011) 'Re-conceptualizing social anchors in community development: Utilizing social anchor theory to create social capital's third dimension'. *Community Development*, *42*(1): 70–83.

Deaux, K., Reid, A., Mizrahi, K. and Ethier, K.A. (1995) 'Parameters of social identity'. *Journal of Personality & Social Psychology*, *68*: 280–91.

Eagly, A.H. and Chaiken, S. (1993) *The psychology of attitudes*. Fort Worth, TX: Harcourt, Brace & Jovanovich.

Funk, D.C. and James, J.D. (2001) 'The Psychological Continuum Model: A conceptual framework for understanding an individual's psychological connection to sport'. *Sport Management Review*, *4*: 119–50.

Gurin, P. and Townsend, A. (1986) 'Properties of gender identity and their implications for gender consciousness'. *British Journal of Social Psychology*, *25*: 139–48.

Heere, B. and James, J.D. (2007a) 'Sports teams and their communities: Examining the influence of external group identities on team identity'. *Journal of Sport Management*, *21*: 319–37.

Heere, B. and James, J.D. (2007b) 'Stepping outside the lines: Developing a multi-dimensional team identity scale based on social identity theory'. *Sport Management Review*, *10*: 65–91.

Heere, B., James, J.D., Yoshida, M. and Scremin, G. (2011) 'The effect of associated group identities on team identity'. *Journal of Sport Management*, *25*: 606–21.

Heere, B. and Katz, M. (2014) 'Still undefeated: Exploring the dimensions of team identity among fans of a new college football team'. *Journal of Applied Sport Management*, *6*(1): 25–43.

Heere, B. and Newland, B. (2013) 'Moving beyond the female spectator as a demographic: Measuring the salience of gender identity and its effect on team identity'. *Journal of Contemporary Athletics*, *7*(3): 197–207.

Heere, B., Walker, M., Gibson, H., Thapa, B., Geldenhuys, S. and Coetzee, W. (2013) 'The power of sport to unite a nation: The social value of the 2010 FIFA World Cup in South Africa'. *European Sport Management Quarterly*, *13*: 450–71.

Heere, B., Walker, M., Yoshida, M., Ko, Y., Jordan, J.S. and James, J.D. (2011) 'Brand community development through associated communities: Grounding community measurement within social identity theory'. *Journal of Marketing Theory & Practice*, *19*: 407–22.

Henderson-King, D. and Stewart, A. (1994) 'Women or feminists? Assessing women's group consciousness'. *Sex Roles, 31*: 505–16.

James, J.D., Kolbe, R.H. and Trail, G.T. (2002) 'Psychological connection to a new sport team: Building or maintaining the consumer base?' *Sport Marketing Quarterly, 11*(4): 215–25.

Katz, M. and Heere, B. (2013) 'Leaders and followers: An exploration of the notion of scale-free networks within a new brand community'. *Journal of Sport Management, 27*: 271–87.

Kwon, H.H. and Armstrong, K.L. (2002) 'Factors influencing impulse buying of sport team licensed merchandise'. *Sport Marketing Quarterly, 11*(3): 151–63.

Lock, D., Funk, D.C., Doyle, J.P. and McDonald, H. (2014) 'Examining the longitudinal structure, stability, and dimensional interrelationships of team identification'. *Journal of Sport Management, 28*: 119–35.

Luhtanen, R. and Crocker, J. (1992) 'A collective self-esteem scale: Self-evaluation of one's social identity'. *Personality & Social Psychology Bulletin, 18*: 302–18.

Mael, F. (1988) 'Organizational identification: Construct redefinition and a field application with organizational alumni'. Unpublished doctoral dissertation. Wayne State University, Detroit.

Mael, F.A. and Tetrick, L.E. (1992) 'Identifying organizational identification'. *Educational & Psychological Measurement, 52*: 813–24.

Muñiz, A.M. and O'Guinn, T.C. (2001) 'Brand community'. *Journal of Consumer Research, 27*: 412–32.

Phinney, J.S. (1992) 'The multigroup ethnic identity measure: A new scale for use with diverse groups'. *Journal of Adolescent Research, 7*: 156–76.

Pritchard, M.P., Havitz, M.E. and Howard, D.R. (1999) 'Analyzing the commitment-loyalty link in service contexts'. *Academy of Marketing Science, 27*: 333–48.

Schau, H.J., Muñiz Jnr, A.M. and Arnould, E.J. (2009) 'How brand community practices create value'. *Journal of Marketing, 73*(5): 30–51.

Snyder, C.R., Lassegard, M.A. and Ford, C.E. (1986) 'Distancing after group success and failure: Basking in reflected glory and cutting off reflected failure'. *Journal of Personality & Social Psychology, 51*: 382–88.

Tajfel, H. (1978) *Differentiation between social groups: Studies in the social psychology of intergroup relations*. London: Academic.

Tajfel, H. (1981) *Human groups and social categories*. Cambridge, England: Cambridge University Press.

Trail, G. and James, J.D. (2001) 'An analysis of the sport fan motivation scale'. *Journal of Sport Behavior, 24*: 108–27.

Wann, D.L. (1995) 'Preliminary validation of the Sport Fan Motivation Scale'. *The Journal of Sport & Social Issues, 20*: 377–96.

Wann, D.L. and Branscombe, N.R. (1990) 'Die-hard and fair-weather fans: Effects of identification on BIRGing and CORFing tendencies'. *Journal of Sport & Social Issues, 14*: 103–17.

Wann, D.L. and Branscombe, N.R. (1991) 'The positive social and self concept consequences of sports team identification'. *Journal of Sport & Social Issues, 15*: 115–27.

Wann, D.L. and Branscombe, N.R. (1993) 'Sports fans: Measuring degree of identification with their team'. *International Journal of Sport Psychology, 24*: 1–17.

Wann, D.L., Brewer, K.R. and Royalty, J.L. (1999) 'Sport fan motivation: Relationships with team identification and emotional reactions to sporting events'. *International Sports Journal, 3*(2): 8–18.

Wann, D.L., Melnick, M.J., Russell, G.W. and Pease, D.G. (2001) *Sport fans: The psychology and social impact of spectators*. New York: Routledge.

Wann, D.L., Schrader, M.P. and Wilson, A.M. (1999) 'Sport fan motivation: Questionnaire validation, comparisons by sport, and relationship to athletic motivation'. *Journal of Sport Behavior, 22*: 114–39.

Warner, S., Kerwin, S. and Walker, M. (2013) 'Examining Sense of Community in sport: Developing the multidimensional "SCS" Scale'. *Journal of Sport Management, 27*: 349–62.

Woolf, J., Heere, B. and Walker, M. (2013) 'Leveraging charity sport events as "brandfests" to develop a brand community'. *Journal of Sport Management, 27*: 95–107.

Yoshida, M., Gordon, B., Nakazawa, M. and Biscaia, R. (2014) 'Conceptualization and measurement of fan engagement: Empirical evidence from a professional sport context'. *Journal of Sport Management, 28*: 399–417.

Yoshida, M., Heere, B. and Gordon, B. (in press) 'Predicting behavioral loyalty through community: Why other fans are more'. *Journal of Sport Management*.

Applying team identity theory

Daniel Lock[1]

I became aware of the conceptual thrust of Heere and James' (2007) work after reading Heere's (2005) doctoral study in 2006 while I was undertaking my PhD at the University of Technology, Sydney. During my PhD, it became evident that team identification researchers painted a simplistic view of sport consumer identity processes. I was observing more complex identity processes, which consisted of multiple groups and pre-existing identities that shaped consumption – beyond the team identity. This drew me to Heere and James' (2007) work, which explored how organisations could align with external group identities to increase resonance beyond the team identity (e.g., ethnic, religious, gender, etc.). This theoretical process aligned closely with the process of social identification I was observing in Australia at the time (Lock, Taylor and Darcy, 2011; Lock, 2009).

In my research since, the major application of Heere and James' (2007) contribution concerns the ways in which consumers use multiple social groups to structure and supplement their consumption experiences. Existing research on team identification (e.g., Boyle and Magnusson, 2007; Branscombe and Wann, 1991) focuses on one-group membership. This work illustrates that team identification influences a range of consumption behaviours. However, it does not provide an explanation of other groups that shape sport consumption.

Heere and James (2007) applied social complexity theory to elaborate on this mono-group perspective. While focusing on external group memberships in their published work (Heere, James, Yoshida and Scremin, 2011; Heere and James, 2007), Heere and James (2007) illustrated that multiple group memberships can shape consumption behaviours. Acknowledging this conceptual point, they intimated that groups within and beyond the team identification may shape behaviour, which underpins the current attention dedicated to the role of subgroups (i.e., groups that exist within a team identity) on consumption behaviour (Bernache-Assollant, Bouchet, Auvergne and Lacassagne, 2011; Tyler, 2013). In this vein, I am currently using Heere and James' (2007) study to develop understanding of how sport consumers use subgroups to supplement team identification.

Moving forward, I foresee three cogent areas to apply and elaborate this work. First, there is a need to develop understanding of how and why consumers use different identity groups. Advancement in this area will inform organisational efforts to design marketing activities that capitalise on the complex nature of consumer identities. Second, there is a need to understand how different group memberships interact and influence one another. While Heere *et al.* (2011) provide initial data on this topic, there is scope for additional explorations to forge understanding of the structure (cf. Roccas and Brewer, 2002) and interactions between group memberships. Third, the multiple-group perspective invokes complex methodological challenges in terms of how best to develop understanding of the complex relationships between consumer identities. While qualitative (Tyler, 2013) and quantitative work (Heere *et al.*, 2011) exists, there is a need to develop and utilise new and innovative methodological approaches to explore multiple group memberships in sport.

In summary, Heere and James (2007) broadened the landscape of team identification research, opening sport management research to the reality that multiple-group memberships influence team identification. This approach provides a rich arena to advance understanding of consumer behaviour from inside and outside of team identities in the future.

Note

1   Daniel Lock is with the Department of Tourism, Sport and Hotel Management at Griffith University.

References

Bernache-Assollant, I., Bouchet, P., Auvergne, S. and Lacassagne, M. (2011) 'Identity crossbreeding in soccer fan groups: A social approach. The case of Marseille (France)'. *Journal of Sport & Social Issues,* 35: 72–100.
Boyle, B. and Magnusson, P. (2007) 'Social identity and brand equity formation: a comparative study of collegiate sports fans'. *Journal of Sport Management, 21*: 497–520.
Branscombe, N. and Wann, D. (1991) 'The positive social and self concept consequences of sports team identification'. *Journal of Sport and Social Issues, 15*: 115–27.
Heere, B. (2005) 'Internal and external group identities of a sport team: The development of a multi-dimensional team identity scale' Unpublished PhD thesis. Florida State University, Talahasse.
Heere, B. and James, J. (2007) 'Sports teams and their communities: Examining the influence of external group identities on team identity'. *Journal of Sport Management, 21*: 319–37.
Heere, B., James, J., Yoshida, M. and Scremin, G. (2011) 'The effect of associated group identities on team identity'. *Journal of Sport Management, 25*: 606–21.
Lock, D. (2009) 'New team identification: Sydney FC, a case study'. Unpublished doctoral thesis. University of Technology, Sydney.
Lock, D., Taylor, T. and Darcy, S. (2011) 'In the absence of achievement: The formation of new team identification'. *European Sport Management Quarterly, 11*: 171–92.
Roccas, S. and Brewer, M. (2002) 'Social identity complexity'. *Personality and Social Psychology Review, 6*: 88.
Tyler, B. (2013) *Fan communities and subgroups: Exploring individuals' supporter group experiences.* University of Massachussetts, Amherst.

19

SPORT CONSUMER BEHAVIOUR[1]

Galen T. Trail

Overview

There are billions of people worldwide who are interested in sport as fans and spectators, specifically consuming sport from a non–participatory standpoint. People attend sport events as spectators; consume sport through variety of mediums (TV, internet, smartphones, radio); purchase merchandise representing teams, leagues and countries; consume concessions at the games and matches; and discuss it with family, friends and complete strangers; among many other behaviours. Men's Soccer World Cup 2014 attendance exceeded 3.4 million people in sixty-four matches (FIFA World Cup, 2014) and 111.5 million people watched the 2014 Super Bowl on TV (Super Bowl XLVIII, 2014). Sport spectating can bring people to the highest of highs (an estimated 700,000 fans lining the streets of Seattle in February for a parade for the Super Bowl champion Seattle Seahawks; Bien, 2014) to the lowest of lows (Brazilian men's soccer fans being absolutely devastated when the home team lost 7–1 at home to Germany in the semi-final of the World Cup in 2014; Borden, 2014). What, however, explains all of this behaviour? What explains why people consume sport?

The specific constructs and key propositions

We proposed a model and framework to explain why people spectate and consume sport (Trail, Anderson and Fink, 2000). In 2003, we first tested the model (Trail, Fink and Anderson, 2003), and the model has evolved since then (Harrolle, Trail, Rodriguez and Jordan, 2010; Trail, Anderson and Fink, 2005; Trail and James, 2011). Parts of it have been examined for nuances and potential additions (James and Trail, 2008; Kim and Trail, 2010; Kim and Trail, 2011; Kim, Trail and Magnusen, 2013; Kwon, Trail and Anderson, 2005; Kwon, Trail and Lee; 2008; Lee and Trail, 2011a; Shapiro, Ridinger and Trail, 2013; Trail, Kim, Kwon, Harrolle, Braunstein-Minkove and Dick; 2012; Woo, Trail, Kwon and Anderson, 2009). The original model showed that sport consumption behaviour could be predicted by the interaction of six general constructs: motives; identification (with the team); expectancies about the experience/outcome (whether it was attending a game, watching on TV, or whatever); the confirmation or disconfirmation of those expectancies; self-esteem responses (Basking in Reflected Glory – BIRGing and Cutting Off Reflected Failure – CORFing); and the affective state of the individual (positive and negative mood, and level of satisfaction). These six factors were arranged sequentially and all were supposed to predict future consumption behaviour either directly or indirectly (See Figure in Trail *et al.*, 2003). I will give a brief overview of each of the constructs.

Motives reflect 'the energizing force that activates behavior and provides purpose and direction for that behavior' (Hawkins, Best and Coney, 2004, p. 354) and are based on social and psychological needs (Trail *et al.*, 2000). Sloan (1989) suggested a variety of theories that explain specific motives and how each may be applicable to sport, and we provided a fair amount of support for the proposed relationships between the different motives and team identification (Fink, Trail and Anderson, 2002; Trail *et al.*, 2000; Trail *et al.*, 2003) and motives and expectations (Trail *et al.*, 2000; Trail *et al.*, 2003).

We defined *identification* as 'an orientation of the self in regard to other objects including a person or group that results in feelings or sentiments of close attachment' (Trail *et al.*, 2000, pp. 165–6). The basis for team identification has been attributed to both identity theory and social identity theory, but we view it from the identity theory prospective. As Jeff James and I noted:

> the reason that we have chosen identity theory rather than social identity theory is because social identity theory does not explain variance within the collectivity; in other words, it does not explain why fans act differently from each other ... [F]ans act differently because the identity standard (role identity) is specific to the individual and varies to the extent that the individual wants it to vary relative to the perceived situational meanings.
>
> *(Trail and James, 2013, p. 58)*

Although we tested the proposed relationship between identification and expectancies, the amount of variance explained in expectancies by identification was less than four per cent, indicating that identification was not a good predictor of expectancies (Trail *et al.*, 2003).

Both Goldstein (1989) and Zillmann, Bryant and Sapolsky (1989) indicated that fans and spectators typically have *expectations* about their potential experiences, learned either through prior experiences or through communications from others. These expectations can be about the venue, the outcome of the game, experiences during the game, etc. According to Madrigal (1995) these expectancies are either confirmed or disconfirmed positively or negatively. How the expectancies are confirmed or disconfirmed, and whether positively or negatively, then impacts how people feel (affective state) and their self-esteem responses. We tested the relationship between expectancies and the confirmation or disconfirmation of expectancies and determined that there was no significant relationship between the two (Trail *et al.*, 2003). On the face of it, the results did not make sense, but as one investigates more thoroughly, it is readily apparent that no relationship should exist. Expectancies prior to the event can be either confirmed or disconfirmed by the event experiences and whether they are or are not depends entirely on the person. Thus for each person who had their expectations confirmed, there could be another who had them disconfirmed. If there are sufficient numbers equally balanced, then the correlation between the two variables would be zero, as we observed.

Affective state is composed of feelings (positive mood or negative mood) and level of satisfaction (Trail *et al.*, 2000). When someone's expectancies are positively confirmed (team wins when expected to) or positively disconfirmed (team wins when they weren't expected to) then that person feels happy (positive mood) and the person feels satisfied. On the other hand, when the expectancies are negatively confirmed (team loses when expected to lose) or negatively disconfirmed (team loses when they were expected to win), then that person feels sad or upset, and usually dissatisfied. We found support for this hypothesised relationship as (dis)confirmation of expectancies explained thirty-two per cent of the variance in affect (Trail *et al.*, 2003).

The (dis)confirmation of expectancies was also hypothesised to impact *self-esteem responses*. We proposed that self-esteem responses included BIRGing and CORFing (Trail *et al.*, 2000). Basking in Reflective Glory typically occurs when a favourite team wins and an individual wants to promote the association with a successful other by, for example, wearing team apparel, or telling people how big a fan he or she is of the team. This allows that individual to feel successful through the association. However, people who have a high need for achievement and typically search for it vicariously will often Cut Off Reflected Failure if they are not highly identified with the team and the team starts losing. However, the hypothesised relationship between (dis)confirmation and self-esteem behaviours was minimal at best, as only three per cent of the variance in BIRGing and CORFing was explained.

The result of the interaction of all of these variables is, theoretically, an increase in behavioural consumption intentions (conative loyalty). *Conative loyalty* means that fans intend to consume the product or service in the future and in our model this was focused on attending future games, purchasing team merchandise, buying team-related clothing and supporting the team (Trail *et al.*, 2003). However, intentions often do go astray and actual future behaviour tends to be considerably less than is typically intended. Approximately ten per cent of the variance in future behaviour was explained by all of the aforementioned variables in the model.

Boundary conditions

The reason that conative loyalty does not predict actual behaviours as well as expected is because of constraints, barriers or obstacles. *Constraints* are 'factors that impede or inhibit an individual from attending a sport event' (Kim and Trail, 2010, p. 191), but can also be applied to any type of consumption behaviour, including media and merchandise consumption. Constraints can be either internal or external to the individual. We defined internal constraints as 'internal psychological cognitions that deter behavior' (p. 194) and external constraints as 'social or environmental aspects that prevent or decrease the likelihood of the individual performing the behavior' (Kim and Trail, 2010, p. 194). Both internal (perceptions that significant others have no interest in the sport or team) and external constraints (cost, weather, lack of transportation) may impact individuals differentially and maybe overcome if the motivation to consume the product is sufficient. However, we did not include constraints in the original depiction of the model of sport consumer behaviour (Trail *et al.*, 2003).

Application

As noted above, we tested the originally proposed model (see Figure 1 in Trail *et al.*, 2003) and determined that only ten per cent of the variance in behaviour intentions (conative loyalty) was explained (Trail *et al.*, 2003). In addition, several of the predicted paths were not supported to the extent expected. These somewhat disappointing results led to us proposing three competing models based on our previous results, and coupled with identity theory and satisfaction theory (Trail, Anderson and Fink, 2005; see Figures 1–3 therein). Based on identity theory, the left-hand portion of Model A depicted team identification impacting self-esteem responses (BIRGing and CORFing), which directly impacted conative loyalty. On the right-hand side of the model, satisfaction theory supported the relationships from (dis)confirmation of expectancies to mood (affective state) and then to conative loyalty. Model B:

> is an extension of Model A, but guided by research in the sport consumer realm, in
> addition to the consumer satisfaction and identity theory models. In this model,

(dis)confirmation leads to mood. Mood and identification both directly lead to self-esteem responses (BIRGing and CORFing), and self-esteem responses lead to conative loyalty.

(Trail et al., 2005, p. 101)

Finally, Model C, a direct effects model, was also proposed and tested. In this model, all variables have a direct influence on conative loyalty, with no indirect effects. Model B was chosen as the best fitting model as almost fifty per cent of the variance in conative loyalty was predicted by the model and it integrated identity theory, satisfaction theory and prior results from sport-related research.

Process

Activities that spurred our interest in the topic

The genesis of the idea of a sport consumer behaviour model came about through a doctoral level class at The Ohio State University taught by Bob Madrigal. Janet Fink, Jeff James and I were all in that class discussing research on motives, satisfaction, expectancies, team identification and so on. Each of us had to individually write a term paper synthesising a chosen set of articles that we had covered in that class, plus additional research in the particular area that we were most interested in. I had been impressed with Madrigal's (1995) paper on cognitive and affective determinants of fan satisfaction with sporting event attendance and thought it was a good starting point. In addition, Wann's (1995) and Sloan's (1989) work on motives contributed quite a bit to my thought process; as did Wann and colleagues' (Branscombe and Wann, 1991; Wann and Branscombe, 1993) work on identification. I also used Cialdini *et al.*'s (1976) and Snyder, Lassegard and Ford's (1986) work on BIRGing and CORFing. Many other works contributed as well, obviously.

Based on the aforementioned research, I started synthesising the empirical relationships that appeared across all of the research and determining consistencies therein. For example, much of the research indicated relationships among motives and team identification. Furthermore, a variety of research also showed relationships among team identification and a variety of other variables such as satisfaction, BIRGing/CORFing, and behavioural intentions. Using all of the above information, I proposed a model of consumer behaviour for the class term paper. Dr Madrigal provided some critical feedback when he handed back the paper. Nothing came from those efforts for a couple of years as I focused on my dissertation (which was not on this topic). After graduating and getting my first tenure-track position at Iowa State University, the pressure to publish became quite apparent, and I started thinking back to some possibilities. I dug up the term paper, approached Dr Dean Anderson, my mentor at ISU, and Dr Janet Fink who was at Texas at the time, and asked them if they wanted to be part of this project. Both agreed and a good collaboration was born. In addition, Dr Jeff James and I continued to work on the motives of sport fandom and a variety of projects came from that, the most well-known being the Trail and James (2001) paper. The work that Dr James and I did on motives contributed substantially to the original model proposed in 2000 (Trail *et al.*, 2000) and tested in 2003 (Trail *et al.*, 2003).

The largest failing of the term paper, as Dr Madrigal pointed out, was that I had not included very much (read 'any') theoretical justification for the relationships among the variables or even the inclusion of the variables in the proposed model. Although Madrigal (1995) had included Oliver's (1993) work on satisfaction theory in his article, I had not used it in support of our model, which was certainly a failing. Madrigal suggested that I include it, which eventually we did. In addition, this is where Drs Anderson and Fink provided their valuable contributions to the research. Dr Anderson provided considerable theoretical support for the idea of identification and the relationships proposed therein; whereas Dr Fink suggested self-esteem theory for supporting the BIRGing and CORFing ideas and relationships. These ideas and theories started to appear in our first two papers (Trail *et al.*, 2000; Trail *et al.*, 2003). Then, as we further developed our ideas, we incorporated identity theory, satisfaction theory and self-esteem theory into the justification of our model much more effectively than we had initially (Trail *et al.*, 2005). Thus, we did not start with a sufficient theoretical basis and then build the model; we proposed the model and later we added theory to support the model tenets. This is the wrong (and ineffectual) way to propose a model. In addition, this is quite probably why the first model only explained ten per cent of the variance in the sport consumer behaviour intentions and why the later models, modified and supported by theory, explained considerably greater amounts of variance in consumer behaviour. In addition, as we incorporated values theory, constraint theory and the theory of planned behaviour, and incorporated additional variables suggested by those theories, larger amounts of variance was explained and new relationships examined.

Extensions and applications

We have continued to build on the foundational models of sport consumer behaviour from 2000, 2003 and 2005. For instance, in a project with Harrolle and colleagues (Harrolle *et al.*, 2010), we slightly modified the 2005 model by creating two components of disconfirmation of expectancies (quality of performance and outcome) and tested it on two different samples of potential fans and spectators (Latino and non-Latino). The model fit both samples adequately with 44.5 per cent of the conative loyalty variance explained in the Latino sample and 73.5 per cent in the non-Latino sample, providing additional support for the sport consumer behaviour model.

Various other research projects have tested aspects of the model. For example, Robinson and I (2005) expanded the idea of team identification to incorporate many different points of attachment (the team, the players, the coach, the community, the sport, the university and the level of sport) and looked at the relationships among points of attachment and motives. In a collaboration with Woo and colleagues (Woo, Trail, Kwon and Anderson, 2009), we expanded the model around those relationships, proposing second-order factors for both motives and points of attachment. In one longitudinal study, we examined how past attendance behaviour impacted current team identification and attendance intentions, which in turn predicted actual attendance behaviour (Trail, Anderson and Lee, 2006), while in another longitudinal study, we built on those findings to show that past behaviour impacted future behaviour both directly and indirectly through points of attachment (Shapiro *et al.*, 2013). Other extensions include examining (a) the relationships among vicarious achievement (a motive), team identification, and BIRGing and CORFing (Kwon *et al.*, 2008; Trail *et al.*, 2012); (b) patterns among internal and external motivators and constraints on attendance (Kim and Trail, 2011), which was then extended to sport media consumption intentions (Larkin, Fink and Trail, 2014); and (c) a modification and extension of the model to focus specifically on athletic team merchandise (Lee and Trail, 2011b, 2012; Lee *et al.*, 2013). In our latter work, additional variables such as personal values, previous product experience, product attributes, attitude towards the brand and attitude towards the product were included in this model, which explained almost eighty-six per cent of the variance in intentions to purchase team-licensed merchandise in the future (Lee *et al.*, 2013).

Besides our own work that has applied, extended and modified the model, other researchers have used aspects of it. Most research has focused on the motivation aspects or identification aspects of the 2003 model. However, there have been several exceptions. Gau, Gailliot and Brady (2007) used both the 2003 and 2005 models to examine motives, team identification, service quality and satisfaction. Gray and Wert-Gray (2012) used aspects of the 2003 model to examine the effects of team identification and satisfaction with team performance on four sport consumption behaviours: in-person attendance, media-based attendance, purchase of team merchandise and word of mouth. Shapiro, Drayer and Dwyer (2014) used many of the relationships in support of their proposed model of fantasy sport participation. Santos (2012) also used aspects of the 2003 model to investigate the impact of motives, satisfaction, perceived service quality, subjective norms, attitude and control on purchase intention.

The work has also informed teaching and practice. The sport consumer behaviour model soon became the foundation for a class on sport consumer behaviour that has been taught at Iowa State University, University of Florida, The Ohio State University, Florida State University and Seattle University, among others. In addition, the model was the basis for the *Sport consumer behavior* book that Jeff James and I wrote (Trail and James, 2013). We cover an overview of a variety of sport consumer behaviours; theories and models (other than just ours) applicable to sport consumer behaviour; socialisation into fandom; market segmentation; culture and sub-culture; needs, values and goals; motives; consumer perceptions; market demand characteristics; expectancies, (dis)confirmation and satisfaction; BIRGing, CORFing, Blasting, BIRFing and CORSing. Using the model and the textbook provides an excellent basis for the sport consumer behaviour class, which focuses on the application of market research for specific sport organisations. That is, based on the model, the students in the class do market research for a specific sport organisation (e.g., Seattle Thunderbirds). The students create a survey that includes the variables discussed in class from the model and then collect data from fans and spectators of the sport organisation. Using a cluster analysis technique, they segment the data and then, using the model, the students examine the relationships among the variables to proposed marketing and communication recommendations to the sport organisation.

Future directions

Theoretical or empirical extensions

The model has continued to develop as we add more relationships and variables, and as we see that certain relationships previously proposed and tested are not sufficient. In addition, we have expanded the theories we use for the theoretical base of the model as we add more variables and proposed new relationships. For example, we now include self-determination theory (Deci and Ryan, 2008), Means-End-Chain theory (MEC – Gutman, 1982), attitude theory (Eagly and Chaiken, 1993), the theory of planned behaviour (Azjen, 1991) and self-esteem theory (Cast and Burke, 2002), in addition to identity theory (Stryker and Burke, 2000) and satisfaction theory (Oliver, 1977) that we originally included. Jeff James and I modified the model slightly for the textbook and then proposed a new model at the American Marketing Association Summer Marketing Educators Conference in 2011 (Trail and James, 2011). Since then, we have continued to work on it and are currently preparing a paper for submission. However, I will give a brief overview here as to the current edition of the Sport Consumer Behavior Model (Figure 19.1).

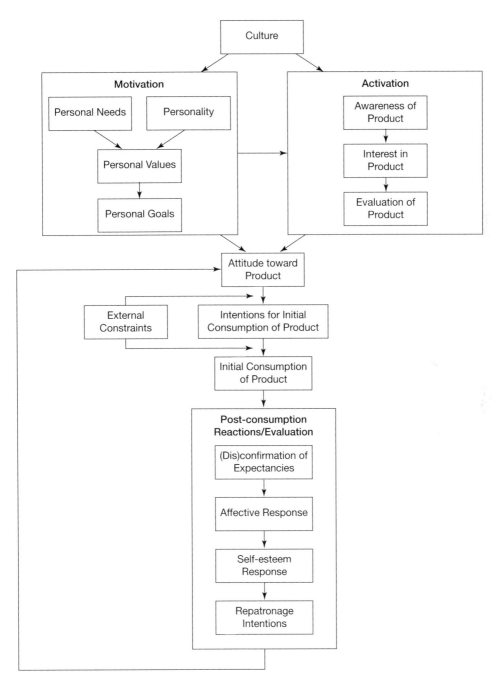

Figure 19.1 Model of Sport Consumer Behavior from Trail and James (2011)

As depicted in Figure 19.1, we propose that culture (and subculture aspects) will interact with internal motivators and external activation to socialise people into being sport consumers. We have organised culture into four dimensions including shared contexts, shared cognition, shared affect and shared behaviours (Trail and James, 2013). Within these dimensions, cultural determinants create opportunities for people to become interested in consuming sport or being a fan through internal motivating characteristics and external activating situations.

Internal motivators include personal needs, personality characteristics, personal values and personal goals. These four categories of motivators obviously vary considerably across individuals, but for the consumption of sport to occur, at least one motivation, in one of these categories, must exist. For example, some people have the need for achievement and for some, it is most easily fulfilled vicariously through some successful other. So, for this individual, the need for vicarious achievement requires some outside entity to fulfill this need; that is, there must be an external activation that elicits and then potentially fulfills that need.

External activation occurs when the individual perceives that a product/service exists. The perception process consists of becoming aware of the product/service, becoming at least somewhat interested, and then initially evaluating the product/service. This perception process influences the attitude towards the product/service. However, we propose that it is the interaction between the internal motivator and the external activation that is critical for an attitude to form about a sport product/service. Using our example from above, both the need for vicarious achievement must exist and the successful other (winning team) must become salient to potentially fulfill that need, for an attitude about that team to come into being.

An attitude 'is a psychological tendency that is expressed by evaluating a particular entity with some degree of favor or disfavor' (Eagly and Chaiken, 1993, p. 1). As Eagly and Chaiken posited, attitudes are developed through cognitive learning as people gain information about the attitude object through both indirect and direct experiences. The direct experiences are derived from exposure to the object and experience with it, whereas the indirect experiences can be through others such as friends, family or the media. As the attitude toward the sport product or service comes into being, intentions to consume (or not) that product/service occur. As noted in an earlier section of the document, the intentions to consume the product may or may not lead to actual consumption, typically predicated on constraints.

As depicted in Figure 19.1 we hypothesise that external constraints can impact the individual at two points in the model: the first is between the attitude-to-intentions relationship, and the second possibility is between the intentions-to-action relationship. An individual may have a very positive attitude towards a team, but because of geographical constraints, have no intentions of buying tickets to a home game. For example, I like FC Barcelona and would like to see them play at their home venue, but considering that I live in Seattle and I will not fly, it would be rather difficult to overcome those constraints. Thus, I do not intend on attending a home Barca match. Therefore, the constraint has impacted the attitude-to-intentions relationship for me. However, if Barca comes to Seattle to play Seattle Sounders FC I would intend on going to that match. A constraint might prevent me from going even if I intended to though if I could not get a ticket.

The rest of the model is the same as our 2005 model in that, after the consumption of the product, expectancies are either confirmed or disconfirmed, which lead to an affective response. The affective response, if positive, leads to BIRGing and if negative could potentially lead to CORFing. These self-esteem related responses then impact whether there are any repatronage intentions and whether there is an adjustment in the attitude towards the product/service or brand.

This newly proposed model has not been tested yet and the biggest questions that need to be answered are (a) whether or not the cultural socialisation factors impact internal motivation, or perhaps more likely, external activation, and (b) whether the interaction between internal motivation and external activation will explain more variance in the model than each individually. That has yet to be determined.

Conclusion

In sum, the original work we did (Trail *et al.*, 2003), has created a foundation for anyone interested in investigating sport consumer behaviour. Although we have come a long way since that first model, there are many areas that still need further research. There also is considerable applicability to the industry and to the profession. We hope that as people see the value of this area of research the impact will spread and more sport organisations will benefit. We hope that academicians and their students that have the skills and expertise will help organisations investigate their own consumers and implement changes based on that research.

Note

1   This chapter is a reflection on Trail, Fink and Anderson (2003), and the work related to it.

References

Ajzen, I. (1991) 'The theory of planned behavior'. *Organizational Behavior and Human Decision Processes*, 50: 179–211.

Bien, L. (2014, 5 February) 'Seahawks Super Bowl parade: Crowd estimated at 700,000, larger than Seattle population'. *SBNATION*. Retrieved from www.sbnation.com/nfl/2014/2/5/5383424/seattle-seahawks-super-bowl-parade-attendance (accessed on 1 September, 2014).

Borden, S. (2014, 8 July) 'Goal, Goal, Goal, Goal, Goal, Goal, Goal, and Brazil's Day Goes Dark'. *The New York Times*. Retrieved from www.nytimes.com/2014/07/09/sports/worldcup/world-cup-2014-host-brazil-stunned-7–1-by-germany-in-semifinal.html?_r=0 (accessed on 1 September, 2014).

Branscombe, N.R. and Wann, D.L. (1991) 'The positive social and self-concept consequences of sports team identification'. *Journal of Sport & Social Issues*, 15: 115–27.

Cast, A.D. and Burke, P.J. (2002) 'A theory of self-esteem'. *Social Forces*, 80: 1041–68.

Cialdini, R.B., Borden, R.J., Thorne, A., Walker, M.R., Freeman, S. and Sloan, L.R. (1976) 'Basking in reflected glory: Three (football) field studies'. *Journal of Personality & Social Psychology*, 34: 366–75.

Deci, E.L. and Ryan, R.M. (2008) 'Self-determination theory: A macrotheory of human motivation, development, and health'. *Canadian Psychology*, 49: 182–5.

Eagly, A.H. and Chaiken, S. (1993) *The psychology of attitudes*. Fort Worth, TX: Harcourt Brace Jovanovich.

FIFA World Cup Record – Organization (2014) Retrieved from www.fifa.com/worldfootball/statisticsandrecords/tournaments/worldcup/organisation (accessed on 1 September, 2014).

Fink, J.S., Trail, G.T. and Anderson, D.F. (2002) 'An examination of team identification: Which motives are most salient to its existence?' *International Sports Journal*, 6: 195–207.

Gau, L.S., Gaillot, M.T. and Brady, M. (2007) 'A model examining relationships among team identification, sport spectator's motives, perceived service quality, and satisfaction'. In J.D. James (ed.) *Sport marketing across the spectrum: Research from emerging, developing, and established scholars* (pp. 81–97). Morgantown, WV: Fitness Information Technology.

Goldstein, J.H. (1989) 'Violence in sports'. In J.H. Goldstein (ed.) *Sports, games, and play: Social & psychological viewpoints* (second edn, pp. 279–97). Hillsdale, NJ: Lawrence Erlbaum Associates.

Gray, G.T. and Wert-Gray, S. (2012) 'Customer retention in sports organization marketing: Examining the impact of team identification and satisfaction with team performance'. *International Journal of Consumer Studies*, 36: 275–81.

Gutman, J. (1982) 'A means-end chain model based on consumer categorization processes'. *Journal of Marketing*, 46: 60–72.

Harrolle, M.G., Trail, G.T., Rodríguez, A. and Jordan, J.S. (2010) 'Conative loyalty of Latino and Non-Latino professional baseball fans'. *Journal of Sport Management*, 24: 456–71.

Hawkins, D.I., Best, R.J. and Coney, K.A. (2004) *Consumer behavior: building marketing strategy*. McGraw-Hill/Irwin series in marketing. Boston, MA: McGraw-Hill Irwin.

James, J.D. and Trail, G.T. (2008) 'The relevance of team identification to sport consumption behavior intentions'. *International Journal of Sport Management*, 9: 427–40.

Kim, Y.K. and Trail, G.T. (2010) 'Constraints and motivators: A new model to explain consumer behavior'. *Journal of Sport Management*, 24: 190–210.

Kim, Y.K. and Trail, G.T. (2011) 'Factors influencing spectator sport consumption: A case of NCAA women's college basketball'. *International Journal of Marketing & Sponsorship*, 13: 60–82.

Kim, Y.K., Trail, G.T. and Magnusen, M.J. (2013) 'Transition from motivation to behavior: Examining the moderating role of identification on the relationship between motives and attendance'. *International Journal of Sport Marketing & Sponsorship*, 14: 190–211.

Kwon, H., Trail, G.T. and Anderson, D.F. (2005) 'Are multiple points of attachment necessary to predict cognitive, affective, conative, or behavioral loyalty?' *Sport Management Review*, 8: 255–70.

Kwon, H.H., Trail, G.T. and Lee, D. (2008) 'The effects of vicarious achievement and team identification on BIRGing and CORFing in a winning vs. losing situation'. *Sport Marketing Quarterly*, 17: 209–17.

Larkin, B., Fink, J. and Trail, G.T. (2014) 'Does the living room become the fantasy front office? A cognitive evaluation of the consumption habits of fantasy sport users'. North American Society of Sport Management Conference. Pittsburgh, PA.

Lee, D. and Trail, G.T. (2011a) 'The influence of personal values and goals on cognitive and behavioral involvement in sport'. *Journal of Sport Management*, 25: 593–605.

Lee, D. and Trail, G.T. (2011b) 'A theoretical model of team-licensed merchandise purchasing (TLMP)'. *ICHPER-SD Journal of Research*, 6: 62–7.

Lee, D. and Trail, G.T. (2012) 'Confirmatory analysis of the athletic team merchandise model'. *Measurement in Physical Education & Exercise Science*, 16: 101–18.

Lee, D., Trail, G.T., Lee, C., Schoenstedt, L. and Choi, H. (2013) 'Exploring structural relationships among the factors that affect purchase intention of athletic team merchandise'. *ICHPER-SD Journal of Research*, 8: 27–35.

Madrigal, R. (1995) 'Cognitive and affective determinants of fan satisfaction with sporting event attendance'. *Journal of Leisure Research*, 27: 205–27.

Oliver, R.L. (1977) 'Effect of expectation and disconfirmation on postexposure product evaluations: An alternative interpretation'. *Journal of Applied Psychology*, 62: 480–6.

Oliver, R.L. (1993) 'Cognitive, affective, and attribute bases of the satisfaction response'. *Journal of Consumer Research*, 20: 418–30.

Robinson, M. and Trail, G.T. (2005) 'Relationships among spectator gender, motives, points of attachment, and sport preference'. *Journal of Sport Management*, 19: 58–80.

Santos, M. (2012) 'An attendance behavior model at sports events: Comparison and contrast of two models'. *Sport Science Review*, 21: 21–42.

Shapiro, S., Drayer, J. and Dwyer, B. (2014) 'Exploring fantasy baseball consumer behavior: Examining the relationship between identification, fantasy participation, and consumption'. *Journal of Sport Behavior*, 37: 77–93.

Shapiro, S., Ridinger, L. and Trail, G.T. (2013) 'An analysis of multiple spectator consumption behaviors, identification, and future behavioral intentions within the context of a new college football program'. *Journal of Sport Management*, 27: 130–45.

Sloan, L.R. (1989) 'The motives of sports fans'. In J.H. Goldstein (ed.) *Sports, games, and play: Social & psychological viewpoints* (second edn, pp. 175–240). Hillsdale, NJ: Lawrence Erlbaum Associates.

Snyder, C.R., Lassegard, M. and Ford, C.E. (1986) 'Distancing after group success and failure: Basking in reflected glory and cutting off reflected failure'. *Journal of Personality & Social Psychology*, 51: 382–8.

Stryker, S. and Burke, P.J. (2000) 'The past, present, and future of an identity theory'. *Social Psychology Quarterly*, 63: 284–97.

Super Bowl XLVIII most-watched TV Program in U.S. History. (2014, February 27). Available at www.nfl.com/superbowl/story/0ap2000000323430/article/super-bowl-xlviii-mostwatched-tv-program-in-us-history (accessed on 1 September, 2014).

Trail, G.T., Anderson, D.F. and Fink, J.S. (2000) 'A theoretical model of sport spectator consumption behavior'. *International Journal of Sport Management*, 1: 154–80.

Trail, G.T., Anderson, D.F. and Fink, J.S. (2005) 'Consumer satisfaction and identity theory: A model of sport spectator conative loyalty'. *Sport Marketing Quarterly*, *14*: 98–112.

Trail, G.T., Anderson, D.F. and Lee, D. (2006) 'Determinants of attendance: The Predictive value of team identification, past attendance, and attendance intentions'. Sport Marketing Association Conference. Denver, CO.

Trail, G.T., Fink, J.S. and Anderson, D.F. (2003) 'Sport spectator consumption behavior'. *Sport Marketing Quarterly*, *12*: 8–17.

Trail, G.T. and James, J.D. (2001) 'The Motivation Scale for Sport Consumption: Assessment of the scale's psychometric properties'. *Journal of Sport Behavior*, *24*: 108–27.

Trail, G.T. and James, J.D. (2011, August) 'Model of spectator sport consumption'. American Marketing Association Summer Marketing Educators Conference. San Francisco, CA.

Trail, G.T. and James, J.D. (2013) *Sport consumer behavior*. Seattle, WA: Sport Consumer Research Consultants LLC.

Trail, G.T., Kim, Y.K., Kwon, H.H., Harrolle, M.G., Braunstein-Minkove, J.R. and Dick, R. (2012) 'The effects of vicarious achievement and team identification on BIRGing and CORFing: Testing mediating and moderating effects'. *Sport Management Review*, *15*: 345–54.

Wann, D.L. (1995) 'Preliminary validation of the Sport Fan Motivation Scale'. *The Journal of Sport & Social Issues*, *19*: 377–96.

Wann, D.L. and Branscombe, N.R. (1993) 'Sports fans: Measuring degree of identification with their team'. *International Journal of Sport Psychology*, *24*: 1–17.

Woo, B., Trail, G.T., Kwon, H.H. and Anderson, D.F. (2009) 'Testing models of motives and points of attachment'. *Sport Marketing Quarterly*, *18*: 38–53.

Zillmann, D., Bryant, J. and Sapolsky, B.S. (1989) 'Enjoyment from sport spectatorship'. In J.H. Goldstein (ed.) *Sports, games, and play: Social & psychological viewpoints*. (second edn, pp. 241–78). Hillsdale, NJ: Lawrence Erlbaum Associates.

Applying the Sport Consumer Behavior Model

Brian A. Turner[1]

Since graduating with my PhD in 2001, I have taught Sport Marketing every year. When I first began preparing for these classes, one name that consistently showed up in the literature was Dr Galen Trail. As a fellow Ohio State alumnus, I had the opportunity to meet and interact with Dr Trail many times early in my academic career. I was especially impressed with his work on sport spectators and always read what he published in this area. In 2003, along with Drs Janet Fink and Dean Anderson, he published an article titled 'Sport spectator consumption behavior' (Trail, Anderson and Fink, 2003). In the article, the authors tested Trail, Anderson and Fink's (2000) theoretical model of sport spectator consumption behaviour and were able to explain eleven per cent of the variance in sport consumption intentions.

During the 2007–08 school year, Dr Trail and I were colleagues at Ohio State. Since our offices were next to each other, we had many great academic discussions that year. He mentioned that he was in the process of writing a sport consumer behaviour textbook (along with Dr Jeff James). Dr Trail left for a position at Seattle University after that year, so I 'inherited' the Sport Consumer Behavior Seminar. I knew right away that I wanted to use his new textbook, *Sport Consumer Behavior* (Trail and James, 2012), in my new seminar class.

I was initially attracted to the model in Trail *et al.* (2003) because it was one of the few that truly attempted to explain why individuals consume sport by including multiple psychographic variables. Students often struggle with understanding complex models (even doctoral students);

however, Trail and James (2013) explain each of the model's components (and others) in a sequential and logical manner that students can comprehend.

The Trail *et al.* (2003) article is really the foundation for my Sport Consumer Behavior Seminar. While Dr Trail has expanded his initial model, the variables in the 2003 article provide a solid framework for the course. We have great class discussions each week on each of the variables in this study. In particular, I believe the students have the liveliest debates on the topic of disconfirmation of expectancies for experience/outcome. Students invariably follow a variety of teams and all have expectations for their performance. Some assume their favourite teams may only win a few games a year, while others expect their team to win every game they play. Every student can give an example of a game they expected their team to win, but ultimately lost and how they felt afterwards. They can also describe the euphoria when their team pulled off a big upset when they were expecting the team to lose. The students absolutely love exploring this component of Trail *et al.*'s (2003) model. In fact, after taking my seminar, one doctoral student included (dis)confirmation of outcomes in a larger study on basking in reflected glory (BIRGing) (Jensen, Turner, Greenwell, McEvoy and Walsh, 2014).

One year in the seminar we conducted research for our athletic department. Using the Trail *et al.* (2003) article as a foundation, students (in small groups) had to develop an instrument examining why spectators attend events, collect data at a sporting event, analyse the data, present the results in class and submit the findings to the athletic department. The model was an invaluable resource that enabled the students to successfully develop and use an instrument within considerable time constraints (i.e., we were on quarters at the time and only really had about seven to eight weeks to complete the entire project).

I plan on continuing to use the Trail *et al.* (2003) article as the guiding framework for my consumer behaviour seminar. I look forward to seeing how Dr Trail further develops his theories of sport spectator consumption behaviour in the coming years. Finally, I also anticipate more students developing research projects based on this line of research.

Note

1   Brian A. Turner is an Associate Professor and co-ordinator of the Sport Management in the College of Education and Human Ecology at The Ohio State University.

References

Jensen, J.A., Turner, B.A., Greenwell, T.C., McEvoy, C.D. and Walsh, P. (2014, May). 'BIRGing 40 years later: A replication of Cialdini's seminal study'. Paper presented at the annual meeting of the North American Society for Sport Management (NASSM), Pittsburgh, PA.

Trail, G.T., Anderson, D. F. and Fink, J.S. (2000) 'A theoretical model of sport spectator consumption behavior'. *International Journal of Sport Management*, 1: 154–80.

Trail, G.T., Fink, J.S. and Anderson, D.F. (2003) 'Sport spectator consumption behavior'. *Sport Marketing Quarterly*, 12: 8–17.

Trail, G.T. and James, J.D. (2012) *Sport consumer behavior*. Seattle, WA: Sport Consumer Research Consultants LLC.

20

BRAND EQUITY IN SPORT

Conceptualisation, advancement and extensions[1]

Jay Gladden

There has to be more than winning!

Growing up in the Chicagoland area, I spent my childhood following the hapless Chicago Cubs. As I grew older, though, and began to focus on a career working in sport, I was struck by the fact that while fluctuations in the Cubs' won-loss record had some impact on attendance at games, it was not as dramatic as one might expect. During my early career as both a master's student and then working for an agency primarily conducting fan/audience research around sport events, I was struck by how professional teams and college athletic departments exclusively focused on winning as a driver of revenues. This seemed misguided and myopic – there had to be more to the financial success of a sport team or organisation than winning. Or, was the Cubs situation an anomaly? Given the entirely inconsistent outcomes in competition, even for the most revered franchises over time, there seemed to be a need for a new outlook or approach. To some degree, I left industry and entered a doctoral programme to develop a deeper understanding of the team sport environment, and more specifically what caused some sport organisations to be financially successful over time, even when performance was not at a championship calibre.

I was fortunate. I found a useful literature base while sitting in a doctoral seminar early in my PhD studies. This doctoral course, taught by Dr George Milne at the School of Management, University of Massachusetts, focused on marketing and was structured to expose students to some of the most important work in the discipline. Each week the course covered a different literature base and during this particular week we had some great conversations about branding theory. This led to a discussion after class in which Dr Milne encouraged me to consider the possibilities of applying the branding literature to sport. A review of the sport literature revealed that there had been no attempts to apply branding theory to the sport setting.[2] Given the lack of research, Dr Milne and I were excited about the opportunities to conceptualise how branding applied to sport, and then later to test those conceptualisations.

What is brand equity?

People unfamiliar with brand management assume it refers to the management of the logo and marks of a particular company or product. While a brand is a name, often a logo, and sometimes even a slogan or positioning statement, the development of brand equity is a much more involved process. The brand provides a connection point – it is what the organisation does, both purposely and inadvertently, to develop strong connections to the brand that ultimately result in loyalty. The brand provides distinctiveness and provides the product/organisation a point or points of difference in comparison with competitors (Aaker, 1991). This resonated with me. The Cubs did not win much, but they had a unique stadium in a wonderful Chicago neighbourhood, which allowed for a completely unique attendance experience.

Two of the early and foremost thought leaders on the topic of brand equity were David Aaker and Kevin Keller, and some of their early work on brand management heavily influenced my initial efforts developing branding theory in sport. Aaker's (1991) book, *Managing brand equity: Capitalizing on the value of a brand name*, remains one of the most often cited pieces on branding. The book offers, then discusses, a conceptual framework for brand equity that suggests five components to be managed: perceived quality, brand awareness, brand associations, brand loyalty, and other proprietary brand assets (Aaker, 1991). The first four components received most of the attention in the book and thus became the foundation for my initial work in the sport setting. This framework was appealing in that it both addressed the driver most often thought to influence revenue in sports – quality – but it also captured other elements, such as brand awareness and brand associations. Another intriguing element of the Aaker framework was its attention to loyalty as a component of equity. Perhaps the most interesting element of Aaker's model as it applied to sport was the concept of brand associations. Generally defined as the connections that one has when a brand name is mentioned, this seemed to be very appropriate for spectator sport, where the product was experiential and intangible. For example, Wrigley Field would present a strong, unique and favourable association with the Chicago Cubs.

Keller (1993) further developed the concept of brand association, conceiving 'consumer-based brand equity' as being composed of brand awareness and brand image. In Keller's (1993) conceptualisation of brand image, brand associations combined to create the image. Furthermore, Keller (1993) argued that there were three types of associations – attributes, benefits and attitudes – and it was strong, unique and favourable brand associations that led to the generation of brand image. This conceptualisation seemed particularly appropriate given there are basic elements of a sport brand, such as the logo, the players, the coaches, the owners and so on (Gladden and Funk, 2002). There are also benefits provided by the sport brand, such as nostalgia or identification with a group of people following the team (often referred to as fan/team identification; Gladden and Funk, 2002). The third form of association, attitudes, measured the strength of the association by gauging people's knowledge about a brand or the importance that people attach to the brand (Gladden and Funk, 2002).

Early work: conceptual framework based on the work of Aaker

Our first attempt at applying brand equity to sport (Gladden *et al.*, 1998) utilised Aaker's (1991) conceptual framework as a foundation for better understanding intercollegiate athletics (see Figure 20.1). Focusing on the four main components of Aaker's framework (awareness, perceived quality, associations and loyalty), we identified potential antecedents that would lead to brand equity. While we liked the broader structure presented by Aaker's framework, we sought to add to the understanding by identifying the precursors, or creators of brand equity in sport. I started with intercollegiate sport, because that was the setting of greatest interest to me at the time. To identify potential antecedents of brand equity, I perused both the academic literature and the popular press for evidence or conjecture of elements outside of winning that might lead to a stronger brand or positive marketplace outcomes. I also spent considerable time discussing these potential constructs with Dr Milne and Dr William Sutton. Once I identified a variety of potential antecedents, Dr Milne suggested that we organise the potential antecedents based on common factors. As a result, we categorised them into three areas: team-related (coach, star player, success), organisation-related (management, tradition, conference/schedule and product delivery) and market-related (competitive forces, local/regional media coverage, geographic location and team support/following).

Another addition to the application of the Aaker model was a recognition that the creation of brand equity resulted in marketplace outcomes. Consequences, such as merchandise sales, national media coverage, corporate support, atmosphere at games and ticket sales, were also all potentially visible and measurable outcomes. Finally, we realised that some of the consequences, and the resulting marketplace perception, could lead to the enhancement of antecedents of brand equity. For example, increased ticket sales could impact the product delivery and entertainment package (an antecedent of brand equity). As a result, we built a feedback loop into the framework depicting the potential impact of the consequences on the antecedents and brand equity. The connection of factors creating brand equity that also resulted in positive marketplace outcomes provided the deeper explanation, which had driven my initial motivation for doctoral studies. This first work provided the foundation for my doctoral dissertation and was published in the *Journal of Sport Management* (Gladden *et al.*, 1998).

A logical follow-up to the conceptual framework piece was to empirically test the framework, and this became the mission of my doctoral dissertation. Before testing the model, we decided

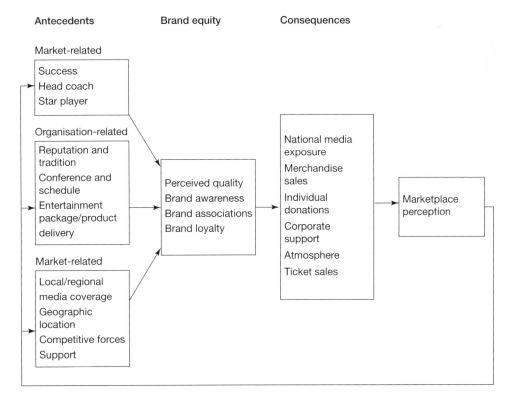

Figure 20.1 Conceptual framework for assessing brand equity in Division I college athletics
Source: Reprinted, by permission, from Gladden, Milne and Sutton, 1998.

to broaden the model so it could be applied to a variety of spectator sport settings, including professional sport. To do so, some modifications to the initial framework were necessary. Specifically, logo design and stadium/arena were added as organisation-related antecedents. Additional revenues, such as those realised through brand extensions (e.g. merchandise stores or practice facilities that generate revenue and fuel brand equity), were added as a consequence of brand equity. In my first empirical exploration of brand equity, I sought to validate a broader working hypothesis: that brand equity matters. It was clear that winning led to positive outcomes, but did brand equity also matter in the development of these positive marketplace outcomes? To answer this, my doctoral dissertation compared the predictive abilities of brand equity and team success on a variety of potential marketplace outcomes. This work established that *both* brand equity and success were predictive of positive marketplace outcomes, thus supporting the notion that winning is *not* everything. As a follow-up, Milne and I (Gladden and Milne, 1999) documented and discussed the results of regressing brand equity and success on merchandise sales.

Concurrent to the work above, I also developed ways in which the theory could be used in the classroom. Because the framework expressed clear antecedents and consequences of brand equity, the utilisation of this model to analyse the position of a brand was a natural extension. Along with Glenn Wong, we published a case study in McDonald and Milne's (1998) *Cases in Sport Marketing* that challenged students to apply the brand equity framework to a better understanding of the University of Massachusetts Athletic Department during a time of transition around their basketball programme (Gladden and Wong, 1998). The use of the model beyond the team sport setting was also possible. The Aaker (1991) framework provided the foundation for an analysis of New Balance's brand management efforts. As a niche competitor in the highly competitive athletic footwear industry, New Balance employed various strategies to create awareness, associations, a perception of quality and loyalty (Gladden and McDonald, 1999). This case study was designed to illustrate how an athletic footwear and apparel company focused on brand management. In doing so, the case was intended to be used as a teaching tool for both students and executives to better understand brand management in a sport setting that did not focus on teams.

Customer-based brand equity – towards a deeper understanding

While my initial work based on Aaker's (1991) model was rewarding, I felt as if we were only beginning to understand brand equity in sport. Prior to entering a PhD programme, my work led me to travel all over North America collecting fan and consumer perceptions related to sport brands and sponsors. I knew that while very clear trends could be identified, each individual's consumption experience and relationship with the team/organisation was unique. Thus, as I started my work as an Assistant Professor, I sought a better understanding of the fan's perception of sport brands. To do so, I moved towards Keller's (1993) conceptualisation of customer-based brand equity as a useful base. In his pivotal *Journal of Marketing* piece, Keller explained customer-based brand equity as 'conceptualized from the perspective of the individual consumer and a conceptual framework is provided of what consumers know about brands and what such knowledge implies for marketing strategies' (p. 2). There were two very appealing aspects to this approach. First, Keller explicitly focused on the consumer's experience, and second, the goal of his work was to yield insights that would drive marketing strategy. Given the inconsistency of the sport product, where success cannot be guaranteed, this orientation seemed particularly relevant. Under Keller's (1993) conceptualisation, brand equity is dependent on consumer's knowledge of the brand, where knowledge is composed of brand awareness and brand associations. Unlike Aaker (1991), who conceptualised brand awareness, associations, loyalty and perceived quality together, Keller (1993) argued that, 'high levels of brand awareness and a positive brand image should increase the probability of brand choice, as well as produce greater consumer (and retailer) loyalty' (p. 8). In essence, if there are high levels of awareness and strong brand associations, then loyalty can result. Applied to sport, if people are aware of a team brand and hold strong associations toward that brand, then it would make sense that the brand would be stronger.

Using Keller's (1993) model, initial work with Dr Dan Funk focused on conceptualising the potential set of brand associations in sport and then empirically testing the relevance of the model. The wealth of sport research provided an excellent foundation to identify potential brand associations. We conducted a thorough literature review and identified a list of potential brand associations. Then, focus groups were conducted with graduate students to determine if any potential associations were missing. Next, it was important to empirically validate the model and demonstrate the link to brand loyalty. The result was the Team Association Model, which presented an empirically validated model that included attributes, benefits and attitudes towards a sport team (Gladden and Funk, 2002). The model was extended to examine the relationship between attributes and benefits and loyalty to a professional sport team. At the same time, Dr Funk and I (2001) demonstrated how the Team Association Model could account for the variance in brand loyalty, thus validating the notion that if a team is successful in creating brand associations, that team will realise some degree of brand loyalty.

As my work in the area continued, and I could point to empirical validation of the theoretical application and development, I also observed a number of early conversations and efforts within the sport industry that focused on developing team brands. Additionally, some of the trends at the time (e.g., acquisitions and extensions, and early efforts around customer relationship management) suggested that this foundation and perspective would be relevant for the industry. This provided the foundation for a prospective piece with Dr Bill Sutton and Dr Dick Irwin, where we argued that the development of brand equity would be a central focus of North American professional team sport between 2000 and 2010 (Gladden, Irwin and Sutton, 2001). This piece suggested that teams would employ two broad strategies to develop brand equity: the acquisition of assets and the development of customer relationships. While some of the specific directions suggested within these categories were not fully realised, the two broad strategies turned out to be quite accurate.

Extending the initial work

Following the four-year period (1998–2002) that included the publications based on the work of Aaker (1991) and Keller (1993), I increased my efforts to fully understanding brand equity in sport. In collaboration with Dr Matthew Robinson, we altered the conceptual framework focused on team brand equity to apply to the intercollegiate recreation and intramural sports environment (Robinson and Gladden, 2003). This paper took into account the unique facets of recreation and intramural sports on a university campus and identified ways that brand equity could be developed in that setting.

As the focus on globalisation intensified between 2000 and 2010, there was also a need to consider how technology significantly enhanced the reach of sport teams across international borders. Accordingly, a collaboration with Dr Anthony Kerr resulted in a paper that revised the initial framework to conceptualise team brand equity in the global marketplace (Kerr and Gladden, 2008). Central to this piece was the addition of antecedents to brand equity that would lead a sports consumer in one country to start following or think highly of a brand in another country. For example, the concept of a star player was expanded to identify three potential types of star players (ambassadors, magicians, icons) based on how they helped a team develop brand equity across borders. Another interesting addition was sponsor alignment, which argued that those teams that had major global brands as naming sponsors had a better chance of developing brand equity. The final addition to the antecedents was the concept of brand community. The revised framework applied the concept of brand community (McAlexander, Schouten and Koenig, 2002), where people formed social bonds around a brand and linked it to the creation of brand equity.

Brand associations in sport – A flurry of activity

While the initial work based on the Aaker model (Gladden *et al.*, 1998; Gladden and Milne, 1999) stimulated a few studies attempting to extend the theory, the initial studies on brand associations (Gladden and Funk, 2001; 2002) have seen a much more significant cascade of follow-up from a variety of researchers. Most notably Stephen Ross and a variety of colleagues have spent considerable effort extending the understanding of brand associations. Ross' (2006) first publication on the topic offered an alternative conceptual model that included elements of both Aaker's (1991) and Keller's work, as well as elements of our initial work on brand equity. In this first paper, Ross argued that organisation-induced, market-induced and experience-induced antecedents led to spectator-based brand equity (composed of brand awareness and brand associations). In turn, the brand equity resulted in consequences similar to those articulated in the work of Gladden *et al.* (1998) and Gladden and Milne (1999) around intercollegiate and professional sport. Soon thereafter, Ross, James and Vargas (2006) published a second paper proposing an alternative means to measure brand associations in the team sport setting. Rather than using a literature review to develop the range of brand associations, Ross *et al.* started by eliciting brand associations from a free-thought listing technique from thirty-seven undergraduate students. The result was the Team Brand Association Scale (TBAS).

There were several differences between the TAM and TBAS. First, the TAM identified sixteen potential associations whereas the TBAS identified eleven. Second, nearly all of the TBAS associations could be classified as attributes (either product-related or non-product related), whereas the TAM identified attributes, benefits and attitudes. In addition, there were significant correlations between eight TAM constructs and seven TBAS constructs suggesting significant overlap between the two models (Ross *et al.*, 2006). A third study, by Ross, Russell and Bang (2008), expanded the TBAS to include two measures of brand awareness to create the spectator-based brand equity model. Brand equity research following Ross *et al.* (2008) has used a combination of our initial work and the work of Ross. To date, there is no clarity as to which model/framework is the most widely accepted. This is likely due to the similarities between a number of the proposed associations in each.

In addition to the work of Ross and colleagues, other authors have attempted to further develop the understanding of brand associations, particularly in reference to team sport. Kaynak, Guletkin Salman, and Tatoglu (2008) argued that the most appropriate conceptual framework for brand equity would include attributes, benefits and attitudes creating brand associations which, in turn, would result in loyalty. This piece drew heavily on our earlier work in attempting to provide a comprehensive discussion of brand association and brand loyalty in professional sport. Bauer, Stockburger-Sauer and Exler (2008) advanced the literature when they conceptualised and demonstrated the empirical links between brand equity elements. They suggested that attribute-based associations lead to benefits, which result in strong attitudes, psychological commitment and ultimately brand loyalty. This study follows the framework work of Gladden and Funk (2001, 2002), but suggests some different associations. This study is of particular note because it suggests and validates the linkage between basic associations (attributes), more complex associations (benefits and attitudes) and brand loyalty, and in doing so demonstrates a process where one element causes another.

Another interesting extension focused on how a professional sport league could develop brand associations. Kunkel, Funk and King (2014) employed a free-thought listing technique (similar to Ross *et al.*, 2006) to identify a potential set of league brand associations and then empirically validated these constructs in the Australian professional sport context. This paper identified seventeen different potential associations for a sport league, a number of which (e.g., star player, tradition, nostalgia, logo, management) were similar to the team-based constructs but were applied to the league. However, there were some new and interesting associations identified through this work. For example, player development (the league helps develop young athletes) and education (following the league expands the consumer's knowledge of the sport) were both identified as unique brand associations with a league.

Other applications and extensions of brand equity in sport

One other substantive piece of work conceptualising brand equity in sports adopted a significantly different approach in comparison with our conceptualisations. In 2007, Boyle and Magnusson suggested social identity creation was central to the development of brand equity. They argued that the groups with which people self-identify are at the core of brand equity formation (Boyle and Magnusson, 2007). Their research built upon initial work by Underwood, Bond and Baer (2001), who proposed the social-identity brand equity model. The work of Boyle and Magnusson, and of Underwood and colleagues, focused on social identity as a driver of brand equity. While my initial brand association work identified the related concept of fan identification as one of many sources for salient brand associations, this work focused on multiple dimensions of social identity. While the work of Boyle and Magnusson identified strong links between social identity and brand equity among students, alumni and the general public who supported an intercollegiate athletics programme, the results were more mixed across groups related to what led to the creation of social identity. For example, the history of a university's basketball programme was an important factor leading to social identity formation for alumni and the general public, but not for students. Watkins (2014) extended the social-identity brand equity model as a basis for understanding brand equity by looking at the fans of an NBA team. This research discovered that salient group experience (participating in spectating with a group of people), community group experience (how the team represents the city) and the venue in which the team plays were all significant factors leading to fan/social identification. Interestingly, history/tradition was not a significant factor leading to fan identification.

Unfinished business: still much more can be done

Our initial work around brand equity in sport has clearly sparked conversation, interest and study from a variety of different standpoints. However, I do have one regret to date. I am unaware of any circumstances where a brand equity framework is utilised by a team or athletic department. It is gratifying to see how teams and athletic departments have increasingly focused on managing relationships with their fans and providing the best possible experience for their fans. In both cases, such a focus can lead to stronger and more favourable associations. However, when branding is discussed by industry, it is still usually focused on logos, team colours, team names or advertising slogans. There is still a great opportunity to further develop our understanding of brand equity such that there is widespread adoption of consistent measures of the phenomena. Granted, there are available measures, such as *Forbes'* annual valuation of franchises, but none of these measures has a specific focus on brand equity.

The lack of widespread adoption by teams and leagues might be overcome via two strategies. First, the research using brand associations as a framework for understanding brand equity has advanced to the point that we have empirical support that associations can lead to brand loyalty. These studies provide an excellent understanding of the range of potential associations, but at the same time may have offered too many potential associations for any one organisation to manage. Narrowing the pool of associations to those that can actually be influenced by the organisation may help ease adoption and utilisation. However, this task could prove to be quite challenging. For example, in our 2002 work on brand associations, we found that benefits such as fan identification and nostalgia were more predictive of brand loyalty than attributes. Yet, the work by Bauer and colleagues (2008) demonstrates that attributes impact the creation of benefits. Thus, the complexity of these relationships would challenge any effort to reduce the number of factors.

Additionally, there is likely a need to identify one-item measures for the various associations so organisations can deliver shorter instruments and increase response rates. While some accuracy may be compromised, this could help stimulate adoption. A second strategy would specifically examine the linkage between a select set of associations and loyalty. For example, product-related attributes could be examined: To what degree does a head coaching change, recruitment or acquisition of a star player, or renovation of a stadium impact brand equity over time?

Thus, while our understanding of brand equity in sport has advanced significantly, we still have much to do. It appears a bridge to industry must still be built. The adoption of brand equity research by practitioners as they make organisational decisions is a goal for which we should strive.

Notes

1 This chapter is a reflection on Gladden, Milne and Sutton, (1998), and the work related to it.
2 Late in 1995, the first work to examine brand equity by Boone, Kochunny and Wilkins appeared in *Sport Marketing Quarterly*.

References

Aaker, D.A. (1991) *Managing brand equity: Capitalizing on the value of a brand name*. New York: The Free Press.

Bauer, H.H., Stokburger-Sauer, N.E. and Exler, S. (2008) 'Brand image and fan loyalty in professional team sport: A refined model and empirical assessment'. *Journal of Sport Management*, 22: 205–26.

Boone, L.E., Kochunny, C.M. and Wilkins, D. (1995) 'Applying the brand equity concept to Major League Baseball'. *Sport Marketing Quarterly*, 4: 33–42.

Boyle, B.A. and Magnusson, P. (2007) 'Social identity and brand equity formation: A comparative study of collegiate sports fans'. *Journal of Sport Management*, 21: 497–520.

Gladden, J.M. and Funk, D.C. (2001) 'Understanding brand loyalty in professional sport: Examining the link between brand associations and brand loyalty'. *The International Journal of Sports Marketing & Sponsorship*, 3: 45–69.

Gladden, J.M. and Funk, D.C. (2002) 'Developing an understanding of brand associations in team sport: Empirical evidence from consumers of professional sport'. *Journal of Sport Management*, 16: 54–81.

Gladden, J.M. and McDonald, M.A. (1999) 'The brand management efforts of a niche specialist: New Balance in the athletic footwear industry'. *The International Journal of Sports Marketing & Sponsorship*, 1: 168–84.

Gladden, J.M. and Milne, G.R. (1999) 'Examining the importance of brand equity in professional sport'. *Sport Marketing Quarterly*, 8: 21–9.

Gladden, J.M. and Wong, G.M. (1998) 'The creation and maintenance of brand equity: The case of University of Massachusetts Basketball'. In M.A. McDonald and G.R. Milne (eds) *Cases in sport marketing* (pp. 281–304). Sadbury, MA: Jones & Bartlett.

Gladden, J.M., Irwin, R.L. and Sutton, W.A. (2001) 'Managing North American major professional sport teams in the new millennium: Building, sharing, and maintaining equity'. *Journal of Sport Management*, 15: 297–317.

Gladden, J.M., Milne, G.R. and Sutton, W.A. (1998) 'A conceptual framework for assessing brand equity in Division I college athletics'. *Journal of Sport Management*, 12: 1–19.

Kaynak, E., Gultekin Salman, G. and Tatoglu, E. (2008) 'An integrative framework linking brand association and brand loyalty in professional sports'. *Brand Management*, 15: 336–57.

Keller, K.L. (1993) 'Conceptualizing, measuring, and managing customer-based brand equity'. *Journal of Marketing*, 57: 1–22.

Kerr, A. and Gladden, J.M. (2008) 'Extending the understanding of professional team brand equity to the global marketplace'. *International Journal of Sports Management & Marketing*, 3: 58–77.

Kunkel, T., Funk, D. and King, C. (2014) 'Developing a conceptual understanding of consumer-based league brand associations'. *Journal of Sport Management*, 28: 49–67.

McAlexander, J.H., Schouten, J.W. and Koenig, H.F. (2002) 'Building brand community'. *Journal of Marketing*, 66: 38–54.

McDonald, M.A. and Milne, G.R. (1999) *Cases in sport marketing*. Sudbury, MA: Jones & Bartlett.

Robinson, M.J. and Gladden, J.M. (2003) 'Thinking strategically about marketing: A conceptual framework for understanding brand equity in recreation and intramural sports'. *Recreational Sports Journal*, 27: 7–19.

Ross, S.D. (2006) 'A conceptual framework for understanding spectator-based brand equity'. *Journal of Sport Management*, 20: 22–38.

Ross, S.D., James, J.D. and Vargas, P. (2006) 'Development of a scale to measure team brand associations in professional sport'. *Journal of Sport Management*, 20: 260–79.

Ross, S.D., Russell, K.C. and Bang, H. (2008) 'An empirical assessment of spectator-based brand equity'. *Journal of Sport Management*, 22: 322–37.

Underwood, R., Bond, E. and Baer, R. (2001) 'Building service brand via social identity: Lessons from the sports marketplace'. *Journal of Marketing Theory & Practice*, 9: 1–13.

Watkins, B.A. (2014) 'Revisiting the social identity – brand equity model: An application to professional sports'. *Journal of Sport Management*, 28: 471–80.

Applying the brand equity in sport model

Artemisia Apostolopoulou[1]

I had the good fortune and privilege to have Dr Jay Gladden as my PhD advisor at the University of Massachusetts, Amherst. I was first introduced to his work on brand equity in the summer of 1999 while reviewing literature on brand management and brand extensions. This article caught my attention because it made sense! In a very effective manner, it reviews mainstream research on brand equity and applies it to the sport setting with examples. The list of antecedents and consequences identified in the article is comprehensive, while the connection of each of those elements with the four components of brand equity validates the relevance of the framework to collegiate sport. Beyond that, I consider the ability to apply with relative ease this framework to a number of settings within the sport industry a major strength. Whether the sport property is a professional team, a governing body or an event, the proposed brand equity framework can serve as a tool for assessment and growth.

Over the past twelve years I have regularly assigned this article, as well as subsequent branding-related work by Dr Gladden, as required reading in my undergraduate and graduate sport marketing classes. No matter how much has been written since about the management of sport brands, I find this work to be theoretically sound, easily adapted and timeless. And the feedback I have received from my students supports that. The framework provides a starting point from which students are called to assess a sport property's awareness, perceptions of quality, associations tied to the brand and levels of sport consumer loyalty. In addition, students are trained to think of sport properties as brands, to identify ways to strengthen each component of equity and to apply the framework to settings other than collegiate sport. I have also used this theory to discuss with students their own brand and what they need to do in order to achieve high levels of personal equity. This article has provided me with the necessary theoretical platform for those discussions and has greatly contributed to my students' learning.

This theory has informed my own research, too, particularly my writings on the branding of sport properties and on sport licensing (Apostolopoulou and Biggers, 2010; Apostolopoulou, Papadimitriou and Damtsiou, 2010; Apostolopoulou, Papadimitriou, Synowka and Clark, 2012; Clark, Apostolopoulou, Branvold and Synowka, 2009; Giannoulakis and Apostolopoulou, 2011; Papadimitriou, Apostolopoulou and Dounis, 2008). Introducing extension products or services is largely dependent on the existence of a strong parent brand. Sport properties are no exception. Realising the factors that influence the equity of a property is important in order to strengthen and further develop it via the introduction of line and brand extensions. The brand equity framework has provided me with a solid understanding of how branding principles apply to sport properties and how extensions can be used in the brand building process. Furthermore, my own research on licensing connects well with the discussion on brand associations since it positions licensed products as vessels of meaning that can impact consumer behaviour and consequently the equity of a sport brand.

I fully expect that Gladden's work will continue to inform and inspire my teaching and research in the future.

Note

1   Artemisia Apostolopoulou is a Professor of Sport Management in the School of Business at Robert Morris University.

References

Apostolopoulou, A. and Biggers, M. (2010) 'Positioning the New Orleans Hornets in the "Who Dat?" city'. *Sport Marketing Quarterly, 9*: 229–34.

Apostolopoulou, A., Papadimitriou, D. and Damtsiou, V. (2010) 'Meanings and functions in Olympic consumption: A study of the Athens 2004 Olympic licensed products'. *European Sport Management Quarterly, 10*: 485–507.

Apostolopoulou, A., Papadimitriou, D., Synowka, D. and Clark, J.S. (2012) 'Consumption and meanings of team licensed merchandise'. *International Journal of Sport Management & Marketing, 12*: 93–110.

Clark, J.S., Apostolopoulou, A., Branvold, S. and Synowka, D. (2009) 'Who knows Bobby Mo? Using intercollegiate athletics to build a university brand'. *Sport Marketing Quarterly, 18*: 57–63.

Giannoulakis, C. and Apostolopoulou, A. (2011) 'Implementation of a multi-brand strategy in action sports'. *Journal of Product & Brand Management, 20*: 171–81.

Papadimitriou, D., Apostolopoulou, A. and Dounis, T. (2008) 'Event sponsorship as a value creating strategy for brands'. *Journal of Product & Brand Management, 17*: 212–22.

21

THE PSYCHOLOGICAL CONTINUUM MODEL

An evolutionary perspective[1]

Daniel C. Funk and Jeffrey D. James

Introduction

The study of consumer behaviour in sport management emphasises the role of consumer experiences and how these experiences influence perceptions and preferences towards sport products and services. A decision to attend or watch a sporting contest, participate in a recreational event, use a mobile device to gather sport information, or purchase and wear a sport branded T-shirt is based on a number of external and internal forces, among which attitudes are particularly influential. This chapter provides a review of a theoretical framework, the Psychological Continuum Model (PCM), that outlines how an individual's attitude towards a sport object (e.g., team, player, sport, activity) initially forms and may change based on social-psychological principles. Over the past fifteen years, the framework has been developed and refined to advance our understanding of the decision-making process that guides motivations and behaviours in various sport and related contexts, and in different countries. The PCM has been used extensively as a theoretical foundation to guide sport consumer research in order to assist in the development of management actions useful in designing and promoting the optimal consumer experience. In this chapter we explore the PCM from an evolutionary perspective across three important time periods: the Conceptual Period (2001–09), the Operational Period (2009–15) and the Contextual Period (2015-onwards). The Conceptual Period includes an overview of the PCM along with revisions and refinements to the framework. The Operational Period presents empirical results utilised to validate and apply the framework in various contexts. The Contextual Period is a look forward at the role of context in the future development of the PCM.

The Conceptual Period (2001–09)

The Psychological Continuum Model was introduced in 2001 as a conceptual framework to organise literature from various academic disciplines and as a guide to advance our understanding of the psychology of sport consumer behaviour (Funk and James, 2001). The PCM utilised a hierarchical approach with four stages – Awareness, Attraction, Attachment and Allegiance – to categorise relevant literature applicable to attitudinal outcomes at each stage. We proposed that sport consumers would move through each stage, with each symbolising a different stage of attitude formation (i.e., connection) toward a sport object (see Figure 21.1). The basic premise of the PCM's hierarchy was that an individual would initially develop an attitude towards a sport object and his/her attitude would progressively grow stronger, and the attitude formation could be deconstructed into four stages. In other words, an individual who never played golf nor watched a professional sport team would not go to bed one night and then wake up the next morning and suddenly be an avid golfer or diehard fan. We proposed that various individual and sociological processes would facilitate or inhibit the stage-based movement toward a stronger psychological connection to the sport object. The following section provides a brief review of the stages and progression using a connection with the Philadelphia Eagles of the National Football League as an example.

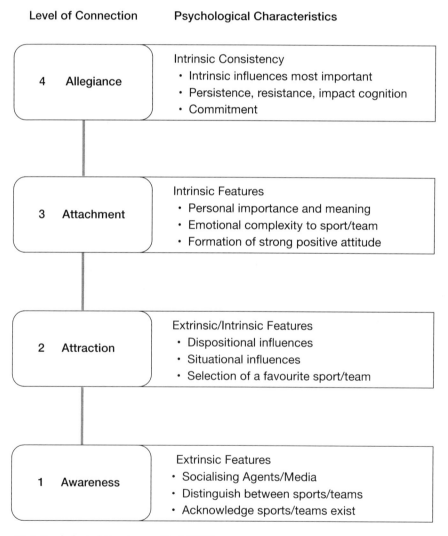

Level of Connection   **Psychological Characteristics**

4   Allegiance

Intrinsic Consistency
• Intrinsic influences most important
• Persistence, resistance, impact cognition
• Commitment

3   Attachment

Intrinsic Features
• Personal importance and meaning
• Emotional complexity to sport/team
• Formation of strong positive attitude

2   Attraction

Extrinsic/Intrinsic Features
• Dispositional influences
• Situational influences
• Selection of a favourite sport/team

1   Awareness

Extrinsic Features
• Socialising Agents/Media
• Distinguish between sports/teams
• Acknowledge sports/teams exist

Figure 21.1 Psychological Continuum Model 2001
Source: Funk and James, 2001.

The hierarchical structure of the PCM detailed in Figure 21.1 illustrates a bottom-up vertical progression. As the individual progresses to a higher stage, the psychological connection becomes incrementally stronger. The progression is analogous to an elevator with four floors corresponding to Awareness, Attraction, Attachment and Allegiance, and each floor represents a unique stage of psychological connection between an individual and the Philadelphia Eagles.

Awareness

The lowest stage at the bottom of Figure 21.1, the Awareness stage, represents the point at which an individual becomes aware that the football team exists. At this stage the individual has a general level of knowledge (i.e., I know there is a Philadelphia Eagles football team). The awareness occurs from the influence of socialising agents that operate as external forces that introduce the team and shape the initial attitude towards the team. Socialising agents vary by culture and context and typically are parents, relatives, peers, mass media, schools and sport organisations. At the Awareness stage, the individual is aware of the team but has not yet considered engaging in some form of consumption behaviour such as attending or watching an Eagles game. As socialising agents continue to influence the individual and attitude formation is stimulated, an individual is expected to move upward to the second stage: Attraction.

Attraction

The Attraction stage is reached when positive affect towards the team occurs. This positive emotion is triggered when the individual realises that hedonic and dispositional needs can be fulfilled through some form of consumption behaviour related to the team. The individual begins to consider watching and/or attending a game, reading information or talking about the team to acquire psychological benefits ranging from socialising with friends and family, enjoying the performance of athleticism and game strategy, excitement surrounding the event spectacle, self-esteem derived through vicarious achievement, and/or the ability to escape the normal routines of daily life. The Attraction stage is indicative of positive attitude formation towards the team, which manifests through an increased psychological connection (e.g., 'I like the Eagles'). Within the Attraction stage, socialising agents continue to operate as important external forces to create positive associations. As the psychological connection strengthens, subsequent attitude formation and change is driven more by individual psychological processes rather than sociological processes, and movement occurs from Attraction to Attachment.

Attachment

The Attachment stage denotes the formation of a meaningful psychological connection with the football team. This connection forms as the team is internalised into the individual's self-concept and aligned with core values held by the individual. Individual processes of integration and individuation that occur over time and across situational contexts govern internalisation. Integration occurs when an individual attempts to join with similar others who support the team, while individuation occurs when the individual attempts to differentiate his/herself from non-supporters. These self-developmental tasks create a more stable connection with the team based on emotional, functional, and symbolic meaning and lead to identification (e.g., 'I am an Eagle'). Attitude formation at the Attachment stage is based on an amalgamation and collective streng-thening of associations that provides more stability to the connection. If the relationship with the team continues, this connection continues to strengthen and leads to the Allegiance Stage.

Allegiance

The Allegiance stage represents the strongest psychological connection on the vertical continuum. Allegiance is reached when the attitude toward the team becomes durable and impactful, leading to commitment, loyalty and devotion (e.g., 'I live for the Eagles'). Individuals at this stage possess a highly formed attitude that is resistant to change, stable across context and time, influences cognitive processing of information, and is predictive of behaviour. The next section includes a description of a revision to the PCM that occurred to clarify what potential forces would cause movement within the continuum.

Revisions to the PCM

The PCM was revised in 2006 to outline movement between stages (Funk and James, 2006) (see Figure 21.2). The developmental progression within the vertical framework was advanced through the introduction of a sequence of inputs, processes and outputs that operate within each of the stages. The inputs represent internal and external determinants previously identified in the literature that would potentially influence an individual's psychological connection. The internal determinants were categorised into personal and psychological characteristics while the external determinants were suggested as stemming from a broad range of environmental factors. Three processes – labelled awareness, attraction and attachment – were positioned as a continuum of processes in order to illustrate how internal and external inputs form unique outcomes at each stage. Overall, the revision of the PCM provided greater clarity as to how the psychological connection between an individual and a sport object progressively forms through particular internal social-psychological mechanisms.

Subsequent revisions to the PCM occurred in 2008, serving to refine and extend its scope. Funk (2008) conceptualised the sequence of inputs, processes and outputs as operating similarly to the consumer decision-making process (see Figure 21.3). This revision introduced a hierarchical decision-making approach in which the inputs, processes and outputs sequence also contains a recursive feedback loop that operates within each stage and contributes to movement to adjacent stages. This perspective equated the decision-making recursive sequence as the internal mechanism that controlled movement within and between stages to account for the formation and change of the psychological connection. Funk also offered new insight into stage-based outcomes by conceptualising behavioural engagement as increasing in complexity at each of the four PCM stages through the breadth, depth and frequency of consumption-related actions.

The second revision that occurred in 2008 was offered by Beaton and Funk (2008). The authors argued the PCM should be conceptualised as a stage-based framework rather than a continuum model. Beaton and Funk argued the PCM has a structure composed of statements and concepts that should be viewed as the systematic and detailed explanation that accounts for the *how* and *why* individuals engage in leisure activities. As a framework, the PCM would provide the foundation and rationale for developing and testing new theories in five important ways. First the stage-based structure has the ability to address the complexity and non-linear patterns of human behaviour, which overcomes a criticism of continuum models that treat individuals as either engaging in a behaviour or not. Second, with the stages concept individuals may be assigned to a specific stage according to certain characteristics that differ from other stages. Third, if different stages do exist, then different forces maybe be at work between the stages. Fourth, movement through the four stages is not governed by a prescribed time function, so individuals may have different trajectories, as time spent in a specific stage may differ and movement may occur in either direction. Finally, as a stage-based framework the PCM would allow researchers

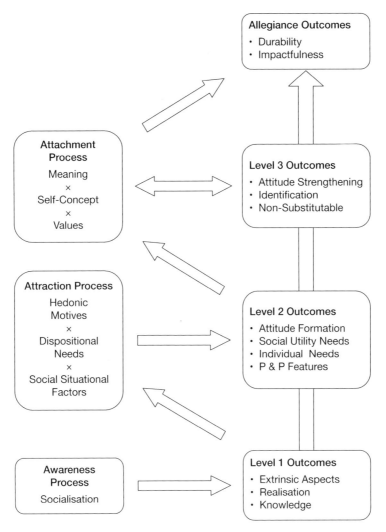

Figure 21.2 Psychological Continuum Model 2006
Source: Funk and James, 2006.

to utilise various concepts and constructs to develop and empirically test a theory to explain how a phenomenon works, and the information could be related back to the overall framework serving to advance knowledge in a programmatic manner. This revision highlighted a unique characteristic of the PCM in that it integrates the advantages of both stage-based models and continuum models to create a theoretical hybrid; a stage-based continuum model that serves as a framework to study the developmental progression of a psychological connection to a sport, sport-based object or leisure activity.

The introduction and revisions comprise an important period in the conceptual development of the PCM. This Conceptual Period occurred over a decade, which generally ran from 2000–09, and provided the foundation for the development of a sound theoretical framework that could

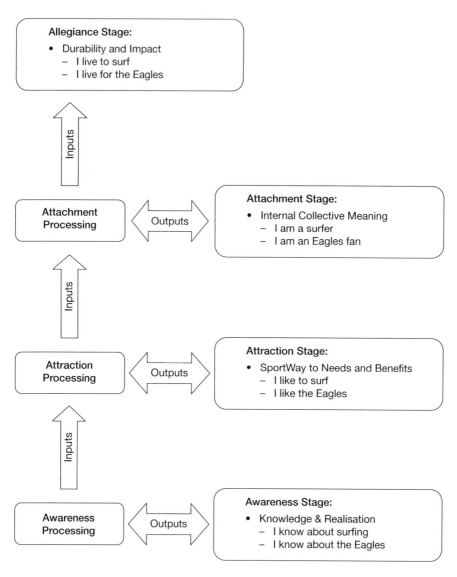

Figure 21.3 Psychological Continuum Model 2008
Source: Funk, 2008.

be used to study sport consumer behaviour and generate new knowledge. Researchers utilised the PCM to examine attitudes and behaviours in a variety of sport environments, including professional, collegiate and international sport, recreational and organised events, non-profits and fitness facilities. In addition, this research was conducted across numerous countries, including the US, Canada, Australia, Japan and Greece. The use of the framework in teaching undergraduate and graduate students studying sport marketing and sport consumer behaviour also began to emerge during this period. In 2009, the PCM entered into a second period of its evolution, which ran from 2009–15, as research was primarily devoted to empirically validating the stages and applying the PCM to other leisure contexts. This Empirical Period provided a means to operationalise the PCM and lead to a second generation of knowledge.

The Operational Period (2009–15)

An important contribution to the PCM was published in the work of Beaton, Funk and Alexandris (2009), prompting a new direction of research devoted to using the PCM as a stage-based framework. The advancement produced a second generation of knowledge largely influenced by limitations and new insight that occurred during the Conceptual Period. A key limitation of the PCM was that a mechanism or staging procedure did not exist to place an individual into one of the four stages. The ability to stage individuals becomes paramount in order to test and falsify propositions regarding personal, psychological and environmental determinants, as well as internal processes that may influence or inhibit movement. In addition, some type of staging mechanism would need to be based on a theoretical approach, which would make it applicable to all contexts. In response to this limitation, Beaton *et al.* (2009) developed and empirically tested a method to position individuals within the four PCM stages (see Figure 21.4).

The staging protocol or 'staging tool' utilises a three-step procedure based on the original tenets of the PCM framework published in 2001, proposing the use of involvement facets to distinguish between stages. The first step is to measure three facets of involvement (i.e.,

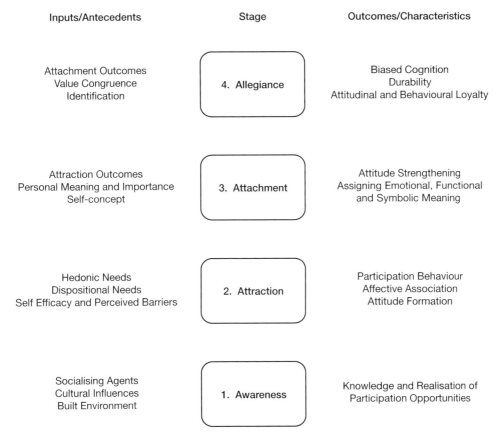

Figure 21.4 Psychological Continuum Model 2009
Source: Beaton, Funk and Alexandris, 2009.

pleasure, centrality and sign) and calculate mean scores for each facet (see Figure 21.5). Step two utilises predetermined cut points on the seven-point Likert scales to develop profiles of high, medium and low on each involvement facet (see Figure 21.5). The third and final step employs a qualitative algorithm based on an a priori theoretical configuration of twenty-seven unique profiles to allocate stage membership (see Figures 21.6 and 21.7). The authors validated the staging tool for the Attraction, Attachment and Allegiance stages with empirical data collected from rugby participants in Australia and recreational skiers in Greece. The results provided initial evidence that the staging procedure could accurately place individuals into three stages that revealed intra-stage similarities and inter-stage differences on involvement and resistance to change. In addition, the diversity of samples provide a robust assessment that the staging procedure could be employed across different sport or leisure contexts, and provide a useful tool for both researchers and practitioners.

The Operational Period ushered in a substantial amount of research applying the PCM framework to various research contexts and domains. The PCM has been used as a theoretical

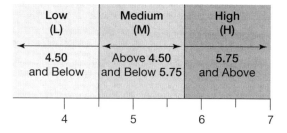

Figure 21.5 Staging procedure the Psychological Continuum Model
Source: Beaton, Funk and Alexandris, 2009.

Awareness			Attraction			Attachment			Allegiance		
*P	C	S	P	C	S	P	C	S	P	C	S
[a]L	L	L	M	L	L	L	L	M	M	H	H
			H	L	L	L	L	H	H	H	M
						L	M	L	H	M	H
						L	M	M	H	H	H
						L	M	H			
						L	H	L			
						L	H	M			
						L	H	H			
						M	L	M			
						M	L	H			
						M	M	L			
						M	H	L			
						M	M	M			
						M	M	H			
						M	H	M			
						H	L	M			
						H	M	L			
						H	M	M			
						H	L	H			
						H	H	L			

*: P=Pleasure Facet; C=Centrality Facet; S=Sign Facet
a: may be Awareness if a non-participant, or Attachment if a participant

Figure 21.6 Theoretical distribution of involvement profiles across PCM stages
Source: Beaton, Funk and Alexandris, 2009.

and empirical diagnostic tool to conceptualise and empirically validate attitudes and behaviours in sport management, recreation, event management and tourism contexts. The staging procedure has been applied to sport spectators and fans of collegiate and professional sport teams and leagues, recreational running, golf, skiing, rugby, tennis, softball, organised event participants in road races and triathlons, and tourists travelling to participate in events. Research has been conducted in numerous countries, including the US, Australia, Greece, Iran, Japan, New Zealand, South Africa and South Korea. Taken together, this body of works provides evidence to the ecological validity of the framework. In addition, the PCM framework has now been integrated into a number of texts and chapters, as well as content for students in various countries. Industry adoption of the framework has seen it applied to mass-participation sport events, horse racing, collegiate and professional spectator sports, charity events, analysis of collegiate alumni donations

Using the involvement profile ratings, complete the actions below **IN ORDER** until stage is determined

> ➢ Action 1:   If **Pleasure** facet is rated low (L),
>
>   stage = Awareness (non-participants), Attachment (participants);
>
>   If condition not satisfied then

> ➢ Action 2:   If **Both** Centrality and Sign facets are rated low (L),
>
>   stage = Attraction;
>
>   If condition not satisfied then

> ➢ Action 3:   If **Either** Centrality and Sign facets are rated low (L),
>
>   stage = Attachment;
>
>   If condition not satisfied then

> ➢ Action 4:   If **Any Two** facets are rated as high (H),
>
>   stage = Allegiance;
>
>   If condition not satisfied then

> ➢ Action 5:   **All** remaining,
>
>   stage = Attachment.

Figure 21.7 Staging algorithm for the Psychological Continuum Model
Source: Beaton, Funk and Alexandris, 2009.

and longitudinal studies in youth sports development. The industry application has largely utilised the PCM as a segmentation tool to create consumer profiles and tracking movement between stages to determine conversion rates and cost of marketing investment.

The Operational Period also witnessed two notable extensions to the PCM that served to provide an alternative approach to conceptualise and operationalise the boundaries of the framework. The first occurred in 2011 when Funk and colleagues conceptualised and empirically verified the four stages as a linear continuum that represented the relationship between attitudinal and behavioural engagement to recreational golf (see Figure 21.8; Funk, Beaton and Pritchard, 2011). A positive relationship between the degree of attitudinal engagement and the frequency and complexity of behaviours was depicted as a linear regression slope of stages. However, the authors argued that if attitude and behaviours were not consistent, a quadric slope pattern would likely occur. A second extension utilised this relational stage approach to develop a new perspective on sport brand architecture. Kunkel, Funk and Hill (2013) utilised the PCM segmentation procedure to place individuals into one of the four PCM stages, but did this process for both a professional league and team playing in that league, and compared stage place-ment consistency (see Figure 21.9). Three types of consumer groups were found to exist: (a) co-dominant group in which the individual was equally involved with the league and team (i.e., placed in equal stages of the PCM for both team and league); (b) a team dominant group in which the team stage placement was one or more higher than the league stage placement; and (c) a league dominant group in which the league stages was higher by one stage or more than the team stage placement. The results provided new evidence that the brand relationship of leagues and teams is perceived differently by consumers based on their psychological connection, and that the professional league can operate as an external force.

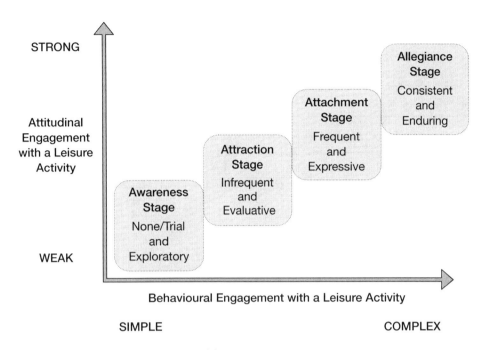

Figure 21.8 Psychological Continuum Model 2011
Source: Funk, Beaton and Pritchard, 2011.

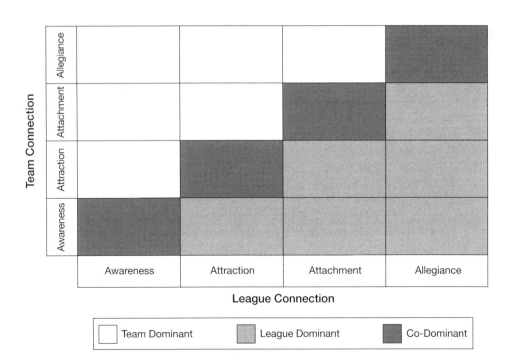

Figure 21.9 Psychological Continuum Model 2013
Source: Kunkel, Funk and Hill, 2013.

The Operational Period provided a substantial body of empirical evidence in support of the PCM framework. However, this evidence and research also revealed several limitations and situations in which the PCM did not account for a particular phenomenon or did not operationalise the entire population correctly. For example, in empirical studies, up to ten to twenty per cent of the participants could be miss-specified into the wrong stage. Attitudinal and behavioural stages were not consistent for a segment of the population. The question as to why a small group of individuals or a subset of the population did not follow theoretical predictions has become a fruitful area for future study. Also, the relative influence of external factors (environmental forces) on the psychological connection as well as movement remains theoretical, especially within the lower stages of attraction and awareness. Taken together, the conceptual and empirical support for the PCM combined with the limitations and criticisms directed at the framework, suggest that the emergence of a third period of research will now begin. A period in which context matters as an important step to spur future research and advance the PCM. This period will be called the Contextual Period.

The Contextual Period: 2015 to present

Previous research has shown the utility of PCM across many contexts and empirically supported the stage-based framework with quantitative and qualitative evidence. The Contextual Period will embrace an exploration of the nuances of the consumer context. The Contextual Period will primarily focus on the environmental experience in order to better understand what influences stage placement as well as transitions between stages. This should be driven by a service experience design approach in which the consumer experience is considered a journey through which many interactions occur between an individual and a sport organisation. This interaction is a management function. From this perspective, an interaction represents a touch point in which a consumer encounters information, a physical element, or any type of external stimuli managed by the organisation through various channels (e.g., email, advertising, website, parking, venue atmosphere). The touch points equate to a series of potential consumption points that have both temporal and geographical parameters that operate in a system. Research in the Contextual Period should include examinations of these consumption touch points as they operate in a service system design framework. This information will generate new knowledge on managerial and social determinants but will require a change in research approaches.

In the Contextual Period, a premium will be placed on research designed to investigate unique experiences in order develop new insight on service design to advance the PCM framework. We have been able to explain the perceptions of service by consumers, but not how the design of the service works. Given that services are largely based on the interactions between organisations and the motivations and behaviours of consumers, understanding people will be a key aspect. Such research will require both qualitative and quantitative techniques to examine the breadth and depth of consumption points, as well as the nuances of the experience as a design system. Initially, the focus will likely be context dependent with in-depth fieldwork to deliver new insight, and generalisability of results will be a secondary consideration. This will require researching the experience as it happens, as the use of post-event surveys or online panels about an experience can suffer from memory decay. Efforts will be needed to map out a behavioural system or sequencing of behaviours and testing prototypes of simulated behaviour. Without this approach, it will be difficult for researchers to create a comprehensive and customised blueprint of consumption points to measure and capture the complexities of the experiential journey, which includes the service design. Segmentation should also occur at the consumer journey level to understand the timeline of the experience and relative influence of consumption points (i.e., pre-event, event, post-event). In addition, the temporal segmentation approach can be used in conjunction with the PCM staging procedure to examine key interactions (i.e., Time × PCM × Consumption Point). This information will provide valuable insight for our understanding of the relative influence of how consumption points operate as inputs in the decision-making sequence within the PCM stage-based framework. This information is expected to generate new understanding of a specific context and differences across contexts. For example, if one experience design system works in one context (e.g., basketball) but not another (e.g., baseball), identifying the reason or mechanism to explain divergent results will lead to new knowledge and theory testing.

The Contextual Period will also require revisiting developments that occurred within the Operational Period. For example, the allocation procedure used to stage individuals into one of the four stages of the PCM will require further work in three important ways. First, the involvement dimensions of pleasure, centrality and sign used to calculate profiles to employ the algorithm will require psychometric development and testing to ensure discriminant validity. The original items used to measure the involvement facet were adapted from existing scales in recreation and future work would be well advised to develop these survey items 'from scratch' using established scale-development procedures. While the adapted scales have performed adequately, a fresh approach drawn from the perspective of sport participants and sport spectators would likely add contextual richness to prospective measures. It is also possible that participants and spectators may provide ideas that are unique to each context, which should be included in prospective measures of the involvement constructs. Second is the use of the sign dimension with its strong identification component. This may require a reconceptualisation using a divergent approach of two types of self-definitions of identity: internal (how I define myself) and external (how I perceive others defining me). Third is the use of analytic work on the pre-determined cut-points in Figure 21.5 to: (a) create context specific profiles and (b) create transitional stages. The context-specific work should consider making it more difficult to achieve a 'high' profile on a specific involvement dimension (e.g., moving the cut-point from 5.5 to 6.0). The transitional-stage work should focus on creating boundaries that overlap two of the existing PCM stages; for example, a boundary stage that contains the upper portion of the Attraction stage and the lower portion of the Attachment stage. This could be done to create three additional transitional stages using the existing cut-points. These boundaries could be used to identify individuals ready to transition upward or downward to a new stage. If it is possible to capture such transitional staging, further insight and knowledge may be acquired as to what mechanisms, and how such mechanisms, drive transitions among the stages.

The Contextual Period will highlight the service design elements that collectively define the sport management context. Ultimately what sport management is selling is an experience through a system of consumption points. Funk (2008) noted, 'Sport consumer behaviour is about the journey not the destination' (p. 4), to describe how watching or participating in a sport event is about an experiential journey. As part of this journey, the individual encounters a management system that utilises particular functions to provide information about how a specific service or product satisfies internal needs, and how a particular experience may deliver desired benefits to the consumer. Researchers working with the PCM who adopt the concept of consumer experience design approach will provide new information for successful operations since sport management is the result of the effective amalgamation of service marketing and management strategies.

Conclusion

No matter where in the world one may travel, no matter the cultures with which one may interact, a common denominator is sport. Whether one's interest is participating in some type of sporting event, watching sporting events played by family members, amateur athletes or professional athletes, we cannot escape the prominent place of sport in societies. Said another way, people all around the world connect with and through sport. Funk and James (2001) started out to develop a mechanism with which 'to guide our understanding of the underlying social-psychological process accounting for an individual's shift from initial awareness of a sport or team to subsequent allegiance' (p. 120). A keen observer will be able to recognise that the connection with or interest in sport and related objects (e.g., teams, players, activities) varies from the person with the casual knowledge that a professional football team exists, for example, to the individual who 'lives and dies' for his or her team.

The PCM (Funk and James, 2001) originally provided a means by which researchers could better understand the different types or stages of connection. From that point, it was a natural progression to identifying and striving to understand the mechanism or processes operating at different stages and along the continuum. The revisions to the PCM and advances in our understanding have moved us beyond just assessing how an individual's attitude toward a sport object initially forms and may change, to utilising a stage-based continuum model that serves as a framework to study the developmental progression of a psychological connection to a sport, sport-based object or leisure activity. As noted, the PCM is now utilised to advance our understanding of the decision-making process that guides motivations and behaviours.

As we move forward, the time for closing the knowledge loop is on the horizon. In many ways we have come full circle in the study of sport consumer behaviour. Very early research focused on activities within the control of management, such as pricing, packaging and distribution, as critical activities. We have progressed to periods in which we have sought to focus more on the consumer rather than the product; the evolution of the PCM provides an illustration of our journey to better understand the individual consumer's perspective and perception. As we look to the Contextual Period, we return to mental and physical elements, to touch points that are within the control of management. We do not, however, abandon our knowledge of the consumer; rather, through frameworks such as the PCM we recognise the importance of understanding both the individual and the context in which consumption takes place, the internal and external factors that influence consumer behaviour. We continue striving to further develop the PCM as a means by which to better understand the complex, dynamic subject that is sport consumer behaviour.

Note

1   This chapter is a reflection on Funk and James (2001) and the work related to it.

References

Beaton, A.A. and Funk, D.C. (2008) 'An evaluation of theoretical frameworks for studying physically active leisure'. *Leisure Sciences, 30*: 53–70.

Beaton, A.A., Funk, D.C. and Alexandris, K. (2009) 'Operationalizing a theory of participation in physically active leisure'. *Journal of Leisure Research, 41*: 177–203.

Funk, D.C. (2008) *Consumer behaviour for sport and events: Marketing action.* Elsevier: Jordon Hill, Oxford UK.

Funk, D.C., Beaton, A.A. and Pritchard, M. (2011) 'The stage-based development of physically active leisure: A recreational golf context'. *Journal of Leisure Research, 43*: 268–9.

Funk, D.C. and James, J.D. (2001) 'The Psychological Continuum Model: A conceptual framework for understanding an individual's psychological connection to sport'. *Sport Management Review, 4*: 119–50.

Funk, D.C. and James, J.D. (2006) 'Consumer loyalty: The meaning of attachment in the development of sport team allegiance'. *Journal of Sport Management, 20*: 189–217.

Kunkel, T., Funk, D.C. and Hill, B. (2013) 'Brand architecture, drivers of consumer involvement, and brand loyalty with professional sport leagues and teams'. *Journal of Sport Management, 27*: 177–92.

Applying the Psychological Continuum Model

Kevin Filo[1]

I initially became aware of the Psychological Continuum Model (PCM; Funk and James, 2001, 2006) as a master's student at the University of Texas at Austin. I had enrolled in a Sport Consumer Behavior seminar convened by one of the framework's co-creators (Daniel C. Funk) and Funk and James (2001) was a required reading for the course. The final assignment for the class required students to apply course content to the development of an explanation for how consumers connect with a sport object within a specific context. I incorporated the PCM framework into an examination of how content on an organisation's official website influenced sport fans' connection with the team. Dan and I extended the idea behind this assignment into a journal article (cf. Filo and Funk, 2005). Technological advances (e.g., social media) have significantly impacted the timelessness of this particular piece of research, but this initial application of the framework facilitated better understanding of consumers' psychological connection within sport.

I have since come to appreciate the balance struck between the specific guidance provided for how a psychological connection forms among sport consumers, alongside a more broad and open invitation to explore, extend and advance the PCM. Researchers have the opportunity to further develop the inputs, processes and outcomes across each stage. For instance, team identification (e.g., Lock, Taylor, Funk and Darcy, 2012) has been successfully incorporated into the framework to come to a better understanding of sport consumers. My work with Lock (Lock and Filo, 2012) represents just one of several examples of how stages and processes within the framework can be dissected. The PCM framework can be favourably compared to open-source software wherein the platform (i.e., the PCM framework and its guiding principles) is provided, allowing new insights and innovations to be made by users.

In my own career, the framework provided instruction that factors such as motives, values and self-concept lead to a charity sport event taking on emotional, symbolic and functional meaning. Using these ideas, we were able to uncover select recreation motives and motives for charitable giving (Filo, Funk and O'Brien, 2008) and demonstrate that these factors contribute to an event taking on emotional, symbolic and functional meaning (Filo, Funk and O'Brien, 2011, 2014). In addition, our research unearthed communitas as an outcome within the attachment stage (Filo *et al.*, 2008). We feel that these findings can be extended across a number of different contexts.

A better understanding of the processes across each stage represents the most notable area for future development. Researchers are encouraged to pursue longitudinal investigations of sport consumers drawing upon not only quantitative and qualitative methods for data collection, but also experimental design. The data tracking built into new media technologies provides an additional avenue for investigation and application. Finally, the integration of the PCM outside of the sport context for comparison across industries can further understanding.

Note

1   Kevin Filo is with the Griffith Business School at Griffith University.

References

Filo, K. and Funk, D.C. (2005) 'Congruence between attractive product features and virtual content delivery for Internet marketing communication'. *Sport Marketing Quarterly, 14*: 112–22.

Filo, K., Funk, D.C. and O'Brien, D. (2008) 'It's really not about the bike: Exploring attraction and attachment to the events of the Lance Armstrong Foundation'. *Journal of Sport Management, 22*: 501–25.

Filo, K., Funk, D.C. and O'Brien, D. (2011) 'Examining motivation for charity sport event participation: a comparison of recreation-based and charity-based motives'. *Journal of Leisure Research, 43*: 491–518.

Filo, K., Funk, D.C. and O'Brien, D. (2014) 'An empirical investigation of the role of camaraderie, cause, competency, and participation motives in the development of attachment to a charity sport event'. *Managing Leisure, 19*: 245–62.

Funk, D.C. and James, J.D. (2001) 'The Psychological Continuum Model: A conceptual framework for understanding an individual's psychological connection to sport'. *Sport Management Review, 4*: 119–50.

Funk, D.C. and James, J.D. (2006) 'Consumer loyalty: The meaning of attachment in the development of sport team allegiance'. *Journal of Sport Management, 20*: 189–217.

Lock, D. and Filo, K. (2012) 'The downside of being irrelevant and aloof: Exploring why individuals do not attend sport'. *Sport Management Review, 15*: 187–99.

Lock, D., Taylor, T., Funk, D. and Darcy, S. (2012) 'Exploring the development of team identification'. *Journal of Sport Management, 26*: 283–94.

22

SPORT FAN SOCIALISATION

Becoming loyal to a team[1]

Jeffrey D. James

Introduction

If you think about the hours and hours of sports programming available on television, over the radio and via the internet, it is easy to conclude that people enjoy sports. If you review the reports of sales of sporting goods in just the United States alone, it is easy to conclude that people enjoy participating in sports. Taken together, the interest in following sports passively, as spectators, and the interest in participating in sports, provide anecdotal evidence that sport is prominent in our society and something we value. The prominence of sport is further illustrated through the various metaphors people use when speaking. For example, in a business setting it would not be unusual to hear someone say, 'Give me a *ballpark* figure', or, 'The *ball is in our court*', or, 'Be careful not to *jump the gun*'. We like to watch sports, we like to play sports and we like to talk about sports. Sports are important to us, but why is this so?

The role or place of sport in society is not the focus of this work. That content is best left for another treatise. What will be focused on with this work is the idea that the importance of, or the value placed on, sport is a part of our society. As such, we communicate the importance from one generation to the next and include sport in some way, shape or form in our everyday lives. The focus of this work is *socialisation* and the importance of this concept for the advancement and study of sport management. More specifically, the focus is on our interest in following sports teams and the strong psychological connection so many form with sports teams. These are the folks we refer to as allegiant or loyal team fans. It seems evident that people who wear team apparel, that schedule their activities so nothing interferes with their attending or watching 'the game', who talk about their favourite team, who go so far as to define themselves as part of a team and proclaim, 'I bleed scarlet and grey' (or add your favourite team's colours), have developed a very strong psychological connection to a sports team (Funk and James, 2001, 2006).

It is important to recognise that a person does not just 'wake up' one day and realise she or he is a loyal team fan. Start at the beginning, your very beginning – birth. When you were born, you had no knowledge about, understanding of, or interest in any particular sport or a sports team. You learned, through various influencing agents, about sports, teams and athletes, and developed (or not) an interest in sports. We go through a *process* to reach the point at which we like sports and want to follow sports teams.

263

The notion of process, of being socialised into sport, was illustrated for me earlier in my career. While working as a marketing director for a minor league baseball team, I watched a couple bring their three-day-old – yes, three-day-old – daughter to her first baseball game. They were so excited to begin teaching her about baseball and their favourite team. The young couple helped me understand that there is a process by which people form connections with a sports team. The preceding is one episode that influenced my desire to study socialisation as a process by which people may become loyal team fans (James, 2001).

Overview

As a starting point, some background pertaining to socialisation in general should be considered. Socialisation is a process through which people learn the attitudes, values and actions appropriate for individuals that are members of a particular society (Kenyon and McPherson, 1973). Another way to think about socialisation is that it is the means by which we learn behaviours, or roles, that are essential for participation in society (Hughes and Kroehler, 2012). In essence, socialisation is the process through which we learn what it means to be part of society and how to live and act within a given society. Socialisation is about more than sport, but socialisation is a critical process through which we as members of society learn, not just about sport and about watching and/or participating in sporting activities, but why we come to value sport and to value the roles associated with sport.

What is meant by the idea of, 'roles associated with sport?' Kenyon and McPherson (1973) refer to primary and secondary sport roles. A primary role includes being an athlete or playing a sport. Secondary roles include watching sporting events as a spectator, reading about sports and/or listening to sports. Such behaviours are associated with the role of sport consumer. Being a coach, referee, sporting goods retailer or a sports promoter are examples of other secondary roles, what Kenyon and McPherson refer to as producer roles. One way to think about the various sport roles, whether primary or secondary, is that our interest in sport can manifest in numerous ways. Critical questions remain to be addressed, however, including 'how does the process of socialisation occur?' 'When does socialisation occur?' 'How has the concept of socialisation been studied within sport management?' In the remainder of this chapter, I discuss (a) the process of socialisation in general and the theories of socialisation as background for better understanding (b) sport and socialisation and (c) previous work that has been done on sport and socialisation, which leads to (d) my specific study of becoming a loyal team fan. The final section includes suggestions and ideas for future work with the topic.

Process

Socialisation in general

To better understand socialisation in general it is important to address two elements: theories of socialisation and agents of socialisation. The theories are important for understanding the process of socialisation. The latter include understanding what socialising agents are and how various agents facilitate the socialisation process. Both elements are important for understanding how socialisation occurs.

Theories of socialisation

Three theories commonly associated with socialisation are social learning theory (Bandura, 1971), cognitive development theory (Piaget, 1970) and symbolic interactionism (Hughes and Kroehler, 2012). With social learning theory there is an emphasis on conditioning and observational learning as mechanisms through which various attitudes, values and roles develop. Those emphasising cognitive development theory purport that socialisation proceeds differently based on the stage or phase of development. Symbolic interactionists focus on symbolic (subjective) meanings imposed on objects, behaviours and events; from this view attitudes, values and roles are socially constructed.

It is not within the scope of this work to review the three theories. Instead, I emphasise how social learning theory and cognitive development theory served as the guiding framework for the study of socialisation in sport contexts. I incorporated tenets of social learning theory in my work because it seemed obvious from a review of previous research on socialisation in general, and sport socialisation specifically, that elements of learning and modelling would be important to understanding becoming a loyal team fan. I focused on cognitive development theory as a result of 'dissecting' loyalty. With even a brief review of previous research pertaining to loyalty (c.f., Day, 1969; Jacoby, 1971), you would recognise the multi-dimensional nature of loyalty, notably the attitudinal and behavioural dimensions. Thinking about what is involved in forming attitudes, and attitudes influencing behaviour, I recognised that cognitive development would play a role in becoming a loyal team fan. With a reasonable understanding of socialisation, including the theoretical tenets that would frame my work, the next step was to consider the role of various agents in the socialisation process.

Socialising agents

The individuals, groups and institutions that are part of, and which create, the social context in which we learn attitudes, values and roles, are socialising agents. Socialising agents help us learn what the values and norms are in a particular society, and the roles or positions within the social structure, including being a fan of a sports team. The socialising agents commonly identified include family, peers, school (education) and media. To better understand the impact of socialising agents, think about your favourite sports team. How did that team become important to you? Did your father or other family members teach you about the team? Do you have the same favourite team as your father or other family member? Think about the sports you like to participate in – how did you learn about a particular sport? Did a sibling or peer play that sport? Did you learn about a sport in school? Our engagement with family, friends and the media contributes to what we think and believe and how we behave.

One other point to consider regarding socialising agents, and the process of socialisation overall, is that agents influence us throughout our life, which, said another way, simply means that socialisation occurs throughout one's life. We learn about the attitudes, values, norms and roles of our society, literally, from the day we are born through to the day we die. Much of our socialisation regarding core beliefs, norms and values occurs early in life. That does not preclude, however, learning about new roles (e.g., progressing from being an elementary school student, to a middle school student, to a high school student, to a college student), accepting new norms (e.g., communicating in shorthand via texting) and changing one's attitude towards a subject (e.g., rules governing the administration of college athletics began in part to address the idea that students competing as athletes should not be paid; today advocates are lobbying to pay students involved in college athletics). Socialisation is applied to many topics, including sport. So, what about sport and socialisation?

Sport and socialisation

For anyone involved in the study of sport and socialisation, there is an understanding that the elements are generally considered from one of two perspectives: socialisation through sport and socialisation into sport. The former involves the use of sport as a tool or platform through which a person learns values and norms that are important within one's society. For example, values associated with sport include learning the importance of teamwork, learning to deal with defeat, learning discipline, the value of hard work, just to name a few. Socialisation into sport encompasses the study of how individuals come to value sport, better understanding the place and importance of sport in one's society. The latter topic is our primary focus: better understanding of how people come to value sport in general and sports teams more specifically.

What do we mean when we write about or say that 'sport is important to someone?' Think about the following example. I know a man for whom baseball is really important: seriously, really, really important. During one of the seasons I worked as a marketing director for an AA baseball team, this man, who was a season ticket holder and had been since the team first began playing, had a son who scheduled a summer wedding. The wedding date was set before the baseball schedule was released. Upon learning the team's schedule, there was recognition that there was a conflict; the wedding was scheduled the same evening as a home baseball game. The father gave the couple three choices: (a) change the time of the wedding; (b) change the date of the wedding; or (c) have the wedding without him. Being at the baseball game was important to that man. When we say that a sport or team is important to someone, what we generally mean is that the sport or team is something that a person thinks about, spends time participating in or following, something a person talks about and invests his or her resources in (e.g., spending money to buy team merchandise or game tickets).

As noted earlier in the chapter, it is important to recognise that a person does not just 'wake up' one day and realise she or he is a loyal team fan. I believed (and still do) there is a process by which people become loyal team fans. We are influenced, throughout our life, through a process of socialisation. By the way, the wedding date and time were changed. So, how is socialisation involved in people thinking of sport and sports teams as an important element in their life? What have we learned about socialisation into sport?

Previous research

Scholars have studied the topic of socialisation into sport for several decades. Kenyon and McPherson (1973), and McPherson (1976) provide information about the impact that various socializing agents had on individuals becoming sport participants. For example, Kenyon and McPherson learned that during elementary school years individuals were encouraged to participate in sports primarily by family members. For those participating as college athletes, peer reinforcement was found to be very important (Kenyon and McPherson, 1973). These studies deal with people participating in sports. McPherson also studied sport consumers – those who watch sports – and found that, among high school students, peers had a strong impact on whether males followed sports teams, while parents were more influential for female high school students.

The study of sport socialisation from the 1970s through the 1980s was conducted primarily with college students and adults. Information was based on the memories and recollections of participants in the respective studies. While other research was conducted regarding socialisation and other contexts (e.g., leisure socialisation, Hoff and Ellis, 1992; consumer socialisation, Bahn, 1986) there was essentially no other substantive work[2] on sport socialisation until the late 1990s, going into the new millennium.

The late 1990s provided a unique opportunity to study loyal team fans. The owner of the then Cleveland Browns decided to relocate the franchise to Baltimore, Maryland. There was a void in Cleveland: no professional football team. But there were still Browns fans. I met Dr Richard Kolbe at a consumer psychology conference and we discussed my work on becoming a loyal team fan. As a Cleveland Browns fan, he lamented the team's move to Baltimore and wondered what would happen with the Browns fans.

When an announcement was made by the National Football League that there would be another Cleveland Browns football team, we recognised the opportunity to study those who were Browns fans, how they became Browns fans and whether they would be loyal fans of the 'new' team. Rick and I (Kolbe and James, 2000) conducted a study of Browns fans in an effort to better understand the factors influencing people to become fans of professional sports teams. We sought to provide answers to two questions: which people and things most strongly influence an individual's decision to become a team fan; and in what age period does an individual typically become a team fan? Similar to previous research (e.g., McPherson, 1976), adults were surveyed and asked to think back on people, events or other agents that influenced their becoming a team fan. Participants were also asked to report at what age they thought they became a 'true' team fan.

We found that among individuals reporting that they became a team fan early in life, prior to the teenage years, fathers had the most influence (Kolbe and James, 2000). Those who reported becoming a team fan during their adult years noted that players and coaches for the particular team were important influences. One challenge with the earlier research, continuing with the Kolbe and James work, is the reliance on recall from adults. While there is certainly merit to the information individuals may provide, there is also a question as to the impact of various socialising agents that may not be remembered after five, ten or more years. Recognising the limitations with previous research is part of what drove me to want to better understand the process of becoming a team fan from a different approach. I realised that if our knowledge was to advance, we had to try to learn about becoming a team fan during the process, not just after the fact. To develop theory about becoming a loyal team fan would require a differ-ent approach. To address the concerns I had with previous work, and to explore the early development of team loyalty, I sought to examine when children may first begin to demonstrate team loyalty and what socialising agents influenced the initial development of team loyalty (James, 2001).

Through my research, I was trying to better understand the impact of socialising agents on the initial development of team loyalty. Additionally, I was trying to ascertain when a child would be capable of demonstrating team loyalty based on stage of cognitive development. Think back to the earlier information provided about theories of socialisation. Through my early work I incorporated both social learning theory and cognitive development theory in a study of sport socialisation. As I have already noted, being loyal to a specific sports team does not occur on a whim. Loyalty results when one has a strong psychological connection to an object, a sports team, that is persistent and resistant to change; 'becoming loyal to a team requires a minimum level of thought and reasoning, a minimum level of cognitive development' (James, 2001, p. 236).

The ideas I sought to test regarding cognitive development came together in large part from my thinking about the multi-dimensional nature of loyalty. I agree with the premise that loyalty is multi-dimensional (Jacoby, 1971) and, further, that in order for someone to have a strong attitude towards a sports team, there would have to be a minimum level of cognitive development. I really centred on cognitive development because I was trying to address some of the limitations with earlier research. I believed that working with individuals as they are learning about sports teams, I could better understand the process of becoming a loyal team fan.

Instead of relying on recall information from adults about their childhood, I interviewed children ages five to six and eight to nine to learn whether they had a favourite sports team and, if so, whether various socialising agents influenced a child's preference for a particular team. With respect to loyalty, I assessed whether children demonstrated psychological commitment (based on cognitive complexity, resistance to change and volition, elements that require having reached a particular level of cognitive development) and behavioural consistency. I talked with the children about their interest in a variety of topics, including playing sports and following sports teams. The interviews included questions about various socialising agents (e.g., parents, siblings, friends) to determine whether children were aware of the preferences of others and to gauge the way(s) in which various agents may have influenced a particular child's socialisation into sport, to following a specific team.

I learned that children in both age groups were aware that family members or friends did have a favourite sports team. Children on average reported knowing their father's favourite team more so than other family members or friends. While not all children indicated they had a favourite sports team, among those that did have a favourite team, the influence of a father was most prominent. As part of the research, I attempted to sort out the manner in which fathers influenced or socialised their children. Fathers were found to influence the children by talking about a favourite team, watching the team on television and taking children to a game. While the results in and of themselves were not particularly surprising, the research provided the most direct evidence of socialisation in action in the sense that children were able to provide information about the formation of their preferences and team loyalty during the period in life that they were being influenced as opposed to recall studies. This type of work provides a snapshot of what particular socialising agents had an impact on development of loyalty to a particular sports team, and also the manner in which a particular agent (e.g., a father) influenced a child.

In terms of theory development, a key outcome from my preliminary work was proposing a theory about the initial development of team loyalty. Based on cognitive development theory and social learning theory, I proposed that the development of team loyalty occurs through a five-stage process: (a) introduction to sports and teams, (b) preference formation, (c) preference strengthening, (d) emerging commitment and (e) identification with a team (James, 1997). Within the theory I advanced ideas about the impact of various socialising agents and the impact of stage of cognitive development. In the initial research I learned about the importance of 'person factors' in sport socialisation: specifically, the influence of family members on the initial development of team loyalty. From the work by Kolbe and James (2000), I was also aware of the role of non-persons (e.g., team history, community connection). In a later project (James, Walker and Kumina, 2009) I sought to learn more about the non-person factors.

Extensions and applications

In the 2009 project,[3] and consistent with earlier studies, I surveyed adult sport consumers about factors influential to the development and continuation of their sport fandom. An additional element in the work was grouping respondents based on the degree to which they had internalised the team as part of their identity. Consistent with previous research, I assessed the importance of persons, specifically family members, coaches and players. In a different vein, I also assessed the importance of non-person factors, such as a team's history, style of play and connection with the community, as socialising agents. A third element in this work included assessment of factors that were believed to influence one's continued connection with the sports team, i.e., the ongoing socialisation process.

The results were consistent with previous work; the person reported to have the most impact on someone becoming a fan of a particular team was a father. The agent next identified, at a much lower percentage, was a friend. The finding reinforced what had been consistently reported in research dealing with sport socialisation; that family members are a primary influence early in an individual's life. The inclusion of non-person factors in the 2009 project is an example of advancing the study of sport socialisation. This facet illustrated for us that socialising agents, particularly in a sports context, may come in a variety of forms. I learned that the tradition of a team had an important influence on people thinking of the team as their favourite. The team as a representation of a particular city ('my hometown team') was also influential. Findings such as these help us understand on some level why people come to value sports and a particular sports team. The notions of tradition and a hometown team both provide a source of collective identity, a sense of belonging, which is a fundamental need that may be satisfied through a psychological connection with a sports team. Heere and James (2007), among others, write about the proposition that sports teams may be representative of other group identities such as one's hometown, and provide a mechanism for satisfying a need for belonging. This latter point illustrates how my earlier ideas provided a foundation from which others developed new ideas pertaining to the connections people have with sports teams.

There is continued interest in the topic of sport socialisation. One recent project was a study of the topic across national boundaries; Parry, Jones and Wann (2014) compared the influence of socialising agents in samples from the United Kingdom, Greece, Australia, Norway and the United States. They collected information from a sample in the United Kingdom and compared the results with previous research from other countries. Parry *et al.* (2014) specifically examined the extent to which parents, friends/peers, school and community contributed to a person's socialisation into the sport fan role. Consistent with previous research efforts, they asked people to rate how much influence the respective agents had on their decision to be a sport fan. The participants were also asked to complete an open-ended response item noting the most influential person or entity in their choice to be a sport fan.

The findings were consistent with previous research; in all countries, fathers were reported to have the most influence on someone becoming a sport fan, with friends cited second in terms of frequency (though at a much lower level). A notable difference was that friends were noted as more influential in Greece, Australia and Norway than family. At a minimum, such findings should lead us to question what other differences there may be in sport socialisation in different nations, or perhaps what differences there may be across cultures.

Future directions

So, where do we go from here? Is sport socialisation an area that merits continued attention by sport management scholars? Since it is not likely that the importance of sport and sports teams will diminish in the near future, it is important to continue our study of how people become interested in sports and teams, how loyalty forms and the impact of loyalty over time. Another issue to consider is the notion of degradation. On one hand, loyalties formed early in life are believed to persist. On the other hand, who has not noticed a change in their interest in sports and teams? Perhaps it is not one's loyalty that changes, just one's behaviours in relation to a sports team. Is there a lifecycle to team loyalty? If so, what might that entail?

Sport socialisation is a topic that merits our attention. To really understand what socialisation agents influence people and how, longitudinal research is needed. Efforts are needed to talk with and observe individuals as they are being influenced, similar to my early work. When constraints prohibit such labour and time-intensive work, we can focus on more in-depth research with existing team fans. We must talk to people, listen to people telling their stories, share their memories as fans and think about their current situations and what influences them to continue as loyal team fans. Sports and sports teams are important to people; they will continue to be important to people. We would be remiss if we did not continue to advance our understanding of why we are enamored with sports and teams, and the processes by and through which we continue to pass along our interest to future generations. If you are not sure what to do next, think about two questions: Who is your favourite team? Why do you have a favourite team? Let the answers guide you into the research.

Notes

1   This chapter is a reflection on James (2001) and the work related to it.
2   Space constraints prevent an exhaustive review of all sport socialisation research. Particular works were selected in order to address specific points for discussion.
3   The James, Walker and Kuminka (2009) article was a report on research I conducted in 2002, but did not write up for publication until 2008–09, with the help of two (now former) doctoral students.

References

Bahn, K.D. (1986) 'How and when do brand perceptions and preferences first form? A cognitive developmental investigation'. *Journal of Consumer Research, 13*: 382–93.

Bandura, A. (1971) *Social learning theory.* Morristown, NJ: General Learning Press.

Day, G.S. (1969) 'A two dimensional concept of brand loyalty'. *Journal of Advertising Research, 9*: 29–35.

Funk, D.C. and James, J.D. (2001) 'The Psychological Continuum Model: A conceptual framework for understanding an individual's psychological connection to sport'. *Sport Management Review, 4*: 119–50.

Funk, D.C. and James, J.D. (2006) 'Consumer loyalty: The meaning of attachment in the development of sport team allegiance'. *Journal of Sport Management, 20*: 189–217.

Heere, B. and James, J.D. (2007) 'Stepping outside the lines: Developing a multi-dimensional team identity scale based on social identity theory'. *Sport Management Review, 10*: 65–91.

Hoff, A.E. and Ellis, G.D. (1992) 'Influence of agents of leisure socialization on leisure self-efficacy of university students'. *Journal of Leisure Research, 24*: 114–26.

Hughes, M. and Kroehler, C.J. (2012) *Sociology: The core* (eleventh edn). New York: McGraw-Hill.

Jacoby, J. (1971) 'A model of multi-brand loyalty'. *Journal of Advertising Research, 11*: 25–30.

James, J.D. (1997) 'Becoming a sports fan: Understanding cognitive development and socialization in the development of fan loyalty'. Doctoral dissertation. Retrieved from ProQuest, UMI Dissertations Publishing (9731644).

James, J.D. (2001) 'The role of cognitive development and socialization in the initial development of team loyalty'. *Leisure Sciences, 23*: 233–62.

James, J.D., Walker, M. and Kuminka, W. (2009) 'Becoming a professional football team fan: Differences based on level of team internalization'. *International Journal of Sport Management, 10*: 14–34.

Kenyon, G.S. and McPherson, B.D. (1973) 'Becoming involved in physical activity and sport: A process of socialization' (pp. 303–32). In G.L. Rarick (ed.) *Physical activity: Human growth and development.* New York: Academic Press.

Kolbe, R.H. and James, J.D. (2000) 'An identification and examination of influences that shape the creation of a professional team fan'. *International Journal of Sports Marketing & Sponsorship, 2*: 21–37.

McPherson, B.D. (1976) 'Socialization into the role of sport consumer: A theory and causal model'. *Canadian Review of Sociology & Anthropology, 13*: 165–77.

Parry, K.D., Jones, I. and Wann, D.L. (2014) 'An examination of sport fandom in the United Kingdom: A comparative analysis of fan behaviors, socialization processes, and team identification'. *Journal of Sport Behavior, 37*: 251–67.

Piaget, J. (1970) 'The stages of the intellectual development of the child'. In P. Mussen, J. Conger and J. Kagan (eds) *Readings in child development and personality* (pp. 291–302). New York: Harper and Row.

Applying sport fan socialisation theory

Haylee Uecker Mercado[1]

The central mission of scholars is to conduct research that contributes knowledge to a scientific discipline, on the one hand, and to apply that knowledge to the practice of management as a profession, on the other (Simon, 1967). To do this well, we need to design our research so that it provides an intimate understanding of the practical problems facing the profession. Equally important, we need to appreciate and strengthen our skills in developing good theory so that research conducted about these problems will advance the knowledge that is relevant to both the discipline and the profession.

About a decade ago, I began to explore the relationships between culture and socialisation into sport. The impetus for this research came from several sources. First, as I began my pursuit of doctoral programmes in sport management, I encountered Dr Jeffrey James and his work on team loyalty and socialisation into sport. I was subsequently accepted into the programme with Dr James as my advisor. One of the first doctoral seminars I took was a sport marketing seminar that exposed me to various theories and provided me with ways in which theories were developed, in particular sport socialisation. A second reason for connecting to this theory was through a Hispanic marketing course that opened my eyes to an emerging, yet highly misunderstood, segment of the population. Finally, I was immersed into this segment through personal and professional relationships that allowed me to see the value of this line of research. I realised that there was a need to design research so that it would provide a deeper understanding of the practical problems facing the sport industry. Equally important, there was a need to appreciate and strengthen our skills in developing good theory so that research conducted about cultural problems would advance the knowledge that was relevant to both the discipline and the profession.

Application

The goal of my research agenda is to investigate the primary sport socialisation agents for multiple generations of individual Hispanic subcultures (i.e., Cuban, Puerto Rican, etc.). More specifically, the theory was used to provide insight into similarities and differences in sport socialisation among multiple generations within particular Hispanic subcultures. I used the socialisation theory as I began to look at how sport socialisation was impacted by culture, level of acculturation and generation. This line of research has served me well in varying aspects of research, teaching and practice. I have used culture as a basis for marketing, managerial and event management lectures and have been asked to speak to several professional organisations on the impact of culture on their employees and stakeholders based on their socialisation into and through sport on varying generational and acculturation levels. For example, I found that reverse socialisation occurs in this segment where the third generation most often introduces the first generation to sport in cases where there are low acculturation levels (Mercado, 2008).

While sport socialisation research has made strides recently, it remains an area of study that is under-developed. The current literature does not fully address the creation of a sport spectator or the values that are transferred through sport participation. Further, I am not aware of any qualitative studies that ascertain whether the current sport socialisation agents being studied are exhaustive. These might include the influence of media, video games and the internet. Additionally, there has been little effort to look at the sport socialisation process from a generational or subcultural perspective, as my research initially explored.

Note

1   Haylee Uecker Mercado is an Assistant Professor at the University of South Carolina.

References

Mercado, H.U. (2008) 'Market segmentation based on subcultural socialization: A case study'. Unpublished doctoral dissertation, Florida State University.
Simon, H.A. (1967) 'The business school: A problem in organizational design'. *Journal of Management Studies*, 4: 1–16.

23

WHAT ATTRACTS FANS TO A VENUE?[1]

Kirk Wakefield

Introduction

The study of person, place and situation-based factors influencing sport consumption behaviours is now a relatively rich field of research. Yet, until the early 1990s, limited empirical evidence existed beyond aggregate economic models of fan attendance to explain fan behaviour. These models (e.g., Noll, 1974) did little to explain why small town markets (e.g., St Louis Cardinals) or perennial losers (e.g., Chicago Cubs) could continue to attract millions of fans. What is it about these places that attracts proportionately more fans than economic models would predict? Clearly, something besides population size, competition, prices, income levels and team performance influences attendance.

The basic research question then and now is: what attracts individuals to places? Such a fundamental question provides researchers with the proper scope to examine literature in relevant fields to build upon and enhance theory. The question is not, 'what drives fan attendance?' – although this is the practical, managerial question addressed. Such a narrow scope would limit the application, influence and impact to be field specific.

Overview of the sportscape

The sportscape refers to the built or fixed elements of the physical environment of a sporting event that remain the same from game to game. The sportscape includes every tangible element fans encounter as they approach the exterior of a facility, enter and navigate through the interior of the facility, and subsequently exit. The exterior layout includes the facility's design and location of parking lots and the aesthetic appeal of the facility architecture. The interior layout and design includes (a) layout accessibility, which is a function of wayfinding signage and space allocation, (b) seat comfort and (c) scoreboards.

In work done with Sloan, we investigated the response of individuals to other elements of the (football) stadium experience that may be more transient, including food service quality and variety, fan control, cleanliness and perceived crowding (Wakefield and Sloan, 1995; see also Harrell, Hutt and Anderson, 1980; Stokals 1972). Later, Blodgett and I (Wakefield and Blodgett, 1996) examined the effects of layout, aesthetics, seating, electronic displays and cleanliness on individuals' overall perceptions of facility quality and subsequent satisfaction and behavioural intentions in both football, baseball stadiums and casinos. We also examined the effects of the physical environment (building design, décor and equipment), adding the effects of ambience (cleanliness, temperature, employee appearance) and service quality (Parasuraman, Zeithaml and Berry, 1988) experienced at sporting events (hockey) to predict attendance (Wakefield and Blodgett, 1999). These findings also applied to other entertainment settings, including movie theatres and recreation centres. In a shopping centre setting, Baker and I investigated the effects of the layout, interior design and décor, but also examined ambient effects of music, lighting and temperature on individual's response to the environment (Wakefield and Baker, 1998). Hence, the elements of the physical environment examined within the sportscape also apply within other shopping and entertainment settings.

Figure 23.1 illustrates an S-O-R (stimulus-organism-response) framework with all of the elements of the physical environment and service environment individuals encounter attending a sporting event, and subsequent cognitive, affective and behavioural responses. The organism – the individual fan – may respond differently to various sportscape stimuli dependent upon individual characteristics (e.g., loyalty to the team; season ticket holder vs. individual ticket buyer) and situations (e.g., regular season vs. playoffs).

Little work has been done in the area of individual and situational moderating variables that explain why fans can look at the same place but perceive it in entirely different lights. Strombeck and I (2008), for example, found that individuals evaluated the physical environment and service quality differently dependent upon the stage in the service delivery – from approach and entrance throughout the experience until exit – and the service received at each stage. Such effects are likely in sportscape settings where individuals may gain relatively negative or positive perceptions at each step of the fan journey:

Parking lot → Admission → Food service → Seating → Restrooms →
Team store → Facility exit → Parking exit

Thus, although we know the physical environment has predictable influences, across a wide variety of sports and service settings, on how individuals perceive places and respond emotionally and behaviourally, we know less about the boundaries under which these effects might vary rather dramatically. Since the sportscape and much of the servicescape research is conducted in relatively hedonic environments, we are less certain how the same individual who responds to stimuli in these settings is more or less influenced by the environment in more utilitarian settings (see Wakefield and Blodgett, 1994).

Process

The St Louis Cardinals organisation was one of the first professional sports teams to take a truly market-oriented approach (viz., Kohli and Jaworski, 1990) to serving fans. As fate would have it, my dissertation at Saint Louis University (1991) on control systems for the market-oriented firm coincided with a stint working as a secret shopper for the St Louis Cardinals. The secret shopper programme was aimed at providing and measuring excellent customer service at every point in the experience, from the appearance of the parking lot facilities, to entering old Busch Stadium, to sitting in the seats, to timing each food service line, to checking on the cleanliness of the restrooms in the seventh inning, to the exit from the parking facilities. The practice of the secret shopper programme directly applied to the subject of my dissertation – how to maintain a customer-oriented service approach. While completing the PhD, I determined to explore these variables and anything else that might predict fan satisfaction and attendance.

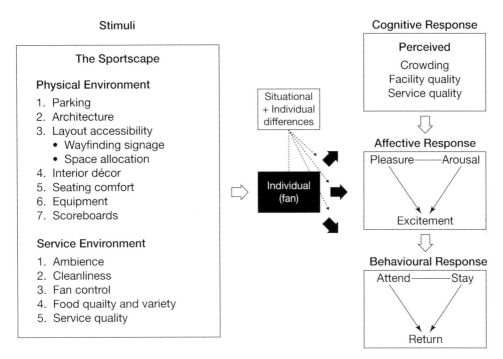

Figure 23.1 Sportscape S-O-R framework

Gaining co-operation

Upon arriving at Ole Miss to begin my academic career, spurred on by co-author Hugh Sloan, we made an initial visit to the athletic department to explore collaborative research opportunities. With the help of the athletic director, we gained support from a number of Southeastern Conference programmes to explore the influence of the stadium experience on fan attendance. Keys to gaining co-operation were (a) familiarity and experience in the field, and (b) asking interesting research questions with direct application to the bottom line. While not everyone can be a major league secret shopper, many have retailing and other experiences directly applicable that provide credibility.

Gaining expertise

One way to gain expertise and credibility is to proactively build a network of relationships and experiences that provide insight to others in the industry. I did this in two ways.

First, as part of a video-experimental design, a road trip was in order to videotape every aspect of five stadiums each from the same vantage points – from St Louis to Pittsburgh (Three Rivers Stadium), Cincinnati (Riverfront Park), Cleveland (Municipal Park) and Detroit (Tiger Stadium). Fan interviews revealed what they liked and didn't like about the parks. Meetings with executives for each team provided more insight. The result of the videotaped experiments using the Cincinnati and Cleveland videos for contrast is reported in our first publication on the subject (Wakefield and Blodgett, 1994).

Second, any minor league team within a few hours driving distance, including the Memphis Chicks (AA), Memphis Redbirds (AAA), Memphis Maddogs (CFL, defunct), Huntsville Stars

(AA), Memphis Riverkings (CHL) and Jackson Generals (AA), became familiar locations for student projects and research studies. Integrating fan research into courses, using on-campus and nearby venues, became common practice to help students understand consumer behaviour and as a way to collect unique data. The teams benefited by understanding what aspects of the venue experience needed improvement and understanding the relative role of facilities on attendance. In one case, the CHL used data collected among fans in the DFW area to maintain the Ft Worth franchise (the Fire, who played in the Fort Worth Convention Center) and to close the Dallas (Freeze) franchise that played at the dark and dank Fair Park Coliseum.

These studies were often combined with another study of practical interest to the team, such as a service quality survey. The key in working with teams is to first help solve a pressing problem. Sometimes this was as simple as learning where fans searched for information about games or preferred starting times. Other times, the problems were more complex, which led to other fan research regarding social influence (Wakefield, 1993), promotion value (Wakefield and Bush, 1998), promotion proneness (Wakefield and Barnes, 1996), sponsorship recall (Wakefield, Becker-Olsen and Cornwell, 2007; Wakefield and Bennett, 2010) and dysfunctional fans (Wakefield and Wann, 2006).

Gaining theory

Environmental psychology provides the theoretical background for research regarding approach-avoidance in physical environments, yet we must dig a much deeper theoretical hole to understand its source. Doing so provides a richer understanding of why processes and relationships work as they do and offers avenues to conduct research that potentially impacts broader disciplines including psychology, sociology, business and economics.

The built elements of the sportscape, inclusive of the interior and exterior layout and design of a stadium, are derived from the more general study of how individuals respond to servicescapes (Bitner, 1992) as the tangible component of the service delivery (viz., Baker, 1986; Parasuraman *et al.*, 1988). The foundation for studying service environments, sport or otherwise, lies within the approach-avoidance framework of Russell and Mehrabian (1976; Mehrabian and Russell, 1974). The approach-avoidance framework originated from studies measuring the psychological and emotional responses to a variety of stimuli via semantic differentials (Osgood and Suci, 1955), applied specifically to elements of the physical environment. The use of semantic differentials to measure the response to stimuli emerged from the work of Osgood (1952) and his colleagues' (Karwoski, Odbert and Osgood, 1942) study of 'synesthetic thinking' that explains the process of translating musical stimuli to visual responses – such that when one hears music (or other stimuli) one assigns meaning along a continuum of polar opposites. The result of their work was the first use of semantic differentials to measure the meanings people assign to stimuli they experience. Figure 23.2 illustrates the theoretical progression leading to the study of the sportscape.

Study of the built environment in services marketing is also heavily reliant upon the work within marketing on atmospherics and other tangible cues that influence individual behaviour. In particular, Harrell *et al.* (1980) examined the causal links between one's feeling that others are intruding upon one's space – psychological crowding (Stokols, 1972) – and physical density (the number of others in a given space) to learn that individuals employ adaptive strategies (e.g., deviate from plans, [in]complete purchases) that influence key outcomes (e.g., satisfaction and enjoyment associated with the experience).

Applying the same theory to the physical environment of sporting events, we would expect that fans feeling confined or closed in due to cramped space in the corridors, aisles or seats

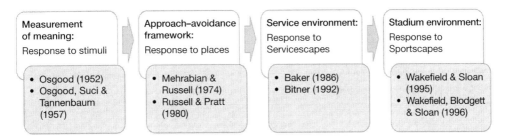

Figure 23.2 Theoretical evolution from stimuli to sportscapes

might deviate from the time they planned to spend at an event, forego merchandise purchases they intended to make, and decide then and there not to return again. Alternatively, in facilities with a more open design that reduces physical density and allows for free movement to reach one's desired destination, we can expect fans to spend more time, purchase more, enjoy the experience and want to frequently return. In short, this is what our series of sportscape-related studies have found.

As with any meaningful research stream, the contribution of these servicescape and sportscape studies is threefold in terms of theory, method and practice. First, the broader services literature was dominated by SERVQUAL (Parasuraman *et al.*, 1988) throughout the 1990s with an emphasis on service quality provided by employees, but with scant attention to the influence of the environment on consumer cognitions, affect and behaviour. Studies in the sportscape setting established that the physical environment is often as much or more important than employee service in determining consumer behaviour. This work includes studies regarding sporting events but positioned in terms of hedonic consumption (Wakefield and Barnes, 1996) and then applied in other retail environments such as movie theatres and casinos (Wakefield and Blodgett, 1999) and shopping centres (Wakefield and Baker, 1998). Without substantive consideration of the tangible, built environment, the conceptualisation and measurement of an organisation's service delivery is incomplete and would offer less reliability in predicting affective and behavioural outcomes associated with the service experience.

Second, from a methodological perspective, elements of the sportscape are delineated, defined and measured with reliable and valid scales to predict affective and behavioural responses to the environment. The sportscape scales allow researchers and practitioners to discriminate between relative effects of seating comfort, scoreboard quality, layout design, space allocation, wayfinding signage, interior décor and design, and parking accessibility to determine which of these influences consumer response in a given setting. Prior servicescape and service quality research lacked specificity and combined unrelated elements observed in the physical environment, including the appearance of personnel, physical facilities and equipment (see Parasuraman *et al.*, 1988).

In many ways, the relative effects of the tangible and intangible aspects of service delivery remain poorly understood, as researchers continue to ignore appropriate measurement and inclusion of key service environment factors in hotels (e.g., Sánchez-Hernández, Martínez-Tur, Peiró and Ramos, 2009), hospitals (e.g., Piligrimiene and Rutelione, 2013), retailing (e.g., Meng, Summey, Herndon and Kwong, 2009), high tech services (He and Li, 2011), sport tourism (e.g., Costa, Glinia and Drakou, 2004) and managing sports (e.g., Theodorakis and Alexandris, 2008). The two mistakes common to these (and more) studies is the omission of elements likely to influence perceptions of the environment and treating general elements (appearance of personnel, physical facilities, etc.) as one generic 'tangibles' construct that includes anything that doesn't involve employee–customer interaction.

Third, as a practical matter, the stream of research launched from study of the sportscape has offered some guidance through further replication, extensions and adaptations in the field of sport management. Thomson-Reuters Web of Science can map a stream of research looking forward from the original article (Wakefield, Blodgett and Sloan, 1996). Most of the article's subsequent (140+) citations appear in the sport management literature, including many in the *Journal of Sport Management* and *Sport Management Review*. Some reach into the broader services and business literature and links to the downstream impact stemming from this research into the fields of services and retailing (e.g., Wakefield and Baker, 1998; Wakefield and Blodgett, 1999).

Extensions, applications and future research

The importance of the sportscape in determining fan satisfaction has been incorporated into a variety of extensions and applications. Relevant findings of three key studies are summarised here, followed by suggestions for future research relevant to each study. I conclude with a summary of a fourth study incorporating the sportscape, making methodological recommendations for future studies.

Extending sportscape

League brand associations

In building a conceptual understanding of consumers' perceptions of a league's brand associations, Kunkel, Funk and King (2014) incorporate the quality of the atmosphere in the league's stadiums. As these authors note, 'the atmosphere surrounding games is one of the most important motives to attend league games . . . as consumers do not take anything away from games other than memories of their experience' (p. 59).

In general, investigating perceptions of brand attributes associated with leagues is fertile ground for future research, as most empirical work regarding fan perceptions focuses on teams, venues or players. With respect to understanding the effects of physical surroundings on perceptions of leagues, opportunity exists to develop multiple-item scales amenable to understanding how fans holistically view the quality of various leagues. For example, perceptions of minor leagues may be proportionately more influenced by the quality of the facilities than by the other brand associations studied by Kunkel *et al.* (2014). In particular, minor league baseball appears to have enhanced brand perceptions due to the influx of fan-friendly stadiums managed by customer-centric owners such as Mandalay Entertainment.

In contrast, facilities hosting dirt track racing (itself an under-studied venue and fan base) may suffer from poor perceptions of facilities that hinder expansion to attract new customers. Alternatively, unknown are the reasons some fans are willing to attend venues with relatively uncomfortable seats, cramped spaces and overall poor amenities, as are often found at racing facilities.

Fan satisfaction

Aimed at explaining overall fan satisfaction (FANSAT) at the venue level for soccer clubs, Sarstedt, Ringle, Raithel and Gudergan (2014) incorporated and compared elements of the sportscape with other antecedents of fan satisfaction, such as team characteristics, competitor characteristics, stadium security, peripheral services, fan-based activities and club characteristics. Results of their field studies indicated that, relative to these other factors, the sportscape is the strongest predictor of fan satisfaction and subsequent attendance. While we might expect this to be the case, an interesting question is whether the sportscape matters more or less across different venues where season ticket holders would be expected to spend more or less time.

The number of regular season home games for NCAA football (six), NFL (eight), MLS (17), NHL and NBA (41), and MLB (81) might suggest that the importance of the sportscape would increase where frequent fans would spend more time. While difficult to accomplish, no research to date has attempted to determine the relative importance of the built environment relative to other services across the various sportscapes. One way to assess such effects would be to keep the venue the same, but study fans attending different events. For example, some facilities may host NBA, NHL, arena football, rodeos and concerts. Administering otherwise identical surveys, such as the FANSAT to representative samples across these settings, may reveal differences across single-event buyers to season ticket holders who attend every game, but one must also account for overlap among patrons at each event. The latter issue, attendance at the same venue for multiple purposes and accounting for cross-selling of events, offers another avenue for research.

Further, as Sarstedt *et al.* (2014) note, analysis accounting for the heterogeneity among fans, by clustering or segmenting them, may reveal differences in the relative influence of factors on fan satisfaction. In particular, one might expect that the sportscape is perceived differently by season ticket holders versus other segments. Similarly, fan categories, such as those identified by Harris and Ogbonna (2008), might differ in sportscape perceptions and relevant influences on satisfaction and attendance. For example, among the seven fan categories of English Premier League fans (armchair supporters, social fans, oldtimers, leisure switchers, antifans, club-connected supporters and die-hard fanatic) identified, we might expect the 'oldtimers' to perceive the venue differently from 'antifans'.

Sensoryscape

One explanation for why some individuals are willing to endure objectively inferior facilities (i.e., those that are visually unappealing or physically uncomfortable), is that other elements of the sensoryscape – sounds, smells and tastes – may compensate. Lee, Heere and Kyu-soo (2013) expanded upon the early work on sportscapes (Wakefield and Sloan, 1995; Wakefield, Blodgett and Sloan 1996) to include other sensory elements such as the (a) sounds of the cheering, music and scoreboard, (b) smells of the stadium, crowd, food and tailgating and (c) the tastes of the food and drinks.

Lee *et al.* (2012) found that the overall sensoryscape has the strongest influence on fan satisfaction compared with the effects of social interaction and one's sense of the place feeling like home to them. However, it may be that for some fans in some venues – again, perhaps in some sports – the relative effects of social interaction and being on home turf is enough to make up for poor facilities. That said, we would expect superior facilities to capitalise on such strong social ties and community feelings.

As Lee and colleagues (Lee *et al.*, 2013; Lee *et al.*, 2012) suggest, we know little regarding how teams might take advantage of the spectators themselves to enhance the stadium experience. Within the United States, fans observing World Cup, Premiere League and Major League Soccer matches seem to be adopting the more active fan behaviours (e.g., chanting, singing, costumes, etc.) and practising them at other non-soccer events. Organisations that facilitate such practices may be able to increase fan satisfaction in relatively cost-efficient ways compared with investing in physical facilities.

On a more micro-level, exploring the effects of the senses on individual consumers in sports settings offers a fruitful line of enquiry. For example, the work of Peck and her associates (Peck and Childers, 2003a,2003b; Peck and Wiggins, 2006; Peck and Johnson, 2011; Peck, Barger and Webb, 2013) on haptic information – or information attained by touching with the hands – suggests that perhaps just the way a hotdog feels in the hands of a fan might matter. Its texture, hardness, temperature and weight (not to mention tastes) are all aspects of haptics that could influence fan responses to concession experiences.

A common experience at sporting events, and of importance to teams and corporate partners, is physical interactions with brands, such as automobile displays where fans are invited to touch, sit, inspect and then interact with staff and others in the venue regarding the automobile. Peck *et al.* (2013) found, for instance, that simply touching an object creates feelings of ownership and that even imagining touching may have similar effects. Such findings extended to sponsors of interactive displays at sports venues may offer added value to such partnership packages.

Methodological and modelling? Considerations

Yoshida and James (2010) incorporate the sportscape into a model of relationships between service satisfaction and game satisfaction that determines fan behavioural intentions. Their work emphasises a key principle of sport marketing – that customer service consists of the core service (aspects related to the game) and ancillary services controlled by management (facility and service quality). We might argue that game atmosphere is partially controlled by management and is partially uncontrollable owing to heterogeneous fan behaviour at sporting events. Based on studies conducted among Japanese professional baseball and United States football spectators, the authors found game satisfaction to strongly influence behavioural intentions, but service satisfaction only influenced behavioural intentions in the Japanese baseball setting.

Yoshida and James' (2010) work offers the opportunity to raise important theoretical and modelling issues. In their work, they found that facility space had no significant effect on service satisfaction. However, this should be expected as, in the original sportscape model (Wakefield

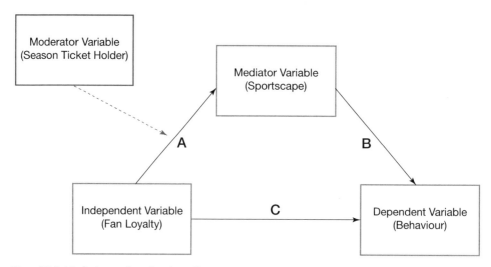

Figure 23.3 Mediation and moderation effects

et al., 1996; see Figure 23.3), space allocation influences fans' perceptions of layout accessibility, which in turn influences perceived crowding and subsequently influences pleasure (or satisfaction) and behavioural responses. Hence, the ultimate effects of some sportscape elements may be mediated by other perceptions and affective responses.

First, care must be taken to appropriately model the relationships between perceptions of the physical environment and psychological constructs such as perceived crowding and affective responses (Russell and Pratt, 1980). Failing to do so may underestimate the indirect effects.

Second, care must be taken to include some measure of fan loyalty (Wakefield and Sloan, 1995) to account for other motives. Yoshida and James (2010) tested another hierarchical model controlling for game attendance, thereby better accounting for the variance explained by service and game satisfaction.

Third, little effort has been made in the sport management literature to formally test mediating and moderating effects. In fact, studies in the sport domain in sport-dominant journals have done little to follow common experimental methods. As Lynch *et al.* (2012) argue, the modal approach in consumer research may sacrifice relevance for the value of complexity (Lehmann, McAlister and Staelin, 2011). Consumer researchers may have gone overboard in testing hypothesised relationships using experiments, aimed at providing process evidence through a series of moderation and mediation tests. However, research in sport-related contexts has made little effort to consider the appropriate psychological processes by which fans respond to stimuli – such as those encountered in sports facilities. Hence, we could use more of an experimental approach in our approach to understanding sports fans.

None of the studies reported in this chapter have taken an experimental approach to separating out the individual effects and the underlying processes. For example, do the perceptions fans have regarding the sportscape mediate or moderate the effects of passion fans have for the team and their desire to attend and stay at games?

We (Wakefield and Sloan, 1995) suggest that team loyalty moderates sportscape-related effects on desire to stay and intentions to attend, but this was not tested. As Figure 23.3 illustrates, we might find that loyalty to the team directly influences perceptions of the sportscape (path A) and directly influences behaviour (path C), and that the sportscape also directly influences behaviour (path B). In this case, we would expect complementary mediation, where the mediated effect (A × B) and the direct effect (C) are significant. Appropriate tests for mediation using a bootstrap test of the indirect effect (A × B) can be found in Zhao, Lynch and Chen (2010).

Alternatively, we might believe another variable moderates the strength of the relationships in the model. For example, the team loyalty→sportscape (path A) could be tested to determine if length of time one has been a season ticket holder moderates the path such that the longer one has a season ticket the stronger the effect of loyalty on perceptions of the sportscape. Further, the moderating effect may be negative (positive), such that the longer one is a season ticket holder the worse (better) the attitude towards the physical facilities. In a structural equation model using software such as Smart PLS, these interaction effects are easily constructed (see Ringle, Wende and Will, 2005).

Conclusion

In many ways, our understanding of the processes by which physical surroundings determine individuals' responses in sports settings remains at a basic level. We know the stadium and its various sportscape components – including the built and service environment – influence affective and behavioural responses among fans. What we don't know much about is *how* individual elements of the sportscape (tangibles and intangibles) influence response.

We know at a general level that the *appearance* of various sportscape and service components influences perceptions and subsequent affective responses. Yet, we don't know how it influences these responses.

For example, the work of Russell and his colleagues (Widen, Christy, Hewett and Russell, 2011; Yik, Widen and Russell, 2013) finds that individuals may identify emotions of disgust, shame, embarrassment, compassion and contempt by observing others' facial expressions. However, age or other factors may lead individuals to interpret what the majority view as the 'disgust' face as anger (Widen and Russell, 2008). In a sport service setting where staff must deal with complaining behaviour, how are their facial expressions interpreted by fans? How might service personnel say ('No problem, we will clean that mess right up') with facial expressions? Studies investigating such issues provide deep insight into broader consumer behaviour while also informing sport management regarding recruitment, selection, training and retention of service personnel.

Similar in-depth studies could be conducted with virtually each element of the sportscape, delving into the deeper psychological and physiological reactions to stimuli in the sport environment.

Note

1   This chapter is a reflection on Wakefield, Blodgett and Sloan (1996) and the work related to it.

References

Baker, J. (1986) 'The role of the environment in marketing services: the consumer perspective'. *The Services Challenge: Integrating for Competitive Advantage*, 1(1): 79–84.

Bitner, M.J. (1992) 'The impact of physical surroundings on customers and employees'. *The Journal of Marketing*, 56(2): 57–71.

Costa, G., Glinia, E. and Drakou, A. (2004) 'The role of empathy in sport tourism services: A review'. *Journal of Sport & Tourism*, 9: 331–42.

Harrell, G.D., Hutt, M.D. and Anderson, J.C. (1980) 'Path analysis of buyer behavior under conditions of crowding'. *Journal of Marketing Research*, 17(1): 45–51.

Harris, L.C. and Ogbonna, E. (2008) 'The dynamics underlying service firm: Customer relationship insights from a study of English Premier League soccer fans'. *Journal of Service Research*, 10: 382–99.

He, H. and Li, Y. (2011) 'Key service drivers for high-tech service brand equity: The mediating role of overall service quality and perceived value'. *Journal of Marketing Management*, 27(1/2): 77–99.

Karwoski, T.F., Odbert, H.S. and Osgood, C.E. (1942) 'Studies in synesthetic thinking: II. The role of form in visual responses to music'. *Journal of General Psychology*, 26: 199–222.

Kohli, A.K. and Jaworski, B.J. (1990) 'Market orientation: the construct, research propositions, and managerial implications'. *Journal of Marketing*, 54(2): 1–18.

Kunkel, T., Funk, D. and King, C. (2014) 'Developing a conceptual understanding of consumer-based league brand associations'. *Journal of Sport Management*, 28: 49–67.

Lee, S., Heere, B. and Kyu-soo, C. (2013) 'Which senses matter more? The impact of our senses on team identity and team loyalty'. *Sport Marketing Quarterly*, 22: 203–13.

Lee, S., Lee, H., Seo, W. and Green, C. (2012) 'A new approach to stadium experience: The dynamics of the sensoryscape, social interaction, and sense of home'. *Journal of Sport Management*, 26: 2–505.

Lehmann, D., McAlister, R. and Staelin, R. (2011) 'Sophistication in research in marketing'. *Journal of Marketing*, 75: 155–65.

Lynch, J.G., Alba, J.W., Krishna, A., Morwitz, V.G. and Gürhan-Canli, Z. (2012) 'Knowledge creation in consumer research: Multiple routes, multiple criteria'. *Journal of Consumer Psychology*, 22: 473–85.

Mehrabian, A. and Russell, J.A. (1974) *An approach to environmental psychology.* Cambridge, MA: M.I.T. Press.

Meng, J., Summey, J.H., Herndon, N.C. and Kwong, K.K. (2009) 'Some retail service quality expectations of Chinese shoppers'. *International Journal of Market Research*, 51: 773–96.

Noll, R.G. (1974) 'Attendance and price setting'. In R.G. Noll (ed.) *Government and sports business*. Washington, DC: Brookings Institution.

Osgood, C.E. (1952) 'The nature and measurement of meaning'. *Psychological Bulletin*, 49: 197–327.

Osgood, C.E. and Suci, G.J. (1955) 'Factor analysis of meaning'. *Journal of Experimental Psychology*, 50: 325–38.

Osgood, C.E., Suci, G. and Tannenbaum, P. (1957) *The measurement of meaning*. Urbana, IL: University of Illinois Press.

Parasuraman, A., Zeithaml, V.A. and Berry, L.L. (1988) 'Servqual: a multiple-item scale for measuring consumer perception of service quality'. *Journal of Retailing*, 64(1): 12–40.

Peck, J. and Childers, T.L. (2003a) 'To have and to hold: the influence of haptic information on product judgments'. *Journal of Marketing*, 67(2): 35–48.

Peck, J. and Childers, T.L. (2003b) 'Individual differences in haptic information processing: The "need for touch" scale'. *Journal of Consumer Research*, 30: 430–42.

Peck, J. and Johnson, J. (2011) 'Autotelic need for touch, haptics, and persuasion: The role of involvement'. *Psychology & Marketing*, 28: 222–39.

Peck, J. and Wiggins, J. (2006) 'It just feels good: Customers' affective response to touch and its influence on persuasion'. *Journal of Marketing*, 70: 56–69.

Peck, J., Barger, V.A. and Webb, A. (2013) 'In search of a surrogate for touch: The effect of haptic imagery on perceived ownership'. *Journal of Consumer Psychology*, 23: 189–96.

Piligrimiene, Z. and Rutelione, A. (2013) 'Dual sides of health care service quality: What is really important for patients?' *Economics & Management*, 18: 112–23.

Ringle, C.M., Wende, S. and Will, A. (2005) 'SmartPLS 2.0 (M3) beta'. Hamburg. Available at www.smartpls.de (accessed on 1 September, 2014).

Russell, A. and Pratt, G. (1980) 'A description of the affective quality of environments'. *Journal of Personality & Social Psychology*, 38: 311–22.

Russell, J.A. and Mehrabian, A. (1976) 'Environmental variables in consumer research'. *Journal of Consumer Research*, 3(1): 62–3.

Sánchez-Hernández, R.M., Martínez-Tur, V.V., Peiró, J.M. and Ramos, J.J. (2009) 'Testing a hierarchical and integrated model of quality in the service sector: Functional, relational, and tangible dimensions'. *Total Quality Management & Business Excellence*, 20: 1173–88.

Sarstedt, M., Ringle, C.M., Raithel, S. and Gudergan, S.P. (2014) 'In pursuit of understanding what drives fan satisfaction'. *Journal of Leisure Research*, 46: 419–47.

Stokols, D. (1972) 'A social-psychological model of human crowding phenomena'. *Journal of the American Planning Association*, 38(2): 72–83.

Strombeck, S.D. and Wakefield, K.L. (2008) 'Situational influences on service quality evaluations'. *Journal of Services Marketing*, 22: 409–19.

Theodorakis, N.D. and Alexandris, K. (2008) 'Can service quality predict spectators' behavioral intentions in professional soccer?' *Managing Leisure*, 13(3/4): 162–78.

Wakefield, K.L. (1993) 'Redefining the market concept for the 1990s'. *Journal of Marketing Theory & Practice*, 1(1): 1–16.

Wakefield, K.L. and Baker, J. (1998) 'Excitement at the mall: Determinants and effects on shopping response'. *Journal of Retailing*, 74: 515–39.

Wakefield, K.L. and Barnes, J.H. (1996) 'Retailing hedonic consumption: A model of sales promotion of a leisure service'. *Journal of Retailing*, 72: 409–27.

Wakefield, K.L. and Bennett, G. (2010) 'Affective intensity and sponsor identification'. *Journal of Advertising*, 39: 99–111.

Wakefield, K.L. and Blodgett, J.G. (1994) 'The importance of servicescapes in leisure service settings'. *Journal of Services Marketing*, 8(3): 66–76.

Wakefield, K.L. and Blodgett, J.G. (1996) 'The effect of the servicescape on customer's behavioral intentions in leisure service settings'. *Journal of Services Marketing*, 10(6): 45–61.

Wakefield, K.L. and Blodgett, J.G. (1999) 'Customer response to intangible and tangible service factors'. *Psychology & Marketing*, 16(1): 51–68.

Wakefield, K.L. and Bush, V.D. (1998) 'Promoting leisure services: Economic and emotional aspects of consumer response'. *Journal of Services Marketing*, 12: 209–22.

Wakefield, K.L. and Sloan, H.J. (1995) 'The effects of team loyalty and selected stadium factors on spectator attendance'. *Journal of Sport Management*, 9: 153–72.

Wakefield, K.L. and Wann, D.L. (2006) 'An examination of dysfunctional sport fans: method of classification and relationships with problem behaviors'. *Journal of Leisure Research*, 38: 168–86.

Wakefield, K.L., Becker-Olsen, K. and Cornwell, T.B. (2007) 'I spy a sponsor: The effects of sponsorship level, prominence, relatedness, and cueing on recall accuracy'. *Journal of Advertising*, *36*(4): 61–74.

Wakefield, K.L., Blodgett, J.G. and Sloan, H.J. (1996) 'Measurement and management of the sportscape'. *Journal of Sport Management*, *10*: 15–31.

Widen, S.C. and Russell, J.A. (2008) 'Children's and adults' understanding of the "disgust face"'. *Cognition & Emotion*, *22*: 1513–41.

Widen, S.C., Christy, A.M., Hewett, K. and Russell, J.A. (2011) 'Do proposed facial expressions of contempt, shame, embarrassment, and compassion communicate the predicted emotion?' *Cognition & Emotion*, *25*: 898–906.

Yik, M., Widen, S.C. and Russell, J.A. (2013) 'The within-subjects design in the study of facial expressions'. *Cognition & Emotion*, *27*: 1062–72.

Yoshida, M. and James, J.D. (2010) 'Customer satisfaction with game and service experiences: Antecedents and consequences'. *Journal of Sport Management*, *24*: 338–61.

Zhao, X., Lynch, J.G. and Chen, Q. (2010) 'Reconsidering Baron and Kenny: Myths and truths about mediation analysis'. *Journal of Consumer Research*, *37*(2): 197–206.

Applying sportscape

T. Christopher Greenwell[1]

The sportscape concept developed by Kirk Wakefield and colleagues has been influential in understanding how the different elements of sports facilities influence various sport consumer behaviours. I was initially introduced to this work in 1999 as a doctoral student. Prior to beginning my doctoral studies, I had worked in college athletics where I was responsible for meeting attendance goals for multiple sports playing at five different facilities. Not having any control over the quality of the teams I marketed, I became keenly aware of the role other elements, such as the facility, played in driving attendance. As such I was interested in researching how sports facilities contributed to whether or not consumers would attend various events. Considering the changing environment in spectator sports (new facilities, rising customer expectations, increased demands on event marketers) it was becoming more important to understand the role of the sport environment.

At the time, the understanding of the influence of sport facilities was incomplete. While many scholars had addressed the role of the facility, results were often limited as they tended to use incomplete measures to address perceptions of sport facilities. Further, much of the research in this area had suggested that sports facilities had little influence on spectators' enjoyment or consumption behaviours. Research on the sportscape was different in that it included a more complete set of facility factors and multiple outcomes to provide a more comprehensive understanding of the various elements of sport venues and how those elements influenced sport consumers. The sportscape, therefore, became a key piece of my research agenda.

In my own research, I was able to utilise Wakefield's sportscape research to address some of the aforementioned controversies in the sport management literature. Specifically, by employing the sportscape, we were able to understand the role of the facility relative to other elements of the service encounter. We found the sportscape had a significant influence on customer satisfaction. Customer demographic profiles and levels of team identification also affected these dynamics. The multidimensional nature of the sportscape was also confirmed in later research into the critical aspects of service encounters. In this research, my colleagues and I were able to illustrate how the various aspects of the facility could influence both satisfaction and dissatisfaction with a sport experience.

This research has also been valuable in my work with local sport organisations. Working mostly with organisations that would fall under the banner of niche sports, my colleagues and I have been able to illustrate what organisations, who typically don't have star players, can do with their facilities to provide a great experience for their consumers. Similarly, this concept has been an important element of the courses I teach on sport marketing and event management. Considering sport consumers may spend hours in the facility and the importance this generation's sports consumers place on facilities, it is vital for students to understand the various elements of the sportscape and how these elements can be managed to maximise customer satisfaction.

Note

1   T. Christopher Greenwell is with the Department of Health and Sports Sciences at the University of Louisville.

24

THE SPORTS PRODUCT[1]

Daniel Mason

Overview

It is always interesting to reflect back on work that one has done in the past. This chapter is based on some of my earlier work (Mason, 1999), where I presented an integrated framework that pulled together various concepts and assumptions appearing in different bodies of literature. I would like to make clear that marketing was/is not my background or academic area of focus, although the paper appeared in a special issue on sports marketing. In the call for papers I saw an opportunity to draw upon the literature I was familiar with and make some general statements about the sports product, which I had hoped would be useful for those in the marketing field. In many respects, the paper represents an amalgam of assembled ideas, and I have been surprised and flattered by the number of scholars who have cited it in their work.

In addition, instead of inspiring specific empirical studies, it has been used more as a jumping-off point for scholars doing research in different fields, including sports economics, marketing and consumer behaviour, to frame the context of their research. Thus, scholars from a variety of disciplines, including economics, marketing, management, tourism, communication, public policy, and even history, have cited the article in a rather eclectic group of journals. Later in this chapter, I make some suggestions about extending the framework. I would also like to note that many scholars have explored this topic and again, I am simply trying to pull together some ideas into one framework. As a result, I hope that I have not overlooked the contributions that some may have already made to this area of study.

Interestingly, the one discipline that has not cited this paper widely is the one that influenced the paper the most: the sports law literature. The other field that provided a starting point for the paper was the economics literature, specifically the foundational work of Neale (1964) and Rottenberg (1956). That work inspired a number of studies in the sports economics literature that have examined determinants of demand and whether the closeness of competition between teams influences game attendance. It was the notion of the uncertainty of game outcomes between two different entities (teams) – the core product – and a dialogue in the legal literature surrounding the legal status of leagues as joint ventures or single entities, that provided a starting point for me.

The sports economics literature had already established that the core product for sports leagues was the uncertainty of game outcomes. The logic here is that, in the absence of a team to compete against or a series of games that lead to a championship, an individual team cannot produce a product. However, this did not seem to capture the complexities of the sports fan consumption experience or the manner through which cities clamoured to serve as hosts of major league professional sports franchises. As a result, I chose to develop a way to describe and frame the different stakeholders who consumed the professional sports league product, how they consumed it, and the nature of the relationship between the stakeholder and the league itself. Thus, the core product had evolved into different things for different consumers. Not only that, but sports fans represented only one type of consumer; cities, corporations and media companies also consumed the sports product, albeit for different reasons.

Process

At the time I wrote the paper, I was putting together my reading list for my comprehensive exams and candidacy for my doctorate. At the University of Alberta, comprehensive examinations and candidacy take place at the same time. The student takes the written exam over two days and then meets with the doctoral committee approximately one week later for an oral defense of both the exam answers and the proposed dissertation research. As a result, I was heavily immersed in both reading related directly to my dissertation and with the broader literature. However, the ideas that appeared in the paper were rooted in the reading I had done during the course of my master's degree studies. At that time, I was fortunate to have had the opportunity to take a sports law class in the Faculty of Law of my university. A professor who also was a practising lawyer with considerable experience working in the professional sport industry taught the course. As part of my coursework, I had to write a term paper looking at a legal issue related to sport. I chose to examine agent problems, including corruption, recruitment and mismanagement, in professional sport. This work would later be the foundation for my doctoral research (Mason and Slack, 2001a, 2001b, 2003).

In preparing this assignment, I spent a significant amount of time in the law library, where it turns out a considerable amount of material had been published in law journals on the subject. As I read more on the subject, I discovered that there were many interesting legal arguments being made, on a number of subjects, in this literature. Thus, although my term paper was concerned with agent regulation, I read more widely on legal issues related to the sport industry, including franchise relocation. Later, my doctoral research employed a theory from the organisational economics literature – agency theory – and examined the development and regulation of player agents (Mason and Slack, 2005). Part of my preparation involved background reading on the market structure of professional sports, and I returned to the sports law literature. At that time, much of the operations of professional sports leagues were more mysterious; for example, the National Hockey League (and National Hockey League Players' Association) had only recently begun making the players' salaries public. However, I found that whenever a sports league was involved in any legal wranglings, they were forced to 'open the books' and reveal financial information about their operations. For this reason, I found law journals to be a treasure trove of not just arguments about the fundamental operations of sports leagues, but basic financial information on league operations.

As I was re-immersing myself in this literature, I became aware of a call for papers for a special issue on sports marketing to be published in the *European Journal of Marketing*. This was a fairly open call and, perhaps naively, I thought that some of the ideas that I was throwing around could be shaped to fit the call. At that time in the legal literature there was much debate over how to define professional sports leagues, as this would have implications for the manner through which leagues would be considered cartels, monopolies, joint ventures and/or single business entities (cf. Goldman, 1989; Grauer, 1983; 1989; Gray, 1987; Gray and Walters, 1988;

Jacobs, 1991; Roberts, 1984; Ross, 1989). The most high-profile case involved the relocation of the National Football League's (NFL) Oakland Raiders to Los Angeles (Kurlantzick, 1983). In this case, the Raiders' owner, Al Davis, elected to move the team and receive some substantial financial benefits for doing so. However, for a number of reasons, including vacating the second largest market in the US and undermining the stability of franchises in local markets, the NFL voted not to allow the move (Davis also alleged that there were personal reasons for the League not allowing him to move; Harris, 1986).

This case raised some fundamental questions surrounding what leagues were, how individual franchises related to them and the rights individual teams had in making business decisions that might compromise the interests of other league teams. In reading through this material, I found that my own interest was not in which party (the league or the franchise) had the legal right to decide where franchises could be located; rather, it was in how each side was crafting arguments about what the business entity itself was. The argument from the Raiders was that, as a separately owned legal business entity, the team should be considered the relevant business enterprise; thus, a decision to move a team was within the rights of the individual team owner. The NFL's counterargument was that the league itself was the relevant business entity, with the need for franchises to be privately owned in order to preserve perceptions of the integrity of the games being played (fans might question game outcomes where one entity owned and controlled all players). I realise that this discussion is grossly oversimplifying the many different arguments that were being made; however, what I took from this debate was that the most interesting argument being waged was about exactly *what* was being produced and that this would lead to an understanding of the relevant level of analysis at which professional sport should be examined (i.e., the league or franchise level).

For this reason, reading these articles made me think about exactly what was being consumed as a product and who was doing the consuming. In other words, while the legal debate was concerned with whether or not leagues should be considered single business entities, or groups of independent businesses combining to produce a product, could I move a step further by discussing who was doing the consuming? At this point, the product could be defined as a series of games with an uncertain outcome that led to an eventual league champion (also with an uncertain outcome). The key to the single entity argument of the NFL was that, in the absence of a league, an individual franchise could not produce the core product, and interest in the team would not be the same in the absence of the league. Imagine, if you will, the Dallas Cowboys existing, but without the other NFL teams to play against or a Super Bowl to challenge for. There would still be Cowboys fans, but interest in, and the value of, the franchise would be substantially diminished.

While the argument was logical, what was missing here was an explanation of the intricacies of the ways in which fans experience the NFL. For example, while someone might be drawn to watching football (or any other sport) due to the excitement of the contest (particularly a close or uncertain one), fans develop their own unique relationships with their sports, teams and players. We know now that fans cheer for teams because they are fans of a given sport, a specific sports league and/or always support a local team. Some fans follow certain players as they move from team to team, while others only cheer for 'their' team (Borland and Macdonald, 2003). Others cheer for the local team and would stop supporting a team if it moved (Foster and Hyatt, 2007), and would start following a new team that began playing locally (Hunt, Bristol and Bashaw, 1999; Lewis, 2001). There has been a considerable amount of scholarship that has teased apart these relationships, several of the authors of which are also contributing to this volume. Given that I am not a sport marketing expert, I will defer to their expertise to explain these nuances in greater detail.

With this background, I sought to develop a discussion that used this literature to say something about how fans consumed the professional sport product. However, this discussion would not capture the other business operations of sports leagues, where revenues were increasingly driven by revenues derived from media and/or corporations, and lucrative subsidies offered by cities to relocate (or remain) in a given market. For this reason, I assumed that, while the uncertainty of game outcomes remained the 'core' product produced by leagues, this did not completely capture the other types of business relationships leagues had and what the media sought in return. For example, while close contests and many teams challenging for a championship would enhance overall interest in a given league, the cities that sought franchises were likely looking for something else. This would mean that the league 'product' would vary depending on the consumer.

To address this, I reflected on the revenue streams that leagues generated. Clearly, fan interest had driven demand for professional sports leagues as a televised product. The result had been exponentially growing league-wide media contracts. However, while viewers were motivated to watch games on television for a number of different reasons, television and other media providers were purchasing something else: content. In other words, while providers obviously would prefer close contests, they were only interested insofar as sports leagues generated a large enough audience to sustain their own revenue streams (from sponsors, advertisers, etc.). Thus, the media were interested in a product that would garner more viewers than the programming options offered by competing providers. In addition, there might also be other benefits, such as the prestige associated with showing league or championship games, that the media could receive by virtue of affiliating with a given league or sport.

In the course of developing my broader research programme, I was also interested in franchise relocation (Mason and Slack, 1997) and the notion that cities were seeking status affiliations by hosting major league sports teams. In the two decades leading up to the writing of the 1999 paper, there had been a period of 'franchise free agency' in North American professional sport, where teams moved more freely (and in the wake of the Raiders' case where the team was allowed to move without permission of the parent league; Euchner, 1993). This saw cities increasingly offering lucrative lease agreements and other incentives for teams to relocate, or to keep local teams from moving (Rosentraub, 1997). Examining this issue led to the conclusion that, although it was the uncertainty of game outcomes that gave sport its unique character, leading to its importance to local citizens, the cities that bid for teams were consuming some-thing else. This manifested itself in terms of economic benefits, where cities anticipated new jobs and investment by virtue of hosting a team (the veracity of which has been questioned by independent assessment). In addition, other intangible benefits are sought by cities, found in the form of 'big league' status and psychic income (Crompton, 2004). Cities were less interested in uncertainty of outcome and more with the prospects of basking in the reflected glory of team successes and affiliating with other host cities.

Finally, I identified one other group of consumers: corporations. They pay to affiliate with sports leagues and teams, but not because the outcome of games is uncertain. It is because they look to leverage their links to sport to serve their own business interests. This can be achieved in a number of ways, including sponsorships, owning teams outright, advertising and/or using games as a site to conduct business (using luxury boxes or other seating).

Extensions and applications

Since its publication, the paper has been used conceptually to undergird research in two areas: sports economics and sport marketing. The framework has not been extended *per se*; rather, it is typically used to help describe the research context for other studies (Funk and Pritchard,

2006), frame hypotheses (Pritchard and Funk, 2010) or develop scales (Marticotte and Carrier, 2009). In the sports economics field, the discussion of the uncertainty of game outcomes as the core product has been cited in reviews of demand (Borland and Macdonald, 2003), tanking in professional sport (Price, Soebbing, Berri and Humphreys, 2010) and influences of game outcomes on team stock prices (Demir and Rigoni, in press).

Marketing, however, remains the field where the paper is cited most frequently. In many cases, the framework is cited in order to describe the complex market for sport as part of the broader entertainment industry (Breitbarth and Harris, 2008; Dale, van Iwaarden, van der Wiele and Williams, 2005; Pritchard and Kharouf, in press) and credited as being 'an attempt to clarify the sport product in greater detail' (Bauer, Sauer and Schmitt, 2005, p. 499). Described as 'an extensive literature review' (Dale *et al.*, 2005, p. 472), the paper has been positioned as a foundational citation for many papers. For example, it has often been the lead-in citation to studies (Chih-Hung Wang, Jain, Ming-Sung Cheng and Kyaw-Myo Aung, 2012; Farrelly, Quester and Clulow, 2008; Kunkel, Funk and Hill, 2013; Madichie, 2009; McDonald, Karg and Vocino, 2013; Pritchard, Funk and Alexandris, 2009), or been part of the introductory discussion in an article (Farrelly and Quester, 2003; Funk and Prichard, 2006; Kunkel, Doyle and Funk, 2014; Polonsky and Speed, 2001; Pritchard and Funk, 2006; Smith and Stewart, 2007). Thus, the framework appears to serve as a jumping-off point for conceptualising issues related to: corporate social responsibility (Blumrodt, Desbordes and Bodin, 2013; Walker and Parent, 2010); brands, brand equity and brand communities (Bauer *et al.*, 2005; Devasagayum and Buff, 2008; Kunkel, Doyle and Funk, 2014); sponsorship (Cliffe and Motion, 2005; Farrelly, 2010; Farrelly and Quester, 2003; Polonsky and Speed, 2001); and fans, fan consumption and media (Funk and Prichard, 2006; Pritchard and Funk, 2006; Pritchard *et al.*, 2009).

More recently, Kunkel and colleagues have used the framework as a starting point to examine *brand architecture*, which has led to the ability to segment spectators (Kunkel *et al.*, 2013; Kunkel, Funk and King, 2014). This work serves as a good representation of how the framework has been used. Although nothing new was introduced in the framework that hadn't been discussed variously in different literatures, in bringing these (at times) disparate concepts together, the paper has become a convenient starting point for work in other areas. Thus, the contribution that the framework seems to make is in articulating the complexities of how sports leagues, as products, are marketed, which has been used by scholars to introduce their own unique and novel ideas related to the various subjects listed above.

Future directions

Although the framework has been used as a foundation for other work, this does not mean that it could not be built upon in the future. In terms of future directions and applications, a modest proposal follows. Because the original paper was targeted for a marketing journal, I focused solely on the consumer of the sports product: those to whom the product would be marketed. As a follow up, I suggest that future work examine what is being produced as a result of the consumption of the product, and extend it beyond professional sports leagues to other levels of organised sport.

Producing the 'product'

As a starting point, I would like to reflect on the process through which the core sports product gets made. What I would like to discuss now is what is produced as a result of that consumption process. In other words, in the course of producing the sports product, what else is being made? For the purposes of elaboration, I divide the discussion into three basic categories – the *production of athletes*, the *production of participation opportunities,* and the *production of achievement.*

The production of athletes

While people participate in sport for fun and recreation, one consequence of training and playing is the production of athletes of varying skills. Viewed in this way, we can see how, at various levels, competing and participating in sport provides an opportunity for the production of the athlete-as-product. The ways in which we see this product are determined by the level at which the production occurs. These are described in more detail below.

YOUTH/GRASSROOTS SPORT AND PLAYER DEVELOPMENT

Children of all ages become involved in organised sport for a variety of reasons. Regardless of the rationale, an outcome of participation, coaching and other factors is an incremental improvement in athletic or playing ability. Thus, many people see grassroots sport as a vehicle to produce better players; athletes who will go on to be successful in other leagues, or even professionally. This is not to say that participating in sport is not a reward on its own (see below); rather, the delivery system for high-performance sport views participation as a necessary step to reaching higher levels of competition. Seen in this way, the product is athletic ability and the consumer is the participant, the parent who signs the child up, or higher levels of the delivery system in a given sport.

There are also those who feel that, in addition to simple incremental improvements in athletic ability, athletic participation has the potential to yield very desirable personal attributes, such as teamwork, working with others and leadership. In this sense, the athlete is the desired end product, but not simply as a talented player who will move on to another level of competition; rather, the end product is the athlete as a desirable individual who may make valuable contributions in other life endeavours based on the knowledge/experience gained through playing sport. Seen in this way, a product of grassroots sport development is the desirable traits that athletes (and, possibly by extension, coaches and other affiliated stakeholders) garner through participation. This would also be consumed (or enjoyed) by participants and/or their families and the deliverers of that given sport.

ORGANISED, COMPETITIVE SPORT

The rationale described above for grassroots sport holds true for more organised, competitive sport, but the stakes are higher. By the time a player makes it to this level, the athlete has risen above the level of many others who continue to play, but only recreationally. This affords the athlete additional possibilities for advancement, such as: (a) playing professionally (where applicable); and (b) representing region, province/state, or even country in elite competition. In this way, the participant becomes an athletic product that can be used to produce an entertainment product (such as a professional brand of a sport, e.g., 'NHL hockey'), and also a product that can be used to produce regional or even national sentiment. This is the level at which there is a potential for fans to become consumers of the product.

SPORTS CAMPS

Sports camps are small business operations that operate primarily during the off-season and provide an opportunity for players – more frequently in their developmental stages – to improve their skills through additional coaching and instruction. Typically, camps feature prominent current and former players and coaches. Many parents send their children to camps as a way of improving their skills, ideally to increase their chances for advancement. Thus, the fundamental goal of, say, ice hockey camps is to produce an elite (or at least improved) athlete. At the higher levels, more specialised camps are offered where athletes hone specific skills and techniques in order to refine their games.

The production of participation opportunities

Contrary to the goals for involvement in sport described above, many people play sport purely for its intrinsic value as a form of recreation, leisure and play. Thus, one of the foundational goals of sport, at a variety of levels, is to produce an environment that creates an opportunity for meaningful leisure experience to occur.

YOUTH/GRASSROOTS PARTICIPATION IN SPORT

Thus, while some players, coaches and parents see youth/grassroots sport as a means through which to train children for the purposes of advancement, others are simply seeking a rewarding social and physical experience.

SPORTS CAMPS

While some parents and participants attend sports camps to develop their skills, others are more geared towards providing a fun, social experience. These rationales are not mutually exclusive and camps will tend to gravitate towards one or the other, with more specialised camps catering to skill development for specific sports. The key means to differentiate lies in the motivations for participation, rather than what is provided as a camp experience.

The production of achievement

Participation in sport results in an *outcome*. As described above, it can be manifested in athletic ability and/or leisure experience. However, the outcome also has broader implications for different stakeholders.

COMMUNITY, REGIONAL, NATIONAL OR INTERNATIONAL SUCCESS

The results of an athletic event have meaning to its participants, viewers and other stakeholders. There are numerous examples of where the outcome of a game has impacted many outside of the production of the event itself. This can occur on a more local level, such as a local minor sport team winning a championship, or on a larger scale, such as the 1980 gold-medal winning US Men's Olympic hockey team.

The delivery system for this kind of achievement has become much more rationalised and streamlined; as a result, many sport bodies have created highly sophisticated talent identification systems and have developed age-specific elite development programmes in their respective sports.

INDIVIDUAL ACHIEVEMENT

While athletic exploits can garner widespread attention, participants and their immediate stake-holders may also seek specific outcomes from participation. This could include setting personal bests, losing weight or beating rivals.

COLLECTIVE ACHIEVEMENT

Other aims could be realised from athletic achievement, such as increasing participation numbers, reducing obesity or raising the profile of a given sport. Any number of these can be realised simultaneously and vary according to the goals of the stakeholder.

Conclusions

In sum, I am honoured and flattered to have been offered the opportunity to submit a chapter to this volume. As I have shown, my work on the sports product is likely different from many of the other contributions, in that it has provided more of a foundation for studies and research in other areas, rather than a theory that has since been tested and/or extended. I hope that my discussion above has shed light on the process through which ideas emerge and are synthesised into new work. I also hope that my brief extension may provide some foundation for further understanding the complexities of the ways in which sport, as a product, is produced and consumed.

Note

1   This chapter is a reflection on Mason (1999) and the work related to it.

References

Bauer, H.H., Sauer, N.E. and Schmitt, P. (2005) 'Customer-based brand equity in the team sport industry: Operationalization and impact on the economic success of sport teams'. *European Journal of Marketing*, *39*: 496–513.

Blumrodt, J., Desbordes, M. and Bodin, D. (2013) 'Professional football clubs and corporate social responsibility'. *Sport, Business and Management: An International Journal*, *3*: 205–25.

Borland, J. and Macdonald, R. (2003) 'Demand for sport'. *Oxford Review of Economic Policy*, *19*: 478–502.

Breitbarth, T. and Harris, P. (2008) 'The role of corporate social responsibility in the football business: Towards the development of a conceptual model'. *European Sport Management Quarterly*, *8*: 179–206.

Chih-Hung Wang, M., Jain, M., Ming-Sung Cheng, J. and Kyaw-Myo Aung, G. (2012) 'The purchasing impact of fan identification and sports sponsorship'. *Marketing Intelligence & Planning*, *30*: 553–66.

Cliffe, S.J. and Motion, J. (2005) 'Building contemporary brands: A sponsorship-based strategy'. *Journal of Business Research*, *58*: 1068–77.

Crompton, J. (2004) 'Beyond economic impact: An alternative rationale for the public subsidy of major league sports facilities'. *Journal of Sport Management*, *18*: 40–58.

Dale, B., van Iwaarden, J., van der Wiele, T. and Williams, R. (2005) 'Service improvement in a sports environment: A study of spectator attendance'. *Managing Service Quality: An International Journal*, *15*: 470–84.

Demir, E. and Rigoni, U. (in press) 'You lose, I feel better: Rivalry between soccer teams and the impact of Schadenfreude on stock market'. *Journal of Sports Economics*.

Devasagayam, P.R. and Buff, C.L. (2008) 'A multidimensional conceptualization of brand community: An empirical investigation'. *Sport Marketing Quarterly*, *17*(1): 20–9.

Euchner, C.C. (1993) *Playing the field: Why sport teams move and cities fight to keep them*. Baltimore, MD: Johns Hopkins University Press.

Farrelly, F. (2010) 'Not playing the game: Why sport sponsorship relationships break down'. *Journal of Sport Management, 24*: 319–37.

Farrelly, F. and Quester, P. (2003) 'The effects of market orientation on trust and commitment: The case of the sponsorship business-to-business relationship'. *European Journal of Marketing, 37*: 530–53.

Farrelly, F., Quester, P. and Clulow, V. (2008) 'Exploring market orientation and satisfaction of partners in the sponsorship relationship'. *Australasian Marketing Journal (AMJ), 16*(2): 51–66.

Foster, W.M. and Hyatt, C. (2007) 'I despise them! I detest them! Franchise relocation and the expanded model of organizational identification'. *Journal of Sport Management, 21*: 194–212.

Funk, D.C. and Pritchard, M.P. (2006) 'Sport publicity: Commitment's moderation of message effects'. *Journal of Business Research, 59*: 613–21.

Goldman, L. (1989) 'Sports, antitrust, and the single entity theory'. *Tulane Law Review, 63*: 751–97.

Grauer, M.C. (1983) 'Recognition of the National Football League as a single entity under Section 1 of the Sherman Act: Implications of the Consumer Welfare Model'. *Michigan Law Review, 82*(1): 71–116.

Grauer, M.C. (1989) 'The use and misuse of 'Consumer Welfare': Once more to the mat on the issue of single entity status for sports leagues under Section 1 of the Sherman Act'. *Tulane Law Review, 64*(1): 1–59.

Gray, J.A. (1987) 'Section 1 of the Sherman Act and control over NFL franchise relocations: The problem of opportunistic behavior'. *American Business Law Journal, 25*: 123–59.

Gray, J.A. and Walters, S.J.K. (1988) 'Is the NFL an illegal monopoly?' *University of Detroit Law Review, 66*(5): 5–32.

Harris, D. (1986) *The League: The rise and decline of the NFL.* Toronto, Ontario: Bantam Books.

Hunt, K.A., Bristol, T. and Bashaw, R.E. (1999) 'A conceptual approach to classifying sports fans'. *Journal of Services Marketing, 13*: 439–52.

Jacobs, M.S. (1991) 'Professional sports leagues, antitrust, and the single-entity theory: A defense of the status quo'. *Indiana Law Journal, 67*(1): 25–58.

Kunkel, T., Doyle, J.P. and Funk, D.C. (2014) 'Exploring sport brand development strategies to strengthen consumer involvement with the product – The case of the Australian A-League'. *Sport Management Review, 17*: 470–83.

Kunkel, T., Funk, D.C. and King, C. (2014) 'Developing a conceptual understanding of consumer-based league brand associations'. *Journal of Sport Management, 28*: 49–67.

Kunkel, T., Funk, D. and Hill, B. (2013) 'Brand architecture, drivers of consumer involvement, and brand loyalty with professional sport leagues and teams'. *Journal of Sport Management, 27*: 177–92.

Kurlantzick, L.S. (1983) 'Thoughts on professional sports and antitrust laws: Los Angeles Memorial Coliseum Commission v. National Football League'. *Connecticut Law Review, 15*: 183–208.

Lewis, M. (2001) 'Franchise relocation and fan allegiance'. *Journal of Sport Social Issues, 25*: 6–19.

Madichie, N. (2009) 'Management implications of foreign players in the English Premiership League football'. *Management Decision, 47*: 24–50.

Marticotte, F. and Carrier, S. (2009) 'The aftermath of the latest labour conflict in the National Hockey League: the impact on brand equity'. *International Journal of Sport Management and Marketing, 5*: 38–54.

Mason, D.S. (1999) 'What is the sports product and who buys it? The marketing of professional sports leagues'. *European Journal of Marketing, 33*: 402–18.

Mason, D.S. and Slack, T. (1997) 'Appropriate opportunism or bad business practice? Stakeholder theory, ethics, and the franchise relocation issue'. *Marquette Sports Law Journal, 7*: 399–426.

Mason, D.S. and Slack, T. (2001a) 'Evaluating monitoring mechanisms as a solution to opportunism by professional hockey agents'. *Journal of Sport Management, 15*: 107–34.

Mason, D.S. and Slack, T. (2001b) 'Industry factors and the changing dynamics of the player-agent relationship in professional hockey'. *Sport Management Review, 4*: 165–91.

Mason, D.S. and Slack, T. (2003) 'Understanding principal-agent relationships: Evidence from professional hockey'. *Journal of Sport Management, 17*: 38–62.

Mason, D.S. and Slack, T. (2005) 'Agency theory and the study of sport organizations'. *Sport in Society, 8*: 48–64.

McDonald, H., Karg, A.J. and Vocino, A. (2013) 'Measuring season ticket holder satisfaction: Rationale, scale development and longitudinal validation'. *Sport Management Review, 16*: 41–53.

Neale, W.C. (1964) 'The peculiar economics of professional sports'. *Quarterly Journal of Economics, 78*: 1–14.

Polonsky, M.J. and Speed, R. (2001) 'Linking sponsorship and cause related marketing: Complementarities and conflicts'. *European Journal of Marketing, 35*: 1361–89.

Price, J., Soebbing, B.P., Berri, D. and Humphreys, B.R. (2010) 'Tournament incentives, league policy, and NBA team performance revisited'. *Journal of Sports Economics, 11*: 117–35.

Pritchard, A. and Kharouf, H. (in press) 'Leisure consumption in cricket: devising a model to contrast forms and time preferences'. *Leisure Studies.*

Pritchard, M.P. and Funk, D.C. (2006) 'Symbiosis and substitution in spectator sport'. *Journal of Sport Management, 20*: 299–321.

Pritchard, M.P. and Funk, D.C. (2010) 'The formation and effect of attitude importance in professional sport'. *European Journal of Marketing, 44*: 1017–36.

Pritchard, M.P., Funk, D.C. and Alexandris, K. (2009) 'Barriers to repeat patronage: The impact of spectator constraints'. *European Journal of Marketing, 43*: 169–87.

Roberts, G.A. (1984) 'Sport leagues and the Sherman Act: the use and abuse of Section 1 to regulate restraints on intraleague rivalry'. *University of California at Los Angeles Law Review, 32*: 219–301.

Rosentraub, M.S. (1997) *Major league losers: The real cost of sports and who's paying for it.* New York: Basic Books.

Ross, S.F. (1989) 'Monopoly sports leagues'. *Minnesota Law Review, 73*: 643–760.

Rottenberg, S. (1956) 'The baseball players labor market'. *Journal of Political Economy, 64*: 242–58.

Smith, A.C. and Stewart, B. (2007) 'The travelling fan: Understanding the mechanisms of sport fan consumption in a sport tourism setting'. *Journal of Sport & Tourism, 12*: 155–81.

Walker, M. and Parent, M.M. (2010) 'Toward an integrated framework of corporate social responsibility, responsiveness, and citizenship in sport'. *Sport Management Review, 13*: 198–213.

Applying the sports product framework

Thilo Kunkel[1]

I first discovered Mason's (1999) article in 2007 when I was writing a literature review for my honours thesis. In the thesis, I investigated what factors influence the attractiveness of professional sport leagues from a consumer perspective. Consumer behaviour research in relation to sport leagues was scarce, and most academic sport consumer behaviour publications focused on sport teams, whereas research focused on leagues was mainly positioned in the economic area of competitive balance. However, Mason's article was an exception and provided a starting point for my research project of investigating sport league consumers.

I was attracted to this article because it provides a basis to understanding the consumption of sport leagues. In particular, the article outlines the unique relationship between leagues and their teams, the nature of sport fans, the different ways sport is consumed and the different income streams for sport organisations. Throughout the article, Mason highlights that consumers are the most important stakeholder group and that other groups, such as media and sponsors, would not be attracted to professional (spectator) sport organisations without the interest of end consumers. Understanding the importance of consumers and their influence on other stakeholder groups and the target sport organisation is imperative for sport management researchers. Therefore, the article provided me with a solid foundation for research related to sport leagues and connected parties, and as a result has significantly influenced my own research agenda of sport league branding.

In my research, I investigate strategic brand development for sport organisations, with a focus on sport leagues. Mason emphasised that sport league marketing is complex because decision-making needs to consider the league as well as the affiliated teams, which highlights the close relationship between leagues and teams. To investigate this relationship, my colleagues and I first examined the brand architecture of sport leagues and teams from a consumer's perspective. Findings demonstrated that consumer brand loyalty is influenced by both the league and the team for a majority of consumers (Kunkel, Funk and Hill, 2013). In subsequent inquiries, we observed seventeen unique brand associations consumers link with sport leagues. These brand associations were correlated with behavioural outcomes related to sport leagues (Kunkel, Funk and King, 2014). We then examined strategies sport leagues can utilise to develop their brand and positively influence consumer involvement with the league and its teams. Identified strategies can be used to position league brands and influence consumers' brand associations (Kunkel, Doyle and Funk, 2014). Overall, my research has extended Mason's conceptual foundation of sport league marketing by investigating the unique relationship between leagues and teams from a consumer perspective.

As Mason has highlighted, sport organisations, such as teams, are evaluated with a broader context in mind; in this case the influence of the consumer's perceptions of the league. Therefore, I envision future research based on Mason's (1999) article to further investigate the relationships between sport leagues and their related stakeholders. Examples are to investigate the influence sport leagues have on their teams, the players within the league and sponsors of these entities. Given the advancement of technology, future sport league consumer research should also investigate how leagues can use technologies to foster consumer involvement and the internationalisation of sport leagues.

Note

1   Dr. Thilo Kunkel is an Assistant Professor in the School of Tourism and Hospitality Management at Temple University.

References

Kunkel, T., Funk, D.C. and Hill, B. (2013) 'Brand architecture, drivers of consumer involvement, and brand loyalty with professional sport leagues and teams'. *Journal of Sport Management, 27*: 177–92.
Kunkel, T., Funk, D.C. and King, C. (2014) 'Developing a conceptual understanding of consumer-based league brand associations'. *Journal of Sport Management, 28*: 49–67.
Kunkel, T., Doyle, J.P. and Funk, D.C. (2014) 'Exploring sport brand development strategies to strengthen consumer involvement with the product – The case of the Australian A-League'. *Sport Management Review, 17*: 470–83.
Mason, D.S. (1999) 'What is the sports product and who buys it? The marketing of professional sports leagues'. *European Journal of Marketing, 33*: 402–18.

PART IV

Sociocultural theories

25

THE GENDERING OF LEADERSHIP IN SPORT ORGANISATIONS

Post-structural perspectives[1]

Annelies Knoppers

Overview

Gender continues to be one of the most frequently used categorisations in societal and organisational life and is often a focus for researchers and policymakers as they strive to reduce gender inequities in organisations, including those in sport (e.g., Hoeber, 2007; Pfister and Radtke, 2009). Gender equality and empowerment of women is one of the eight Millennium Development Goals that the United Nations developed in 2000. Today that goal is still relevant (Grown, Rao Gupta and Kes, 2005). The Olympic Charter (IOC, 2013) states that 'Any form of discrimination with regard to a country or a person on grounds of race, religion, politics, gender, or otherwise is incompatible with belonging to the Olympic Movement' (p. 12). Yet women continue to remain relatively under-represented in positions of leadership, including those in sport (see Burton, 2015, for a summary of the research).

Much of my life as a scholar has been devoted to looking for clues and untangling a tangled clew (ball of yarn) that could help understand dynamics of gender such as these, especially in organisational life and leadership. Such understandings are needed, not only because gender inequality is unacceptable, but also because much of the inequality in society is produced in organisations (Acker, 2006). Although scholars have used a variety of scholarly perspectives to explore this topic, I argue that the gendering of leadership in sport organisations has generally been under-theorized. In this paper, I describe my search for clues that began long before I wrote the 1992 article (Knoppers, 1992), which might add to the theorizing about gender and especially to that about gender in sport organisations.

Process

The article I wrote in 1992, its critique of an individual and of a structural approach, and its advocacy of a relational perspective to investigate the relative lack of women in positions of leadership, does not stand alone; its development was part of a long process involving my personal and scholarly life. My mother was one of the first female theology students in the Netherlands and my father was involved in the underground resistance during World War II. Together they imparted to me sensitivity to injustice. Due to a combination of circumstances, I attended a girls' high school in Montreal. I had only female teachers; the high school had its own gym meaning that girls had every opportunity to be involved in sport. The gym was ours every afternoon! I considered this to be normal. When I subsequently attended college in the USA, I was shocked to discover that there were few opportunities for women to compete and be recognised for their accomplishments in sport and other subjects. As a coach, I had to literally smuggle a volleyball team off campus so we could compete in a regional tournament. There was no money for such outings by women athletes and we were assumed not to be interested in, or able to handle, such competition. I worked primarily in physical education and athletic departments of colleges and universities where women in positions of leadership were rare. As a faculty member, I experienced first-hand how much of my behaviour and that of my few female colleagues was attributed to being a woman. In contrast, my male colleagues tended to be described as scholars/faculty members/coaches first. As a developing scholar in the social sciences in the 1980s, I wanted to understand why so many people thought this situation was normal, why it continued and why it was difficult to effect change.

I began to read scholarly research on the subject, thinking that somewhere I could find the clue that would give me *the* explanation. Although a great deal of research on gender and organisations/leadership had emerged by then, at that time it was still possible to read much of it! Through my reading, I discovered that scholars approached gender in various ways. Much of the scholarship I read in the 1980s saw gender as a dichotomous category consisting of women and men and used theories about individuals (human capital) and/or structure to explain the absence of women in male-dominated occupations. The individualist approach suggested that the lack of women could be attributed to their lack of qualifications and overall work behaviour. For example, since women had not played men's football they were assumed to be unqualified to coach it. Or, women might experience role conflict between their femininity and the masculine orientation required to be a good coach (e.g., Wrisberg, 1990). I had written a conceptual critique of masculinity, femininity and androgyny as fixed categories earlier, so I was rather critical of the explanatory power of the individual approach (Knoppers, 1980). In addition, women were moving into positions of leadership in other organisational sectors, suggesting women were qualified to take on high-level jobs, but sport lagged behind in this regard. Moreover, men who had never played a women's sport were hired to coach such sports. How could they be seen as qualified if experience in the sport was an important criterion? I therefore began to look for explanatory theoretical explanations or clues with a focus on the clew of structure. I focused first on Kanter's (1977) theory about structure as a possibility in explaining this under-representation of women.

Kanter (1977) argued that not individual characteristics, but ostensibly gender-neutral structural determinants of opportunity, power and tokenism in organisations could explain the under-representation of women. I explored the role these structural determinants might play in explaining the lack of women in coaching. I presented and discussed these determinants and what they might mean for research on coaches in a conceptual article (Knoppers, 1987). I subsequently engaged in an empirical quantitative project of collegiate coaches to compare women and men on these determinants (Knoppers, Meyer, Ewing and Forrest, 1989, 1990, 1991). Statistical differences between women and men for each of these determinants did partially explain the under-representation of women. In other words, the results suggested that gender differences were more a function of structure than of attributes of individual women and men.

The findings also raised more questions, however. Research by others (e.g., Ott, 1989; Zimmer, 1988) suggested that structure itself is not gender neutral. Men and women were treated differently within the same structure. Thus, the structure of 'structure' tended to favour men. I began to realise that gender was much more complex than only a categorical concept that reduces it to a static dichotomy of women and men or of fixed ideas about femininity and masculinity. I also understood that the focus on only essentialist categorisations of individuals or on structure ignored the complex and layered dynamics of gender and perhaps explained why relatively little change in this dominance was occurring. I began to read scholarship in the literature on gender, organisations and leadership that saw gender not so much as a category or as a structural outcome but as a complex relational construct. This idea seemed to hold many potential fruitful insights that might help explain some of the ways in which gender manifested itself in organisations.

This realisation was not as straightforward as it sounds. Although I wanted to focus on this complexity, I did not know what that complexity might contain or where my search to unravel any part of this complexity might lead me. I wrote the 1992 article as a summary of what I had read and as a way to offer another way of looking at gender other than the individual or structural approach. I argued that when scholars and policymakers tended to reduce women's under-representation in leadership positions in sport organisations to a structural problem and/or to a problematic deficit in skills women needed to perform well on the job, they ignored part of the bigger picture. I therefore proposed that gender should be seen and explored as a relational practice that varies by time and place. The foundations for that article were laid by my earlier conceptual articles, one that critiqued the notion of sex roles and the other that explored what a focus on structure of organisations might mean for research on gender and coaches. In addition, my empirical research on structure led me to the realisation that although structural theories might have some explanatory power, they were based on assumptions that the latest literature showed were not gender-neutral. These research projects therefore led me to gender as a relational concept, an idea I tried to develop in the 1992 article. After I had written that article I wondered how I could capture this concept at least partially in empirical research.

Fortunately, the tools available for exploring gender evolved a great deal since 1992 and allowed me access to theoretical sophistication that gave me greater insight into the failure of sport organisations to reduce gender inequalities significantly (see also Connell, 2005; Knoppers and McDonald, 2010; Sterk and Knoppers, 2009). Various experiences helped me realise that capturing the complexity of gender required other ontologies and epistemologies than the positivist approaches and quantitative methodologies I had used until then. I needed additional tools to capture invisible dynamics of processes. A pivotal moment was a course I audited in Qualitative Research Methods that was grounded in cultural anthropology and social constructionism. The contents of this course made me realise how much of what individuals think and do is based on their social constructions and assumptions about reality. The concept that organisations, gender and leadership were all social constructions was an exciting eye-opener for me. It opened up vistas of possibilities for research and for change since it assumes that individuals are active social beings, who shape and are shaped by structures. The idea of agency suggested there was room for transformation and also that structures could be changed. At that time, scholars such as Ann Hall, Nancy Theberge and Susan Birrell had already begun to pay attention to and uncover the relationality of gender in sport. Other scholars, such as R. Connell, Mike Messner and Don Sabo, began to focus on masculinities not as static categorisations but as constructions embodied in practices. These conceptual tools and the way these scholars employed various methodologies not only inspired me but also gave me other ways of looking at gender and leadership in sport organisations than I had used in the past.

I therefore chose to focus on gendered organisational processes and underlying assumptions using qualitative methodologies rather than looking at gender differences and quantifiable outcomes. Through (more!) extensive reading about gender in organisations and in the critical sociology of sport and attending various conferences such as North American Society for the Sociology of Sport, I discovered two possible perspectives that could give me further insight in gender as a relation: a processual approach based on the work of Joan Acker and a discursive approach based on the work of Michel Foucault.

Extensions and applications

Acker (1990, 1992) has argued that organisations consist of often invisible processes that together gender an organisation. This gendering of organisational processes occurs at minimally four levels: (a) gendered identity work that employees do to fit in the organisation and enables them to do the job; (b) informal interactions between employees in which gender is always involved; (c) definitions and assignment of tasks that lead to a gendered division of labour; and (d) a gendering of organisational culture and images. In other words, gender is 'done' and embedded in an organisation through its culture and images, its division of labour and tasks, the content of formal and informal interactions, and the identity work of organisational members. Together these (overlapping) processes describe an organisation and its work and how it is gendered. I found this approach to be helpful in making visible some of the complexities of (categorical) gender segregation in sport organisations and specifically of the gendering of leadership.

We (Knoppers and Anthonissen, 2005, 2008; Claringbould and Knoppers, 2007, 2008) used Acker's approach to study how men and women in senior positions in management and governance in sport organisations negotiated gender. We found, for example, that women who served on boards of national sport organisations did their best not to be seen as feminist because that was associated with being bitchy; they wanted to be seen as competent as defined by the male defined norm. In other words, they were doing identity work in their interactions with others so that they might be constructed or seen as acceptable leaders who fit the norm informed by images of men as managers and leaders. These practices constructed or reinforced images that suggested who was suitable for which position and consequently produced a gendered division of labour. Specifically, I discovered that the four interdependent processes produced regimes of gender inequality that were invisible, tended to be legitimised and accepted as normal or common sense and helped explain how men could dominate positions of leadership in sport organisations. Such processes resulted in complex organisational patterns of 'advantage and disadvantage, exploitation and control, action and emotion, meaning and identity' (Acker, 2006, p. 146; see also Acker, 2012; Benschop and Doorewaard, 2012). In other words, gender was more than a categorisation but was also a verb, a relational process involving both women and men.

I thus expanded on the ideas I discussed in 1992, especially that of gender as a social relation, but also now saw structure and deficits/capital as social constructions. This insight into the layeredness of gender as a social constructed relation helped me, therefore, to identify several clues in my search for explanations why the conditions described at the beginning of this chapter continue to exist. I continue to find Acker's approach useful in untangling questions of gender in organisations. The prevalence of these processes means that even when sport organisations strive for gender equality by focusing on reducing the male to female ratio, they continue to (re)produce social relations based on gender. The explanatory power of this approach did not mean I had completely unraveled the ball of yarn or clew that explained gender inequality in sport organisations.

Insight into these complex processes did not help me to explain how and why these often invisible regimes of inequalities (Acker, 2006) continue to exist and how they had become common sense, despite organisational commitment to equality and fairness and laws and policies, such as those of the IOC and UN that forbid discrimination. These results led me to focus especially on the process of the production of culture and images and to ask questions about possible sources of common sense, ideologies on which assumptions are based and why some assumptions become known as truths. The preparation of my inaugural address for a chair in the pedagogy of sport at the University of Utrecht, extensive reading and discussions with colleagues led me to post-structural perspectives based on the work of Michel Foucault. In preparation for my inaugural address I read Foucault's (1977) *Discipline and punish* and Markula and Pringle's (2006) translation of his work to sport, because I wanted to understand possible sources of underlying assumptions people have about the pedagogies of sport participation. As I read his work, I realised that several Foucauldian concepts could give me more insight into the complexity of gender in (sport) organisations although Foucault did not write about either.

A Foucauldian framework suggests that language and discourses often serve as sources of common sense and of invisible underlying assumptions and are seen as truths, that are internalised by individuals and become embedded in organisational processes and structures. These notions gave me an awareness of the role that language and seemingly invisible ideologies form organisational discourses that may play a role in the gendering of leadership in sport. Organisational discourses are formal and informal rules that shape what are considered to be good, appropriate and bad management practices and organisational behaviour. In other words, discourses are knowledge and a source of power because they shape thought and practices (see also Markula and Pringle, 2006; Mills and Denison, 2013). This approach assumes, therefore, that practices are based on discourses and vice versa. To understand how I could use such Foucauldian insights to explain gendering of sport leadership, I again to turned to scholarly literature but this time that which was based on a post-structural perspective that often relied on such insights. This extensive reading included the critical management studies literature in which Foucauldian notions are often used. According to Foucault (1977, 1980), discursive practices shape reality. In other words, practices are rooted in dominant discourses. I realised that this includes gendered organisational processes and that I needed to move from a focus on men and women in these processes to concentrate on practices.

Future: post-structural perspectives

The use of a post-structural lens led me to questions such as: What is considered the implicit norm for managerial work/sport leadership and how is it constructed? Which practices sustain it? On what is this norm based? How congruent are assumptions about this norm with social constructions of masculinity and femininity? In other words, I began to see Acker's processual approach through a discursive lens. Specifically, I understood that gender as a social relation was constructed by discourses about gender that informed ways in which identity work was done, shaped organisational culture and images, impacted divisions of labour and was embedded in interactions. I now saw all of these as practices. Colleagues and I undertook a series of studies with a focus on how discursive practices about masculinity and diversity might limit diversity in sport management (Knoppers, 2011; Knoppers and Anthonissen, 2003, 2005, 2008; Knoppers, Claringbould and Dortants, 2014). The results suggested that assumptions about the ideal manager or director were associated with practices of heroic masculinity that included a competitive sport background and ability to give 24/7 to the job, and that such descriptions of managerial work were seen as neutral and common sense.

So what might the individual, structural and relational approaches I discussed in 1992 look like from a post-structural perspective? A post-structural perspective would require a scrutiny of expressions used to describe aspects of capital (and the words 'capital' and 'deficit') and structure. For example, my finding (Knoppers, 2011) that senior managers in non-profit organisations value someone with a competitive sport background as fitting the profile of an ideal manager could be seen as a statement about 'capital' needed for the job. This emphasis on competitive sport background as part of the profile of an ideal manager can be seen as a possible deficit for women aspiring to high positions of leadership, especially in sport organisations. Women will rarely be able to build enough capital or might be constructed as being deficient because they rarely participate in men's sport. Instead of accepting this deficit as a fact and then looking for ways women could compensate their exclusion from men's competitive sport, however, a post-structural approach would require researchers to explore what exactly it is about a competitive sport background that is assumed to qualify men for a top position. How could such a qualification be deconstructed? What do those hiring managers associate with a competitive sport background? Which images and skills are associated with that? Hovden (2000) used this approach by looking at the practice of selection of high-level positions in governance of sport and found that although members of selection committees assumed criteria for selection were neutral, they implicitly wanted candidates who embodied what they saw as heroic masculinity. Similarly, Shaw and Hoeber (2003) used discourse analysis to explore assumptions held by staff in national sport organisations about positions. They found that jobs associated with discursive practices of femininity tended to be marginalised, while senior management positions that were associated with discourses of heroic masculinity were valued. This research made me realise that post-structural perspectives could provide a lens that enables researchers such as myself to look at such assumptions and to draw attention to the multiplicity and complexities of gender in sport organisations.

Claringbould and I (2013) drew on the empirical literature to explore the under-representation of women managers/directors in sport organisations by combining a post-structural discursive approach with Acker's processual theory of gender in organisations. We attempted to show how discursive practices informed each of the four processes. We also tried to break new ground by suggesting several practices that may not explicitly be part of Acker's four processes, such as use of liminality (unawareness), privilege and societal discourses. In addition, my relatively recent work suggests that embodiment or bodywork in (sport) organisations also merits attention (Knoppers and Van Amsterdam, 2014), since it also may play a role in the privileging of certain practices. This, however, needs further research.

These ideas about the use of post-structural theorizing are not meant to be exhaustive, nor do I mean to say that other approaches that might capture complexity are not legitimate. Yet a post-structural focus on discourse as knowledge and power, and their possible use to explore which knowledges about gender, work, sport and organisations are produced, problematised and challenged in different settings, is needed (Bacchi and Rönnblom, 2014). It can produce new and needed insights about the ways in which leadership is gendered and how that gendering is maintained, produced and challenged in sport organisations. I recognise that although I have paid some attention to the intersectionality of social relations (Knoppers and Anthonissen, 2001, 2005), it is my theorizing that more work is needed that includes it. Gender is not a universal construct. I understand that practices of masculinity and of femininity are embedded in practices of whiteness, ableness, class privilege and of heteronormativity and that this intersectionality also needs more attention and theorizing from sport management scholars including myself (see for example, Bendl, Fleischman and Walenta, 2008; King, 2008; Kitchin and Howe, 2013; Knoppers and McDonald, 2010; McDonald and Toglia, 2010).

I see my own research development, especially with respect to theoretical perspectives, as fluid and as continually going one step further, often without being able to see what is ahead.

It is as if each time I focus on one thread of the complex clew that comprises gender in organisations, other threads become visible or are created. Developing theories and explanations is a dynamic process. I assume there is no grand theory that will eventually explain how gender works in sport organisation. Yet, I do believe that research can reveal different dimensions that may have been invisible, and that may generate ideas for organisational transformations that may reduce inequalities produced in sport organisations.

Note

1   This chapter reflects on Knoppers (1992) and the work related to it.

References

Acker, J. (1990) 'Hierarchies, jobs, bodies: A theory of gendered organizations'. *Gender & Society*, 4: 139–58.

Acker, J. (1992) 'Gendering organizational theory'. In A.J. Mills and P. Tancred (eds) *Gendering organizational analysis* (pp. 248–62). Newbury Park, CA: Sage Publications.

Acker, J. (2006) 'Inequality regimes: Gender, class, and race in organizations'. *Gender & Society*, 20: 441–64.

Acker, J. (2012) 'Gendered organizations and intersectionality: Problems and possibilities'. *Equality, Diversity and Inclusion: An International Journal*, 31: 214–24.

Bacchi, C. and Rönnblom, M. (2014) 'Feminist discursive institutionalism—a poststructural alternative'. *NORA-Nordic Journal of Feminist and Gender Research*, 1–17.

Bendl, R., Fleischmann, A. and Walenta, C. (2008) 'Diversity management discourse meets queer theory'. *Gender in Management: An International Journal*, 23: 382–94.

Benschop, Y. and Doorewaard, H. (2012) 'Gender subtext revisited'. *Equality, Diversity and Inclusion: An International Journal*, 31: 225–35.

Burton, L.J. (2015) 'Underrepresentation of women in sport leadership: A review of research'. *Sport Management Review*, 18: 155–165.

Claringbould, I. and Knoppers, A. (2007) 'Finding a 'normal' woman: Selection processes for board membership'. *Sex Roles*, 56: 495–507.

Claringbould, I. and Knoppers, A. (2008) 'Doing and undoing gender in sport governance'. *Sex Roles*, 58: 81–92.

Claringbould, I. and Knoppers, A. (2013) 'Understanding the lack of gender equity in leadership positions in (sport) organization'. In Leisink, P., Boselie, P., Hosking, D.M. and van Bottenburg, M. (eds) *Managing social issues: A public values perspective* (pp. 162–82). Cheltenham, UK: Edward Elgar Publishing.

Connell, R. (2005) *Masculinities*. Cambridge: Polity Press.

Foucault, M. (1977) *Discipline and punish: The birth of a prison*. New York: Pantheon Books.

Foucault, M. (1980) 'Truth and power'. In C. Gordon (ed.) *Power/Knowledge: Selected interviews and other writings 1972–1977* (pp. 109–33). London: Tavistock.

Grown, C., Reo Gupta, G. and Kes, A. (2005) *Taking action: Achieving gender equality and empowering women*. UN Millennium Project, London: Earthscan Publications.

Hoeber, L. (2007) '"It's somewhere on the list but maybe it's one of the bottom ones": Examining gender equity as an organizational value in a sport organization'. *International Journal of Sport Management and Marketing*, 2: 362–78.

Hovden, J. (2000) 'Gender and leadership selection processes in Norwegian sporting organizations'. *International Review for the Sociology of Sport*, 35: 75–82.

International Olympic Committee (IOC) (2013) *Olympic charter 2013*. Lausanne: IOC.

Kanter, R.M. (1977) *Men and women of the corporation*. New York: Basic.

King, S. (2008) 'What's queer about (queer) sport sociology now? A review essay'. *Sociology of Sport Journal*, 25: 419–42.

Kitchin, P.J. and Howe, D.P. (2013) 'How can the social theory of Pierre Bourdieu assist sport management research?' *Sport Management Review*, 16: 123–34.

Knoppers, A. (1980) 'Androgyny: Another look'. *Quest*, 32: 184–91.

Knoppers, A. (1987) 'Gender and the coaching profession'. *Quest*, 39: 9–22.

Knoppers, A. (1992) 'Explaining male dominance and sex segregation in coaching: Three approaches'. *Quest*, 44: 210–27.

Knoppers, A. (2011) 'Giving meaning to sport involvement in managerial work'. *Gender, Work & Organization, 18*: e1–e22.

Knoppers, A. and Anthonissen, A. (2001) 'Meanings given to performance in Dutch sport organizations: Gender and racial/ethnic subtexts'. *Sociology of Sport Journal, 18*: 302–16.

Knoppers, A. and Anthonissen, A. (2003) 'Women's soccer in the United States and the Netherlands: Differences and similarities in regimes of inequalities'. *Sociology of Sport Journal, 20*: 351–70.

Knoppers, A. and Anthonissen, A. (2005) 'Male athletic and managerial masculinities: Congruencies in discursive practices?' *Journal of Gender Studies, 14*: 123–35.

Knoppers, A. and Anthonissen, A. (2008) 'Gendered managerial discourses in sport organizations: Multiplicity and complexity'. *Sex Roles, 58*: 93–103.

Knoppers, A., Claringbould, I. and Dortants, M. (2014) 'Discursive managerial practices of diversity and homogeneity'. *Journal of Gender Studies*: 1–16.

Knoppers, A. and McDonald, M. (2010) 'Scholarship on gender and sport in *Sex Roles* and beyond'. *Sex Roles, 63*: 311–23.

Knoppers, A., Meyer, B.B., Ewing, M. and Forrest, L. (1989) 'Gender and the salaries of coaches'. *Sociology of Sport Journal, 6*: 348–61.

Knoppers, A., Meyer, B.B., Ewing, M. and Forrest, L. (1990) 'Dimensions of power: A question of sport or gender?' *Sociology of Sport Journal*: 369–77.

Knoppers, A., Meyer, B.B., Ewing, M. and Forrest, L. (1991) 'Opportunity and work behavior in a male dominated occupation'. *Journal of Sport and Social Issues, 15*: 1–20.

Knoppers, A. and Van Amsterdam, N. (2014) 'Making the body visible in sport organizations/research'. Paper presented at the annual conference of the North American Society for Sport Management (June). Pittsburgh, OH.

Markula, P. and Pringle, R. (2006) *Foucault, sport and exercise: Power, knowledge and transforming the self.* London and New York: Routledge.

McDonald, M.G. and Toglia, J. (2010) 'Dressed for success? The NBA's dress code, the workings of whiteness and corporate culture'. *Sport in Society, 13*: 970–83.

Mills, J.P. and Denison, J. (2013) 'Coach Foucault: Problematizing endurance running coaches' practices'. *Sports Coaching Review, 2*: 136–50.

Ott, E.M. (1989) 'Effects of the male–female ratio at work'. *Psychology of Women Quarterly, 13*: 41–57.

Pfister, G. and Radtke, S. (2009) 'Sport, women, and leadership: Results of a project on executives in German sports organizations'. *European Journal of Sport Science, 9*: 229–43.

Shaw, S. and Hoeber, L. (2003). '"A strong man is direct and a direct woman is a bitch": Gendered discourses and their influence on employment roles in sport organizations'. *Journal of Sport Management, 17*: 347–76.

Sterk, H.M. and Knoppers, A. (2009) *Gender, culture, and physicality: Paradoxes and taboos.* Lanham, MD: Lexington Books.

Wrisberg, C.A. (1990) 'Gender-role orientations of male and female coaches of a masculine-typed sport'. *Research Quarterly for Exercise and Sport, 61*: 297–301.

Zimmer, L. (1988) 'Tokenism and women in the workplace: The limits of gender-neutral theory'. *Social Problems*: 64–77.

Applying the three-tiered approach to male dominance and sex segregation in coaching

Marlene A. Dixon[1]

I first became aware of Knopper's (1992) work during my master's degree programme at the University of Texas. In conjunction with Janet Fink, Maureen Fitzgerald and Dorothy Lovett, I was developing a literature review on burnout in coaches, and female coaches in particular. This literature review was both personally and professionally motivated as I was also coaching college volleyball and basketball at the time.

What initially drew me to this work, along with her earlier pieces on coaching, was the articulation in theory of what had been happening in practice for many years, especially within college and professional sport. That is, she articulated that the rules of the game and the basic assumptions within the coaching profession were fundamentally different for men than for women. She also argued that the policies, norms and work cultures surrounding the management of coaches typically operated on the assumptions of the men's rules, which, consequently, did not always fit well for the management of women. Finally, without explicitly using the term, she outlined a multi-level approach (individual, structural and socio-cultural), which I have also utilised heavily in my own work. I have found this work, over the past twenty years, to be of profound influence on my research, teaching and practice.

I relied heavily on Knopper's (1992) work in the development of mine and Jennifer Bruening's (2005) multi-level model for work–family conflict in coaching mothers, as well as the subsequent empirical testing of that model (Bruening and Dixon, 2007; Dixon and Bruening, 2007; see Chapter 15 of this volume). Several tenets of Knopper's (1992) work were particularly salient to my own exploration of the coaching lives of mothers.

First, and most strongly, Knoppers argued that the traditionally masculine model of coaching was built upon structural assumptions that impact the management of coaches. For example, she argued that it is assumed that coaches (men) have a full support system for their non-work/family life, and thus can devote their full time and effort just to coaching. This assumption has profound implications for mothers who are coaches, because they do *not* necessarily have those resources to support their non-work lives or coaching careers, yet their administrators manage them as if they do. This leads to early burnout and exit for many women coaches.

Second, she argued that coaching and administration could be distinguished by traditional assumptions about men's and women's abilities and roles in the workplace. In our work on gender roles within college athletics administration (Bruening and Dixon, 2007), this line of thinking has been valuable for exposing stereotypes about women's interests and capabilities that keep them from advancing in administrative roles in particular.

This framework will continue to have application in many ways. In my own work, it is already showing value, as I begin exploring the work–life interface of coaching fathers (Graham and Dixon, 2014). That is, men also work within a traditionally masculine coaching culture that is generating increasing tension with changing socio-cultural notions of fatherhood and dual-earner families. As men confront the powerful culture of coaching, they will encounter these structural and socio-cultural assumptions that will continue to shape both families and coaching as a career.

Note

1 Marlene A. Dixon is a Professor at Troy University.

References

Bruening, J.E. and Dixon, M.A. (2007) 'Work–family conflict in coaching II: Managing role conflict'. *Journal of Sport Management, 21*: 471–96.

Dixon, M.A. and Bruening, J.E. (2005) 'Perspectives on work–family conflict in sport: An integrated approach'. *Sport Management Review, 8*: 227–53.

Dixon, M.A. and Bruening, J.E. (2007) 'Work–family conflict in coaching I: A top down perspective'. *Journal of Sport Management, 21*: 377–406.

Graham, J.A. and Dixon, M.A. (2014) 'Coaching fathers in conflict. A review of the tensions surrounding the work–family interface'. *Journal of Sport Management, 28*: 447–57.

Knoppers, A. (1992) 'Explaining male dominance and sex segregation in coaching: Three approaches'. *Quest, 44*: 210–27.

26

INCLUSIVE MASCULINITY THEORY[1]

Eric Anderson

Overview

In the summers of 2011–14, I returned to visit a Southern California high-school cross-country team I had coached in 1990. Composed of forty-three members, the team has Korean, Chinese, Caucasian, Mexican, Egyptian and African-American athletes; alongside atheists, and those of the Jewish, Christian, Buddhist, Mormon and Muslim faith, and a coach who is a Jehovah's Witness. One team member wears black every day and sports half a dozen piercings, while another wears preppy clothes and does ballet. Two have been voted the school's homecoming King in the last few years, several play musical instruments to a high standard or are in bands, and some of the athletes maintain high grade point averages while others maintain grades just sufficient to compete. One was arrested for breaking into a school and stealing computers and a few are Eagle Scouts. Some have special social, educational or physical needs, and others maintain high social, athletic, or sexual capital. Perhaps most significantly, there are two openly gay male athletes, and another publicly declares that he will just fall in love with whomever he falls in love.

Despite this diversity, social groupings on the team are diverse and fluid. Race, intelligence, religion and sexuality are not important variables in establishing friendship patterns. No athlete on the team reports being bullied, on or off the team. Yet, when I taught at this school twenty-three years earlier, matters were different.

Back then the school was ruled by football players and this negatively impacted the school's general population. The runners, for example, feared the football team (Anderson, 2000). Football players hated gays, femininity and all 'lesser masculine' sports. Thus, when students started a Gay–Straight Alliance in 1993, football players started a heterosexual club, even picketing the gay club with homophobic signs.

But now as the runners on the team run past the football players (lined up to do drills), they sometimes stop to have short conversations, discussing homework or forthcoming shared social engagements. Or, as the football players walk to get water, they stop to talk to the stretching runners. It is evident that their friendship networks overlap. The two gay male athletes on the cross-country team are no exception. They have friends on the football team. The openly gay freshman football player has friends on the cross-country team.

As the team runs on the far side of the field, they pass the school's marching band, whose members possess less athletic capital than the runners. This is a group that, in 1990, the runners themselves marginalised. Yet today's runners do not mock band members. Just as with the football players, the runners stop to chat with them, too.

Highlighting this, a fully-geared freshman football team walks by the runners on the way to their first football match. Walking side-by-side, holding hands with the player adjacent, I ask one of them why they are holding hands, he responds that it is tradition (it wasn't a tradition in 1993). Another says, 'It shows brotherhood'. None of the runners on the cross-country team comment about the hand-holding. From my perspective, this homosocial tactility is amazing; from their perspective, it is uneventful.

At a pre-race spaghetti dinner the following night, two of the straight male runners stood chatting to other runners. From behind, one rested his head on the other's shoulder, wrapping his arms around the other's waist – a standing cuddle. I timed it from another table: it lasted for eleven minutes and thirty-seven seconds. Furthermore, eight of the runners on this team made what can only be described as a highly provocative Harlem Shake video, which included nudity and featured one of the gay members mock-humping one of the straight team members. At one of the runner's birthday parties, five of the athletes took a photo in which they stood behind each other, each with their hand in the front pocket of the guy in front of them. The boy in the middle is openly gay and each team member in the picture is of a different racial ethnic group. These are examples of bountiful similar occurrences for the boys on this team.

When I made my final goodbye to the team this summer, a number of the boys called out, 'We love you', as I drove away. They gave me shirts for my one-year-old twins as a going away gift. In rainbow colours the shirts had printed on them, 'Two dads are better than one'. These youth celebrated the fact they had an openly gay coach who is married to his husband and the proud father of two baby boys. 'When you return next summer I will be the first to give a big hug', one straight runner messaged me on Facebook.

The gendered behaviours of these young men on this high school team are radically different from 1990. Seeing the change in one city is powerful, but it is also what I see in my dozens of studies in both the US, and even more so in the UK – studies that I detail in my (2014) book *21st century jocks: Sporting men and contemporary heterosexuality*. Their attitudes towards diversity, homosexuality, femininity, same-sex touch and the expression of love for another male are that of inclusion and plurality. In 1990, their attitude was one of exclusion of anything different from the jock-norm. But this school is no longer run by jocks. Friendship patterns today are fluid and the gendered behaviours of the boys in the school are highly feminized, at least by 1990 standards.

Inclusive masculinity

The type of masculinity exhibited by the youth I report upon here is starkly different from what the dominant paradigm of the previous generations suggested about young men, which maintained that they are homophobic, sexist, violent, emotionally repressed and afraid of physical contact with other males. The most important theoretical tool for understanding this social stratification of men and their masculinities has come through Connell's (1995) concept of hegemonic masculinity, which also embedded in it the archetypical man as being homophobic, stoic, violent and macho.

Developed from a social constructionist perspective in the mid 1980s, hegemonic masculinity theory articulated two social processes. The first concerned how all men benefit from patriarchy; however, it is the second social process that has been heavily adopted by the masculinities literature. Here, Connell's theoretical contribution was particularly adopted for its conceptualisation of the mechanisms by which an intra-masculine hierarchy is created and legitimised. It is only this aspect of his theory that I address and ultimately reject.

In conceptualising intra-masculine domination, Connell argued that one hegemonic archetype of masculinity is esteemed above all other masculinity types, so that boys and men who most closely embody this one standard are accorded the most social capital, relative to other boys and men. Some of the characteristics of hegemonic masculinity concern variables that are earned, such as attitudinal depositions (including the disposition of homophobia), while other variables concern static traits (e.g., Whiteness, heterosexuality and youth). Connell argued, however, that regardless of body mass, age, or even sporting accomplishments, gay men are at the bottom of this hierarchy. Furthermore, Connell maintained that straight men who behave in ways that conflict with the dominant form of masculinity are also marginalised. It was for these reasons that I have argued homophobia has traditionally been an effective weapon to stratify men in deference to a hegemonic mode of heteromasculine dominance (Anderson, 2005). Connell theorized (1995) that the power of a hegemonic form of masculinity was that those subjugated by it nonetheless believed in the right. Instead of disputing their marginalised position, they revered those at the top. Accordingly, researchers found that team sport players generally controlled youth spaces (Plummer, 1999).

I argue that hegemonic masculinity theory was precise in its ability to predict masculine configurations in the 1980s, and it likely continued to be useful throughout the 1990s. However, the level of homophobia among youth peaked in 1988 (Anderson, 2009), mainly because of decreasing hysteria around HIV's association with gay men. The high level of homophobia and hypermasculinity of the mid 1980s had, however, serious implications for not only attitudes towards gay men, but also for how straight men performed their gender (Peterson and Anderson, 2012). Thus, hegemonic masculinity theory is historically contextualised within its own temporal moment. Specifically, it existed in a culture that I call 'homohysteric' (Anderson, 2009).

Using data from both the US and the UK, I developed the concept *homohysteria* (Anderson, 2009; McCormack and Anderson, 2014a) to explain the power dynamics of changing homophobia on the masculinities of heterosexual men. Theorizing the inter-relations between homosociality, masculinity and homophobia, I adopted earlier scholarship that demonstrated that high levels of cultural homophobia influence individuals to distance themselves from social suspicion of homosexuality through the avoidance of gender atypical behaviours (Floyd, 2000; Ibson, 2002). I augmented this by situating this scholarship within specific social and historical conditions, arguing that homophobia only operates this way in *homohysteric* settings. In other words, homophobia does not necessarily influence males' gendered behaviours; it only does so when specific cultural conditions are met. Homohysteria thus adds a historical analysis to the existing theorizing of the influence of homophobia on males' behaviours and attitudes.

There are three social conditions that must be met for a homohysteric culture to exist: (a) widespread awareness that male homosexuality exists as an immutable sexual orientation within a significant portion of a culture's population; (b) high levels of homophobia in that culture; and (c) an association of gender atypicality with homosexuality. These varying levels of social conditions help explain various social trends concerning masculinities, including: improving attitudes towards homosexuality among heterosexual men (Adams, 2011); the changing cultural experiences of gay men (Anderson, 2011c); and the various meanings of discourse related to sexualities (McCormack, 2011).

Homohysteria itself is a concept that can apply to both men and women. Both Worthen (2014) and Anderson and Bullingham (in press) have used the theory on women, thus far. For men, with the basic understanding of homohysteria as a cultural force that implores men to avoid certain behaviours in order to avoid social homosexualization, *inclusive masculinity theory* is simple: it maintains that as homohysteria decreases, men no longer need to position themselves as hypermasculine in order to be thought heterosexual. As homohysteria decreases, the vertical, hegemonic, stratification that Connell described is no longer accurate, as it shifts (horizontally) to permit multiple types of masculinities to exist without hegemony of any. Should cultural matters change, and homohysteria were to again rise in a culture, the ordering of men would likely return to the way Connell conceptualised.

Specific constructs and propositions

In research on White, middle class, former high school football players, I (Anderson, 2005) first used the term inclusive masculinity to theoretically describe the social process concerning the emergence of an archetype of masculinity that undermines the principles of orthodox (read hegemonic) masculine values – yet one that is also esteemed among male peers. Although this theory is formalised in my (2009) book, *Inclusive masculinity: The changing nature of masculinities*, its tenets, and the empirical motivation for a new theorizing of masculinity, are elucidated here.

Its genesis began in 2005, where I described how a reduction of cultural homophobia challenged the dominance that hegemonic masculinity maintained over heterosexual university athletes. I found two esteemed versions of masculinity: I labelled one orthodox masculinity (which includes extreme homophobia and misogyny) and the other inclusive masculinity (which does not). However, two oppositional masculinities, each with equal influence, co-existing within one setting is not consistent with Connell's (1987, 1995) theorizing. Connell suggested that multiple masculinities do exist within any organisation, institution or culture; and she certainly argues that any one hegemonic archetype of masculinity will be challenged and perhaps replaced by another. However, she described hegemonic masculinity as a hegemonic process by which only one form of institutionalised masculinity is 'culturally exalted' above all others (Connell, 1995, p. 77). Then, according to Connell, men are compelled to associate with this one dominant form (i.e., men looking up the hierarchy).

One of the many forms of masculinity Connell described is protest masculinity. This form of masculinity, she argues, contests the current hegemonic form for dominance. However, the resolution of this struggle is simply that a new, singular, version of a (hegemonic) dominating masculinity emerges. I (Anderson, 2009) suggest that, in periods of high homophobia, Connell was correct: Only one dominating, hegemonic version of masculinity will exist (and it will have homophobia at its core). This is because homophobia is fundamental to the production and stratification of men as an ordered system of valued or subjugated individuals in a highly homophobic culture (Ibson, 2002).

However, inclusive masculinity theory suggests that something different emerges in a culture of diminishing homohysteria. Here, men are permitted increased social freedom in the expression of attitudes and behaviours that were once highly stigmatized. In a moment of decreasing cultural homohysteria, two archetypes will consume most men's membership.

Inclusive masculinity theory next maintains that, as cultural homohysteria further diminishes, multiple forms of masculinity can exist in a horizontal (not stratified) alignment. Here, one or more forms of inclusive masculinity are shown to dominate numerically, but they are not hegemonically dominating (McCormack, 2011). In other words, when inclusive masculinity (as an archetype) proliferates, it does not seem to also dominate. This is something I found in a number of university settings in the previous few years (Anderson, 2005, 2008, 2009). Importantly, if there is no hegemony, there can also be no hegemonic masculinity. Thus, inclusive masculinity theory serves as a social-constructionist theory that simultaneously incorporates and expands upon Connell's (1987) theorizing.

Inclusive masculinity thus supersedes hegemonic masculinity theory because it is a more flexible theory that can be used to explain the social dynamics of settings with both high *and* low levels of homohysteria. When Connell devised hegemonic masculinity theory in the mid 1980s, there was no such thing as a Western culture low in homohysteria. But the significant changes that have occurred since then means that Connell's theory is no longer applicable in many organisational, institutional and geographical locales today.

Boundary conditions

Inclusive masculinity theory was founded upon Anglo-American research. It emerged from the data, instead of superimposing theory over data. This means that matters might vary cross-culturally. I make no pretense that homophobia has reduced globally; instead, it is rife in many parts of the world, and homosexuality is still illegal in eighty-one countries. Because homophobia varies, so will the product of that homohysteria.

More precisely, there are varying combinations of (a) the awareness of homosexuality; (b) antipathy or inclusion towards it; and (c) the culturally coding of certain behaviours as feminine, and thus gay, will vary. These three cultural traits will undoubtedly determine unique outcomes for men's gendered behaviours. For example, in a highly religious theocracy, homosexuals are likely socially perceived extraordinarily rare or perhaps non-existent. While this culture would be considered highly homophobic it is not homohysteric because they don't readily believe that others are gay. Accordingly, men in many Islamic countries are permitted to engage in physical and emotional intimacy (not sex) without threat to their publicly perceived heterosexual identities – if homosexuality does not exist, one cannot be thought gay for holding another's hand.

Opposite to this, a homohysteric culture (like Jamaica) comes through a high measure of cultural homophobia alongside high awareness that homosexuality exists in significant numbers. This is in a culture that both loathes homosexuals but knows they lurk among us. Because homosexuality is mostly invisible, it means that in this culture, all men (of all sexual orientations) must distance themselves from anything coded as gay; otherwise, they will be homosexualized and treated accordingly. In a homohysteric culture, men therefore value the most extreme representations of masculinity, and they equally maintain highly homophobic attitudes, all in attempt to distance themselves from being thought gay. Essentially, in a homohysteric culture, men are attempting to escape social stigma by avoiding being perceived as gay.

The greater the homohysteria within a culture, the more effective homophobia is in limiting the gendered components of masculinity. This will likely influence the social organisation of masculinity types differently in differing cultures.

Empirically validating the theory

Although inclusive masculinity theory (IMT) was first explicated in 2009, scholars are rapidly adopting it as a theoretical framework. For example, in ethnography of a US soccer team, Adams (2011) used IMT to show high levels of homosocial bonding and pro-gay attitudes. He documented multiple examples of straight athletes adopting social behaviours once coded as feminine or gay, where they embrace the opportunity to openly value friendship and the expression of emotional intimacy. Peterson (2011) applied IMT to examine the changing gender dynamics of British university dance floor settings, documenting heterosexual men dancing together in highly sexualized ways without concern as to how strangers perceive their sexual identity. Roberts (2013) shows that young, working-class men working in retail express inclusive masculinities. Cashmore and Cleland (2012) used IMT to document an erosion of homophobia among British soccer fans; Magrath, Anderson and Roberts (in press) used it to show pro-gay attitudes among academy-level British soccer players; Dashper (2012) adopted IMT to show that middle-aged British men enact inclusive masculinities in the sport of dressage; and Morris and Anderson (in press) use it to show how popular male YouTube vloggers display inclusive masculinity.

The theory has been utilised in populations apart from White, British men as well. Cavalier (2011) used IMT to show the changing relationships in older men towards hegemonic masculinity in Canada; Anderson (2011b) uses it in American soccer players; and Southall *et al.* (2009) as well as Southall *et al.* (2011) show that some athletes of colour in the US exhibit inclusive masculinities. Here, they show that while White athletes in the US maintain more inclusive attitudes than African-American athletes, there is a significant decrease in homophobia among both these groups of men; a similar finding to Dean (2013) showing anti-homophobia from Black and White American men. I have further evidenced this argument by examining the social dynamics of young men in the UK – where the change in masculine configurations of practice has been more pronounced. Here, pro-gay attitudes and the promotion of inclusive masculine behaviours are documented among British soccer players (Adams, Anderson and McCormack, 2010) and field-hockey teams (Anderson, McCormack and Lee, 2012). McGuire and I (Anderson and McGuire, 2010) use IMT to explain results of intra-masculine dynamics and homosocial bonding among British rugby players, and in other research (Anderson, Adams and Rivers, 2012), we use IMT to explain how it is that 89 per cent of heterosexual male undergraduates have kissed another male on the lips without being homosexualized by this activity; Drummond, Filiault, Anderson and Jeffries (in press) show this number to be 29 per cent in Australia. Anderson and McCormack (in press) show that cuddling in bed is common for straight male, undergraduate friends in Britain, too.

Inclusive changes are also reflected in the way sport media reports upon gay male athletes (Kian and Anderson, 2009; Kian, Anderson, Vincent and Murray, in press), heterosexual soccer players (Vincent, Kian and Pedersen, 2011), as well as how sport media reports upon the softening of masculinity in the National Football League (Anderson and Kian, 2012).

It is significant that scholars use the theory to explain inclusive findings within the institution of sport, as competitive, organised sports are traditionally associated with a socially conservative form of gendered expression. However, these changes are not limited to sport – they are also found in educational settings. I document similar behaviours among sixteen-year-old British working-class youth (Anderson, 2011a), American fraternity men (Anderson, 2008), and among British men who dance (Peterson and Anderson, 2012). Gottzén and Kremer-Sadlik (2012) even show inclusive masculinities developing among young fathers in America.

McCormack (2012; McCormack and Anderson, 2010) documents even more significant shifts in the masculine dynamics in British high schools. Using IMT, he demonstrates that there has been an erosion of homophobia and a softening of masculinity among sixteen to eighteen-year-old boys. In addition to documenting the inclusion of LGBT students, he finds that boys engage in a great deal of homosocial tactility, and that they esteem acts of social inclusion. He also develops a class analysis to show that while class does act as a dampener on progressive attitudes, it does not prevent them (McCormack, 2014). Thus, he supports IMT's central argument that these changes are the result of a substantial decrease in homohysteria in the broader youth culture.

Processes

My first masculinities research (on gay male athletes) used hegemonic masculinity theory (Anderson, 2002). I did not desire to use this theory, because my data did not fit in with the theory. However, I was compelled to use hegemonic masculinity theory by the reviewers.

A few years later, in research on White, middle-class, former high school football players, I (Anderson, 2005) first used the term *inclusive masculinity* to theoretically describe the social process concerning the emergence of an archetype of masculinity that undermines the principles of orthodox (read hegemonic) masculine values – yet one that is also esteemed among male peers. I described how a reduction of cultural homophobia challenged the dominance that hegemonic masculinity maintained over heterosexual university athletes, showing two esteemed versions of masculinity: one I labelled as orthodox masculinity (which includes extreme homophobia and misogyny) and the other inclusive masculinity (which does not). However, because two oppositional masculinities, each with equal influence, co-existing within one setting is not consistent with Connell's (1987, 1995) theorizing, it set me to theorize my findings by looking outside of hegemonic masculinity theory.

Over the next few years I conducted a great deal of research on young straight and gay male athletes, and formalised my theory in my (2009) book, *Inclusive masculinity: The changing nature of masculinities.* It was *very* late into the writing of that book in which I conceptualised the notion of homohysteria.

Extensions and applications

Theoretical alterations

My original formulation of both inclusive masculinity theory and homohysteria have not significantly altered since their 2009 conception. However, in 2014 I teamed up with Mark McCormack (McCormack and Anderson, 2014a, 2014b) to thoroughly explore the concept of homohysteria and its utility. We published a lengthy exploration of the concept in a *Sex Roles* forum. Here, four other authors critically examined the concept; one applying it to women (Worthen, 2014).

Crucially, in this reconfiguration we noted that independent operating levels of the two social variables of the awareness of homosexuality and attitudes towards it can create three different cultures. The first concerns high homophobia but low awareness of its existence within that given culture. In such a culture men can be tactile with each other because it's not possible for them to be thought gay because homosexuality is not widely believed possible. We call this a culture of homoerasure. Next is homohysteria: where both a high awareness and antipathy towards homosexuality exist; and finally a culture of inclusivity. Here, awareness remains high, but homophobia low. Within this culture men can return to their homosocial tactile behaviours as they did in a culture of homoerasure. Thus, the model can serve as both a macro-theoretical tool for understanding a given culture within a given timeframe, as well as a tool for explaining cross-cultural comparison. For example, men can walk hand in hand in many Islamic cultures without homosexual suspicion. These ideas are illustrated in Figure 26.1.

While there has been a rapid and expansive uptake of inclusive masculinity theory, criticism also exists (see Roberts, 2014). The criticism around the theory, however, generally regards whether one believes that such a gay-friendly culture exists among young men. Some have tried to disprove the theory by showing that homophobia still exists. But this is accountable by

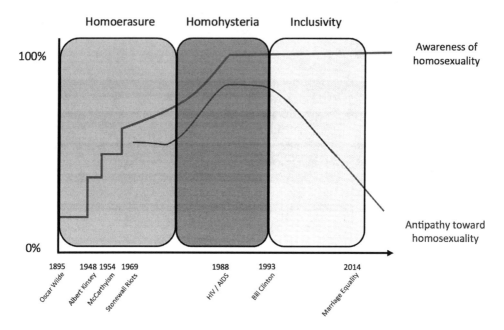

Figure 26.1 Patterns of homohysteria
Source: © Eric Anderson, used with permission.

the theory, which specifically articulates that in locations of high homohysteria, hegemonic theory is correct; but in locations of low homohysteria, inclusive masculinities proliferate.

Theoretical extensions

Finally, I made inclusive masculinity theory simplistic by intention. It was my desire to avoid inaccessible, and oftentimes vague, theorizing by grand theorists. To me a social theory should be simple and have the ability to make a prediction. I shun academic-elitism. Thus, I have made an open invitation to other scholars to examine my theory and add to it (hoping they do so in accessible and practical ways).

McCormack (2011, 2012, 2014) is one scholar who has met this challenge. He recently contributed to inclusive masculinity theory by explicating how popularity is achieved in cultures where bullying and marginalisation are not present. McCormack shows that what makes boys popular is not regulating others, but instead being inclusive and having charisma. Unique to a homohysteria-free culture, he shows that males value the ability to socialise with boys from other groups, including gay youth. Thus, hegemony is replaced by heterogeneity.

Praxis

Inclusive masculinity theory is more of a heuristic tool for understanding the social organisation of masculinity types than it is a tool for making public policy or other practical changes. However, McCormack (2012) has used the concept to argue that our approach towards the attempted eradication of once-homophobic phrases, like 'that's so gay' are ill-fated because they fail to account for the shift towards inclusion of gay youth; and they fail to account for intent of language use. He argues, for example, that telling youth that they are being homophobic for using phrases which they contextualize as having nothing to do with homosexuality engenders homophobia.

Finally, in my book, *21st century jocks: Sporting men and contemporary heterosexualities*, I argue that the evidence of inclusive masculinities is so abundant that to now assume jocks as homophobic is to make a prejudicial statement. Without evidence, the accusation of homophobia is to 'pre-judge' a population; and that is the root of prejudice. This is another attempt to critique the theory. When presenting about my theory at conferences scholars routinely say, 'Well, you collect your data on mostly White, middle class men and that's a small segment of society.' To this I respond that, first, this is not a small, but instead a large majority (in the UK) of society; but second, I ask them: 'So you are saying that Black or lower class boys are more homophobic? Because without evidence to support your proposition that is both racist and classist.' The point is: inclusive masculinity theory emerged from evidence and must therefore be critiqued through an evidence-based approach.

Future directions

While this chapter has provided an exposition of inclusive masculinity theory and its key concept of homohysteria, there are several areas where the theory and concept can be developed further:

1   Homohysteria developed as a concept from empirical research on White male youth, so further research is needed to examine for the influence of race on the relation between decreasing homophobia and heterosexual males' gendered behaviours.
2   Homohysteria was developed on the influence that heterosexual males' attitudes towards homosexual males has on their gendered behaviours. Research investigating the influence of heterosexual women's attitudes and their impact on homohysteria among women would be timely and significant (c.f. Worthen, 2014).
3   While homohysteria conceptualises the links between homophobia and heterosexual men's gendered behaviours, it does not examine the operations of heterosexism or heteronormativity in a culture of inclusivity. If heterosexism conceptualises the social and structural privileging of heterosexuality, and heteronormativity refers to the normalisation of a particular kind of (e.g., White, able-bodied) heterosexual, the intersection of homo-hysteria with these issues requires further research. It seems unlikely that homohysteria is independent of these mechanisms of heterosexual privilege; yet, further qualitative research is needed to understand these intersections.
4   The decline of homophobia in the West is not matched by other parts of the world (Kohut, 2013). Further examination of the simultaneity of these processes to provide a compre-hensive theory about shifting homophobias in a global context would be a significant development. We may, for example, find that increasing gender regulation in countries that are aggressively criminalising homosexuality.
5   We know that (in the UK) young males show high degrees of inclusive masculinity (including kissing, cuddling and loving other men in a homosocial fashion) but the masculinities of younger boys have not been investigated. This calls for more research.

Note

1   This chapter is a reflection on the changing nature of heterosexual masculinities and how we theorize them, including an emphasis on Anderson (2009).

References

Adams, A. (2011) '"Josh wears pink cleats": Inclusive masculinity on the soccer field'. *Journal of Homosexuality*, 58: 579–96.

Adams, A., Anderson, E. and McCormack, M. (2010) 'Establishing and challenging masculinity: The influence of gendered discourses in organized sport'. *Journal of Language and Social Psychology*, 29: 278–300.

Anderson, E. (2000) *Trailblazing: America's first openly gay high school coach*. Hollywood, CA: Alyson Press.

Anderson, E. (2002) 'Openly gay athletes contesting hegemonic masculinity in a homophobic environment'. *Gender & Society*, 16: 860–77.

Anderson, E. (2005) 'Orthodox and inclusive masculinity: Competing masculinities among heterosexual men in a feminized terrain'. *Sociological Perspectives*, 48: 337–55.

Anderson, E. (2008) 'Inclusive masculinity in a fraternal setting'. *Men and Masculinities*, 10: 602–20.

Anderson, E. (2009) *Inclusive masculinity: The changing nature of masculinities*. London: Routledge.

Anderson, E. (2011a) 'Inclusive masculinities of university soccer players in the American Midwest'. *Gender and Education*, 23: 729–44.

Anderson, E. (2011b) 'The rise and fall of western homohysteria'. *Journal of Feminist Scholarship*, 1(1): 80–94.

Anderson, E. (2011c) 'Updating the outcome: Gay athletes, straight teams, and coming out in educationally based sport teams'. *Gender & Society*, 25: 250–68.

Anderson, E. (2014) *21st century jocks: Sporting men and contemporary heterosexuality*. London: Palgrave Macmillan.

Anderson, E., Adams, A. and Rivers, I. (2012) '"I kiss them because I love them": The emergence of heterosexual men kissing in British institutes of education'. *Archives of Sexual Behavior*, 41: 421–30.

Anderson, E. and Bullingham, R. (in press) 'Openly lesbian team sport athletes in an era of decreasing homohysteria'. *International Review for the Sociology of Sport*.

Anderson, E. and Kian, E.M. (2012) 'Examining media contestation of masculinity and head trauma in the National Football League'. *Men and Masculinities*, 15: 152–73.

Anderson, E. and McCormack, M. (in press) 'Cuddling and spooning heteromasculinity and homosocial tactility among student-athletes'. *Men and Masculinities*.

Anderson, E., McCormack, M. and Lee, H. (2012) 'Male team sport hazing initiations in a culture of decreasing homohysteria'. *Journal of Adolescent Research*, 27: 427–48.

Anderson, E. and McGuire, R. (2010) 'Inclusive masculinity theory and the gendered politics of men's rugby'. *Journal of Gender Studies*, 19: 249–61.

Cashmore, E. and Cleland, J. (2012) 'Fans, homophobia and masculinities in association football: Evidence of a more inclusive environment'. *The British Journal of Sociology*, 63: 370–87.

Cavalier, E.S. (2011) 'Men at sport: Gay men's experiences in the sport workplace'. *Journal of Homosexuality*, 58: 626–46.

Connell, R.W. (1987) *Gender and power: Society, the person and sexual politics*. Palo Alto, CA: Stanford University Press.

Connell, R.W. (1995) *Masculinities*. Berkeley, CA: University of California Press.

Dashper, K. (2012) '"Dressage is full of queens!" Masculinity, sexuality and equestrian sport'. *Sociology*, 46: 1109–24.

Dean, J.J. (2013) 'Heterosexual masculinities, anti-homophobias, and shifts in hegemonic masculinity: The identity practices of Black and White heterosexual men'. *The Sociological Quarterly*, 54: 534–60.

Drummond, M.J., Filiault, S.M., Anderson, E. and Jeffries, D. (in press) 'Homosocial intimacy among Australian undergraduate men'. *Journal of Sociology*.

Floyd, K. (2000) 'Affectionate same-sex touch: The influence of homophobia on observers' perceptions'. *The Journal of Social Psychology*, 140: 774–88.

Gottzén, L. and Kremer-Sadlik, T. (2012) 'Fatherhood and youth sports: A balancing act between care and expectations'. *Gender & Society*, 26: 639–64.

Ibson, J. (2002) *Picturing men: A century of male relationships in everyday American photography*. Washington, DC: Smithsonian Institution Press.

Kian, E.T.M. and Anderson, E. (2009) 'John Amaechi: Changing the way sport reporters examine gay athletes'. *Journal of Homosexuality*, 56: 799–818.

Kian, E.M., Anderson, E., Vincent, J. and Murray, R. (in press) 'Sport journalists' views on gay men in sport, society and within sport media'. *International Review for the Sociology of Sport*.

Kohut, H. (2013) *The analysis of the self: A systematic approach to the psychoanalytic treatment of narcissistic personality disorders*. Chicago, IL: University of Chicago Press.

Magrath, R., Anderson, E. and Roberts, S. (in press) 'On the door-step of equality: Attitudes toward gay athletes among academy-level footballers'. *International Review for the Sociology of Sport*.

McCormack, M. (2011) 'Hierarchy without hegemony: Locating boys in an inclusive school setting'. *Sociological Perspectives*, *54*(1): 83–101.

McCormack, M. (2012) *The declining significance of homophobia: How teenage boys are redefining masculinity and heterosexuality*. Oxford, UK: Oxford University Press.

McCormack, M. (2014) 'The intersection of youth masculinities, decreasing homophobia and class: An ethnography'. *The British Journal of Sociology*, *65*: 130–49.

McCormack, M. and Anderson, E. (2010) '"It's just not acceptable any more": The erosion of homophobia and the softening of masculinity at an English sixth form'. *Sociology*, *44*: 843–59.

McCormack, M. and Anderson, E. (2014a) 'The influence of declining homophobia on men's gender in the United States: An argument for the study of homohysteria'. *Sex Roles*, *71*: 109–20.

McCormack, M. and Anderson, E. (2014b) 'Homohysteria: definitions, context and intersectionality'. *Sex Roles*, *71*: 152–8.

Morris, M. and Anderson, E. (in press). '"Charlie is so cool like": Authenticity, popularity and inclusive masculinity on YouTube'. *Sociology*.

Peterson, G.T. (2011) 'Clubbing masculinities: Gender shifts in gay men's dance floor choreographies'. *Journal of Homosexuality*, *58*: 608–25.

Peterson, G.T. and Anderson, E. (2012) 'The performance of softer masculinities on the university dance floor'. *The Journal of Men's Studies*, *20*(1): 3–15.

Plummer, D. (1999) *One of the boys: Masculinity, homophobia, and modern manhood*. London: Routledge.

Roberts, S. (2013) 'Boys will be boys . . . won't they? Change and continuities in contemporary young working-class masculinities'. *Sociology*, *47*: 671–86.

Roberts, S. (ed.) (2014) *Debating modern masculinities: Change, continuity, crisis?* London: Palgrave Macmillan.

Southall, R.M., Nagel, M.S., Anderson, E., Polite, F.G. and Southall, C. (2009) 'An investigation of male college athletes' attitudes toward sexual-orientation'. *Journal of Issues in Intercollegiate Athletics*, *2009*: 62–77.

Southall, R., Anderson, E., Southall, C., Nagel, M. and Polite, F. (2011) 'An investigation of the relationship between college athletes' ethnicity and sexual-orientation attitudes'. *Ethnicity and Racial Studies*, *34*: 293–313.

Vincent, J., Kian, E. and Pedersen, P.M. (2011) 'Flying the flag: Gender and national identity in English newspapers during the 2006 World Cup'. *Soccer & Society*, *12*: 613–32.

Worthen, M.G. (2014) 'The cultural significance of homophobia on heterosexual women's gendered experiences in the United States: A commentary'. *Sex Roles*, *71*: 141–51.

Applying inclusive masculinity theory

Jamie Cleland[1]

While inclusive masculinity theory researchers have tended to focus on a fairly narrow age group of sixteen- to twenty-five-year-old young men, my research has sought to widen this scope to show that men of all ages are holding more liberal and inclusive views towards sexuality in professional football. To contextualise a shift in the culture of football from the 1980s to more contemporary times, the homohysteric environment that Anderson (2009) refers to in the 1980s was present within football when black British footballer, Justin Fashanu, became the first professional to come out in 1990. Not only did he receive racist abuse in a period of heightened racism, but he was also ostracised by fans, the media, teammates and even his own brother, John, who was also a professional footballer. This case illustrated how football was a homophobic (as well as racist) institution: a place where manhood seemed to be in constant need of revalidation.

I first became aware of inclusive masculinity theory in 2010 after analysing the findings of 3,500 football supporters and players towards the presence of gay footballers. This was in response to the English Football Association dropping a campaign focusing on homophobia as it was deemed that the game was not ready for one to take place. This decision provided an opportunity to analyse the perception that the authorities, fans, clubs, agents, media and the players were part of a homophobic environment that placed barriers on accepting gay footballers. Rather than demonstrate orthodox views towards sexuality, however, 93 per cent of the participants highlighted a decreasing culture of homophobia in football by expressing their support for a gay player who should only be judged on his performance on the field of play (Cashmore and Cleland, 2012). Since then, subsequent research on sexuality in professional football has found similar evidence of decreasing cultural homophobia in online football fan forums (Cleland, 2015) and within the print media that reflected on Anton Hysén (a lower league semi-professional player in Sweden) coming out in March 2011 (Cleland, 2014).

Inclusive masculinity theory has therefore provided a theoretical context to my findings that have outlined how boys and men hold more liberal views and behavioural attitudes than had previously been the case. A change in culture has also been illustrated by a small number of professional players following Hysén and coming out to widespread support. For example, Robbie Rogers initially retired aged twenty-five when he came out in January 2013 after being released by Leeds United (he has since reversed this decision and plays in Major League Soccer for LA Galaxy in the United States), while in January 2014, former German midfielder Thomas Hitzlsperger announced that he was gay. Despite notable progress since the 1990s, however, there continues to be examples of orthodox views remaining in the culture of football as the need to retain masculine capital continues to play a prominent role in the everyday practice for some individuals. When examples like this occur, it provides another opportunity where inclusive masculinity theory can be applied to further outline significant cultural changes that render these views obsolete in what many refer to as the people's game.

Note

1   Jamie Cleland is with the Department of Social Sciences at Loughborough University.

References

Anderson, E. (2009) *Inclusive masculinity: The changing nature of masculinities.* New York: Routledge.

Cashmore, E. and Cleland, J. (2012) 'Fans, homophobia and masculinities in association football: Evidence of a more inclusive environment'. *British Journal of Sociology, 63:* 370–87.

Cleland, J. (2014) 'Association football and the representation of homosexuality by the print media: A case study of Anton Hysén'. *Journal of Homosexuality, 61:* 1269–87.

Cleland, J. (2015) 'Discussing homosexuality on association football fan message boards: A changing cultural context'. *International Review for the Sociology of Sport, 50:* 125–40.

27

THIS WAY . . . THIS EXPLAINS MY REALITY

Critical Race Theory in sport and leisure[1]

Kevin Hylton

Introduction

In 2005 Michael Banton wrote a retrospective on fifty-five years of research in sociology (Banton, 2005). In particular his work focused on ethnic and racial studies. Widely regarded as one of the leading international sociologists, his reflections on his approaches to the sociology of 'race' and ethnic relations was published in the same year that I was challenging academics in the sociology of sport and leisure to engage in a more inclusive and critical exposition of racialised phenomena (Hylton, 2005). Some of the questions that I was asking included: (a) at what point will those in the field recognise that a narrow academic focus will leave them with charges of repetition and theoretical myopia; (b) do academics in the field recognise that even critical theories with a social justice focus can ignore 'race'; and (c) are academics in the field willing to incorporate other marginalised ideas and voices to address these imbalances? In regards to the academy, my ire was focused on how sport and leisure studies, a necessarily multidisciplinary field, marginalised specific issues of 'race' and racism.

My paper focusing on Critical Race Theory (CRT) in *Leisure Studies* (Hylton, 2005) consisted of three sections, concluding with 'a call to sport and leisure theorists and policymakers to centralize "race", racism, and race equality in their everyday considerations' (p. 94). The first part of the paper explored the shared racial justice agenda of CRT and other areas of ethnic and racial studies. The paper unpacked the fundamentals of CRT's precepts as a useful introductory point for readers new to the framework. As a device to emphasise how a critical 'race'-centered approach can strengthen social theorizing, the paper then moved on to the second section that mapped out the flawed analogous developments of critical theory in sport and leisure sociology and the North American based critical legal studies, as both were inconsistent in their treatment of 'race' in their analyses. In the final part of the paper CRT is advanced as:

> A worthy theoretical framework from which to interrogate issues of 'race', and to refocus the theoretical lens onto anti-oppressive theory, race equality, and related areas in sport and leisure studies.
>
> *(Hylton, 2005, p. 82)*

I haven't shifted from this position, though I wish to make the point firmly that in attempting to develop theoretically informed interventions one is bound to make mistakes (Banton, 2005). I also wish to make a few brief related points: (a) CRT is *not a theory* but a *framework*, which I outline in this paper, and elsewhere, through the use of precepts or tenets (Hylton, 2009, 2012); (b) though 'race' and racism are central, CRT has a larger anti-essentialist focus to contest other forms of subordination; and (c) CRT uses the term 'race' that incorporates discourses of ethnicity and urges all to use racialised terminology politically, pragmatically and under advisement.

In many ways, I have seen CRT gain a foothold and flourish at conferences, in academic journals and postgraduate studies across a plethora of disciplines; indeed, *BritCrit*, the substantive application of CRT in the UK, has become more conspicuous (Gillborn, 2011). Yet there will still remain criticism of the place of intersecting identities and forms of oppression that are being de-centred, or worse, devalued in opposition to 'race'. Even though CRT is an anti-essentialist framework that embraces intersectionality and all forms of social justice agendas, there will inevitably be complaints of topics that have not yet *significantly emerged* in some areas using this *emerging framework*.

In 2005 I summarised precepts of CRT as: (a) the centralising of 'race' and racism at the same time as recognising their connection with other forms of subordination and oppression; (b) challenges to traditional dominant ideologies around objectivity, meritocracy, colourblindness, race-neutrality and equal opportunity; (c) a clear commitment to social justice that incorporates elements of liberation and transformation; (d) centralising the marginalised voice; and (e) necessarily transdisciplinary. These are not exhaustive precepts, though are popular in most theorizing of this framework. If sociology has taught us anything it is that 'race' has no foundation in science and remains a social construction. However, if history has taught us anything it is that 'race' is a lived reality, and it is this fundamental point that forces CRT to recognise its constructed nature while pragmatically putting racialisation and racism in the sights of these activist scholars. CRT is distinctive because it centres 'race' and racism where other critical perspectives are more circumspect in their pursuits of social justice. Critical race theorists ensure that the salience of 'race' is recognised and racism is disrupted so as to ensure racial justice or even racial transformations become goals in the way we *do business* (Delgado and Stefancic, 2001).

CRT's starting point is that society is ridden with racisms that have been explained historically, politically, culturally, economically and epistemologically. Foundational writers Richard Delgado and Jean Stefancic (2001) are typical of critical race theorists' expositions on racism when they state that racism is 'Ordinary, not aberrational–"normal science," the usual way society does business, the common, everyday experience of most people of color' (p. 7; see also Crenshaw, Taylor, Gillborn and Ladson-Billings, 2009; Dixson and Rousseau, 2006; Gillborn, 2009). Similarly, MacPherson's (1999) conclusion at the end of his enquiry into racism in the London Metropolitan Police reinforced a CRT viewpoint when he stated that, 'there must be an unequivocal acceptance that the problem actually exists as a prerequisite to addressing it successfully' (p. 652). For social transformation to occur, this must be understood.

Simple conceptions of racism as, for example, overt and covert, do not fully engage the sophistication of its manifestations in society; ergo sport and leisure. These racial processes and formations (Omi and Winant, 1994; Winant, 2001) are experienced discursively, materially or affectively, ranging from actual events to those that are felt. Racisms can be viewed simply as perceived or more comprehensively as a cancerous social concern that affects all of us. Though this intellectual debate must be taken seriously it is important that scholarly gymnastics make us limber in a practical sense to challenge historical racialised inequalities in the everyday. Like Macpherson (1999) cautioned, it is imperative not to be stymied by these debates and to,

'Take the view that the important issue now is to stop arguing about definitions and do something about the racism' (p. 650).

Racism in sport

Racism in sport is a serious contemporary issue and one that, on any given day, is likely to produce multiple examples of global controversies. Today it is the turn of Italy's FA President, Carlo Tavecchio, to be banned from any position within European football body UEFA as a result of making racist remarks in his campaign for the FIGC presidency. Reuters reports that his remarks were based upon a fictitious African player when he said:

> In England, they identify the players coming in and, if they are professional, they are allowed to play [. . .] Here instead we get 'Opti Poba', who previously ate bananas and then suddenly becomes a first-team player with Lazio.
>
> *(Homewood, 2014)*

Other recent and sensational events that fall into this category include NBA Clippers owner Donald Sterling, fined $2.5 million USD and banned from owning an NBA franchise because of the cynical racism he inadvertently divulged to the world via a telephone conversation with his partner (Barrabi, 2014). The presence of racism in sport and society is obvious to many, and Bondy (2014), of the *New York Daily News*, argues that they know of at least ten of the 'most egregious examples still plaguing the athletic field and the boardrooms'. I have summarised Bondy's arguments in Table 27.1.

It is overly simplistic to suggest that racism is only the vestige of the far right and/or hooligans, though we should be clear that there were periods where their presence was much more conspicuous. One thing we see less of in the professional domain internationally, but specifically where it comes to football in the UK, is the racist violence that blighted stadia in the 1970s–80s. However, a review of the Runnymede Trust's[2] bulletin reports reveals the inter-generational prevalence of 'race' and racism in sport, leisure and society. One year after the European Parliament's Committee of Enquiry into the rise of fascism and racism in Europe, we witnessed horrific scenes in the Heysel stadium in Brussels where thirty-nine people died, fuelled by such bigotry (RunnymedeTrust, 1985a). Football stadia, the recruiting grounds for neo-Nazis such as the National Front (NF), found the NF distributing racist literature urging their followers to 'kill the n>**s' (RunnymedeTrust, 1987). Some of the leaflets they distributed at Heysel were asking questions of supporters that are disturbingly being heard today. 'One leaflet at Heysel entitled *Unemployment* asked, "Have you been thrown on the scrapheap by foreign imports?"' (RunnymedeTrust, 1985a, p. 7).

Politics of 'race' shift over time, though it may disturb some how closely aligned elements of the far-right NF discourse from the racist violence in sport from the 1980s are still with today's major political parties. Labour wish to secure borders, crack down on immigrants undercutting British workers, and the Tories wish to implement a new hardline immigration strategy. The notion of sport as a prism on society becomes clearer at these times.

The mingling of British neo-Nazis and Italian fascists before Liverpool v. Juventus at Heysel in 1985 should not be lost on those in football today who feel that fascism is acceptable. It was the Tyneside and District Antifascist Association in 1985 that called for a total ban on the National Front at football matches, as these activities had been ignored for so long, yet it was on neighbouring Wearside in 2013 when an openly fascist manager was taken on by Sunderland Football Club. The controversy following Paolo Di Canio's management contracts at both

Table 27.1 Current examples of racism in sport

Issue	Explanation
1	Ice hockey fans on the internet – the abuse that black players endure on social media is something relatively new, and truly disgusting. When Wayne Simmonds was creating problems for the Rangers in the first round of the playoffs, a torrent of racist tweets hit the web.
2	Lack of translators for Spanish-speaking players.
3	Redskins – The NFL's franchise in Washington continues to churn out public relations releases, citing surveys that indicate Native Americans don't really mind the obviously offensive nickname.
4	Graduation rate for black college athletes – Top college basketball and football programmes continue to recruit and then exploit black athletes without proper academic counselling. The majority who don't make it will need to find a different profession – without a college degree. At Wisconsin they reported a 100 per cent graduation rate among its white basketball players and a 0 per cent rate among its black players.
5	Stereotypes of Asian players – Asians and Asian Americans are pigeonholed too often by sport. They're supposed to be good at golf, baseball, tennis and figure skating, but not at basketball or football.
6	The coverage of black players in the media – The cultural gap remains huge between the largely white media that cover professional sport and the largely black population of players in football and basketball.
7	Owners – Until ownership of professional sports teams becomes more diverse there can never be a trickle-down effect. Too many white owners employ too many white vice presidents who employ too many white general managers.
8	Upper management in baseball
9	Cleveland Indians baseball team mascot
10	European football fans – Football supporters in Spain, Italy, Holland and all over Eastern Europe have demonstrated over the years they are the most ignorant bunch of all. Crowd behaviour was awful at Euro 2012 in Poland and Ukraine. Then last year, players from AC Milan courageously walked off the field in Lombardy after spectators there uttered derisive chants at Ghanian-German player Kevin-Prince Boateng. Most recently, Barcelona's Dani Alves tried to defuse matters by picking up a banana thrown at him by a Villarreal fan (who was arrested), peeling it and eating it before he took a corner kick.

Source: Based on summary of Bondy (2014).

Swindon FC and Sunderland were prompted by those unwilling for history and politics to remain forgotten in the direction they pointed their moral compass. The European Union Fundamental Rights Agency's (FRA, 2010) study on racism, ethnic discrimination and exclusion of migrants and minorities in sport found that racism, anti-Semitism and anti-gypsyism were consistent across all twenty-seven-member nations. As we go back and forwards in decades, and as the social and political climate change, we can see that racism and policy responses in and through sport tangle with recurrent issues. Integration, Xenophobia, Far Right Politics, Racist Violence and even Fascism reminds us that the genealogy of these ideas and politics metamorphosise into new discourses. For example, in 1985 The Runnymede Trust (RunnymedeTrust, 1985b) reported on an article in the *Telegraph* that a Chelsea fan was fined £100 for wearing a T-shirt that read: 'Chelsea's Yid-busters Coming Soon to Rid The World'.[3]

This was an obvious anti-Semitic dig at rivals Tottenham Hotspur (Spurs) whose history of attracting Jewish fans has made them a target for rivals. Twenty-nine years later in 2014 the tensions continue and are more complex, as Spurs fans express a fondness for the use of self-identifying chants such as *Yid Army!* and *Yiddo!* that could easily be read as anti-Semitic. Spurs are in the middle of a heated debate as to who can use the word Yid; is it offensive when reclaimed by Spurs fans? Spurs fans in 2014, as well as rival supporters, risk being prosecuted for anti-Semitic chants just as the Chelsea fan was two decades earlier. Prime Minister David Cameron added to the debate that it was acceptable for Spurs fans to chant the word, even after the Football Association warned that fans could face criminal charges and long banning orders (Johnson, 2013; TelegraphSport, 2013). Here, two major stakeholders in the race equality landscape of sport are at complete odds and are another example of the significance and complexities of 'race' and racism in sport. Furthermore, sport demonstrates here how contemporary racialised issues of terminology, identities, politics/policy and racist intent in the use of language abound as ideas are constructed and reworked.

In an example where intent was unequivocal, Norman Tebbit used sport as a starting point for another famous discussion on integration in 1990 as he argued, 'if you don't support the national team where you are living then you couldn't be integrated into that society' (RunnymedeTrust, 1990). Tebbit used the sport of cricket to make this point and in particular targeted south Asian communities to challenge their validity as productive and integrated citizens. This *Loyalty Test* was not well received, yet it further demonstrates that over the years sport and leisure spaces have emphasised the broader divisions we see every day while, as with the Spurs chants, not necessarily resolving them. Racial abuse in sport is still rife and the Runnymede Trust has recorded many incidents and responses to them. For example, soon after 1993, when the Commission for Racial Equality launched its *Let's Kick Racism Out of Football* campaign (now Kick it Out), Derby County players Gary Charles and Paul Williams were substituted at Millwall after receiving racist abuse (RunnymedeTrust, 1994); a BNP councillor had also just been elected in the Isle of Dogs.[4] Interestingly, Brendan Batson, spokesperson for the Professional Footballers Association, felt that taking the players off was a backward step and that the players should have been kept on the pitch. However, two decades later in 2013 many ex-players and football governing bodies, lauded as heroic the action by Kevin Prince Boateng who walked off the pitch for being racially abused by spectators as he played for AC Milan against Pro Patria. Ideas and tolerances shift and move on yet 'race' and racism remain significant.

In 1999, I wrote a paper for *The Leisure Manager* entitled 'Where are the Black leisure managers?' (Hylton, 1999). I am disappointed that over fifteen years later the same questions are being asked. As Chelsea football club manager, Jose Mourinho, is roundly condemned by FIFA for saying there is no racism in football (Ackerman, 2014), his naivety and White privilege become exposed. The discourse of 'race' in sport has retained the equivalence of Guinier and Torres' (2003) 'Miner's Canary' as it continues to be reiterated in discussions of leadership, management and coaching, the media, local government, pedagogy, science, migration and research, to name a few. A miner's canary was used in the past to detect levels of poisonous gasses in mines and the presence of the canary meant the presence of this danger. The continued presence of 'race' as a starting point to focus critical 'race' scholars on such projects, as CRT's key writings develop fluidly to engage new and challenging racialised phenomena in sport, denotes the pernicious presence of racism in society that permeates it. The resilience of 'race' and more specifically, racialised issues, processes and formations to manifest themselves inter-generationally, internationally, intersectionally, culturally, politically, economically and socially force a constant revisioning of ways to disrupt their insidious onslaught.

Leading up to and subsequent to the *Leisure Studies* paper in 2005, part of my challenge has involved balancing the development of CRT as a theoretical framework to explain and challenge more complex subjects. In the vein of Banton's (2005) urgings that sociologists need to make their theories less abstract and to consider more diligently 'the adequacy of the explanations of problems that can be derived from theories' (p. 466), I have developed and applied CRT in my work through examinations of theories of education and 'race' (Hylton, Pilkington, Warmington and Housee, 2011; Pilkington, Housee and Hylton, 2009); 'race' and culture in tourism and events (Hylton and Chakrabarty, 2011); social capital and social integration (Hylton, 2008, 2010b); football studies (Hylton, 2013, 2014; Long, Hylton, Welch and Dart, 2000); Olympism (Hylton and Morpeth, 2009, 2012, 2014); antiracism, sport, and its development (Hylton, 2010a, 2011); migration (Long, Hylton and Spracklen, 2014; Spracklen, Long and Hylton, 2014); methodologies (Hylton, 2012); and Whiteness (Hylton and Lawrence, 2015; Long and Hylton, 2002). At the same time, it is important not to lose sight of the *fact of racism* and the constant need to restate the issues for new generations of policymakers, practitioners and students that often require 'old wine in new bottles'. Hence, my policy- and practice-oriented research informed by CRT have included studies for a range of national governing bodies, government departments and local authorities. The difficulty of continuing any sociological development is the requirement to engage intellectual pursuits while ensuring they are couched in lived realities. Critical Race Theory's movement towards social justice cannot be purely theoretical, even though theoretical debates can be had, neither can it be purely interventionist because of our need to observe thoughtful action.

Academics with an interest in ethnic and racial studies in sport and leisure would draw similar conclusions to me in the *Leisure Studies* paper that:

> The resultant outcome of using a CRT perspective is likely to lead towards a resistance to a passive reproduction of the established practices, knowledge and resources, that make up the social conditions that marginalize 'race' as a core factor in the way we manage and experience our sport and leisure.
>
> *(Hylton, 2005, p. 81)*

Research and writing informed by CRT have become widespread and more common than in the 2000s. They definitely outstrip the foundations that I based my initial ideas on in the 1980s and that developed into the application of CRT in my doctoral studies in the 1990s (Hylton, 2003). For many, CRT's attraction comes from its ability to articulate and explain the lived realities of racialised and minoritised actors. Just as other theoretical standpoints enable a more accurate and honest telling of social relations from the perspective of the classed, gendered or disempowered in other ways, CRT offers a pragmatic critical framework that facilitates different uses and approaches. This framework can be encapsulated in what I referred to as precepts, sometimes tenets, and it is to these issues that I now turn.

Critical race theory

I often describe journeys to CRT in ontological terms. CRT is a way to say *this way . . . this explains my reality . . . these realities*. CRT's framework enables an articulation of issues that reflect a lived experience. A lived experience where activist scholars, such as Derek Bell (Bell, 1987), Patricia Williams (Williams, 1997), Gloria Ladson-Billings (Ladson-Billings, 1997) and Charles Mills (Mills, 1997), begin much of their work. From such an experiential starting point, they then apply razor-sharp critiques to challenge embedded racial inequalities in the law and wider society (Bell), colourblindness (Williams), racialised inequalities in education (Ladson-Billings) and 'race' and White racism (Mills). Similarly, my doctoral thesis emerged out of my unease at the glass ceiling in the local authority that I was working in as an innercity community sport development officer, and a desire for social justice and transformation. I had few Black role models in my authority and felt further isolated in meetings in and out of my organisation. In conducting graduate degree research across a number of authorities, I found, scattered across other local authorities, similar stories from Black officers where 'race' and racism affected their opportunities and well-being in the workplace. Yet at the same time I needed to establish what institutionalised processes framed and perhaps even caused these racial formations. At that point I began my PhD journey.

Using CRT, I was able to explore issues that were being ignored or marginalised, thus enabling me to challenge orthodoxies in sport and leisure settings. The very process of asking new questions from a particular social location, identifying the power-to-knowledge dynamic, theoretical and methodological colourblindness forced an uncomfortable framing of the academic landscape and persuasive reasons for change. Change for the academy was matched by the demystifying of ideas concerning sport for all and meritocracy in local government as equal opportunities and race equality policies failed to be implemented in practice, thus impacting minoritised participants and practitioners in terms of access, recruitment, retention and progression (Hylton, 2003). The work had to cross existing theoretical fields in a transdisciplinary fashion. Though not exhaustive, it included the policy sciences, sociology, community studies, ethnic and racial studies, critical Whiteness studies, Black feminism and gender studies, urban studies and human resource management. Using CRT to centre 'race' meant that a transdisciplinary critique enabled a more persuasive need for research on 'race'. Here the limitations of the past were surpassed by a theoretical approach that shifted the marginalised voice of Black academics and 'race' research from the margins to the centre.

My thesis and subsequent work for an antiracism in sport organisation, Kick it Out, forced me to more diligently consider the place of Whiteness, White privilege and White supremacy in sport and leisure (Hylton, 2009; Hylton and Lawrence, 2015; Long and Hylton, 2002; Long *et al.*, 2000). Related applied research on the nature and extent of racism in grassroots football revealed processes that privileged Whiteness in local government that systematically ignores historical inequalities and made apparent the snowy peaks at senior levels. This ranged from the Whiteness of league officials and disciplinary panels, county officers and racism on and off the pitch that went unpunished, often leading to the internalisation of racism by Black players. For instance some predominantly Black teams would not represent themselves at disciplinary hearings because they knew that they would feel alienated as they would not see anyone who looked like themselves across the table, and therefore faced a double-jeopardy (i.e., if they defend a fine and are found guilty they receive an additional fine). However, if they do not turn up for a disciplinary hearing, the panel will deem them guilty. The perception of racial hierarchies and racialised inequalities were 'accepted' and the 'game played' accordingly to the detriment of Black and minoritised players.

A concern with racism and the regular suspicion towards its nature and extent from academic, practitioner and policy circles has led me to aim to be more specific about not only naming racism(s) but also it is imperative to explain the specific conditions under which particular forms of racism thrive in sport and leisure arenas. For example, in *'Race' and sport: Critical Race Theory* (Hylton, 2009: 86), I move to illustrate how racial practices are recreated while naming their specific incarnations as (a) racialisation and mediated racial identities, (b) Whitecentrism, (c) the myth of difference and mimetic accuracy and (d) the myth of assimilation and enlightened racism. Though not mutually exclusive, my use of a CRT lens enabled an analysis able to persuasively explain how the print media reproduced racialised ideologies while naming the different techniques. Similarly a critique of the London 2012 Olympic Games through the lens of interest convergence (Hylton and Morpeth, 2012) enabled a telling of how state and White interests merged with those Black and minoritised communities in East London who were overdue infrastructure improvements and employment opportunities (see Bell, 1980; Gillborn, 2009). Such observations caution against superficial approaches to sport policymaking where hubris and plain idealism with a one-off event alone cannot purport to address the embedded racialised inequalities in sport and wider society.

Conclusion

As I continue to develop ideas that use CRT and its related concepts, I find it imperative to work through processes of naming, describing and disrupting 'race', racialisation and racism in relation to how they are experienced; for example, as microaggressions in the everyday (Burdsey, 2011; Hylton, 2010a, 2011). As a reflexive and non-dogmatic framework, CRT encourages a critique of those on the political Left as much as they do on the Right. To this end, I utilise microaggressions as a descriptive and explanatory technique to critique loose approaches to anti-racism. The question *'Anti-What?'* in context of challenging antiracists to be clear about *what they are against* shores up the efficacy of their campaigns and interventions as they use thoughtful action against racism rather than the less focused knee-jerk responses we sometimes witness. Being critical of those on the Left as well as the Right strengthens our activist-scholarship, antiracist interventions, and continues the agenda to undermine racism.

I agree with Banton that in attempting to develop theoretically informed interventions, one is bound to make mistakes (Banton, 2005). As we work reflexively and critically we cannot escape our subjectivities. As we make decisions to research and write we are also making inadvertent decisions to exclude subjects that could potentially be incorporated into these analyses. Yet it is this process of trying to improve explanations that, 'Obliges scientists to improve their conceptual armoury . . .' (Banton, 2005, p. 466).

Notes

1 This chapter is a reflection on Hylton (2005) and the work related to it.
2 The UK's foremost Black think-tank.
3 'Yid' is an abbreviation of the word 'Yiddish', a language used by Jews in central and Eastern Europe. The term is often used in the shortened version as a derogatory term.
4 Millwall is an area in London, in the Isle of Dogs, in the London Borough of Tower Hamlets.

References

Ackerman, N. (2014, 9 October, 2014) 'Jose Mourinho blasted for racism stance by FIFA vice-president Jeffrey Webb'. Available at http://bleacherreport.com/articles/2225671-jose-mourinho-blasted-for-racism-stance-by-fifa-vice-president-jeffrey-webb (accessed on 10 October, 2014).

Banton, M. (2005) 'Finding, and correcting, my mistakes'. *Sociology, 39*: 463–79.

Barrabi, T. (2014) '7 quotes from Donald Sterling's interview with Anderson Cooper about racism, Magic Johnson and V. Stiviano'. Available at www.ibtimes.com/17-quotes-donald-sterlings-interview-anderson-cooper-about-racism-magic-johnson-v-stiviano-1583621 (accessed on 1 September, 2014).

Bell, D. (1980) '*Brown v. Board of Education* and the interest convergence dilemma'. *Harvard Law Review, 93*: 518–33.

Bell, D. (1987) *And we are not saved: The elusive quest for racial justice.* New York: Basic Books.

Bondy, P. (2014) '10 places where racism is still a major issue in sports'. Available at www.nydailynews.com/sports/bondy-10-places-racism-major-issue-sport-article-1.1778178 (accessed on 1 September, 2014).

Burdsey, D. (2011) 'That joke isn't funny anymore: Racial microaggressions, colour-blind ideology an the mitigation of racism in english men's first class cricket'. *Sociology of Sport Journal, 28*: 261–83.

Crenshaw, K., Taylor, E., Gillborn, D. and Ladson-Billings, G. (2009) *Foundations of Critical Race Theory in education.* New York: Routledge.

Delgado, R. and Stefancic, J. (2001) *Critical Race Theory: An introduction.* New York: New York University Press.

Dixson, A.D. and Rousseau, C.K. (2006) *Critical Race Theory in education: All God's children got a song.* New York: Routledge.

FRA (2010) *Racism, ethnic discrimination and exclusion of migrants and minorities in sport: A comparative overview of the situation in the European Union.* Schwarzenbergplatz 11: European Union Agency for Fundamental Rights.

Gillborn, D. (2009) *Racism and education: Coincidence or conspiracy?* London: Routledge.

Gillborn, D. (2011) 'Once upon a time in the UK: Race, class, hope and Whiteness in the Academy (personal reflections on the birth of "BritCrit")'. In K. Hylton, A. Pilkington, P. Warmington and S. Housee (eds) *Atlantic crossings: International dialogues on Critical Race Theory* (pp. 21–38). Birmingham: CSAP/Higher Education Academy.

Guinier, L. and Torres, G. (2003) *The miner's canary: Enlisting race, resisting power, transforming democracy.* Cambridge, MA: Harvard University Press.

Homewood, B. (2014) 'Italian FA chief barred from UEFA over "banana" comment'. Available at http://uk. reuters.com/article/2014/10/07/uk-soccer-italy-racism-idUKKCN0HW1GM20141007 (accessed on 1 September, 2014).

Hylton, K. (1999) 'Where are the Black leisure managers?' *The Leisure Manager, 17:* 32–4.

Hylton, K. (2003) 'Local government, "race" and sports policy implementation: Demystifying equal opportunities in local government'. PhD thesis, Leeds Metropolitan University, Leeds.

Hylton, K. (2005) 'Race, sport and leisure: Lessons from Critical Race Theory'. *Leisure Studies, 24:* 81–98.

Hylton, K. (2008) 'Race, equality and sport networks: Social capital links'. In M. Nicholson and R. Hoye (eds) *Sport and social capital* (pp. 257–83). Oxford, UK: Elsevier.

Hylton, K. (2009) *'Race' and sport: Critical Race Theory.* London: Routledge.

Hylton, K. (2010a) 'How a turn to critical race theory can contribute to our understanding of "race", racism and anti-racism in sport'. *International Review for the Sociology of Sport, 45:* 225–354.

Hylton, K. (2010b) 'Social integration through sport'. In B. Houlihan and M. Green (eds) *Routledge international handbook of sports development* (pp. 100–13). London: Routledge.

Hylton, K. (2011) 'Too radical? Critical Race Theory and sport against racism Ireland'. In J. Long and K. Spracklen (eds) *Sport and challenges to racism* (pp. 229–46). London: Routledge.

Hylton, K. (2012) 'Talk the talk, walk the walk: Defining Critical Race Theory in research'. *Race, Ethnicity and Education, 15:* 23–41.

Hylton, K. (2013) '"Race", racism and international football'. In P. Mason (ed.) *Encyclopedia of 'race' and racism.* Detroit, MI: MacMillan Reference.

Hylton, K. (2014) '"Race", racism and football'. In J. Hyughson, J. MacGuire, K. Moore and R. Spaaij (eds) *Routledge handbook of football studies.* London: Routledge.

Hylton, K. and Chakrabarty, N. (2011) '"Race" and culture in tourism, leisure and events. *Journal of Policy Research into Tourism Leisure and Events, 3*(2): 105–08.

Hylton, K. and Lawrence, S. (2015) 'Reading Ronaldo: Contingent Whiteness in the football media'. *Soccer and Society, 16:* 765–82.

Hylton, K. and Morpeth, N.D. (2009) '"Race", East London and the 2012 Olympics'. In I. MacRury and G. Poynter (eds) *Olympic cities – 2012 and the remaking of East London* (pp. 219–29). London: Ashgate.

Hylton, K. and Morpeth, N.D. (2012) 'London 2012: "Race" Matters, and the East End'. *International Journal of Sport Policy & Politics, 4*(2): 1–18.

Hylton, K. and Morpeth, N.D. (2014) '"Race" Matters, and the East End'. In D. Bloyce and A. Smith (eds) *The 'Olympic and Paralympic' effect on public policy.* London: Routledge.

Hylton, K., Pilkington, A., Warmington, P. and Housee, S. (eds) (2011). *Atlantic crossings: International dialogues on critical race theory.* Birmingham: CSAP/Higher Education Academy.

Johnson, D. (2013, 3 October) 'Tottenham Hotspur and West Ham United supporters could be arrested for chanting "Yid", Met warns'. *The Daily Telegraph.* Available at www.telegraph.co.uk/sport/football/teams/tottenham-hotspur/10353969/Tottenham-Hotspur-and-West-Ham-United-supporters-could-be-arrested-for-chanting-Yid-Met-warns.html (accessed on 1 September, 2014).

Ladson-Billings, G. (1997) 'Just what is Critical Race Theory, and what's it doing in a *nice* field like education?' *Qualitative Studies in Education, 11*(1): 7–24.

Long, J. and Hylton, K. (2002) 'Shades of White: An examination of Whiteness in sport'. *Leisure Studies, 21:* 87–103.

Long, J., Hylton, K. and Spracklen, K. (2014) 'Whiteness, Blackness and settlement: Leisure and the integration of new migrants'. *Journal of Ethnic & Migration Studies, 40*(11): 1779–97.

Long, J., Hylton, K., Welch, M. and Dart, J. (2000) *Part of the game: An examination of racism in grass roots football.* London: Kick it Out.

MacPherson, S.W.o.C. (1999) 'Report of the Stephen Lawrence inquiry'. London.

Mills, C. (1997) *The racial contract.* Ithaca, NY: Cornell University.

Omi, M. and Winant, H. (1994) *Racial formation in the United States: From the 1960s to the 1990s.* London: Routledge.

Pilkington, A., Housee, S. and Hylton, K. (eds) (2009) *Race(ing) forward: Transitions in theorising 'race' in education.* Birmingham: CSAP/Higher Education Academy.

RunnymedeTrust (1985a, July) 'Football violence'. *Runnymede Trust Bulletin, 181.*

RunnymedeTrust (1985b, May) 'National front and football violence'. *Runnymede Trust Bulletin, 179.*

RunnymedeTrust (1987, December) 'Fascism and football violence'. *Runnymede Trust Bulletin, December.*

RunnymedeTrust (1990, June) 'Tebbit cricket loyalty test'. *Runnymede Trust Bulletin, 236.*

RunnymedeTrust (1994, June) 'Racism and football'. *Runnymede Trust Bulletin, 276.*

Spracklen, K., Long, J. and Hylton, K. (2014) 'Leisure opportunities and new migrant communities: challenging the contribution of sport'. *Leisure Studies, 40*: 1779–97.

TelegraphSport (2013, 19 September) 'Andre Villas-Boas welcomes David Cameron's support for Tottenham fans' "Yid" chants'. *The Daily Telegraph.* Avaialble at www.telegraph.co.uk/sport/football/teams/tottenham-hotspur/10319722/Andre-Villas-Boas-welcomes-David-Camerons-support-for-Tottenham-fans-Yid-chants.html (accessed on 1 September, 2014).

Williams, P.J. (1997) *Seeing a colour-blind future: The paradox of race.* London: Virago Press.

Winant, H. (2001) *The world is a ghetto: Race and democracy since world war II.* New York: Basic Books.

Applying Critical Race Theory

Daniel Burdsey[1]

It goes without saying that unearthing and engaging with the ideas, insights and theories of others is one of the many pleasures and privileges of life in the academy. The routine nature of such processes makes them no less enlightening or fulfilling when they occur. Then there are those special occurrences when, even in relatively small sub-disciplines – for instance, the social science or management of sport – a new contribution exhibits the potential to facilitate a significant step-change within the field. It is within this category that Professor Kevin Hylton's application of Critical Race Theory (CRT) to sport and leisure resides (e.g., Hylton 2005, 2009, 2010).

Over the last decade, Hylton's CRT-influenced scholarship has offered a hugely valuable addition to the literature on the sociology and management of sport and leisure. On a personal note, this work has been among the most important influences on my own research. I remember distinctly discovering Hylton's (2005) article in *Leisure Studies* a decade ago, and feeling a mixture of excitement, curiosity and even relief about the opportunity to explore and apply this three-letter acronym with which I was hitherto unfamiliar. I recognised immediately how its application could benefit my teaching, research and activism. I was familiar with the critical tradition in sociology and ethnic and racial studies, and the cultural Marxism and feminism of my mentors and colleagues influenced me significantly. Crucially, Hylton's work provided me (and many others) with a toolkit to combine these standpoints into a race-specific epistemology and praxis with which to understand and interrogate critically racialised phenomena, and to strive for social justice, in sport and leisure.

The immediate appeal of the article lay in various components. These include Hylton's (2005) insistence that issues of racial subordination in sport should 'stay at the centre of [researchers'] investigations or lens, rather than at the comfortable rim' (p. 85); his call for academics 'to make their research political rather than neutral, transformatory rather than merely critical' (p. 88); and his identification that 'mainstream epistemologies and research agendas make up part of the forces of oppression' (p. 90). I have since sought to embed the CRT approach outlined by Hylton in my own work on race, ethnicity, sport and popular culture, using it primarily as a means of illuminating the experiences of British Asian male cricketers and analysing racist episodes in English men's football (e.g., Burdsey, 2011, 2014). In addition to its specific topic relevance, it also holds methodological pertinence, linking race to important aspects of ethical and conscious research, including reflexivity, awareness of responsibilities and power relationships, and an appreciation of how knowledge is generated and legitimated (Sampson, Bloor and Fincham, 2008). CRT has also compelled me to reflect critically on my own subjectivity, as a White, male academic. Recognising the contentious relationship between dominant subjectivities and this emancipatory standpoint (Gillborn, 2008), CRT has enabled me to problematise and destabilise my Whiteness; to strive for more equal power relationships in research encounters; and to elevate minority voices in the design, undertaking and analysis of research.

Ten years on from Hylton's article, the racial inequalities and injustices of the contemporary neoliberal (sporting) conjuncture suggest that its influence and importance to the critical study of sport and leisure will be just as important for the next decade.

Note

1 Daniel Burdsey is with the School of Sport and Service Management at the University of Brighton.

References

Burdsey, D. (2011) 'That joke isn't funny anymore: Racial microaggressions, colour-blind ideology and the mitigation of racism in English men's first-class cricket'. *Sociology of Sport Journal*, 28: 261–83.

Burdsey, D. (2014) 'One week in October: Luis Suárez, John Terry and the turn to racial neoliberalism in English men's professional football'. *Identities: Global Studies in Culture and Power*, 21: 429–47.

Gillborn, D. (2008) *Racism and education: Coincidence or conspiracy?* Abingdon: Routledge.

Hylton, K. (2005) 'Race, sport and leisure: Lessons from critical race theory'. *Leisure Studies*, 24: 81–98.

Hylton, K. (2009) *'Race' and sport: Critical Race Theory.* Abingdon: Routledge.

Hylton, K. (2010) 'How a turn to critical race theory can contribute to our understanding of "race", racism and anti-racism in sport'. *International Review for the Sociology of Sport*, 45: 335–54.

Sampson, H., Bloor, M. and Fincham, B. (2008) 'A price worth paying? Considering the "cost" of reflexive research methods and the influence of feminist ways of "doing"'. *Sociology*, 42: 919–33.

28

GATEKEEPING AND SPORT COMMUNICATION[1]

Steve Bien-Aimé and Marie Hardin

Introduction

Perhaps no other issue has frustrated, with good reason, women's sports advocates over time more than this: the vexing and persistent practice of mediated sports producers – no matter the platform, no matter the time period – to ignore and marginalise female sports competitors. But *why?* There is, of course, more than one answer to this question, which has been pondered by mostly by scholars of sport sociology, who have looked at the issue through a variety of feminist lenses and through Gramsci's (1971) notion of hegemony.

As scholars of journalism and mass communication, we have taken a different approach to the question, adding theories from our field to understand decision-making by media producers around women's sport. In this chapter, we discuss *gatekeeping* and how this concept has been applied to questions about (non)coverage of women's sport. We provide an overview of gatekeeping, discuss how it has been integrated into research involving sports journalists and newsrooms, and review the impact gatekeeping practices have had on how sports news is covered. We then suggest ways research might further address sexism in coverage.

Overview of gatekeeping and journalism

Sport journalists receive a great deal more information than they ever disseminate to the public, even in the age of social media. In fact, it could be surmised that all individuals, as a matter of practicality, do not blindly regurgitate every piece of information they receive; there is a filtering process that occurs. In mass communications, this phenomenon is called gatekeeping (Shoemaker, 1991; Shoemaker and Vos, 2009). Scholars (e.g., Singer, 2001; Shoemaker, 1991; Sundar and Nass, 2001) have traced the concept of gatekeepers to social psychologist Kurt Lewin (1947). Lewin theorized about how families made decisions regarding food consumption. He looked at the different channels – food growers and food consumers – in decision-making about eating (p. 145). Lewin wrote, 'Gate sections are governed either by impartial rules or by "gate keepers." In the latter case an individual group is "in power" for making the decision between "in" and "out"' (p. 145). In the cases of food growers and consumers, some dominant person or group must decide what crops are produced, and another dominant person or group must decide what foods are suitable for a family to consume. Farms do not all grow the same crops and households do not purchase every item found in a supermarket. Instead, these entities are subject to a process whereby filtering occurs through a number of channels, involving economic, environmental and social factors, among others.

White (1950) is widely credited as being the first scholar to apply gatekeeping to mass communications, or more specifically to journalism (e.g., Cassidy, 2006; Hoskins and O'Loughlin, 2011; Shoemaker, 1991; Toledo Bastos, Galdini Raimundo and Travitzki, 2013). White wanted to understand how an editor selected stories from various wire services to run in a newspaper. 'Mr Gates', as the editor was dubbed, was essentially the sole arbiter in deciding which articles to accept and reject. Near the conclusion of the article, White (1950) wrote: 'It begins to appear . . . that in his position as "gate keeper" the newspaper editor sees to it . . . that the community shall hear as a fact only those events which the newsman, as the representative of his culture, believes to be true' (p. 390).

There are various models of gatekeeping, depending on the contextual setting (Shoemaker, 1991; Shoemaker and Vos, 2009). For sport communications scholars, Abraham Z. Bass's notion of gatekeeping could prove beneficial. Bass (1969) examined the news decisions made at United Nations Radio. He saw the gatekeeper function performed twice, once in 'news gathering' and again in 'news processing' (p. 72). Editors were not the only individuals who decided what news was disseminated to the public; reporters also acted as gatekeepers. Editors do not leave newsrooms and acquire information. They can only 'process' the information reporters gather. Therefore, there is a lot of power in the hands of reporters both in terms of whom they talk to and whom they ignore, and how reporters frame the information they receive. Editors also have gatekeeping power; thus, there are two sets of gates.

There are various factors that influence gatekeepers' decisions. While people make personal decisions about what information is shared and what information is excluded, institutions do shape gatekeepers' choices (Shoemaker, 1991; Shoemaker and Vos, 2009). For instance, a social media manager for a sports team most likely will not post information criticising a star player, even if that star player performed poorly. Institutionally, there are most likely norms (whether spoken or unspoken) that would discourage disparaging information to pass through the gate of that particular team.

An individual's background cannot be ignored as also influential. A person's educational level, childhood and experiences help form a certain worldview. In addition, one's race, sexual orientation and other socially constructed identities work to place that individual in a unique position in society. Berry, Jay and Lynn (2010) combine the importance of background and identity by stating, 'We are not only the sum of our parts but also the sum of our experiences' (p. 6). Shoemaker and Vos (2009) relate an individual's complexities to how that person would function as a gatekeeper: 'An African-American heterosexual woman from a middle-class background who graduated from an Ivy League university may go through a different decision-making process than a white gay man who comes from a working-class background and attended a small state university' (p. 43).

Influences outside of reporters and editors could also impact gatekeepers' decisions. The audience (or perceived audience) for information is one example of a possible external pressure, although scholars differ on whether the audience does impact news choices (Shoemaker, 1991). However, journalists have relied upon their knowledge of their 'audiences' to justify their decisions. In terms of how Dutch sport journalists portrayed women and reported on female athletes, Knoppers and Elling (2004) found that these journalists based their decisions on what they perceived to be audience desire. Knoppers and Elling also reported that the perceptions of audience desires and tastes seemed to reflect the journalists' own views.

Exploring the role of 'audience' in gatekeeping

As former practising journalists, we bring to our research a first-hand understanding of the phenomena that Knoppers and Elling (2004) explained in their research: An understanding of 'audience' that permeates the practice of newsgathering and reporting, making its way – often without explicit acknowledgement – into the decision-making process about content. There is no question that the rise of the internet, social media and digital technologies has taken much of the guesswork out of understanding audience demographics and consumption patterns, but that has certainly not always been the case, as it was not in 2005, when Hardin (2005) launched the first survey to link gatekeeping and sport coverage. Furthermore, as a White woman (Hardin) and Black man (Bien-Aimé), both of us are part of under-represented groups in the sport-media workplace; thus, we are interested in the way identity and the gatekeeping process are linked.

It was with those interests and background that Hardin (2005) surveyed 285 newspaper sport editors in the southeastern United States, exploring the relationship between the gendered identities of sports editors (primary decision-makers about coverage), their understanding of reader interests and gatekeeping. She found that sport editors were overwhelmingly White men. Although almost 90 per cent of editors felt confident they knew what their readers wanted, only 42 per cent had a formal way (such as monitoring calls to the sports department or conducting informal focus groups with individuals recruited by reporters) to assess audience interest. From the data, Hardin reached a similar conclusion to that of Knoppers and Elling (2004): journalists perceive they know what their audiences want, and they judge these interests to be aligned with their choice to predominantly cover professional men's sports and provide scant coverage of women's sports. Hardin (2005) concluded that editors' 'sense about audience interest is driven, at least in part, by personal beliefs and hegemonic ideology about women's sports' (p. 72). The reliance on intuition, not hard data, could have significant implications for how women's sports are covered. About 44 per cent of respondents said reader interest was low or non-existent for women's sports; that hunch could lead editors to block stories regarding female athletes and competition from being published (Hardin, 2005).

Hardin (2005) also sought to gauge sports editors' perceptions on the quality of female athletes. For instance: do editors view female athletes as equal to their male counterparts? About one-third of editors surveyed believed women to be athletically inferior to men and that women were not as interested in sports compared with men. These same editors might use these personal beliefs to justify ignoring women in sport because more attention should be given to the supposedly superior male athletes (Hardin, 2005).

The results were not surprising, given our own newsroom experience and understanding of the dynamics that permeate the sports beat – perhaps best explained for the uninitiated in *Inside the sports pages* (Lowes, 2000), which, though dated, still captures the general dynamics in sport beat reporting. Although 'objectivity' has long served as the holy grail in newsrooms and, more recently, in sports departments as they sought to lose the 'toy department' image and be perceived as legitimate journalistic enterprises, this research seemed to confirm that the personal beliefs of sports editors (often driven by their identities, no doubt; as we discuss later, male and female journalists express different beliefs about the value of women's sport), along with their unsubstantiated assumptions about 'reader interest' both drove, then justified, their decisions about content.

Applying gatekeeping to sport coverage

Modern sport has been viewed as a place for men to dominate (Burstyn, 1999; Cahn, 1994). The mentality is based upon sport being a place for men to demonstrate their masculinity and supposed physical superiority. Under this framework, women are often treated as substandard to men in sport. Understanding *how* sport journalists reify the idea of sport as male is important to us as mass communication scholars; as we understand how it occurs, we can work to address attendant newsroom practices and priorities.

Evidence for case studies is not difficult to find. The case of Becky Hammon provides an opportunity to demonstrate how even in celebrating an achievement, sport journalists continue to reinforce sport as masculine. Hammon has been ranked as one of the top fifteen players in the history of the Women's National Basketball Association (NBA, 2014). However, it is only when Hammon was hired to be the assistant coach for the National Basketball Association's San Antonio Spurs that she received significant media coverage. Pay attention to how journalists described the news. CNN.com began its story this way: 'In what many sports fans view as a historic move, the reigning NBA champion San Antonio Spurs announced the hiring of Becky Hammon as assistant coach' (Martin, 2014). ABCNews.com went in a similar direction: 'Becky Hammon has made history as the first full-time female assistant coach in the NBA, but she says that was never her intent' (ABC News, 2014). Few, if any, journalists have found it particularly newsworthy that men coach women successfully (see Gino Auriemma of the University of Connecticut women's basketball team or Bill Laimbeer, formerly of the Detroit Shock). However, journalists found it especially newsworthy and groundbreaking that Hammon, a sixteen-year professional and former Olympian, is coaching men as an assistant.

Most journalists covered this story similarly; again, we find gatekeeping instructive as a lens. Shoemaker (1991) would likely view the similarities in the Hammon coverage as another form of gatekeeping; the socialisation of journalists into a 'pack mentality', where reporters essentially follow each other so as to not deviate from the path and potentially look foolish to their peers. To put this in a simpler way: If we all do it, we all can't look bad if we're wrong. Referring back to Hammon, it would appear that the gatekeepers are acknowledging they view the Women's National Basketball Association as inferior to the National Basketball Association and/or female basketball players as inferior to male basketball players.

Of course the most obvious evidence of journalists' tendency to devalue female athletes, based on a number of gatekeeping factors, is in the amount of media coverage women's sport competition receives. There is no shortage of studies that document the persistent disparity (Cooky, Messner and Hextrum, 2013; Fink, in press). A longitudinal study of television coverage on local network news and on ESPN's *SportsCenter* shows that female athletes get very little – miniscule is not too strong a descriptor – airtime (Cooky *et al.*, 2013). This has been the case for decades, across college and professional sports, and across print, broadcast and online media. For instance, in a 1998 examination of the sports sections of *The New York Times* and *USA Today*, and the content of *Sports Center* and CNN's sports television shows, Eastman and Billings (2000) reported that female athletes received less than 10 per cent of television coverage and less than 20 per cent of the newspaper coverage. In an analysis of newspaper (print and online) coverage during the 2006 NCAA men's and women's basketball tournaments, Kian (2008) found that the men's tournament received an overwhelming amount of the coverage.

If female athletes receive significantly less media attention than male athletes, then it is important to examine the sex composition of sport newsrooms. Richard Lapchick has analysed the racial and gender breakdowns of selected sport departments for years, assigning grades for departments' commitment to diversity. In the 2012 assessment, Lapchick and his co-authors again gave newsrooms an F for gender diversity. Women comprised 14.6 per cent of staffs and only 9.6 per cent of sports editors (Lapchick *et al.*, 2013). The substantial disparity could help begin to explain why female athletes receive so little media coverage. As Hardin argued (2005), if men have little direct experience with female sport, then men might have more of an inclination to dismiss it.

Understanding the gatekeeping role in sport is critical because reality is socially constructed (e.g., Berger and Luckmann, 1967; Ferri, 1988; Lindgren and Packendorff, 2009; Parker and Easton, 1998). Individuals' perceptions of the world are shaped by their environments and what they are taught to believe. Journalists often provide the lenses by which the public sees events, *mediating* reality. How stories are written, how videos are produced and who is included and excluded go a long way in determining how society views sport. This is not to disregard agency on the part of media consumers. Furthermore, this is not to discount the role of audience desires and demands – by virtue of clicks, downloads and screen-time – all of which can be measured, taking the guesswork out of what media producers can be certain will draw individuals and, thus, be sold to advertisers. However, if the gatekeeping process consistently and broadly produces homologous content, audiences may not know what they are missing and dominant paradigms (in this case, an understanding of the superior athletic body as masculine) go unchallenged.

Extensions and applications of gatekeeping in sport communication

While not explicitly mentioning gatekeeping, Hardin and Whiteside (2009) described gatekeeping's negative effects for female sport journalists. Hardin and Whiteside interviewed female sport journalists to understand how they navigated the industry. They found that female sport journalists were readily made aware of their marginalised status and were often told they were unqualified by their colleagues. In addition to feeling they constantly had to validate themselves to men, the female journalists expressed frustration in working a grueling schedule without the possibility of moving to the top ranks. The sexist conditions and overwork pushed some women out of sport journalism. Hardin and Whiteside (2009) explained:

> The women who left and those who considered leaving presented their decisions as individual, free choice. They acknowledged barriers such as the time demands and what they called a 'boys-will-be-boys' culture, but did not see these barriers as institutionally constructed. Instead, they accepted them as natural and immutable. Jane, the copy editor who was verbally abused on the copy desk, did say that supervisors needed to 'do a better job of overseeing everything' (i.e. spotting and stopping harassment), but did not see the sports-journalism environment, which privileges men, as part of the problem.
>
> *(p. 643)*

If men create the structure by which sport must be practised, then it is through this paradigm that one must view the status of female sport journalists. There is a gendered gate preventing women from practising sport journalism in an environment that acknowledges them entirely as equals to men.

Hardin (2013) has suggested that the lack of women in the sport media workplace could be linked to content that excludes female athletes and, certainly, gatekeeping as a theoretical lens would support this suggestion. Research already points to differing attitudes among women and men in sports journalism towards Title IX and women's sports. Surveys of journalists across print, broadcast and online formats have demonstrated that women put a higher value on coverage of female athletes and generally believe the women's sport does not receive enough coverage

(Hardin). Content analyses examining differences in the ways women and men cover sport confirm that women cover female athletes in more positive terms than their counterparts (for instance, see Kian and Hardin, 2009).

Gatekeeping has also been extended to examine decisions made by sport-talk radio programming directors. We surveyed directors from across the United States to explore demographics and programming decisions (Hardin, Antunovic, Bien-Aimé and Li, 2013). The directors were overwhelmingly white men and many directors believed their listeners had little interest in female sport. We surmised the following:

> [T]he lack of programming directed at female listeners suggests that directors are either not concerned about attracting them or they presume that female listeners are interested in the same content as male listeners . . . It is implied, based on these estimates, that if female listeners are interested in the station's programming, they are interested in sports associated with masculinity and packaged in a way to appeal to a particular male target demographic.
>
> *(Hardin et al., 2013, p. 417)*

Sports information has also been examined with gatekeeping as a theoretical backdrop, with the understanding that the availability of information sources, such as those provided by sports information operations, impact decision-making by gatekeepers (Shoemaker, 1991; Shoemaker and Vos, 2009). If information is hard to obtain, journalists must put forth the effort to seek it out; on the other hand, when the information is readily available it is easier to disseminate. Because we already know that media operations dedicate far more resources towards reporting on men's sports, the availability of information and material on women's sports by those responsible for providing it on behalf of sports organisations (such as universities) becomes critical for coverage.

In that light, Hardin, Whiteside and Ash (2014) surveyed sport information directors, the individuals who provide much of athletic programmes' information to the news media, to gauge their attitudes on gender-related issues. They found that sport information directors did not believe female athletes needed additional resources from schools. This viewpoint 'may reflect a sincere belief that female athletes already have equal resources, or – more problematic – a belief that while the values of equity and fairness are just and good, women have not necessarily earned the right to those resources' (Hardin *et al.*, 2014, p. 57). They speculated that sport information directors normalise the disparity in coverage between male and female sports. Further, many sport information directors did not object to assigning staff based on gender (i.e., men assigned to men's sports and women assigned to women's sports):

> Such logic, however, necessarily puts women at a tremendous disadvantage in the sports information workplace, virtually guaranteeing their inability to climb through the ranks in athletic departments in any kind of critical mass because of their lack of access to high-visibility assignments (such as men's basketball and football), which are considered essential for promotion.
>
> *(Hardin et al., 2014, p. 58)*

If women are precluded from reaching the highest levels of gatekeeping, this could help explain the treatment of women within sport.

Future directions for gatekeeping

Although gatekeeping in sport media has been examined both in media composition and in overall media coverage, gatekeeping should be explored on a more fundamental level. There are many ideological assumptions that enter the sport media lexicon that are rarely challenged. For example, the practice of asymmetrical gender marking (Billings, Halone and Denham, 2002; Halbert and Latimer, 1994; Messner, Duncan and Jensen, 1993) – using women to describe one league, but not using men to describe the other league, a Women's National Basketball Association in contrast to the National Basketball Association – might be better explained through a personalised level of gatekeeping. Shoemaker and Vos (2009) ask, 'How much autonomy and power do individual gatekeepers have to impose their own agendas on media content? What conditions are conducive to the exercise of personal judgment over more structural constraints?' (p. 134). If an editor wanted to make it a practice to call the National Basketball Association, the *Men's* National Basketball Association, would that be allowed/tolerated by the publishers?

Gatekeeping must also be examined more deeply at the source level. As Cooky *et al.* (2013) indicated, professional sport leagues and universities play a role in promoting their athletes to the media. Hardin *et al.* (2014) examined attitudes of sport information directors. However, further understanding the decision-making process as to which sports and which athletes receive more resources towards media engagement could yield much beneficial information for sport communication.

Note

1   This chapter is a reflection on Hardin (2005) and the work related to it.

References

ABC News (2014, 18 August) 'Becky Hammon talks locker rooms, history-making role and inspiration'. Available at http://abcnews.go.com/Sports/beckyhammon-talks-locker-rooms-history-making-role/story?id=25016415 (accessed on 22 August, 2014).

Bass, A.Z. (1969) 'Refining the "gatekeeper" function: A UN Radio case study'. *Journalism Quarterly*, 46: 69–72.

Berger, P.L. and Luckmann, T. (1967) *The social construction of reality: A treatise in the sociology of knowledge.* New York: Doubleday.

Berry, T.R., Jay, M. and Lynn, M. (2010) 'Introduction: Thoughts and ideas on the intersectionality of identity'. *The Journal of Educational Foundations*, 24(1–2): 3–9.

Billings, A.C., Halone, K.K. and Denham, B.E. (2002) '"Man, that was a pretty shot": An analysis of gendered broadcast commentary surrounding the 2000 men's and women's NCAA Final Four basketball championships'. *Mass Communication & Society*, 5: 295–315.

Burstyn, V. (1999) *The rites of men: Manhood, politics and the culture of sport.* Toronto: University of Toronto Press.

Cahn, S.K. (1994) *Coming on strong: Gender and sexuality in twentieth-century women's sport.* New York: Free Press.

Cassidy, W.P. (2006) 'Gatekeeping similar for online, print journalists'. *Newspaper Research Journal*, 27: 6–23.

Cooky, C., Messner, M.A. and Hextrum, R.H. (2013) 'Women play sport, but not on TV: A longitudinal study of televised news media'. *Communication & Sport*, 1: 203–30.

Eastman, S.T. and Billings, A.C. (2000) 'Sportscasting and sports reporting: The power of gender bias'. *Journal of Sport and Social Issues*, 24: 192–213.

Ferri, A.J. (1988) 'Perceived career barriers of men and women television news anchors'. *Journalism Quarterly*, 65: 661–7.

Fink, J.S. (in press) 'Female athletes, women's sport, and the sport media commercial complex: Have we really "come a long way, baby"'? *Sport Management Review*.

Gramsci, A. (1971) *Selections from the prison notebook*. New York: International Press.

Halbert, C. and Latimer, M. (1994) '"Battling" gendered language: An analysis of the language used by sports commentators in a televised coed tennis competition'. *Sociology of Sport Journal*, *11*: 298–308.

Hardin, M. (2005) 'Stopped at the gate: Women's sports, "reader interest," and decision making by editors'. *Journalism & Mass Communication Quarterly*, *82*: 62–77.

Hardin, M. (2013) 'Want changes in content? Change the decision makers'. *Communication & Sport*, *1*: 241–5.

Hardin, M., Antunovic, D., Bien-Aimé, S. and Li, R. (2013) 'The status of women in sport-talk radio: A survey of directors'. *International Journal of Sport Communication*, *6*: 409–22.

Hardin, M. and Whiteside, E. (2009) 'Token responses to gendered newsrooms: Factors in the career-related decisions of female newspaper sports journalists'. *Journalism*, *10*: 627–46.

Hardin, M., Whiteside, E. and Ash, E. (2014) 'Ambivalence on the front lines? Attitudes toward Title IX and women's sports among Division I sports information directors'. *International Review for the Sociology of Sport*, *49*: 42–64.

Hoskins, A. and O'Loughlin, B. (2011) 'Remediating jihad for western news audiences: The renewal of gatekeeping'. *Journalism*, *12*: 199–216.

Kian, E.M. (2008) 'Study examines stereotypes in two national newspapers'. *Newspaper Research Journal*, *29*: 38–49.

Kian, E.M. and Hardin, M. (2009) 'Analyzing content based on the sex of sports writers: Female journalists counter the traditional gendering of media coverage'. *International Journal of Sport Communication*, *2*: 185–204.

Knoppers, A. and Elling, A. (2004) '"We do not engage in promotional journalism": Discursive strategies used by sport journalists to describe the selection process'. *International Review for the Sociology of Sport*, *39*: 57–73.

Lapchick, R., Burnett, C., Farris, M., Gossett, R., Orpilla, C., Phelan, J., Sherrod, T., Smith, S., Thiel, S., Walker, C. and Snively, D. (2013) 'The 2012 Associated Press Sports Editors racial and gender report card'. *The Institute for Diversity and Ethics in Sport*. Available at www.tidesport.org/rgrc/ 2012/2012_apse_rgrc.pdf (accessed on 15 April, 2014).

Lewin, K. (1947) 'Frontiers in group dynamics: II. Channels of group life; social planning and action research'. *Human Relations*, *1*: 143–53.

Lindgren, M. and Packendorff, J. (2009) 'Social constructionism and entrepreneurship: Basic assumptions and consequences for theory and research'. *International Journal of Entrepreneurial Behaviour & Research*, *15*: 25–47.

Lowes, M.D. (2000) *Inside the sports pages*. Toronto: University of Toronto Press.

Martin, J. (2014, 6 August) 'San Antonio Spurs hire Becky Hammon as assistant coach'. *CNN*. Available at http://edition.cnn.com/2014/08/05/us/spurs-becky-hammon-coach/ (accessed on 22 August, 2014).

Messner, M.A., Duncan, M.C. and Jensen, K. (1993) 'Separating the men from the girls: The gendered language of televised sports'. *Gender & Society*, *7*: 121–37.

NBA (2014, 5 August) 'Spurs name Becky Hammon assistant coach'. Available at www.nba.com/ spurs/spurs-name-becky-hammon-assistant-coach (accessed on 20 August, 2014).

Parker, R. and Easton, D. (1998) 'Sexuality, culture, and political economy: Recent developments in anthropological and cross-cultural research'. *Annual Review of Sex Research*, *9*: 1–19.

Shoemaker, P.J. (1991) *Communication concepts 3: Gatekeeping*. Newbury Park, CA: Sage.

Shoemaker, P.J. and Vos, T.P. (2009) *Gatekeeping theory*. New York: Routledge.

Singer, J.B. (2001) 'The metro wide web: Changes in newspapers' gatekeeping role online'. *Journalism & Mass Communication Quarterly*, *78*: 65–80.

Sundar, S.S. and Nass, C. (2001) 'Conceptualizing sources in online news'. *Journal of Communication*, *51*: 52–72.

Toledo Bastos, M., Galdini Raimundo, R.L. and Travitzki, R. (2013) 'Gatekeeping Twitter: Message diffusion in political hashtags'. *Media, Culture & Society*, *35*: 260–70.

White, D.M. (1950) 'The "gate keeper": A case study in the selection of news'. *Journalism Quarterly*, *27*: 383–90.

Applying the gatekeeper influence in sport communication model

Erin Whiteside[1]

I often refer to my career before entering academia as my prior life. During that time, I worked in sports media, an industry largely dominated not simply by men, but by an ideology that provides the logic for marginalising women and women's sports. While there, I understood that girls and women faced challenges in earning credibility and respect, particularly when it came to garnering media coverage. Still, it was not until encountering the scholarship of Marie Hardin (2005) that I finally acquired a toolkit with which to interpret my experiences and observations, and develop ideas for addressing systemic inequities related to gender in sports media.

Hardin's work (2005) represents a major contribution to sports media literature, as it demonstrates the social construction of sports media through various influences in the gatekeeping process. Sports media is a key space in which shared cultural meanings are negotiated, contested and affirmed, and thus analyses of coverage are critical in understanding the ways in which sports media contribute to the maintenance of invisible social hierarchies. Still, too often scholars focus solely on critiquing content itself and ignore the modes of production that give rise to that content. Hardin's article and other research exploring how attitudes among gatekeepers may explain trends in content (e.g., Hardin, 2013; Hardin and Shain, 2005a; Hardin and Whiteside, 2009a; Hardin, Whiteside and Ash, 2014) take into consideration the processes of sports media production, thus offering insight into how and where change may occur, a goal that is at the heart of all critical (and feminist) sports studies scholarship.

In my own work, I have incorporated the concept of the social construction of sports news to offer both an explanation for *why* we see certain trends in content, and *how* various attitudes towards girls and women manifest themselves in sports media. For example, in a study in which we analysed high-school basketball coverage, we found that girls competing at that level are not presented in overly feminine frames, and that they also receive similar resources to boys when they do receive coverage (Whiteside and Rightler-McDaniels, 2013). Along with arguing that the coverage we analysed may function in liberating ways by offering a more agentic vision of female athletes to readers, we also drew from ideas grounded in the social construction of news to consider *why* we observed these trends and what factors may have been part of the gatekeeping process. Still, such studies offer an incomplete picture of how gender identities are constituted through sports media discourses. To that end, we have continued to survey sports media professionals about their attitudes toward women's sports and Title IX, as part of a wider project aimed at understanding *how* these concepts are negotiated and, ultimately, presented to the public (Hardin and Whiteside, 2009a; Hardin *et al.*, 2014).

The social construction of news is a multi-faceted process mediated by numerous gatekeepers and influences. Surveys can measure attitudes among key individuals in that process and thus demonstrate how those attitudes may shape content. Ideologies, however, do not exist in a vacuum. In other work, Hardin has interviewed sports media professionals on some of these issues (e.g., Hardin and Shain, 2005b, 2006; Hardin, Shain and Schultz-Poniatowski, 2008; Hardin and Whiteside, 2008, 2009b, 2009c, 2012; Whiteside and Hardin, 2011). Scholars should similarly employ an ethnographic approach to further illuminate the complexities in the sports media production process, including how gender-related attitudes function in everyday decision-making.

Doing so will ultimately provide a more detailed picture of how various trends in content manifest themselves and where change may be most likely to occur.

Note

1   Erin Whiteside is an Assistant Professor in the School of Journalism and Electronic Media at the University of Tennessee.

References

Hardin, M. (2005) 'Stopped at the gate: Women's sports, "reader interest," and decision making by editors'. *Journalism & Mass Communication Quarterly, 82*: 62–77.

Hardin, M. (2013) 'Want changes in content? Change the decision makers'. *Communication & Sport, 1*: 241–45.

Hardin, M. and Shain, S. (2005a) 'Strength in numbers? The experiences and attitudes of women in sports media careers'. *Journalism & Mass Communication Quarterly, 82*: 804–19.

Hardin, M. and Shain, S. (2005b) 'Female sports journalists: Are we there yet? No'. *Newspaper Research Journal, 26*: 22.

Hardin, M. and Shain, S. (2006) 'Feeling much smaller than you know you are. The fragmented professional identity of female sports journalists'. *Critical Studies in Media Communication, 23*: 322–38.

Hardin, M., Shain, S. and Shultz-Poniatowski, K. (2008) 'There's no sex attached to your occupation: The revolving door for young women in sports journalism'. *Women in Sport & Physical Activity Journal, 17*: 68–80.

Hardin, M. and Whiteside, E. (2008) 'Maybe it's not a generational thing: Values and beliefs of aspiring sports journalists about race and gender'. *Media Report to Women, 36*: 8–15.

Hardin, M. and Whiteside, E.E. (2009a) 'Sports reporters divided over concerns about Title IX'. *Newspaper Research Journal, 30*: 58–80.

Hardin, M. and Whiteside, E. (2009b) 'Through the revolving door: Narratives of young women in U.S. sports journalism'. *Journalism, 10*: 627–46.

Hardin, M. and Whiteside, E. (2009c) 'Token responses to gendered newsrooms: Factors in the career-related decisions of female newspaper sports journalists'. *Journalism, 10*: 627–46.

Hardin, M. and Whiteside, E. (2012) 'Consequences of being the "team mom": Women in sports information and the friendliness trap'. *Journal of Sport Management, 26*: 309–21.

Hardin, M., Whiteside, E. and Ash, E. (2014) 'Ambivalence on the front lines? Attitudes toward Title IX and women's sports among Division I sports information directors'. *International Review for the Sociology of Sport, 49*: 42–64.

Whiteside, E. and Hardin, M. (2011) '"I don't feel like I'm up against a *wall* of men!" Negotiating difference, identity and the glass ceiling in sports information'. *Journal of Intercollegiate Sport, 4*: 210–26.

Whiteside, E. and Rightler-McDaniels, J. (2013) 'Moving toward parity? Dominant gender ideology vs. community journalism in high school basketball coverage'. *Mass Communication & Society, 16*: 808–28.

29

THE CONTINUUM THEORY

Challenging traditional conceptualisations and practices of sport[1]

Mary Jo Kane

We get interesting theory when we . . . allow our minds to roam freely and creatively . . . Theory is insightful when it surprises, when it allows us to see profoundly, imaginatively, and unconventionally into phenomena we thought we understood.

(Mintzberg, 2005, p. 361)

Background and overview

In the early-to-mid 1990s, I was publishing articles on the interconnections among sport, gender and power. I was contributing to a growing and sophisticated body of knowledge that had moved beyond descriptive studies examining women's sports participation – and their continued second-class citizenship in spite of the progress made in the wake of Title IX – to one grounded in critical feminist theory.[2] This particular analytic framework examines the fundamental role sport plays in (re)producing and maintaining dominant ideologies and structures related to gender. Central to this critique is the deeply embedded belief that 'biology is destiny' whereby individuals are assumed to fall into unambiguous and oppositional bipolar categories of 'male' and 'female'. Numerous scholars contested the notion (and practice) of biological reductionism by demonstrating how there are no 'natural' immutable categories of female and male because conceptions of 'woman' and 'man' are never removed from broader social and political realities (Bartky, 1988; Frye, 1983).

Essential to this analysis was an understanding of how sport becomes an ideal setting for establishing and articulating the 'assumption that there are two, and only two . . . bipolar, mutually exclusive sexes' (Birrell and Cole, 1990, p. 3). Sport also serves as an ideal site for the connection between gender and power relations because it vigilantly maintains gender difference as hierarchically ordered and, more importantly, *grounded in the physical body and thus perceived as biologically, meaning inherently based.* More than any other institution, sports centre around – and richly reward – measurable, physical differences between the sexes where heights, scores and distances are relentlessly recorded and compared (Bryson, 1990). These differences provide the basis for common sense, apparent empirical proof that men are naturally superior to women (Kane, 1998). As I mentioned in the original article, sport scholar Paul Willis makes precisely this point:

Sport and biological beliefs about gender difference combine into one of the few privileged areas where we seem to be dealing with unmediated 'reality,' where we know 'what's what' without [listening] to the self-serving analyses of theorists, analysts, political groups. Running faster, jumping higher, throwing farther can be *seen*—not interpreted.

(1982, p. 117)

It should be emphasised that any set of beliefs and practices that can claim a biological basis is a particularly effective tool for a dominant group's (e.g., men's) ability to maintain a stranglehold of power. What is equally important to note, however, is how much cultural support is invested in men's athletics. Far from being biologically based, there is great urgency surrounding sport as a masculinizing *practice*. As Whitson points out: 'What such effort and concern immediately belie is any notion of biological destiny. If boys simply grew into men and that was that, the efforts described to teach boys how to be men [through sports] would be redundant' (1990, p. 22).

How (and why) I developed the continuum theory

The discussion outlined above is a delineation of the central arguments I made in the 1995 article as a preamble to my point of departure, meaning even though I agreed with the overall critique of the interplay among sport, gender and relations of power – and how that interplay demonstrated the role of sport in 'proving' male superiority as biologically based – I was increasingly concerned that scholars (myself included) were unwittingly contributing to the very stereotypes about gender difference we were so forcefully arguing against. For example, one strategy advanced for changing the power dynamic between women and men was to elevate the status of those sports outside the traditional male pantheon such as running, swimming and wilderness activities. Whitson (1990) supported this approach because 'the demonstrable achievements of *women in such sports* . . . have helped to weaken the popular association between sport and masculinity' (p. 28, emphasis added). Whitson also argued that gender-neutral sports created 'opportunities open to people who do not typically shine in confrontational team games, *to smaller men, and to women*' (p. 28, emphasis added).

What troubled me about Whitson's well-intentioned analysis is that he not only reinforced traditional notions of gender – and biological imperatives associated with size and strength – he failed to mention women's achievements in traditionally male-identified team sports such as basketball and hockey. Women's entrance into these kinds of sports on any serious level would surely pose a significantly greater threat to men's dominance than would emphasising their accomplishments as runners and swimmers. In essence, Whitson confined women (and 'smaller' men) to sports that, by definition, had less status and power while leaving the impression that these 'lesser' sports were the only ones in which women could compete.

During the time I was immersed in this research I came across a related body of knowledge that was also being critiqued through the lens of critical feminist theory – the muscle gap literature. This ideological construct refers to the degree of difference that exists when comparing women's and men's performance in the same sport or physical activity. Scholars such as Ann Hall (1990) and Lois Bryson (1990) were arguing that culturally embedded assumptions about the muscle gap disadvantaged females because superior athleticism was routinely defined in ways that privileged physical skills and social attributes traditionally identified with males. These comparisons provided the framework for gender (i.e., muscle gap) differences whereby females are systematically shown to be inherently inferior athletes (Nelson, 1994). As with the biology-is-destiny literature previously cited, I agreed with the overall analysis, but was increasingly aware that this line of discussion, which effectively demonstrated the oppressive impact of the so-called muscle gap, was also unintentionally reinforcing that very same dualistic ideology. I say this because feminist critiques of the muscle gap frequently explained and defended performance differences as predictable outcomes of patriarchal ideologies, practices and structures surrounding sports. Such an approach locked any analysis into a dualistic framework where one could logically say, 'Of course men outperform women. Look at all the advantages they have both physically and in terms of social support and access to resources.' While this is certainly the case, it nevertheless reconfirms gender as separate and distinct categories. Doing so obscures any acknowledgement of sport as a continuum where there is a range of performance differences *among* individual females and males. As a result, even when scholars quite rightly defended performance differences they did so within a framework that included only one gender comparison, only one muscle gap.

So how did all of my reading of the literature – and the theoretical constructs embedded within – allow my rather perplexed and confused mind to, as Mintzberg's quote at the beginning of this paper suggests, 'roam free' and 'see profoundly, imaginatively and unconventionally into phenomena' I thought I understood. Or as the editors of this text posed to the authors: 'Describe the process for developing [your] theory . . . [D]iscuss the events or activities that spurred your interest in the topic.' Reflecting on this interesting question, I realised that I began to formulate the sport-as-continuum theory because of two experiences in my life outside the academy. The first involved the Twin Cities marathon. I had never lived in areas like Boston or New York where marathons took on legendary status. But in Minneapolis, where I moved in 1989 to become a faculty member at the University of Minnesota, the Twin Cities marathon (considered in the top ten of marathons nationwide) was an annual event of great civic pride. The marathon literally ran in front of my house and my neighbours would hold annual gatherings to cheer on the runners. It was my first experience seeing elite runners up close and I was reminded that the marathon was one of the few sporting activities where women and men competed on the same course at the same time.

While cheering on the runners I noticed how much of the conversation was dominated by well-meaning muscle gap comparisons and how great everyone thought it was that women were closing the performance gap with each new generation. But what I also noticed was that the best female runners were outperforming many – indeed most – of the male runners and not just the stragglers at the end. During the same time period when I was analysing a body of knowledge that failed to recognise the possibility of many muscle gaps, in my personal life I was witnessing the *reality* that there actually were. In short, I became acutely aware that the results of the marathon were framed using a single overall comparison, meaning the first male to cross the finish line versus the first female. This one – and only one – comparison is a critical point I will return to later in the manuscript.

The second experience had to do with professional football. I grew up in central Illinois and, along with all of my family members, passionately followed college and pro football. I was intimately familiar with the Black and Blue division of the NFL – the Bears, Vikings, Packers and Lions. I knew the records of the teams as well as the individual performances of the players. Shortly after I arrived in Minnesota I met a recently retired NFL player and then record holder for one of the Black and Blue division teams. I was rather startled because this player was much smaller in height (approximately 5'8") and build than I had anticipated. My assumption was that although there are obvious size differences between, for example, quarterbacks and defensive linemen, I also assumed that *every* athlete would have a physical presence that was overpowering. They were, after all, members of the NFL.

I left this encounter thinking that I knew a number of females who were taller and in all likelihood physically stronger than was this former player. Yet conventional notions about gender difference based on physical size and strength precluded any possibility that females would be big and strong enough to play sports like professional football. Yet I had just experienced a situation where that was obviously not the case. Just like the marathon, I began to connect my scholarly readings of biological determinism – and critiques that such dualistic thinking was perfectly suited for a sport setting – with real life experiences that were quite to the contrary. Perhaps some females could compete with and against some males, particularly in those sports not grounded in the most extreme possibilities of male size and physical strength (Messner, 1988). Maybe this notion of 'women's' and 'men's' sports, where we assume that all men will outperform all women – especially at elite levels of competition – was obscuring a far greater reality: rather than organising sports into two mutually exclusive categories based on what we assume are inherent (i.e., biological) gender differences, we could think about sports as a continuum of physical activity where women and men fall along a range of performance differences. It was within this intersection of my professional and personal lives that the continuum theory was born.

Central tenets and ramifications of the sport continuum theory

The title of my 1995 manuscript is, 'Resistance/Transformation of the oppositional binary: Exposing sport as a continuum'. I was beginning to understand that analysing sport as a continuum would allow scholars to critique sports as a gendered binary without falling into the same unintentional traps I outlined above. But why the use of the verb 'exposing' and how was that connected to resisting – and even transforming – sports? Here was my point of departure from previous research: I argued that confining our analysis to categories of 'men's' and 'women's' sports suppressed knowledge of sport as a continuum. I further argued that as long as we constructed sports in this manner, females would be forever seen as engaging in 'lesser' sports and thus, by definition, be considered inferior athletes when measured against their male counterparts. This is precisely why exposing sport as a continuum would be profoundly threatening to established conventions of power because it would provide evidence that some women can (and do) outperform some men, even in 'men's' sports (e.g., basketball), and that they also possess physical attributes such as strength and speed in greater capacities than do many men. In sum, 'the acknowledgement of such a continuum provides a direct assault on traditional beliefs about sport, and gender itself, as an inherent, oppositional binary that is grounded in biological difference' (Kane, 1995, p. 193).

Based on your own lived experience participating in and watching sports, you may be wondering – even resisting – how I could possibly make the claim that 'women outperform men' in a variety of sports and physical activities. To address this issue I return to the muscle-gap literature. Recall that earlier in the paper I cited Paul Willis who brilliantly made the point that, '[Men] running faster, jumping higher, throwing farther can be *seen*—not interpreted' (1982, p. 117). But what Willis did not say – and here is the key to the continuum – is that it is *only men who are seen* jumping higher, running faster and throwing farther. If, however, we conceptualised sport as a continuum of performance difference we would witness many women running faster, jumping higher and throwing farther than many men. This is precisely why we rarely (if ever) see women performing in such a manner.

None of my arguments refute the fact that there are biological – and performance – differences between women and men, though it must be emphasised that cultural factors clearly exaggerate those differences. For example, traditional definitions of what it means to 'be a man' are synonymous with what it means to be an athlete; while females, until recently, were stigmatised for participating in sports, particularly team sports at elite levels (Cooky, Wachs, Messner and Dworkin, 2010; LaVoi and Kane, in press). Given this background, it stands to reason that we have routinely emphasised muscle-gap comparisons such as the average female versus the average male. But if we reframed our analysis to conceptualise sport as a continuum, we would see a very different reality – a *range of performance differences* among women and men that would reveal not just one, but many muscle gaps. As I pointed out in the original paper:

> [Although] males, as a class, tend to have an advantage in strength and size over women, as a class, it is equally true that the 'range of difference among individuals in both sexes is greater than the average difference between the sexes.'
>
> *(Rathe, as cited in Kane, 1995, p. 201)*

Containing/suppressing knowledge of the continuum: the role of gender segregation

If males, as the dominant group, are to maintain their position of power and privilege, sports must be perpetuated as a taken-for-granted binary. One way this is accomplished is to ensure there is rarely (if ever) any overlap, that we never witness females outperforming males, particularly in sports traditionally associated with men. In the original paper I highlighted how much cultural effort goes into maintaining the sport binary while simultaneously suppressing evidence of the continuum. Central to my thesis was that a key to obscuring any notion (or reality) of performance overlap was to prevent women and men from competing with and against each other. This is done first and foremost by organising sports as 'women's' and 'men's' sports. What's important to note, however, is that most women participate in the same sports that men do, but because they rarely compete head-to-head, we never imagine the existence of a continuum, meaning the possibility that many sports can be constructed as a gender-neutral activity where numerous individuals – some of whom are male and some of whom are female – have varying degrees of ability and performance outcomes that frequently include overlap.

To clarify my argument, let me use tennis as a case in point. I am in no way suggesting that, for example, Serena Williams could beat the top-rated male professional tennis players. That is an uncontested fact. But here is an equally uncontested fact: Serena Williams could beat the vast majority of all males who play tennis. What is important to note about these two sets of facts, and how they relate to the continuum, is not that we shouldn't emphasise – or even prioritise – the first set over the other, *it's that we never even consider the latter.* Under current conceptualisations of sports – where we glorify one gendered outcome and totally erase the other – we end up with the following punchline: 'No matter how good a woman is, she can never beat a man.' But imagine how we would think about sports and its 'gendered nature' if we included an additional punchline: 'Some women can beat almost all men, even in the same sport.' Such a conclusion allows us to see why segregating women and men is so essential to suppressing sport as a continuum.

Mechanisms that contain the continuum

I argued in the original piece that there are a number of what I referred to as mechanisms of containment that limit any evidence of a sport continuum. Due to space limitations, I will highlight just two of them: selective gender comparisons and re-gendering. Central to understanding how these containment mechanisms play out is to analyse the totally arbitrary – and artificial – imposition of structural variables and rules that strictly enforce the oppositional binary. As mentioned above, obscuring evidence of a continuum is relatively easy because females and males rarely compete against each other. But there is one popular sport where they not only compete in the same event, but are on the same course at the same time – the marathon. This sport offers a particularly graphic and powerful example of how evidence of a continuum is artificially suppressed. We literally witness a range of performance difference stretched out for miles where men and women are running simultaneously, interspersed along the same course.

Even though one race is taking place, it is artificially constructed as two separate races based on sexual difference. As a result, performance differences between women and men become a primary focus of the event. Racing statistics and media coverage reinforce this oppositional categorisation: the cameras focus on the first runners to cross the finish line and talk about the winner of the men's race. It is usually at this point where the emphasis shifts to the front-running female(s) and the ensuing discussion of who will win the women's race. I am not suggesting that the marathon shouldn't be covered in this fashion. What I am suggesting is to consider why this gender comparison becomes the only one that is ever made. And who benefits when this happens? As I pointed out in the original piece, we select – and then emphasise – one gender comparison while ignoring all others:

> [O]nce the first female crosses the finish line, gender comparisons regarding the rest of the race vanish from the television landscape—she is compared only to the men who have finished ahead of her. We are not told that this same woman has just outperformed all of the other men who have yet to cross the finish line.
>
> *(1995, p. 209)*

The arbitrary decision to focus exclusively on who finished ahead of the female who won the women's race instead of (or in addition to) who finished behind her, automatically ensures that we will never see women beating men even though we literally just witnessed it. Such artificially imposed conventions teach us to read these performance differences only (and always) in ways that privilege men. There is an additional point to be made regarding how selective gender comparisons in general, and the marathon in particular, suppress any evidence of women outperforming men. In the 2013 Twin Cities Marathon, 4,924 men and 3,931 women finished the race. The women's winner finished 45th overall. Even though forty-four men finished ahead of her, 4,879 men finished behind her. Given this rather remarkable result, it's not surprising why some gender comparisons are emphasised over others.

A second mechanism of containment refers to what I called re-gendering, which is a particularly insidious form of binary reinforcement. Re-gendering occurs when females display superior athleticism in a skill or a sport traditionally associated with males. The female in question is re-gendered because when she exhibits such athletic prowess, her own gender becomes temporarily erased while she is being simultaneously recast as male. The sporting world is replete with examples of re-gendering. In Little League we may witness a young girl crushing a baseball and, when we do, a familiar retort is 'she hits just like a man'. This seemingly reasonable response reinforces two important components of the oppositional binary: it confirms that superior athleticism belongs exclusively to males – especially in those sports that 'matter' most – while subverting any notion that females can (and do) possess such physical skills in such capacities. Re-gendering is insidious because, on the surface, it gives the impression that female athleticism is not only accepted but enthusiastically supported – such retorts are, after all, usually meant as a supreme compliment. But we need to remember that the young girl or woman who exhibits such athletic competence is not being supported as a female: 'What re-gendering reveals is that in order to receive this kind of praise she must be (temporarily at least) considered anything but female' (Kane, 1995, p. 208).

Application and impact of the sport continuum

With respect to its application, the continuum theory is not designed to be empirically tested using classic scientific methods as when a scholar develops formal axioms, postulates and theorems (Punch, 2013). It is more in the tradition of theorizing advanced by Mintzberg, who argues that as scholars and educators, our obligation is to develop a set of ideas that stimulates 'pondering, wondering, thinking . . . not knowing [the truth]' (2005, p. 356). There are, however, tangible, real-world ways where the sport continuum has been applied both in measurable and anecdotal terms. These range from scholarly lines of enquiry resulting in publications to classroom settings where (I am told) my article is included in course syllabi and serves as a basis for lively discussions with students. Over the years, my colleagues have mentioned how much the sport continuum has informed their work. And I am always deeply honoured, even a bit surprised and humbled, when a newly minted PhD tells me that my work in general, and the continuum paper in particular, formed the basis of their research studies.

The same can be said for my own work twenty years removed from my original conceptualisations. How ideologies and practices perpetuate gendered relations of power within a sport context remain at the centre of my empirical investigations ranging from media coverage of women's sports (Fink, Kane and LaVoi, 2014; Kane, LaVoi and Fink, in press) to occupational employment patterns related to women's leadership positions in intercollegiate athletics (Kane, 2001). Using more scientific 'measures of impact', a search on Google Scholar indicated that the article has been cited 143 times. One final measure of the theory's influence relates to an experience I had this past summer. I direct an interdisciplinary research centre at the University of Minnesota. As I was preparing to write this manuscript, I asked one of our interns to compile a list of more recent publications. She had just completed her undergraduate work and would soon pursue her graduate studies. She told me she had already read the continuum paper as it was assigned in one of her undergraduate classes. This anecdote alone speaks volumes to perhaps the theory's greatest impact: seeing one's work passed on to a new generation is a legacy that would make any scholar proud.

Extension and future directions

As with measuring impact, the continuum theory cannot be extended in a formal, scientific way. Yet Mintzberg's approach to theorizing led me to this particular train of thought: in the two decades since I first introduced the sport continuum, women have made unprecedented participation and achievement gains across a wide variety of sports including ice hockey, lacrosse and extreme sports (Kane, 2012). These developments appear to provide significantly more opportunities to reveal sport as a continuum, but the record is pretty clear that traditional gender arrangements about how sports are conceptualised and practiced remain firmly entrenched as an oppositional binary.

That said, let us theorize for a moment and examine what would happen if the continuum were extended as we move further into the twenty-first century and as women's participation continues to increase. I was (and remain) keenly aware that the logical extension of the theory would be to fully integrate the sporting enterprise where we would no longer use gender as a centrepiece to practice sports. Such an outcome is no more on the radar screen today than it was twenty years ago. But there is a reason for this and it lies at the heart of the theoretical underpinnings of the continuum. Recall that I emphasised the essential role sex segregation plays in suppressing evidence of the continuum and thereby reinforcing male power and privilege. Because 'women's' and 'men's' sports are deeply entrenched within a biology-is-destiny framework, we have learned from generation to generation that segregating sports is a well-meaning and practical approach designed to encourage females to participate, but to do so in ways that protect them from being injured if they compete against men (Theberge, 2000). Examples range from Little League Baseball, where attempts to integrate the sport in the early 1970s were met with medical claims that girls' bones were more susceptible to fractures (Goodman, 1989), to assertions that females would be hopelessly overmatched if they were allowed to compete against males and doing so would jeopardise the very integrity of sports (Kidd, 1990). However, one could argue that it is actually men who are being protected by segregating sports, because if females really are naturally inferior athletes, wouldn't they automatically fail if given the opportunity to compete against men? Wouldn't such head-to-head competitions give men the very evidence they would need to empirically advance their claims?

Given such circumstances, it's important to ask why there has been a history of resistance to women's desires to compete with and against men. Perhaps it's because men are concerned that women can outperform them even in sports they have claimed as their own. Putting forth such an argument in no way suggests that women can outperform men at the most elite levels of competition, particularly in sports like football, basketball and hockey that are organised around the most extreme physical capacities of the male body and where a central component of the sport is to physically subdue one's opponent. But there are some sports, even at the most elite, high-stakes levels, where we cannot only imagine such possibilities, but where women actually *have* outperformed their male counterparts. Two such examples involve Olympic sports – rifle shooting and ski jumping. Women were first allowed to compete in shooting – and in head-to-head competitions against men – at the 1968 Olympics in Mexico City and did so until the 1996 Games in Atlanta. Why the switch? According to McDonagh and Pappano (2008), segregating rifle shooting occurred because of what took place at the 1976 Montreal Olympics where Margaret Murdock tied with her male teammate in the 50-metre three-position shooting event. In a controversial decision, judges broke the tie, giving Murdoch the silver medal, though both athletes stood on the gold medal stand during the awards ceremony. Murdoch believed that her unprecedented performance spurred officials to seek separate (and different) shooting events in future Olympics because '[M]en didn't like having a woman beat them' (p. 12).

After this controversial finish, the IOC not only segregated the sport, but enforced arbitrary and artificial rules where women, by definition, could not be considered equal – let alone superior – athletes. From 1996 on, women have competed in six shooting events compared with nine for men. And in those events where they engage in the same skill (e.g., skeet), women shoot at seventy-five targets versus 125 targets for men. A similar pattern of women outperforming men – and which also resulted in sex segregation where arbitrary rules were imposed – occurred in ski jumping. For decades women were banned from competing in the Olympics because, according to IOC officials, there were not enough females around the globe who could jump at elite levels, and where as late as 2005, an IOC member stated that he opposed women's entrance because it 'seems not to be appropriate from a medical point of view' (Clarke, 2014, para. 7). But after a series of lawsuits and international pressure, women were finally allowed to compete for the first time at the 2014 Olympics in Sochi, Russia, though not against men and in fewer overall events (Women's Ski Jumping USA, n.d., para. 10).

Though these are powerful and reality-based examples of females outperforming males in the same sport at the highest levels, I am well aware that attempts to integrate sports would, at least for the foreseeable future, harm females in very profound ways. We would, for example, have only one basketball, hockey, tennis, golf, swimming team. In such circumstances, very few females would make the overall team. But it doesn't automatically follow that we can't discontinue *any* current practices where rules are artificially changed to guarantee that males will always outperform females. As a society, we have the ability to reintegrate rifle shooting at the Olympic Games, to remove 'ladies tees' from golf, or to change tennis so that women also play three out of five (versus two out of three) sets to win a match.[3] Practising some sports as a continuum would directly challenge those assumptions – repeated in mantra-like fashion – that women can outperform only lesser-skilled males or can only excel in so-called women's sports. If the continuum were to take hold, even in a limited fashion, we would begin to see an erosion of segregationist policies and practices where females are denied opportunities because of deeply entrenched beliefs that they possess innately inferior capacities.

Dream a little dream

You won't be surprised to learn that when I introduce the sport continuum to my students – and challenge them to follow it to its logical conclusion of integrating sports – I am met with a great deal of resistance, at least when it comes to its practical implications. It will also come as no surprise that females resist such ideas just as much if not more so (for obvious reasons) than do males. I am very aware that attempts to integrate sports, especially team-oriented combat sports, would fall into the realm of being removed from reality. But remember that it was many generations ago when young girls who had aspirations to play sports were repeatedly told that such desires – and opportunities – were 'just a dream'. For these generations of pre-Title IX girls, playing sports at all – let alone at such elite levels – seemed (and were) far-fetched. So let me close with a suggestion that seems equally far-fetched: that unless and until young girls of the next several generations grow up dreaming of becoming a star basketball player, not a star *girls'* basketball player, they will forever be consigned to a 'lesser than' status. It is only when we unconditionally commit to sport as a continuum – where young girls and women have similar amounts of social support and access to resources – that sports, fully integrated and transformed, will no longer exist as an oppositional binary. Theoretically speaking.

Notes

1 This chapter is a reflection on Kane (1995) and the work related to it.
2 Critical feminist theory posits that society is structured around a series of inequitable relationships of power whereby women are systematically devalued and marginalised (Kane and Maxwell, 2011).
3 The rationale for this gender difference is that women lack the endurance capacities of men. It is particularly ironic because if there is any physical attribute that women possess (on average) in greater capacities than men it's endurance (Kane, 1995).

References

Bartky, S.L. (1988) 'Foucault, femininity and the modernization of patriarchal power'. In I. Diamond and L. Quinby (eds) *Feminism and Foucault: Reflections on resistance* (pp. 61–86). Boston, MA: Northeastern University Press.
Birrell, S. and Cole, C.L. (1990) 'Double fault: Renee Richards and the construction and naturalization of difference'. *Sociology of Sport Journal*, 7: 1–21.
Bryson, L. (1990) 'Challenges to male hegemony in sport'. In M.A. Messner and D.F. Sabo (eds) *Sport, men and the gender order* (pp. 173–84). Champaign, IL: Human Kinetics.

Clarke, L. (2014, 3 February) 'Sochi 2014: Women's ski jumpers ready to prove their Olympic mettle'. Available at www.washingtonpost.com (accessed on 1 September, 2014).

Cooky, C., Wachs, F.L., Messner, M.A. and Dworkin, S.L. (2010) 'It's not about the game: Don Imus, race, class, gender and sexuality in contemporary media'. *Sociology of Sport Journal*, 27: 139–59.

Fink, J.S., Kane, M.J., LaVoi, N.M. (2014) 'The freedom to choose: Elite female athletes' preferred representations within endorsement opportunities'. *Journal of Sport Management*, 29: 207–19.

Frye, M. (1983) *The politics of reality. Essays in feminist theory*. Trumansburg, NY: Crossing Press.

Goodman, M. (1989, September) 'Little League: American as apple pie (but not as sweet)'. *Z Magazine*, 2: 68–9.

Hall, M.A. (1990) 'How should we theorize gender in the context of sport?' In M.A. Messner and D.F. Sabo (eds) *Sport, men, and the gender order* (pp. 223–40). Champaign, IL: Human Kinetics.

Kane, M.J. (1995) 'Resistance/transformation of the oppositional binary: Exposing sport as a continuum'. *Journal of Sport & Social Issues*, 19: 191–218.

Kane, M.J. (1998) 'Fictional denials of female empowerment: A feminist analysis of young adult sports fiction'. *Sociology of Sport Journal*, 15: 231–62.

Kane, M.J. (2001) 'Leadership, sport and gender'. In S.J.M. Freeman, S.C. Bourque and C.M. Shelton (eds) *Women on power: Leadership redefined* (pp. 114–46). Boston, MA: Northeastern University Press.

Kane, M.J. (2012) 'Title IX at 40: Examining mysteries, myths and misinformation surrounding the historic federal law'. *President's Council on Fitness, Sports & Nutrition Research Digest*, 13: 2–9.

Kane, M.J. and Maxwell, H.D. (2011) 'Expanding the boundaries of sport media research: Using critical theory to explore consumer responses to representations of women's sports'. *Journal of Sport Management*, 25: 202–16.

Kane, M.J., LaVoi, N.M. and Fink, J.S. (in press) 'Exploring elite female athletes' interpretations of sport media images: A window into the construction of social identity and "selling sex" in women's sports'. *Communication & Sport*.

Kidd, B. (1990) 'The men's cultural centre: Sports and the dynamic of women's oppression/men's repression'. In M.A. Messner and D.J. Sabo (eds) *Sport, men, and the gender order* (pp. 31–44). Champaign, IL: Human Kinetics.

LaVoi, N.M. and Kane, M.J. (in press) 'Sport sociology for sport management'. In P. Pedersen, L. Thibault and J. Quarterman (eds) *Contemporary sport management* (fourth edn). Champaign, IL: Human Kinetics.

McDonagh, E. and Pappano, L. (2008) *Playing with the boys: Why separate is not equal in sports*. Oxford University Press.

Messner, M.A. (1988) 'Sports and male domination: The female athlete as contested ideological terrain'. *Sociology of Sport Journal*, 5: 197–211.

Mintzberg, H. (2005) 'Developing theory about the development of theory'. In K.G. Smith and M.A. Hitt (eds) *Great minds in management: The process of theory development* (pp. 355–72). Oxford University Press.

Nelson, M.B. (1994) *The stronger women get, the more men love football: Sexism and the American culture of sports*. New York: Harcourt Brace.

Punch, K.F. (2013) *Introduction to social research: Quantitative and qualitative approaches*. Los Angeles, CA: Sage.

Theberge, N. (2000) *Higher goals: Women's ice hockey and the politics of gender*. Albany, NY: SUNY Press.

Willis, P. (1982) 'Women in sport and ideology'. In J. Hargreaves (ed.) *Sport, culture and ideology* (pp. 117–35). London: Routledge & Kegan Paul.

Whitson, D. (1990) 'Sport in the social construction of masculinity'. In M.A. Messner and D.F. Sabo (eds) *Sport, men, and the gender order* (pp. 19–30). Champaign, IL: Human Kinetics.

Women's Ski Jumping USA (n.d.) 'Our Olympic story'. Available at www.wsjusa.com/olympic-inclusion (accessed on 1 September, 2014).

Applying sport continuum theory

Cheryl Cooky[1]

My first introduction to Mary Jo Kane's (1995) ground-breaking article was as a master's student in sport studies at Miami University. The article was assigned for one of my classes, 'Women and Sport', then taught by Mary G. McDonald. As a first year graduate student developing expertise in the area of gender and sport, I liked the article but unfortunately lacked the necessary background to fully appreciate Kane's theoretically innovative arguments. Moreover, I lacked the professional experience and insight to recognise the powerful ways in which such conceptual frameworks challenged dominant gender ideologies reproduced in sport, and the potential of such to challenge the common sense assumptions students and the general public have regarding men's presumed physical superiority in sport. As a published researcher, experienced teacher and a scholar that engages the media, I now have a deep appreciation for this article as Kane provides an accessible yet nuanced understanding of gender and sport, one that moves beyond binary perspectives. What is even more impressive is that the article was published in 1995, yet still has a high degree of relevance in contemporary theorizing on gender and sport. Indeed, I have utilised Kane's article in my own research and it continues to be a required reading each semester that I teach my own 'Gender Issues in Sport' class.

Some of my research focuses on mainstream news media frames of female athletes. My colleagues and I published several articles on the media framings of Caster Semenya, the South African track and field athlete who underwent a very public 'gender verification' testing in 2009 (see Cooky, Dycus and Dworkin, 2013; Dworkin, Swarr and Cooky, 2013). We also published several position papers that examine notions of fair play and the belief of sport as a level playing field, both of which inform the rationale governing bodies use to implement sex testing policies (Dworkin and Cooky, 2012; Cooky and Dworkin, 2013). Central to our analysis was that the sex/gender binary is socially constructed, but that sport maintains the notion of natural, categorical gender difference, as vividly illustrated in sex-testing discourse wherein only female athletes are required to undergo 'gender verification'. Moreover, we asserted that female athletes who do not fit into traditional Western expectations of femininity are more likely to have their 'biological standing as female athletes called into question' (Kane, 1995, p. 210). We utilised Kane's conceptual framework, which argues for the recognition of sport performance as a continuum, rather than a binary, to offer a feminist critique of the sex/gender binary in sport so as to challenge the rationale offered by governing bodies to justify the need for sex testing/gender verification in women's athletics.

At the time of this writing, it has been nearly twenty years since Kane's article was published. According to Google scholar, the article has been cited in 143 publications. Given the enduring usefulness of Kane's conceptual framework for understanding issues pertaining to gender and sport, I am certain this article will retain its relevance for feminist sports studies scholars for another twenty years to come.

Note

1   Cheryl Cooky is an Associate Professor of Women's, Gender and Sexuality Studies at Purdue University.

References

Cooky, C. and Dworkin, S.L. (2013) 'Policing the boundaries of sex: A critical examination of gender verification and the Caster Semenya controversy'. *Journal of Sex Research, 50*: 103–11.

Cooky, C., Dycus, R. and Dworkin, S.L. (2013) '"What makes a woman a woman?" vs. "Our First Lady of sport": A comparative analysis of Caster Semenya in U.S. and South African news media'. *Journal of Sport & Social Issues, 37*: 31–56.

Dworkin, S.L. and Cooky, C. (2012) 'Sport, sex segregation, and sex testing: Critical reflections on this unjust marriage'. *American Journal of Bioethics, 12*: 1–3.

Dworkin, S.L., Swarr, A.L. and Cooky, C. (2013) '(In)Justice in sport: The treatment of South African track star Caster Semenya'. *Feminist Studies, 39*: 40–69.

Kane, M.J. (1995) 'Resistance/transformation of the oppositional binary: Exposing sport as a continuum'. *Journal of Sport & Social Issues, 19*: 191–218.

PART V

Economic theories

30

SPORT AND ECONOMIC REGENERATION IN CITIES[1]

Chris Gratton, Simon Shibli and Richard Coleman

Introduction

The focus of our work (Gratton, Shibli and Coleman, 2005) was the economic regeneration potential for cities from major sports events. The use of sport for urban regeneration first emerged as a policy in the USA in the early 1980s, most notably in Indianapolis. In the late 1980s and early 1990s a few British cities, in particular Sheffield, Birmingham and Glasgow, adopted a similar strategy. In this chapter, we will look at the theoretical rationale behind such strategies and how this has changed in recent years.

Overview: sport and urban regeneration

The study of hallmark events or mega-events became an important part of tourism literature in the 1980s. Since then the economics of sports tourism at major sports events has become an increasing part of this event tourism literature. Many governments around the world have adopted national sports policies specifying that hosting major sports event is a major objective. The justification of such policies was initially the potential that such events had to generate direct economic impact benefits for the host city and host country.

The hosting of major sports events is often justified by the host city in terms of long-term economic consequences, directly or indirectly, resulting from the staging of the event (Mules and Faulkner, 1996). These effects were primarily justified in economic terms, by estimating the additional expenditure generated in the local economy as the result of the event, in terms of the benefits injected from tourism-related activity and the subsequent re-imaging of the city following the success of the event (Roche, 1992). Although economic impact was the main focus of the sports event literature initially, emphasis moved to a broader range of economic benefits that hosting events could generate.

Cities staging major sports events have a unique opportunity to market themselves to the world. Increasing competition between broadcasters to secure broadcasting rights to major sports events has led to a massive escalation in fees for such rights, which in turn means broadcasters give blanket coverage at peak times for such events, enhancing the marketing benefits to the cities that stage them.

Such benefits might include a notional value of exposure achieved from media coverage and the associated place marketing effects related to hosting and broadcasting an event, which might encourage visitors to return in future. Or there may be related sports development impacts, which may encourage young people to get more involved in sport. Collectively these additional benefits could be monitored using a more holistic Balanced Scorecard approach to event evaluation, as outlined in Figure 30.1.

In theory, then, there is a wide diversity in the range of economic benefits that sports events can generate. Kasimati (2003) summarised the potential long-term benefits to a city of hosting major sports events such as the summer Olympics: newly constructed event facilities and infrastructure, urban revival, enhanced international reputation, increased tourism, improved public welfare, additional employment and increased inward investment. In practice, however, there is also a possible downside to hosting such events including: high construction costs of sporting venues and related other investments in particular in transport infrastructure, temporary congestion problems, displacement of other tourists due to the event, and underutilised elite sporting facilities after the event that are of little use to the local population.

Despite there being a strong theoretical case in favour of urban regeneration benefits from investment in sporting infrastructure in order to host major sports events, there are also strong arguments that the negative impacts of such investment may match or even outweigh these benefits. The evidence of the net balance between the positive and negative economic benefits to cities from hosting sports events has tended to be different in the USA and the rest of the world, in particular in Europe and Australia.

City sports strategies in North America

Over the last two decades many cities in the United States have invested vast amounts of money on sports stadia on the basis of arguments relating to economic benefits to the city from such investment. Most of these strategies have been based on professional team sports; in particular, American football, baseball, ice hockey and basketball. Unlike the situation in Europe, professional teams in North America frequently move from city to city.

Since the late 1980s, cities have offered greater and greater incentives for these professional teams to move by offering to build new stadia to house them, costing hundreds of millions of

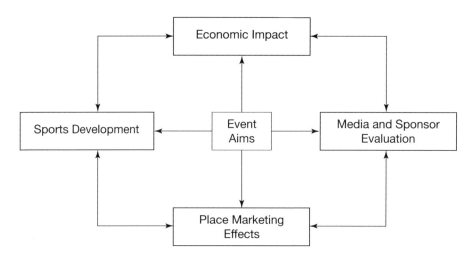

Figure 30.1 The 'balanced scorecard' approach to evaluating events
Source: Gratton *et al.*, 2005, p. 988.

dollars. The teams just sit back and let cities bid up the price. They either move to the city offering the best deal or they accept the counter offer invariably put to them by their existing hosts. This normally involves the host city building them a brand new stadium to replace their existing one, which may only be ten or fifteen years old.

Baade (2003) indicates how, since the 1980s, escalating stadium construction costs have increased the size of stadium subsidies:

> The number of stadiums that have been built since 1987 to the present is unprecedented. Approximately 80 per cent of the professional sports facilities in the United States will have been replaced or have undergone major renovation during this period of time. The new facilities have cost more than $19 billion in total, and the public has provided $13.6 billion, or 71 per cent, of that amount. In few, if any, instances have professional teams in the United States been required to open their books to justify the need for these subsidies. Rather, teams have convinced cities that to remain competitive on the field they have to be competitive financially, and this, teams claim, cannot be achieved without new playing venues.
>
> *(p. 588)*

This use of taxpayers' money to subsidise profit-making professional sports teams seems out of place in the North American context. The justification for such public expenditure is an economic one: the investment of public money is a worthwhile investment as long as the economic impact generated by having a major professional sports team resident in the city is sufficiently great. Economic impact refers to the total amount of additional expenditure generated within a host city (or area), which could be directly attributable to the staging of a particular event. Only visitors to the host economy as a direct result of an event being staged are eligible for inclusion in the economic impact calculations (i.e., the expenditure by people resident in the host area is not included on the basis that they would spend money locally irrespective of whether an event is taking place).

Baade (1996), Noll and Zimbalist (1997), and Coates and Humphreys (1999), however, showed no significant direct economic impact on the host cities from such stadium development. Crompton (1995, 2001) also argues that economic impact arguments in favour of such stadium construction using public subsidies have been substantially exaggerated.

Schimmel (2001) and Davidson (1999) analyse how sport has been used in Indianapolis for economic regeneration of the city. Indianapolis is a mid-western US city that in the mid 1970s was suffering from the decline of its heavy manufacturing base, in particular its car industry. Local politicians were keen to develop a new image of the city. As Schimmel indicates, the problem was not that the city had a bad image, but rather that the city had no image at all. The strategy was to target the expanding service sector economy in an attempt to redevelop the city's downtown area by using sport as a catalyst for economic regeneration and building a national image. From 1974 to 1984, a total of $1.7 billion USD in public and private resources was invested in inner-city construction (Schimmel, 2001), of which sporting infrastructure played a major role. The strategy included investment in facilities in professional team sports but added to this a strategy of hosting major sports events in the city.

Between 1977 and 1991, 330 sports events were hosted by Indianapolis. Davidson (1999) attempted to measure the economic contribution of sport to the city in 1991. He found that, in 1991, eighteen sport organisations and nine sport facilities in the city employed 526 employees. In addition, thirty-five sports events held in the city in 1991 generated additional spending of $97 million USD. He estimated the total economic contribution of sport organisations, facilities and events in Indianapolis in 1991 to be $133 million USD. Although Indianapolis was an early example, the strategy of using sports events as a catalyst for urban regeneration became popular in the UK in the 1980s and 1990s.

Sport and economic regeneration in cities in the UK

Several cities in the UK (Sheffield, Birmingham and Glasgow) have used sport as a lead sector in promoting urban regeneration and these three cities were awarded National City of Sport status in 1995 partly because of this. They have all invested heavily in their sports infrastructure so that each has a portfolio of major sporting facilities capable of holding major sports events.

In addition to facilities, each city has a supporting structure of expertise in event bidding and management to ensure quality bids with a high probability of success and to guarantee high-quality event management. Events are a major vehicle for attracting visitors to the city and hence contributing to urban regeneration. However, these cities are also involved with developing sport in the cities through performance and excellence programmes (e.g., training, squad preparation, coaching) and in community sports development, so that the local population benefits from the investment in sports infrastructure.

These and other cities have made a specific commitment to public investment in sport as a vehicle for urban regeneration. However, the quantity and distribution of returns to such public sector investment in sport, predominantly from local government, have been largely under-researched and remain uncertain. Often such investment attracts criticism because of media attention on a specific event, such as the World Student Games in Sheffield in 1991, and there has been little research on the medium- and long-term returns on such investment.

Sport and economic regeneration in cities in other parts of the world

One of the first major studies in this area was the study of the impact of the 1985 Adelaide Formula 1 Grand Prix (Burns, Hatch and Mules, 1986). This was followed by Richie's in-depth study of the 1988 Calgary Winter Olympics (Richie, 1984; Richie and Aitken, 1984, 1985; Richie and Lyons, 1987, 1990; Richie and Smith, 1991). In fact, immediately prior to these studies, it was generally thought that hosting major sports events was a financial liability to host cities following the large debts faced by Montreal after hosting the 1976 Olympics. There was a general change in attitude following the 1984 Los Angeles Olympics, which made a clear profit.

Mules and Faulkner (1996) point out that even with such mega-events as Formula 1 Grand Prix races and the Olympics, it is not always an unequivocal economic benefit to the cities that host the event. They emphasise that, in general, staging major sports events often results in the city authorities losing money even though the city itself benefits greatly in terms of additional spending in the city. Thus the 1994 Brisbane World Masters Games cost the city A$2.8 million to organise but generated a massive A$50.6 million of additional economic activity in the State economy. Mules and Faulkner's basic point is that it normally requires the public sector to finance the staging of the event and incurring these losses in order to generate the benefits to the local economy. They argue that governments host such events and lose taxpayers' money in the process in order to generate spillover effects or externalities.

It is not a straightforward job, however, to establish a profit-and-loss account for a specific event. Major sports events require investment in new sports facilities and often this is paid for in part by central government or even international sports bodies. Thus, some of this investment expenditure represents a net addition to the local economy since the money comes in from outside. Also such facilities remain after the event has finished, acting as a platform for future activities that can generate additional tourist expenditure (Mules and Faulkner, 1996).

Sports events are increasingly seen as part of a broader tourism strategy aimed at raising the profile of a city and therefore success cannot be judged on simply profit-and-loss basics. Often the attraction of events is linked to a re-imaging process and, in the case of many cities, is invariably linked to strategies of urban regeneration and tourism development (Bianchini and Schwengel, 1991; Bramwell, 1995; Loftman and Spirou, 1996; Roche, 1994). Major events, if successful, have the ability to project a new image and identity for a city. The hosting of major sports events is often justified by the host city in terms of long-term economic and social consequences, directly or indirectly resulting from the staging of the event (Mules and Faulkner, 1996).

Process

Our initial interest in the economic impact generated by hosting major sports events came from Sheffield City Council commissioning the Sport Industry Research Centre (SIRC) to estimate the economic impact of the games played in Sheffield as part of the 1996 European Football Championships (EURO 96). Those responsible for organising the EURO 96 tournament were mainly concerned with security issues and economic impact was not something they had really considered. The results from the research indicated that the economic impact in each of the eight host cities was substantial and overseas visitors alone contributed over £120 million additional expenditure to the local economies of the host cities during the tournament.

These results for the EURO 96 football championships generated major interest in the economic impact on host cities from staging sports events. In 1997, UK Sport was set up with one of its priorities to bring major sports events to the UK. This was initially called the World Class Events Programme. The main policy behind this was to give UK elite athletes the opportunity to have top-level competition on their own home soil. However, if bringing such events to the UK could also generate economic benefits then this justified subsiding UK national governing bodies to bring events such as World and European championships to the UK. Consequently, over the following decade UK Sport commissioned research around the international events that came to the UK to assess the economic impact of these events. SIRC won many of these research contracts and the economic impact of major sports events became a major focus for our research programme.

In a report commissioned by UK Sport, *Measuring success 2: The economic impact of major sport events* (UK Sport, 2004), SIRC presented an overview of the findings from sixteen economic impact studies of major sports events undertaken since 1997, many of which took place in Sheffield, Glagow or Birmingham, the three National Cities of Sport, and all but three (Spar Europa Cup, World Cup Triathlon, World Indoor Athletics) of which were carried out by SIRC. This consolidated piece of research built on the original *Measuring success* (UK Sport, 1999a) document published by UK Sport in 1999, which recognised and demonstrated the potential of major sports events to achieve significant economic impacts for the cities that host them.

These sixteen studies were conducted using essentially the same methodology as those published by UK Sport in 1999 entitled *Major events: The economics – A guide* (UK Sport, 1999b). This therefore provides a dataset in which the events are directly comparable and we concentrated on these comparisons. Key findings from the research are outlined in Table 30.1, commencing with the impact of each event.

Overall, the findings confirm that major sports events can have significant economic impacts on host communities. These impacts ranged from the £0.18m of additional expenditure attributable to the half-day IAAF Grand Prix Athletics staged on a Sunday in Sheffield in June

Table 30.1 Economic impact of sixteen major sports events

Year	Event	Host city	Event days	Impact (£)	Impact per event day (£s)
1997	World Badminton	Glasgow	14	2.22m	0.16m
1997	European Junior Boxing	Birmingham	9	0.51m	0.06m
1997	1st Ashes Test – Cricket England v Australia	Birmingham	5	5.06m	1.01m
1997	IAAF Grand Prix 1 Athletics	Sheffield	1	0.18m	0.18m
1997	European Junior Swimming	Glasgow	4	0.26m	0.06m
1997	Women's British Open Golf	Sunningdale	4	2.07m	0.52m
1998	European Short Course Swimming	Sheffield	3	0.31m	0.10m
1999	European Show Jumping	Hickstead	5	2.20m	0.44m
1999	World Judo	Birmingham	4	1.94m	0.49m
1999	World Indoor Climbing	Birmingham	3	0.40m	0.13m
2000	Flora London Marathon	London	1	25.46m	25.46m
2000	Spar Europa Cup – Athletics	Gateshead	2	0.97m	0.48m
2001	World Amateur Boxing	Belfast	8	1.49m	0.19m
2001	World Half Marathon	Bristol	1	0.58m	0.58m
2003	World Cup Triathlon	Manchester	1	1.67m	1.67m
2003	World Indoor Athletics	Birmingham	3	3.16m	1.05m

Source: (Gratton *et al.*, 2005, p. 991)

1997, to the £25.5m attributable to the Flora London Marathon in April 2000. Moreover, other events, most notably the World Cup Triathlon, World Indoor Athletics and Test Cricket, attracted additional expenditure per day in excess of £1m. Junior events (e.g., European Junior Swimming and Junior Boxing) had the least significant daily impacts, mainly because they rarely attract considerable numbers of spectators. It is interesting to note that the two events generating the highest economic impacts, the London Marathon and a cricket Test Match, were domestic events that take place annually, do not need to go through a bidding process and do not require new sporting infrastructure investment.

Economic impact is not UK Sport's rationale for attracting major events to the UK, but it is a useful device by which to justify funding an event in economic terms. The evidence suggests that, as a general rule, it is the expenditure by visitors to an event that contributes the majority of any additional expenditure, rather than spending by the organisers of an event.

Spectators contributed the majority of the additional expenditure at ten of the sixteen events, and such events are termed spectator driven. Further analyses revealed a strong correlation between the number of spectator admissions and the absolute economic impact of an event, which suggests that the absolute number of spectators is the key driver of economic impact.

Extensions and applications

The main extension of the theory in recent years has been the broadening out of the benefits beyond simply economic impact. A broad range of benefits has been suggested for both the country and the host city from staging major sports events including: urban regeneration legacy benefits, sporting legacy benefits, tourism and image benefits, and social and cultural benefits. The direct economic impact benefit, however, is the reason most cities have put forward for their desire to host events. It is well known that cities and countries compete fiercely to host the Olympic Games or the soccer World Cup. However, over recent years there has been increasing competition to host less globally recognised sports events in a wide range of other sports where spectator interest is less assured and where the economic benefits are not so clear cut.

Figure 30.2 outlines the broad range of benefits that hosting an event may generate. In addition to the benefits in Figure 30.1, we have added legacy and the value of the event to residents of the host city. As indicated earlier, economic impact has been the main focus of impact over the recent past but this is now changing to a focus on these two benefits, legacy and the value of the event to residents of the host city.

The argument on why cities bid to host major events in the 1980s and 1990s was based on the economic development paradigm. That is, events will influence people living outside the host city and country to visit or invest in the city or country either during the event itself or in subsequent years because the place marketing effects of seeing the event on television will generate more tourism in the longer term.

The American sport economics literature, however, has argued consistently that no evidence exists to suggest such economic benefits from hosting events ever actually materialise. As Crompton (2004) states:

> The prevailing evidence is that substantial measurable economic impact has rarely been demonstrated. This is causing the focus of the argument for public subsidy to be redefined, away from economic impacts and economic development towards the psychic income benefits. This is the new frontier.
>
> *(p. 55)*

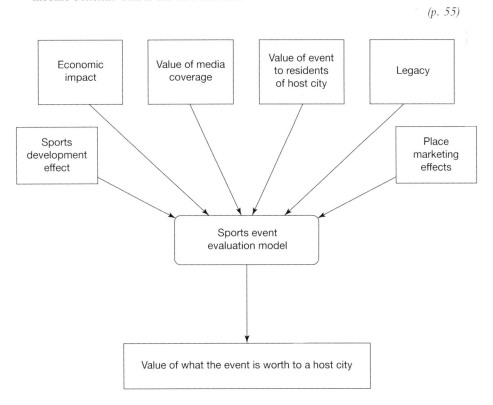

Figure 30.2 Towards an event evaluation model

This literature is mainly concerned with the economic impact of teams in the major four American team sports: American football, ice hockey, baseball and basketball. Other economists have shown that major events do generate substantial economic impact. The soccer World Cup in Germany in 2006 generated an economic impact of 2.56 billion euros, with an average of 40 million euros from each match (Preuss, Kurscheidt and Schütte 2009).

There is little evidence to suggest that the Olympics, summer or winter, generate a significant economic impact of the size of the World Cup. During the period July to September 2012 there were 4 per cent less visits to the UK by overseas residents than in the same period in 2011. A similar pattern was observed in Beijing in 2008, Athens in 2004 and Sydney in 2000.

In contrast to the economic argument, which focuses on audiences external to the host city or country, psychic income focuses *internally* on the host city or host country residents, and refers to the emotional and psychological benefit residents receive from hosting as indicated in Figure 30.3.

Gratton and Preuss (2008) also identified such emotional benefits as an important part of the legacy of major events. In addition, in the last few years, sport economists have adopted the methodology developed in the economics of happiness literature to analyse the effect of hosting major events on national pride and social well-being. Some studies have examined the willingness to pay (WTP) for both hosting sports events and success at sporting events and found that WTP can be substantial. Atkinson, Mourato, Symanski and Oxdemiroglu (2008) explored the willingness of citizens of London, Manchester and Glasgow to host the 2012 London Olympic Games. They found the average WTP was highest among Londoners (£22), about twice as much as in London and Manchester, and was £2 billion for the UK population as a whole. Sussmuth, Heyne and Maennig (2010) found similar levels of WTP for German citizens for the 2006 World Cup. Wicker, Hallman, Breuer and Feiler (2012a) and Wicker, Prinz and von

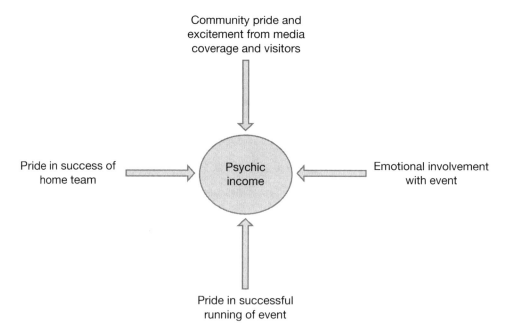

Figure 30.3 Psychic income paradigm
(Adapted from Crompton, 2004)

Hanau (2012b) found significant levels of willingness to pay for both Olympic success and World Cup success among German citizens.

Kavetsos and Szymanski (2010), using Eurobarometer data for twelve European countries, showed that hosting major events had a significant impact on national pride. Kavetsos (2012), using Eurobarometer data for sixteen countries, also found significant effects on national pride from hosting major events. De Nooij, Van den Berg and Koopmans (2013), using a social cost–benefit analysis of the Netherlands World Cup bid, found that a greater sense of happiness, national pride, harmony and national identity were the main economic benefits to the hosts from staging a World Cup rather than economic impact.

Jing (2012) carried out an exploratory study of Chinese young people to estimate the impact of Beijing 2008 on national pride and self-esteem four years on. A sample of 184 university students aged from eighteen to twenty-four were asked whether they agreed or disagreed with the statement: China's hosting of the Beijing 2008 Olympic Games created a strong sense of national identity; 86.4 per cent either agreed or strongly agreed. Responding to the statement, 'I am proud at China's performance in topping the medal table in Beijing', 90.8 per cent agreed or strongly agreed. This study was carried out four years after the staging of the Beijing Olympics, indicating that psychic income can be an important part of the legacy of hosting major events.

Future directions

The previous focus on the direct economic benefits of hosting major sports events has now changed. Most economists in the United States have questioned whether such benefits ever existed. In the rest of the world, most economists would argue that they can exist in the right circumstances. The last two Olympics, in Beijing and London, undoubtedly led to substantial urban regeneration, but this was not the result of visitors spending huge amounts either during the event or through subsequent visits as a result of the Olympics. The urban regeneration came from internal investment from the host nations. The economic paradigm, however, is still relevant as witnessed by the huge economic impact of the World Cup in 2006 in Germany. Also many smaller events generate can generate significant economic impact.

It is the case though that the emphasis now is on the other benefits that hosting major sports events can bring to a city and a country. We have argued in this chapter that perhaps the major benefit is a psychological one: psychic income. This argument also fits with new developments in economics. Over the last few decades, economic studies have shown that increasing wealth as measured by GDP does not lead to increasing happiness. A new area of economics has emerged – the economics of happiness – looking at the factors that make people in a country happy. The future of this area of event economics is to assess how important hosting major sports events is in contributing to the happiness of a nation.

Note

1   This chapter is a reflection on Gratton, Shibli and Coleman (2005) and the work related to it.

References

Atkinson, G., Mourato, S., Symanski, S. and Oxdemiroglu, E. (2008) 'Are we willing to pay to "back the bid?" Valuing the intangible impacts of London's bid to host the 2012 summer Olympic Games'. *Urban Studies*, *45*: 419–44.

Baade, R.A. (1996) 'Professional sports as catalysts for economic development'. *Journal of Urban Affairs*, *18*: 1–17.

Baade, R.A. (2003) 'Evaluating subsidies for professional sport in the United States and Europe: A public sector primer'. *Oxford Review of Economic Policy, 19*: 585–97.

Bianchini, F. and Schwengel, H. (1991) 'Re-imagining the city'. In J. Comer and S. Harvey (eds) *Enterprise and heritage: Crosscurrents of national culture* (pp. 214–34). Routledge: London.

Bramwell, B. (1995) 'Event tourism in Sheffield: A sustainable approach to urban development?' Unpublished paper, Centre for Tourism, Sheffield Hallam University.

Burns, J.P.A., Hatch, J.H. and Mules, F.J. (eds) (1986) *The Adelaide Grand Prix: The impact of a special event.* Adelaide: The Centre for South Australian Economic Studies.

Coates, D. and Humphreys, B. (1999) 'The growth of sports franchises, stadiums and arenas'. *Journal of Policy Analysis, 18*: 601–24.

Crompton, J.L. (1995) 'Economic impact analysis of sports facilities and events: Eleven sources of misapplication'. *Journal of Sport Management, 9*: 14–35.

Crompton, J.L. (2001) 'Public subsidies to professional team sport facilities in the USA'. In C. Gratton and I.P. Henry (eds) *Sport in the city: The role of sport in economic and social regeneration* (pp. 15–34). Routledge: London.

Crompton, J.L. (2004) 'Beyond economic impact: An alternative rationale for the public subsidy of major league sports facilities'. *Journal of Sport Management, 18*: 40–58.

Davidson, L. (1999) 'Choice of a proper methodology to measure quantitative and qualitative effects of the impact of sport'. In C. Jeanreaud (ed.) *The economic impact of sport events* (pp. 9–28). Neuchatel, Switzerland: Centre International d'Etude du Sport (CIES).

de Nooij, M., Van den Berg, M. and Koopmans, C. (2013) 'Bread or Games? A social cost-benefit analysis of the World Cup bid of the Netherlands and the winning Russian bid'. *Journal of Sports Economics, 14*: 521–45.

Gratton, C. and Preuss, H. (2008) 'Maximising Olympic impacts by building up legacies'. *International Journal of the History of Sport, 25*: 1922–38.

Gratton C., Shibli, S. and Coleman, R. (2005) 'Sport and economic regeneration in cities'. *Urban Studies, 42*: 985–99.

Jing, Z. (2012) 'An evaluation of Chinese young people's perceptions of the 2008 Beijing Olympic Games'. MSc Sport Business Management thesis, Sheffield Hallam University.

Kasimati, E. (2003) 'Economic aspects and the Summer Olympics: A review of related research'. *International Journal of Tourism Research, 5*: 433–44.

Kavetsos, G. and Szymanski, S. (2010) 'National well-being and international sports events'. *Journal of Economic Psychology, 31*: 158–71.

Kavetsos, G. (2012) 'National pride: War minus the shooting'. *Social Indicators Research, 106*: 173–85.

Loftman, P. and Spirou, C.S. (1996, September) 'Sports stadiums and urban regeneration: The British and United States experience'. Paper presented to the conference, Tourism and Culture: Towards the 21st Century, Durham.

Mules, T. and Faulkner, B. (1996) 'An economic perspective on major events'. *Tourism Economics, 12*: 107–17.

Noll, R. and Zimbalist, A. (eds) (1997) *Sports, jobs and taxes.* The Brookings Institution: Washington, DC.

Preuss, H., Kurscheidt, M. and Schütte, N. (2009) *Ökonomie des Tourismus durch Sportgroßveranstaltungen: Eine empirische Analyse zur Fußball-Weltmeisterschaft 2006.* Wiesbaden: Gabler Verlag.

Ritchie, J.R.B. (1984) 'Assessing the impact of hallmark event: conceptual and research issues'. *Journal of Travel Research, 23*: 2–11.

Ritchie, J.R.B. and Aitken, C.E. (1984) 'Assessing the impacts of the 1988 Olympic Winter Games: the research program and initial results'. *Journal of Travel Research, 22*(3): 17–25.

Ritchie, J.R.B. and Aitken, C.E. (1985) 'OLYMPULSE II – evolving resident attitudes towards the 1988 Olympics'. *Journal of Travel Research, 23*(Winter): 28–33.

Ritchie, J.R.B. and Lyons, M.M. (1987) 'OLYMPULSE III/IV: a mid-term report on resident attitudes concerning the 1988 Olympic Winter Games'. *Journal of Travel Research, 26* (Summer): 18–26.

Ritchie, J.R.B. and Lyons, M.M. (1990) 'OLYMPULSE vi: a post-event assessment of resident reaction to the XV Olympic Winter Games'. *Journal of Travel Research, 28*(3): 14–23.

Ritchie, J.R.B. and Smith, B.H. (1991) 'The impact of a mega event on host region awareness: a longitudinal study'. *Journal of Travel Research, 30*(1): 3–10.

Roche, M. (1992) 'Mega-event planning and citizenship: Problems of rationality and democracy in Sheffield's Universiade 1991'. *Vrijetijd en Samenleving, 10*(4): 47–67.

Roche, M. (1994) 'Mega-events and urban policy'. *Annals of Tourism Research, 21*(1): 1–19.

UK Sport (1999a) *Major events: The economics*. London: Author.

UK Sport (1999b) *Major events: The economics – A guide*. London: Author.

UK Sport (2004) *Measuring success 2: The economic impact of major sports events*. London: Author.

Schimmel, K.S. (2001) 'Sport matters: Urban regime theory and urban regeneration in the late Capitalist Era'. In C. Gratton and I.P. Henry (eds) *Sport in the city: The role of sport in economic and social regeneration* (pp. 259–77). London: Routledge.

Sussmuth, B., Heyne, M. and Maennig, W. (2010) 'Induced civic pride and integration'. *Oxford Bulleting of Economics and Statistics*, 72: 202–20.

Wicker, P., Hallman, K., Breuer, C. and Feiler, S. (2012a) 'The value of Olympic success and the intangible effects of sports events – A contingent valuation approach in Germany'. *European Sport Management Quarterly*, 12: 337–55.

Wicker, P., Prinz, J. and von Hanau, T. (2012b) 'Estimating the value of national sporting success'. *Sport Management Review*, 15: 200–10.

Applying the balanced scorecard approach to evaluating events

Larissa Davies[1]

Gratton, Shibli and Coleman (2005) examine the rationale and justification for investments in sport infrastructure to generate wider economic benefits for cities. The authors introduce the theory of using a balanced scorecard approach to evaluating events and use empirical evidence from sixteen major sports events and a case study of the Commonwealth Games in Manchester 2002 to assess the evidence for the success of such strategies. I first became aware of this work when I was teaching undergraduate geography students about sport, leisure and tourism in the mid 2000s. Subsequently, I have used this article with undergraduate and postgraduate sport business management students to illustrate the wider contribution of major events to local communities. The article was of particular interest to me at the time as it was one of the earlier academic articles published in a multidisciplinary journal, which attempted to create and articulate the linkages between sport and wider local economic development.

The article utilises the theory of the balanced scorecard, developed by Kaplan and Norton (1996, 2005) of Harvard Business School. The balanced scorecard was originally presented as a technique for performance management in business organisations and considers performance from four perspectives: financial; internal business process; learning and growth; and customer perspective. Gratton *et al.* (2005) suggest using an adaptation of the balanced scorecard as an approach to evaluating the wider economic benefits of events, with the four perspectives translating to economic impact; media and sponsor evaluation; place marketing effects; and sports development. I found the article and the theory useful for encouraging students to consider the broader dimensions of event impact and evaluation. The article was one of the earliest contributions in the field to report beyond direct economic impact and to include perspectives such as the media profile of events. The events utilised in the article (for example the 1998 European Short Course Swimming Championships), demonstrate the potential economic value of exposure achieved from media coverage and the associated place marketing effects related to hosting and broadcasting a major event, which might encourage visitors to return or visit in the future. The theory in the article thus helped me to demonstrate to students the potential synergies between sport and economic benefit more widely.

Gratton *et al.*'s article (2005) continues to serve as an early attempt by scholars to conceptualise the wider benefits of sports events, and I will use the article in future teaching to illustrate how event evaluation has developed historically. I will continue to encourage students to consider holistic evaluation frameworks for measuring event impact in my teaching, and I envisage future applications of the theory presented in the article to include, but not be limited to, testing the validity of the model with more recent empirical data from major events.

Note

1   Dr Larissa Davies is a Reader in Sport Management at the Sport Industry Research Centre and Academy of Sport and Physical Activity, Sheffield Hallam University.

References

Gratton, C., Shibli, S. and Coleman, R. (2005) 'Sport and economic regeneration in cities'. *Urban Studies, 42*: 985–99.

Kaplan, R.S. and Norton, D.P. (1996) *The balanced scorecard: Measures that drive performance*. Boston, MA: Harvard Business School Press.

Kaplan, R.S. and Norton, D.P. (2005) 'The balanced scorecard: Measures that drive performance'. *Harvard Business Review, 83*(7): 172–80.

31

TOWARDS A NEW THEORY OF SPORTS-ANCHORED DEVELOPMENT FOR REAL ECONOMIC CHANGE[1]

Stephanie Gerretsen and Mark S. Rosentraub

Introduction

Some social and management science scholars might not regard the sustained findings that sports venues produce neither regional economic development nor fiscal returns for investor cities as a theory. Yet Abraham Kaplan (1973) defined a theory as a sustained relationship *if* it allows one to make 'sense of a disturbing situation so as to allow us more effectively to bring to bear our repertoire of habits, and even more importantly, to modify habits or discard them altogether, replacing them by new ones as the situation demands' (1973, p. 295). The research by numerous scholars produced in the 1990s sustained the view that the public investments in arenas, ballparks and stadia produced no real changes in regional economic development. Their findings became a principle of public policy for sport management. The research sustained Kaplan's definition of a theory in that the research identified an undesirable outcome for taxpayers and the public sector that warranted a change. The changes prescribed included (a) a ban on public investments in the venues used by professional sports teams, (b) a change in laws, making it possible for professional sports leagues to limit the number of teams and (c) the use of eminent domain to allow governments to seize franchises that threatened to relocate when the public sector did not acquiesce to demands for a subsidy for a new venue (Kennedy and Rosentraub, 2000; Rosentraub, 1997).

Other scholars, however, positioned different theories that suggested each of these policy recommendations were fraught with practical, legal and political hurdles that made implementation unlikely. Olson (1965) identified the barriers to the collective action required to get all cities, states and provinces to agree to ban subsidies when a single city or governments could reap benefits from the knowledge that no other was likely to offer a subsidy. His work also helped identify the benefit that exists for cities already home to teams to support the leagues' ability to restrict expansion. Doing so ensured that cities with teams continue to enjoy a special status that would deteriorate if many more cities were home to a franchise. Last, in the aftermath of *Kelo v. New London* (545 U.S. 469), in which the US Supreme Count sustained public takings for economic development, several states passed laws making it more difficult to seize property to advance a government's agenda (Ely, 2009).

In light of these theories and observations that effectively eliminated the proposals to change undesirable outcomes for cities dealing with the demands from teams, what path remains for the practice of sport management? If another theory or path does not exist, are we relegated to the position where there is no alternative to the conclusion that cities that deal with teams are destined to be 'major league losers' (Rosentraub, 1997)? Through this chapter our goal is to posit a different theory to create a new habit or practice that creates pecuniary (real financial) benefits for teams *and* the public sector. That objective can be achieved when a public/private partnership for a venue includes a real estate development strategy to build a new neighbourhood anchored by an arena, ballpark or stadium (Rosentraub, 2014). This new theory creates major league winners from a legacy of major league losers.

What turned the public sector into major league losers?

There has been a degree of hegemonic control established by economic and political elites to subvert competitive or free-market forces that produced the extremely profitable environment of those owning teams in the four major sports leagues. Note, the owners of teams in Major League Soccer or other leagues, such as lacrosse or women's leagues, among others, have not yet enjoyed that benefit. Federal laws in the US and Canada have granted the leagues the ability to control the supply of teams and then to enter into contracts with all of the leading media outlets to reduce the ability of a start-up league to secure a lucrative system to distribute their games or product (Low, Halladay and Opashinov, 2012; Noll and Zimbalist, 1997; Quirk and Fort, 1992; Scully, 1995). This subversion of market forces led to the use of public subsidies to secure the presence of the limited supply of teams that, in turn, elevate profits. Numerous scholars have argued that public subsides of arenas, ballparks and stadiums have contributed to the elevated value of teams and the profits earned by owners (even if those profits are only secured when franchises are sold). At the same time, the initial wave of studies on the use of tax money to help pay for venues could not identify any tangible returns for the public sector. The four older professional sports leagues,[2] working with civic and economic elites, have secured non-market control (Noll and Zimbalist, 1997; Vroom, 2012) of a valuable asset (professional sports). This might seem as an incorrigible situation in which involved parties could never be encouraged to change outcomes.

Can this environment be changed?

We suggest a solution set can be established independent of changes in governance of the major sports leagues.[3] Those solutions, policies and practices can ensure that taxpayers and the public sector enjoy economic returns from their investment in sports venues. Central cities can work with teams and business leaders to ensure that their fiscal position is dramatically enhanced. Indeed, a declaration that behaviour cannot be changed is a failure to recognise Kaplan's (1973) insight into the importance of theory. A theory exists to permit the correction of undesired outcomes and the formulation of other theories to create a more beneficial outcome.

Following this introduction, the second part of the chapter is an exploration of the theory that precisely describes a distributing situation regarding the relationship between teams and the fiscal returns to the public sector for their investments in venues. Much of the existing literature sustains a view of the hegemonic control of a scarce resource – professional team sports – that skews economic returns away from the public sector. The failure to use another theory – discussed in the third part of the chapter – can lead to desirable changes for the public sector. Prodded by Kaplan's (1973) perspective we join theories to posit an alternative course of action that produces substantial pecuniary benefits for the public sector. The last part of our paper uses brief summaries of two cases where the public sector secured important pecuniary gains.

A prevailing theory of teams, venues and economic development: the unending era of major league losers

For decades independent and academic analysts have not found meaningful positive regional economic changes as a result of (a) the presence of a professional sports team or (b) the public sector's investment in venues for teams. Among one of the earliest assessments of the inability of cities to capture the benefits of venues and teams was Rosentraub and Nunn's (1978) study of outcomes in Arlington (Texas Rangers) and Irving (Dallas Cowboys). They concluded that the suburban cities investing in venues were unable to capture sufficient economic activity to realise a positive pecuniary return. A few years earlier, Okner had already concluded 'the benefits from publicly owned sports facilities probably accrue disproportionately to the moderate-income or well-to-do citizens in the community at the expense of the poor' (1974, p. 374). His research was a cautionary note that without very different policies a stage was being set for the formation of practices that would benefit the wealthy at the expense of the poor if the public sector continued to invest in venues. With the launching of Indianapolis' downtown revitalisation efforts anchored by sports venues in the 1970s and 1980s and the building of several new venues in the 1980s and 1990s, scholars began to carefully analyse what the wide-ranging public investments meant for regions and taxpayers.

Led by Baade and Dye's work (1988, 1990) numerous studies affirmed the same basis observation (Baade, 1996; deMause and Cagan, 2008; Coates and Humphreys, 1999; Euchner, 1993; Noll and Zimbalist, 1997; Quirk and Fort, 1992; Rosentraub, 1997; Rosentraub and Swindell, 1991; Whitford, 1993). The presence of stand-alone venues for professional sports teams did not enhance regional economic development. City officials seemed convinced that jobs in the construction sector or at sports venues would lead to lower unemployment levels, higher general wage levels, increased revenues for local businesses and higher tax collections for local governments. Yet the sport management research performed concluded that isolated sports venues would not generate economic growth. Sports-related employment might rise, but those positions were too small or few in number to change regional economic patterns. Humphreys (2001) bluntly cautioned that while cities might enjoy marketing and image benefits there would be little 'job creation, higher earnings [or] additional tax revenues' (2001, p. 37). Coates and Humphreys (1999) even found that sports facilities had a negative impact on regional economies due to high levels of public debt and government funding used to subsidise the construction of professional sports facilities.

Long (2005) added a new dimension to this stream of research by urging a calculation of forgone property taxes, the cost for acquiring land and the public sector's costs for the provision of needed infrastructure to sustain sports venues (and the traffic it generates). Her work augmented research by Nelson (2002) that highlighted the observation that aggregate spending within metropolitan areas did not seem to change when teams were present. That research underscored the concerns of many scholars that spending for sports was simply a shift of regional consumption patterns from one form of discretionary spending to another. The plethora of work sustaining these observations continued into the twenty-first century with new studies produced by Siegfried and Zimbalist (2000, 2002), Chapin (2002), Matheson (2002), Coates and Humphreys (2003), Zimbalist and Long (2006) and Long (2013).

There have been numerous other studies but this incomplete listing sustains the theory that teams playing in stand-alone venues do not change regional economic activity. An obvious question, however, is why with such a theory emerging did mayors, county officials or governors continue to chase professional sports teams and build venues as part of their economic development strategies? Recent events in Minneapolis, Sacramento and Seattle underscore why sport management has to continue to develop theories that help the public sector better manage outcomes from their investments in sports venues.

With four games remaining in their 2011 season the Minnesota Vikings exercised their option to and informed local and state officials that the team would not agree to continue to play their home games in the covered stadium that opened on 3 April, 1982. In effect the team was declaring itself a 'free agent'. With Los Angeles along with a private investor having recently agreed to a plan for new downtown stadium, fear was rampant that the Vikings were headed west. There were reasons to doubt the viability of the Los Angeles option. *First*, the downtown stadium would be built by Anschutz Entertainment Group/AEG Worldwide, meaning that terms would have to be negotiated that could include selling a portion or the entire team to Phil Anschutz. *Second*, relocation would require the payment of a relocation fee to the NFL. Both of these factors made relocation unlikely unless the Wilf family wanted to sell the team. Regardless, the public sector agreed to invest $498 million for a new iconic stadium. With construction costs likely to exceed $1 billion, the team's share of the cost will exceed the support from Minnesota and Minneapolis. Nevertheless, there was no guaranteed new real estate investment from the team or its owner in exchange for the substantial investment being made by the public sector. The team will enjoy substantial new revenue streams in the new venue; the economic gains to the public sector are far more speculative.

Sacramento's mayor, Kevin Johnson, a former NBA star, worked to ensure that the Kings (NBA) would not be sold to new owners intent on relocating the team to Seattle. Mayor Johnson convinced a group led by Mr Vivek Ranadive to purchase 65 per cent of the team (which was valued at $534 million) and invest $255 million towards the cost of an anticipated $475 million arena. The public sector would pay the rest of the cost.

Seattle was willing to invest in a new arena, where a NBA and NHL franchise would play their home games, near a new ballpark, SAFECO Park, and stadium, Century Link Field. In September of 2012, the Seattle City Council approved Chris Hansen's plan for a $490 million arena with $200 million of the cost paid by the public sector. The public sector's investment was conditional on the attraction of an NBA or NHL franchise. If franchises from both leagues were secured, the entire $200 million would be invested by the public sector. If only an NBA team relocated or was created for Seattle arena, the public sector investment would be $120 million.

With a theory suggesting there was little to no value for a region's economy from the public sector's investment in sports venues, why do communities still support higher taxes to ensure the presence of teams? There are two distinct possibilities. One possible explanation for the long-lasting attraction of elected leaders to sports for urban development could be a commitment to advancing the interests of local economic elites. Squires (1989, p. 3) observed that the beneficiaries of many public/private partnerships were 'large corporations, developers, and institutions because the tax burden and other costs [for urban revitalisation] were shifted' away from them to consumers and residents. At the same time these institutions also became contributors to the political campaigns of those individuals who would perpetuate a long-standing policy of government support for business above the interests of lower-income individuals (Krumholz, 1991). It was these wealthy interests that dictated what governments would do, and what services they would not provide through their control of urban politics and elections (Lindblom, 1977). There were a large number of scholars who analysed urban development and concluded that subsidies to businesses produced little for the residents of cities. As Cummings (1988) noted, since the 1980s and the reduced availability of Federal funds for large-scale urban revitalisation, cities are more dependent on private capital.

Second, the infatuation with sports teams could be a result of public officials wanting to use the popularity of sports in an effort to attract investment in a city. Some might take exception with a preference for sports as a tool for advancement, preferring instead to encourage investments in education. Responding to that valuable suggestion, many would note that state governments were indeed making substantial investments in human capital through higher education, primary and secondary schools. Yet, the well-educated students were leaving for areas with a large set of amenities and jobs. These migration patterns suggested to some that cities had to offer more amenities to attract and retain well-educated individuals. Hosting teams and entertainment centres was one way to compete with other job centres where well-educated young people flocked.

Regardless of the forces driving the interest in sports, the public sector's investments must be guided by a theory that does not mean capitulation to interests that are contrary to those of residents of the central cities. Before turning our attention to that objective in the context of public investments in sports venues for professional franchises, there is another change that is taking place that might also explain why leaders are focused on using sports to overcome undesirable outcomes for urban centres. Indeed, these patterns could well explain why sports have become important for urban revitalisation strategies.

Another theory describing a disturbing outcome

Central city leaders have been dealing with the effects of the decentralisation of economic activity for decades. While it was thought that the surging population of the US would sustain both central and suburban cities, by the 1970s it was clear that people and businesses preferred newer cities. Economic segregation became commonplace with central city residents having median household incomes far below those found in suburban areas. As more and more businesses followed the middle and upper classes to the areas surrounding the former engines of the American economy, central cities had to adapt to declining tax bases. As revenue sharing between governments declined, the fiscal stability of central cities deteriorated (Nunn and Rosentraub, 1996). An era of 'fend for yourself federalism' (Herbers, 1987) required central city leaders to figure out the best possible ways to attract and retain all forms of capital. With reduced revenues service levels declined and those households that could relocate moved from central cities to other suburban communities.

At the same time that some scholars were studying the lack of regional economic change from sports teams and venues, others were analysing the changing economic and demographic patterns in metropolitan areas. Sternlieb and Hughes concluded in 1983 that central cities were no longer the growth nodes for American society. Rusk's *Cities without suburbs* (1993) highlighted the greater economic stability for central cities that had more expansive boundaries that permitted them to include the suburban communities with areas with older neighbourhoods. In contrast those cities with more limited geographic boundaries would be destined to experience far more dramatic challenges. The industrial age had lasted for a century, but now people and cities were being asked to adjust to a new set of changes within a generation and a half. Communities, leaders or residents had never before experienced this rate of change. These changes have had extraordinary geographic implications, including the creation of polycentric urban regions with numerous job centres and even multiple downtown areas. In some metropolitan areas, suburban areas built their own town centres or downtown areas to compete with those found in traditional central cities.

Central cities across North America have been challenged by a phenomenon of socioeconomic restructuring, the polarisation of social intercourse, and corporate and household relocations. The movement away from monocentric forms of urban space to a polycentric structure with multiple job centres accelerated a widening gap between the rich and poor and between central and suburban cities. As metropolitan regions become more polycentric, smaller but more abundant downtown centres formed in independent suburban cities. Furthermore, with the world becoming more interconnected through the newest technological innovations and economic integration, it is no longer necessary for individuals or firms to locate in any one city. Maintaining a company's manufacturing factories and operations in one centralised location has become obsolete. Between 2007 and 2010, job location and employment change for jobs in manufacturing and construction have declined by 20 and 30 per cent within 35 miles of downtown centres in 100 of the largest metropolitan areas (Kneebone, 2013).

Polycentric urban forms have had rapid and dramatic implications for urban centres. Wilson (1996) notes one tragic consequence has been the loss of jobs for inner city residents. While poverty has always been linked to central cities, within the last decades there has been a disappearance of ladders of opportunity and the loss of tax revenue. Central cities must envision new responses to poverty and joblessness. Squires (2002) summarised the effects noting:

> Between 1950 and 1990, metropolitan areas expanded from 208,000 square miles housing 84 million people to 585,000 square miles housing 193 million people. Population in these communities grew by 128 percent while the land area on which they resided grew by 181 percent . . . More significant than these demographic shifts is the growing inequality associated with spatial developments. In 1960, per capita income in cities was 105 percent of their surrounding suburbs. By 1990, that ratio fell to 84 percent . . . Cities tended to gain lower-income households and lose upper-income residents.
>
> *(pp. 5–6)*

If central cities are to reverse economic segregation, social and economic activity within their deteriorating urban space has to be enhanced. Central cities can no longer depend on revenue infusions from state governments that face their own fiscal challenges. Suburban governments are also not inclined to share revenues with central cities. As a result, central cities now have to develop their own policy responses to the challenge of generating revenues and new theories are needed to guide these efforts.

These observations sustain a theory of economic decentralisation that, in Kaplan's (1973) terms, creates another regrettable or unfortunate set of outcomes (or 'habits'). As revenues decline, a city cannot provide residents with the quality and quantity of urban services needed. The deterioration of urban services is an issue all too familiar to residents of many central cities and the businesses that struggle to remain in those communities. To respond to the loss of economic activity, central cities must forge partnerships with capital that produce the revenues needed to pay for needed urban services (Rosentraub, 2014). Can sports help reverse undesirable outcomes from economic decentralisation?

A new theory to guide the partnership between cities and teams

How does a central city amid decentralising economic patterns attract or deflect regional economic activity back into its taxing borders? What activity attracts a large number of visitors each and every year and is also an activity that suburban cities cannot duplicate or also offer? An answer is sports.

Cities tried festival marketplaces to bring economic activity back into central cities long after the era of classical downtown department stores ended. But those efforts were easily duplicated by suburban cities. Some central cities tried to popularise their downtown areas without changing the mix of amenities, but those efforts were also duplicated as suburban cities built or renovated their own town centres or built lifestyle retail centres that offered an antiseptic if 'faux downtown'.

Ballparks hosting MLB teams attract more than 2 million visits each season. An arena can be expected to generate a million visits if (a) it is home to either an NBA or NHL team (or both), and (b) also hosts numerous other entertainment events (concerts, family shows, etc.). A stadium home to an NFL team can be expected to enjoy 700,000 visits each season. If several of these venues are located near each other, it is not unreasonable to expect 4 million visits to an entertainment district. If a city could reliably expect several million visits each year to a specific part of its downtown area, how could the surrounding real estate be developed to produce profits for a team's owner and new tax revenues for a city? The answer to that question drives the research that is establishing a new theory for sport management.

Major league spectator sports do not substantially change regional economic development levels. But sports do change *where* in a region economic activity occurs. If that activity produces new tax revenues for a city striving to deflect wealth back into its borders – and the revenues received exceed the costs of an investment – then sports can enhance a city's budget. If a city strategically uses sports for *anchored* development projects rather than stand–alone facilities, sports can enhance urban revitalisation efforts by relocating regional economic activity. Nelson (2002) and Rosentraub (1997) were among the first to assert and demonstrate that locating major league stadiums in a city's central business district *could* make a difference in changing the distribution of economic wealth and had the potential to enhance revenue streams for a central city. What would define whether or not there was a positive or net increment to a central city's revenue portfolio would be determined by the structure of the financial planning for the new venue. If the central city's taxpayers invested more than they received in new revenues, the net return would be negative. If, however, there were investments by other governments and a plan for new real estate development was implemented, a central city could enjoy new revenue growth. Why would teams be interested in locating in downtown areas when large numbers of their fans live in suburban areas?

First, downtown areas are often at the juncture of numerous transportation links. This means access to venues can be easily accommodated. *Second*, downtown areas often have the space that offers teams the ability to develop complementing real estate that has the potential to substantially increase the leveraged profits a franchise can produce. Those revenues are not subject to any form of revenue sharing with other owners or players. *Third*, development styles that emphasise 'new urbanism' can be easily adapted to and be included in remaking or revitalising a downtown area. New urbanism has become increasingly popular and underscored by the creation of new 'lifestyle malls' and town centres in suburban cities.

As defined by the founders of the Congress for the New Urbanism (CNU, 2014), new urbanism 'stands for the restoration of existing urban centers and towns within coherent metropolitan regions, the reconfiguration of sprawling suburbs into communities of real neighbourhoods and diverse districts, the conservation of natural environments, and the preservation of our built legacy.' Some of the most relevant principles include:

> Architectural design[s that] shall [be] derive[d] from local, time-honored building typologies. Building shells must be designed to be enduring parts of the public realm. The balance of jobs, shopping, schools, recreation, civic use, institutions, housing, areas of food production and natural places shall occur at the neighborhood scale, and with these uses within easy walking distances or easy access to transit.
>
> *(Congress for the New Urbanism,*
> *Canons of Sustainable Architecture, 2014)*

These broad principles, subject to the creativity and interpretation of urban designers, planners and architects, have resonated with consumers (Song and Knapp, 2003). Restoring downtown areas into mixed-use developments anchored by sports facilities has generated communities in high demand (Cantor and Rosentraub, 2012; Freshwater, 2014; Reindl and Gallagher, 2014), even in cities with declining population levels.

There are a growing number of studies about the influence of sports venues on property values that suggest a new theory is evolving or has emerged (in Kaplan's, 1973, sense or view of epistemology). Reviews of that literature have to consider the extent to which the venue is part of the neighbourhood concept that emphasises principles of new urbanism. Some arenas, ballparks and stadiums have not been incorporated into a neighbourhood plan and therefore it would be anticipated that those venues might have a very different effect on the performance of real estate values. Tu (2005) looked at the short- and longer-term effects of FedEx Field (Washington Redskins). While that venue was not part of a master-planned new urbanism neighbourhood, the venue did have a positive long-term effect on home values. AT&T Stadium in Arlington, Texas (Dallas Cowboys), a spectacular venue, was also not incorporated into any neighbourhood, and Dehring, Depken and Ward (2007) found that average property values declined by 1.5 per cent. Such an outcome was hardly surprising given the failure to include any ideas or buildings that would be considered part of a new urbanism approach or development. Ahlfeldt and Maennig (2010) also found positive effects from sports arenas on land values in Berlin, even when the venues were not part of a new urbanism community. Feng and Humphreys (2012) established that median house values in census blocks located closer to a venue were statistically higher, especially in Columbus' Arena District. The area surrounding the Nationwide Arena can be considered one of the most successful applications of new urbanism to sports-anchored development. San Diego's Ballpark District, the downtown area adjacent to the Staples Center and LA LIVE, Cleveland's East 4th Street, and downtown Denver are other examples of the linkage of sports venues to the concepts of new urbanism. In each instance, the gains for central cities are evident.

Huang and Humphreys (2014) used data involving fifty-six venues to continue researching the effects of sports venues on real estate development. This very important study, however, did not separate new urbanism communities from those efforts where a sports venue was simply built in a downtown or inner city area without any attention to a detail master plan. As many urban planners would note, in any area with decentralising tendencies failing to have an effective plan, it would be unlikely to see positive changes that would be otherwise detailed in master plans that adhere to the principles of new urbanism. Joining the two different approaches (those with and without a master plan adhering to principles of the new urbanism) is destined to find far less effects from sport venues. Along with presenting evidence that stand-alone facilities and venues that are not part of integrated plans are less likely to have an effect on real estate development, Huang and Humphreys suggest that sports venues have far less effect on real estate values. Their work stands in sharp contrast to insights offered by Cantor and Rosentraub (2012) in their study of San Diego's Ballpark District.

Evidence from case studies

Too few studies concerning the effects of sports venues on downtown development and central city finances exist to sustain a theory. Sufficient evidence, however, does exist to suggest important insights have been identified to warrant and orient future research. Indeed, a goal of this chapter has been to identify an emerging new theoretical framework that can guide the practice, teaching and study of sport management. We turn to two case studies to illustrate outcomes that have been valuable for teams and cities.

Indianapolis

No city was as focused on sports (combined with culture and entertainment) for a master-planned redevelopment of a downtown area as Indianapolis. Indianapolis' plan emphasised many of the principles of new urbanism, including the incorporation of historical facades and building into its revitalisation efforts. The plan was conceived in the early 1970s and then carefully followed by four different mayors (three Republicans and one Democrat). The City/County Council supported the strategy through periods of both Republican and Democratic majorities and leadership from the Black and White communities. A total of $11.6 billion (in constant 2013 dollars) was invested in the downtown area in an effort to confront the decentralising trends common to most central cities. Investments were made by Indianapolis, the suburban counties surrounding the city, Indiana, and the non-profit sector (Lilly Endowment). The private-sector investment accounted for slightly less than half of the funds committed to the revitalisation strategy. Slightly more than a third of the total investment was from Indianapolis. The original stadium (Hoosier Dome) and arena (Market Square Arena) have been replaced by second-generation venues, illustrating Indianapolis' on-going commitment to the downtown strategy. What has Indianapolis gained?

Indianapolis has been able to slow decentralisation trends, but decentralisation has not been abated. Manufacturing positions and jobs in wholesale trade migrated to suburban areas (to take advantage of lower land prices). Finance and insurance jobs were retained in the downtown area even as some information sector jobs relocated. Yet, in 2002 there were 42,464 private-sector jobs in the downtown area; in 2011 there were 40,922. A loss of 3.6 per cent of the private-sector job base in the downtown area is an accomplishment as the downtown area is still home to a large employment base (95,013 workers). In 2002 there were 79,708 workers in the downtown area.[4] Why did the total number of jobs increase? Downtown Indianapolis is home to a large complex of hospitals associated with Indiana University, the growing campus of Indiana University-Purdue University Indianapolis, and Indiana's state government complex. These employees generate income and sales taxes for Indianapolis. In summary, then, relative to employment levels, the revitalisation strategy has encouraged on-going employment opportunities that sustain a level of vitality for Indianapolis and its downtown area.[5]

The number of people living in the downtown area has almost doubled since 1990. There are now approximately 28,000 people living in downtown Indianapolis and almost 500 homes were bought in the past two years (Rosentraub, 2014). There are other factors, despite decentralising trends, that have complicated Indianapolis' strategy or success. First, suburban cities have aggressively joined the effort to create their own downtown centres that are committed to the principles of the new urbanism. Downtown Indianapolis has to compete with suburban cities trying to offer the same urban experience in the midst of economically homogenous areas. Second, the venues built in downtown Columbus, Cincinnati and Louisville are sufficiently close to Central Indiana and those venues compete for events that at one time always played at Indianapolis' arena. With fewer events coming to downtown Indianapolis, maintaining the financial viability of the arena and other amenities has become more difficult. While imitation (by other central cities and suburban areas) is indeed a salute to Indianapolis' early success, too much duplication has weakened Indianapolis' market position. The sustained vitality and success of downtown Indianapolis, however, does illustrate what a detailed plan, embracing precepts of new urbanism and anchored to sports venues, can achieve.

San Diego

Without a substantial commitment from the owner of the San Diego Padres to develop the area now known as the Ballpark District, there would be no partnership with the public sector for a new venue. John Moores agreed that, through his company, more than $450 million of new development would take place in the Ballpark District. At the end of the building process more than $2.87 billion was invested in the area. More than 3,000 market-rate residential units were built in the Ballpark District. In 2000, throughout all of downtown San Diego there were 16,000 residential units. The City now anticipates 53,000 units will exist by 2030.[6] While the Ballpark District is the location for only a portion of these residences, its success has helped transform downtown San Diego in ways that few anticipated. To join the Ballpark District partnership, the City of San Diego also required that the team owner build 1,000 hotel rooms. By 2012 more than 1,200 new hotel rooms were added in the Ballpark District. The Ballpark District adhered to many of the principles of the new urbanism and is location of a new urban park and numerous other amenities. These amenities help sustain property values even during the recession when other communities in Southern California suffered through a severe collapse in housing prices and homeowner equity (Cantor and Rosentraub, 2012).

The extraordinary success of the Ballpark District and the property taxes generated, however, became a focal point for statewide debate. When the plans for the Ballpark District were formulated, few envisioned that it would be as successful as it became. The idea of using sports venues to anchor urban development was in its infancy, and in an era when any notion that sports could enhance a city's finances, it was believed that the ballpark district plan could be a new gimmick on the old game of getting subsidies for sports venues. The new property taxes that would be generated were transferred to the Centre City Development Corporation, not the City of San Diego. Assigning new taxes to authorities had been a usual practice with the objective of ensuring that some money would exist to help sustain infrastructure and seed other projects.

As the Ballpark District's success grew, the funds accruing to the development corporation grew. Those funds continued to grow even as the financial challenges for the City of San Diego increased as a result of unfunded liabilities for its pension funds. Rather than seeking support to transfer funds from the development authority to the City's general revenue fund, a political crisis emerged. In effect, the City of San Diego had made an investment in a ballpark that anchored development. But that development produced revenue for another entity. Jerry Brown adopted this issue in his campaign for the governorship of California and today the former development authority is now part of the City of San Diego's Civic San Diego. San Diego now receives all property taxes and can use those revenues to meet any of its needs, including the facilitation of the future development of downtown San Diego. Putting aside the administrative issues associated with the use of development authorities, what is critical to this chapter is that the Ballpark District, anchored by PETCO Park and built with a master plan adhering to new urbanism principles, was quite successful (Cantor and Rosentraub, 2012). Its success offers a blueprint for other communities regarding what should be done if indeed sports venues are to enhance urban space and the finances of central cities.[7]

An agenda for a new theory of economic development and sport management

Epistemologists correctly note that substantial empirical work is required to sustain a relationship as a theory. That standard was met with regard to the role of sports in regional economic development and for the effects of economic decentralisation on central cities. Important insights into the effect of sports on repositioning regional economic activity – to the advantage of central cities – exists. Far more work is needed, however, to sustain the position that venues as part of master planned new neighbourhoods emphasising elements of the new urbanism can benefit teams and central cities. Yet sufficient evidence does exist to suggest that future students and researchers focused on sport management have to broaden their focus and recommendations to community leaders and team owners.

Notes

1   This work is a reflection and extension of Rosentraub's (1997) book, *Major league losers*.
2   The National Basketball Association (NBA), The National Football League (NFL), the National Hockey League (NHL) and Major League Baseball (MLB) constitute the four older leagues. A newer league, Major League Soccer (MLS), has not yet established a market position similar to the one enjoyed by the other leagues.
3   It has been argued that only if anti-trust laws and regulations were applied to the sports leagues could the public sector, taxpayers and fans be protected from the excesses resulting from the free-market protections available to teams (Rosentraub, 1997; Kennedy and Rosentraub, 2000). Political and legal battles to change or apply anti-trust laws are not needed. Within the existing structure and system, as it will be argued, the public sector can use real estate development practices to achieve returns that produce very desirable outcomes.
4   Employment data were calculated from information available from the US Bureau of the Census' online database, *On The Map*.
5   It could be argued that the State of Indiana would have employed people in the downtown area, as would have Indiana University hospitals, even if there were no effort to revitalise the area. Indeed, that is a possibility. It cannot be determined if leadership of those institutions would have been as focused on the downtown area if deterioration trends had continued. It is possible that if the area continued to decline patients would have been reluctant to venture downtown and that Indiana would have spread its government offices into suburban areas. The observation that state governments and universities would remain in downtown areas regardless of development patterns or trends is beyond the scope of this chapter. It is appropriate, however, to recognise that different outcomes could have resulted.
6   www.sandiegodowntown.org/flash/development.pdf
7   www.civicsd.com/

References

Ahlfeldt, G.M. and Maennig, W. (2010) 'Impact of sports arenas on land values: Evidence from Berlin'. *The Annals of Regional Science*, *44*: 205–27.
Baade, R.A. (1996) 'Professional sports as catalysts for metropolitan economic development'. *Journal of Urban Affairs*, *18*: 1–17.
Baade, R.A. and Dye, R.F. (1988) 'An analysis of the economic rationale for public subsidization of sports stadiums'. *The Annals of Regional Science*, *22*(2): 37–47.

Baade, R.A. and Dye, R.F. (1990) 'The impact of stadium and professional sports on metropolitan area development'. *Growth & Change, 21*(2): 1–14.

Cantor, M.B. and Rosentraub, M.S. (2012) 'A ballpark and neighborhood change: Economic integration, a recession, and the altered demography of San Diego's Ballpark District after eight years'. *City, Culture & Society, 3*: 219–26.

Chapin, T. (2002) 'Beyond the entrepreneurial city: Municipal capitalism in San Diego'. *Journal of Urban Affairs, 24*: 565–81.

Coates, D. and Humphreys, B.R. (1999) 'The growth effects of sports franchises, stadia and arenas'. *Journal of Policy Analysis and Management, 14*: 601–24.

Coates, D. and Humphreys, B.R. (2003) 'The effect of professional sports on earnings and employment in the services and retail sectors in US cities'. *Regional Science & Urban Economics, 33*: 175–98.

Congress for the New Urbanism (2014) *Canons of sustainable architecture and urbanism.* Available at www.cnu.org/sites/files/Canons.pdf (accessed on 29 August, 2014).

Cummings, S. (ed.) (1988) *Business elites and urban development.* Albany, NY: State University of New York Press.

Dehring, C.A., Depken, C.A. and Ward, M.R. (2007) 'The impact of stadium announcements on residential property values: Evidence from a natural experiment in Dallas-Fort Worth'. *Contemporary Economic Policy, 25*: 627–38.

DeMause, N. and Cagan, J. (2008) *Field of schemes: How the great stadium swindle turns public money into private profit.* Lincoln, NE: University of Nebraska Press.

Ely, J.W., Jnr (2009) 'Post-Kelo reform: Is the glass half full or half empty?' *Supreme Court Economic Review, 17*(1): 127–50.

Euchner, C. (1993) *Playing the field: Why sports teams move and cities fight to keep them.* Baltimore, MD: Johns Hopkins University Press.

Feng, X. and Humphreys, B.R. (2012) 'The impact of professional sports facilities on housing values: Evidence from census block group data'. *City, Culture, & Society, 3*: 189–200.

Fort, R. and Quirk, J. (1995) 'Cross-subsidization, incentives, and outcomes in professional team sports leagues'. *Journal of Economic Literature*: 1265–99.

Freshwater Newsletter (2014) 'No vacancy: With more residents moving downtown occupancy rates reach 95 percent'. Available at www.freshwatercleveland.com/features/downtownliving082511.aspx. (accessed on 29 August, 2014).

Herbers, J. (1987) 'The new federalism: Unplanned, innovative, and here to stay'. *Governing.* Available at www.governing.com/topics/mgmt/new-federalism-unplanned-innovative-here-to-stay.html (accessed on 7 August, 2014).

Huang, H. and Humphreys, B.R. (2014) 'New sports facilities and residential housing markets'. *Journal of Regional Science, 54*: 629–63.

Humphreys, B. (2001) 'The myth of sports-led economic development'. *Economic Development Commentary, 25*(1): 34–7.

Kaplan, A. (1973) *The conduct of inquiry: Methodology for behavioral science.* New York: Harper & Row.

Kennedy, S.S. and Rosentraub, M.S. (2000) 'Public-private partnerships, professional sports teams and the protection of the public's interests'. *The American Review of Public Administration, 30*: 436–59.

Kneebone, E. (2013) *Job sprawl stalls: The Great Recession and metropolitan employment location.* Washington, DC: Brookings Institution.

Krumholz, N. (1991) 'Equity and local economic development'. *Economic Development Quarterly, 5*: 291–300.

Lindblom, C.E. (1977) *Politics and markets: The world's political-economic systems.* New York: Basic Books.

Long, J.G. (2005) 'Full count: The real cost of public funding for major league sports facilities'. *Journal of Sports Economics, 6*(2): 119–43.

Long, J.G. (2013) *Public/private partnerships for major league sports facilities.* New York: Taylor and Francis.

Low, D.M., Halladay, C.W. and Opashinov, M. (2012) 'Canada: Cartel regulation'. Available at www.mondaq.com/canada/x/175544/Antitrust+Competition/Cartel+Regulation+2012 (accessed on 2 November, 2014).

Matheson, V.A. (2002) 'Upon further review: An examination of sporting event economic impact studies'. *The Sport Journal, 5*: 1–4.

Nelson, A.C. (2002) 'Locating major league stadiums where they can make a difference: Empirical analysis with implications for all major public venues'. *Public Works Management & Policy, 7*(2): 98–114.

Noll, R.G. and Zimbalist, A.S. (eds) (1997) *Sports, jobs, and taxes: The economic impact of sports teams and stadiums*. Washington, DC: Brookings Institution Press.

Nunn, S. and Rosentraub, M.S. (1996) 'Metropolitan fiscal equalization: Distilling lessons from four US programs'. *State & Local Government Review*. 90–102.

Okner, B. (1974) 'Subsidies of stadiums and arenas'. In R. Noll (ed.) *Government and the sports business*. Washington, DC: Brookings Institution.

Olson, M. (1965) *The logic of collective action*. Cambridge, MA: Harvard University Press.

Quirk, J. and Fort, R.D. (1992) *Pay dirt. The business of professional team sports*. Princeton, NJ: Princeton University Press.

Reindl, J.C. and Gallagher, J. (2014, January) 'Downtown Detroit apartment rents spiking higher, even pricing out middle class'. *Detroit Free Press*. Available at www.freep.com/article/20140126/BUSINESS04/301260081/Rents-rising-Detroit-downtown-Midtown-Corktown (accessed on 29 August, 2014).

Rosentraub, M.S. (1997) *Major league losers: The real cost of sports and who's paying for it*. New York: Basic Books.

Rosentraub, M.S. (2014) *Reversing urban decline: Why and how sports, entertainment, and culture turn cities into major league winners*. Boca Raton, FL: CRC Press/Taylor and Francis.

Rosentraub, M.S. and Nunn, S. (1978) 'Suburban city investment in professional sports: Estimating the fiscal returns of the Dallas Cowboys and Texas Rangers to investor communities'. *American Behavioral Scientist*, *21*: 393–414.

Rosentraub, M.S. and Swindell, D. (1991) 'Just say no? The economic and political realities of a small city's investment in Minor League Baseball'. *Economic Development Quarterly*, *5*(2): 152–67.

Rusk, D. (1993) *Cities without suburbs*. Washington, DC: Woodrow Wilson Press.

Scully, G. (1995) *The market structure of sports*. Chicago, IL: University of Chicago Press.

Siegfried, J. and Zimbalist, A. (2000) 'The economics of sports facilities and their communities'. *The Journal of Economic Perspectives*, *14*(3): 95–114.

Siegfried, J. and Zimbalist, A. (2002) 'A note on the local economic impact of sports expenditures'. *Journal of Sports Economics*, *3*: 361–6.

Song, Y. and Knapp, G. (2003) 'New urbanism and housing values: A disaggregate assessment'. *Journal of Urban Economics*, *54*: 218–38.

Squires, G. (ed.) (1989) *Unequal partnerships: The political economy of urban redevelopment in postwar America*. New Brunswick, NJ: Rutgers University Press.

Squires, G.D. (2002) 'Urban sprawl and the uneven development of metropolitan America'. In G.D. Squires (ed.) *Urban sprawl: Causes, consequences, and policy responses* (pp. 1–22). Washington, DC: The Urban Institute.

Sternlieb, G. and Hughes, J.W. (1983) 'The uncertain future of the central city'. *Urban Affairs Quarterly*, *18*: 455–72.

Tu, C.C. (2005) 'How does a sports stadium affect housing values? The case of FedEx Field'. *Land Economics*, *81*: 379–95.

Vroom, J. (2012) 'The economic structure of the NFL'. In K.G. Quinn (ed.) *The economics of the National Football League* (pp. 7–31). New York: Springer.

Wilson, W.J. (1996) *When work disappears: The world of the new urban poor*. New York: Knopf.

Whitford, D. (1993) *Playing hardball: The high-stakes battle for baseball's new franchises*. New York: Doubleday.

Zimbalist, A. and Long, J.G. (2006) 'Facility finance: measurement, trends, and analysis'. *International Journal of Sport Finance*, *1*(4): 201–11.

Applying Rosentraub's economic development theories

Laura Misener[1]

I became aware of the work of Mark Rosentraub as I was preparing my dissertation proposal and my comprehensive exam-reading list. As an emerging critical scholar, I was struggling with the ways in which sport was uncritically being held up to such acclaim in the urban development context as a driver of civic and economic growth. I admired the work of the critical urban scholar Jane Jacobs (1969, 1984, 2000) for advocating for the mindful development of cities and the empowerment for citizens to become advocates for their place in these development activities. It appeared to me from my work on urban sporting projects that there was often a lack of this type of thoughtful development when it came to context of sporting developments. I then read Mark Rosentraub's book, *Major league losers: The real costs of sports and who's paying for it* (1999). Herein, I was drawn into this work critiquing the ways in which cities were co-opting urban space in the name of sporting developments for so-called economic gains, without taking account of the social and community-based milieu of these environments. In particular, I was attracted to the complex understanding of sport and economic development as a not merely a commodity-based activity befit to urban elites, but how there was a complex interplay in the social, political and economic structures of sporting developments that was often poorly understood by those in the sport sectors. However, in this I still felt that there was more to be understood about the ways in which cities could effectively utilise sport as a driver of development if connected intimately to the social, community and political structure driving the process. Most importantly, as my work on sporting events and urban development has emphasised, community-centred values and citizen input need to be at the centrepiece of these development-related efforts, which has been the foundation to all of my work on sport and urban development.

Dr Rosentraub's follow-up book, *Major league winners: Using sports and cultural centers as tools for economic development* (2009), drew together the theoretical insights about the cultural value of sports for development with the need to be mindful of citizen rights and responsibilities in the process. The theoretical approach to sport-driven urban economic development remains a central part of my research programme aimed at ensuring that sport events are not merely 'Spectacle', but rather become intimately intertwined with the political, economic and social factors that shape the developments (Misener and Mason, 2008, 2009). From this perspective, I also ensure that my students understand the value of interdisciplinarity in their work. Much of Dr Rosentraub's work has demonstrated the need for sport managers to understand the nuances of politics, architecture, governance, finance, media relations and tourism. It is only through these complex theoretical lenses that we can ensure that sport and our sport-related research remains critically connected to the context in which these sporting practices occur. Hence, my future work focuses on those often excluded from the development-related projects and aims to ensure greater levels of accessibility are apparent in sporting and urban economic developments.

Note

1   Laura Misener is with the Faculty of Health Sciences at the University of Western Ontario.

References

Jacobs, J. (1969) *The economy of cities*. New York: Vintage Books.

Jacobs, J. (1984) *Cities and the wealth of nations*. New York: Random House.

Jacobs, J. (2000) *The nature of economies*. New York: Modern Library.

Misener, L. and Mason, D. (2008) 'Towards a community centred approach to corporate community involvement in the sporting events agenda'. *Journal of Management & Organisation, 16*: 495–514.

Misener, L. and Mason, D.S. (2009) 'Fostering community development through sporting events strategies: An examination of urban regime perceptions'. *Journal of Sport Management, 23*: 770–94.

Rosentraub, M.S. (1999) *Major league losers: The real cost of sports and who's paying for it*. New York: Basic Books.

Rosentraub, M.S. (2009) *Major league winners: Using sports and cultural centers as tools for economic development*. Boca Raton, FL: CRC Press.

32

FORT AND QUIRK

A look back and a look forward at competitive balance theory[1]

Rodney Fort

Introduction

I have been asked to look back to my paper with James Quirk, 'Cross-subsidization, incentives, and outcomes in professional team sports' (Fort and Quirk, 1995, henceforth FQ95), and at the subsequent work related to it. I am honoured to do so and to have the article recognised this way. FQ95 marked the beginning of my journal contributions on sports economics.[2] It is annually my most cited journal article by a long shot and my most cited piece of work. (Oh to be younger again.) Many colleagues tell me it has had a significant impact on their work, and that is most gratifying.

There had been two other works that employed mathematical theoretical modelling of sports leagues decades before FQ95 (El Hodiri and Quirk, 1971; Quirk and El Hodiri, 1974), but they used a different modelling approach and could not have foreseen the variety of cross-subsidy mechanisms that came after. There also was other mathematical modelling aimed solely at individual questions (e.g., Atkinson, Stanley and Tschirhart, 1988). Unbeknown to us, John Vrooman was working on his version of a mathematical model of talent distribution in leagues at the same time, and his paper appeared in print at the same time as ours (Vrooman, 1995). In retrospect, FQ95 and Vrooman are complementary pieces.

There were two motivations for the work. First, we were asked to put the article together by then-editor of the *Journal of Economic Literature*, John Pencavel. We were fortunate to have such an opportunity. Second, around that time, academic and popular interest in rigorous explanations of sports team owner behaviour was on the rise. Labour unrest was clearly on the horizon and would come to Major League Baseball in the form of the 'mother of all strikes' just as we submitted the piece in 1994. There was much to discover and, it ends up, much that we could say about current events circa the early 1990s.

FQ95 was decidedly American-centric, and other work on world sports league models was happening as well. Stefan Kesenne (1996) was working on win maximisation models and a bit later Szymanski (2003) included some 'questions' about FQ95 with full-blown critiques appearing from Szymanski (2004) and Szymanski and Kesenne (2004) shortly thereafter. Thankfully, the lines of enquiry in North America and Europe did come to terms, producing a more general theoretical approach to sports leagues.

The chapter proceeds in four more sections. The next section is an overview including the topic of interest, specific constructs, key propositions, careful identification of assumptions and their limitations, and tests that we performed. Subsequently, I describe the process for developing the theory; that is, the events that spurred our interest and the manner in which the thoughts were developed. Following that I present 'FQ95', which is all about where we took the theory and where other people took it. Finally, speculation on future directions for the theory is offered.

Overview

In our formal mathematical characterisation of the equilibrium talent distribution in a professional sports league, we were interested in all of the major cross-subsidisation mechanisms among teams in a league. Owners of larger-revenue teams ostensibly subsidise their smaller-revenue counterparts in the name of the survival of smaller-revenue franchises and in the name of competitive balance; that is, enhancing the competitiveness of smaller-revenue teams on the field. Our theoretical model, as it turns out, suggested that while the cross-subsidy mechanisms do aid the profitability of smaller-revenue teams, they could not be relied upon to enhance competitive balance. Indeed, under some reasonable characterisations in the model, larger-revenue teams are simultaneously more profitable. Thus, in place of the idea of cross-subsidy is a suggestion that these mechanisms were more about the redistribution of value away from players towards owners.

We freely admitted that some of these ideas harkened back to the non-mathematical economic theory applications by Rottenberg (1956). Indeed, our model (a) included his suggestion that fan preferences include outcome uncertainty and (b) typically generated implications consistent with his invariance principle.[3] The latter would end up a bone of contention in the international co-generation and extension of league theory mentioned above and covered below. Interestingly, and quite the contrary to the way our work was portrayed later, while our model typically generated results consistent with his invariance principle, we never set out to champion Rottenberg.

Instead, our aim was to understand the impacts of cross-subsidy mechanisms brought to bear in three ways by leagues. First, the reserve option clause, payroll caps and player drafts provide cross-subsidies when imposed in the input market for player talent. Second, gate, local and national revenue sharing provide cross-subsidies through co-operative arrangements among team owners. Third, subsidies can be produced by carefully managing league expansion and team relocation through physical territory protection.[4]

Our approach was to formally model the decisions by individual owners and the effects of imposing cross-subsidy mechanisms on league profits, team owner profits, player compensation and the distribution of talent in the league. We also offered (very) elementary empirical evidence as a basic check on the theory and as a guide to future work.

Ours was a league of profit maximising team owners. In choosing their level of talent, team-owner gate revenue depended on differential winning chances (closeness of competition) and market size. Local revenue and national revenue were also included. Our focus on these last was TV; local TV revenue depended on closeness of competition and market size, just like gate revenue.

Strictly aimed at North American leagues of the time, we modelled a closed league. The only way for one owner to improve her or his chances was to buy talent from another owner so changes in winning percentages had to be zero-sum. We excluded scale effects; that is, in our model a unit of talent increased winning the same regardless of how much the team currently was winning. We normalised the impact to unity, which resulted in equivalence between choosing winning percentage and choosing talent itself. We further assumed a balanced schedule so that sum of winning percentages equals half the number of teams (referred to by all after this as the league adding up constraint). We ignored roster restrictions. With all of this, cross-effects of an increase in talent by one owner on the other owners just became a constant equal to the inverse of one less than the number of teams. Since we ignored everything else, the only cost was the price per unit talent, assumed constant.

Ours was a static model (that is, at a point in time) even though the earlier mathematical theory work on sports leagues was dynamic (that is, adding decision-making over time; El Hodiri and Quirk, 1971; Quirk and El Hodiri, 1974). With revenues and costs specified, we maximised profits in an n-team league, found individual team optimality, and a gate-sharing equilibrium. In the optimisation problem, at first, only gate and national TV are shared. We then extended the model to sharing of other types of local revenue (TV) and the imposition of other cross-subsidy mechanisms.

While the model determined equilibrium in the n-team case, it was easier to demonstrate our key propositions using a two-team diagram we had popularised earlier.[5] Adding in that one team was a strong-drawing team at the gate and on TV, the fundamental equilibrium result was equal marginal revenues across all teams in the league at the same marginal cost of a unit of talent. At this equilibrium, the stronger-drawing team had a higher winning percentage than the weaker-drawing team.

From there, we added the reserve-option clause touted by owners during its use as necessary for league survival, lest all the talent go to larger-revenue market owners. Rottenberg of course suggested otherwise and our model predictions coincided with his (and with the earlier findings in El Hodiri and Quirk, 1971, and Quirk and El Hodiri, 1974). Since the reserve-option clause only reduces the marginal cost of talent, while the marginal value of talent does not change, then the market can only clear at the same talent distribution as before. However, the savings would be divided between both types of owners and profits rise for both by the relative redistribution away from players. Weaker-drawing teams are buoyed by the reserve-option clause, as per the claims of the time, but not through any form of talent redistribution toward weaker-drawing teams. The reserve option clause was simply a taking from what would otherwise be player pay.[6]

The model also predicted that a hard payroll cap (i.e., no loopholes and fully enforced) would drive a league to parity. That is, with equal amounts to spend, the only outcome consistent with spending those equal amounts on payroll occurs when teams choose talent so that their winning percentages are all equal to 0.500. Restrictions on the size of the cap needed to raise league profits, as well as raise profits for both types of teams, were also provided. However, the most important observation was that a payroll cap is a *disequilibrium* outcome and all incentives are to violate the cap, moving back toward the pre-cap talent distribution. Thus, a third party must enforce the cap.

The model predictions for the rookie draft followed in exactly the same way as the reserve option clause and began with precisely the same logic. If anything but the profit-maximising distribution of talent were to occur under a draft, then there would be incentives for smaller-revenue team owners to move talent to larger-revenue owners; the distribution of talent should be invariant with respect to the imposition of the draft.[7] This key proposition echoed Rottenberg on the Rule 5 (Minor League) Draft that was the only one in place at his writing but for the reverse-order-of-finish draft of incoming players in place at our writing.

Unlike the draft, which we handled strictly as a descriptive continuation of the reserve option clause using the two-team diagram, we moved on to explicitly handle revenue sharing in the rigorous format of the n-team model. Interestingly, we arrived again at the invariance principle.

By way of intuitive description of the model results, consider equilibrium in our model, that is, equal marginal revenues across all teams in the league at the same marginal cost of a unit of talent. Now, what does revenue sharing do? For all team owners, the marginal value of talent falls by precisely the same amount *at the margin*, namely, by the percentage of talent's value that must be shared. Given that the marginal value of talent falls for all owners by the same amount at the margin, then there can be no rearrangement of talent among the owners! All that can happen is that the price of talent falls by the amount of sharing at the margin.

Quite simply, the amount of revenue that each owner puts in the pot for sharing comes from precisely the reduction in price of talent shared by all owners. The way that it is shared among the owners is irrelevant to the outcome. Total pay to players falls by the amount of the revenues that are shared and there is no change in the distribution of talent across the league[8].

Just for the sake of completeness (and because we had a previous interest in the topic; see Quirk and Fort, 1992), we also discussed rival leagues, expansion and franchise moves to round out the paper. This is not really driven at all by the model, *per se*, other than to carry forward the implications of profit maximisation for the behaviour of owners in leagues towards rival leagues and how expansion and the movement of franchises would keep those rivals, real in some cases and potential in others, at bay.

The primary limitations were later revealed to be in two important areas. First, we excluded scale effects, that is, a unit of talent increases winning the same regardless of how much the team currently wins; and since we made that assumption the marginal impact was normalised to unity. While this led to the simplification that choosing winning percentage was the same thing as choosing talent, it also confused later theoretical development. Second, our assumptions allowed us to gloss over the management input (on and off the field) and the entire talent-generation market. In perhaps the most important move forward in the modelling of sports leagues, it would later be pointed out (see 'After FQ95', below) that this modelling choice made it impossible to have either open or closed leagues and Nash conjectures at the same time in the talent market (which our model could not) as well as Nash equilibrium (which our model did). Nash conjectures in the talent market just means that every owner ignores the talent choice of the rest of the owners in making their own choice. These limitations and their role in the further development of the theory are the subject of the next section. Before moving on to that, another charge for this chapter is following through on the empirical tests that we did.

That there are relatively stronger and weaker teams was apparent and should be today. So we didn't test the obvious. In addition, we had no profit data to test any of the cross-subsidy profit implications of the model, but we could check on competitive balance. We proceeded to do so for the theoretical predictions for each of the cross-subsidy mechanisms. Our approach was pretty much the same in each case. We examined the distribution of winning percentages around natural experiments represented by the historical imposition of one of the mechanisms using both descriptive statistic observation and a regression analysis adjusting for expansion. We also examined the behaviour of the Gini coefficient on league championships around these natural experiments.

Owner fears that balance would worsen in the absence of the reserve option clause were not realised. The standard deviation of winning percentages in either the American or National Leagues in Major League Baseball did not increase with its demise after the famous Messersmith/McNally arbitration decision in 1975. Neither did the Gini coefficient applied to championships indicate that they became more concentrated after the end of the reserve option clause.

Turning to the model implications for a payroll cap, we did not find the predicted decline in balance in the National Basketball Association after the cap was introduced following the

1983/84 season.[9] This rejected the 'hard' version of the cap employed in our theory and put the focus back on our other observations about payroll caps. The results suggest that the NBA cap was soft rather than hard and/or that there was insufficient enforcement of the disequilibrium that results from the payroll cap. We provided evidence of both. Further, the Gini coefficient on championships also suggested that they became a bit *more* concentrated after the imposition of a payroll cap, hardly in keeping with an improvement in balance.

Data on the rookie draft were not as kind to the model predictions. In support of the theory, we could not reject the hypothesis of equal balance before and after the National Football League draft (in place to effect the 1936 season) or for the National League of Major League Baseball before and after that draft (in place to effect the 1966 season). However, there was a statistically significant *decline* in the standard deviation of winning percentages (improved regular season balance) in the American League after the imposition of the baseball draft.[10] There were also declines of 20 per cent and 22 per cent in the Gini coefficient on championships (improved playoff balance) in the National and American Leagues in Major League Baseball, respectively. Thus, in the Major League Baseball draft, there are important contradictions to the theory we developed. Why this should be true in baseball compared to football remains unanswered as far as I know.

There were no natural experiments on revenue sharing at the time of our writing.[11] However, comparative statics from our model provided predictable differences among leagues in their revenue sharing arrangements. More equal drawing potentials among markets in the NFL is consistent with their historical bent towards more sharing than occurs in other leagues.

The process

The process of creating FQ95 was completely unremarkable. The setting was the beginning of what could foreseeably be the stoppage of baseball and was eventually for parts of the 1994–5 seasons, including the 1994 playoffs and World Series. Popular claims about the importance of outcome uncertainty were flying around and claims counter to the dictates of the invariance principle were common (e.g., baseball needed more revenue sharing or even a payroll cap to balance competition). James Quirk and I had been corresponding about the entire lack of any theory-driven tests of any of this speculation. Apparently, we were not alone. John Pencavel, the editor at the *Journal of Economic Literature* at the time, contacted Quirk and requested a piece on sports economics.

So, there was much to discover and, it ends up, much that we could say about current events of the time. We both knew the original Rottenberg ideas well, and James Quirk is one of the most adept applied modellers in economics. He was my PhD thesis advisor at California Institute of Technology, and I was just a few years on the job as an assistant professor at Washington State University. We had worked together before on *Pay Dirt* (Quirk and Fort, 1992). So we put our heads together. There was nothing remarkable about the form of the collaboration either. Quirk began the modelling, I commented and added on, and the paper took shape.

The road to the final product was not smooth. Our first attempt was sent back to us. It was too much directed at only theory rather than suggesting the road to empirical application. So we took a second shot, identifying explicitly what the empirical implications were and adding the empirical investigation of the impacts of cross-subsidies. This led naturally enough to some 'first take' simple empirical assessment of the model implications. And that was the final product that appeared in print.

After FQ95

Since ours was neo-classical economics, it was natural to take the model into the areas that were still uncharted. The usual first extension is to move from static modelling to dynamic modelling, but El Hodiri and Quirk (1971) and Quirk and El Hodiri (1974) had already done that. The remaining directions to take any neo-classical model are, for the more mathematically inclined, into questions about the existence of equilibrium and just what type of equilibrium it represented, as well as an exploration of the social welfare implications of the model.

In Fort and Quirk (2007), we tackled the theoretical formalities that had to do with the existence of equilibrium and whether or not such equilibrium was of the rational expectations variety. Existence was established (with a little help from Quirk's colleague, Mohamed El Hodiri), and we did show that equilibrium was of the rational expectations variety.

Turning to social welfare, in Fort and Quirk (2010), we employed a standard welfare function in economics (the sum of consumers' and producers' surpluses) for its implications relative to profit maximisation choices in a league dominated by single-game ticket sales, like Major League Baseball. We did the same for a league dominated by season-ticket sales, like the National Football League, in Fort and Quirk (2011). One virtue of the neo-classical approach to welfare does shine through: even though the results are somewhat 'messy', the conditions we derive rest on empirically tractable measures like elasticities. However, to my knowledge, these have yet to be approached empirically.

The original FQ95 theory stood for exactly one year before the limitations acknowledged above were laid bare in the international league context. I think it is safe to say that there were two main thrusts in the international context. First, there was the long line of work on win maximisation from Stefan Kesenne. While there is a long line of journal articles there, beginning with Kesenne (1996), I refer the reader to his excellent compilation text instead where they are all brought together (Kesenne, 2014) along with a few other issues in the theory. The main argument was that European team directors are taken to pursue wins rather than profits, and Kesenne runs his model through the entire gamut of possible competitive balance interventions, from revenue sharing to payroll caps. Fort and Quirk (2004) was our response, and I leave that interaction to the interested reader.

The second main thrust laid bare the full implications of the simplifying assumptions we used. Szymanski (2003) previewed the issues but the full thrust of the insights came in Szymanski (2004) and Szymanski and Kesenne (2004). Renaming the FQ95 approach the 'Walrasian Fixed-Supply Conjecture Model', the elements of the criticism were that our model had both logical and a theoretical malfunctions. On the logical side, our assumption that made the choice of talent the same as the choice of winning percentage essentially produced a 'no choice' model! Once one team made its choice, the other was stuck with what was left. Our rejoinder to this was in Fort and Quirk (2007). This is simply a misunderstanding of how a tatonnement process works; it is *not* that one team chooses and the other is stuck; rather, it is that the price that confronts owners given their choices must clear the market. While subtle, this is an essential issue in the theoretical attainment of equilibrium.

However, the other part of the criticism really hit the mark straight on. Our assumptions (including the reduction of the talent choice to the winning percentage choice) removed a dimension of the decision problem that rendered our characterisation inconsistent with Nash conjectures among owners as they made their talent choice. Quite simply, our model could not have both a closed league and Nash conjectures in the talent market, even though it did have Nash equilibrium. Any violation of Nash is simply a death sentence in modern industrial organisation modelling, despite the FQ95 model's previous usefulness and empirical relevance.

The answer, of course, was to fully include the underlying talent market in the model. Szymanski and Kesenne (2004) suggested it must be done and Jason Winfree and I did so in Winfree and Fort (2012). There was a follow-up rejoinder to Szymanski (Winfree and Fort, 2013) with added insight from Paul Madden (in press). The result appears to be a model of profit maximising owners, with Nash conjectures in the talent market, and the flexibility to handle either an open or closed talent market, and still have Nash equilibrium.[12]

I was also charged with comments on the place of the theory in teaching. It does appear as a mainstay in my undergraduate textbook (Fort, 2011), but in the next edition it will be a special case of a more general treatment for students that allows them to see the importance of the characterization of open/closed leagues and Nash conjectures. This was the important observation on teaching that was offered by my now-colleague Stefan Szymanski (2004), and I will follow it. I also know that the model receives treatment in textbooks aimed at students studying world football (e.g., Downward, Dawson and Dejonghe, 2009). Finally, as far as I know, graduate students interested in sports leagues are led through this entire literature here at Michigan and in a variety of universities in Europe.

The future

If theoretically minded colleagues are as relentless as they have been in the past, then no doubt there are more modern dynamic treatments and solution concepts remaining to be applied to sports league models. Even though El Hodiri and Quirk (1971) and Quirk and El Hodiri (1974) were dynamic treatments, they were of the operations research variety at the leading edge in their time where talent is treated like an optimal inter-temporal inventory problem.

Another area that occurs to me is applications under uncertainty. This is a nearly untouched area and no doubt expected utility of wealth analysis will generate other interesting key propositions about the denizens of sports leagues. In a sense, this handwriting is already on the wall since there has been a distinct movement towards utility maximisation approaches to sports league modelling (see note 12).

Empirically, there are still a couple of issues. First, just what did happen during the draft in Major League Baseball (contradicting the theory in FQ95) as distinct from the National Football League (failing to contradict the theory)? Second, the way to move on to an assessment of league welfare generation relative to a social welfare function has been shown. Again, while messy, the components in the mess are empirically tractable. Who knows, perhaps analysis in this direction will eventually make its way to an assessment of the costs of market power as exercised by pro sports leagues. Come to think of it, I think I'll go back and re-read Arnold Harberger (1954) . . .

Notes

1 This chapter is a reflection on Fort and Quirk (1995) and the work related to it.
2 While *Pay Dirt* (Quirk and Fort, 1992) was on the shelves earlier, as was another monograph (Fort, 1992), I had no other sports publications in journals prior to FQ95.
3 Space allowed precludes coverage of the fundamental importance of Rottenberg (1956). See Fort (2005) and Sanderson and Siegfried (2006).
4 Protecting local TV markets for some leagues could also be added but such was only just beginning to be an issue when we were writing.
5 The diagram first appeared in an appendix in *Pay Dirt* (Quirk and Fort, 1992) even though almost all later citations attributed it to FQ95. We could have done a better job on making this clearer in FQ95.

6   This, along with Rottenberg's similar earlier observation, would forever later be labelled as a version of Coase's straw man theorem. However, Rottenberg wrote well before Coase and our results simply put formal clothes on his intuition (on this issue, see Fort, 2005).

7   An important early debate concerned whether the world was 'frictionless' without significant transactions costs interfering with this outcome (Daly, 1992; Daly and Moore, 1981). We handle this point in the paper as well.

8   We allow for, and discuss, that the marginal value of talent at the gate may be different from the marginal value of talent on local TV and what the conditions would need to be for the same invariance result to hold in this case. We have observed these effects, but it ends up that later work has completely ignored this distinction.

9   While the NFL cap was in place at the time of our writing, there was not a sufficient 'after' period. The NHL cap came much later after the 2004–05 lockout.

10 We chalked the American League result up to the extraordinary situation of CBS's ownership of the Yankees right at the 1964 juncture in the data, but that has not been examined subsequently in any work that I know.

11 Major League Baseball would go from only gate to pooled local sharing, including local TV, in 1991 and again there was no 'after' period for analysis. It would take until 2001 for the National Football League to move its gate sharing arrangement to pooled sharing. The major sharing in the National Football League occurs by centralising the entire TV contract and sharing it equally, which had been done since the inception of the league.

12 There is another stream in the literature that is loosely based on some of the ideas in FQ95 and subsequent work that takes the model into a utility maximisation direction. In my opinion, this is ultimately where to go and leads us right back to Sloane (1971) and Quirk and El Hodiri (1974). I review this evolution and suggest directions in Fort (forthcoming).

References

Atkinson, S., Stanley, L. and Tschirhart, J. (1988) 'Revenue sharing as an incentive in an agency problem: An example from the National Football League'. *Rand Journal of Economics*, *19*: 27–43.

Daly, G. (1992) 'The baseball player's labor market revisited'. In P. Sommers (ed.) *Diamonds are forever: The business of baseball* (pp. 11–28). Washington, DC: Brookings Institution.

Daly, G. and Moore, W.J. (1981) 'Externalities, property rights and the allocation of resources in Major League Baseball'. *Economic Inquiry*, *19*: 77–95.

Downward, P., Dawson, A. and Dejonghe, T. (2009) *Sports economics: Theory, evidence, and policy*. London: Routledge.

El Hodiri, M. and Quirk, J. (1971) 'An economic model of a profesional sports league'. *Journal of Political Economy*, *79*: 1302–19.

Fort, R. (1992) 'Pay and performance: Is the field of dreams barren?' In P. Sommers (ed.) *Diamonds are forever: The business of baseball* (pp. 134–62). Washington, DC: Brookings Institution.

Fort, R. (2005) 'The golden anniversary of "The baseball players' labor market"'. *Journal of Sports Economics*, *6*: 347–58.

Fort, R. (2011) *Sports economics* (third edn) Upper Saddle River, NJ: Prentice Hall.

Fort, R. (forthcoming) 'Managerial objectives: A retrospective on utility maximization in pro team sports'. *Scottish Journal of Political Economy*.

Fort, R. and Quirk, J. (1995) 'Cross-subsidization, incentives, and outcomes in professional team sports leagues'. *Journal of Economic Literature*, *33*: 1265–99.

Fort, R. and Quirk, J. (2004) 'Owner objectives and competitive balance'. *Journal of Sports Economics*, *5*: 30–42.

Fort, R. and Quirk, J. (2007) 'Rational expectations and pro sports leagues'. *Scottish Journal of Political Economy*, 54: 374–87.

Fort, R. and Quirk, J. (2010) 'Optimal competitive balance in single-game ticket sports leagues'. *Journal of Sports Economics*, *11*: 587–601.

Fort, R. and Quirk, J. (2011) 'Optimal competitive balance in a season ticket league'. *Economic Inquiry*, *49*: 464–73.

Harberger, A.C. (1954) 'Monopoly and resource allocation'. *American Economic Review*, *44*: 77–87.

Kesenne, S. (1996) 'League management in professional team sports with win maximizing clubs'. *European Journal for Sports Management, 2*: 14–21.

Kesenne, S. (2014) *The economic theory of professional team sports: An analytical treatment.* Cheltenham, UK: Edward Elgar.

Madden, P. (in press) '"Walrasian fixed supply conjecture" versus "contest-Nash" solutions to sports league models: Game over?' *Journal of Sports Economics.*

Quirk, J. and El Hodiri, M. (1974) 'The economic theory of a profesional sports league'. In R. Noll (ed.) *Government and the sports business* (pp. 33–80). Washington, DC: Brookings Institution.

Quirk, J. and Fort, R. (1992) *Pay dirt: The business of professional team sports.* Princeton, NJ: Princeton University Press.

Rottenberg, S. (1956) 'The baseball players' labor market'. *Journal of Political Economy, 64*: 242–58.

Sanderson, A.R. and Siegfried, J.J. (2006) 'Simon Rottenberg and baseball, then and now: A fiftieth anniversary retrospective'. *Journal of Political Economy, 114*: 594–605.

Sloane, P.J. (1971) 'The economics of professional football: The football club as a utility maximizer'. *Scottish Journal of Political Economy, 18*: 121–46.

Szymanski, S. (2003) 'The economic design of sporting contests'. *Journal of Economic Literature, 41*: 1137–87.

Szymanski, S. (2004) 'Professional team sports are only a game: The Walrasian fixed-supply conjecture model, contest-Nash equilibrium, and the invariance principle'. *Journal of Sports Economics, 5*: 111–26.

Szymanski, S. and Kesenne, S. (2004) 'Competitive balance and gate revenue sharing in team sports'. *Journal of Industrial Economics, 52*: 165–77.

Vrooman, J. (1995) 'A general theory of professional sports leagues'. *Southern Economic Journal, 61*: 971–90.

Winfree, J. and Fort, R. (2012) 'Nash conjectures and talent supply in sports league modeling: A comment on current modeling disagreements'. *Journal of Sports Economics, 13*: 306–13.

Winfree, J. and Fort, R. (2013) 'Reply to Szymanski's "Some observations on Winfree and Fort 'Nash Conjectures and Talent Supply in Sports League Modeling: A Comment on Some Current Modeling Disagreements'"'. *Journal of Sports Economics, 14*: 327–9.

Applying competitive balance theory

Scott Tainsky[1]

The irony in reflecting on competitive balance (hereafter CB) for the *Routledge Handbook of Theory in Sport Management* is that much of the contemporary research is in this area has grown atheoretical. Branches of the CB research entail discovering new and clever ways of measuring league balance – and even making the argument for one tell-all measure of CB. The roots of CB research can be traced to Rottenberg (1956), an insightful narrative of MLB rules that somewhat incidentally proposed the importance of outcome uncertainty, often synonymous with CB. It is impossible for me to reflect on Rottenberg without hearing Fort's voice, not solely for his meticulous review of the paper (Fort, 2005), but also for his ability to capture the underlying significance implicit in Rottenberg – that microeconomic *theory* can be used to explain competitive balance as well as remedies for imbalance, supposed and actual.

Although the empirical quality of Fort's work is no less sophisticated than those whose purpose is strictly applicative – in fact Fort was the first or among the first to create metrics for the dispersion of winning percentages across a league; compare the dispersion across multiple leagues; adjust for season length, and so on – his work is indeed the appropriate reference for the handbook of theory on CB. Invariably reflective of history, policy and, foremost, the theory that explains the actions of sport managers and owners, it is fair to say that Fort has written the *books* on competitive balance in sport. I first read (and re-read) *Pay Dirt* (Quirk and Fort, 1992), which illuminated how baseball was, paradoxically, anti-competitive. Although far more comprehensive than the topic of CB, the origins of the book *15 sports myths and why they're wrong* (Fort and Winfree, 2013) can be seen in *Cross-subsidization, incentives, and outcomes in professional team sports leagues* (Fort and Quirk, 1995). The latter certainly requires a great deal of advanced economics to grasp the intricacies; however, the thread of real versus imagined impact of sports policy on the sports product, and particularly CB, has been there since the beginning.

Fort (w/Maxcy, 2003) and others (Borland and MacDonald, 2003) have reviewed the literature on CB, but it is Fort's voice loudest that compels scholars to push the boundaries when, to whom, and why competitive balance matter. For example, in the context of college football, Salaga and I (in press) found that uncertainty of outcome is not solely confined to the game itself, but also the outcome relative to *ex ante* expectation. The extension of seasonal balance's impact on consumption of out-of-market games (Tainsky, Xu, Salaga and Mills, 2014) and study of short-run demand (w/Winfree, 2010) are an homage to Fort's amplification of distinguishing between game, championship and consecutive uncertainty, and an effort to explore the areas between and within those constructions.

Future directions may entail reconsidering the comparison of CB between sports given differences in the contest success function (B.M. Mills, personal communication, 27 February, 2014). The extent to which new policies ostensibly designed to produce competitive balance are theoretically and empirically effective is an enduring question so long as there are leagues.

Note

1   Scott Tainsky is with the Department of Recreation, Sport and Tourism at the University of Illinois.

References

Borland, J. and MacDonald, R. (2003) 'Demand for sport'. *Oxford Review of Economic Policy, 19*: 478–502.

Fort, R. (2005) 'The golden anniversary of the baseball players' labor market'. *Journal of Sports Economics*, 6: 347–58.

Fort, R. and Maxcy, J. (2003) 'Competitive balance in sports leagues: An introduction'. *Journal of Sports Economics, 4*: 154–60.

Fort, R. and Quirk, J. (1995) 'Cross-subsidization, incentives, and outcomes in professional team sports leagues'. *Journal of Economic Literature*: 1265–99.

Fort, R. and Winfree, J. (2013) *15 sports myths and why they're wrong.* Palo Alto, CA: Stanford University Press.

Quirk, J. and Fort, R. (1992) *Pay dirt: The business of professional team sports.* Princeton, NJ: Princeton University Press.

Rottenberg, S. (1956) 'The baseball players' labor market'. *The Journal of Political Economy, 64*: 242–58.

Salaga, S. and Tainsky, S. (in press) 'The effects of outcome uncertainty, scoring, and pregame expectations on Nielsen Ratings for Bowl Championship Series Games'. *Journal of Sports Economics.*

Tainsky, S. and Winfree, J.A. (2010) 'Discrimination and demand: The effect of international players on attendance in Major League Baseball'. *Social Science Quarterly, 91*(1): 117–28.

Tainsky, S., Xu, J., Salaga, S. and Mills, B.M. (2014) 'Spillover benefits to local enthusiasm: Increases in league-wide interest as a consequence of local sports team competitiveness'. *Journal of Economics and Business, 74*: 1–10.

PART VI

Conclusion

33

THEMES AND DIRECTIONS FOR THEORY IN SPORT MANAGEMENT

Alison Doherty, Janet S. Fink and
George B. Cunningham

Introduction

In drawing from the perspectives of leaders across a range of disciplinary foci, our aim with this collection was to consider the place of theory in our field and relate how our sport management colleagues have engaged in the theory building process. The compilation of chapters represents a range of sport management contexts and theoretical premises. This serves to highlight the diversity of our field.

In this concluding chapter we draw together some apparent common themes across the chapters in this book that help to highlight key aspects of theory and theory development in sport management. To begin, each of the works focused on explaining some phenomenon in the sport context by outlining the key constructs and relationships among them so that one may understand 'how, when, why, and under what conditions phenomena take place' (Cunningham, 2013, p. 1). As noted in the opening chapter to this book, this is what good theory should do. As the authors' accounts indicate, the theories presented here add value to scholarship, education and practice (they have utility; Bacharach, 1989), and they can be (and have been) rigorously scrutinised and empirically examined (Popper, 1959). Notably, several authors provide direction for future research that must (continue to) 'test' their theory, not being content to settle with what they have derived thus far.

The works reported here, and similar efforts, represent strong scholarly currency (Corley and Gioia, 2011) that our colleagues have invested in the advancement of our sport management discipline (Doherty, 2013). Although the level of sophistication of a theory – its refinement and complexity – may be a marker of its value and contribution to a field (cf. Colquitt and Zapata-Phelan, 2007; Shilbury and Rentschler, 2007), this is not something we feel the need to assess, at least not at this point. Nonetheless, the authors' descriptions of the evolution of their theorizing suggest increasing sophistication as that work has unfolded (see, for example, the chapters by, Funk and James; Gerretsen and Rosentraub; Kane; Knoppers; Parent; Preuss). Importantly, the chapters provide several examples of theory testing and expansion that represent what may be described as a ripple effect, as the introduction of a given theory or framework stimulates and shapes further research and knowledge building, as well as theory refinement. For example, Mahony's theorizing about organisational justice in the intercollegiate athletics setting informed his own and other scholars' related research, in turn shaping his original framework as it continued to evolve. Interestingly, Mahony relates how he then took that framework to yet another context – namely, educational administration – as another example of the continued influence of his theoretical work. Heere's theory of team identification continues to unfold, with his most recent conceptualisation proposed within his chapter here; further theorizing that acknowledges advances in research on team identity by himself, his colleagues, and other scholars since it was first examined. Cornwell describes the ripple effect of her conceptualisation of sponsorship-linked marketing on research pertaining to sponsorship-linked advertising and internal marketing. She anticipates still further extensions of sponsorship-linked marketing to the critical phenomena of social media and corporate social responsibility. The application chapters have proven quite useful in highlighting this ripple effect, as colleagues describe how and why they picked up a particular theory/perspective to facilitate their own research (e.g., Donaldson), their teaching (e.g., Davies) and/or their practice (e.g., Dalrymple).

Themes in theory and theory development

'Sport management theories'

As noted, the theories presented in the chapters here represent a range of theoretical premises, including derivation from parent theories and disciplines (e.g., Babiak, Heinze and Wolfe from CSR theory; Chelladurai from leadership theory; de Bosscher from economic competition theory; Wakefield from environmental psychology). In each case, the authors describe the importance of placing theory within the unique context of sport. Chalip's (2006) oft-cited query about sport management as a unique discipline – and whether it is indeed unique – is consistently, albeit not always intentionally, addressed across the chapters. For example, Gladden focused on the four main components of Aaker's (1991) framework for brand equity and brought that into the sport context by identifying the most important antecedents to the development of brand equity in sport. Babiak *et al.* relate that the CSR framework was informed by the general management literature yet grounded in the contextual factors of professional sport that are not present in other industries; namely, fan passion, transparency of management decisions, unique economic support and complex stakeholder management. Notably, Warner relates that the Sport and Sense of Community Theory was prompted to a large extent by her wondering, 'what *is* distinctive about sport?'

Prompting and shaping the theorizing process

When providing guidance regarding chapter structure, we were particularly interested in what spurred authors' interest in the topic and theorizing about it, and what shaped their thinking and the eventual theory. What emerged was a range of stories about what influenced the authors to pursue and formulate a theoretical explanation for a particular phenomenon. Some authors related several influences to their work, and we highlight some of the common themes here. What is notable is that in no instances did any of the authors seek merely to fill a gap in the literature. Rather, they recount various experiences and tensions that prompted their theorizing and research efforts to explain phenomenon and build knowledge in our field.

Need for a way to explain a particular phenomenon

This was the most common impetus to theory development described across the chapters. The need was either based on a belief that no relevant theory existed (e.g., Lyras and Welty Peachy; Parent), or that existing explanations were insufficient (e.g., Hylton; Fink). For example, Kihl could not find existing theory to explain micro-level consequences of corruption on organisational stakeholders and so developed her work on post-corruption experiences in the sport setting. De Bosscher, along with her colleagues, noted 'the lack of an empirically-grounded, coherent theory on the factors determining international sporting success' (including a method to compare nations and consider the complicated question of the relationship between elite sport policy and success). In contrast, Knoppers was not satisfied with the existing explanations presented about the lack of female leaders in sport, feeling that the individual and structural explanations put forth to that point were insufficient to explain what was happening in that context. Similarly, Kane was dissatisfied with how the literature was explaining the hierarchical gendered power relations in sport. James reports feeling that the existing literature and methods were not sufficiently addressing the *process* of developing fan loyalty. Rather than relying on recall information from adults, he talked with children in different cognitive stages and different levels of fan loyalty to gain a better understanding of the development of fandom. Mason's theorizing about the nature of the sport product was prompted by a sense that the establishment, in the sports economics literature, 'that the core product for sports leagues was the uncertainty of game outcomes . . . did not seem to capture the complexities of the sports fan consumption experience'. These authors, and many others who indicated that theory was insufficient or non-existent to explain their sport phenomenon of interest, were prompted to push the envelope in terms of considering new and different ways of explanation. Their struggles in this regard are apparent in their stories, which nonetheless reveal the opportunity they took to develop new knowledge.

Need for synthesis of a range of concepts

Several authors describe how their theory development process involved synthesising a variety of concepts, and more concrete constructs, into a model that they felt would at least begin to capture the explanations they were trying to generate about a phenomenon. For example, Skille felt compelled to integrate what turned out to be 'very different theories' in order to arrive at a framework that would enable him to explain the implementation of sport policy at the grassroots level. 'Chella' Chelladurai also combined theories, each of which he felt were insufficient on their own, to explain sport leadership. Fink drew on a range of concepts in the literature and 'slowly the framework began to take form' in a way that aligned with her personal musings about diversity management in the sport context. Trail endeavoured to develop a more complete explanation of sport consumer behaviour and in doing so integrated numerous variables (e.g., motives, identification, self-esteem responses) using a variety of theoretical premises (e.g., theories of satisfaction and self-esteem) to build and justify the model. Funk and James' hierarchical Psychological Continuum Model 'organise[s] literature from various academic disciplines', drawing particularly on psychological and sociological processes to explain sport consumer behaviour through attitude formation. These examples highlight two key points: theory is often not simple, but rather involves a collection of constructs that are considered important to (begin to) explain a phenomenon; and those constructs are integrated, rather than hanging alone, as together they propose a (more) meaningful explanation. Parent describes a senior colleague advising her that 'if [she] could illustrate in one image the various theories and concepts to be examined in [her] study, then [she] was on the right track'.

Emerged from empirical work

While some authors developed their theories conceptually (e.g., Cornwell; Kane; Lyras and Welty Peachy; Mason), several describe the empirical derivation of their framework. This suggests both typology and taxonomy approaches to theorizing (cf. Slack and Parent, 2006) within the field. Examples of empirically-derived theories include both Warner and Kihl, who each used a grounded theory approach to explore the meaning of sense of community in the sport context and post-corruption experiences in sport, respectively. Relatedly, Ferkins and Shilbury used developmental action research undertaken in the field to uncover their ever-developing explanation of strategic board capability in non-profit sport organisations. In contrast, de Bosscher presents the extensive process she and her colleagues have gone through in both the initial development of the SPLISS, as well as its subsequent versions. As another example, Rod Fort describes how he and Quirk used economic theory and data from various leagues to develop and refine their theory of competitive balance. Gratton, Shibli and Coleman's theorizing about the economic impact of major sport events was prompted, and heavily informed, by the findings of commissioned research in several host cities. From multiple studies (and data sets) they developed their theory of key correlates of income generation in this context. Interestingly, their work has evolved recently to acknowledge other important benefits of hosting, including *psychic* income.

Personal experience in the industry

Several authors note that their theorizing was prompted and further informed by their personal experience in the sport industry; encountering circumstances that, in retrospect, were not able to be sufficiently or satisfactorily explained by existing literature. For example, Gladden's experience in the sport industry prompted him to better understand and explain why some sport organisations could remain financially successful during extended years of poor perform-ance. Bien-Aimé and Hardin describe how Hardin's first-hand experience as a female journalist afforded her the opportunity to explain how (untested) media gatekeepers' perceptions of the media audience influences what is covered in the sport news, particularly with regard to women's sport. Meanwhile, Dixon and Breuning relate that their personal experience as college coaches, and leaving the profession because of anticipated work–family conflict, resonated with their theory building on work–life balance; 'this experience motivated us to find new pathways for career and life success for ourselves and others'. Of note, they also relate that such personal experiences 'created challenges for remaining objective as scholars', and prompted them to continuously check their thinking and writing. Chelladurai also relates how his theorizing on leadership 'has been based on my own experiences as a player and coach'. Interestingly, when examining the literature he found a 'disconnect' between what he was learning and his reality. This disconnect prompted his further enquiry and ultimate theorizing about sport leadership. Relatedly, Mahony experienced an inconsistency between his real life experience as an athletic administrator and what research was indicating about stakeholders' perceptions of organisational justice in athletics. Like Chelladurai, this disconnect prompted Mahony's efforts to explain the phenomenon. Heere's theorizing about team identification was prompted by his personal experience as a spectator (from another country) at NBA and college sports games, and a need to reconcile the similarities and differences between the American and European professional sport experience. Meanwhile, Anderson's experience as a coach, and his connections with both athletes and administrators, shaped his theory of inclusive masculinities. He outlines these experiences in his chapter, noting the changes he observed on a track and field team from the time he served as coach to a decade later when he visited the team once more as an academic. Many of the authors let their passion and their personal questions drive and inform their theorizing.

Emerged from conversations with others

Another influence on the theory development process for several authors was engaging in conversations, typically with colleagues, about the phenomenon of interest. Both Warner and Kihl consider that conversations with colleagues provided encouragement, insight and opportunity for building their work. Ferkins and Shilbury relate that their 'specific curiosity emerged as a result of wide-ranging discussions with sport practitioners'. They note that these conversations were not part of any fieldwork but were a critical part of the preliminary process of understanding the sport governance issues in the field. Cornwell relates that an exchange with a corporate executive at a professional sport event resonated with her and stimulated further theorizing about marketing through sport sponsorship. This theme reinforces the influence of personal experiences and connections with others in shaping our theorizing, as we talk through ideas and 'bounce' them off of others. Theory building is rarely undertaken in a vacuum.

Extending, revising and tweaking theory

Most of the chapter authors describe how they, and others, have engaged in extending their original work, often right away as they continue their line of enquiry. Typically this is prompted by the theory being refuted, an enhanced understanding of the phenomena, or simply changing times and contexts, resulting in changes to the relationships among constructs. For example, while Rosentraub notably wrote about how cities hosting professional sports teams in the 1990s were 'major league losers', in this volume he and Gerretsen outline ways in which those very cities can leverage their relationships with the team to further their economic, social and cultural capital. Like Rosentraub, Preuss put forth his original theory of event legacy in 2007 and a much more sophisticated version in 2015; he describes the development of both, including how the most recent version extends from the original, in his chapter. De Bosscher also outlines, in considerable detail, how she and her colleagues continued to evolve the SPLISS (from version 1.0 to 2.0) with the extension of the framework to still other nations' elite sport systems and drilling down further to understand the critical success factors. This continued work was prompted by what de Bosscher describes as still insufficient explanations of the relationship between national sport policies and international sporting success. Ferkins and Shilbury also describe their progressive efforts and 'milestones' in developing an explanation for board strategic balance in the sport context. They illustrate their research flow and the evolution of their theorizing over time. While they share their most current modelling in the chapter, they also note that it is still *emerging* theory, as it is yet to be rigorously tested by others. In this way, they presume that it will continue to evolve.

In fact, all of the authors (perhaps at our prompting), acknowledge that theirs is a work in progress that will – and should – continue to evolve as it is adopted, tested, refined and extended by themselves and by others. Of note, Kirk Wakefield presumes that theorizing about the sportscape will be extended even further. In describing its ripple effect so far with respect to league brand associations, fan satisfaction and sensoryscape, he derives from those empirical efforts still further directions for research and refinement of the sportscape framework. Mason proposes several directions for research that examine the *production* of the sport product (including athletes, participation opportunities and achievement as products). Kihl notes that her work must now move from 'substantive' to 'formal' theory, through rigorous testing and broader application that 'would be at a higher level of abstraction that extends beyond a specific stakeholder group and/or organisation to generalise across a discipline'. The authors who have developed the theory presented in this book have not settled (nor will they) with the explanations they have generated.

Theory in practice

A few authors relate how their work has been picked up by practitioners, highlighting a theory-practice linkage. De Bosscher's framework of elite sporting success has been adopted by policymakers around the world who have used it to evaluate their nation's effectiveness on the international sport scene. Ferkins and Shilbury describe how their action research in the field has resulted in major changes to the governing structure of sport organisations, changes to board activity and individual board member perspectives along the way. Perhaps as a consequence, they have been contacted by CEOs and board members of national and state sport organisations in a selection of nations with similar sport systems. The impact of their work in practice is evidenced in the testimony of Neil Dalrymple of Bowls Australia in the application that accompanies their chapter. Lyras and Welty Peachy also describe the direct impact of Sport-for-Development Theory, through its application to a sport event, on a subsequently 'revamped competition structure . . . [that] de-emphasised winning, and focused much more on the educational and cultural aspects of the event'. Hylton's work with critical race theory has informed others' scholarship, but has also impacted how they teach their classes and engage the sport enterprise. Further, Fink describes how her diversity management framework (Fink and Pastore, 1999) framed the guidelines for an NCAA 'diversity in athletics' award aimed at honouring and thus bringing attention to diversity management practices in intercollegiate athletic departments. As Fink notes, 'the establishment of the award is a great exemplar of bridging scholarship and practice'.

Concluding comments

Many of us, our colleagues and our students may be prompted by a felt need to explain some phenomenon; maybe in response to a crisis, like Kihl experienced, or a personal disconnect between the literature and one's reality, as Chelladurai describes. A perceived lack of sufficient or satisfactory explanation may be – and should be – an impetus for 'someone [to] do research on this, maybe even me' (Parent). Building theory is not an easy task and, as can be gleaned from the authors' accounts in this book, it may be fraught with frustration, road blocks, inconclusive findings and a need to 'get back to it'. Ferkins and Shilbury emphasise that, although the work presented in their chapter and illustrated graphically indicates a 'chronological sequence in terms of publication dates, in reality, there were many hills and dales, peaks and troughs, and perhaps it is only in hindsight that we have been able to plot the milestones of this journey with any real clarity'. We wish you the best on your journey with theory in sport management.

References

Aaker, D.A. (1991) *Managing brand equity: Capitalizing on the value of a brand name*. New York: The Free Press.

Bacharach, S.B. (1989) 'Organizational theories: Some criteria for evaluation'. *Academy of Management Review*, *14*: 496–515.

Chalip, L. (2006) 'Toward a distinctive theory of sport management'. *Journal of Sport Management, 20*: 1–21.

Colquitt, J.A. and Zapata-Phelan, C.P. (2007) 'Trends in theory building and theory testing: A five-decade study of the Academy of Management Journal'. *Academy of Management Journal, 50*: 1281–303.

Corley, K.G. and Gioia, D.A. (2011) 'Building theory about theory building: what constitutes a theoretical contribution?' *Academy of Management Review, 36*: 12–32.

Cunningham, G.B. (2013) 'Theory and theory development in sport management'. *Sport Management Review, 16*: 1–4.

Doherty, A.J. (2013) 'Investing in sport management: The value of good theory'. *Sport Management Review, 16*: 5–11.

Fink, J.S. and Pastore, D.L. (1999) 'Diversity in sport? Utilizing the business literature to devise a comprehensive framework of diversity initiatives'. *Quest, 51*: 310–27.

Popper, K. (1959) *The logic of scientific discovery*. New York: Harper and Row.

Shilbury, D. and Rentschler, R. (2007) 'Assessing sport management journals: A multi-dimensional examination'. *Sport Management Review, 10*: 31–44.

Slack, T. and Parent, M.M. (2006) *Understanding sport organizations: The application of organization theory*. Champaign, IL: Human Kinetics.

INDEX

Please note: UK spelling is used in this index.

Printed in the United States
by Baker & Taylor Publisher Services